INDIA EDUCATION REPORT

Contributors

A. Mathew	National Institute of Adult Education, New Delhi
A. S. Seetharamu	Institute for Social and Economic Change, Bangalore
Alok Mathur	Sandhan Research Centre, Jaipur
Anita Dighe	Indira Gandhi National Open University, New Delhi
Anita Rampal	National Literacy Resource Centre, Mussoorie
Anuradha De	Collaborative Research and Dissemination, New Delhi
C. Seshadri	Regional Institute of Education, Mysore
C. J. Daswani	United Nations Educational, Scientific and Cultural Organisation, New Delhi
Claire Noronha	Collaborative Research and Dissemination, New Delhi
Disha Nawani	Gargi College, University of Delhi, Delhi
Geetha B. Nambissan	Jawaharlal Nehru University, New Delhi
Jandhyala B. G. Tilak	National Institute of Educational Planning and Administration, New Delhi
Juhi Shah	Sandhan Research Centre, Jaipur
K. Sujatha	National Institute of Educational Planning and Administration, New Delhi
M. N. G. Mani	Sri Ramakrishna Mission Vidyalaya College of Education, Coimbatore
M. S. Yadav	Educationist, New Delhi
Manabi Majumdar	Madras Institute of Development Studies, Tamil Nadu
Meenakshi Bhardwaj	International Concepts, New Delhi
Meera Samson	Collaborative Research and Dissemination, New Delhi
Mona Sedwal	National Institute of Educational Planning and Administration, New Delhi
Neeti Gaur	National Institute of Educational Planning and Administration, New Delhi
P. Radhakrishnan	Madras Institute of Development Studies, Tamil Nadu
R. Akila	Madras Institute of Development Studies, Tamil Nadu
R. Govinda	National Institute of Educational Planning and Administration, New Delhi
S. Hom Chaudhuri	Pachhunga College, North-Eastern Hill University, Aizawl
Sharada Jain	Sandhan Research Centre, Jaipur
Shobhita Rajgopal	Sandhan Research Centre, Jaipur
Sudesh Mukhopadhyay	National Institute of Educational Planning and Administration, New Delhi
Sumitra Chowdhury	Department of Industries, Government of India, New Delhi
Usha Nayar	National Council of Educational Research and Training, New Delhi
Vandana Chakrabarty	SNDT Women's University, Bombay
Venita Kaul	World Bank, New Delhi
Vimala Ramachandran	Educational Research Unit, Jaipur
Vinod Raina	Eklavya, Bhopal

INDIA EDUCATION REPORT

Edited by
R. GOVINDA

National Institute of
Educational Planning and
Administration

United Nations
Educational, Scientific
and Cultural Organization

OXFORD
UNIVERSITY PRESS

OXFORD
UNIVERSITY PRESS

YMCA Library Building, Jai Singh Road, New Delhi 110 001

Oxford University Press is a department of the University of Oxford. It furthers the
University's objective of excellence in research, scholarship, and education
by publishing worldwide in

Oxford   New York

Auckland   Bangkok   Buenos Aires   Cape Town   Chennai
Dar es Salaam   Delhi   Hong Kong   Istanbul   Karachi   Kolkata
Kuala Lumpur   Madrid   Melbourne   Mexico City   Mumbai   Nairobi
São Paulo   Shanghai   Singapore   Taipei   Tokyo   Toronto

with an associated company in Berlin

Published in India
By Oxford University Press, New Delhi

First published 2002

ISBN 019 565795 0

The views expressed in this book belong to the individual authors
and may not represent those of NIEPA or UNESCO

Typeset in CG Times 10.5/12.5
by Excellent Laser Typesetters, Pitampura, Delhi 110 034
Printed at Roopak Printers, Delhi 110032
Published by Manzar Khan, Oxford University Press
YMCA Library Building, Jai Singh Road, New Delhi 110 001

Foreword

Over fifty years ago the UNESCO constitution identified *Education For All* as a key aspiration of the fledgling organization. Sadly, progress towards this goal, in India and elsewhere, proved to be much slower than anticipated. Independence raised expectations without increasing the means to satisfy them, particularly in a period of rapid population growth. In 1990 the international community renewed its commitment to *Education For All* at the Jomtien Conference, which initiated a decade of intense activity, at both global and national levels, to promote the development of basic education. In particular, education came to be seen not simply as an instrument of social and economic development, but as a basic human right.

As the decade of the 1990's drew to a close it became clear that progress was still disappointing. Another world forum on *Education For All*, preceded by an assessment of unprecedented thoroughness, was convened in Dakar in 2000. India took this opportunity to review and reflect on all aspects of its education system. This book contains the outcome of this admirable work, which records both the achievements and the unfinished agenda in a candid fashion.

Learning from the experience of the Jomtien Conference, the Dakar Forum was more deliberate in setting out quantitative goals, precise deadlines and a detailed strategy for achieving *Education For All*. UNESCO was asked to be the co-ordinator and catalyst of an international effort to be conducted over the first fifteen years of the new millennium. The Dakar Forum set global targets but the action to achieve them must take place at the national and grassroots levels. Only the commitment of UNESCO's member states and their citizens can make the dream of *Education For All* a reality.

That is why it is such a pleasure to welcome this excellent volume describing India's experience. Because of its democratic and intellectual traditions, not to mention its sheer size, the advancement toward *Education For All* in India will be a vital indicator of progress in the world as a whole. Happily, the two years that have elapsed since the Dakar Forum have seen a heightened sense of commitment to education within individual member states, as well as greater cooperation across the international community. All now recognize that *Education For All* means not merely the provision of primary schooling but a new philosophy of life-long learning for all. As this book demonstrates so well, *Education For All* is an intellectual challenge as well as a political and administrative ambition. The aim is an era of learning without frontiers of geography, age, class, creed and nationality. It is to promote a learning that will reveal the treasure within each human being expressed through the four processes of learning to be, learning to learn, learning to do, and learning to live together.

Progress toward *Education For All* is at a critical juncture in India. This is a country of paradoxes. India has emerged as a global player in the information and communications technology revolution—yet it is home to millions of illiterates and out of school children. In recent years, the country has begun to unlock its tremendous potential to achieve economic progress and to liberate its people from the misery of poverty. The political and economic leaders understand the critical role of basic education in this effort and have taken significant steps to make it a reality for all. However, putting the country on course to achieve the goals of *Education For All* presupposes a realistic assessment of the current situation, not only in quantitative terms but also in the analysis of trends, of causes and effects, and of previous policies. This is precisely what the present volume has attempted to do.

In the 1990s, although India made good progress in adult literacy and saw a tremendous expansion of educational facilities and school enrolment, the journey is far from over. Achieving the goals of *Education For All* in India by 2010, as proposed in its recent policy documents, will not be an easy task. The challenge is one of both scale and complexity. This book shows that the core problem of *Education For All* in India is one of equity. Some parts of the country have galloped towards the goals but others continue to make only slow progress. Some sections of the population have benefited from the education system and now form part of the global elite, but many more remain on the fringes of society with no schooling at all. Bridging this educational gap is even more urgent in our fast expanding digital world.

A second major challenge for education in India is quality. The studies presented here show that quality improvement has not kept pace with the expansion of the system, partly because resources have been in short supply. The authors recognize that ignoring the issue of quality in the public education system will further aggravate the problem of inequity as the poor continue to depend on publicly funded schools. The aim must be to break the insidious link between quality and exclusivity.

Nations in both the developed and the developing worlds now seek to enhance the role of civil society in the governance and management of education. This has been achieved in different ways around the world. The *India Education Report* records how India has participated in this changing process. In particular, the management of education has been decentralized across the country through transfer of powers to the *panchayati raj* bodies. Here, as elsewhere, progress is uneven across the states but the signs from the field seem to be quite positive. Decentralization has been coupled with increased attention to the creation of partnerships between government bodies and non-governmental organizations.

A key feature of the papers in this book is that they are written by independent experts who present a critical but purposeful analysis of the situation. They not only serve as useful and objective benchmarks on the status of *Education For All* but also provide new perspectives on educational development in India.

I congratulate NIEPA for completing such a massive task of documentation at this critical juncture and I am delighted that UNESCO has been an active partner in this exercise. The book provides a splendidly comprehensive complement to the largely quantitative *Education For All 2000* assessment carried out in preparation for the Dakar Conference. Experience has shown that international dialogue can be helpful in refining the strategies and tactics that will deliver *Education For All*. This report is a powerful contribution to that dialogue and I commend it to a wide readership.

SIR JOHN DANIEL
Assistant Director-General for Education
UNESCO

Preface

India began its endeavour to establish a system of mass education more than fifty years ago. The Constitution of the country made it obligatory for the state to provide basic education for all up to the age of 14, within a period of ten years. It was soon realized that the task was not an easy one, particularly with the fast pace at which population increase was overtaking the expansion of the education system. While literacy rates and school enrolments increased consistently, the number of illiterates also continued to rise. However, persistent efforts to reach the goal of education for all seem to have begun paying results in recent years. The increase in literacy figures in the 1990s showed a significant jump and consequently, for the first time, there was a decrease in the absolute number of illiterates in the country. Female literacy showed a faster increase than the male literacy rates, though we still have a long way to go in fully bridging the male-female gap. Participation of children in the school also showed a positive trend with school dropout rate among girls showing a significant decrease in the 1990s. Nevertheless, the field reality amply demonstrates that the task is not yet complete.

As is well documented, the 1990s marked a significant period in the progress of EFA not only in India but also at the global level following the first global meet on EFA held in 1990 at Jomtien, which culminated in the second meet at Dakar in 2000. The Dakar Conference required that a comprehensive review of the progress in EFA be made in each country according to the guidelines issued by UNESCO. In India, the exercise was expanded to include a series of critical reviews by independent experts on different subthemes of EFA. The whole exercise was jointly carried out by NIEPA in collaboration with the Ministry of Human Resource Development, Government of India. The review papers not only highlighted the innovative efforts and strategies made during the last decade of the century but also pointed to the persisting gaps and problems and indicated the areas that need priority action. The present volume is an abridged version of selected review papers from that series which has been ably edited by Professor R. Govinda.

I am thankful to UNESCO for funding the original exercise of preparing various review papers as part of the EFA 2000 assessment process and thereafter putting together this volume for publication. I am also thankful to the Ministry of Human Resource Development, Government of India, for not only assigning the task of coordinating the review for the Dakar Conference but also permitting NIEPA to publish the material in the form of a concise volume. I hope that the volume will serve as a useful benchmark and guide future course of action at national and state levels.

December 2001
New Delhi

B. P. KHANDELWAL
Director
National Institute of Educational
Planning and Administration

Acknowledgements

The genesis of the volume lies in the elaborate exercise carried out by Ministry of Human Resource Development and NIEPA with financial support from UNESCO which resulted in a series of review papers on the status of basic education in India. UNESCO has again provided generous financial support for the publication of the present volume. All the papers included in this volume, except the one on basic education among Dalit children, have been selected from the earlier series. These are essentially abridged versions of the original papers. I am grateful to all the authors for allowing NIEPA to use the original papers to bring out this volume. Dr Mona Sedwal's contribution to the entire exercise was enormous. She coordinated a variety of activities, apart from contributing substantially to the editorial work. I would like to express my special gratitude to Mr Abhimanyu Singh, currently leading the EFA Follow-up Cell at UNESCO, whose constant help and guidance was instrumental in the conception and execution of the work. I gratefully acknowledge the critical and unquestioned support from Professor B. P. Khandelwal, Director of NIEPA, without which this project could not have been completed. I am also grateful to the editorial staff of Oxford University Press for their patience and cooperation in bringing out this volume.

December 2001   R. GOVINDA
New Delhi   *Editor*

Contents

Tables

Boxes

Figures

Abbreviations and Acronyms

AIES	All India Education Survey
AIPSN	All India People's Science Network
AKES	Aga Khan Education Service
AKF	Aga Khan Foundation
APPEAL	Asia Pacific Programme of Education for All
ARC	Association of the Rights of the Child
AS	Alternative Schooling
AW	*Anganwadi*
AWC	*Anganwadi* Centre
AWW	*Anganwadi* Worker
BAS	Baseline Assessment Survey
BCC	Building Construction Committee
BEMC	Block Education Management Committee
BEP	Bihar Education Project
BGVS	*Bharat Gyan Vigyan Samiti*
BJVJ	*Bharat Jan Vigyan Jatha*
BRC	Block Resource Centre
BSG	Block Steering Group
CABE	Central Advisory Board of Education
CACL	Campaign Against Child Labour
CAPART	Council for Advancement of People's Action and Rural Technology
CAPE	Comprehensive Access to Primary Education
CBR	Community Based Rehabilitation
CBSE	Central Board of Secondary Education
CDPO	Child Development Project Officer
CE	Continuing Education
CEMD	Centre for Educational Management and Development
CIET	Central Institute of Educational Technology
CRC	Cluster Resource Centre
CSIR	Council of Scientific and Industrial Research
CSWB	Central Social Welfare Board

CSWI	Committee on the Status of Women in India
CTE	College of Teacher Education
DAE	Department of Adult Education
DIET	District Institute of Education and Training
DoE	Department of Education
DPEP	District Primary Education Programme
DTERT	Department of Teacher Education, Research and Training
DWCD	Department of Women and Child Development
DWCRA	Development of Women and Children in Rural Areas
EAS	Employment Assurance Scheme
ECCD	Early Childhood Care and Development
ECCE	Early Childhood Care and Education
ECD	Early Childhood Development
ECE	Early Childhood Education
Ed.CIL	Educational Consultants India Limited
EFA	Education For All
EGS	Education Guarantee Scheme
ET	Educational Technology
ETT	Elementary Teacher Training
GDP	Gross Domestic Product
GER	Gross Enrollment Ratio
GNP	Gross National Product
GoI	Government of India
HDI	Human Development Index
HDSA	Human Development in South Asia
HPS	Higher Primary School
HSTP	Hoshangabad Science Teaching Programme
HRD	Human Resource Development
HSLC	Higher Secondary School Leaving Certificate
IASE	Institute of Advanced Studies in Education
IATE	Indian Association of Teacher Educators
ICAR	Indian Council of Agricultural Research
ICDS	Integrated Child Development Services
ICMR	Indian Council of Medical Research
IEDC	Integrated Education of Disabled Children
IER	Indian Educational Review
IFAD	International Fund for Agricultural Development
IGNOU	Indira Gandhi National Open University
IIE	Indian Institute of Education
IIT	Indian Institute of Technology
IMR	Infant Mortality Rate
IPC	Indian Penal Code
IPCL	Improved Pace and Content of Learning

IPER	Institute of Psychological and Educational Research
IRDP	Integrated Rural Development Programme
IT	Information Technology
ITV	Interactive Television
IYDP	International Year of Disabled Persons
JBT	Junior Basic Training
JRY	*Jawahar Rozgar Yojana*
JSN	*Jan Shikshan Nilayam*
JSS	*Jan Shikshan Sansthan*
KSPS	*Khand Stariya Shiksha Prabandhak Samiti*
KSSP	*Kerala Shastra Sahitya Parishad*
KSSWF	Karnataka State Student Welfare Fund
KSTBF	Karnataka State Teachers' Benefit Fund
LJ	Lok Jumbish
LJP	Lok Jumbish Parishad
LPS	Lower Primary School
MAS	Mid-term Assessment Survey
MBSE	Mizoram Board of Secondary Education
MCD	Municipal Corporation of Delhi
MHIP	Mizo Hmeichhe Insuihkhawm Pawl
MHRD	Ministry of Human Resource Development
MIS	Management Information System
MLC	Mass Literacy Campaign
MLL	Minimum Levels of Learning
MPK	*Mahila Prashikshan Kendra*
MS	*Mahila Samakhya*
MVF	M.Venkatarangaiyya Foundation
NAEP	National Adult Education Programme
NAR	Net Attendance Ratio
NBT	National Book Trust
NCAER	National Council of Applied Economic Research
NCERT	National Council of Educational Research and Training
NCLF	National Child Labour Fund
NCSW	National Commission for Self-Employed Women and Women in the Informal Sector
NCTE	National Council for Teacher Education
NER	Net Enrollment Ratio
NFE	Non-Formal Education
NFTW	National Foundation for Teachers' Welfare
NGO	Non Governmental Organization
NIAE	National Institute of Adult Education
NIEPA	National Institute of Educational Planning and Administration
NIPCCD	National Institute of Public Cooperation and Child Development
NLM	National Literacy Mission

NLMA	National Literacy Mission Authority
NMIMS	Narsee Monjee Institute of Management Studies
NPAE	National Programme of Adult Education
NPE	National Policy on Education
NRF	National Renewal Fund
NSS	National Sample Survey
NSSO	National Sample Survey Organization
OB	Operation Blackboard
OBC	Other Backward Castes
OECD	Organization for Economic Cooperation and Development
ORG	Operations Research Group
PA	Private Aided
PL	Post-Literacy
PLC	Post Literacy Campaign
POA	Programme of Action
PRI	*Panchayati Raj* Institution
PROBE	Public Report on Basic Education
PTC	Primary Teacher Certificate
PTR	Pupil–Teacher Ratio
PUA	Private Unaided
RCI	Rehabilitation Council of India
REDS	Ragpickers' Education and Development Scheme
RGI	Registrar General of India
RIE	Regional Institute of Education
RVREC	Rishi Valley Rural Education Centre
SACCS	South Asian Coalition of Child Servitude
SC	Scheduled Caste
SCERT	State Council for Educational Research and Training
SDAE	State Directorate of Adult Education
SDP	State Domestic Product
SEWA	Self Employment Women's Association
SIDA	Swedish International Development Agency
SIEMAT	State Institute of Educational Management and Training
SIERT	State Institute of Educational Research and Training
SK	*Shiksha Karmi*
SLM	State Literacy Mission
SLMA	State Literacy Mission Authority
SMC	School Management Committee
SNDT	Shreemati Nathibai Damodar Thackersey Women's University.
SNP	Special Nutrition Programme
SOPT	Special Orientation for Primary Teachers
SPARC	School for Potential Advancement and Restoration of Confidence
SSA	*Sarva Shiksha Abhiyan*

SSLC	Secondary School Leaving Certificate
SSN	Social Safety Net
ST	Scheduled Tribe
STC	Senior Teacher Certificate
SWRC	Social Work and Research Centre
TASH	Technology and Social Health Foundation
TCH	Teacher's Certificate Higher
TINP	Tamil Nadu Integrated Nutrition Project
TLC	Total Literacy Campaign
TLE	Teaching Learning Equipment
TPR	Teacher–Pupil Ratio
TPS	Teachers Per School
TTC	Teacher Training Certificate
TWD	Tribal Welfare Department
UEE	Universalization of Elementary Education
UGC	University Grants Commission
UNDP	United Nations Development Programme
UNESCO	United Nations Educational, Scientific and Cultural Organization
UNICEF	United Nations International Children's Education Fund
UPE	Universalization of Primary Education
UPS	Upper Primary School
VAEC	Village Adult Education Committee
VA	Voluntary Agency
VEC	Village Education Committee
VER	Village Education Register
VO	Voluntary Organization
VRC-H	Vocational Rehabilitation Centre for the Handicapped
WDC	Women's Development Corporation
WDP	Women's Development Programme
YMA	Young Mizo Association
YUVA	Youth for Unity and Voluntary Action
ZSS	*Zilla Saksharata Samiti*

1

Providing Education For All in India
An Overview

R. Govinda

India began its journey towards the goal of universal and free basic education little more than fifty years ago with the Indian Constitution stating, 'The State shall endeavour to provide, within a period of ten years from the commencement of this Constitution, for free and compulsory education for all children until they complete the age of fourteen years'. The struggle to meet this basic commitment began forthwith. But conditions then were really dismal. The overall literacy rate was 18 per cent and female literacy rate was only 9 per cent. The gross enrolment ratio at primary stage (classes I–V covering the age group 6–11) was 43 per cent, the corresponding figure for girls was only 25 per cent. At upper-primary stage (classes VI–VIII and age group 11–14) only 1 of 8 children was enrolled in school; among girls, only 1 of 20. Over five decades, there has been phenomenal growth in coverage. Today nearly 4 of 5 children in the age group 6–14 are in school. Two of 3 persons are functionally literate. Thus in the last fifty years, several milestones in this regard have been crossed and the progress achieved is by no means small. But it falls short of meeting the goal of Education For All (EFA). This chapter presents a quantitative picture characterizing the basic education scenario in the country.[1] It highlights the various measures initiated by the government during the last fifty years, focusing on the goal of universalizing elementary education (UEE). Yet what is it that ails the system and because of which we have been unable to meet this basic constitutional commitment? Figures and official accounts do not, perhaps, reveal the whole story.

The latter part of the chapter raises a number of critical questions on the status of the system based on the various chapters included in the volume.

THE CONTEXT

The review presented in this volume was carried out as part of an international effort coordinated by the United Nations Economic, Social and Cultural Organization (UNESCO) to review the status of basic education in different parts of the world. The exercise focusing on selected quantitative indicators of basic education was to specifically capture the progress made during the last decade of the twentieth century, euphemistically referred to as the EFA decade following the global conference on Education For All held at Jomtien in 1990. In India, apart from compiling data on quantitative indicators, effort was also made to carry out a qualitative review of the situation in a more comprehensive and objective manner with the help of independent reviewers. The chapters included in the volume represent this comprehensive effort.

In delineating the broad contours of the review process, developments in basic education during the EFA decade were kept in the main focus. However, it was felt that in the Indian context, the natural time period for any such review was post the launching of the National Policy on Education (NPE) in 1986. It is not difficult to find the rationale for this decision. In India's not so smooth journey towards the goal of UEE, the NPE stands out as a significant landmark. The NPE had been formulated after conducting a prolonged nationwide debate on the problems and issues confronting the education system in the country.

---

[1] The initial part of this chapter draws extensively from the publication, *EFA 2000 Assessment: India Country Report* (brought out by MHRD and NIEPA, New Delhi) and sets out the perspective of the Government of India on the subject.

Further, along with the formulation of the policy a Programme of Action (POA) was adopted which clearly outlined the strategies and processes to be pursued for achieving UEE. This was followed by a framework of partnership between central and state governments on a massive scale through a number of centrally sponsored schemes. With this as the backdrop, any review of EFA would virtually be a reflection on the implementation of recommendations made by the NPE. Thus, for the present qualitative review, though the 1990s remain the focus, developments in the post-NPE period form the larger canvas.

As is well known, the 1990s saw the primary education scene opening up to external assistance on a fairly large scale. Possibly, as part of the commitments made by the international donor community at the Jomtien Conference, the country saw the emergence of a large multi-state programme for EFA under the banner of the District Primary Education Programme (DPEP). Alongside this, Rajasthan initiated a fairly large programme of EFA under the name of Lok Jumbish (LJ). In the changed scenario, primary education in India truly became a subject of international scrutiny. The EFA projects have been in operation, gradually expanding to cover half the country, for the last 6 to 8 years. These EFA initiatives, coupled with various centrally sponsored schemes, have undoubtedly made the 1990s the most intensive period of primary education development in India. Meanwhile, the literacy scene also got galvanized with mass literacy campaigns (or Total Literacy Campaigns—TLC) stretching across the length and breadth of the country through the National Literacy Mission (NLM). Therefore, the assessment exercise would also throw light on the performance of these initiatives.

Another development in the last decade that forms a part of the backdrop for the review is the Supreme Court judgment which, interpreting the constitutional provisions, declared basic education as a fundamental right of every citizen, requiring the state to make necessary provisions as a basic obligation. Currently, a bill to amend the Constitution is under consideration in Parliament to incorporate education up to 14 years as a fundamental right of every citizen. Simultaneously, at an international level, basic education found a prime place in the development discourse as a component of the Human Development Index (HDI) brought out by the United Nations Development Programme (UNDP). These national and international developments have transformed the status of UEE from merely a public sector activity of the state to that of a legal obligation, societal responsibility, and moral commitment. The extent to which these have been operationalized will be reflected in the review of the situation.

DO WE HAVE ADEQUATE NUMBER OF SCHOOLS?

Providing elementary education for all, with an ever-burgeoning population, has not been an easy task. However, the network of primary schools has expanded significantly. An estimated 95 per cent of the rural population living in 826,000 habitations has access to a primary school within a radius of 1 km and about 85 per cent of the population has an upper-primary school within a radius of 3 km. Though there are nearly 150 million children currently enrolled in primary schools, there were an estimated 35 million children who were not going to school in 1997; the number is likely to have increased to around 40 million by 2000.

There has been substantial expansion of primary and upper-primary schools in the country in the recent decades. The number of primary schools increased nearly three times between 1951 and 1991. The increasing trend has continued during the last decade (see Table 1.1). This has, no doubt, helped spread basic education in some of the remote corners of the country. However, this may not imply that the entire population and habitations in India have been adequately covered/served by basic schooling facilities within reasonable distance, as prescribed for the children of these age groups. In fact, rural habitations not served by primary sections in 1993 stood at 16.64 per cent (see Figure 1.1), which meant that 176,523 habitations had still to be provided access to the facility of primary schooling. Of these unserved habitations, about 40,000, each with a population of 300 or more, need to be provided with primary schools as per existing norms. Thus, the establishment of primary schools in small unserved habitations became a major concern during the 1990s and considerable success could be achieved in this regard in some of the states.

TABLE 1.1
**Number of Primary/Upper-Primary Schools
1990–7**

Year	Primary	Increase	Upper-Primary	Increase
1990	560,935	57,172	151,456	29,079
1991	566,744	5809	155,926	4470
1992	571,248	4504	158,498	2572
1996	598,354	27,106	176,772	18,272
1997	610,763	12,409	185,506	8734

Sources: • Education in India. Ministry of Human Resource Development, Government of India, Department of Education, New Delhi, 1992.
• Selected Education Statistics 1997–8. Ministry of Human Resource Development, Government of India, Department of Education, New Delhi, 1998.

The changing ratio of upper-primary schools to lower-primary also indicates improvement in the availability of

Per cent population served by a primary school

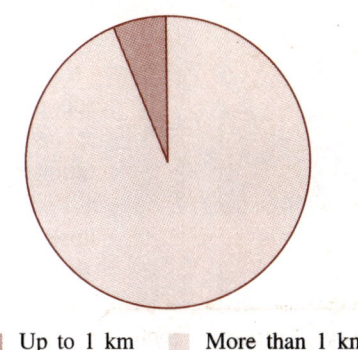

■ Up to 1 km   ■ More than 1 km

Per cent habitations served by a primary school

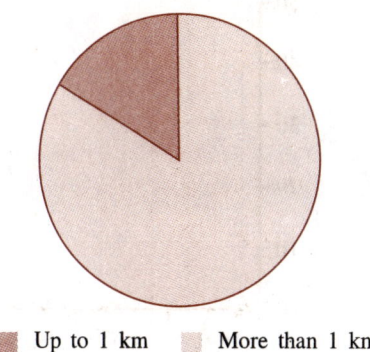

■ Up to 1 km   ■ More than 1 km

Per cent population served by an upper-primary school

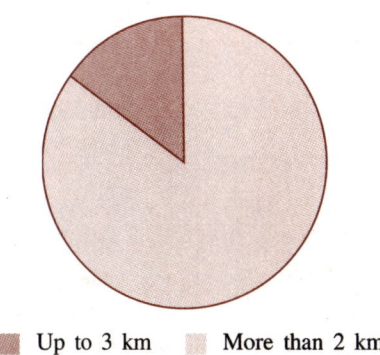

■ Up to 3 km   ■ More than 2 km

Per cent habitations served by an upper-primary school

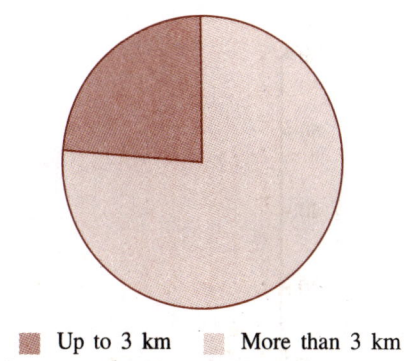

■ Up to 3 km   ■ More than 3 km

FIGURE 1.1: Rural habitations/population in India served by primary and upper-primary schools (1993)
Source: NCERT (1998, vol. 1).

schooling facilities. In 1957, there was only one upper-primary school for every six lower-primary schools, but this situation has gradually improved. In 1987, the ratio was 4:1, which further improved to 3:1 by 1993. This also indirectly indicates an increase in demand for upper-primary education and an improvement in transition rates from lower-primary to upper-primary classes. The goal is to further improve the situation and provide at least one upper-primary school to every two lower-primary schools.

ARE ALL CHILDREN ENROLLED IN SCHOOLS?

According to a recent assessment, the country has achieved near universal enrolment as indicated by the gross enrolment ratios. However, examined against participation of age-specific population, there is still a sizeable gap in the net enrolment ratios. Yet, low enrolment ratio is not a problem in all parts of the country. Several states show a net enrolment ratio of more than 80. Even traditionally underdeveloped states such as Madhya Pradesh show a significantly high net enrolment ratio of 79.2. Yet some states such as Bihar, Jammu and Kashmir, Nagaland, Rajasthan, Uttar Pradesh, and West Bengal seem to face a serious problem demanding immediate attention.

Although female enrolment has shown a significant increase during the last few years, gender disparity does not seem to have reduced. Figures show that there are at least as many girls outside school as there are inside in the age group of 6–14 years. Particular attention in this regard is required in some states such as Bihar, Jammu and Kashmir, Rajasthan, and Uttar Pradesh. In fact, not even 4 out of 10 girls in Uttar Pradesh belonging to the age group of 6–11 years are in primary school.

HOW MANY CHILDREN REALLY COMPLETE THE BASIC EDUCATION CYCLE?

Measures to improve access and enrolment should be coupled with suitable measures to retain children in school long enough for them to complete the full cycle of primary education. Though most states of India have done well in enrolling more and more children in schools, their inability to retain them has been a problem. Considerable efforts have been made during the last decade to ensure that children do not drop out of school after initial enrolment.

There has been a significant decline in dropout rates between 1991 and 1999 (see Figure 1.2). This is

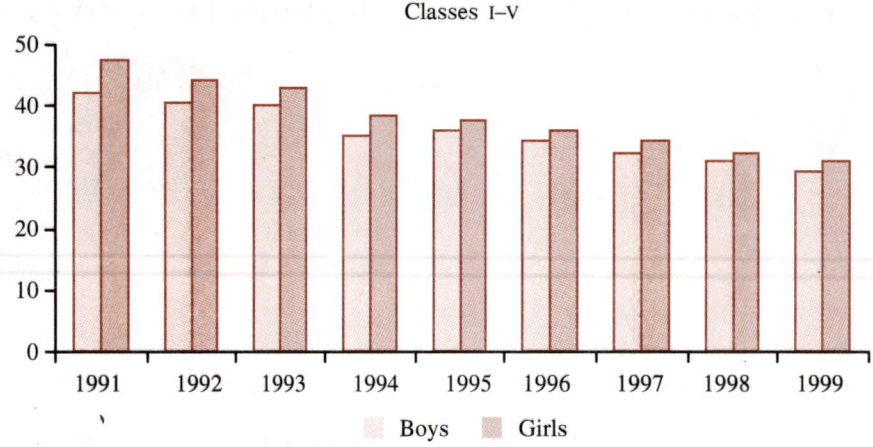

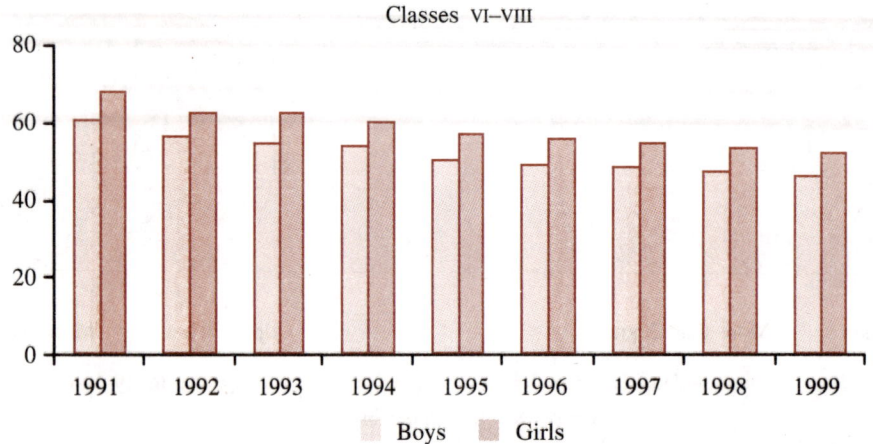

FIGURE 1.2: Dropout Rates at Primary and Upper-Primary Stages

Source: Department of Education (1995–6).

particularly pronounced in the case of girls. Between 1991 and 1995 the dropout rate for girls declined from about 48 per cent to 38 per cent at primary stage (classes I–V). If the same trend continues, as estimates indicate, 7 out of 10 girls who joined primary school in 1999 are likely to remain in the system for at least five years. It can also be observed that the difference between boys and girls is narrowing, though the situation is not quite encouraging with respect to upper-primary stage.

Himachal Pradesh, which has recorded quick progress in recent years, shows a lower dropout rate for girls in comparison to that for boys. This reinforces the well-recognized fact that progress in EFA goals demands special focus on education for girls. The transition rates also point out that girls are at a disadvantage. Though overall dropout figures do not show any significant gender difference, one finds a fairly large difference between boys and girls with regard to the proportion of children moving from lower-primary to upper-primary classes.

Recent figures indicate that more children are staying in the system for longer number of years. However, the situation is not fully satisfactory. The following issues need particular attention:

● As in the case of enrolment, there are wide disparities among different states with regard to the efficiency with which the school system functions. One can identify certain states which have remained chronically difficult.

● The situation as it stands now shows that girls are at a disadvantage. However, a positive feature is that a reduction in the dropout rate has been faster in the case of girls than in the case of boys in recent years. This is possibly due to the special attention paid, over recent years, to education for girls in general, and to all the EFA projects in particular.

● There is an urgent need to improve the transition rates. This problem gets compounded when viewed in conjunction with the problem of unenrolled children and the extent of dropout in lower-primary classes. Here again education for girls needs special attention.

STRATEGIES THAT HAVE BROUGHT MORE CHILDREN TO SCHOOL

Recognizing the problems of regional and gender disparities, the central and state governments have initiated several special measures to ensure no one is deprived of access to basic education. The following points in this regard need specific mention, though it may take longer to witness a measurable impact of these strategies and specific measures:

• Modifying traditional distance norms: The decision to modify traditional distance and population size norms, and the establishment of primary education facilities in smaller habitations have yielded positive results as revealed by the figures for Madhya Pradesh or, to some extent, even Andhra Pradesh where high proportions of people live in small habitations located in hilly and tribal areas. This clearly establishes that non-enrolment is not only due to physical distance but also often due to social and cultural barriers.

• Participatory-school mapping and micro-planning: Another major effort that seems to have succeeded in bringing more children into the fold of education is that of participatory-school mapping and micro-planning (see Box 1.1), as demonstrated by the LJ project in Rajasthan. This is being implemented in many parts of the country under DPEP as well as other EFA projects.

Box 1.1
School Mapping in the LJ Project

The technique of 'school mapping' is Lok Jumbish's special contribution to the task of mobilizing people for education. This begins with LJ workers (or those from a local NGO) building a rapport with members of the community who are interested in improving education standards in the village. These members, also called the *prerak dal* (inspirational group), are given a short training for the task of mapping, which they undertake along with the LJ workers or the NGO. School mapping refers to the exercise of visually depicting every household in the village on a simple map. Small symbols indicate the schooling status of every household member in the 5–14 age group. The whole exercise is an occasion for interacting with the community. When the map is ready, it is possible to see which household needs special help, and to discuss the schooling facilities required in the village. The *prerak dal* and the local community draw up a set of proposals based on mapping data. The proposals usually relate to two issues: the need for new schools and non-formal centres, and the improvement of the existing ones. These proposals are then sent to a block level committee, which is the sanctioning authority.

School mapping allows the ordinary, even non-literate villager to participate in a field survey and make proposals—a tremendous capacity-building exercise. Prompt follow-up of these proposals further builds up the confidence of the community.

Village 'Chausla', Police Station Kaleda, Distt. Kekri, Ajmer

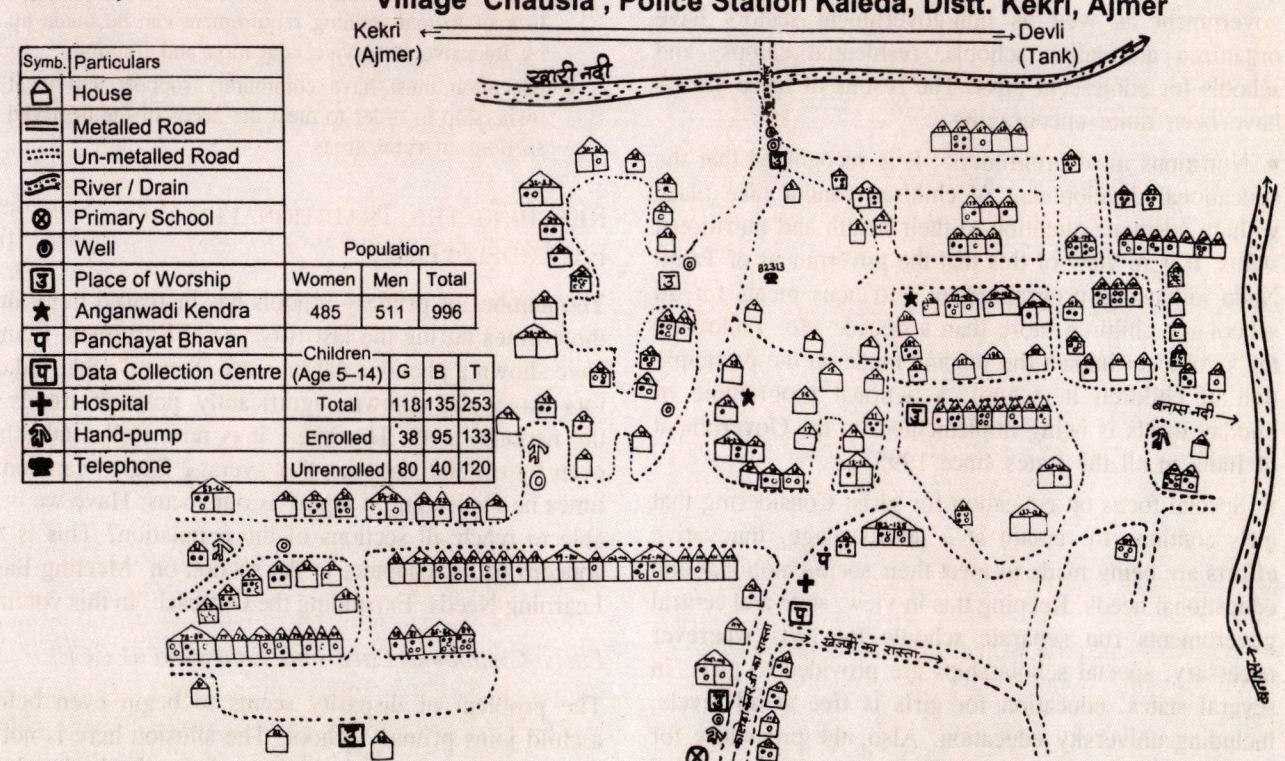

Symb.	Particulars
🏠	House
═	Metalled Road
⋯	Un-metalled Road
〜	River / Drain
⊗	Primary School
◉	Well
[ज]	Place of Worship
★	Anganwadi Kendra
[प]	Panchayat Bhavan
[ध]	Data Collection Centre
✚	Hospital
🚰	Hand-pump
☎	Telephone

Population		
Women	Men	Total
485	511	996

Children (Age 5–14)	G	B	T
Total	118	135	253
Enrolled	38	95	133
Unrenrolled	80	40	120

Source: **PROBE** Team (1999).

• Orchestrating local demand for schooling: The 1990s have witnessed significant efforts in many states to establish local community structures such as village education committees, mother–teacher associations, and local core teams and women's groups. This has helped in mobilizing local demand for schooling and reducing the apparent distance between the community and the school. This has also led to shifting the approach from 'supply-based to demand-based' strategies for providing educational facilities.

• District planning: Another strategy being adopted for increasing enrolment and attendance of children in primary education and reducing inter-regional disparity is that of decentralized planning. Recognizing that there are wide disparities within each state and that state-level planning may not be able to fully respond to local considerations, the DPEP, which covers more than 200 districts, has adopted a district-specific approach to planning primary education.

• Establishing part-time and alternate schools: Children who have yet to enrol for schooling at a primary stage constitute a more difficult group in terms of their socio-economic and cultural background. This is more so for the girl child and the problem is more acute and complex at the upper-primary stage, as clearly indicated by the combined gross enrolment ratios for this stage. These complexities demand more innovative methods for providing primary education through formal and non-formal channels. With this in view, several programmes in the government as well as non-government sectors have organized alternative schools, residential camps, and schools for adolescent girls. The results of these efforts have been quite encouraging.

• Nutritious meal programme: It is recognized that the educational development of children cannot take place without adequate attention to their health and nutritional status. It is in view of this that the government of Tamil Nadu initiated a programme of nutritious meals for all school-age children more than a decade ago. Following the significant impact the scheme made on the participation of children in school, a national programme of midday meals is being implemented by the Government of India in all the states since 1995.

• Special focus on education for girls: Considering that girls continue to remain at a disadvantage, innovative efforts are being made to meet their socio-emotional and educational needs. Keeping this in view, state and central governments run separate schools for girls wherever necessary; special scholarships are provided to girls; in several states, education for girls is free at all levels, including university education. Also, the procedure for recruiting teachers in almost all the states envisages that at least 50 per cent positions are filled by women teachers.

• Tackling the problem of schools in remote habitations: Another problem faced by schools located in small remote habitations is that of the reluctance of teachers to work in such schools. To meet the requirement of such schools a novel experiment called Shiksha Karmi Project has been tried out in Rajasthan (see Box 1.2). Successful during the initial years, the project has expanded to cover a large number of habitations in the state. Since the problem is not unique to Rajasthan, several other states are beginning to adopt this model on a fairly large scale.

BOX 1.2

Shiksha Karmi—The Barefoot Teacher of Rajasthan

To overcome the problem of teacher absenteeism in remote localities, the concept of 'barefoot teachers' was introduced by the Shiksha Karmi Project (SKP) which is being implemented in Rajasthan since 1987 with financial assistance from the Swedish International Development Agency (SIDA). The idea was to substitute the absentee primary school teacher by a 'local educational worker'. The project aims at universalization and qualitative improvement of primary education in remote and socio-economically backward villages in Rajasthan, with primary attention being given to girls. The project works on the assumptions that:

• a 'barefoot teacher' belonging to a local community can work effectively to reach every child in the locality

• if a person is willing to work as a social worker, the lack of formal training requirement can be made up by intensive in-service education and training

• education must have community support and local ownership in order to meet the needs of the deprived sections in rural areas

---

REACHING THE TRADITIONALLY EXCLUDED GROUPS

The number of primary schools has increased more than three times during the last fifty years. Enrolment figures have shown a phenomenal increase. Several other indicators have also shown significantly positive trends at the national level. However, it is now well established even by official statistics that average figures can sometimes be misleading if equity is our focus. Have we been able to reach all sections of the population? This is the concern of the chapters in the section on 'Meeting Basic Learning Needs: Expanding the Outreach' in this volume.

Early Childhood Care and Education (ECCE)

The problem of disparity seems to begin even before a child joins primary school. The allusion here is not to the unequal social and economic home backgrounds of children but to the incomparable institutional arrangement provided for meeting their basic needs at the early childhood stage. Venita Kaul's chapter on 'Early Childhood Care and Education' examines this issue in detail. The chapter questions the probability of the goal of EFA being attained, as expected, if the early years of a child's life, preceding entry to primary school, are left unattended. This is important since, according to official figures, less than one-fifth of the children receive any kind of preschool education in the country. The Integrated Child Development Services (ICDS) is the largest programme that attempts to reach basic development inputs to children prior to the school-entry age of 6 years. However, the early childhood education component of the scheme continues to remain one of its weakest since its focus is more on health and nutritional aspects. The chapter discusses the potential and limitations of this programme to become the main platform for meeting the pre-school education needs of the country.

Educating the Girl Child

Many consider that the problem of UEE in India is essentially a problem of girls' education. Although a positive change has been visible in recent years with regard to the decreasing gender gap in school enrolment, are we doing enough about education for girls? This issue is addressed by Usha Nayar in the chapter 'Education of Girls in India: An Assessment'. The chapter, while sounding positive, highlights the long distance yet to be traversed for achieving the goal of UEE for girls and for addressing the issue of gender equity in education. Based on the official statistics available for 1997–8, it is estimated that around 11 million girls within the age group 6–11 remain unenrolled in school, accounting for nearly 88 per cent of all unenrolled children from the same age group. The corresponding figure for the 11–14 age group is around 16 million girls, constituting 58 per cent of all unenrolled children in the age group. Several factors seem to be impeding the education of girls. Girls are doubly affected by the absence of effective early childhood education programmes as they are invariably burdened with the responsibility of taking care of younger siblings. Distance norms for opening middle schools work against the interest of girls as often they are not allowed to go out of the village for schooling. Further provision of basic infrastructure and women teachers in schools could considerably influence the situation through various EFA projects as indicated by recent efforts.

Schooling for Scheduled Castes (SCs) and Scheduled Tribes (STs)

The constitution of independent India acknowledged centuries of social, economic, and educational deprivation suffered by the SCs and STs, and incorporated specific provisions to protect these communities from discrimination as well as to facilitate their development. Where education is concerned, the Constitution directs the states to 'promote with special care the educational and economic interests' of these groups. What has been the status of basic education among these traditionally excluded groups? This question is addressed in two chapters, one on education of SCs and the other on education of STs. Examining the status of education among SCs, Geetha Nambissan and Mona Sedwal conclude that at the end of the 1990s, the gap between the constitutional commitment of UEE for children up to the age of 14 and the actual participation of Dalit (SC) children in schools remains large and is likely to continue. The paper emphasizes the need to look beyond aggregate concerns and towards adopting a framework of social justice which focuses on qualitative concerns about what educational experiences mean for identity and self-worth as well as for life in the future. The chapter on STs by K. Sujatha expresses similar views on the status of basic education among tribals. Both chapters highlight the positive impact of formal education on the life of these groups.

> One of the critical factors for economic betterment of Dalits in the post-independenence period has been formal education. Education has facilitated occupational diversification and mobility, particularly through reservations, for a small section of the Dalit population who are now in public sector jobs. This in turn has lessened their dependence on the higher castes bringing with it some modicum of social dignity.

Nevertheless, there is disparity within disparity: education of girls lags even among these groups. Treating SCs and STs as two homogeneous entities in framing incentive systems does not seem to have helped overcome intra-group disparities. There is also wide variation among states in the educational development of SCs and STs. Poverty continues to be the major hindrance. While it is important to hold schools accountable for educational backwardness of social groups such as the Dalits, the fact of poverty and its implications for schooling must be underscored. In an economy dominated by a struggle for survival, options are limited. Since education does not provide any visible and immediate benefit and tribals do not see beyond their present state, the participation of tribal children in the process of education also becomes limited. Another reason for low participation is the opportunity cost involved, as the majority of non-enrolled children are either required to work in households or follow family occupations. Even if the economic contribution of children is indirect, they certainly facilitate the participation of parents in economic activity. Several studies have highlighted the language barrier as a factor impeding the progress of formal schooling among tribals. Interestingly, the Constitution of India allows the use of tribal dialect (mother tongue) as the medium of instruction in case the population of a tribe is more than 100,000. But this has not been adopted on the pretext of feasibility and viability of introducing and sustaining such a change. Notwithstanding these persistent problems,

> micro-level evidence shows that interventions and initiatives like the midday meal scheme, creation of self-help women's groups, environment-building programmes under different projects, appointment of local tribal teachers, and developing partnership between school and village communities in school management have helped tribals realize the importance of education and adopt a positive attitude towards the education of their children.

Education of the Urban Deprived

Figures reveal that the population living in urban areas is expanding at a very fast rate, currently accounting for more than one-third of the total population. Even though urban areas present a relatively better education scene, in the midst of affluence and globalization languishes a burgeoning population of impoverished children. Rural–urban disparities in education development are well documented in the traditional literature on regional disparities but not much attention has been paid to the high level of disparities within the urban sector. Surprisingly, successive policy documents on education have made no mention of the problems of education among the urban disadvantaged. Consequently, there is no coherent perspective on tackling the problems of education of such children, and nor is there adequate information on the educational provisions reaching disadvantaged children in urban areas. The chapter by Vandana Chakrabarty gives a broad picture of the status of basic education reaching urban disadvantaged children. Apart from focusing on the appalling status of basic education facilities provided to the underprivileged in urban areas, the chapter highlights the fact that urban centres are host to a number of NGOs and present a variety of innovative efforts in basic education. Recent years have also witnessed a rising interest among corporate houses to support basic education in urban areas.

Reaching the Out-of-School Children

A problem closely related to UEE is that of out-of-school children, many of whom end up as working children or child labourers. According to the 1991 census, there are 11.28 million child workers (6.18 million boys and 5.10 million girls) in the age group 5–14. About 91 per cent of these children are concentrated in rural areas. Of the 11.28 million working children, 9.08 million are classified as main workers and another 2.2 million as marginal workers. Besides, nearly 7 million children are enumerated as involved in household duties; 88 per cent of these are girls. Household duties could mean anything from assisting at the family farm or in any other family occupation, besides household chores like cooking, taking care of children, and fetching water and fuel. Thus, if a comprehensive definition of work is taken, the total incidence of child workers is quite substantial and merits serious attention. It is to meet the educational needs of this massive group of out-of-school children that the Government of India and several state governments have been running non-formal education (NFE) centres for nearly two decades. What has been the outcome of these efforts and to what extent have we been able to arrive at a reasonable strategy for reaching basic education to the out-of-school children? This is the theme of the chapter 'Children: Work and Education' by Sharada Jain. The chapter highlights the controversies surrounding the task of identifying how many children are out of school and how many are working children. Precious effort has been invested in gathering the right data, but every new attempt has yielded a new figure, further muddling the issue. Also, the chapter considers that 'the dichotomization of education from work is unwarranted'. This is closely linked to debates on appropriate strategies for reaching out-of-school children. For some, education is the key to the elimination of child labour. They believe that only by making education universal and compulsory can parents be made to free children from work. These groups also reject the non-formal systems of education and are concerned with upgrading the quality of the formal system. However, there are others who give weight to the economic circumstances that force children's participation in the labour market and argue for an educational system that takes cognizance of these circumstances. They suggest that work is not necessarily opposed to learning, but lay stress on distinguishing between hazardous and non-hazardous forms of work. This position also attaches importance to NFE interventions coexisting with the formal system. Underpinning these different positions are some fundamental debates about the meaning and value of education, about who should take decisions on children's needs, interests, and well-being. Apart from highlighting such core issues, the paper also presents an overview of a number of innovative initiatives in the NGO sector to meet the challenge of reaching basic education to the out-of-school children (see Box 1.3).

Box 1.3

M.Venkatarangaiyya Foundation (MVF) of Andhra Pradesh

The MVF is now well known for its pioneering work in providing basic education to working children. The MVF believes that formal education, especially in the formative years of 6–14 has an intrinsic value that cannot be provided by other means. Therefore, to provide basic education, MVF emphasizes the strengthening of government schools rather than creating alternative avenues through non-formal education (NFE). The approach adopted by the MVF consists of:

- convincing parents and children about the need for basic education through advocacy measures
- developing confidence in children that they too can join their peers and study in regular formal schools
- taking children away from their homes and away from their workplace
- bridging the gap between these children and schoolgoing children in terms of academic abilities through bridging courses/summer camps on a full-time basis

The MVF programme which began with three villages in Andhra Pradesh in 1990 had expanded to 500 villages in 1999, covering ten *mandals* in the Ranga Reddy district and six *mandals* in other districts. More than 80,000 children in 500 villages have benefited from the MVF programme which begins with withdrawing children from work and finally enrolling them in government schools. About eighty-five villages have been made child labour free and in more than 400 villages all children below the age of 11 years are in formal regular schools. As a result of the implementation of the MVF programme, an attitudinal change among community members, parents, employers, and teachers has been perceived, and this is clearly reflected in the community's support for the programme and also in the sacrifices made by individuals to ensure that their children receive education. Also noticed are changes in the perception of the institution of girls' marriage and other social and cultural practices. The programme has emerged not only as a programme of basic education but also an endeavour to bring about social change.

Education of Children with Special Needs

Inclusive education has become a common theme of all discourses on basic education the world over. The 1989 UN Convention on the Rights of the Child to which India is a signatory, states that disabled children have the right to 'achieve participation in the community and their education should lead to the fullest possible social integration and educational development'. Taking a cue from international trends, India has also got into the act and incorporated its intent through a number of policy documents, legislations, and programme strategies. Yet are we doing enough? Do we even know the exact magnitude and nature of the problem? These questions have been addressed in the chapter by Sudesh Mukhopadhyay and M. N. G. Mani. The chapter presents vital information on the theme and attempts to identify the problems and issues involved. In 1993, it was estimated that there were 12.59 million children in the school-going age, and with disabilities, for whom provisions had to be made. The proportion of the disabled is estimated to be around 1.82 to 2 per cent. But the actual participation of children with disabilities in schools does not seem to go beyond 88,000 even with most liberal assessments. It is not that the country has not recognized the problem. For instance, the Rehabilitation Council of India (RCI) Act was adopted in 1992 and the Persons With Disabilities (Equal Opportunities, Protection of Rights and Full Participation) Act was passed on 22 December 1995. With this, necessary legal instruments have been created to deal with the situation. But the progress on the ground seems to be quite inadequate. It is in this context that the authors raise the question, 'Is India ready for accelerated action?'

BUILDING PARTNERSHIPS WITH THE COMMUNITY FOR UEE

With independence from colonial control more than fifty years ago, the government took upon itself the task of providing basic education for all as directed by the Constitution. But how was this to be done? Was it to be pursued purely as a government-controlled phenomenon? Should community members have any role in this? Should the government only be a provider of funds and facility, leaving the management of schools entirely to the people? Who would represent the community in school governance? Though these questions had been examined several times in the past, the 1990s brought them to centre stage again. The chapter by Vinod Raina on 'Decentralization in Education' attempts to address some of these issues, keeping in view the emerging framework of Panchayati Raj for governance of education in many states. Raina argues that exploring the question of decentralization of education is a superficial exercise unelss one delves into its political and developmental linkages. He states that generally three major institutions of social coordination can be distinguished for the purpose. The state and the market are the two key institutions of social coordination. The third, community, is always a residual category in comparison with the state and market and is conceptualized differently, according to the conception of the state and market. One observes that during the last decade, fairly vigorous attention has been paid to the problem of management and control of education, both at the policy and implementation levels. Additionally, there has been greater advocacy for the need to involve communities in the process of school education through decentralization. In particular, there is in evidence a noticeable desire to decentralize primary education and literacy in the country.

Will decentralization necessarily lead to genuine empowerment, if equity concerns are not kept in view? Raina cautions that

> in the state, market, community triad, marketization of education for greater public choice is also a form of decentralization, but it clearly lacks equity. A clear policy articulation is necessary in India that spells out the kind of decentralization the state and civil society ought to promote, keeping in view rampant caste, class, and gender disparities.

Whether privatization is considered a form of decentralization or not, there is enough evidence to show that the number of schools under private management is increasing in an unprecedented manner. Is this a positive development bringing in a greater sense of partnership between the government and private providers of primary education? What has prompted this trend in recent years? Is this trend visible throughout the country? Does it signify a positive move towards rationalizing public and private expenditure on primary education by allowing those who can afford it to source education through payment? Or will it lead to greater inequity and social divide, as some scholars fear? These are some of the questions addressed in the chapter on 'Private Schools and Universal Elementary Education' by Anuradha De and others. Available evidence indicates that private schools have been expanding rapidly in recent years. They now include a large number of primary schools which charge low fees and have also apparently spread to rural areas according to both macro- and micro-level data. Does this indicate that private schooling has come of age, contributing towards the goal of UEE? 'A priori, nothing definite can be said about the influence of private schools on the achievement of UEE.' The situation is too varied among different states to make any generalizations without further state-specific explorations. Data at macro level reveals that it is the massive government school system on which the poor still rely, but here too, the cost of schooling is often too much to bear. In response to the familiar question of 'who goes to private schools?', the authors observe that disaggregation on the basis of caste, region, and gender has demonstrated considerable biases in the clientele of private schools. There are more private schools for boys, for upper castes, and for urban areas than government schools. In other words, attending a private fee-paying school is likely to be a mark of social privilege. Some studies have also reported an exodus from the government school system to private schools. This is largely attributed to two factors: rise in demand for education and fall in quality of government schooling. The growth of private schools, more especially fee-paying ones, is in itself a symptom of rising demand for education, but it is rising demand in the face of falling quality of government schools which appears most important. It is often argued that private schools have the advantage of operational efficiency—lower running costs, and higher achievement. It is on this count that government–private partnership is generally talked about. In this regard, it is felt that though the sharing of responsibility between the two will continue to grow in quantitative terms, on the qualitative plane, it is perhaps difficult to marry the operational advantages of the narrow private sector with the more egalitarian amplitude of the government school system.

It is difficult today to carry on any discourse in education without referring to the emerging partnership between the government and NGOs, particularly in the field of basic education. In fact, NGO coalitions have emerged as major actors even at a global level through their intensive advocacy campaigns and focused field-level action programmes in developing countries. What is the role and contribution of NGOs to the field of basic education in India? This question has been explored by Disha Nawani in her chapter on the subject. The chapter highlights the enormous variety that passes off as the NGO sector in a monolithic fashion. This is even more complicated in the Indian context because of a long historical tradition of voluntary contribution in the field of education as well as the government's own programme of supporting and promoting programmes through NGOs. There is a general perception that NGOs represent the organized front of civil society at large and the local community where they work in particular. While this general perception may not be contested, the relationship between the government and NGOs may not always present a picture of perfect collaboration and synergistic partnership in achieving the goal of UEE. It is with this backdrop in mind that the author examines the nature of NGOs dealing with education in the country, the kind of relationship they share with the government and other organizations, the way they generate funds for running their activities, and the overall contributions they are making to the development of basic education in the country. The chapter also presents interesting insights into the functioning of NGOs through specially conducted case studies of selected NGOS working in the area of basic education. The government in India is itself a major source of funds for NGOs but it is observed that there is a relationship of 'control' and 'mistrust' between the two and not one of 'trust' and 'support'. However, it is difficult to make generalizations about the role of NGOs or their relationship with the government.

> NGOs represent a plurality of efforts whereas the official education structure in India is essentially a uniform mono-lithic structure that finds it difficult to respond to differences which exist among people. It is this heterogeneous nature of Indian society and democratic nature of its polity, which makes the role of NGOs even more significant, for only small, local efforts of this kind, which the community closely identifies with, can make education a personal and enriching experience for everyone.

Considering that the government continues to occupy a major part of the educational space in India and the total NGO sector is still too small in comparison with the massive educational enterprise, it would be unreal-istic to expect that NGOs could significantly contribute to the goal of UEE in quantitative terms. Rather, as the chapter concludes, 'NGOs' role is neither to wipe out illiteracy completely nor to ensure that all children go to school but essentially to play a catalytic role in mobilizing people and providing innovative thrusts in the education system.'

MEETING QUALITY CONCERNS IN ELEMENTARY EDUCATION

The elementary education system has always been dominated by government schools though the country had always provided space for private schooling, even offering grants to private schools. However, government schools were never marked as of especially poor quality in comparison with their private counterparts as is done today with little exception. After the proclamation to establish a mass education system in the country, it took national planners around thirty years to specify distance and population norms for opening new primary schools so that access is not denied to children due to physical distance. But establishing a school meant no more than posting a teacher to work in the school. Thus, the quality of the schools was never a primary concern, even in terms of infrastructure, and the government schools grew in number, often with no school building or classrooms and with no academic support material. It took another 15–20 years to specify, under the Operation Blackboard (OB) project, the minimum requirement for a primary school—at least two classrooms, at least two teachers, basic learning kits, and at least some rudimentary in-service orientation for teachers. It took a few more years

to indicate the essential learning output one would expect from every child at the end of the primary schooling cycle. But this happened at the national level only in the 1990s. Considering that around 9 out of 10 primary schools are financed and managed by the government, what is the current status of infrastructure and other facilities in the schools? Quality, of course, cannot be determined only in terms of the infrastructure provided. Rather, more critical questions are: What is taught at school? How is it taught? How much do children really learn? And how are teachers prepared to carry out their tasks? These are some of the questions examined by a set of four chapters included in the volume.

The Question of Relevant Curriculum and Textbooks

The NPE categorically stated that one of the major weaknesses in the attempts to bring about curricular reform in the past has been the lack of a comprehensive plan to link curricular changes with the processes of teaching, learning, teacher training, and examination reform. What have we done since then, and particularly during the last decade? The chapter 'Texts in Context: Development of Curricula, Textbooks and Teaching–Learning Materials' by Anita Rampal takes a compre-hensive view of the whole gamut of activities in recent years connected with curriculum making and textbook preparation, covering both formal school and non-formal adult education sectors. Quoting from the Yashpal Committee Report, Rampal points out:

> Barring exceptions, our textbooks appear to have been written primarily to convey information or 'facts', rather than to make children think and explore.... The distance between the child's everyday life and the content of the textbook further accentuates the transformation of knowl-edge into a load. Neither the mode of communication, nor the selection of objects depicted, nor the language conveys the centrality of the child in the world constructed by the text.

This lack of relevance to the life of the child seems to be the major problem with the school curriculum in the country. The author acknowledges that several major efforts have taken place in recent years to correct this problem, particularly under the auspices of primary education projects. However, 'curriculum development and textbook preparation must remain an important ongoing and creative activity, which involves most teachers in some way or the other, in order to ensure their motivation in the process of teaching, and their sense of ownership.' It is argued that curriculum and textbook preparation have to be further decentralized if a sense of ownership has to emerge among the teachers. This is a significant point as over a period of time curriculum framing and textbook production in most states have become routine bureaucratic exercises. How involvement of local talent can inject creativity into the exercise was clearly demonstrated, not only by primary education projects, but also by literacy campaigns. In this context, Rampal also calls for a more open, pluralistic perspective of the state by providing adequate space for NGOs and other structures outside the government to present alternate curricular materials. Unfortunately, 'linkages of such agencies have only remained tenuous and have tended to snap at the smallest pressure or jolt.' It is pointed out that 'recognition of local and indigenous knowledge systems, with emphasis on learning in a contextual manner' has generally been outside the purview of curriculum renewal processes. A question that remains unanswered in the midst of these arguments for decentralization is: who will lead such decentralized curriculum framing? Is it realistic to expect that state agencies which possess centralized control over the process and are led mainly by urban middle class interest groups could take such initiatives? It is interesting to note that while government schools catering to relatively poorer sections are under obligation to use state-prescribed textbooks, private schools enjoy much greater freedom in this regard, particularly at the elementary stage. This, of course, does not imply that private schools use more relevant learning material and adopt child-friendly transaction methods. The problem, therefore, is not merely of freedom to choose, but of non-availability of creative learning material in the market to choose from. It is high time that state agencies, instead of treating textbook writing as a state monopoly, promote and overtly support creative initiatives in preparing relevant learning material. Another question related to curriculum and textbooks that is often undermined is the backwash effect of a centralized system of examination, which only tests the memorizing capacity of the students. Will curriculum framing and textbook preparation ever become creative endeavours under the overbearing shadow of such an examination system?

How Well Equipped are Our Schools?

Whatever the curriculum and textbooks prescribed, under what conditions do children learn in primary schools and how much do they learn? These are core concerns of any meaningful discourse on quality. The chapter, 'Learning Conditions and Learner Achievement in Primary Schools' by M. S. Yadav and others examines these concerns. It may be noted that the NCERT periodically brings out All-India Educational Survey Reports on schools in the country which provide benchmarks to assess the status of learning conditions characterizing

primary schools. A few other large-scale studies conducted recently also give an idea of the situation at the macro level. It was mentioned earlier that the OB scheme, launched more than ten years ago, defined the broad parameters determining basic educational facilities in primary schools. How far have these specifications been implemented? Available empirical evidence indicates that the situation is far from satisfactory. Around 5 per cent primary schools do not have any classrooms at all and another 15–20 per cent have only one. If safe drinking water and separate toilet facilities for girls are taken as basic indicators of the quality of infrastructure in schools, the situation is alarming. In about 40 per cent schools, children have no access to safe drinking water, and separate toilet facilities for girls are available in only 15–20 per cent schools. Further, according to a recent national evaluation of the OB scheme, if only 4 of the 15 items—2 classrooms, 2 teachers, basic learning kits, and teacher training orientation for using the learning material—specified under the OB scheme are considered, only 15 per cent of government schools are provided with them.

While enrolment figures have significantly increased, has the number of teachers increased proportionately? The number of teachers has not kept pace with increase in enrolment. In fact, the 1990s saw massive recruitment of teachers in order to fill posts offered under the OB scheme to convert single-teacher schools into at least two-teacher schools. Yet, the number of pupils per teacher increased during the period. Several factors seem to have contributed to this. First, some of the state governments have slowed down the pace of filling vacant teaching posts while using the OB posts which were funded by the Government of India. Second, new schools are opened by state governments without meeting the basic norms. Third, and perhaps the most important factor, is the irrational deployment of teachers. Posting and transfer of teachers seems to depend on the political connections and clout the teacher has. State-level average pupil–teacher ratio does not reveal the real position. Should the practice of appointing teachers to the system and not to particular schools continue at all? The issue is debated repeatedly, but centralized control over the posting and transfer of teachers is so powerful a political tool that no state government seems ready to act. At the same time, there is also a lack of application of the mind to the problems at state level. The question of equipping every school with adequate material and human resources should be determined on the basis of local parameters such as the size and location of the school. For instance, many schools located in small habitations function with not more than 20–5 children on any given day. Such schools need more teaching–learning material—crayons, slates, drawing and writing material, play material for small children, and so on—not additional classrooms, and perhaps, not even additional teachers. Similarly, supplying one set of learning kits to a large school with 4 or 5 teachers and more than 200 children can do very little towards improving the quality of the school. What is the value, under such conditions, of pan-Indian solutions such as the OB scheme?

How Much Do Our Children Learn in State Supported Schools?

The chapter by Yadav and others dealing with this issue highlights the fact that the NPE, and thereafter, the specification of minimum levels of learning (MLLs) at the national level played an important role in bringing the issue of quality to the attention of all concerned. 'One can state that, notwithstanding critical observations on the MLL programme, the initiative played a major role in focusing the attention of planners and policy makers as well as administrators and practitioners all over the country on the issue of learner achievement.' But has it made a sustainable impact on the way teachers teach and children learn? No study has really looked at this issue. Most of the projects implemented, following the publication of the MLLs, appeared to endorse the specifications wholesale and focused on measurement of learning outcomes rather than on making teachers internalize the principle underlying the concept of learning competencies. There have been plenty of discussions and discourses on the MLLs.

Some large-scale external testing has been conducted, mainly as part of the DPEP, to assess the achievement status of children in primary schools. But these surveys as well as some others which can be used to draw some broad observations have very little in common. The tests used for the various surveys also do not conform to any basic common parameters, nor are they standardized norm-referenced tests. Comparing or subjecting the results of these tests to any meta analysis, therefore, seems far-fetched. In fact, some of the findings such as those based on paper–pencil tests given to 7- or 8-year-old children studying in class II can have no technical validity. It should be remembered that these are not general ability tests; they are tests of school-based learning. Scholastic testing is meaningful only in the context of what has been taught and on the assumption that children have learnt what has been taught. But how valid are these assumptions?

With respect to learner achievement levels, though the chapter by Yadav and others presents a somewhat positive picture based on some large-scale studies, closer scrutiny reveals that the situation is quite diasappointing.

First of all, the tests used for measuring learner achievement are too rudimentary and do not comprehensively represent the learning inputs provided. A 40 per cent or 60 per cent mark on such a test can hardly be taken as an effective indicator of mastery of basic knowledge and skills. Second, such large-scale external testing has drawn attention away from the importance of strengthening internal evaluation by teachers on a regular basis. Can quality improvement be achieved by merely conducting external testing programmes? Evidence from experience does not seem to support such an assumption. In fact, in the entire effort to improve quality through EFA projects, the school and its machinery seems to be receiving little attention. The focus has mainly been on the conduct of centralized teacher training at block and district levels. The core question that remains unaddressed is: can quality of education improve if schools do not improve significantly? Having conducted a number of national- and state-level testing exercises during the last decade, do we know what and how much our children in government schools are learning? The answer is, we know very little; not more than was known earlier. The obvious reason is that we know very little of what is taught in school and how it is taught. Is external testing not the wrong end to begin improving the quality of education?

How are Our Teachers Prepared for their Professional Work?

The Education Commission (1964–6) wrote: 'Destiny of our nation is being shaped in our classrooms.' It is obviously teachers who are the key players in this process of shaping the nation's destiny. With the expansion of the school system, gone are the days when teaching was considered a 'calling' pursued by a select few. It has become a job opportunity like other. This has made teacher education a very important phenomenon. How is this important activity being carried out in the country? Expansion of the system has also brought people from a variety of socio-economic backgrounds into the teaching profession. In fact, there has been considerable dismay over the falling status of teachers in the public eye over many years. In this context, how would one describe the current status of elementary school teachers? These vital issues related to teachers and teacher education have been dealt with in two chapters included in the Report.

With respect to teacher education, the 1990s saw elaborate action, both in terms of institutions of teacher training and of regulatory mechanisms for quality improvement. The scale of investment made in creating or strengthening teacher education institutions in the form of IASEs, CTEs, DIETs, BRCs, and CRCs was unprecedented. The establishment of the National College of Teacher Education gave a new dimension to the teacher education endeavour in the country. It is difficult to judge the full impact of these developments on the teacher education scene in the country, though initial euphoria seems to be gradually giving way to studied scepticism, if not to a sense of despair in some aspects, while enthusiasm still continues in certain aspects, particularly related to in-service training.

To what extent have all these developments changed the public image and quality of teacher education? Realization is dawning that mere establishment of a regulatory framework and supply of infrastructure cannot make a real difference. The core issue is: what happens in teacher education institutions? What value do they add to educational development in the country? The chapter on teacher education by C. Seshadri points out that 'Initial training suffers from isolation, a low profile and poor visibility.' Several factors seem to contribute to this as highlighted in the chapter. One important issue is that of our failure to redirect the thrust of teacher education to the overarching concern of UEE. Considering the context in which our elementary education system functions, it is essential to bring in initial teacher education as a deliberate strategy to deal with the unfinished UEE agenda. A second factor debilitating elementary teacher education is its being a non-degree programme administered by a government department. The B.El.Ed. programme of Delhi University has presented a unique model for moving in this direction. A yet more important issue relates to the nature of the teacher training curriculum itself. There is a

need to contextualize the curriculum and integrate theoretical learning with practical experience instead of bifurcating the two. Theoretical insights deriving from a psychological and socio-cultural study of how children learn and grow, for example, should feed into the development of pedagogical practices or professional competencies through solid field training. Teacher trainees should be given every opportunity to experience real schools, real classrooms, 'real' children, and also try alternate ways of using pedagogical skills to develop their professional capability. The knowledge base of pedagogy is built through such reflective practice.

But do our teacher training programmes provide adequate space for such reflective thinking? Seshadri laments,

Primary teacher education reform actions carried out so far have been in the form of grand, pan-Indian programmes and schemes emanating from the centre. It is disquieting that a climate has not been created for the emergence of context-specific initiatives at state and sub-state levels towards the reform of teacher training structures and processes.

Examining the issue of the status of elementary school teachers, A. S. Seetharamu identifies a variety of factors that have contributed to the changing social profile and status of teachers in independent India. Many of these factors relate to the working conditions characterizing the education system in general and schools in particular. He also identifies other related factors such as autonomy, professionalism, and ownership which influence the status of teachers. Interestingly, except for teachers in some selected states, all others possess prescribed professional training qualifications. Has this helped raise the status of the teaching profession as a whole? What really are the core issues? One of the core factors seems to be the earning levels of teachers.

In many parts of the country, teachers receive lower salaries than upper division clerks, revenue inspectors, trained nurses, and pharmacists.... Variation among the states is glaring.... In 75 per cent cases teachers retire at the same position at which they had joined but with a higher salary as commensurate with their length of service in the profession.

Seetharamu points to another phenomenon which seems to seriously affect the professional status of teachers.

Even when qualified and trained teachers are available, the state government may not have the resources or compulsion to spend on an adequate number of teachers for primary education. For all these reasons, several state/UT governments have resorted to employing unemployed educated youth as teachers at the elementary level.... They are given various titles: 'para-teachers', 'shiksha karmis', 'contract teachers', and 'vidya upasaks'. Information about these teachers is very limited. They are paid consolidated salaries which vary between one-tenth and one-fifth of the salary of a regular elementary school teacher, across different regions of India.

This is paradoxical because the NCTE, which bears statutory responsibility to ensure that fully qualified people are engaged as teachers in schools, has prepared detailed norms for teacher qualification and recruitment. Thus, indirectly, the level of investment by the state government in elementary education becomes an important determinant of teacher status.

Does society really bother about these developments and the consequent deterioration in the status of teachers?

The value of a person or his activity/occupation/profession is unconsciously measured by society on the basis of its perception of the contribution the person makes to the furtherance of the society's goals. What is the contribution that elementary teachers make to the society?

Are teachers conscious of the need to prove their value to the community in which they function? This becomes meaningful only if an effective system of public account-ability operates. Unfortunately, teachers are not chosen by the community to serve them, and therefore, they do not seem to feel a sense of accountability towards the community. Moreover, teachers are appointed by the government. Will we ever get out of this trap? And why does the teaching profession not establish and enforce its own framework of accountability? There is no doubt that it is professional standards of work that, in the final analysis, determine the value the community attaches to the profession and thereby contribute to the elevation of the social status of teachers. No amount of political bargaining by itself is likely to change the public image of the profession.

MANAGING THE LITERACY JUGGERNAUT

Apparently, increase in literacy rates during the 1990s has been significantly higher than in the previous decades. As per the 2001 census, the literacy rate for India (7+ age group) stands at 65.38 per cent. Though gender disparity remains pronounced, for the first time it shows a converging trend. The male–female literacy gap, which was to the tune of 25 per cent in 1991, has been reduced to around 20 per cent in 2001. As Figure 1.3 shows, the 1990s have also demonstrated a converg-ing trend between rural and urban literacy rates.

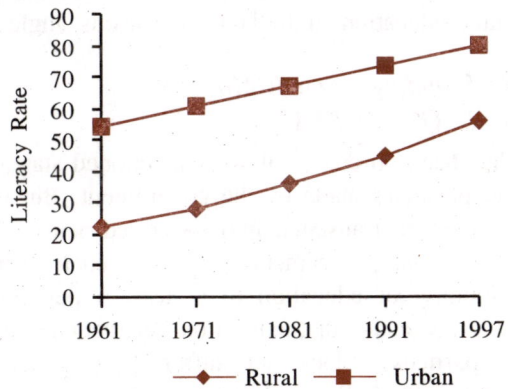

FIGURE 1.3: Rural–Urban Literacy Rates (%)

However, these figures may not tell the whole story of what we have been doing with the problem of adult illiteracy in the country. The adult education enterprise has grown into a nationwide phenomenon, particularly with the launching of the NLM in the late 1980s. But what has been the contribution of the NLM in moving towards the goal of basic EFA? This has been a constant refrain from many quarters.

There is no doubt that the mass literacy campaigns of the NLM changed the common perception of adult education programmes and established that if done in the right manner they can influence the scene significantly.

But what has been the ground reality? What has happened beyond literacy campaigns? Many scholars consider that the value of the literacy campaigns lies not so much in imparting reading and writing skills to adult illiterates but in their capacity to influence the quality of life of the people. There are four chapters that deal with these themes: 'Indian Engagement with Adult Education and Literacy', 'Literacy Campaigns and Social Mobiliza-tion', 'Education and the Status of Women', and 'Chang-ing Concepts and Shifting Goals: Post-literacy and Continuing Education in India'. Together, the chapters provide a retrospective overview of the concepts in-volved, a review of the progress made, and also take a critical look at the processes adopted.

Examining the evolving phenomenon of mass literacy campaigns during the last decade, Mathew, in his chap-ter, 'Indian Engagement with Adult Education and Lit-eracy', highlights the failure of the NLM to make a significant dent in the life of the people in the tradition-ally underdeveloped states of the Hindi belt. This is in spite of the fact that the Arun Ghosh Committee which carried out a mid-course assessment of the programme in 1994, called for revamping the strategy and giving up the undue emphasis on declaring districts as totally literate, besides revamping it to also deal with the apparently intransigent situation in the Hindi belt. After all, this is not confined only to the literacy programme. Studies have also revealed that the majority of out-of-school children are concentrated in a few states of northern India. Can we really aspire to achieve improve-ment in the literacy status of these states without viewing the problems of adult education and primary schooling in an integrated perspective? Has any effort been made to evolve such a combined programmatic perspective at the national level? The programme framework and man-agement structure for implementation indicate the con-trary. There is very little evidence either in the national programme or in its implementation at the local level that such ideas are even reflected upon. For instance, the DPEP makes no reference in any of its documents to programmes for dealing with adult illiteracy, as though the educational status of parents of the children in schools is irrelevant to the progress of primary education. The NLM programmes also do not make any effort to interface with formal schooling.

Two factors have been perceived as central to the idea of literacy campaigns: social mobilization and women's empowerment. The process of social mobilization is not seen merely as an instrument of environment build-ing, but also as the driving force throughout the campaign process. This is the theme of the paper by Anita Dighe who also expresses disappointment that the process could not make any headway in the northern states, except for some sporadic short-term efforts. The chapter also presents several success stories in varying contexts which led to collective action in areas of wider social concern such as the anti-arrack agitation in Nellore. The cases of successful mobilization bring into the forefront two important features, namely the overwhelming spirit of voluntarism at field level and the critical role played by women in successful campaigns. It is well recognized that education of women holds a key place in influencing the spread of basic education. In fact, NPE (1986) pointed out that the problem of girls' education cannot be dealt with in isolation from the broader questions of women's status. This also led to the launch of special programmes addressing the issue of women's empowerment such as Mahila Samakhya. If the national leadership views improvement in the status of women as so critical for educational development, what has really happened during the last 10–15 years? Vimala Ramachandran presents a comprehensive review of this important area. The NPE (1986) asserted,

> Education will be used as an agent of basic change in the status of women. In order to neutralize the accumulated distortions of the past, there will be a well-conceived edge in favour of women. The National Education System will play a positive, interventionist role in the empowerment of women.... The removal of women's illiteracy and obstacles inhibiting their access to, and retention in elementary education will receive overriding priority, through provision of special support services, setting of time targets, and effective monitoring.

To what extent this rhetoric has been made a reality needs to be carefully examined.

The NLM has always claimed that the TLC is not an end in itself. It is only the beginning of an effort to improve the quality of life of the people by opening up a new vista of opportunities. The programmes of post literacy (PL) and continuing education (CE) are supposed to meet this goal. What does evidence from the field indicate in this regard? C. J. Daswani, in his critical chapter on the policies of the government, castigates the national leadership for its lack of focus and uncertain approach in dealing with the subject. In line with successful trends elsewhere in the world, the NLM also defined literacy programmes as looking beyond the acquisition of reading and writing skills, linking them effectively with economic and social dimensions. Some of the documents even went on to set lofty goals of empowering the people for self-determination in directing their own as well as the life of the community. Yet, when it came to actual programming, the NLM placed all activities beyond imparting literacy and numeracy skills on the backburner, defining the strategy in a linear fashion as consisting of TLCs, followed by post literacy

campaigns (PLC), and CE programmes in that order. In many districts years passed before any semblance of a post literacy programme was in place, allowing the neo-literates to lapse into illiteracy; and CE which is supposed to explicitly focus on the social and economic life of the people remains almost a non-starter till today in many parts of the country. Do we really have a long-term perspective on the course of action to be initiated in the field of literacy and CE? What place will the community have in such a perspective? How does that link with concerns for poverty alleviation and improvement in quality of life of the people? These questions have remained unaddressed.

Financing Elementary Education

The common reason given for the country's inability to provide EFA is that the country is poor and the government does not have any money to spend on elementary education. This is a dangerous alibi if it is read along with the fact that those who get left out of the purview of education are only poor people. Does it imply that 'we are poor and therefore we cannot educate our poor'? No egalitarian democratic society can take shelter under such a plea. It is essential that we face the question more squarely: 'Are we spending enough money to provide quality education for all?' The chapter by J. B. G. Tilak presents an analysis of the pattern of financing of elementary education in India from various angles.

Are We Spending Enough Money to Provide Quality EFA?

There has been no dearth of well-intentioned statements and bold promises made by the government. But intentions have to be translated into concerted action. Consecutive national governments have pledged to increase public funding of education to at least 6 per cent of national income, so that education—elementary education in particular—does not suffer from paucity of financial resources. But in 1990–1, only 4.9 per cent of GDP was invested in education in India. And

> ever since, it has been rather consistently declining. It should be noted that it would be a stupendous task to reach a level of 6 per cent of GNP by the end of the Ninth Five Year Plan, as promised by the government, from the current level of 3.6 per cent. Among the countries of the world on which such data are available, India ranked 115th with respect to this indicator of national efforts on education, and amongst countries with a population of 100 million or more, India figures at the bottom, except Bangladesh. The need to raise this proportion considerably cannot be emphasized enough. Almost all—from laymen to researchers—plead for the same, though there are no detailed estimates on what should be the desirable and feasible proportion of GNP. Further, Tilak points out that while UEE has been becoming an

increasingly tougher task, causing repeated postponement of the goal, the relative priority given to elementary education in the total educational expenditures has gradually declined over the successive Five Year Plans. Not only has the relative importance given to education in Plan expenditure gradually declined until the Sixth Five Year Plan, but also the relative share of education in any Five Year Plan, including the Seventh and the Eighth Five Year Plans, has been the lowest, despite the hymns sung in praise of education in every Plan document.

Is Expansion of Private Sector Schooling the Solution?

How well founded is the impression created that the country is short of resources to achieve the goal of UEE? In response to this Tilak points out, 'Finding resources to finance UEE is an urgent task as well as, contrary to popular fears, an entirely achievable task.' This does not imply that funds are readily available and our leadership is not forthcoming with them. In this context another popular notion being discussed in recent years is the question of mobilizing private investment in elementary education. This idea seems to have emerged due to the apparent increase in private schools in recent years. However, closer examination of the ground reality shows that

> it would be unrealistic to assume that the private sector in education would provide any financial relief to the government.... The unaided primary schools do provide some financial relief, but at huge social and economic cost. The adverse effects include accentuating dualism, elitism, and class inequalities.... At the same time, its relative size cannot also increase significantly, as the benefits attached to private schooling are mostly due to scarcity of places in private schools, and the benefits get reduced with expansion of the private sector. It has also been found that the private sector has already reached 'optimum' levels in India, the 'optimum' levels being defined in terms of the share of private sector in developed countries like the US.

Yet if one accepts that the share of private schools is expanding, even if it is a short-term phenomenon, how are we responding to it in readjusting the government-sponsored sector? As argued in another chapter included in the volume, if government-sponsored institutions fail to respond to quality concerns, how should the people react? In fact, evidence shows that in the face of low quality of government schools, many are squeezing their family budgets to pay for private education of their children.

International Aid and UEE

The 1990s saw the opening of the primary education scene to external assistance on a fairly large scale. 'While there are no detailed and comprehensive estimates of trends in external aid for education, according to the available data, external assistance accounts for about Rs 10,000 million (in the 2000–1 Union Budget).' Did we need to mobilize external funding for UEE which is a constitutional commitment? To what extent will this ease the problem of resources for primary education? Opinions seem to differ in this regard. But Tilak considers that the decision to bring in international money to support primary education in the country is not a desirable one. In the last couple of years, allocations to elementary education have been increased. But a substantial part of the increase in the outlay for elementary education is accounted for by external aid, leading many to warn that the growth in public expenditure on elementary education is largely 'borrowed growth'.

The debate on private sector investment in primary education and the appropriateness of depending on external funding will not only continue but even intensify in the years to come. There is no evidence to believe that external assistance including borrowing from the World Bank for education has disappeared from the scene after short-term involvement in any country and there is no reason to believe that the Indian case will be any different. In fact, the situation may become even more complex with the action shifting from indirect national-level involvement to more direct involvement of international agencies with several states. Will this not further accentuate regional disparities which are already a serious problem? There is no doubt that these and other debates on elementary education during the 1990s have brought more pressure on the government 'to accord a high priority to UEE. At the same time, it is now being realized that the government's capability in funding education has reached saturation point.' Perhaps, the capability of the government has to be seen not only in terms of availability of resources but also in terms of the capacity to raise resources from the community, to attract contributions for educational development from charitable sources, and most importantly, to efficiently utilize the funds. It is paradoxical that questions of inadequacy of resources are continuously discussed while official records indicate that allocations from both domestic and external sources are not fully utilized year after year. This raises the question: Even if the entire Rs 136.9 thousand crore, as estimated by the Expert Group, is made available, will the government implementation machinery be able to utilize all that money and bring dramatic improvement in the system? If the government machinery cannot, who will make it happen?

RECOUNTING SOME SUCCESS STORIES: ARE WE LEARNING FROM EXPERIENCE?

School education was originally included in the 'State List' in the Indian Constitution, making it the responsibility of state governments to provide UEE. Under that arrangement, the national government did not have any direct role to play in developing the school education sector as a whole, and primary education in particular. At the policy level the situation changed with the constitutional amendment made in the mid-1970s, placing school education in the 'Concurrent List'. Thus, UEE became a shared responsibility of the national and state governments. Recognizing its increased and direct responsibility, the national government has been investing substantially, particularly following the NPE adopted in 1986, in the development of elementary education to correct existing imbalances.

It is, however, fully recognized that sustainable change and development in basic education are highly conditioned by state-specific contexts. Mere funds and schemes from the Centre will not guarantee the achievement of the UEE goal. It is highly dependent on the traditions and values of the local people; commitment and enthusiasm of state-level educational leadership; and capacity to adopt innovative approaches. Viewed from such a perspective, authentic accounts of UEE achievement would demand understanding the processes, problems, and prospects of achieving UEE in every state independently.

It has to be acknowledged that even in the midst of a huge number of illiterate adults and out-of-school children, there are states that have marked remarkable progress in innovating in the system and moving towards the goal of UEE. These state-level success stories clearly demonstrate the possibilities of moving forward at an increased pace by adopting the right policies and implementation practices. It is with this in view that the volume presents brief accounts of in-depth analysis of the situation carried out in four selected states, namely Himachal Pradesh, Mizoram, Rajasthan, and Tamil Nadu. From the UEE process and achievement point of view, the four states get self-selected, though several other states could also have been included. The success of Himachal Pradesh came to light with the PROBE survey (1999) which pointed out how the state has forged ahead of some of its neighbours with whom it had shared disappointing statistics of educational development till recently. The chapter on Himachal Pradesh which is aptly entitled: 'Primary Education in Himachal Pradesh: Examining a Success Story', captures the factors contributing to the relatively quick progress made by the state. The chapter on Mizoram: 'From a Script-less to a Literate Society: The Story of Mizoram's Uphill Journey' brings out the unique role played by local youth and women organizations within the background of pioneering work done by religious organizations. The progress of Mizoram is truly remarkable, as the hilly state inhabited by several tribal communities did not even have a script of its own till just about 100 years ago. But today it occupies the top rank in terms of literacy rate. The Tamil Nadu case 'Progress Towards Education for All: The Case of Tamil Nadu', presents a success story of a different kind. The overt social policies and programmes of the state, including the famous Nutritious Noon Meal Scheme, are said to have made a significant impact on school enrolment in the 1980s. Subsequently, with its apparent success in controlling population growth, the state has got the opportunity to pursue quality concerns of EFA in an effective manner. Rajasthan cannot stake claim to join the company of the other three states just mentioned, based on quantitative progress in EFA. In the league table of states of India, Rajasthan continues to occupy a very low rank. The chapter on Rajasthan, however, takes a look at exemplar practices adopted in two major programmes contributing to EFA goals, namely Shiksha Karmi and Lok Jumbish.

The findings of these case studies conclusively demonstrate that there are plenty of learning opportunities within the country. But are other states, which have remained chronically backward in educational development indicators looking for such learning opportunities? Is the national government making adequate effort to facilitate such inter-state learning processes?

POSTSCRIPT

Most authors reviewing different facets of elementary education in this volume acknowledge the NPE-1986 as a major landmark. It has to be recognized that in the aftermath of the NPE, particularly in the 1990s, there was very intensive activity in the field of literacy and elementary education, unprecedented in post independent Indian history. Questions of adult literacy and elementary education entered public discourse as never before. It is therefore natural to pose the question: 'Are we nearer to the goal of UEE today than before?' Theoretically, the answer is 'yes', and that the distance has certainly reduced. However, the time required to reach the target of UEE is relative to population growth on the one hand and the efforts made by the country on the other. Leaving theory apart, when could one expect to reach the goal of providing EFA as committed in the Constitution? This takes us towards the exercise of target setting and follow-up which has a long history. The story in fact is one of shifting targets and broken promises.

The first effort to indicate how long it would take for India to ensure that all children receive primary education goes back to little before Independence. The Sargeant Commission suggested a forty-year period for achieving the goal. But soon after that, when the

Constitution makers began discussing the issue, it was felt that the country could not wait forty years to reach the goal of UEE. After considerable deliberation, Article 45 was inserted, promising that the state shall provide free and compulsory education for all children upto the age of 14 within a period of ten years. But follow-up action essentially entailed the establishment of more schools. The promise did not materialize. National leadership deliberated again on the issue towards the end of the 1950s and, with much anguish at failure, reiterated the commitment. The follow-up entailed not only opening new schools but also providing incentives to children in order that they did not drop out.

The next exercise was undertaken as part of the Education Commission 1964–6, which realized the complexity of the task with population pressure moving the target farther, demanding increased effort. As though acknowledging the unrealistic nature of the target date specified in the Constitution, and the more reasonable nature of the Sargeant Committee recommendation, the Commission spelt out a period of twenty years, implying 1985 as the date by which the target of UEE could be reached. As a follow-up measure, the Commission recommended expension of the delivery framework and adoption of non-formal education methods including part-time schools for the purpose. Though more primary schools were opened, not much was done to follow-up on other recommendations of the Commission.

The constitutional amendment made in 1976 placing school education in the Concurrent List brought the central government more directly into the picture. As though pricked by conscience, and in view of the approaching deadline of 1985, a major exercise was initiated across the country in 1978 consisting of statewise assessment of the situation and preparing a ten-year perspective plan for each state to reach the goal of UEE. The exercise brought out the unevenness of progress made across the country, recognizing regional (inter-state) disparity as the central feature of the problem. Based on the exercise, nine states were identified as educationally backward states and were chosen for special dispensation from the central government. A massive programme of NFE was also launched. The national government also launched the National Adult Education Programme in 1978. How political uncertainty and change of government influenced the course of action as India entered the 1980s is well documented.

The next major milestone was the NPE 1986 which made a very candid analysis of the situation in the pre-policy publication, 'Challenges of Education'. But surprisingly, having analysed the ground reality, the NPE came out with perhaps the most absurd target dates for achieving the goal. This also marked the beginning of openly splitting the target into two parts. The target year for achieving universal primary education (age group 6–11 corresponding to classes I–V) was fixed as 1990 and 1995 for UEE (age group 6–14 corresponding to classes I–VIII). What made the leadership set such unrealistic targets? Was it political compulsion or a general sense of non-seriousness? Had we crossed the 'barrier of conscience' so that breaking the promise did not bother us any more? Was it because by then the dual track system of government schools for the poor and private ones for the not-so-poor had got well entrenched and there was no direct personal stake for the elite leadership in the government system? Or had the leadership realized, learning from past experience in other sectors, that breaking promises need not have any political or administrative repercussions?

The World Conference on Education at Jomtien called for achieving the goal of 'EFA' by the year 2000. India became a signatory to the Declaration signed by more than 150 countries and supported by all leading international agencies. With the 1990s came a new enthusiasm propelled partly by the literacy campaigns and predominantly by the internationally funded projects. It also brought in a heightened technical discourse. Discussions on decentralization, empowering the *panchayat*, district planning, capacity building, fundamental right to education, and so on took centre stage. The promise of universal primary education by 1990 and UEE by 1995 was altogether forgotten. There was not even an internal review of the progress made vis-à-vis the targets set by the NPE. Questioning the unreasonableness of the targets was considered unwarranted in official circles. The country was gripped by the euphoria of implementing internationally funded projects. The strategies adopted and the priorities followed at national level appeared quite strange. The review prior to the NPE had highlighted the problems of inter-state disparities and the educational backwardness of SCs, STs, and other marginalized sections, as the main hindrances in achieving the goal of UEE. Official statistics clearly showed that a few selected states accounted for more than 75 per cent of the out-of-school children in the country. Yet the planners made an about-turn and decided to begin their campaign from states like Kerala and Tamil Nadu which could never have been the candidates for direct intervention by the central government if equity was the primary goal. In fact, even now current statistics tell the same story—the problem of UEE in the country is mainly that of a few selected states and of the marginalized sections.

Though domestic discussion on broken promises and setting new targets had died down, the Dakar Global Conference on Education in April 2000 brought back to memory the promise made at the international forum in Jomtien. A review of the progress had to be made. It was clear that the country was nowhere near the target of UEE. The assessment highlighted the same old problems—regional and gender disparities, continued low participation of marginalized sections, and poor quality of education provided. But there were positive signals from the field in the form of average statistics. The EFA 2000 Assessment report could refer to such positive features as accelerated growth of literacy rates, the male–female literacy gap showing a convergent trend (though the gap was still large), and participation of girls in schooling showing significant increase. Of course, no regrets were expressed for unkept promises.

The new millennium begins with new promises. The revised framework of the NLM promises to reach a literacy target of 75 per cent by the year 2007. The Sarva Shiksha Abhiyan which is the flagship programme of the national government promises to achieve the goal of universal primary education by 2005 and the goal of UEE by 2010 (five years ahead of the international commitment made at Dakar). This would mean that all children (in all states!) would complete at least five years of schooling (or its equivalent through non-formal means) by the year 2005. All of them would transit to upper-primary schools and complete at least another three years of schooling by 2010. Are these targets reasonable? Can they be achieved without changing the strategy of intervention? Is it not necessary to focus on equity concerns and build state-specific strategies for overcoming regional disparities and meeting the educational needs of the marginalized?

REFERENCES

Department of Education (1992). *Education in India*. Ministry of Human Resource Development, Government of India, New Delhi.

———— (1996). *Selected Educational Statistics*. Ministry of Human Resource Development, Government of India, New Delhi.

———— (1998). *Selected Educational Statistics 1997–98*. Ministry of Human Resource Development, Government of India, New Delhi.

Ministry of Human Resource Development and National Institute of Educational Planning and Administration (2000). *Education for All: India*, New Delhi.

National Council of Educational Research and Training (1998). *Sixth All-India Educational Survey, Volume 1—Educational Facilities in Rural and Urban Areas*. New Delhi.

PROBE (1999). *Public Report On Basic Education in India*. The PROBE team in Association with Centre for Development Economics. Oxford University Press, New Delhi.

I

Meeting Basic Learning Needs
Expanding the Outreach

2 Early Childhood Care and Education

Venita Kaul

This chapter deals with the initiatives needed at pre-primary level if the goal of Education for All (EFA) is in sincerity to be attained. It begins with a discussion of the developmental prerequisites needed by a child for success in school and the corresponding status of children in India. It goes on to explore the crucial role that Early Childhood Care and Education (ECCE) can play with respect to these concerns and discusses policies and programmes that have, over the years, addressed this issue in the country. The chapter also examines the impact of existing ECCE programmes and concludes by raising issues that demand urgent attention.

REACHING THE CHILD IN TIME: IS SIX YEARS TOO LATE?

As one follows up on the progress in the last decade, the goal of universalizing elementary education (UEE) still seems very distant. While gross enrolment rates have, over the years, increased significantly, retention and completion rates are still a cause for concern. Even among those who survive the first five years in school, achievement levels are deplorably low. The National Sample Survey Organization (NSSO) (52nd round) data report that almost 47 per cent of the children who drop out of school cite inability to cope academically and lack of interest in studies as the predominant reasons.

Why are such a large number of children not able to succeed in schooling? While the reasons are often sought in school factors related to facilities and teaching–learning approaches, factors intrinsic to the child himself/herself are rarely considered. Among the various child-specific social and personal variables that influence success at school, a significant variable is the psycho-social and physical readiness of the child to negotiate the demands of primary education. This refers to both formation of personal habits of punctuality, regularity, concentration, etc. as also to the child's active learning capacity, defined as 'a child's propensity and ability to interact with and take optimal advantage of the full complement of resources offered by any formal or informal learning environment' (see Levinger 1994).

The child's status vis-à-vis both habit formation and active learning capacity, on entry into primary school, is influenced to a large extent by what the child actually brings with him/her to school in terms not only of pre-literacy skills, but also nutritional/health status, socio-economic background, extent of parental stimulation, and overall home environment. It is therefore crucial to pay heed to the years of a child's life preceding his/her entry into school which tend to determine the quality and extent of response to school inputs.

The first five years of life have always been considered very significant for habit formation. In terms of cognitive capacity too, a great deal of new evidence has been emerging from the field of neuroscience. Some of this evidence suggests that the period from conception to six years is very significant for brain development. These years provide the base for development of competence and coping skills, which affect learning, behaviour, and health throughout life. According to this research, there are some critical periods in the course of brain development, particularly in the development of binocular vision, emotional control, habitual ways of responding, language and literacy, symbols and relative quality, all of which can impact school learning and achievement (see Mustard 1999). During these critical periods a young child must receive the required stimulation from his/her environment, which would help to establish the neural pathways for the optimal development of these faculties.

Many of these critical periods of development are over or start waning by the time the child enters school, i.e. by six years of age. Once the critical periods have passed, while it may be possible to develop the brain's capacity to compensate,[1] it is difficult to again achieve its full potential.

In addition to the psycho-social stimulation, the nutritional and health status of children also impacts their active learning capacity. For example, capacities for processing, structuring, and classifying information; the ability to ask and answer appropriate questions; short-term memory; and levels of alertness, attention, and concentration are crucial for success in school and these, it has been established, are adversely affected by nutritional and health deficits, thus vitiating the efforts of children to benefit from their classroom instruction (see Levinger 1994).

Significant research reveals that the extent and nature of the impact of nutritional deficiency depends on the timing of the deficiency. While malnutrition that occurs at school age is more reversible and less damaging, early childhood malnutrition, particularly that among under-2s, is most serious and can affect academic aptitude, concentration, and attentiveness on a more permanent basis. To quote Brazelton (1994),

> A child's experiences in the first months and years of life determine whether he or she will enter school eager to learn or not. By school age family and caregivers have already prepared the child for success or failure. The community has already helped or hindered the family's capacity to nurture the child's development.

ARE ALL OUR CHILDREN REALLY READY FOR PRIMARY SCHOOL?

In terms of the readiness variables discussed above, a large number of our children 'live in economic and social environments which impede their physical and mental development. These conditions include poverty, poor environmental sanitation, disease, infection, inadequate access to primary health care, inappropriate child caring and feeding practices' (see Department of Women and Child Development 1999). Despite the fact that crucial human development indicators like infant and child mortality rates have shown some improvement in the last twenty-five years and the most severe form of malnutrition has declined by half, more than 50 per cent of India's children under 4 continue to be moderately or severely malnourished and 30 per cent of newborns are significantly underweight. Malnutrition is largely an outcome of a combination of three key factors—inadequate food intake, illness, and deleterious caring practices. Indian

researchers have also observed the negative impact of malnutrition on the cognitive and physical capacities of children, particularly in the first two years of life (see Natesan and Devdas 1981; Anandlakshamy 1982). The situation of the Indian child, therefore, as regards success in primary school, does not appear potentially very promising.

In terms of psycho-social variables related to school readiness, research in the area of ECCE has consistently shown that a very large percentage of children entering primary school are first generation learners, from poverty settings that do not provide them with the required stimulation in terms of quality adult–child interaction, wide sensory exposure, and provisions for play and learning (see Chakraborty and Kundu 1986). A recent study conducted by the National Council of Educational Research and Training (NCERT) in four regions of the country on a sample of 1495 children admitted in Grade I found the average reading readiness score to be 47 per cent, with marked deficiency in sound discrimination and audio visual matching tasks. In mathematics readiness tasks, 60.8 per cent children performed below 75 per cent. The study concluded that children who come directly to primary schools from their homes do not exhibit the desired levels of readiness. It recommended the provision of good early childhood education programmes while ensuring that children who directly enter primary school benefit from a school readiness programme prior to the curriculum for Grade I (see Upadhyay et al. 1997). Several studies investigating the socio-economic and cultural differential and its impact on perceptual, cognitive, and linguistic abilities of children also lend weight to these observations. Interaction of the author with a large number of primary teachers across the country also endorses the view that children who have not been exposed to any regular, organized programme before they are six years old find it very difficult to meet the discipline-related requirements of a school situation in terms of punctuality and regularity of attendance, and of concentrating on a school task for any length of time. This is likely to impact negatively not only the learning dimension but also adjustment and the consequent retention of children in primary schools.

ECCE—A WAY OUT

ECCE, which addresses children in the age group 0–6 years, has been globally acknowledged as a significant input in the context of the preceding dissension, since it serves to compensate for early environmental deprivations on the home front by providing an appropriately stimulating environment to the child. It facilitates the

---

[1] Provided the child has not experienced extreme neglect.

realization of the goals of UEE by helping children develop necessary readiness for schooling in terms of getting them habituated to regularly attending a centre-based programme away from home, and by developing in them certain pre-reading, pre-writing, and pre-number skills, concepts, and vocabulary which can help them negotiate the primary curriculum better. It is also expected to address their health and nutritional requirements through need-based interventions, which should be part of the programme design. It also indirectly facilitates the participation of the girl child, who is often not able to attend school because of chores like sibling care, through provision of substitute care for siblings.

The NCERT's study of the follow up of cohorts in eight states of the country covering as many as 31,483 children showed that ECCE had a significant impact on retention in primary grades, with children who had been through ECCE demonstrating up to 20.5 per cent better rates of retention (see Kaul *et al.* 1993). An evaluation of the major ECCE programme in the country, namely the Integrated Child Development Services (ICDS), by the NIPCCD in 1992 has also indicated the positive impact of ECCE on enrolment and retention of children in primary schools. A micro-level, longitudinal study by the NCERT which followed a cohort of children from the ECCE stage through five grades of primary education has shown that a quality ECCE programme has a significantly favourable and long-term impact on children's learning, specifically in the area of mathematics (see Kaul *et al.*). Studies by Khosla (1985) and Sood (1987, 1992) showed that in comparison with children who had not been to ICDS centres, those attending the centres scored higher in language and cognitive development and also performed better in first and second grades of primary school.

SCOPE OF ECCE

To ensure developmentally appropriate interventions, ECCE inputs would need to be considered agewise since there is a subtle difference in the educational and developmental needs of children as they grow, even while the emphasis continues to remain on the use of play as a medium for learning and on overall development. The programme would, therefore, range in focus stagewise from a greater component of free and unguided developmentally appropriate play activities for 3–4 year olds, through a shift towards more structured and guided play activities for cognitive and language-related tasks and cooperative play for 4–5 year olds, to a further shift towards school readiness activities for 5–6 year olds linked particularly to reading, writing, and number readiness. There is therefore a need, in terms of planning, to consider 3–4 year olds as one unified group, 4–5 year olds as another, and 5–6 year olds as a third group just ready to enter primary school.

The programme would need to have some component of active parent involvement in it as also a component of parent education regarding developmentally appropriate and responsive parenting so as to ensure both continuity of inputs for the child, and better parental acceptance of the play-based educational programme. For facilitating participation of older children, particularly girls, in primary schools, it would be necessary to:

• provide for custodial care of 0–3 year olds also in the form of a creche or day-care facility, to be coterminous with the primary school, so as to free girls to attend school

• extend timings of ECCE centres also to synchronize with the primary schools to free girls from sibling care for 3–6 year olds

• locate ECCE centres next to or in the premises of primary schools (provided the school is close to the main habitation and has adequate space for children to rest, with facility for an extra meal because of the extended timings).

In conformity with a life-cycle approach to child development it is also desirable to provide for the nutritional, health, and emotional needs of adolescent girls and pregnant women, and also serve as a support programme for women in general. Given the desired scope of ECCE interventions as delineated above, the question that emerges is: what is the status of ECCE in India, and how has it evolved in the country over the years?

ECCE IN INDIA: THE JOURNEY FROM PRESCHOOL TO ECD

In terms of spread, at the time of India's Independence in 1947, preschool education was primarily in the hands of a few voluntary organizations. There was no concerted action by the government to reach out to poor and needy children. The first step taken in this direction by the Government of India was the setting up of a Central Social Welfare Board (CSWB) in 1953. The CSWB set up a committee in 1960 to specifically study the problems of children below six years of age. The committee recommended the evolution of a comprehensive plan for their care and training and suggested that responsibility for starting preschools be left to voluntary agencies with adequate assistance from the government. It also emphasized the importance of training and recommended that a cadre of adequately trained child welfare workers be prepared. The CSWB started a grants-in-aid scheme for voluntary organizations, which were running centres for pre-primary children (see Box 2.1) for the early government stand on prescribed education. In addition to this, the CSWB also sponsored a composite programme of Welfare Extension Projects in rural areas during the First Five Year Plan with the creation of women's groups or *mahila mandals* and *balwadis*. During the Second Plan, these projects were coordinated with programmes for women and children in community development blocks, with education for children up to six years forming an integral part. The CSWB was also instrumental in setting up the Supplementary Nutrition Programme in 1970 and a scheme for Creches for Ailing and Working Mothers in 1974.

Box 2.1
Conflicting Recommendations

The Education Commission (1964–6), while clearly recognizing the significance of preschool education in child development and its critical linkage with enrolment, retention, and learning outcomes at primary level, continued to reiterate the earlier stand that preschool education should be left to voluntary agencies. It, however, did recommend that the government should take on the responsibility for supervision, guidance, setting up of model schools, training, and research. In 1968, the Committee for the Preparation of Programmes for Children (*Ganga Saran Sinha* Committee) recommended, for the first time, that the government invest heavily in education, including preschool education, thereby reversing the earlier trend of leaving it to private agencies. The action taken on this recommendation was, however, limited.

In the course of the Third Plan period the focus gradually shifted to the qualitative aspects of the programmes and to the recognition of the child as an entity with specific developmental needs. Although the CSWB had, by then, added 6000 preschools, their quality left much to be desired. Preschool education in the government system continued to be enmeshed in the child welfare concept. The Fourth Plan brought the Scheme for Family and Child Welfare to rural areas. The objectives of this scheme were to foster all-round development of the preschool child, by providing comprehensive welfare services in all aspects of child development, and to strengthen the family to enable it to contribute to the growth and development of the child.

The Fifth Plan period saw a major breakthrough in the concept of child development with a shift in approach from 'welfare' to 'development' and the formulation of the National Policy for Children in 1974. In pursuance of this policy, it was proposed to set up the Integrated Child Development Services (ICDS). The minimum package of services envisaged in the scheme

did not include any component of preschool education. After extensive deliberations on this subject, the ICDS scheme, launched on an experimental basis in 1975, included non-formal preschool education as a component, along with other components of health and nutrition, and had the enlarged scope of addressing the nutritional and health needs of 0–3 year olds and pregnant women, in accordance with a life-cycle approach.

In 1980, the government constituted an expert group on Early Childhood Education, which examined the problems, particularly with reference to the quality of education, and made detailed recommendations regarding steps to be taken to ensure the effectiveness of preschool education. The expert group suggested viable models both for the training of personnel as well as for providing preschool education to different groups of children—tribal, rural, and urban disadvantaged. Though not much action was taken on these recommendations, an Early Childhood Education Scheme of grants-in-aid for voluntary agencies working in the educationally backward states did emerge out of these efforts and is now in operation.

In the 1970s and 1980s, while there was rapid growth of a variety of programmes for children, there was also a sharp polarization in terms of the target group and content of the programmes. In most cases the government-supported programmes degenerated into mere feeding or custodial centres for children with no attention to their psycho-social needs (see Swaminathan 1999). On the other hand, the private sector flourished, establishing nursery schools, initially only in the urban areas and later extending to semi-urban and now rural areas as well. These tended to be, more often than not, developmentally inappropriate, academically oriented programmes which were essentially a downward extension of the primary curriculum. Unfortunately, these also served as pace-setters or role models in terms of programme content, for the other category.

In 1986, the National Policy on Education (NPE) explicitly recognized the importance of Early Childhood Care and Education (ECCE—nomenclature introduced in the policy itself) and emphasized the need to invest in the development of young children belonging to the poverty group. It envisaged coverage of 70 per cent children in the preschool age by the year 2000. A minimum of 250,000 centres were to be established by 1990 to cover all tribal development blocks and blocks having substantial scheduled caste population as well as urban slums. A target of one million centres by 1995 and two million by 2000 was set. Though most of the coverage was to be through the ICDS, diverse kinds of pre-primary education centres and day care centres were also to be encouraged and supported. However, in 1990, the Acharya

Ramamurti Committee observed that while the target of 250,000 centres had been achieved, only 15 per cent of the target population of 3 to 6 years was able to derive the benefit of preschool education and only 10 per cent of the under-6 age group had been able to receive some element of child care services at all (see Committee for Review of National Policy on Education 1986, 1990).

The Eighth Five Year Plan period from 1992 onwards saw accelerated expansion of the ICDS with a view to universalizing the programme. It was proposed to phase out other government-sponsored programmes gradually and merge these with the ICDS as one uniform model across the country. In 1994, the National Creche Fund was set up which envisages that 25 per cent of the creches assisted under the fund would be ICDS centres extended into creches.

The Ninth Five Year Plan has, under the respective plans for education and women and child development, addressed the issue of early childhood care and education more exhaustively than previous Plans. It has reaffirmed priority to the development of early childhood services as an investment in human resource development. It talks of promoting girls' participation through forging of linkages with primary education and of strengthening the ECCE component of the ICDS. The Plan further stresses involvement of women's groups in the management of ECCE programmes, particularly under the decentralized *panchayti raj* system. While acknowledging the first six years of life to be critical, it recommends the institution of a National Charter for Children which would ensure that 'no child remains illiterate, hungry or lacks medical care' by the end of the Ninth Plan.

As we thus trace the development of the concept of ECCE from a historical perspective, one can detect, to a considerable extent under the influence of global thinking, a definite trend from a unidimensional, sectoral concept to a more holistic and developmentally appropriate definition. This emphasis, and the need to provide meaningfully for all children and throughout the childhood span, has also to some extent opened up possibilities of considering alternatives to centre-based programmes for children in the form of family day care, women's group initiatives, home-based programmes, etc.

PROGRAMMES IN ECCE: AN OVERVIEW

As mentioned in the previous section, a variety of schemes and programmes for ECCE have emerged through government as well as non-government initiatives. This section presents an overview of the various programmes currently under operation in the country (see Table 2.1).

TABLE 2.1
Coverage under Various ECCE Schemes 1996–7

Programmes	Number of centres	Beneficiaries' coverage	Percentage of population in age group 3-6 covered
ICDS (preschool education, age group 3–6) (2424 sanctioned Projects)	4,000,000	11,081,000	18.23
Early Childhood Education (ECE)	4365	153,000	0.27
Creches and day care centres— age group 0–5 (estimated coverage on the basis of 25 children per creche)	14,313	31,000	0.52
Balwadis—age group 3–6 (estimated coverage on the basis of 30 children per Balwadi)	5641	17,000	0.29
Pre-primary schools	38,553	194,000	0.33
Total	–	13,383,000	19.64

Note: The total population in the age group 3–6 years as on September 1996 is estimated on the basis of 7 per cent of the total population in the 1991 census.
Source: Department of Women and Child Development, 1997; Department of Education, 1998.

Integrated Child Development Services (ICDS)

The ICDS, which was launched as a centrally sponsored scheme in 1975, is the largest ECCE programme in the country at present. It is an intersectoral programme, which attempts to directly reach out to children in vulnerable and remote areas and give them a headstart by providing an integrated programme of health, nutrition, and early childhood education. Its package of services includes supplementary nutrition, immunization, health check-ups, referral services, non-formal preschool education, and nutritional and health education for children below six years, and to pregnant and nursing women. The nodal agency for coordination and monitoring of this scheme at the central level is the Department of Women and Child Development, Ministry of Human Resource Development, and its counterpart departments at the state level. Out of the 5614 ICDS projects sanctioned till 1996, 4200 became operational during the Eighth Plan. The process of universalization is continuing during the Ninth Plan until all the 5614 ICDS projects become operational.

The ICDS scheme was evaluated by the Planning Commission of India in 1978 and then again in 1982. The positive results of these evaluations led to further expansion of the ICDS. An independent assessment in 1983 supported by UNICEF reported positive outcomes such as substantial enrolment of scheduled castes and tribal children as beneficiaries (see Sood 1992). Several academic institutions also conducted micro-level impact studies of the ICDS which indicated that while the scheme has a positive impact, its impact can be significantly enhanced through interventions for quality.

In 1992, the Department of Women and Child Development sponsored a comprehensive review of the ICDS at national level with the objective of ascertaining the benefits of the scheme and the differences in implementation and utilization of services in urban, rural, and tribal areas. It also aimed at identifying problems and bottlenecks and ascertaining the degree of community involvement in the implementation of the ICDS. The study found that the ICDS positively impacted the health of preschool children in terms of infant mortality rate (IMR), immunization coverage and nutritional status, and their continuation into primary school with as many as 89 per cent of children with preschool experience continuing in school as compared to 52 to 60 per cent without preschool experience. The mid-term evaluation of the World Bank supporting ICDS projects in Andhra Pradesh also indicated a positive impact as regards IMR and severe malnutrition. However, the gains were not found to be entirely commensurate with investment due to problems of effective targeting, implementation, and coverage. Even more than twenty years into the programme, the ICDS covers less than half the target population, and that too with services that are far from satisfactory (see World Bank 1998–9).

The Early Childhood Education (ECE) or preschool education component of the scheme continues to remain one of its weakest. Since the focus of the scheme was on health and nutritional aspects, these were reflected in the early stages of the monitoring of the programme. In 1983, it was realized that preschool education needed further strengthening. As a first step in this direction a monitoring and evaluation cell was set up in the NIPCCD, to look into the ways and means of monitoring preschool education and community participation in the ICDS projects. The monitoring schedules have now been modified to include these aspects as well. Some effort has also been made to reinforce the preschool education component through revision of training syllabi and organization of short-term refresher training in this area. In this context, as an initiative in convergence, the NCERT, along with ten SCERTs and two State Resource Centres in twelve states of the country, has been

providing support to the ICDS, under a UNICEF-supported Early Childhood Education Project, for improving the quality of its preschool education component through supplementing training and development and dissemination of region-specific resource material for children, teacher workers, teacher educators, and parents. Attempts to select and produce core material for distribution to *anganwadis* (AWs), and to supervisory personnel, to further strengthen their monitoring and guiding capabilities, are being made as well.

Two recent studies conducted at the national level on perception and utilization of the preschool education component of the ICDS (see Upadhyay *et al.* 1998) and on evaluation of the ECE component in the District Primary Education Programme (DPEP) by the NCERT (see Kaul *et al.* 1998) have raised continuing concerns related particularly to quality and have recommended a review of the existing arrangements and provisions from a holistic perspective to ensure quality ECCE for all children.

ECCE under the DPEP

In the last few years, acknowledging the significance of ECCE for universalizing primary education, efforts have also been made under the centrally sponsored DPEP, to strengthen the ECCE component of the ICDS. The DPEP aims at strengthening existing provisions through the ICDS, improving the ECCE–primary school linkage and setting up new centres where the ICDS is not yet in position. In terms of strengthening the existing programme, its focus is on quality improvement through supplementing training in ECCE and through the supply of play materials to centres (in some states). To forge linkage with primary schools and to facilitate the girl child by freeing her from the burden of sibling care, the DPEP has encouraged ICDS centres or AWs to extend their timings to synchronize with primary schools, for which the workers are paid additional honorarium from DPEP funds. The new centres opened under the DPEP are all adjacent to primary schools. Programmatic linkages are also being established between preschool and primary school under the DPEP, by introducing the component of school readiness as an initial part of the primary curriculum and by continuing the play-based methodology in grades 1 and 2. This is particularly necessary since only about 19 per cent children in the 3–6 age group actually avail any kind of preschool education facility.

Evaluation of this component has indicated that, unfortunately, there is little ownership of these in the ICDS (perhaps largely due to inadequate participation of the ICDS in the planning) and consequently, the sustainability of these interventions is very much in doubt. Also, the existing ECCE centres in both the ICDS and DPEP do not provide for care of 0–3 year-old siblings who are actually the greater burden for girls. Interestingly, the evaluation also observed that the DPEP model for ECCE (adjacent to and part of the school) was more effective in providing the children a stimulating environment and a feeling of bonding with the school, as compared to an AW.

Early Childhood Education Scheme

This scheme was introduced in the Sixth Plan as a distinct strategy to reduce the dropout rate and improve the rate of retention of children in primary schools. Under this scheme, central assistance is given to voluntary organizations for running preschool education centres. A major lacuna in this scheme is the total lack of health and nutrition components in its programme. There is also no provision for training of personnel, although this aspect is now being attended to, on a limited scale, in various quarters. The scheme was recently evaluated by the NIPPCD at the request of the Department of Women and Child Development (see Vasudevan 1999). The major feedback on the study was that adequate provisions on a recurring basis for replenishing the infrastructure components and facilities and also for skill development and training of the workers were not there. Delegation of responsibility of management to NGOs was also, in the present form, not very conducive to ensuring quality in the programme since the number of centres with each NGO was not viable for any proper supervision or training system to be instituted.

Creches and Day Care Centres Scheme

This scheme was started in 1975 to provide day care services for children below five years. It caters mainly to children of casual, migrant, agricultural, and construction labourers. The programme, in this scheme, is primarily custodial in nature. While some element of training is being given to the workers, the need to strengthen the early childhood stimulation component is still acute. The scheme is sponsored by the Central Social Welfare Board.

Other ECE Programmes

In addition to these schemes that reach out to rural, urban slum, and tribal areas, there are innumerable private, fee-charging nursery schools which cater to those who can afford them in urban and semi-urban areas, gradually percolating to rural areas as well. Due to mismatch of demand and supply, admission to the more prestigious of these schools is generally done through formal tests which tend to be extremely traumatic and unpleasant experiences for both children and parents. Despite recommendations to the contrary, these nursery schools or kindergartens tend to be mere downward extensions of the primary curriculum, irrespective of the age to which they are catering.

Responding to growing social demand for alternative child care arrangements in urban settings, pre-nursery programmes for under-3s have also surfaced in the private sector and even these tend in most cases to be academically and developmentally inappropriate for children. Since at present there is no system of licensing or 'recognition' of these preschools, they are totally autonomous and no exact estimate can be made regarding their numbers. Municipal Corporations of metropolitan cities like Delhi also run preschools attached to their primary schools.

PROGRAMMES FOR TRAINING OF PERSONNEL IN ECE

Pre-service training programmes essentially prepare student teachers for employment in preschools/nursery schools/nursery classes run by both government and voluntary bodies. Nursery Training Institutes are largely in the private sector with government-supported programmes gradually closing down due to diminishing employment prospects for the trainees. This is because government-sponsored programmes like the ICDS have their own training systems and the other potential employers, i.e. private schools, with no regulatory mechanisms in place, do not consider nursery training an essential qualification while recruiting teachers. The Balsevika Training Programme of the Indian Council for Child Welfare continues to train a cadre of multi-purpose child care workers through its 25 Balsevika Training Institutes running in 12 states of the country. These workers have been getting absorbed under various child care programmes.

The two-year integrated course in Preschool and Early Primary Teacher Education which is being implemented in the recognized nursery teacher training institutes of Delhi was prepared on the recommendation of a Pre-school Teacher Education Committee appointed by the National Council for Teacher Education (NCTE) to address the developmental continuum from preschool stage to primary stage and was planned for teachers of pre-school and grades 1 and 2. While this course is being implemented in some states, it is unfortunate that the trainees who pass out are barred by rigid employment rules from jobs as primary teachers and are accepted only as preschool teachers.

The training scene in ECE demonstrates a wide range of programmes, particularly from the point of view of duration which varies from three months to two years (see Table 2.2). The short-term training programmes are mainly in-service programmes, whereas the long-duration programmes are essentially preservice courses. To meet the diverse needs of the ECE programmes in the country, the need for a multimodel approach in ECE training becomes inevitable. Yet, there is general consensus that to ensure field-relevant training experiences for the trainees, the strategy of an initial training followed by frequent refresher training courses, preferably at field level, is likely to yield best results.

the response of children experienced by trainees while conducting activities helps in bringing about a quicker attitudinal change.

EMERGING ISSUES IN ECCE

While there has been a quantum leap in services and programmes related to ECCE, primarily through universalization of the ICDS, the approach to its implementation has remained largely sectoral. In the context of the ICDS, its education component, being only one of six components, gets divided attention and that too with little focus on quality. The other ECCE programmes are

TABLE 2.2
Current Status of Training for ECCE

Name and nature of course	Minimum qualification for entry	Duration
AW workers' training (job training para-professional)	Varies from state to state-class V–VIII the norm	Three months
Nursery teachers' training/pre-primary teachers' training	Class X	One/two years
Vocational training in child care (+2) of CBSE	Class X	One year
Balsevika training of the Indian Council for Child Welfare	Class X	Two years
Montessori training of Association of Montessori International	Class X	Eleven months
Integrated pre-primary and primary teachers' training (Delhi)	Class XII	One year
Diploma in early graduate childhood education	—	Two years
Middle levels supervisors training (job training)	Varies—Graduate, Postgraduate and promoted from lower cadre	One year/distance education—three months

The curricula for ECE training have, across the various programmes, undergone changes in focus over the years. While initially there was greater emphasis on the theories of ECE and child psychology, this proved ineffective in helping the trainees develop the required skills for a classroom situation. Over the last few years the pendulum has swung fully towards a total emphasis on kit development and activities, as a result of which the trainee is not able to develop an understanding of the linkage between the theoretical and the practical components. The need at present is, therefore, to provide a balance. Some of the more innovative training programmes, for example under the NCERT project, have attempted this balance by building into the training a significant component of 'hands on' internship with children in the settings of ECD centres, using this as a basis for discussions of the theoretical framework of the suggested practice. This has shown very positive results for training of personnel at all levels, particularly since

also very sectoral in concept since they do not address the health and nutrition needs of the child but focus only on education. Also, across all ECCE programmes, the resources—material, financial, and human—available are largely not commensurate with the demands of a quality programme. Training provisions for ECCE also require further strengthening and to be made more professional for improved personnel preparation. While the private sector is making rapid expansion in this area, in the absence of any system of regulation, there are marked distortions in educational programmes, with a great deal of 'mis-education' evident, across the states.

Priority to ECCE in the Context of Elementary Education

At present, only about 19 per cent of children in the 3–6 age group are reported to be actually utilizing the benefit of the available ECCE programmes and the vast majority are entering primary education with a significant disadvantage, or are not going into school at all. Since this stage of education is administered by the Department of Women and Child Development it does not get due attention from the education sector. It therefore becomes imperative for the education sector to assume responsibility for ECCE as an indispensable first step in the total educational continuum and a starting point for interventions aimed at achieving UEE.

There is also a need to further strengthen the linkages of ECCE programmes with primary education. However, initiatives under the DPEP like co-locating ECCE/ICDS centres with schools and synchronizing their timings need to be evaluated and expanded in ways that are contextually relevant and developmentally appropriate rather than 'across the board' solutions. While these have shown positive results in certain contexts, they may become counterproductive if applied universally without taking the context into consideration.

The linkage with primary grades needs to be strengthened as well through ensuring continuity in the curriculum from the preschool to the primary stage in a bottom-up and developmentally appropriate manner to prevent the prevalent reverse trend of a downward extension of the curriculum. Since a large percentage of children are still coming into schools without ECCE experience, and also with most states taking in children into grade I at as young as five years, inclusion of a compensatory school readiness component in the grade 1 curriculum could become an integral part of the programme.

Revisiting the Concept of ECCE

Acknowledging that a child's development is continuous, incremental and holistic and not compartmentalized into health, nutrition, and psycho-social stimulation, it is critical to address the total developmental continuum of the early years from 0–11 in totality, in a planned manner, rather than focus on any one sub-stage exclusively, to the neglect of the others. This is particularly significant in our context where the child development indicators are still very dismal. The 0–3 age group has rarely been addressed in programmes from a perspective of providing psycho-social stimulation. Instances abound in discontinuity of approach from one sub-stage to another.

The total childhood continuum can be addressed stagewise by addressing the needs that are more critical for each of the identified sub-stages, keeping the child and not the programme in focus. Critical developmental indicators for each sub-stage need to be identified for this purpose which should essentially guide programme formulation and monitoring in a continuous and holistic

manner. Within the childhood span there is, therefore, a need to plan for the 0–3 age group as one sub-stage, 3–6 as possibly two sub-stages with 3–4 and 4–6 as separate (to allow for differences in their capacities), and similarly consider 6–8 and 8–11 as two sub-stages within the primary stage. The programme in each sub-stage should, however, cater to overall development of the child and not be limited to academic learning.

Context-Specificity and Cultural Relevance of ECCE Programmes

Given the wide diversities across the country, a relevant question that emerges is—to what extent is the policy to have a centrally sponsored, centrally designed, and uniform programme across the country sound? It is necessary to adopt a more flexible approach which takes local contexts and needs into account and encourages variety in terms of content and management. Models experimented with by different non-governmental organizations can be reviewed in this context.

Any programme in ECCE should also provide space for building upon and bringing in traditional folklore, infant games, and child rearing practices of a region, including nutritional and health care patterns. An exercise by the NCERT of compiling children's games from different states in the country highlighted the availability of a wide variety of infant and children's games in every state which are traditionally played in families but are slowly dying out. Reviving these and basing the ECCE programme on these will not only bring the home and community closer to the programme but will also make for wider availability of local resources. There is also a need to revisit the ECCE and primary curriculum from the perspective of including into the developmental objectives the cultural values and behavioural practices that are a part of Indian tradition.

Mis-education' in the Name of ECCE: Need for Quality Control

There is evidently uncontrolled mushrooming of ECCE centres, particularly in the form of nursery schools, in the private sector, with wrong practices propagated by them in the form of holding tests/interviews for the purpose of admission and insistence on formal teaching of the 3 Rs. This amounts to extending the primary curriculum down to the absurd level of two-year-olds, through pre-nursery classes. This situation is largely the outcome of unbridled social demand for alternative care provisions for the young child in view of the significant increase in the number of women joining the workforce, as also the breaking down of traditional support systems like the joint family. With no licensing requirement, the programmes are generally run by untrained personnel and with inadequate facilities. In the absence of any knowledge or skills related to ECCE these programmes resort to large-scale child-unfriendly 'mis-education' in the name of ECCE. Admission tests for children at this vulnerable age are a further source of trauma and tension for the child. These tests (which often expect academic skills from a child even prior to joining school!) have also influenced the curriculum of nursery schools run by trained personnel since they are seen as preparatory programmes for admission tests to primary schools.

While private investment and initiative need to be encouraged, there is need to institute legal provisions along with persuasive advocacy measures for regulation of quality in these programmes. The NCERT in collaboration with the Indian Association of Paediatrics has considerably advocated this area and some initiatives have been taken by professional associations as well. These efforts have created some awareness of the detrimental influence of these wrong practices on the health and personality development of children. There is, however, a need for these efforts to not only be continued but also expanded through multiple agents, to curb this growing trend which is now percolating unchecked, even to rural areas.

Provision of Minimum Basic Resources for Quality

Research and case studies of good practices in the area of ECCE have consistently indicated that it is not any ECE programme/intervention but a programme of a certain quality that can be expected to impact and facilitate the realization of the UEE goals. Research has also demonstrated that while a resource rich programme may not necessarily be effective, a basic minimum in terms of quality as regards financial, human, and material resources is essential for a programme to meet its objectives. This brings in the debate of quantity versus quality. The ICDS typically provides for one 'overburdened' worker with a helper and very limited facilities in terms of space and resources to conduct any kind of a stimulating programme for the children. The existing policy of large-scale quantitative expansion of this uniform model across the country, which has inevitably to compromise on quality and number of personnel needs to be reviewed in terms of cost-effectiveness of the investment.

The issue here is not only of resource provision but also of optimal utilization of the given resources. To this end there is need to identify input indicators for quality and plan interventions accordingly, so as to derive maximum benefits from the investments. The quality issue would also refer to the developmental appropriateness of the content of the programme and training of

personnel. Mechanisms in place for monitoring and supervision at a systemic level are also relevant in any discussion on quality assurance and maintenance.

Training

Closely related to quality is the issue of personnel preparation and training. In view of the continuing expansion of ECCE services and the corresponding increase in demand for trained personnel at all levels for planning, implementation, and monitoring, the need to professionalize and regulate the quality of training offered in this area becomes significant. ECCE falls under the purview of the NCTE which has drawn up specifications for awarding recognition to the pre-service courses. These specifications, however, need to be reviewed in a participatory mode with the training institutions to arrive at the more feasible and critical indicators for training quality. In view of the absence of any system of recognition or registration for ECCE there is, however, no compulsion for private nursery school managements to recruit only qualified teachers. Since the government sponsored programmes run their own induction training, there are few takers for the recognized nursery training programmes, and in states like Maharashtra and UP training institutions have been compelled to close down.

Another significant issue in this context relates to parity and equivalence across programmes, particularly the distance mode programmes, that are offered by different institutions with little or no coordination among them. While the Indira Gandhi National Open University (IGNOU) offers a Diploma in ECCE after the senior secondary level, the National Open School is also initiating a vocational course after secondary level in the same area. Variations exist in quality of teacher/worker preparation across government-sponsored induction programmes too. An overriding dilemma in this context is that the job requirements/expectations from the products of both the long professional one- two-year training programmes and the short three- six-month programmes are similar (in some cases even greater for the latter!) when in many cases the entry qualifications for the latter are also much less than those of the former. Can the outcomes realistically be expected to be identical?

State-level capacity for ECCE in the government sector is still very negligible. The initiative to set up State Resource Centres for ECCE in the SCERTs in twelve states under the UNICEF-assisted and NCERT-guided Early Childhood Education Project has contributed positively in this context. But with rapid turnovers in staff, the opportunities for consolidating capacity remain very scarce.

Community Involvement and Awareness

To encourage optimal utilization of the existing programmes in ECCE, ensure developmentally appropriate child care and development interventions for all children, as also to eliminate pressures on children due to the 'mis-education' carried out in the name of ECCE, a strong lobby has to be created among parents and the larger community who are the actual beneficiaries of the programmes. This can be done through orientation of the community to the benefits of developmentally appropriate and responsive parenting and ECCE along the entire childhood continuum, and to their own role in it in the form of direct community contact programmes, parent-to-parent programmes, as well as through folk and electronic media. Efforts are also required to develop in the community a sense of ownership of the ECCE programmes, particularly the government-sponsored programmes. It is necessary to evolve a systematic community involvement and mobilization strategy within the framework of decentralization of management under the *panchayati raj.*

Monitoring and Supervision of Programmes

While the community can play a significant role in overseeing and providing support to a community-based ECCE programme, there still remains a need for effective mechanisms for decentralized resource support for academic supervision and monitoring of the programme. The supervisory cadre, already in place, needs to be perceived and trained as facilitators playing this positive role. Experiments in the ICDS in some states, in which supervisors organize monthly meetings of the AW workers in their charge to discuss the theme for the month and related activities for children, as well as help the workers solve their difficulties, have shown good results. Using these cluster meetings as a forum for workers to demonstrate some successful activities has also been found to be effective for sustaining their motivation and enthusiasm. The cluster and block-level structures created under the DPEP can also be utilized for this purpose.

Convergence and Coordination

With ECCE defined as a concept which addresses health, nutrition, and psycho-social development in a holistic and synergistic manner along the childhood continuum, its implementation would inevitably involve shared responsibility across different sectors. While the service delivery may be a shared responsibility at the administrative level with some mechanisms for coordination, the planning needs to be done holistically and in continuity

from one sub-stage to the next and for the child's development as a whole. In view of the observations made by some evaluations in both health and education sectors, and also in view of the critical significance of ECCE for primary education, the present arrangement of ECCE as the exclusive responsibility of the Department of Women and Child Development calls for a review. While the 0–3-year age group need a more home-focused/day care approach with health and nutrition interventions being of relatively higher priority as compared to the later stage, this stage can be covered more meaningfully under a convergent mode by the Department of Women and Child Development. The DPEP experience has, however, demonstrated that 4–6-year olds can benefit more from an ECCE programme organized as part of a primary school set up under the education sector. The advantage is in terms of the child forming a timely bond with, and motivation towards, the primary school. This also facilitates continuity in curriculum through primary school and makes possible adequate attention to and a conducive environment for the educational component, as compared to in the AW model.

In terms of convergence, there is also need to plan holistically for the child, by bringing all the schemes and programmes related to child development and education under one umbrella, as is being conceptualized to some extent under the proposed Sarva Shiksha Abhiyan of the Ministry of Human Resource Development. Schemes like the Midday Meal Scheme, School Health Programme, Non-Formal Education, ICDS, and Mahila Samakhya, have ample scope for convergent and coordinated planning and implementation. Convergence within and across sectors and schemes in terms of implementation on the ground becomes even more feasible and meaningful, given the trend towards the *panchayati raj* dispensation. This will hopefully lead not only to more optimal utilization of resources, but also provide for more integrated development of children, which, in turn, would lead to improved quality of life and opportunities for them in the new millennium.

REFERENCES

Anadalakshmy, S. (1982). *Cognitive Competence in Infancy.* Indian Council of Social Science Research, New Delhi.

Brazelton, T. Berry (1994). *Touchpoints: Your Child's Emotional and Behavioral Development.* Perseus Books Group.

Chakraborty, P. K. and R. Kundu (1986). 'Language Development in Low SES Children'. *Social Change,* 16(1), 34–7.

Committee for Review of National Policy on Education 1986 (1990). 'A Perspective Paper on Education'. Acharya Ramamurthi Committee for Review of National Policy on Education 1986. New Delhi.

Department of Education (1998). *Selected Educational Statistics 1997–98*. Ministry of Human Resource Development, Government of India, New Delhi.

Department of Women and Child Development (1997). *Annual Report 1996–97*. Ministry of Human Resource Development, Government of India, New Delhi.

———— (1999). *Annual Report 1998–99*. Ministry of Human Resource Development, Government of India, New Delhi.

Kaul, V., Chitra Ramachandran and G. C. Upadhyaya (1993). 'Impact of ECE on Retention in Primary Grades'. National Council of Educational Research and Training, New Delhi.

Kaul, V. *et al.* (1996). 'Process Based Intervention for Primary Level Mathematics—A Longitudinal Study'. National Council of Educational Research and Training, New Delhi.

———— (1998). 'Shishu Shiksha Kendras. An UP Basic Education Project Initiative—Evaluation Report'. National Council of Educational Research and Training, New Delhi.

Khosla, R. *et al.* (1985). 'Preschool Education in ICDS an Impact Study.' National Institute of Public Cooperation and Child Development, New Delhi.

Levinger, B. (1994). *Nutrition, Health and Education for All*. Newton Education Development Centre, Mass.

Muralidharan, R. (1990). 'Early Childhood Education: Issues, Policies, Programmes and Actions'. *ICCW News Bulletin*.

Muralidharan, R. and B. Kaur (1984). 'The Impact of Intervention Programme on Language and Cognitive Development of Preschool Children from Urban Anganwadis.' National Council of Educational Research and Training, New Delhi.

Mustard, J. F. *et al.* (1999). *Reversing the Real Brain Drain. Early Years Study—Final Report*. Publications Ontario, Toronto.

Natesan, H. and R. P. Devdas (1981). 'Measurement of Mental Abilities of Well Nourished and Malnourished Children'. *Journal of Psychological Researches*, 25(3), 121–4.

Sahni, S. and S. Agarwal (1984). 'A Study of an Intervention in ongoing ICDS Programme to Promote Cognitive Abilities of Preschoolers'. Unpublished Master's Thesis. Haryana Agricultural University, Hissar.

Sharma, A. (1987). 'Monitoring of Social Components of ICDS: A Pilot Project.' National Institute of Public Cooperation and Child Development, New Delhi.

Sood, N. (1987). 'An Evaluation of Non Formal Pre School Education Component in Mongolpuri ICDS Block'. *Technical Bulletin*. Number 1. National Institute of Public Cooperation and Child Development, New Delhi.

———— (1992). 'Pre School Education in ICDS: An Appraisal.' *Technical Bulletin*. No. 5: National Institute of Public Cooperation and Child Development, New Delhi.

Swaminathan, Mina (1999). *The First Five Years: A Critical Perspective on Early Childhood Care and Education in India*. Sage India.

Upadhyay, G. C. *et al.* (1997). 'Preschool Education Component of ICDS and its Perception and Extent on Utilization by the Community—A Study In Delhi.' National Council of Educational Research and Training, New Delhi.

———— (1998). 'Numeracy and Reading Readiness Levels of Entrants to class I—A Synthesis Report'. National Council of Educational Research and Training, New Delhi.

Vasudevan, Sulochna (1999). 'National Evaluation of the Scheme of Early Childhood Care and Education'. National Institute of Public Cooperation and Child Development, New Delhi.

World Bank *(1999)*. *World Development Report, Knowledge for Development*. Oxford University Press, New York.

3 Education of Girls in India
An Assessment

Usha Nayar*

Education of girls has been high on the national agenda since Independence. Special commissions and committees were set up from time to time to assess the progress of girls' education and propose suitable interventions to promote their participation in education. Several strategies were adopted to promote education of girls as an integral part of the planned socio-economic development of the country. A major conceptual shift is noticed in the last decade in the approach to the education of girls and women. Education of girls is increasingly being seen as a basic human right and a crucial input for national development. Yet gender disparities within the education sector are far from having been overcome. This chapter reviews the progress of girls' education in India during the last five decades with special focus on developments during Jomtien period of the 1990s (1990–2000) and within the framework of education for all (EFA).

THE POLICY FRAMEWORK

Over the last decade, a noticeable shift in the approach to female education has been that education of girls is increasingly being seen as a basic human right and a crucial input for national development. Investment in female education is now considered a development imperative rather than a moral commitment, thus lifting it from the plane of pure ethics to that of sound economics. The problem of girls' education, however, does not stand alone, but is inextricably linked with the status of women and the underdevelopment of rural areas. The national policies are designed to reach out to girls and other disadvantaged groups in remote rural areas.

* The author gratefully acknowledges the assistance given by Ms Anita Nuna in the preparation of this paper.

The National Policy of Education (NPE) 1986 and its Programme of Action (revised in 1992) give education a mandate to work for women's equality and empowerment. There is effort now not only to provide equality of educational opportunity but to transform the entire content and process of education for achieving gender equality and a realignment of gender roles to make them more equitable and harmonious (see Box 3.1).

> ### BOX 3.1
> ### Education for Women's Equality
>
> Education will be used as an agent of basic change in the status of women. In order to neutralize the accumulated distortions of the past, there will be a well-conceived edge in favour of women. The National Education System will play a positive, interventionist role in the empowerment of women. It will foster the development of new values through redesigned curricula, textbooks, the training and orientation of teachers, decision makers and administrators, and the active involvement of educational institutions. This will be an act of faith and social engineering. Women's studies will be promoted as a part of various courses and educational institutions encouraged in taking up active programmes to further women's development.
>
> The removal of women's illiteracy and obstacles inhibiting their access to, and retention in elementary education will receive overriding priority, through provision of special support services, setting of time targets, and effective monitoring. Major emphasis will be laid on women's participation in vocational technical and professional education at different levels. The policy of non-discrimination will be pursued vigorously to eliminate sex stereotyping in vocational and professional courses and promote women's participation in non-traditional occupations, as well as in existing and emerging technologies.
>
> —Department of Education, 1986

The Constitutional Guarantees and Policy Mandate

The Constitution of India not only grants equality to women and forbids any discrimination based on religion, race, caste, sex, or place of birth but also empowers the state to practise protective discrimination in favour of women. Under the protective discrimination clause, the state has passed several social and labour legislations and drawn up special programmes and schemes for the protection, welfare, and development of women and children. Additionally, women have reservations in many educational and training institutions, development schemes, local bodies, and certain categories of government jobs. Theoretically, women have gained equality. India has one of the most impressive sets of laws for women and children/girls and yet little is known about them, either by women themselves or by men.

BOX 3.2

National Plan of Action for the SAARC Decade of the Girl Child AD 1991–2000

Rights can be declared and policies can be formulated to express our collective liberal and humanistic concern, but unless the real life of the girl child in her family and community is touched by tangible efforts and actions, nothing can be achieved, Therefore, a climate has to be created in which she can exercise her rights freely and fearlessly. One has to work for the transformation of those social and cultural values that shackle and constrict the girl child and mould her into stereotypical roles. For this, every forum and every platform should be used to create awareness and stimulate positive action. Along with this, effective implementation of the laws for protecting her and provision of opportunities for her to benefit from them has to be insured.

As is evident, there is a clear mandate for social mobilization to change the social and cultural practices that inhibit development of the girl child (see Box 3.2).

The foregoing presentation on the policy backdrop highlights the positive climate being created for promoting girls' education in the country. Of course, they represent only the necessary condition. Provision of facilities as well as actual participation of girls in education depends on the programmes and their field-level implementation. The next section analyses the progress made and the shortfalls in achievement with respect to girls' education in the country.

EDUCATION OF ALL GIRLS: PROGRESS AND SHORTFALLS

India has the second largest educational system in the world after China with 610,763 primary, 185,506 upper primary and 107,100 high/higher secondary schools, 7199 colleges for general education, 2075 colleges of professional education and 229 universities. In addition there are 290,000 non-formal education (NFE) centres for out-of-school children in the age group 6–14 and a massive volunteer-based literacy programme for adults in the age group 15–35. There are 109 million children enrolled in the primary grades, classes I–V; 39.5 million in classes VI–VIII; 27.3 million in classes IX–XII; and close to 6 million in institutions of higher learning. Girls form 43.62 per cent of those enrolled at the primary level, 40.12 per cent at the middle stage, 37.09 per cent at the higher/higher secondary stage and 36.59 per cent in higher education (1997–8). The system continues to characterized by sharp regional and gender disparities.

Yet, Universal Elementary Education (UEE), a constitutional directive, remains unfulfilled. Six of ten females above 7 years of age were illiterate at the last census count. Secondary and higher education started as an urban-middle-class phenomenon and continues to be so even after fifty years of educational development in independent India. Rural females and urban poor form bulk of the illiterate and out-of-school populations. The National Sample Survey (NSS), 1997, however, indicates a breakthrough in literacy with male–female and rural–urban gaps getting reduced.

Female Literacy

Female literacy is considered to be a more sensitive index of social development compared to overall literacy rates. Female literacy is negatively related with fertility rates, population growth rates, infant and child mortality rates, and shows a positive association with female age at marriage, life expectancy, participation in modern sectors of the economy, and above all, female enrolment. Female literacy rate has grown from 8 per cent in 1951 to 39 per cent in 1991, and the corresponding increase in male literacy during this period was from 25 to 64 per cent. Rural–urban and inter-group disparities were sharp. The rural–urban divide was the sharpest amongst females. Urban females were twice as well off in literacy as compared to their rural counterparts. Scheduled Caste (SC) and Scheduled Tribe (ST) females were at the bottom of the heap.

Literacy Gains During 1991–7

Renewed efforts and heavy resource inputs in the area of primary education and the voluntary-based Total Literacy Campaigns of the National Literacy Mission (set up in 1988) appears to have paid dividends. The

53rd round of the National Sample Survey 1997 indicates that India has achieved a breakthrough in literacy in the 1990s.

• The overall literacy rate has gone up from 52 per cent in 1991 to 62 per cent in 1997.

• The pace has accelerated in that the increase in literacy rate was 8.7 percentage points during 1981–91, i.e. from 43.5 per cent to 52.2 per cent, and there is already a 10 percentage point increase between 1991 and 1997.

• The male–female gap has narrowed. Female literacy has improved by 11 percentage points compared to 9 percentage points increase in the case of males during 1991–7. Female literacy in 1997 stands at 50 per cent though it is still much lower than the male literacy rate of 73 per cent.

• Rural literacy has progressed faster than urban. The gap between rural and urban literacy levels has narrowed. The rural–urban gap was 28.4 percentage points in 1991, the rural literacy rate being 44.7 and urban 73.1. In 1997 the former has reached the 56 per cent mark, only 14 percentage points lower than the urban literacy rate of 80. During the six years between 1991 and 1997, the improvement in rural literacy is to the tune of 11.3 percentage points, which is twice as much as the growth of 6.9 percentage points for urban populations.

• The north-eastern states have registered the biggest improvement and now Mizoram (95 per cent) has overtaken Kerala (93 per cent) to the top of the literacy chart and Assam has shown a remarkable increase from 53 per cent in 1991 to 75 per cent in 1997—a 22 percentage points jump.

• What is heartening is that the 'BIMARU' states are not lagging in effort. Bihar showed an improvement of 10.5 percentage points, Madhya Pradesh of 11.8, Uttar Pradesh of 14.4, and Rajasthan of 16.5 percentage points during 1991–7.

Considerable progress has been made in terms of provision of facilities and enrolment of children in the relevant age group. However, the goal of UEE continues to be elusive. This is largely on account of the inability of the system to enrol and retain girls and children from the disadvantaged groups.

ENROLMENT AT THE ELEMENTARY STAGE

A fairly strong gender focus has resulted in greater participation of girls in elementary schooling but the male–female gap in enrolment ratios and share of girls in total enrolment is below par for the country as a whole and is very marked at middle stage. Intra-female disparities as between rural–urban areas and among general populations, SCs, STs, Other Backward Castes (OBCs), and some minorities are sharp.

Due to persistent efforts, the enrolment of girls at the elementary stage has grown steadily over the last five decades.

• The number of girls at primary stage has gone up from 5.38 million in 1950-1 to 47.45 million in 1997-8.

• The number of girls at middle stage has increased from 0.53 million in 1950-1 to 15.84 million in 1997-8.

FASTER GROWTH OF GIRLS' PARTICIPATION

In fact, the growth rates for girls have always been higher than those for boys, not only because of starting from a much lower base but also on account of sustained state effort to promote education of girls as an important part of planned development.

It may be noted that even during the period 1990–1 to 1998–9, the growth rate for girls at primary stage (classes I–V) is twice as high as that for boys and more than double at middle stage (classes VI–VIII). In absolute terms, enrolment of girls during this period at primary level has increased by over seven million compared to boys whose numbers have increased by four million. At middle stage, the increase in the number of girls during this period is to the tune of 3.3 million compared to 2.2 million for boys.

PERCENTAGE SHARE OF GIRLS TO TOTAL

The percentage share of girls in the total has shown a steady increase since Independence at all levels of education (see Tables 3.1 and 3.2 for the elementary). During 1950–1 to 1997–8, the percentage share of girls among the children enrolled at primary stage went up from 28 per cent to 44 per cent, from 16 per cent to

TABLE 3.1
Percentage of Girls in School Enrolment at Elementary Stage, 1950–1 to 1997–8

Year	Primary stage (classes I–V)	Middle stage (classes VI–VIII)
1950–1	28.1	6.1
1960–1	32.6	23.9
1970–1	37.4	29.3
1980–1	38.6	32.9
1990–1	41.5	36.7
1997–8	43.6	40.1

Source: Department of Education (various years), Ministry of Human Resource Development, Government of India.

40 per cent at middle stage; from 13.3 per cent to 36.7 per cent at secondary/higher secondary level, and from 10 per cent to 36.6 per cent in higher education.

TABLE 3.2
Percentage Girls in Total Enrolment by Groups at Elementary Stage 1997–8

Category	Primary stage (classes I–V)	Middle stage (classes VI–VIII)
All communities	43.62	40.12
SC	42.59	38.49
ST	42.82	37.09

Source: Department of Education, MHRD, GoI.

PERCENTAGE SHARE OF SC/ST CHILDREN

The percentage share of SC, ST girls to total SC, ST children is not very remarkably different from the overall percentage share of girls in the general population at primary stage. At middle stage SC, ST girls are way behind. It is perhaps pertinent to state that the percentage share of SC, ST children to the total is similar to proportion of these groups in the total population at primary stage but the situation is not satisfactory for both ST boys and girls at middle stage (see Table 3.3). The SC and ST population constituted 16.33 per cent and 8.01 per cent respectively at the 1991 census.

TABLE 3.3
Percentage Share of SC/ST Children in Total Enrolment at Elementary Stage in 1997–8

Category	Primary stage (classes I–V)			Middle stage (classes VI–VIII)		
	Boys	Girls	Total	Boys	Girls	Total
SC	17.27	16.60	16.96	14.99	14.01	14.59
ST	8.40	8.13	8.28	6.26	5.52	5.96

Source: Department of Education, MHRD, GoI.

REGIONAL VARIATIONS

In 1997–8, the share of girls to total enrolment varied from 37 per cent in Bihar and Uttar Pradesh to 50 per cent in Meghalaya at primary stage; 31 per cent in Bihar to 53 per cent in Daman and Diu at middle stage; 25 per cent in Bihar to 53.5 per cent in Daman and Diu at secondary/higher secondary stage; and from 19 per cent in Bihar to 59 per cent in Kerala in higher education.

Girls are less mobile than boys on account of parental concern for their personal safety, and thus, utilize educational facilities available within the revenue village or in its sub units or habitations (an average of two habitations per village). For instance, very often a revenue village is spread over several kilometres as in Rajasthan and Madhya Pradesh and the same situation prevails in mountainous and forest regions elsewhere which are often divided by physical and social distance, as observed, between upper-caste- class inhabitants and SCs and STs. The well-off upper castes form the core and disadvantaged sections are at the periphery of a village, while the school is often located in the core part of the village. SC and ST parents are at times intimidated into not sending their children to school in some parts of the northern plains (see Nayar 1993–4).

The educational lag of rural girls is linked to under-development of rural areas in terms of development infrastructure, especially convenient, safe means of transport, drinking water, cheap fuel, sanitation, health, and education infrastructure. The problem is acute in small-sized villages and sparsely populated remote areas. Gender and rural poverty combine to add to the burden of the girl child whose direct and indirect earnings and work are needed by families, whereas little boys are let off and even pampered, being seen as potential breadwinners.

Shortage of women teachers in rural areas is seen as a barrier to girls' participation in education, especially at middle stage and above. The last available figures from the Sixth All-India Educational Survey are not very encouraging with regard to rural areas where the demand for female teachers is the most.

ENROLMENT RATIO

Enrolment ratios moved up constantly upto 1990–1, giving gross figures of 86 for girls and 114 for boys at primary stage and 47 for girls and 77 for boys at middle stage. The enrolment ratios appear to be moving towards net figures in 1998–9, being 81 for girls and 98 for boys at primary level and 50 for girls and 67 for boys at upper primary stage. This is likely on account of improved enrolment at the right age and better retention. However, unless an attempt is made to collect age-specific ratios separately, it would be difficult to come to any conclusion, because girls still continue to enter late and drop out earlier. Overall gender gaps persist and the situation of girls belonging to SCs and STs in terms of gender parity needs much greater attention. It is a matter of great concern that the enrolment ratio of boys is showing a more marked downward trend since 1990–1 at both primary and upper primary levels. Girls show an improvement at upper primary stage. In the union territories of Delhi and Chandigarh, girls' enrolment ratio is better than that for boys at upper primary level. Similar trends were noted by an earlier study for Mumbai and Kolkatta (see Nayar 1993). Tables 3.4, 3.5 and 3.6 present the data on enrolment ratios.

TABLE 3.4
Enrolment Ratio by Stages and Sex 1950–1 to 1997–8

Year	Primary stage (classes I–V)			Upper primary (classes VI–VII)		
	Boys	Girls	Total	Boys	Girls	Total
1950–1	60.8	24.9	42.6	20.8	4.3	12.9
1960–1	82.6	41.4	62.4	33.2	11.3	22.5
1970–1	96.5	60.5	78.6	46.3	19.4	33.4
1980–1	95.8	64.1	80.5	54.3	28.6	41.9
1990–1	113.9	85.5	100.1	76.6	47.0	62.1
1997–8	97.5	81.2	89.7	66.5	49.5	58.5

Source: DoE, MHRD, GoI.

DROPOUT RATE

Over the period 1960–1 to 1997–8, both enrolment and retention have registered improvement (see Table 3.7). The dropout rate for primary stage classes (I–V) has gone down from 62 to 38 per cent for boys and from 71 to 41 per cent for girls. At middle stage the dropout rate has come down from 75 to 51 per cent for boys and from 85 to 59 per cent for girls. The last available figures indicate that the dropout rate for SC/ST children is substantially higher than that for general groups, the same being true of rural girls.

TABLE 3.5
Enrolment Ratio by Stages, Sex, and Caste/Tribes 1998–9

Groups	Primary stage (classes I–V)			Upper primary (classes VI–VIII)		
	Boys	Girls	Total	Boys	Girls	Total
All groups	97.5	81.2	89.7	66.5	49.5	58.5
Scheduled caste	102.25	81.60	92.36	75.84	37.59	56.17
Scheduled tribes	102.93	78.34	90.73	53.03	32.93	43.24

Source: DoE, MHRD, GoI.

TABLE 3.6
Inter-state Disparities in Enrolment Ratio of Girls at Elementary Stage 1997–8

States and Union Territories above and below the National Average of 81% Enrolment Ratio for Girls at Primary Stage (classes I–V) 1998–1999

States/UTs above the national average (23%)	Andhra Pradesh (87); Arunachal Pradesh (82); Assam (104); Gujarat (114); Haryana (84); Himachal Pradesh (83); Karnataka (102); Kerala (89); Madhya Pradesh (89); Maharashtra (110); Meghalaya (86); Mizoram (105); Nagaland (86); Punjab (83); Sikkim (110); Tamil Nadu (107); West Bengal (87); Daman & Diu (89); Delhi (82); Lakshadweep (96); Pondicherry (84); Rajasthan (81); Dadra & Nagar Haveli (81). Range: 81 in Rajasthan/Dadra & Nagar Haveli to 114 in Gujarat.
States/UTs below the national average (9%)	Bihar (59); Goa (77); Jammu & Kashmir (53); Manipur (70); Orissa (76); Tripura (75); Uttar Pradesh (49); Andaman & Nicobar Islands (76); Chandigarh (73). Range: 49 in Uttar Pradesh to 77 in Goa.

States and Union Territories below and above the National Average of 50 per cent Enrolment Ratio for Girls at Middle Stage (classes VI–VIII) in India in 1997–1998

States/UTs above the national average (25%)	Arunachal Pradesh (61); Assam (58); Goa (76); Gujarat (59); Haryana (61); Himachal Pradesh (74); Jammu & Kashmir (51); Karnataka (63); Kerala (93); Madhya Pradesh (50); Maharashtra (80); Manipur (65); Meghalaya (50); Mizoram (69); Nagaland (66); Punjab (63); Sikkim (63); Tamilnadu (89); Tripura (50); Andaman & Nicobar Islands (92); Chandigarh (81); Daman & Diu (65); Delhi (92); Lakshadweep (68); Pondicherry (89). Range: 50 in Tripura to 93 in Kerala.
States/UTs below the national average (7%)	Andhra Pradesh (40); Bihar (24); Orissa (39); Rajasthan (33); Uttar Pradesh (28); West Bengal (40); Dadra & Nagar Haveli (49). Range: 24 in Bihar to 49 in Dadra & Nagar Haveli.

TABLE 3.7
Dropout Rate at Elementary Stage in India
1960–1 to 1997–8

Year	Primary (classes I–V)			Middle (classes I–VIII)		
	Boys	Girls	Total	Boys	Girls	Total
1960–1	61.7	70.9	64.9	75.0	85.0	78.3
1970–1	64.5	70.9	67.0	74.6	83.4	77.9
1980–1	56.2	62.5	58.7	68.0	79.4	72.7
1990–1	40.1	46.0	42.6	59.1	65.1	60.9
1997–8*	38.2	41.3	39.6	50.7	58.6	54.1

* provisional figures.

Source: Selected Educational Statistics (relevent years), DoE, MHRD.

Girls' Enrolment, Retention, and Achievement: EFA Projects

THE DISTRICT PRIMARY EDUCATION PROGRAMME (DPEP)

Aggarwal (1999) notices that the participation of girls has considerably improved in the forty-two Phase I DPEP districts. The share of girls' enrolment has increased from 45.55 per cent in 1995–6 to 46.3 per cent in 1997–8. The index of gender equity is more than 95 for 21 of the 42 districts and between 85 and 95 in another 16. There are five districts of Madhya Pradesh, namely Guna, Tikamgarh, Sidhi, Dhar, and Rajgarh where additional efforts are needed to reduce the

TABLE 3.8
Inter-state Disparities in Female Dropout Rates at Primary Stage 1997–8
(classes I–V) (National Average 41%)

States/UTs above the national average (13%)	Andhra Pradesh (47); Arunachal Pradesh (45); Assam (42); Bihar (62); Manipur (54); Meghalaya (64); Mizoram (52); Orissa (48); Rajasthan (58); Tripura (54); Uttar Pradesh (56); West Bengal (54); Dadra & Nagar Haveli (44). Range: 42 in Assam to 62 in Bihar.
States/UTs below the national average (19%)	Goa (13); Gujarat (34); Haryana (16); Himachal Pradesh (31); Jammu & Kashmir (34); Karnataka (34); Kerala (–6.8); Madhya Pradesh (28); Maharashtra (26); Nagaland (35); Punjab (22); Sikkim (37); Tamil Nadu (16); A&N Islands (21); Chandigarh (–4); Daman & Diu (–0.3); Delhi (28); Lakshadweep (7); Pondicherry (–2). Range: –6.8 in Kerala to 37 in Sikkim

Elementary Stage in India (Classes I–VIII) (National Average 59)

States above the national average (15%)	Andhra Pradesh (75); Arunachal Pradesh (67); Assam (69); Bihar 81; Gujarat (65); Karnataka (61); Madhya Pradesh (60); Manipur (72); Mizoram (71); Orissa (63); Rajasthan (70); Sikkim (68); Tripura (74); West Bengal (71); Dadra & Nagar Haveli (62). Range: 60 in Madhya Pradesh to 81 in Bihar.
States below the national average (17%)	Goa (12); Haryana (36); Himachal Pradesh (26); Jammu & Kashmir (43); Kerala (0.7); Maharashtra (46); Meghalaya (47); Nagaland (36); Punjab (31); Tamil Nadu (35); Uttar Pradesh (57); A&N Islands (21); Chandigarh (–17.9); Daman & Diu (18); Delhi (7); Lakshadweep (24); Pondicherry (10). Range: –17.9 in Chandigarh to 43 in Jammu & Kashmir.

There is very negligible male–female difference in the promotion rate or dropout rate; girls, on an average, take a year longer to complete five years of primary schooling compared to the boys (see Table 3.9).

TABLE 3.9
Rates of Efficiency (Primary Stage)

	Promotion rate	Dropout rate	Years input per graduate
Boys	67.8	25.6	07.2
Girls	67.3	26.0	25.8
Total	67.6	25.8	07.5

Source: (NIEPA and MHRD 2000, Sub-table 18 Core EFA Indicators).

inequities between boys and girls. The strategy of Alternative Schooling is expected to overcome gender-related inequities even in the most educationally backward tribal-dominated districts. The minimization of gender-based inequities in primary education would result in improved female literacy in the DPEP districts which were selected from among the low female literacy districts. The project goal to reduce differences among gender and social groups to less than 5 per cent by the end of the project appears to be in sight. However, he warns against complacency as he feels a lot needs to be done to improve the participation and retention of girls. A variety of innovative and cost-effective strategies need to be evolved to reach out to children in isolated small habitations and habitations with a concentration of ST children, working children, and disabled children. Additionally, locally relevant curriculum and teacher training to handle first-generation learners as also greater interaction between school and community through frequent meetings with Village Education Committees, women's groups, and other community-based agencies, need to be developed.

Srivastava's (1999) study of the internal efficiency of primary education in forty districts of Phase I of the DPEP states that in general the gender difference in respect of internal efficiency is small in most of the districts. In 24 districts, the coefficient of efficiency in the case of girls is not very different from that of boys, the difference between the two being less than three points. In 14 districts where the coefficient for girls is less than that for boys, 10 are in Madhya Pradesh. However, in Raisin and Rewa districts, the coefficient of efficiency for girls is substantially higher than that for boys. As regards the cohort dropout rate, of the 40 districts studied, that of girls exceeds that of boys in 25 districts, is almost equal to that of boys in 5 districts, and is less than that of boys in 10 districts. Only in 11 of 40 districts, the dropout rate of girls is 5.0, or more percentage points.

A Mid-term Learning Assessment Survey (MAS) by the NCERT in 1997 in all 42 districts of Phase I of the DPEP indicated significant improvement in language and mathematics, although a great deal remains to be done. The goal of reducing differences between gender groups to less than 55 has been realized in almost all districts across the classes in both the subjects. The result, however, is not so encouraging with regard to social groups.

SHIKSHA KARMI PROJECT

Launched in 1987 with SIDA assistance, the Shiksha Karmi Project (SKP) of Rajasthan is an innovative community-based primary education experiment for remote and difficult villages with dysfunctional primary schools and endemic teacher absenteeism. The regular teachers are replaced with local teachers, *shiksha karmis,* who are less qualified but are continually trained though pre-service, in-service and refresher programmes by the *shiksha karmi sahyogis* (Field Coordinators) and supervisors who are eternally on the move working with the day schools and the *prehar pathshalas* (evening schools). Besides the improvement of the school environment, augmentation of school infrastructure, and increasing enrollment and retention of all children, the *shiksha karmi* sees education of girls as a serious challenge in the extremely low literacy blocks of Rajasthan. At grassroots level, the SKP works through *panchayat*

samitis, shiksha karmi sahyogis, subject specialists of NGOs, and the village communities. The *prehar pathshalas* provide condensed formal school curriculum and specially designed learning materials to educate out-of- school children who are unable to attend regular school for some reason or the other. Presently 22,359 girls (who form 71 per cent of the learners in these centres) are benefiting from these *prehar pathshalas.* Many of them look overage, and hence, perhaps feel shy about going to day school.

The dedication of SKP personnel is exemplar, to say the least. The SKP villages now have batches of girls who have passed Class V and they and their guardians want these schools to be upgraded to middle stage. The pride of a village visited was the woman *shiksha karmi* who had upgraded her qualifications to high school in the last several years. Currently, the SKP is functional in 125 Blocks spread over the 29 districts of Rajasthan, catering to the needs of 165,000 children of whom a majority are first-generation learners.

LOK JUMBISH

Lok Jumbish (LJ) signifies a vigorous people's movement and views education as an instrumentality of women's equality. The LJ strategies that have evolved over a period comprise of people's participation; decentralization, gender equity; improvement of teacher status; quality in all programmes and activities; HRD; and in-built review and evaluation. Education of Girls is its loadstar and women's empowerment and involvement is seen both as a means to universalization of primary education of eight years and as an end in itself. A highly decentralized block-based village-centred project, women make up half its functionaries at all levels of management. At field level, there are two women functionaries to one male functionary. Processes are very important in this project, and the pace has to be set by the village people, by the learners, by the communities. The highly professionalized LJ staff move into communities, win their confidence, and form them into groups for school mapping, and later, school building committees—women and men in equal numbers. It is hard work at times but ultimately the schools and the schooling of its children become the concern and responsibility of the village itself—the parents, the elected members, and all others. It is really an attempt to return primary education where it belongs—the people and the communities themselves. There is an attempt to make curriculum interesting, relevant, and flexible, leaving a lot of room for the teachers to innovate. Besides working with the regular government schools, a major innovation of LJ is its Sahaj Shiksha (non-formal education programme), in which the main takers are girls and boys from very disadvantaged groups and remote areas. Mahila Shikshan Kendras (women's education centres), Adhyapika Manchs (women teachers' forum), gender training of teachers and teacher educators, Balika Shivirs (girl child camps), and late life skills approach and gender sensitization of boys in similar camps are several innovations of the LJ movement.

The LJ sees educational access for girls as paramount, the educational content and process as a means to enhancing the self-esteem of girls and women for taking hold of their own lives and for participating in all social institutions and processes with dignity and self-confidence. Samvadika (The Core Gender Group) meets regularly to understand all dimensions of gender equity and women's empowerment and for sharing field experiences and forever working out new strategies. The LJ is currently working in 75 blocks in 27 districts of Rajasthan. The state government has decided to start the DPEP in nineteen districts. The remaining thirteen districts will be exclusively covered by the LJ.

Besides, the Saraswati Yojana (SY) has been operational in Rajasthan since 1994–5 in order to keep the education of the Girl Child the focus of all educational activities. Under this scheme, local women who have passed Class VIII are given training and financial assistance to run courtyard schools in their homes. At present, about 1220 SY centres are functional in which about 10,000 children are studying. This scheme is in addition to the centrally sponsored scheme of non-formal education (NFE).

THE BIHAR EDUCATION PROJECT (BEP)

This UNICEF- assisted primary education project has done considerable work to promote the universalization of primary education through formal schools, the NFE, and the very innovative Jagjagi Centres for out-of-school girls and educational and residential economic empowerment programmes run by the Mahila Samakhya complement of the BEP. The transformation of shy, reticent tribal and folk girls into alert and confident young women complete with literacy, health and economic skills, and laced with judo and karate training is something to be seen to be believed.

Women Teachers

The number of teachers at school stage has increased phenomenally. During 1950–1 to 1997–8, at primary stage their number has gone up from 538,000 to 1.9 million; at middle stage their number has gone up from 86,000 to 1.2 million. As regards seconary/higher secondary stage, their number has gone up from 127,000 to 1.5 million (see Table 3.10). Whereas the number of primary teachers has increased more than three times during this period, for middle schools there is an increase of more than ten times, and for high school/higher secondary stage there is an increase of nearly nine times.

The primary stage continues to suffer from shortage of teachers in that the phenomenon of multigrade teachers with two to three teachers managing a primary school is common in rural areas. Under the scheme Operation Blackboard (OB), an attempt was made to phase out single-teacher schools and their number substantially decreased as reported in the Sixth All-India Educational Survey. In the OB scheme, while phasing out single teacher schools, it was mandatory that the

TABLE 3.10
Number of School Teachers by Sex in India 1950–1 to 1997–8

('000s)

Year	Primary			Middle			Secondary/Hr. secondary		
	Total	Male	Female	Total	Male	Female	Total	Male	Female
1950–1	538	456	82 (15)	86	73	13 (15)	127	107	20 (16)
1960–1	742	615	127 (17)	345	262	83 (24)	296	234	62 (21)
1970–1	1080	835	225 (21)	638	463	175 (27)	629	474	155 (25)
1980–1	1363	1021	342 (25)	851	598	253 (30)	926	669	257 (28)
1990–1	1616	1143	473 (29)	1073	717	356 (33)	1334	917	417 (31)
1997–8	1872	1229	643 (34)	1212	775	437 (36)	1521	985	536 (35)

Note: Figures in parenthesis indicate percentage share of female teachers to total teachers at each stage.
Source: Department of Education (relevant years), Annual Report, Selected Educational Statistics.

second teacher to be added under this central scheme would be female in case the earlier teacher was male. Many states made sincere efforts to place women teachers in rural schools under the scheme and even increase their quotas in teacher training institutions at the time of recruitment. This has borne results in that the women teachers have improved their share in the total from 15 to 34 per cent at primary level; 15 to 36 per cent at the middle stage; and 16 to 35 per cent at the secondary/higher secondary stage.

Moreover, in this regard regional disparities are extremely large. In 1997–8, the percentage of female teachers to total in the states and union territories ranged from 19 per cent in Bihar to 96 per cent in Chandigarh at primary stage; 18 per cent in Assam to 92 per cent in Chandigarh at middle level; and 15 per cent in Bihar to 84 per cent in Chandigarh at secondary/higher secondary level.

RURAL–URBAN GAP

Besides, the aggregate picture hides the continued shortage of female teachers in rural areas. While urban schools are overstaffed and crowded with women teachers, the rural schools have both staff shortage and very low presence of female teachers (see Table 3.11). This factor is aggravated in low female literacy states and continues to hamper educational participation of girls, especially post primary stages. As field studies show, there is a clear demand for more women teachers at all levels especially at the post primary stages. Parents do not appear to be averse to co-education but feel that presence of women on the teaching/administrative staff of these schools is a must. During some field visits even the all-male faculty of rural schools expressed that having one or more women teacher is necessary even in primary schools as girls feel shy and do not open up much and are unable to share their problems and anxieties. There was a general feeling that women teachers, especially at post puberty stage, can enhance the self-confidence of girls through systematic counselling, besides being good role models (see Nayar 1996–7).

TABLE 3.11
Percentage Share of Female Teachers to Total by Level and by Rural–Urban Areas 1993

Area	Primary	Middle	Secondary	Hr. sec.
Rural	23.45	24.66	22.72	18.10
Urban	60.25	59.47	53.58	41.25
Total	31.41	35.08	33.92	31.57

Source: NCERT (1998). Sixth All-India Educational Survey.

The acute shortage of women teachers has been an area of concern and debate for more than hundred years. The *Recommendation of Education Commission 1882* to financially support rural girls for teacher training through residential programmes is valid even today, but little has been done on this account. The emphasis has been on recruitment of more women teachers or at best quotas in teacher training which were obviously utilized by urban women. The central scheme to finance additional women teachers for rural areas in the Sixth Plan was withdrawn in the Seventh Plan. The explanation was that urban women get recruited and later manage transfers to their respective urban locations. This is hardly to be faulted considering (a) the Indian male-dominated family structure; (b) poor availability of basic amenities of health, housing, hygiene, and education in rural areas; and (c) lack of quotas for rural women in recruitment and teacher training. The problem is more basic. Secondary and higher education of women continues to be an urban elite middle-class phenomenon. Rural girls do not get as far as secondary/higher secondary education to become eligible for entry into primary teacher training. It is pertinent to state that the proportion of women teachers is very low in the low female literacy belt, and this continues as a vicious cycle. There is a need to increase secondary/higher secondary opportunities for rural girls on a priority basis to end the vicious cycle of rural female illiteracy, low enrolments, and lack of women teachers in rural areas (see Nayar 1993).

Education of Out-of-School Girls

A prime area of concern in the education of the girl child is the formulation of action programmes focusing on the education of out-of-school girls at elementary and secondary levels. A major proportion of girls in the 10–18 age group are out of school.

With respect to UEE; the following figures are to be noted (see Table 3.12):

• The estimated out-of-school children in the age group 6–14 was more than 40 million in 1997–8, of these, 67 per cent were girls.

• In the age group 6–11 (classes I–V), there were more than 12 million children out of school, of whom 89 per cent were girls.

• In the age group 11–14, estimated out-of-school children were to the tune of 28 million, of whom 58 per cent were girls.

• In absolute terms, a total of 27 million girls were out of school, 11 million in the primary age group and 16 million in the upper primary age group.

TABLE 3.12

Estimated Number of Non-enrolled Children by Sex at the Elementary Stage in 1997

('000s)

	6–11 years (classes I–V)			11–14 years (classes VI–VIII)		
	Boys	Girls	Total	Boys	Girls	Total
Estimated population in the age group in 1997	62,759	58,403 (48.20)	121,162	35,580	31,966 (47.32)	67,546
Enrolment in 1997–8	61,329	47,453 (43.62)	108,782	23,646	15,841 (40.12)	39,487
Non-enrolled children in 1997–8	1430	10,950 (88.45)	12,380	11,934	16,125 (57.47)	28,059

Source: Department of Education (relevant years). Selected Educational Statistics.

Note: Figures in parenthesis indicate percentage girls to total.

• Assuming that there are 20–5 per cent overage/underage children in the system, the number of out-of-school children in the specific age groups could even be higher.

The NSSO (1998) data on attendance rate estimates 89.64 million children not attending school in 1995–6; 65.52 million in the age group 6–11 and 24.12 million in the age group 11–14 (quoted in Takroo 1999). The NIEPA (1999) Draft EFA 2000 Assessment on Core EFA Indicators puts the figure at 35.06 million in the age group 6–11 after allowing for 21.54 per cent underage and overage children in classes I–V. Nonetheless, it is clear that the problem exists even if different figures are arrived at by different agencies.

In rural areas, there is continued *shortage of women teachers*. A major study has been completed on the problems related to recruitment and posting of women teachers at the elementary stage in rural areas of the four most populous, low female literacy states of Bihar, Madhya Pradesh, Rajasthan and Uttar Pradesh. The study finds that while some effort is being made to draw more women teachers into teaching at the recruitment point and even in teacher training institutions, the real malaise is the low and extremely poor outreach of rural girls to post primary education in rural areas and these girls are unable to complete higher secondary (12 years) level which is the entry requirement for primary teacher's training. (Nayar 1995–6)

CRITICAL ISSUES AND INTERVENTIONS

Education of girls has been high on the national agenda since Independence. Special commissions and committees were set up from time to time to assess the progress of girls' education and to propose suitable interventions to promote their participation in education. Several strategies were adopted to promote education of girls as an integral part of the planned socio-economic development of the country. Theoretically, all formal and non-formal education and training programmes are open to women. In addition, provision exists for opening of separate institutions or separate wings for women/girls exclusively. Education is free for girls up to the higher secondary stage and several states have made education free for girls right up to university level. Besides free education for all children up to the age of 14, there are incentive schemes like free noon meals, free books, free uniforms, and attendance scholarships for girls and children from disadvantaged groups.

It may be pertinent to remind ourselves that the pro-girl policies and action that have accelerated the educational participation of girls during the 1990s owe it to the steady work of earlier decades, springboard action of the NPE, and the Programme of Action of 1992. It is also important to note the significant impact of the Total Literacy Campaigns and ECCE on demand generation, as well as the contribution of women's movement and focus on women's studies.

There are two clear axes of promotion of girls' education, namely expansion of educational facilities and following the accepted policy of undifferentiated curricula and reorienting the contents and processes of education to make it gender-sensitive and a vehicle of women's equality and empowerment. The post-NPE efforts in the area of girls' education appear to be giving positive results, a major yardstick being the sharp increase in literacy levels and greater retention and transition of girls to successive higher levels of education. In absolute terms, enrolment of girls during this period at primary level has increased by over seven million as compared to boys whose numbers have increased by four million. India has two major successes to report. One is the faster growth of girls' participation at primary level and more importantly the redesigning of the content and the process of education for promoting gender equality and for creating a girl-friendly educational and social environment.

This chapter has reviewed the progress of girls' education in India during the last five decades with special focus on the post-Jomtien period (1990–2000) and within the framework of EFA. Against the broad findings of the review, the following are some important issues and interventions that need consideration.

Issues that Remain

Though significant progress has been made in the provision of education for all girls, the task is not yet complete. There are several issues that need to be seriously addressed by educational planners and policy makers in the years to come. Some of these are:

- provision of post-primary education to girls in remote rural areas and from disadvantaged groups;
- special focus on enrolment and retention of SC, ST, OBC girls;
- absence of data in case of educationally backward minorities;
- education of out-of-school girls in the age group 10–18;
- improvement of quality of state and state-aided schools;
- curricular reforms to make education more meaningful and relevant;
- continued thrust on gender sensitive and gender inclusive curriculum and its transaction;
- further gender inputs into pre-service and in-service education of teachers and teacher educators and textbook writers and textbook production boards;
- higher proportion of women teachers in rural areas;
- building up of intersectoral convergence with respect to education-health-nutrition of children and adolescent girls;
- building up of a functional relationship between the education department and *panchayati raj* institutions;
- lack of regular inflow of rural-urban statistics on girls' education.

Interventions Needed

As already pointed out, the situation with respect to girls' education varies considerably across the country. Therefore, interventions have to be worked out in a contextual manner. However, following are some general proposals that may help in tackling the various issues confronting girls' education in the country.

- A large number of girls from remote and small rural habitations continue to get excluded from primary education. It is necessary to create part or alternative schooling in small unserved habitations.
- It is necessary to upgrade all primary schools to middle schools. Girls do not cross village boundaries ordinarily. The 3 km radial distance for a middle school is forbidding at times due to terrain or reasons of personal safety. Moreover, if all the feeder primary schools are able to retain all entrants in class I and nearly all of them pass out of class V, the present serving middle schools can by no means take in all primary school graduates. Further, there is enough evidence that girls continue on to higher classes wherever there are complete middle/secondary or higher secondary schools within the village.
- Make all weather motorable roads to all villages as a first charge and provide free school bus service to all elementary school children (classes I-VIII) and to girls up to higher secondary level. The trade-off between expenditure on building an additional 2 million classrooms/motorable roads and the large array of the existing incentive schemes needs to be studied.
- Girls' primary-level boarding schools or *ashram shalas* are needed for scattered populations in forests, deserts, mountains, for instance. Successful experiments of the Madhya Pradesh tribal development block and of LJ need to be studied before taking any major policy decision.
- However, it is of prime importance to open exclusive *balika vidya peeths* in every block with provision for general and vocational education up to class XII with residential facilities for girls of the villages of the blocks, which do not have a middle or a high school. Vocational courses could include modern trades, and among others, elementary teacher's training, training as para health workers, *anganwadi* workers, preschool teachers, *gram sevikas*, etc.
- The problem of education of Muslim girls needs to be specially addressed. The census could give out figures about their single-year agewise enrolments/participation rates for developing special strategies on a par with other educationally and economically disadvantaged groups.
- The shortage of women teachers poses a major barrier for girls' schooling in rural areas. Four-year residential courses for middle-pass rural girls should be designed to prepare women teachers for the elementary stage in all three streams (languages, science, and mathematics, social sciences with pedagogical inputs).
- The potential of distance education is immense and needs to be tapped for educating girls living in difficult areas and the large out-of-school girls' population.

• Schemes like Apni Beti Apna Dhan (Haryana), Rajyalakshmi and Saraswati Yojana of Rajasthan, and similar other attempts to secure the fundamental right to life of girls need to be strengthened and linked to education for long-term effects.

• Wherever *panchayats* are even partially functional (even when lacking financial resources) and have taken over their schools, things have improved for children's education in general and for girls in particular.

• Articulation and organization of village women around issues of daily survival include their concern for education of their sons and daughters. *Mahila mandals/samoohs* need to be strengthened and revived as a major plank of rural development and women's empowerment.

• An expanded programme of formal and non-formal vocational training for rural girls in health, employment, etc. needs to be instated. Transition rates for rural girls need improvement both at middle and secondary levels.

• A national programme of strengthening science and maths teaching in all girls' schools along with a scheme to meet shortage of science and maths teachers in girls school needs to be instated. The special focus is to improve access of girls to secondary and technical education in rural areas.

• There is need for adequate MIS on women's education and training and gender-sensitive planning.

REFERENCES

Aggarwal, Y. P. (1999). 'Access and Retention in District Primary Education Programme Districts: A National Overview.' Paper presented at the *International Seminar on Researches in School Effectiveness at Primary Stage*. National Council of Educational Research and Training, New Delhi.

Department of Education (1996). *Selected Educational Statistics*. Ministry of Human Resource Development, Government of India, New Delhi.

———— (1992). *National Policy on Education 1992: Programme of Action 1992*. Ministry of Human Resource Development, Government of India, New Delhi.

———— (1998–9). *Annual Report*. Ministry of Human Resource Development, Government of India, New Delhi.

Government of India (1995). 'Country Paper India' presented in *Fourth World Conference on Women*. Beijing.

Ministry of Health and Family Welfare (1997–8). *Annual Report*. Government of India, New Delhi.

Ministry of Law and Justice (As on 1st June 1996). *The Constitution of India*. Government of India, New Delhi.

National Council of Educational Research and Training (1998). *Sixth All-India Educational Survey*. New Delhi.

National Institute of Educational Planning and Administration and Ministry of Human Resource Development (2000). 'EFA 2000 Assessment: Core EFA Indicators.' New Delhi.

National Literacy Mission (1998). *Literacy Rates: An Analysis Based on National Sample Survey Organisation Survey*. Note circulated by National Literacy Mission, Government of India, New Delhi.

National Sample Survey Organisation (1998). *Attending an Educational Institution in India: Its Level, Nature and Cost*. NSS 52nd round (1996–7) Report No. 439. Department of Statistics, Government of India, New Delhi.

Nayar, Usha (1991–3). 'Factors of Continuance and Discontinuance of Girls in Elementary Schooling (Rajasthan, Orissa, Bombay and Delhi in 3000 households and 7000 girls from rural poverty households, tribal areas, and urban slums)'. Study sponsored by National Council of Educational Research and Training and Ministry of Human Resource Development, New Delhi.

———— (1992–3). 'Study on Causes for Drop out and Non-Enrollment Among Rural Girls in Haryana in Low Rural Female Literacy Block Pundri (District Kaithal), Block Nuh (District Gurgaon) and Block Ballabhgarh (District Faridabad).' Study sponsored by UNESCO, New Delhi.

———— (1993). 'Study on Universalization of Primary Education of Rural Girls in India.' National Council of Educational Research and Training (Commissioned by UNESCO), New Delhi.

———— (1993–4). 'District Primary Education Programme Gender Studies in 44 Low Female Literacy Districts in 8 States, viz., Assam, Maharashtra, Haryana, Madhya Pradesh, Karnataka, Kerala, Tamil Nadu and Orissa'. Study sponsored by National Council of Educational Research and Training and Ministry of Human Resource Development, New Delhi.

———— (1995–6). 'Study on Problems of Recruitment and Posting of Women Teachers in Rural Areas (Bihar, Madhya Pradesh, Uttar Pradesh and Rajasthan).' National Council of Educational Research and Training, New Delhi.

Prakash, Ved, *et al.* (1999). 'An Appraisal of Students' Achievement During Mid-Term Assessment Survey under District Primary Education Programme.' Paper presented at the *International Seminar on Researches in School Effectiveness at Primary Stage*. National Council of Educational Research and Training, New Delhi.

Srivastava, A. B. L. (1999). 'Internal Efficiency of Primary Education in Phase-I District Primary Education Programme Districts.' Paper presented at the *International Seminar on Researches in School Effectiveness at Primary Stage*. National Council of Educational Research and Training, New Delhi.

4

Children, Work and Education
Rethinking on Out-of-School Children

Sharada Jain, Alok Mathur, Shobhita Rajgopal, Juhi Shah

INTRODUCTION

The universalization of elementary education (UEE) is one of the few issues on which all political parties have declared agreement; developmental economists stress the urgency of it; and activists raise it as a demand. It has overall approval of the people. Many myths justifying the neglect of the education of poor children have been explored (PROBE Team, 1999, 14–17). It is significant that issues of child rights, child labour, and educational concerns have now come close enough to generate clarity on what needs to be done.

Yet, the visible scenario in this respect is far from what 'should have been'. It does not require clever tools of measurement to demonstrate that there are millions of children in India who are totally deprived of any education worth the name. And it is not as if they are invisible, remote, and therefore, unreached. They are everywhere in the cities: on the streets, wiping cars at traffic junctions, picking rags in mounds of waste; in the *dhabas* (roadside eateries), in small factories, as cheap labour or domestic help; at 'home' completing household chores. In the villages again they are everywhere, responding to the contextual demands of family work as well as bonded labour. The case of girls not having access to education is not subtle or obscure any more—in fact, they, their parents, and the community they live in all lament their lack of access to education.

INTERVENTIONS

At the policy planning and implementation level, several government documents and legislations indicate the state's concern for children and give an impetus to development services for the welfare of children. The revised National Policy on Education (NPE)–1992 redefined educational priorities and made an attempt to address issues of quantity, quality, and equity in educational process. By ratifying the UN Convention on the Rights of Children (CRC) in 1992, the Government of India also committed itself to creating an appropriate environment for survival, protection, and development of children. More recently, the 83rd Constitution Amendment Bill, 1997 seeks to make free education for all children up to the age of 14 years a Fundamental Right (see Box 4.1). On the other hand, a number of NGOs have demonstrated successful approaches in meeting the needs of disadvantaged children, specially girls, and have influenced mainstream education through replication of their models and through policy dialogue with the government. These experiences have also established that NGOs can and do play a strong role in guiding/assisting the state to complement the public education system and improve its effectiveness.

BOX 4.1

Judgement on Right to Education

The judgement of the Supreme Court in J. P. Unnikrishnan Vs State of Andhra Pradesh, 1993 has already transformed an incremental development goal into an entitlement of all children up to 14 years by pronouncing the Right to Education to be a Fundamental Right derived from the Right to Life itself. As regards determining the extent of the responsibility of the State would have to be as laid down by Article 12 of the Constitution of India which includes, 'the Government and Parliament of India, Government and legislature of each of the States and all local or other authorities within the territory of India or under the control of the Government of India'.

—Department of Education (1999, p. 7)

Who are These Children? Why are They Out-of- School?

At one level, unanimity has emerged in the past decade that a certain section of out-of-school children belong to the group that can be called 'child labour'—children who work in factories, under oppressive conditions, and for long hours. Such a situation can never be acceptable in a democratic state. Hence, effective implementation of laws against bonded and child labour must be demanded.

However, this is not the entire story. Children are also out of school for other reasons:

• Dysfunctional schools—'nothing happens in the school'.
• 'Beating', 'scolding', or having been treated shabbily in school.
• Their family and lifestyles being mismatched with the time, pattern, and requirements of school.
• Their being migratory groups—cattle grazers, cotton pickers, construction labour, etc.
• Education not being really free—the minimal fees coupled with expenditure on books etc. being beyond the capacity of the parents.
• A pervasive cynicism and frustration in the community—loss of motivation for change due to exploitative conditions, a sense of betrayal.
• Sparse habitation, therefore, no school nearby.
• Disability and, therefore, invisibility of children.
• Gender roles for girls.
• Having missed the bus—too old to go to class I.

This section presents an illustrative overview of the significant initiatives that have been implemented during the last ten years through government and non-government efforts to make education accessible to out-of-school children, i.e. child labour/working children, street children, girls, and children from other disadvantaged groups. Four major streams of initiatives can be discerned. At one end are the groups which focus principally on rejection of child labour and take a serious stand on the issue of child rights leading further to education. One step removed are the groups which are actively engaged in Early Childhood Care and Education (ECCE); their primary argument is that if children are kept occupied in collective education/care, school becomes a natural next step. Children are thus, in effect, prevented from getting into a labour situation. The third intervention is to improve the availability of educational centres—schools or non-formal education (NFE). This addresses the 'access' issue, i.e. making it possible for children to reach a school. The fourth broad stream of educational efforts attempts to upgrade the image of the school by focusing on the quality of education, the

improved curriculum, and pedagogy. Here the assumption is that if there is a good school available, parents would definitely put their children there rather than send them out for petty work; and children would like to be there because they find it good. In all the various interventions, there are many intermediate points of action/thought, many overlaps, but they all converge on the broad objective of getting out-of-school children into the educational stream.

Advocacy for Child Rights and Campaigns Against Child Labour

The issues of child labour and child rights have become key topics in the development debate, globally as well as nationally. A number of concerns have risen in the wake of the UN Convention on the Rights of the Child (CRC) and various protagonists have taken diametrically opposed positions on the subject. On the one side of the debate are those who believe that child labour must be defined broadly to include all children who are out of the school system as they are potential child labourers, and hence, deprived of their rights. This view is increasingly being adopted by a range of international agencies as well as some national organizations and researchers. For them, education is the key to the elimination of child labour. They also reject the non-formal systems of education and are concerned with upgrading the quality of the formal system. On the other side, and a more liberal view, is that labour must carefully be distinguished from work. Work and education need not necessarily be dichotomous. They give weight to the economic circumstances that give rise to children's participation in the labour market and argue for an educational system that takes cognizance of these circumstances. They suggest that work is not necessarily opposed to learning, but lay stress on distinguishing between hazardous and non-hazardous forms of work. This position also attaches importance to NFE interventions coexisting with the formal system. Underpinning all these different positions are some fundamental debates about the meaning and value of education, about who decides on children's needs, interests, and well-being[1]

[1] The recent surge of interest in child labour has too often been founded upon—and contributed to—four myths about child labour that it is vital to confront:
• The first is that child labour is uniquely a problem of the developing world.
• The second is that child labour emerges inevitably and naturally out of poverty and it will always be with us.
• The third is that most child labourers are at work in sweatshops producing cheap goods for export to the stores of the rich world.
• And the fourth is that there is a simple solution to the child labour problem—a 'trade sanction' or 'boycott' that will end it once and for all.

(see Kabeer, *et al.*, 1999). A great deal of debate is presently conducted at macro and systemic levels on all these issues.

THE NGO FORUM FOR STREET AND WORKING CHILDREN

The NGO Forum, established in thirteen cities between 1987 and 1992, with more than sixty organizations working with street children, has played an important role in awareness building and empowerment of street children. The primary objectives of this group are to promote networking and coordination among NGOs, groups, and individuals concerned with street children and to initiate and promote a common programme of action in the areas of healthcare, education, awareness-building, etc. Some of the common strategies used by the NGO Forum are: sharing of experiences by member organizations through regular meetings, organizing seminars/workshops on several issues concerning street children and child rights, workshops and camps for children, and newsletters.

CAMPAIGN AGAINST CHILD LABOUR

The Campaign against Child Labour (CACL), initiated in 1992, is a nationwide effort seeking eradication of child labour which is defined as a violation of basic human rights. The major focus of the CACL is on the mobilization of public opinion for the eradication of child labour; establishing linkages with other issues, movements and struggles; and intervening in specific cases of child abuse and violations of child rights. Within the short span of seven years, the CACL has succeeded in building up a network of more than 500 social action groups, voluntary organizations, and activists to work together on the issue of child labour and to advocate the rights of children. A two-pronged advocacy strategy has been adopted by the CACL—that of building public opinion on child labour using both conventional and non-conventional media, and of persuading the government to enforce existing laws and to enact a comprehensive progressive legislation to ensure the rights of children (see Rane and Billimoria 1998, 268).

UDAAN: FORUM OF STREET CHILDREN/YOUTH

In September 1992, YUVA—an NGO working for marginalized children in Mumbai—facilitated the formation of 'Udaan' (meaning flight), a forum of street children and youth, which remained active till June 1994. Udaan was an experiment in developing alternatives for the target group. This forum provided a platform for older boys of around 16 years of age to express themselves and articulate issues of their concern. Udaan enabled the boys to establish a sense of solidarity and belonging, gain an identity, and regain their dignity and self-esteem. The lack of an independent resource base led to the discontinuation of the activities of Udaan.

BACHPAN BACHAO ANDOLAN

The 'Bachpan Bachao Andolan' (Save the Childhood Movement/BBA) came into being during the Uttar Pradesh Legislative Assembly elections in 1993. The Andolan emerged as a strategy by the South Asian Coalition of Child Servitude (SACCS), a Delhi-based NGO, to inject the issue of child labour into the electoral campaign. This group organizes direct action like raids and freeing children from bondage; mobilizing public opinion on the issue and building pressure groups for effective implementation of child labour laws and rehabilitation schemes.

The Andolan is the nodal action wing of SACCS, and has state units in Uttar Pradesh, Bihar, Madhya Pradesh, Rajasthan, Maharashtra, Haryana, and Delhi. The initiative has freed more than 27,000 children from servitude in carpet, glass, brick-kiln, stone, ceramics, construction, and agricultural sectors through raids and with orders from Supreme and High Courts. An independent monitoring and labelling system—RUGMARK—has been developed by the group to certify products made without child labour and provide a positive alternative to consumers and producers. Besides, it has also set up fourteen non-formal education centres for working children and a Mukti Ashram at Delhi for sixty bonded child workers who have been freed.

The foregoing analysis indicates that NGOs/voluntary agencies have played an important role in mobilizing opinion and action against child labour and advocating child rights. However, there has been little effort to evolve a comprehensive strategy on other issues that affect children's lives. The extent of participation varies from campaign to campaign initiated by various groups. It is imperative that a greater degree of participation in initiating and promoting campaigns is elicited from children themselves on issues affecting their lives. The case of the MV Foundation (MVF) working in Andhra Pradesh provides an example of sustained efforts for eradication of child labour.

MVF, ANDHRA PRADESH

The MVF, a private charitable trust, has been working in 500 villages of the Ranga Reddy district of Andhra Pradesh. The main thrust of the MVF's work has been on bringing bonded child labourers and working children into the ambit of school education. Relying mainly on community initiatives, the MVF programme motivates parents and children to utilize the formal school as a medium for advancement. All the activities of the MVF are directed towards two basic inter-linked objectives—that there must be abolition of child labour and that all children must go to school. It works towards breaking the labouring cycle, believing that the only way to eradicate child labour is to send all children to school.

Starting in three villages of the Ranga Reddy district in 1991, the MVF has extricated 80,000 children from work and enrolled them in schools. About 4000 bonded child labourers have been liberated and put in schools. The age group ranges from the very young to adolescents. The MVF now operates in nearly 500 villages and 90 per cent of all children in the 5–11 age group are in school in these villages. The organization has also made a significant dent in the schooling of the more difficult age group of 9–14 years. About 5000 adolescent children have been enrolled into formal schools through camps and bridge courses. Besides, seventy-five villages have been declared free of child labour. (see Jagannathan 1999, 10). While working with these children and their families, the MVF found that poverty is not the primary motivating factor for children to work. It also noted that parents do not depend on their children's earnings for a living and that they are willing to make adjustments to send their children to school.

The MVF uses a series of strategies to put working children in school. While young children are encouraged to join school directly, the older ones, mostly first-generation learners, are conditioned to the process of schooling in long-term camps. The children have, therefore, been classified into three age groups since the needs vary at different ages.

THE AGE GROUP 5–8

Most children in this age group are primarily engaged in domestic work, tending livestock, or non-wage-earning work but some are also idle. The strategy adopted by the MVF for these children is to withdraw them from work and enrol them in local government schools. Intensive motivation and awareness programmes are conducted for this purpose to encourage parents to send their children to schools.

THE AGE GROUP 9–11

These children are already involved in hard-core child labour and many of them worked as bonded labourers. For this group, MVF workers first reach out to each and every parent and try and convince them of the vital importance of educating their children. The child workers are then convinced that it is possible for them to 'get away from the drudgery of work'. Third, the gap between these children and school-going children is filled through bridge courses in summer camps.

THE AGE GROUP 12–14

The children in this age group are put in long-duration camps (of about eighteen months). Other than withdrawing them from work, MVF workers help them pass the class VII examination and join secondary school in class VIII.

One of the key features of the the MVF's intervention is reliance on formal, regular government schools to provide for the education of hitherto working children. The MVF model has been widely replicated by a number of government and non-government agencies to tackle the problem of child labour. One criticism of the MVF approach, however, has been that it has viewed education as having instrumental value (children have to be removed from labour, hence they should be in school) rather than intrinsic value.

PRATHAM MUMBAI EDUCATION INITIATIVE

The 'Pratham Mumbai Education Initiative' uses early childhood education as a stepping stone to universalize primary education in the city of Mumbai. Started with UNICEF initiative, Pratham's defined objective is to ensure that all children in the age group of 3–10 in Mumbai city are enrolled in preschool centres or primary schools. Addressing the total lack of preschool facilities for the urban deprived in Mumbai, a few *balwadis* (preschool centres) were started in 1995. In 1998-9, there were 2800 *balwadis* functioning in different areas of Mumbai with an enrollment of 56,000 children (see Banerjee 1999). Pratham has developed a low-cost model for ECCE that is community based. A small fee is collected from each child, which goes towards the salary of the instructor. Pratham recruits promising youngsters from the slums for the job, provides them with the requisite training, and pays them a small honorarium (see Jagannathan 1999, 14).

From the beginning, Pratham's objective has been to work with the existing municipal primary school system to improve access, increase attendance, and strengthen achievement. After reaching universal preschool coverage, Pratham intends to hand over financial responsibility of these centres to the Municipal Corporation of Mumbai, while retaining the responsibility of management.

Increasing Access

NON-FORMAL EDUCATION (NFE)

The last decade has seen several government-supported initiatives for increasing access to primary education. Special effort has been made in many of these programmes to reach out to working children, girls, and those children who cannot attend full-time school due to socio-economic compulsions and cultural barriers.

The first generation of alternative schooling under government auspices consisted of NFE centres sponsored by the central government. The NFE programme is being implemented since 1979 in twenty three states/union territories through 0.29 million centres. Of these, nearly 0.24 million come under the state sector, while the rest are managed by the voluntary sector. At present, there are 676 voluntary agencies involved in running NFE centres in the country (see Department of Education 1997).

The scheme was revised in 1993 with emphasis on organization, flexibility, relevance of curriculum, diversity in learning, and activity to suit the needs of learners through decentralized management. In spite of the revised perspective, evaluation studies indicate that a large number of the NFE centres continue to be dysfunctional and are beset with problems such as:

- delay in disbursement of funds and honorarium to instructors,
- weak training inputs,
- shortage and irregular supply of teaching and learning materials, and
- lack of interest and commitment of district education officials (see *IDS 1994, 135–6; ORG 1994b, 207–8*).

It is evident that the centrally sponsored NFE centres replicate all the operational problems of the formal schooling system—lack of supervision, poor infrastructure, absence of community participation, and so on. Some NGOs have achieved greater success in the area of alternative schooling based on adequate support and accountability structures.

EDUCATION GUARANTEE SCHEME, MADHYA PRADESH

The 'Education Guarantee Scheme' (EGS) was initiated by the government of Madhya Pradesh in January 1997. Under the EGS, the government guarantees the provision of educational facilities to children in habitations where there is no schooling facility in a 1 km radius, within a period of ninety days of receiving a demand for such a facility by the local community. The Scheme is managed on the principles of decentralization and community participation.

The norms for a viable EGS demand are:

- the demand for an educational facility should come from the local community and must be from a rural area;
- no schooling facilities of any kind should exist, within a 1 km radius of the habitation from where the demand has been made;
- the number of prospective students (6–14 years) for the EGS centre should be at least forty. In tribal areas, the number should be at least twenty-five;

- for the year 1997–8 the children were enrolled in class I. In no case shall children already studying in higher classes be allowed to enrol.

The EGS teacher, designated as *guruji*, is a local person identified and selected by the community and appointed by the 'janpad panchayat shiksha samiti'. The minimum educational qualification for a teacher is higher secondary. The guruji is given an honorarium of Rs 500 per month by the *gram panchayat*. One teacher is provided for a group of forty children, and in tribal areas for a group of twenty-five children. The School Education Department arranges for the training and materials. The estimated cost of running one EGS centre is Rs 8500 per annum. This estimate is for 40 children, one guruji, teaching-learning materials, teacher training, academic evaluation of the children, and contingency fund for the functioning of the EGS centre.

The EGS is an effort by a state government to universalize access to schooling facility, focusing on hitherto unreached sections, in the quickest possible time. The issue of local accountability is critical in the EGS, and it stems from the belief that community involvement in school management and the sense of local ownership of the school in the community is what will make the difference, academic inputs and a teacher with basic educational qualifications being available (see Gopalakrishnan and Sharma 1999).

THE MABADI PROJECT, ANDHRA PRADESH

The beginnings of the 'Mabadi' (Our School) Project can be traced to the initiatives taken by the Village Tribal Development Authority (VTDA) to mobilize community participation in the planning and implementation of International Fund for Agricultural Development (IFAD) watershed programmes in Paderu. As part of community participation activities, the community coordinators of the VTDA set up community schools in these tribal areas. The following criteria are adopted by the Integrated Tribal Development Authority (ITDA) for establishing a Mabadi:

- There are no schooling facilities in the village or in nearby accessible areas.
- The initiative to open a school comes from the villagers.
- The villagers provide a place to run the school, and are willing to contribute a fixed amount per child, per month (approximately Rs 5).
- The villagers find a volunteer to teach their children. They form a committee and open a bank account where the amount collected from the community can be deposited.

In 1990–1 there were fifteen such schools. By 1992–3 the number of Mabadi schools had increased to 500. Presently, there are about 850 such schools functioning in the area. The Mabadi is a full-time school going up to class II. After completion of the course at the Mabadi, the teachers encourage parents to admit their children to nearby *ashram* or residential schools. A local youth who has received education up to class VII is appointed by the village education committee (VEC) to teach in the school.

THE ALTERNATIVE SCHOOLING PROGRAMME, MADHYA PRADESH

The Alternative Schooling Programme (ASP) was conceived by the Rajiv Gandhi Prathmik Shiksha Mission in 1994–5 as a major intervention for children (6–14 years of age) who have no access to formal schooling. This programme attempts to address the limitations perceived in both formal and non-formal systems of education by creating an intermediate model (see Box 4.2).

BOX 4.2

On Alternate Schooling

The Alternate Schooling Programme recognizes the important fact that non-participation of children in schooling is not only due to the physical inaccessibility of a school, often it is the social divisions and cultural distances which lead to non-participation. Data from the field reveals that participation of children has shown unprecedented rise in these localities. In general, there is an increased awareness among the planners on the need for clearly targeted local specific strategies.

Source: Govinda (1999).

• The ASP runs for four hours a day as against NFE, which is designed as a two-hour engagement.

• It has provision for two local teachers—one of whom has to be a woman.

• There is a fixed remuneration of Rs 1000 per month as against the *guruji* in the EGS who gets Rs 500 per month.

• There is provision for a supervisor for every 10 alternative school for proper monitoring and intensive academic support to teachers.

• The involvement of the community is greater so that the responsibility for successful implementation of the programme lies with the VEC, or the school management committee (SMC) in each locality (see Ed.Cil 1999, 43).

The following criteria determine opening of an Alternate School.

• Alternate Schools are opened in tribal areas where the population is less than 250 and in non-tribal regions where the population is less than 300 and there is no school within a 1 km radius from the identified village.

• Schools are also opened in villages where there are formal schools, but the number of working children who are out of school is larger than that of those enrolled in the formal schools.

LOK JUMBISH (LJ): PEOPLE'S MOVEMENT FOR EFA, RAJASTHAN

The LJ project was initiated in June 1992, with the basic aim of universalizing primary education in the state of Rajasthan. The goal of the project is to create a people's movement for education with a view to providing basic education to all, and thereby, generating a stimulus for human development. The LJ project has tried to address the needs of children who have been left out of the mainstream educational system through 'sahaj shiksha kendras' (non-formal learning centres). Initiated in 1993 in various blocks of the LJ, these centres are concerned with children who are not able to participate in formal schooling due to several reasons.

An evaluation study on the functioning of *sahaj shiksha* in 1996 observed that the LJ had been able to reach out to children in remote and inaccessible regions of the state. The profile of learners also revealed that three-fourths of the students enrolled in the sahaj shiksha kendras were girls. It also indicated that almost all the children attending these centres were involved in some form of economic activity apart from studying. The study also pointed out that the academic performance of students of LJ-supported formal schools and sahaj shiksha centres was better than that of students of the state-run schools(ORG 1996, 140–1). For girls who have missed the opportunity of schooling and are not in a position to attend the sahaj shiksha centres, *balika shikshan shivirs* (adolescent girls' camps) have been initiated on the lines of the camps organized by the MVF in Andhra Pradesh. The project has also focused on reaching education to children from minority groups and children with disabilities.

These cases indicate that broadening access to schools is not just a matter of increasing the number of schools. School participation is an interaction of supply, demand, and the learning process. Effective participation of children cannot be taken out of context and treated only in terms of physical presence. It is closely dependent on what is taught and how it is taught. It is, therefore, essential to note that quality education can tilt the balance and re-establish the faith of the community in public education which is essential for achieving the goal of education for all (see Govinda 1999).

UPGRADING THE IMAGE OF THE SCHOOL

A number of educational expansion and reform programmes have concentrated on pedagogy and teaching and learning processes as a means of enhancing quality of education. This 'improved school' concept attempts to respond to people's expectations from education, and thereby gets basic support from the community for access, retention, and achievement in a holistic manner.

SHIKSHA KARMI PROJECT, RAJASTHAN

The Shiksha Karmi Project (SKP) was formally launched in Rajasthan in 1987. The aim of this project is to revitalize and expand primary education in selected, remote, economically backward villages of Rajasthan. The project has been implemented by the Government of Rajasthan in cooperation with a number of NGOs with financial support from the Swedish International Development Agency (SIDA). This project is based on an innovative, sustainable, and cost-effective approach, originally developed in Silora block of Ajmer district by Social Work and Research Centre (SWRC), Tilonia (a voluntary group) and the Government of Rajasthan. The crucial innovation in the project is the substitution of primary school teachers by a team of two locally recruited resident educational workers called *shiksha karmis* (see Box 4.3). By December 1998, the Shiksha Karmi Project had covered 2725 schools in 140 blocks all over Rajasthan. There are now 6085 *shiksha karmis* in service, of whom 695 are women. About 202,000 (2.02 lakh) children are enrolled in the programme all over the state.

BOX 4.3
Who is a Shiksha Karmi?

Shiksha karmis have to have a sense of belonging to their village, to care about the children there and to teach them basics of literacy and numeracy. They must help children to be aware of the immediate world round them and the invisible world beyond. They have to be willing to be held accountable to the families who send their children to be educated, and to the community which provides the psychological support in such an enterprise. The *shiksha karmis* have to value knowledge and to recognise its value in use, and commit themselves to being continuing learners of both content and communication. Working as a team, co-operatively, is essential; in fact identification with the whole programme and being a cohesive part of the group constitutes the foundation of the given training.

Source: Anandalakshmy and Jain, 11.

EKLAVYA

Eklavya has been concerned with developing specific alternatives to the elementary education curriculum, particularly science. Its activities have included textbook and material development, teacher–training, and continued teacher support and evaluation processes. In the 1980s, Eklavya pioneered the concept of activity-based science teaching in a few middle schools through the Hoshangabad Science Teaching Programme in Madhya Pradesh. A science kit, appropriate for rural schools, was developed with the objective of using activity-based teaching as a means to nurture the spirit of enquiry in the child. Starting with a few schools, the science teaching programme now spans 500 schools in fourteen districts of Madhya Pradesh.

In 1987, Eklavya also started an experiment, 'Prashika', for making primary school education fun and developed an integrated curriculum for the primary school, providing literacy, numeracy, and environmental study. The Eklavya package emphasizes active classrooms with confident and articulate children who enjoy their tasks. The teachers are encouraged to relate the subject matter to the environment of the children. The language in textbooks is simple and is close to common speech. Its primary school materials, *seekhna sikhana* and *khushi-khushi*, with a strong accent on joyful learning were adopted for statewide implementation in collaboration with the State Council for Education Research and Training, Madhya Pradesh. More recently, Eklavya is collaborating with the District Primary Education Programme of the Government of India to try a new integrated curriculum with appropriate textbooks for classes I–V in Betul district of Madhya Pradesh (see Jagannathan 1999, 22).

BODH SHIKSHA SAMITI, RAJASTHAN

The Bodh Shiksha Samiti began its work in the 1980s in the slums of Jaipur city, Rajasthan, to provide appropriate education to children of socially marginalized groups. It brought centre stage the need to develop strategies to address the schooling of the urban poor as many of the deprived children were out of school. The Samiti's concept of education for slum children is strongly rooted in aspirations of equity for these children. Its approach to the holistic development of children through schooling encompasses non-discriminatory and egalitarian principles in education. To provide schooling to slum children, the Samiti's identified motivated youth (both women and men)and put them through an intensive training programme. The basic tenet of its teacher-training programme is that the teachers must share the concerns and world-view of the children rather than simply acquire skills. Over the years, it has fine-tuned its model of teacher–training and curriculum transaction based on joyful learning and development of both cognitive and non-cognitive skills among children.

Having expanded to seven slums, the Samiti took up a pilot project in ten municipal schools of Jaipur to demonstrate its model of quality primary education, based on learning as fun. The Samiti's intervention in the municipal schools has been rewarding. The schools have reported a reduction in dropout rates from 60 per cent to less than 20 per cent. There is also reported evidence of improvements in levels of learning and the children gaining both cognitive and non-cognitive abilities.

RISHI VALLEY RURAL EDUCATION CENTRE

The Rishi Valley Rural Education Centre (RVREC) was established in the 1980s with the objective of reaching education to rural children. The centre caters to isolated hamlets that do not have access to schooling, establishing satellite schools in these remote areas. Beginning with a single multi-grade school, the RVREC has established sixteen multi-grade, multi-level satellite schools in Chitoor district of Andhra Pradesh.

The educational kit developed by the RVREC, 'School-in-a-Box', containing 500 laminated cards, is a major innovation in teaching/learning materials for multi-grade schools and replaces conventional textbooks. The education kit is designed for both multi-grade and multi-level teaching, allowing the child her/his own pace of learning. The School-in-a-Box is a patented product and is available in different Indian languages. The group has also developed a supportive teacher education programme and evaluation system. The multi-grade schools have provided a congenial atmosphere for first-generation learners and prevented them from dropping out of school.

The past decade has been a period where efforts for UEE have continued both within the government and non-government sectors. The underlying concern has been to fit education to the situation and environment of the child, rather than forcing the child to fit the standard conventional primary school. The involvement of the local community has been central to most of these initiatives. It is also evident that mainstreaming innovative approaches or models within the larger educational scenario calls for forging enduring links and partnerships between governments, NGOs, and other civil society organizations for greater impact and realization the goals of UEE.

UEE: ISSUES AND TRAPS

The previous section focused on analysing the different initiatives taken within the government and NGO sectors to address the issue of out-of-school children. The present section attempts to highlight the gaps which continue to exist within educational policy/planning and processes

vis-à-vis UEE. The Right to Education as a Fundamental Right derived from the Right to Life is possibly the strongest statement defining state responsibility. However, the state has found it difficult to respond to it in a manner matching people's expectations. The reasons for this are not hard to seek: they lie in an intermix of conceptual dilemmas and administrative compulsions arising out of the age old habits of decision making. An attempt at unravelling some of the knots follows.

Enumeration of Out-of-School Children

A convenient method that is frequently used in planning is to work with figures available from official educational records, viz. gross enrolment ratio and net enrolment ratio. This method is fraught with a variety of problems (see Box 4.4).

BOX 4.4

Out-of-School Children: Magnitude

The gross enrollment ratios of children in the age group of 6–11 years and 11–14 years stood at 102 per cent and 62 per cent, respectively, in 1991–2. However, it is commonly known that about half the children entering class I drop out before reaching class V, and two-thirds do so before reaching class VIII. Regional, gender and community disparities mark the phenomena of enrollment and retention.... Gross enrollment ratios are estimated to be about 25 per cent higher than net enrollment ratios which are adjusted for over and under-aged children. According to this reading of the situation, the actual net enrollment rates in elementary education are likely to be about 75–80 per cent of the 6–14 years' age group. Hence, the number of out-of-school children, based on non-enrollment in the age group of 6–14 years, according to Governmental sources could well be 24 million (2.4 crore).... Lack of systematic data on school attendance further confuses the picture, since out-of-school children would effectively be a cumulation of the non-enrolled, the non-attending and the drop outs.

Source: Saldanha (1998, 389–90).

This estimation differs widely from calculations done with different methods (see Table 4.1).

– The Saikia Committee estimates 63 million (6.3 crore) children, in the 6–14 years' age group, who do not go to school.

– The 1991 Census puts the number of children, in the 6–14 years' age group, not attending school at 75.4 million (7.54 crore) (see Department of Education 1999, 8).

The discrepancies in the numbers of out-of-school children assume confusing proportions when the calculations are made on the basis of statistics of child labourers in India.

TABLE 4.1
Out-of-school Children

S. no.	Description	Source	Number (in million)
1.	6–14 years' out-of-school children	Census of India, 1991	75.4
2.	6–14 years' out-of-school children	Saikia Committee, 1997	63.
3.	Children engaged in full-time work as child labourers	National Herald, 2 January 1997	60
4.	Child labour working 12 hours a day on an average	CACL	70–80
5.	Bonded child labour (forced to work)	Bandhua Mukti Morcha	65

– The official estimates for child labour are 17–18 million (1.7–1.8 crore). On the other hand, unofficial sources say there are an estimated 44 million (4.4 crore) working children in India (see Jagannathan 1999, 1).

According to some other estimates, despite 150 million children being enrolled in 800,000 schools that provide primary education within a 1 km radius to children in 95 per cent of the country, 350 million (35 crore) children remain out of school and an equal number do not complete even five years of schooling (see Jagannathan 1991, 1). The report prepared by the Expert Group constituted by the Union Ministry of Human Resource Development (MHRD) to assess the financial requirement for making elementary education a Fundamental Right is explicit in pointing out the problems in planning and possible ways of overcoming them (see Department of Education 1999, 710).

Equity: A Value Notion Used for Promoting Disvalue

The dominant mode of state-initiated planning rests on the assumption that equity can best be ensured if the intervention is standardized and sameness is ensured for all. This not only contains a simplistic interpretation of what 'equality' entails, but effectively perpetuates inequality in a very systematic manner. From the administrators' point of view, there are a series of explanations which end up asserting, 'We must make guidelines and rules which would govern all alternative schools.'

But would this not amount to formalization of the non-formal/flexible mode? Earlier in 1990, the seventeen-member Committee for Review of National Policy on Education (NPERC) headed by renowned activist-educationist Acharya Ramamurthy had come up with a proposal for very serious revision, suggesting non-formalization of the formal system which would incorporate flexibility and contextual relevance within mainstream education—blurring the sharp distinction between NFE and mainstream schools. This approach could possibly have gone a long way in addressing the problems of dropouts, community dissatisfaction, and large-scale 'failures' existing in the group which has access to education. It, however, meants a rethinking on management styles and instructive mode of government machinery dealing with education. UEE administration, in the name of working for equity, is again promoting those very factors that result in most children being unable to adjust to the delivery system.

NFE: Concept and Practice

NFE, at the conceptual level, attempts to weave the intent, content, pedagogy, and evaluation of education around the children as they are in their specificity. Getting out of prescribed formats and regulations with respect to educational management is in fact a response to the oft-quoted statement: 'If I cannot learn the way you teach why can't you teach the way I learn.' Attempts at evolving curriculum, teaching practices, self-learning materials, and monitoring the progress in this flexible mode have been successful in smaller pockets through NGO efforts all over the country.

Despite being a valuable approach to meet largely differing styles/needs for learning, the notion of NFE has acquired serious disrepute because of the way it is seen and picked up by the government administrative system. What has surfaced in a large number of NFE centres is low-grade education for deprived groups. This entire effort can be revised within the very concept of NFE if the basic assumptions governing the educational engagement are changed. In such an attempt, 'planning' for education would take serious cognizance of differing lifestyles and treat it as a positive feature which carries with it a set of knowledge that is valuable, around which educational activities can be woven. In this framework these very children can be seen as having a unique advantage of their own body of knowledge—tribal people earning their livelihood from forests, desert inhabitants engaged in weaving wool or embroidery, fishermen/groups living close to sea and knowing sea life intimately, shepherds migrating with their flocks of sheep, groups earning their livelihood through music, etc.

The state-run NFE centres, in effect, do not take serious cognizance of what these children already know. And, in the name of equity, even for NFE each state has developed a standardised curriculum, textbooks, a prescribed pattern of support and bureaucratic system of monitoring through reports. This system has led to NFE becoming a meaningless and unsuitable proposition mismatched to the lifestyles of children.

Administrative Resistance to Change

State commitment to UEE effectively implies many changes in the strategies for educational delivery. However, these changes have to be implemented through the existing systems. Institutional habits can have an adverse effect on the actual functioning of the programmes. Radical policies and programmes can be subverted when they are treated as a mere change in terminology, with existing attitudes, modus operandi, and basic philosophies remaining unaltered. Rigorous/sensitive school mapping, for example, in principle is a radical shift from the routine 'survey' that generally forms the groundwork in any educational intervention. But if it is the same people who have been doing routine surveys that are now doing school mapping, then it is most likely that the processes would inadvertently revert to habitual surveys under the new label 'school mapping'.

Government–NGO Interaction

There are two essential aspects to any successful programme: innovation and large-scale delivery of services. The first requires a climate of flexibility in implementation which prevails only in voluntary schemes. The second requires the kind of clout, in terms of finance and political force, that only the government can command. The weaknesses and strengths of the two systems need to be recognized. The strengths of the government system lie in its network and power. Its weaknesses are well known: line-management system; centralized, bureaucratic, rule-governed functioning; and reliance on the codified word rather than personal encounter. All these limit the government's effectiveness in implementing programmes for change.

Non-government bodies tend to have a more direct interface with the people, and are, therefore, able to revise strategies by incorporating the feedback they constantly receive. On the other hand, they are clearly not geared for large-scale interventions. Their financial insecurity may generate competitiveness and suspicion among different groups in the field, and this can be seriously counterproductive. The achievement of UEE demands the strengths of both modes of operation. Some interesting models of government–NGO collaboration in educational management have emerged in the past decade and these are worth looking at in some detail.

• The first and most well-known model has a high profile NGO which is invited by the government to 'join hands' with it. Using its linkages and strengths, the NGO is able to exercise a fair degree of autonomy. It receives financial support as well as recognition/status from the state or central government. Its stature is built on the merit of its work. The NGO, in this model, takes the entire initiative in planning and designing the educational intervention.

This form of partnership may, however, turn out to be a short-lived one. It is dependent on the unpredictable match between political will and NGO ideology!

• In a different and, in some ways, almost contradictory kind of model, the government creates and then supports an NGO to operate in areas where its own functioning has proved ineffective. Here the NGO's activities are entirely dependent on the government, in contrast to the earlier model. The NGO serves as a conceptual alternative to decentralization. Its low-key, non-hierarchical mode has advantages since it allows for a more sensitive outreach to people. A number of such organizations have developed in various parts of the country. The success of such projects largely depends on the quality of personal leadership at NGO level.

• The third model, relatively recent, attempts to coordinate diverse kinds of NGOs through an autonomous body created within a government-initiated project. In this model, the diversity of NGOs is not seen as any hindrance, as long as they follow the basic approach and share the objectives of the project. The NGOs, big and small, with varying degrees of experience, can fulfil a diversity of roles within a project. This kind of association makes heavy demands on the government's ability to evolve a sensitive style of day-to-day functioning. The possibility of developing such a style rests on the value the government places on partnership, continuous dialogue, and review.

This third model has the potential to provide the greatest momentum to a genuine ground-level initiative. It also has the greatest difficulty in sustaining itself for a stretch of time. But all three models can coexist and be mutually supportive.

THE FUTURE

Two propositions emerge clearly from the experience over the past decade:

• the basic responsibility for making education available to all children rests with the state; however,

• the state management system cannot, by itself, sustain the required discipline in planning and necessary flexibility, sensitivity, and innovativeness in implementation.

Also, the reductionist approach of dividing children in strict age groups; treating them as basically 'different' from adults; dichotomization of work and education, play and responsibility, formal and non-formal, creates more barriers than facilitation.

At policy level there seems to be a know-all situation. And yet there are serious information gaps which can be filled only by grassroots action. What is needed now is a fuller, more vibrant, and widely shared educational discourse which in turn would facilitate an identification of roles for a wide range of partners. More people, in different idioms, need to understand why certain groups always remain unserved.

Three sets of reasons would possibly emerge through the deliberation:

• They cannot be reached, i.e. their physical distance, geographical remoteness makes them semi-invisible. The physically disabled, moreover, are often not even seen as 'equals' deserving access to normal services.

• The service is available, but it is rejected by some groups. It is seen as inappropriate for their needs. Hence, there is a mismatch between the delivery package and the lifestyles/economic routines of marginalized groups.

• Stereotypes of gender roles continue to dominate society. The notion of girls as legitimate candidates for receiving education has not yet gained universal acceptance or seen as a priority.

A broad understanding could emerge that this situation is the outcome of inappropriate choices in the design of development intervention. This is essentially a failure at the level of planning and not of 'implementation' as has been the oft-repeated analysis. Planning has not demonstrated the discipline of detail which is of critical consequence in an asymmetrical society. The core learning that has surfaced over the past two decades of sustained efforts at understanding and correcting this situation is that if we are serious about achieving our goals of reaching every single child then the process of planning needs to be reversed. Strengthening the centre with infinite more details about the ground situation has proved to be a frustrating exercise. By definition, this process always remains one step behind the actual situation. And it inevitably leaves out the 'under the layer' facts. Efforts need to made to strengthen capacity building at ground level, facilitating the hitherto unserved groups to gather information,

analyse it, and make choices about interventions which are for them.

This process does not undermine the power base at the centre. It simply changes its mode of operation, i.e. capacity-building at ground level is in itself an educational exercise in which the teacher or the giver becomes effectively strengthened. Also 'planning so that people can plan' requires great coordination, an alert information system to identify bottlenecks and transparency to inspire confidence in the people. It presumes open communication channels to facilitate self-corrective networking. Such a reversal, i.e. transfer of initiatives, produces miraculous results—often in proportion to the extent the momentum of old habits, individual and institutional, that can be checked and controlled consciously by the centralized power base.

UEE requires investments in:

• creating a visible accountable and predictable presence of a team/forum which is close to the ground;

• working with women-facilitating forums for reflection and altered self-image of girls;

• dialogue, listening and understanding of the lifestyle of the people;

• camps for an experience of learning—vision of possibilities, a demonstration effect.

REFERENCES

Anandalakshmy, S. and Sharada Jain (1997). *Shikshakarmi: A Paradigm Shift in Primary Education*, Sandhan Research Centre, Jaipur.

Banerjee, R. (1999). 'Revitalizing Government Provision—Experiences From Municipal Schools in Mumbai.' Paper presented at the Institute of Development Studies, Sussex and JNU, New Delhi, Workshop *'Needs versus Rights': Social Policy from a Child-Centred Perspective*. New Delhi.

Department of Education (1997). *Towards the Next Millennium*. Report presented at Islamabad meeting; Ministry of Human Resource Development, Government of India, New Delhi.

——— (1999). *Report of the Expert Group on Financial Requirements for Making Elementary Education a Fundamental Right*. Ministry of Human Resource Development, Government of India, New Delhi.

Department of Women and Child Development (1998). *Annual Report 1997–98*. Ministry of Human Resource Development, Government of India, New Delhi.

District Primary Education Programme (1999). *Reaching out Further. Para Teachers in Primary Education. An In-Depth Study of Selected Schemes*. Educational Consultants India Limited, New Delhi.

Gopalakrishnan, R. and A. Sharma (1999). 'Education

Guarantee Scheme: What does it Claim?' *Economic and Political Weekly*, vol. 34(1), pp. 726–8.

Govinda, R. (1999). 'Educational Provision and National Goals in South Asia: A Review of Policy and Performance.' Paper presented at the Institute of Development Studies, Sussex and JNU, New Delhi, Workshop '*Needs versus Rights': Social Policy from a Child-Centred Perspective*. New Delhi.

Institute of Development Studies (1990). 'Situational Analysis of Women and Children in Rajasthan'. IDSJ Research Reports, Jaipur.

———— (1994). 'Mehanatkash Bachchon Ke Liye Shiksha: Rajasthan Mein Anaupcharik Shiksha Karyakram Ka Mulyankan.' IDSJ Research Reports, Jaipur.

———— (1998). 'Strengthening Quality and Access to Services in ICDS Programme: A Social Assessment.' IDSJ Research Reports, Jaipur.

Jagannathan, S. (1999). 'The Role of NGOs: New Partnerships for Primary Education—A Study of NGOs in India.' Delegation of the European Union in India, New Delhi.

Kabeer, N., Geetha B. Nambissan and R. Subramanian (1999). 'Needs versus Rights': Social Policy from a Child-Centred Perspective. Background Paper prepared for the Institute of Development Studies, Sussex and JNU, New Delhi, Workshop '*Needs versus Rights': Social Policy from a Child-Centred Perspective*. New Delhi.

Lok Jumbish Parishad (1998). *Lok Jumbish: The Seventh Report*. LJP, Jaipur.

Operational Research Group (1994a). 'Evaluation of the Non-Formal Education Programme in the State of Andhra Pradesh'. New Delhi.

———— (1994b). 'Evaluation of the Non-Formal Education Programme in the State of Uttar Pradesh'. New Delhi.

———— (1996). 'Evaluation of the Non-Formal Education Programme in Lok Jumbish Project'. New Delhi.

PROBE (1999). *Public Report On Basic Education in India*. The PROBE team in Association with Centre for Development Economics. Oxford University Press, New Delhi.

Ramachandran, V. (1998). 'Promises, promises.' *Seminar*, No. 464, New Delhi.

Rane, A. and J. Billimoria (1998). 'Child Rights Advocacy in India'. In Desai, M., A. Monterio and L. Narayan (eds) *Towards People-Centred Development*. Tata Institute of Social Sciences, Mumbai.

Saldanha, D. (1998). 'Literacy Campaigns and Basic Education'. In Desai, M., A. Monterio and L. Narayan (eds) *Towards People-Centred Development*. Tata Institute of Social Sciences, Mumbai.

Singh, A. (1999). 'Decentralized Micro-Planning as A Strategy for Education Development of Under-served Populations in Developing Countries'. Paper prepared for *Creative Associates International*, Washington.

5 Education of Urban Disadvantaged Children

Vandana Chakrabarty

INTRODUCTION

India, which was hitherto considered a primarily rural country, is fast becoming urbanized. In 1901, the urban population of the country was only about 26 million—10.8 per cent of the total population. In 1991, with an eightfold increase, urban population stood at 218 million—25.7 per cent of total population (see Government of India 1992) (see Table 5.1). Data on rural and urban population from 1901 to 1991 show how rapidly the country is becoming urbanized. It is expected that the urban population will be above 30 per cent by 2001 (see Eighth Five Year Plan 1992–7).[1] According to the 1991 Census, in 1951 there were only five cities with 'million plus' population. In 1981, this number increased to 12 and in 1991 we have 23 such cities.

TABLE 5.1
Rural and Urban Population 1901–91

Census year	Population (million)		Percentage of total population	
	Rural	Urban	Rural	Urban
1901	213	026	89.2	10.8
1911	226	026	89.7	10.8
1921	223	028	88.8	11.2
1931	246	033	88.0	12.0
1941	275	044	86.1	13.9
1951	299	062	82.7	17.3
1961	360	079	82.0	18.0
1971	439	109	80.1	19.9
1981	524	159	76.7	23.3
1991	629	218	74.3	25.7

Source: Government of India (1992, Population Tables).

[1] According to the 2001 census, urban areas account for 27.98 per cent of the total population of India (Ed.).

Accelerated industrialization, induced largely by centralized planning, has accentuated the process of urbanization in India. In terms of commonly used indices of quality of life, the average urban dweller is clearly far better off than the average villager. For instance, per capita income in urban areas is far more than per capita income in rural areas. The urban literacy rate is 80 per cent which is much higher than the rural literacy rate of 56 per cent (see National Literacy Mission 1998). Nearly all the institutions of higher learning are concentrated in urban areas. Further, compared to an average city or town school, a village school is an appallingly underprovided place of learning. However, the worst—the poorest of the poor—in the urban sector are far worse than the average in the same sector and their number is not very small.

PROFILE OF URBAN DISADVANTAGED CHILDREN

Who are urban disadvantaged children? Researchers and voluntary organizations refer to deprived children, vulnerable children, children in difficult situations, children at risk, and such other categories. While a variety of classification schemes can be arrived at, it may be worthwhile to focus on the categories of disadvantaged children in urban areas who are being addressed through various programmes at operational level (see Box 5.1).

Street and Working Children

A large number of voluntary agencies have worked with various categories of urban disadvantaged children. The most visible is the work done with street and working children. Lambay and Chavan (1993), in their report on

Box 5.1

Categories of Urban Disadvantaged Children

Children from the urban disadvantaged section needing special attention can be classified under the following seven categories:

- Children living in slums and resettlement colonies, especially those living in unauthorized slums
- Child workers/labourers
- Street children
- Children of prisoners
- Children of sex-workers
- Children living in institutions
- Children of construction workers and other migrant labourers

basic education in Mumbai have found that pavement dwellers are present in all wards of Greater Mumbai. As per the census (1991) data there are about 600,000 pavement dwellers in the city.

In a study of street children in Mumbai carried out in 1989 (see D'Lima and Gosalia 1989) it was found that there were about 100,000 street children in the city of Mumbai. Most of them were on their own or had minimum contact with their families. It was also found that:

- Of the 73 per cent of children below 15 years of age, 54.5 per cent never went to school, 29.6 per cent left school and only 11 per cent continued to be in school. Thus, most of these children, instead of being in school are working and contributing to national economy at a very young age.

- The majority of street children (about 71 per cent) are working and they work for 7–12 hours per day. Most of the children work on daily wages and earn an income ranging from Rs 200 to Rs 1200 per month.

- About 76 per cent of these children are very keen to study and have ambitions of being teachers, doctors, or policemen. About 50 per cent of children expressed the need for vocational training.

Boxes 5.2 and 5.3 detail some voluntary efforts at improving school enrolment of street and working children in Pune and data on street children in Delhi, respectively.

In 1995, the number of children below 14 years of age employed in various economic activities[2] was 17 million (9.5 million males and 7.5 million females),

i.e. every eighth child (in the 5–14 age group) in the country was a worker. Estimates indicate that 21 per cent of the working children are in urban areas. The National Sample Survey reports that 3 to 4 per cent of urban children had worked, mostly as hired labour, and that their work had resulted in economic benefits for their families (NSSO 1997).

Box 5.2

Association of the Rights of the Child's (ARC's) Movement for Enrolment of Street/Slum/Working Children in Pune Municipal schools

In 1992 several voluntary organizations working for children pooled together in efforts to advocate for the rights of the child. This led to the formation of the ARC. The ARC use the following strategies for improving enrolments in schools:

- non-formal educational (NFE) centres as a bridge facility to formal schools;
- school enrolment drives for children below 10 yrs and re-enrolment of dropouts;
- advocacy, lobbying, and use of media to highlight education-related issues and problems, simplification of admission procedures, relaxing the requirement for submission of birth certificates, and improving educational infrastructure;
- facilitating involvement of parents through the Jagruk Palak Parishad.
- using various government schemes such as NCLF, foster care, and sponsorship for providing educational facilities to out-of-school children.

Box 5.3

Street Children in Delhi

Delhi has about 400,000 child workers and about 100,000 street children who arrive in the metropolis from neighbouring states, generally in search of work. The most common work they find is that of helpers in wayside restaurants and tea shops; a large number also work as vendors. Many small industrial units depend heavily on child labour. Street children also work as porters, shoe-shine boys, and rag pickers. Street children can broadly be categorized as:

- children on the street who engage in some street trade but return in the night to some shelter;
- children of the street who live on the street where they seek shelter, livelihood, and companionship;
- abandoned children who are the most vulnerable children, who have no ties with their families and are entirely on their own for material as well as emotional survival.

Source: Department of Education (1992).

---

[2] According to the statement of Union Labour Minister given the Rajya Sabha on 20 March 1995 (*Hindustan Times*, 21 March 1995).

MIGRANT CHILDREN

Many agencies working for street and working children also work with migrant working children and migrant children living on the street, though not much work has been done with migrant children as an exclusive group. A study conducted by the School for Potential Advancement and Restoration of Confidence (SPARC) (1989–90) surveyed 286 families with a total of 695 children. About 60 per cent of the children were above 5 years of ages, of whom 37 per cent were literate. Of these 47 per cent had received kindergarten education, 35 per cent primary education, and 18 per cent secondary education; 30 per cent went to municipal schools and the rest to NFE classes held by mobile crèches. About 58 per cent of the families had children who had dropped out from school.

Delinquent Children

Crimes in India (1997) reports that out of 3517 juveniles arrested under the IPC and the SLL in twenty-three cities 1229 (34 per cent) were illiterate, 1100 (31 per cent) were educated up to primary level, 1020 (29 per cent) were educated above primary but below matric, and 128 (3 per cent) were matric/higher secondary and above. As far as their family backgrounds are concerned, 10 per cent were homeless, 27 per cent lived with guardians, and 62 per cent lived with parents. As far as the income group was concerned it was found that less than 10 per cent families had an income of more than Rs 1000 per month. During 1998–9 the central government has spent Rs 38.584 million on prevention and control of juvenile social maladjustment in all the Indian states taken together. Box 5.4 identifies an effort of government in this field in Delhi.[3]

BOX 5.4

Prayas

'Prayas' Juvenile Aid Centre was founded in 1988 for delinquents and other neglected children. The aim is to prevent the vulnerable young from crimes and delinquency by inculcating a sense of individual dignity and social responsibility through vocational programmes and psychological support. The effort is to build the way for a healthy and productive life Elementary NFE, vocational training, and counselling services are provided to the children. The centre is based in Jahangirpuri, a sprouting urban slum in Delhi.

Children of Prisoners

There is no doubt that removal of an offender, who may be the head of the family, from the family has a very grave and disabling impact on the family. This is what happens to the families of many prisoners. This often leads family members of convicts to take to anti-social modes of behaviour. Children are the worst sufferers. Though there are some NGOs working with such families, the magnitude of this problem is unknown as there is almost no data on prisoners' families. However, there are reasonable grounds to believe that it involves a very large number of prisoners.

Children of Prostitutes

There are seventeen agencies in Uttar Pradesh, Orissa, and West Bengal that work with the children of prostitutes. The central government has released an amount of Rs 3.689 million during 1998–9 for this. A few voluntary organizations in other states are also working with this population without using the government. These children have a variety of impairments and disadvantages that translate into special educational needs. If these special educational needs are not met, these children are often at risk of repeating or dropping out of the school because of poverty, hunger, malnutrition, environmental or cultural reasons, and because of minor impairments that impede their performance. Their educational problems can only be solved by a more sensitive and responsible education system.

PRIMARY SCHOOLS IN URBAN AREAS: AN OVERVIEW

It is clear that urban disadvantaged sections have to depend essentially on the government-provided primary education organized directly or through local bodies. It is therefore worthwhile to examine the expanse of primary and upper primary schools in urban areas and the facilities offered therein (see Box 5.5). The data base presented in this section depends heavily on the All-India Educational Survey conducted by the NCERT in 1993. It is, therefore, a bit dated. However, it should serve to give a broad perspective on the trends of facilities and conditions in urban primary schools. It also highlights the lack of a dependable data base on urban primary education.

As per the Sixth All-India Educational Survey, there are a total of 96,433 primary and upper primary schools in urban areas of the country. Of these 28,112 are managed by government, 30,558 by local bodies, 12,856 are private aided, and 24,907 are private unaided. Since education is free in government schools and schools run by local bodies, it is expected that urban disadvantaged children would enrol themselves in these schools. What is the quality of education in these schools? The facilities available in the schools are important indicators of quality of schooling.

---

[3] 'Prayas' is an NGO based at Delhi.

Box 5.5

Facilities in Urban Primary and Upper Primary Schools

No. of urban primary schools	62,874
No. of urban upper-primary schools	33,559
Estimated enrolment in urban primary school	24,556,253
Estimated no. of girls enrolled in urban primary school	13,085,369 (53.28%)
Estimated enrolment in urban upper-primary schools	12,595,946
Estimated no. of girls enrolled in urban upper-primary school	5,675,496 (45%)
Estimated no. of boys enrolled in urban upper-primary school	6,920,450 (54.94%)
Shortage of blackboards in primary schools run by government and local bodies	22.7%
Shortage of blackboards in upper primary schools run by government and local bodies	10.73%
Primary schools having adequate supply of chalks	67.80%
dusters	58.5%
Upper primary schools having adequate supply of chalks	77.38 %
dusters	67.75%
Primary schools—government and local bodies with libraries	37.72%
Upper-primary schools run by government and local bodies with libraries	59.10%
Primary schools with textbook bank	24.92%
Upper-primary schools with textbook bank	37.28%
Primary schools with playground facility	31.92%
Upper-primary schools with play-ground facility	47.68%
Primary schools arranging medical check-up	41.21%
Upper-primary schools arranging medical check-up	55.17%
Primary schools arranging vaccination	44.05%
Upper-primary schools arranging vaccination	52.75%
Primary schools with midday meals facility	14.02%
Upper-primary schools with midday meals facility	26.66%
Primary schools with free uniform facility	25.46%
Upper-primary schools with free uniform facility	32.73%
Primary schools free textbook facility	53.19%
Upper-primary schools free textbook facility	55.41%
Primary schools with attendance scholarship for girls	18.09%
Upper-primary schools with attendance scholarship for girls	21.84%

Note: All the data given here pertains to urban primary and upper-primary schools run by the government or local bodies.
Source: Sixth All-India Educational Survey, Tables 2S50 to 2S100.

Availability of Rooms and Other Basic Facilities

Following the National Policy on Education (NPE) in 1986, the government of India launched a major scheme called 'Operation Blackboard' to assist quality improvement in primary schools. The scheme had very wide coverage reaching all the states of the country. It aimed at ensuring that every primary school will have at least two classrooms with other physical infrastructure, at least two teachers, and a fairly comprehensive set of teaching–learning equipment. This no doubt resulted in massive augmentation of the existing facilities throughout the country. By 1993, about 87.5 per cent of urban primary schools were fuctioning in at least two rooms. About 97.74 per cent upper primary schools had at least two rooms.

The data on drinking water facilities, urinals, and lavatories reveal that these facilities fall far short of the desired standards. Only 46.87 per cent of government primary schools and 57.07 per cent of local body primary schools in urban areas had drinking water. The situation was a little better in upper primary schools where 65.17 per cent of government schools and 69.43 per cent of local body schools had drinking water facility. Government urban primary schools with urinals were 37.69 per cent and those having lavatories were 24.51 per cent of the total. Among local body schools of the same category, 48.77 per cent have urinals and 37.19 have lavatories. Classrooms in municipal schools are generally dark, tiny, hot, and humid. Many of them lack physical inputs such as furniture in classrooms, boundary walls, toilets, and drinking water (see Banerji 1997). Whatever the reasons for these appalling conditions, it is necessary to step up expenditure on improvement of infrastructure of schools. Surely, functioning toilets, safe drinking water, and well-ventilated classrooms are the minimum facilities to be provided for improving the quality of education.

Availability of blackboard

Whether other equipment is provided or not, no school can function without blackboards and writing material. Surprisingly, the Sixth All-India Educational Survey (NCERT 1998) revealed that primary schools run by government had a serious shortage of even this most basic facility of blackboards, followed by upper-primary schools run by local bodies. As already pointed out, it is these schools which cater to the educational needs of urban deprived children. It was also found that one of two schools managed by government and local bodies in urban areas did not have adequate supply of chalks and dusters. In such schools which do not have even basic support facilities such as blackboards, chalks, and dusters, one wonders how other aids such as maps, charts, toys, play equipment, library books, and equipment for work experience, which are specified as part of Operation Blackboard, would be made available. Figure 5.1 shows graphically the shortage of blackboards in primary and upper-primary schools.

Availability of Qualified Teachers

It is not enough to acquire teaching aids. Adequate provision of qualified teachers and their training and orientation are of paramount importance. It is in line with this thinking that provision of at least two teachers in each school was made an objective of the Operation Blackboard. As per the Sixth All-India Educational Survey, 96.56 per cent of sanctioned posts in primary schools run by government or local bodies are filled. In upper primary schools run by the government and local bodies 96.93 per cent of the sanctioned posts are filled. In these primary schools 58.03 per cent teachers are women whereas in upper primary schools, 56.89 per cent teachers are women. The Annual Report (Department of Education) 1999 mentions that at present 100 per cent central assistance is provided for appointment of an additional teacher in single-teacher schools.

Availability of Libraries and Textbook Banks

Libraries and textbook banks should be considered important facilities, especially for children who cannot afford to buy books. Only 41.6 per cent of primary schools run by the government and 34.4 per cent of those by local bodies have libraries. Among upper primary schools, 62.7 per cent government schools and 54.6 per cent schools run by local bodies have libraries.

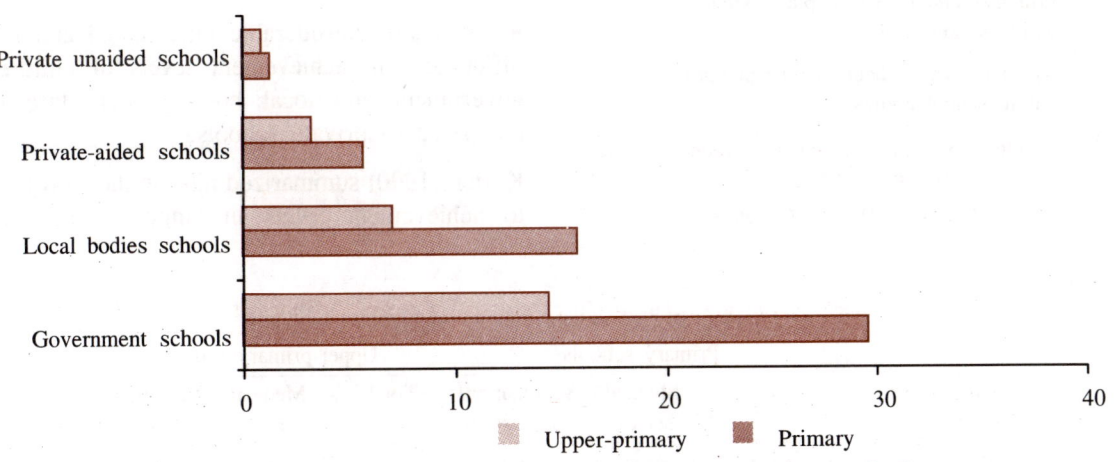

FIGURE 5.1: Shortage of blackboards in primary and upper-primary schools
Source: Table 2S51 Sixth All-India Educational Survey.

The irony is that this situation of shortages is not due to lack of finances. The Annual Report of the Department of Education (1998–9) mentions that several states have unutilized funds sanctioned for teaching–learning equipment under Operation Blackboard (OB) Scheme. The problem of unutilized funds was attributed to lack of sufficient flexibility and decentralized procurement and supply of teaching–learning equipment.

Discussions with some of these school authorities revealed that existing services are not properly utilized. Special effort needs to be made to popularize reading habits amongst schoolchildren. Book banks have proved specially important in government schools to support children from disadvantaged sections in urban areas. Some cities started innovative programmes to attract children to libraries. In Mumbai twenty two library-cum-hobby classes have been started by the education department of the municipal corporation. Four mobile libraries function on Saturdays and Sundays. Twenty nine free municipal reading rooms and libraries have also been made available.

Playground Facility

Playground facilities are absolutely essential in schools, especially in crowded urban areas, to facilitate healthy social and physical development of children. However, it is found that only 25 per cent of government primary schools and less than 40 per cent of upper primary schools have such facilities (see Figure 5.2).

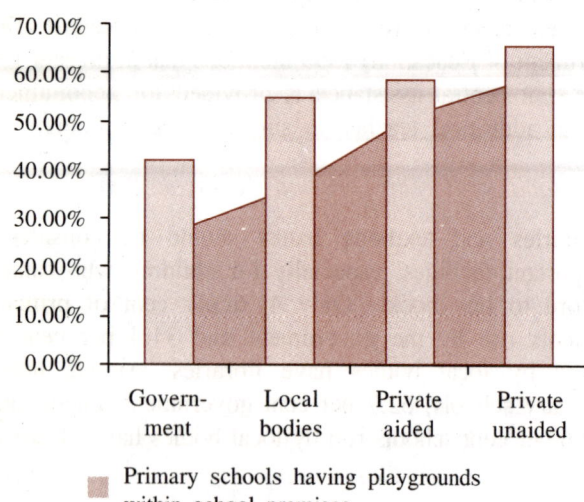

■ Primary schools having playgrounds within school premises

□ Upper primary schools having playgrounds within school premises

FIGURE 5.2: Number of schools having playground facilities within school premises

Source: Table 2S72 of Sixth All-India Educational Survey.

Medical Check-up and Vaccination

The Sixth All-India Education Survey clearly points out that private schools are doing better than the state-run school in arranging medical check-ups and other related facilities (see Table 5.2). This is unfortunate as children attending government-run schools are the ones needing support from schools in terms of medical check-ups and other related matters.

Learner Achivement

Until recently, universal primary education has been equated with mere enrolment and attendance in primary schools. In recent years, however considerable attention has been paid to levels of learning acquired by learners. While fairly extensive baseline studies have been conducted, covering schools in rural areas, not much has been done to assess the situation in urban primary schools. The limited data available in this regard from small-scale studies indicate that:

• Achievement levels of disadvantaged urban primary students are very low when compared to what they are expected to learn;

• While these low levels of learning are first revealed at the lower primary stage, the deficiencies are not rectified at higher primary or secondary stage; and

• There are considerable inter-school and intra-school differences in achievement levels of children. Again government and local body schools fare poorly as compared to private schools.

Kurien (1990) summarized nine studies/ projects relating to achievement levels in language and mathematics

TABLE 5.2

Number of Schools Arranging Medical Check-ups and Vaccination/Inoculation of Students

Management	Primary schools			Upper-primary schools		
	Total	Medical check-up	Vaccination/ inoculation	Total	Medical check-up	Vaccination/ inoculation
Government schools	18648	7715 (41.37)	8493 (45.54%)	9464	4760 (50.29%)	4861 (51.36%)
Local bodies	22832	9382 (41.09%)	9781 (42.83%)	7726	4724 (61.1%)	4207 (54.45%)
Private aided	7079	3541 (50.02%)	3478 (49.13%)	5777	3830 (66.29%)	3617 (62.6%)
Private unaided	14315	9192 (64.2%)	8236 (57.5%)	10592	7649 (72.2%)	6662 (62.89%)
Total	62874	29830 (47.4%)	29988 (47.69%)	33559	20963 (62.46%)	19347 (57.6%)

Source: NCERT (1998, Tables 28 and 96). Sixth All-India Educational Survey.

Notes: Figures in parentheses are percentages.

among urban primary school children. While agreeing with the above, he adds that the situation demands introducion of fundamental changes in pedagogy which should begin by concentrating on major innovations at lower- primary standards (I and II). Several projects have shown that it is possible to bring about improvement thorugh such measures (see Box 5.6). But sustaining the strategies initiated through projects and expanding their coverage has proved difficult.

BOX 5.6

Assessment of the Primary Formal Education System of the MBC

The Primary formal education system of the BMC, not only the largest urban education system of India, perhaps even in the world, introduced environment studies approach in class I where language and mathematics have been identified as key tests in the development of learning skills. The approach is activity centred, student centred, inter-disciplinary, and the emphasis is on growth of learning skills. An evaluation of this approach by Henriques (1987) revealed that it substantially enhanced the learning achievements of students in language and mathematics, the two critical subjects in a child's carreer. It also contributed towards lowering the rate of wastage and stagnation and increasing the rate of attendance in class. The same project was evaluated by Rane (1989) whose findings are congruent with those of Henriques (1987).

Non-Formal Education in Urban Areas

In urban areas, formal school is the preferred means of providing primary education to children. However, the difficult circumstances in which disadvantaged children live compel the use of alternate means of reaching them education so that they are not completely left out of its purview. It is with this perspective that the NFE scheme of the Government of India has been adopted to cover urban slums and areas with concentrations of working children. The extent of coverage under the scheme however appears to be very small.

According to the Sixth All-India Educational Survey (1993), only 6602 NFE centres (5.47 per cent) out of a total of 120,544 are operating in urban areas. Of these 6308 (95.54 per cent) are run by the government and the rest are under voluntary organizations. Even the centres run by voluntary organizations get 100 per cent financial assistance from the central government. Most of the urban centres (93 per cent) run with the help of one instructor. About 2.69 per cent have two instructors and 22 per cent more than two. There are a few centres (2.46 per cent) having no instructors.

DISTRIBUTION OF URBAN NFE CENTRES

The states of Andhra Pradesh and Madhya Pradesh account for around 77 per cent of the urban primary NPE centres. Uttar Pradesh, Gujarat, and Orissa have more than 100 urban centres each. Assam, Bihar, and Tamil Nadu also have a few centres. The scheme was originally sanctioned for the educationally backward states such as Andhra Pradesh, Orissa, Rajasthan, Uttar Pradesh, and West Bengal, and was later extended to backward pockets of other states also.

Though there has been considerable criticism of NFE programmes for children as being of poor quality, there is no doubt that NFE has provided a large number of children in urban areas access to primary education, particularly through non-government organizations. Even if the learning levels are modest, these programmes have helped children from disadvantaged sections improve their self-esteem, confidence and social skills.

Role of Voluntary Organizations in the Education of the Urban Disadvantaged

As has been noted earlier, children of poorer sections of urban society invariably depend on government or municipal schools for their education. However, there are a number of studies pointing to the failure of the government-run schools to meet the educational needs of urban disadvantaged children. It is in this context that the role being played by voluntary organizations occupies a very important place in providing education to disadvantaged groups. This section presents an overview of work done by numerous voluntary organizations which are working to help the urban disadvantaged. The information has been acquired from three main sources: (i) interviews with the coordinators of several NGOs working in the field; (ii) Annual reports and information brochures of the NGOs; and (iii) the Data Bank on Primary Education for the Deprived Urban Children prepared by Sappal and Datta (National Core Group for Deprived Urban Children 1999).

UNDERSTANDING THE TARGET GROUP

Working with special groups of children is not the same as working with the general category of children, specially if the teacher and the taught are from entirely different socio-economic backgrounds. Such a situation calls for special efforts on the part of the teacher/service giver to understand the socio-economic, psychological, physical, and familial circumstances of the group she wishes to reach out to.

A number of voluntary organizations that work with special groups do make serious efforts to understand their target groups. In fact some of them have conducted studies before initiating services. Neelamdana (Chennai) working with children in slum areas conducted a pilot project focusing on slum dwellers, children, and school authorities. The SNDT University's Adult Education sub-centre (Pune), through its programme for street and working children, (see Box 5.7) also conducted a study to understand the profile of these children. Butterflies, a Delhi-based organization working with street children has involved the children themselves in doing research on issues affecting them. Karunalaya (Chennai) did an exhaustive survey on child labour in the Kasimedu fishing area in north Chennai. Based on the results of this survey, it developed and implemented an action programme on child labour in this area, supported by the International Labour Organization. The street children project of the Bangalore Oniyavar Seva Coota (BOSCO) an NGO in Bangalore, was taken up after four years of intense field study and reflection.

Box 5.7
Programme for Street and Working Children, SNDT Women's University, Pune

This project which was started to provide alternate education to twenty-three out-of-school children and went on to look at the problems of these children more comprehensively using the following strategies:

- In-depth understanding of the needs and problems faced by waste-pickers and their children through participant observation.

- Focused attempts to improve the condition of waste pickers and their children.

- Networking with other NGOs, police, municipality, and educational institutions, teachers unions, and trade unions.

- Organizing the waste-pickers to demand better working conditions, education for their children, social security benefits like life insurance and credit facilities.

- Treating the child waste pickers not as beneficiaries of the programme, but as critical participants in changing their own life situations. They were, for instance, involved in enrolling other children in schools and in discussing their needs and problems with others in order to find solutions.

- Social action *dharnas*, public meetings, *morchas*, protests etc. used to demand positive action on their behalf.

Voluntary organizations develop a deep understanding of the disadvantaged groups with which they are working not only through research and analysis of secondary data but also through a large number of volunteers and community workers who are in close touch with the clientele. The Police Child Labour Camps organize educational camps for working children in Hyderabad with the help of volunteers, teachers of the MV Foundation, and local social activists. Neelamdana of Chennai has even started a scholarship scheme to inspire youngsters to volunteer for community service. Navajeevan of Vijaywada has a band of committed volunteers who work with the street children. It is the volunteers who contact the children to save them from the perils of street life and bring them to the Navajeevan shelters. Nanban of Madurai has field development workers who make regular visits to disadvantaged children such as rag pickers, orphans, working children, drug addicts, sexually abused, school dropouts, and aimless drifters. They motivate the children to attend Nanban centres which provide education, skill development, and personality development activities. The students of Social Work and Extension Education and those enrolled in the National Service Scheme not only learn and develop insights into the lives of the disadvantaged, but also improve the organization's understanding of community issues. Loreto Day School of Calcutta has a programme where students of classes V–X regularly tutor street children. For this the regular students are allocated ninety-minute time slots of work education on a weekly basis.

EDUCATION AS A PART OF COMPREHENSIVE SERVICES OFFERED TO THE DISADVANTAGED CHILDREN

A review of services for urban deprived children (see National Core Group for Deprived Urban Children 1999) reveals that education is never offered as a singular, unconnected service to deprived children. It is always part of several other services offered. Therefore, most of the organizations have a multi-pronged approach wherein the intervention strategy consists of different types of services offered simultaneously. Shelter, food, clothing, recreation, medical care are offered along with education in Snehasadan (Mumbai), Navjeevan (Vijaywada), Nanban (Madurai), Krushi (Hyderabad), Jeeva Jyothi (Chennai), and others. Some NGOs offer only night shelters whereas others run 'homes' or offer placement in foster homes. Some offer only nutritious meals, medical care, and recreation along with education. Since many of the urban disadvantaged children are working children, some organizations give importance to saving schemes to instil the habit of saving in working children.

One of the stated objectives of Youth for Voluntary Action (YUVA), Mumbai, is to restore, promote, and defend the rights of the poor in the process of urbanization. It is involved in a number of services such as food, shelter, and health care for working children and street children. NFE is an important service it offers. Likewise, Vatsalaya, Mumbai, also offers a variety of services such as counselling, first-aid and medical facilities, nutrition, recreation, saving and loans, personal care and hygiene, skill training, and children's magazine, along with basic education. Another such effort, again in Mumbai, is that of TASH (see Box 5.8).

Box 5.8
Technology and Social Health Foundation (TASH), Mumbai

TASH Foundation deals with community-based education and health for slum children in two slums in Mumbai. The workers report that preschool education, NFE, and enrichment activities along with mothers' education in the areas of health, nutrition and child rearing help in retaining students in school. There are no drop-outs among the 500 students who have been in TASH schools.

FORMAL EDUCATION—THE PREFERRED ALTERNATIVE

Voluntary organizations working for the urban deprived seem to be convinced that the best route for education is formal schooling. Pratham, Mumbai, conducts bridge courses for older children who are currently out of school, preparing them to join the formal school classes appropriate to their ages. Pratham is, in fact, exploring various models of bridge courses to bring out-of-school children into the mainstream education system.

SNDT's programme for street and working children seeks to address some of the factors which inhibit the participation of children from marginalized groups in the formal education system. Navjeevan (Vijaywada), Nanban (Madurai), Marialaya (Chennai), Jeev Jyothi (Chennai), Door Step School (Mumbai), and many others are successfully preparing and motivating children for enrolment in formal schools.

The education camps of the Hyderabad police are another innovative venture to prepare children for formal school (see Box 5.9).

However, enrolling children in formal schools is not enough. They need to be sustained there. Prerana (Mumbai), an organization working for children of sex workers, not only motivates children to enrol in formal schools, but conducts study and personality development classes for their sustenance. Paraspara (Bangalore) arranges tuition for schoolgoing children from the slums so as to strengthen their academic performance. Pratham arranges remedial classes for those children who are lagging. In SNDT's street and working children's programme, children who perform well in their schools and those who complete SSC are publicly felicitated. Butterflies (Delhi), has a National Open School Study Centre attended by twenty five children. Most NGOs believe that the opportunities for development available to the products of NFE are not comparable to those available to children in formal schools. Therefore, even if the environment in these schools is often alien to street and working children and the curriculum not relevant to their lives, they recognize formal school as the best means of education.

NFE—A NECESSARY SERVICE

However, many urban deprived children are not able to enter or, if admitted, fail to sustain interest in formal schools. Therefore almost all the organizations working with urban disadvantaged children are involved in imparting NFE. The NFE given by them goes beyond the 3Rs. Attempts are made not only to give them the tools of learning but also the knowledge, skills, and attitudes required for dealing with problems of everyday life and for developing into independent persons. This involves creating awareness about rights and responsibilities, health, hygiene, nutrition cleanliness, local and national issues, and many other relevant areas. Often locally developed educational material is used and communicated through participatory techniques such as discussions, discourses, visual inputs, quizzing, co-curricular activities, story telling, dramatics, and arts and crafts. Ankur (Delhi) (see Box 5.10) takes up topics such as rights of the citizens, polluting industries, housing rights, and child labour. Adolescent girls'

Box 5.9
Education Camps of Hyderabad Police

Police Labour Camp of Hyderabad is another innovative initiative started by the police in 1997. Camps are run to wean away a child from labour, using education as a tool. A teacher, police person and local social activist go around a locality, identifying child workers. After identification, the family and the child are convinced about importance of education. The child is motivated to join the camp. At camp, the child is enrolled as a residential student. He is provided with uniform and a place to stay. After she adjusts to the camp and demands education, she is placed in a class according to her/his level (between classes II and VII).

The teacher lives, eats, sleeps, plays, and works with the students. This helps in development of a bond between the teacher and the taught. For the first four months NFE techniques and material are used. In the last two months the students are taught using formal textbooks. At the end of six months students are admitted to formal schools in the vicinity of their homes. It is reported that almost all the children of the first batch chose to join formal schools rather than going back to work.

groups are formed for adolescent education. Intensive effort is made for awareness raising amongst women's groups that become action groups demanding services such as cleaning gutters, admission to schools, greater accountability of teachers, convenient bus routes, electricity, and water supply.

BOX 5.10
Ankur Society for Alternatives and Education

The organization works with children in the community with special reference to alternatives and education. Following are the highlights of the programme:

- Library facility along with discussion on books read, current issues, visits to historical places, museums, etc.
- Classes with one teacher catering to 20 to 25 children of three grades (e.g. classes I, II, III) .
- Participating in campaigns such as rights of citizens, pollution, and other issues affecting their life.
- Adolescent girls' groups have been formed to help them deal with adolescence issues.

Butterflies (Delhi) has developed its own kit with interactive games. SNDT's street and working children project used a kit developed with the help of the children themselves. REDS (Bangalore) also uses specially designed teaching aids and indigenously made kits. Prerana (Mumbai) organizes visits of children of sex workers to hospitals, fire brigade stations, post offices, rural bases, etc. for wider exposure. Some organizations like Marialaya (Chennai) use adult education primers for NFE while others like Karunalaya Social Service Society (Madras) use non-formal primers specially prepared for street and working children by the Madras NGO Forum for Street and Working Children. IPER (Calcutta) is running Open Learning Schools located in the areas where there are large concentrations of children deprived of any facilities of education. They are held sometimes in open streets, sometimes under sheds in parks, and often in local clubs.

School on wheels is an innovative project started by Door Step School to reach out to out-of-school children on the street, at construction sights, working with hawkers, etc. The bus itself provides a classroom wherever out-of-school children are found, where they are taught for two hours at a time convenient to them. The venture was started in 1998 and at present, it serves five locations following a predesigned schedule.

SKILL TRAINING

Skill training for income-generating activities is imparted to those children who do not show an inclination for

formal schooling because they had never been to school or because they cannot cope with the formal school curriculum. For instance, Project Mainstream (Mumbai) not only helps such children in skill development but also extends micro-credits to help them start their own ventures after they complete the vocational training courses. Nanban (Madurai) has different kinds of skill training for girls and boys. Girls unwilling to join formal schools learn karate, Bharata Natyam, sewing, tailoring, batik printing, screen printing, and notebook making. Boys go to auto-rickshaw repair workshops, steel welding units, and agricultural and animal husbandry farms. Jeeva Jyothi (Chennai) is another organization training children in such productive skills as welding, screen printing, and carpentry. Box 5.11 summarizes the skills training programme of REDS for rag pickers.

BOX 5.11
Rag Pickers' Education and Development Scheme (REDS)

REDS was started in Karnataka with the prime concern of helping these children develop an identity of their own. Apart from shelter service, the programme offers training in various trades such as carpentry, electronics, electrical work, tailoring, crafts, painting, screen printing, etc. Placement in white-collar services such as courier and office attendant are also provided. An integrated outreach programme has been developed which includes first aid, literacy, advocacy, recreation, liaison with police, savings, NFE, and solid waste management.

ENROLLING PARENTS AS PARTNERS

It is unlikely that an urban child remains out of school if his parents are convinced about the usefulness of education and take a personal interest in his schooling. Therefore, many NGOs work with parents (if they are available) of out-of-school children. Prerana (Mumbai), which runs programmes for the children of sex workers, has parents' meetings every month. Prajuvala (Hyderabad) working for the same group is running two schools for these children with an enrolment of seventy-five children. These schools are located in the houses owned by sex workers themselves. It has formed a mothers' committee among sex workers that screens and selects children for education and skill training. This small empowerment has not only resulted in voluntary support but has also developed the mothers into active partners in all the activities.

Pratham (Mumbai) runs 3000 *balwadis* covering over 50,000 children of construction workers, rag pickers, beggars, street children, and other such difficult groups. The *balwadis* are in public places or in homes. Parents take interest in the education of their children. In fact, they meet and decide the fees to be paid by them (between Rs 10 and Rs 20 per month). In Balajyothi (Hyderabad), the teachers take great pains to motivate parents to send their children to school. Absenteeism is combated with home visits. In Bodh Siksha Samiti (Jaipur) mothers and older children who have the potential and inclination to work with children are given training as mother-teachers or child-teachers who assist the school-teacher.

SNDT's street and working children programme works closely with parents. The parents have been concientized enough to demand quality education as a right of their children. Palak Parishad (conventions of parents) attended by the Additional Commissioner of Pune municipality, teachers union representatives, trade unionists, etc. are called twice a year.

COMMITTED TEACHERS

In dealing with children from disadvantaged groups, commitment of teachers is the key to success. Keeping this in view, Balajyothi (Hyderabad) appoints teachers from within the community itself, who have readiness to work. They may not be adequately qualified, but are preferred due to their rapport with the community and their attachment to the cause. Krushi (Hyderabad) runs slum schools of 800 children with the help of teachers drawn from the slums themselves.

It is clear that the greater the teacher involvement, the greater is the success of the programme. This is corroborated by the reports of many NGOs. In the Police Child Labour Camps of Hyderabad, teachers remain with the children twenty-four hours. They eat, sleep, play and work with them and through that build a strong rapport with the children. Swadhar in Pune (see Box 5.12) uses several integrated strategies to build up teacher commitment.

CONCLUDING OBSERVATIONS

This chapter brings out several important facts about the status of education of disadvantaged children in urban areas. First of all, it is clear that children from disadvantaged sections in urban areas have to depend mainly on government and local body schools for their basic education. Yet, the data available also indicate that neither the facilities nor the nature of the programmes carried out within these schools are good enough to attract and retain children in schools and ensure their basic education. A positive feature, however, is the existence of a number of field-based voluntary organizations working for the education of urban children in disadvantaged conditions. In quantitative terms, the contribution of voluntary organizations is somewhat limited. But the models evolved with their work in the field stand as good examples for larger emulation. Also, many NGOs have begun to work closely with the government, realizing that universal coverage is possible only through government efforts. In spite of such efforts, the attention received by disadvantaged children is quite inadequate. With urban population burgeoning, it is urgent that serious consideration is given to reaching basic education to poorer sections of society. Following are some pointers for action emerging from the review here.

• The most important task in the area of education for the urban deprived is to make serious efforts for educational planning with alternate scenario building, future projections, and definite financial allocations.

BOX 5.12

Swadhar, Pune

Started in 1998, Swadhar runs 13 classes in different pockets of the city of Pune, including 2 in red-light areas. The aim is to sensitize parents to the need for continuing their child's education, to enrol children in formal schools, to tutor the children so as to enable them to cope with formal school curriculum, to participate in Local Social issues.

To achieve this part-time teachers with good rapport with the community were appointed.

Conscious efforts were made to strengthen the teachers and improve their abilities using the following strategies:

• a continuous training process;
• training innovative methods of reaching out to children and building their self-confidence and sense of worth, specially because these children come from poor strata of society;
• commitment of teachers valued and encouraged;
• close supervision of teachers by the project committee.

This is not an isolated activity, but part of a larger project dealing with other aspects of the lives of school children's families.

Traditional approaches to educational planning do not adequately address the dynamics of urban education which is characterized by high levels of economic divisions.

• The government has the schooling infrastructure that can reach out to all sections of the urban population. Many of the NGO projects have taken their present shape after years of experience, experimentation, review, reflection, and refining. It is therefore necessary that the government and the NGOs work in partnership.

• Parents' associations can play a significant role, not only in ensuring the participation of their wards, but also in mobilizing the support of civil society for the education of the disadvantaged. Currently, parents' associations in many schools are only on paper. This situation has to be changed through suitable action from the government as well as from NGOs. Enlisting the support of local mahila mandals, youth clubs and other community based organizations has been found to be very effective in this regard.

• It is commonly observed that government agencies have viewed the task as mainly of providing physical access in quantitative terms without adequate attention to the quality of education provided. This needs to be rectified. Studies have highlighted that a large proportion of children do not enrol themselves or drop out from schools due to factors essentially related to school. Therefore, the expansion of facilities for schooling should be accompanied by a definite plan of improving the quality of education.

• Educational activities are never isolated. They are a part of comprehensive services offered to deal with many aspects of the lives of disadvantaged children and their families. It is best if education inputs form a part of the package for the well-being of children.

• Flexibility is an important strength of initiatives by NGOs. They often revise their approaches, programmes, and activities to make them more relevant. This is an important point to note in implementing large-scale government programmes and injecting flexibility into their design and implementation process.

• There is need for integration of all levels of education from primary to adult. One cannot look at different levels of education as fragmented, disjointed parts just because they are implemented by different agencies. It is necessary to develop an integrated perspective in dealing with primary education and adult literacy programmes.

• Some voluntary organizations have already demonstrated the possibility of mobilizing resources from corporate houses in the task of basic education. It is necessary to build on this by establishing effective linkages with them in implementing basic education projects.

• Notwithstanding the fast expansion of private education facilities in urban areas, in the final analysis, it is only the government that can reach basic education to all the children from disadvantaged sections. Therefore, efforts should be made to invest in and improve government education system rather than creating small parallel facilities.

REFERENCES

Banerji, R. (1997). 'Why Don't Children Complete Primary School? A case study of Low Income Neighbourhood in Delhi'. *Economic and Political Weekly*, vol. 32, 9–15 August, pp. 2053–63.

Department of Education (1992) *Education for All, The Indian Scene: Widening Horizons*. Ministry of Human Resource Development, Government of India, New Delhi.

———— (1999). *Annual Report, 1998–99*. Ministry of Human Resource Development, Government of India, New Delhi.

D'Lima, Hasel and R. Gosalia (1989). *Situational Analysis of Street Children in Bombay*. UNICEF, Mumbai.

Government of India (1992). *Census of India 1991*, Series 1, India. Paper 2 of 1992. Final Population Totals. New Delhi.

Henriques, Jude (1987). 'Environmental Studies Approach of Parisar Asha in Schools of Bombay Municipal Corporation: An Evaluation.' Tata Institute of Social Sciences, Mumbai.

Kurien, J. C. (1990). 'Levels of Attainment in Language and Mathematics in Primary Schools.' A background paper submitted in the *Workshop on Primary Education for All in Urban Areas*. Jointly organized by BMC-UNICEF at Lonavala.

Lambay, F. and M. Chavan (1993). 'Basic Education in Bombay: A Rapid Appraisal.' UNICEF, Mumbai.

Ministry of Home Affairs (1997). *Crimes in India*. National Crime Records Bureau, Government of India, New Delhi.

National Core Group for Deprived Urban Children (1999). 'Primary Education for the Deprived Urban Children: A Data Bank.' Bodh Shiksha Samiti, Jaipur.

National Council of Educational Research and Training (1998). *Sixth All-India Educational Survey*, vol. 1, New Delhi.

National Literacy Mission (1998). *Literacy Rates: An Analysis Based on National Sample Survey Organisation Survey*. Note circulated by National Literacy Mission, Government of India, New Delhi.

National Sample Survey Organisation (1997). *Economic Activities and School Attendance by Children of India*. NSS 50th Round, Report No. 412. Fifth Quinquennial

Survey. Department of Statistics, Government of India, New Delhi.

Planning Commission (1998). *Eighth Five Year Plan, 1992–97.* Table 2.2: Population Projections 1992–7. Government of India, New Delhi.

Rane, Asha J. (1989). 'Evaluation of Environmental Studies Approach in Municipal Schools in Greater Bombay.' Tata Institute of Social Sciences, Mumbai.

Singh R. P. (1987). *Non-Formal Education—an alternate approach.* Sterling Publishers Private Limited, New Delhi.

SPARC (1989–90). 'Waiting for Tomorrow—A Study on Four Groups of Vulnerable Migrant Children in the City of Bombay, 1989–90'. Sponsored by UNICEF, Department of Social Welfare, Government of Maharashtra, Mumbai.

World Conference on Education for All (1990). *World Declaration on Education for All and Framework for Action to Meet Basic Learning Needs.* Inter-Agency Commission (UNDP, UNESCO, World Bank), New York.

6

Education For All
The Situation of Dalit Children in India

Geetha B. Nambissan and Mona Sedwal

INTRODUCTION

Any effort towards realizing the constitutional commitment of universal elementary education (UEE) for all children must seriously address the constraints that have hitherto excluded large sections of Indian society from basic education. Among the educationally most deprived sections in India are the Dalits,* officially called Scheduled Castes (SCs). According to the 1991 census, there were around 138 million Dalits accounting for 16.5 per cent of the population of India. In the mid-1990s, barely 41.5 per cent of Dalits in rural India were literate and only 62.5 per cent of children in the 6–14 age group had been enrolled in school at some point of time.[1] Attention to the education of their children is, hence, of critical importance. The perspective within which the educational concerns of Dalit communities should be addressed must be one of social justice as Dalit communities have suffered from social discrimination and have traditionally been denied access to learning. A framework of social justice is important in that it goes beyond aggregate concerns of equality in the context of access, participation, and outcomes in education to one which emphasizes qualitative concerns of what educational experiences mean for identity and self-worth as well as for future life chances (see Seceda 1988). It also draws attention to the commitments that educational systems make to the more vulnerable groups and how this bears out in concrete terms.

* In this paper, Dalit is used to specifically refer to Scheduled Caste communities, though today the term is often used to include other oppressed groups as well.

[1] These are literacy and 'ever enrolment' rates from a survey conducted by the National Council of Applied Economic Research (NCAER).

THE CONTEXT OF DEPRIVATION

The roots of educational deprivation of Dalit communities must be traced back to their position as untouchables in the caste structure of traditional Hindu society. These were the most 'polluted' of castes that were hereditarily assigned the most defiling of occupations. They could own no productive assets and were completely dependant on the higher castes whom they served. A number of norms and taboos restricted mobility of Dalits and proscribed certain kinds of behaviour and patterns of interaction. Access to learning was prohibited and Dalits could not enter indigenous schools that taught elementary skills even to lower castes in pre-British India. Though opportunities for education and new occupations that were untied to caste status were opened to the untouchables for the first time during British rule in the mid-nineteenth century, the magnitude of access to such opportunities was limited and only a few Dalit sub-castes, because of their relatively favourable structural location, were able to avail of them. Thus, even in 1961, more than a decade after India's Independence, barely 10 per cent of the Dalit population was literate.

The Constitution of independent India acknowledged the centuries of social, economic, and educational deprivation suffered by the Dalits and specific provisions were incorporated to protect these communities from discrimination as well as to facilitate their development. Where education is concerned, the Constitution directs the states to 'promote with special care the educational and economic interests' of Dalits and other weaker sections (Article 46). However, even in the 1990s, Dalits remained economically extremely vulnerable relative to the general population. In 1993–4, as many as 48.1 per cent of Dalits in rural areas were below the official poverty line in comparison to 31.3 of 'others' (other than Dalit and tribal persons). In urban areas, almost 50 per cent of Dalits were below the poverty line in the same year. Further, almost 70 per cent of rural Dalit households owned an acre or less of land and 61 per cent were wage labour households.[2]

Caste dynamics continue to underlie social and economic relations, especially in rural India where Dalits still occupy the lowest position in the village hierarchy in terms of social and ritual status. The fact that the majority of Dalit households in rural areas own little or no land suggests that these communities continue to be economically dependent on upper and dominant castes, and hence, socially vulnerable as well. They also suffer discrimination from higher castes though this is inadequately documented (see Box 6.1). Dalits still reside in spatially segregated clusters at the periphery of villages, are not allowed access to common village wells, and are prevented from entering temples. Oommen (1984, 46–7) says that Dalits as a group continue to be subjected to what he refers to as 'cumulative

---

BOX 6.1

Dalits and Discrimination

In village after village in rural Andhra, one finds that the Malas and Madigas are made to live outside the village, normally to the east.... The Malas and Madigas find their separate glasses and plates in such hotels. They should buy the eatables only if they are prepared to wash their own plates and glasses and keep them in a separate box meant for them.... The upper castes do not tolerate it if the lower castes wear good clothes put on good chappals as they have to live what is known as the *ayya banchan* life (living at the feet of the upper castes). (Illaiah 2000, 210–11)

In Akramesi village in Tamil Nadu, where the Dalits are numerically an extremely small minority, 'the Pallars were prohibited from fetching water from this (common community) well on the pretext that their vessels and buckets would pollute the water by their touch. The pond used by the caste Hindus for bathing was not even to be approached by the Scheduled Castes.... The Pallars were also prohibited from riding a bicycle'. If the Pallars disobeyed the demands of the caste Hindus, 'the common punishment for such disobedience was nothing less than tying the person to a street lamp post or a tree situated within the village premise and beating him in public till he collapsed'. (Ramaiah 2000, 5–6)

domination' and experience 'multiple deprivations' that stem from 'low ritual status, appalling poverty and powerlessness.'[3]

It is, however, important to remember that Dalits are not a homogenous group. There are more than 400 major caste groups that vary in numerical strength, areas of geographical concentration, and occupations followed. Though around 81 per cent of Dalits are found in rural areas, some sub-castes are more urban based. Socially also Dalits differ in terms of ritual status. Dalit castes such as 'Balmikis' (traditional scavengers) are considered among the most polluted of castes while 'Jatavs' (leather workers) have higher social status. As mentioned earlier, some Dalit castes have had the advantage of early access to education and modern educational opportunities. Post-independence developments such as changes in the agrarian economy, limited land reforms, proximity to cities or actual urban residence, as well as access to education have placed some Dalit sub-castes in a relatively more favourable position to avail of opportunities for economic betterment that have been officially targeted at these communities (see Pai 2000).

Changes in the agrarian economy, new occupational opportunities as well as adult franchise have given some leverage to Dalit communities to defy traditional social norms and taboos. Many parts of India are witness to socio-political mobilization of Dalits who are increasingly demanding land, decent wages, and social dignity. There has been retaliation by the upper castes and reported atrocities against Dalits increased thirty-seven-fold during the period 1970–95 (see Francis 2000).

One of the critical factors for economic betterment of Dalits in the post independent period has been formal education. Education has facilitated occupational diversification and mobility, particularly through reservations, for a small section of the Dalit population who are now in public sector jobs. This in turn has lessened their dependence on the higher castes, bringing with it some modicum of social dignity. It has also been observed that the educated Dalits are less willing to accept the domination of the higher castes and have played an important role in the political and cultural assertion of Dalits witnessed in different parts of the country (see Pai 2000). It is in this larger context of the social and economic realities that Dalits confront, as well as the critical role that education can play in their lives, that we now look at the present situation where schooling of their children is concerned.

---

[2] These are figures from the National Sample Survey (1993–4) cited in Thorat Sukhdeo (1999) 'Social Security in Unorganized Sector in India: How Secure Are The Scheduled Castes?' in *The Indian Journal of Labour Economics*, vol. 42, no. 3, pp. 451–70.

[3] Of course when compared to the past, the social conditions of the Dalits have improved and, as Deliége says, 'the prohibitions are not as strict as they used to be'. However, caste-based discrimination persists and is most acute where Dalits are economically dependent on higher castes (Deliége 1999).

ARE DALIT CHILDREN IN SCHOOL?

The progress of schooling among Dalit children (5–14 years) has been relatively poor compared to that of the general population. As seen in Table 6.1 school attendance rates in rural areas (where almost 90 per cent of the population reside) in 1993–4 was 64.3 per cent for Dalit boys as compared to 74.9 per cent among boys from other (other than Dalit and tribal) social groups. In urban areas, Dalit boys have higher attendance rates (77.5 per cent) but the lag in enrolment rates vis-à-vis other boys continues to be around 10 percentage points. As in the general population, Dalits girls have lower school attendance rates than Dalit boys. The male–female lag in attendance rates is greater in rural areas as compared to urban areas. Poor school enrolment/attendance rates among Dalits relative to the other communities also points to sharp disparities in literacy rates. In the 1981–91 decade, Dalits lagged behind the general population by as much as around 15 percentage point in literacy (37 per cent among Dalits as compared to 52 per cent for the general population). Barely 24 per cent of Dalit women were literate according to the 1991 census.

the educationally most backward states such as Rajasthan and Bihar disparities in school attendance rates between Dalits and other social groups are far sharper.

Also significant is the fact that some states have recorded tremendous progress in school attendance rates between 1987–8 and 1993–4. The performance of Himachal Pradesh is significant. The state which is hailed as the new success story where literacy and schooling are concerned has seen an extraordinary increase in attendance rates especially among Dalit girls in the 5–14 age group. Dalit girls' attendance rates in rural areas have increased from 59.6 per cent in 1987–8 to 82.1 per cent in 1993–4, an increase of 23 per cent in five years (see Table 6.2). Kerala is, as expected, a well-performing state where Dalits are concerned, though states such as Maharashtra and Tamil Nadu have also done well in comparison with the all-India averages for school participation.

Kulkarni (2000) uses NCAER (1994) survey data to compare literacy/school completion rates across age groups in different states to thereby compare the magnitude of inter-state educational disparities over time between other castes (Hindus other than Dalits) and Dalits

TABLE 6.1
School Attendance Rates among Children in the Age Group 5–14 Years for Different Social Groups 1983–94

(per cent)

Social group	School attendance rates among children (5–14 years)											
	1983*				1987–8				1993–4			
	Rural		Urban		Rural		Urban		Rural		Urban	
	M	F	M	F	M	F	M	F	M	F	M	F
Dalit	48.9	25.5	66.7	52.3	49.8*	31.1**	68.2*	53.8*	64.3	46.2	77.5	68.6
Others	59.2	39.2	76.5	69.1	63.4	45.8	78.0	72.6	74.9	61.0	86.8	83.0
All	55.3	34.8	74.8	66.4	58.9	41.1	76.4	69.9	71.0	55.9	85.3	80.7

Note: * Figures correspond to current enrolment rate.
　　　** Neo-Buddhists of Maharashtra are not considered under SC for obtaining the estimates.

Source: National Sample Survey Organisation (1999), *Sarvekshana*, Journal of the NSSO, vol. XXII, no. 4, 79th issue. NSSO Department of Statistics and Programme Implementation, Ministry of Statistics and Programme Implementation, GoI.

Disparities within Dalit communities are significant as seen in inter-state differentials in school attendance rates in the relevant age groups. School attendance rates in rural areas ranged from over 85 per cent for Dalit boys in states such as Himachal Pradesh and Kerala to less than 60 per cent in Bihar, Rajasthan, and Uttar Pradesh in 1993–4. For rural girls, inter-state educational disparities are sharper and range from over 80 per cent in Himachal Pradesh and Kerala to an abysmal 23 per cent in Bihar, and 22 per cent in Rajasthan. What is significant is that in high-performing states such as Kerala and Himachal Pradesh, the participation of Dalits in schools almost equals that of other social groups. However, in

(who are also Hindus). His analysis suggests that in low literacy states such as Rajasthan, Bihar, and Uttar Pradesh, differentials in middle school completion rates between these social groups continued to be significantly high (17–31 percentage points) for rural males in the 15–24 age group. However differentials in high school completion rates for rural males in the 17–24 age group (19–33 percentage points) have actually increased as compared to the older 25–49 age group (16–29 percentage points) pointing to a widening in educational disparities between other castes and Dalits over time in these states. Among women, the gap between these castes has widened in the low literacy states and this is particularly

TABLE 6.2
School Attendance Rates (%) among the Children in the Age Group 5–14 Year

(per cent)

States/UTs	% of Dalits population to total population 1991	1987–8				1993–4			
		Dalits		Others		Dalits		Others	
		M	F	M	F	M	F	M	F
Andhra Pradesh	15.93	55.1	32.1	63.9	42.3	64.3	44.5	71.7	56.0
Assam	7.40	69.9	70.5	63.2	58.7	75.4	70.8	75.9	71.7
Bihar	14.55	24.1	9.3	46.9	27.3	46.0	22.5	63.5	44.1
Gujarat	7.41	70.3	48.6	68.1	53.9	77.5	65.3	78.6	62.6
Haryana	19.75	63.1	49.0	76.9	54.9	76.6	56.6	85.0	71.7
Himachal Pradesh	25.34	76.5	59.6	83.9	69.3	87.6	82.1	91.8	83.9
Jammu & Kashmir	8.31	70.2	53.4	63.3	40.9	87.5	63.9	85.0	75.7
Karnataka	16.38	47.5	29.4	62.5	50.8	65.7	50.5	76.2	67.6
Kerala	9.92	86.1	81.9	89.7	87.5	96.0	88.5	92.9	94.0
Madhya Pradesh	14.55	48.2	25.7	63.0	34.0	57.6	37.0	70.4	52.5
Maharashtra	11.09	66.0(73.3)	43.1(53.1)	77.1	62.5	83.8	72.8	86.4	76.7
Orissa	16.20	46.7	30.9	66.1	51.5	67.9	43.9	76.5	68.0
Punjab	28.31	50.5	41.3	76.3	69.3	68.6	59.2	88.4	83.6
Rajasthan	19.29	49.8	12.3	65.5	27.9	58.1	21.5	76.8	41.1
Sikkim	5.93	60.3	57.3	77.1	74.2	100.0	64.7	89.6	88.4
Tamil Nadu	19.18	72.4	58.1	79.6	63.7	76.9	71.2	85.6	76.6
Tripura	16.36	65.7	63.0	70.6	68.8	87.9	83.2	86.7	86.6
Uttar Pradesh	21.05	43.6	15.1	57.0	33.6	59.7	31.5	69.9	49.4
West Bengal	23.62	47.3	39.0	56.6	52.4	67.9	56.9	71.1	65.9
Chandigarh	16.51	*	*	75.5	98.0	94.8	66.0	99.8	91.4
Delhi	19.05	*	*	88.7	90.1	*	*	89.4	96.2
Pondicherry	16.25	64.7	71.3	89.3	74.3	95.7	100.0	80.5	100.0
All-India[#]	16.37	49.8(68.2)	33.1(52.3)	63.4	45.8	64.3	46.2	74.9	61.0

Note: Figures in brackets relate to neo-Buddhists.
* Results not presented as the number of sample households was less than 20.
[#] All-India figure includes States that have not been listed as their Dalit proportion is very small.

Source: Census of India 1991; National Sample Survey Organisation (1990), Employment Unemployment Situation of Scheduled Caste and Scheduled Tribe Population During late Eighties. NSS 43rd Round, July 1987–June 1988. NSSO, Department of Statistics, Government of India, New Delhi; National Sample Survey Organisation (1997), Economic Activities and School Attendance by Children of India. NSS 50th Round, Report No. 412, Fifth Quinquennial Survey, Department of Statistics, Government of India, New Delhi.

significant where middle and high school completion rates are concerned. Kulkarni (2000, 7) notes 'For females, the gap has widened in some States, probably because earlier the level of education was low among females and has risen faster among other castes than Scheduled Castes'. On the other hand, there has been a narrowing in literacy and school completion rates between other castes and Dalits in states such as Kerala, Himachal Pradesh, and Tamil Nadu.

Data on dropout of children from school also points to significantly poorer school completion rates among Dalits as compared to other social groups. According to the NSSO survey (1993–4) as many as 40.5 per cent of Dalit children in rural areas and 24 per cent in urban areas had discontinued school. The proportion of children who had discontinued school was significantly lower for 'other' social groups (28.8 per cent in rural areas and 13.3 per cent in urban areas). For Dalit girls, dropout from school is as high as 49.9 per cent of the relevant age group as compared to 36 per cent among girls from other social groups in rural areas (NSSO 1997). Government statistics which give dropout rates based on school enrolment records indicate that though the dropout rate of Dalits from school has fallen in the 1990s it still remains fairly high at elementary school stage, around 66.6 per cent among Dalits in 1997–8 as compared to 60.5 per cent for the general population (see Planning Commission 2000).

The discussion thus far highlights disparities in school participation between Dalits and other social groups. It also points to the need to look beyond literacy and school enrolment/attendance rates to actual school completion rates in order to asses, in concrete terms, the progress in education among Dalits relative to other groups. On the other hand, what also emerges is that an analysis of disparities in schooling between Dalits and other groups at aggregate level glosses over the uneven spread of education within Dalit communities themselves: between boys and girls, rural and urban areas, as well as between states. Of concern is that not only do a significant proportion of children from Dalit communities continue to remain out-of-school, but also that there is still a hard core of children who may have never been to school at all.

POLICY PERSPECTIVES

The 1986 National Policy on Education (NPE) aimed at universal enrolment of all Dalit children in the 6–11 age group and 75 per cent enrolment in the 11–14 age group as well as the successful completion by them of primary and middle school stages by 1990.[4] These targets have been reiterated in the revised programme of action in 1992. The educational scene in the 1990s has been dominated by the District Primary Education Programme (DPEP), which placed special emphasis upon improved access, participation, and achievement of children from mar-ginalized groups. In addition, the 'Sarva Shiksha Abhiyan' (SSA) announced in 2000 emphasizes the involvement of Dalit communities in the ownership of school committees, setting up of alternative schooling facilities in unserved habitations, using community teachers, monitoring attendance and retention of Dalit children, and so on. Strategies laid down to universalize primary/elementary education among Dalits are concerned with:

● Expanding school provisioning at primary and middle stages. In predominantly Dalit (and tribal) habitations, distance norms are relaxed so as to facilitate easy access to elementary education. Hostel facilities are also recommended to facilitate learning.
● Subsidizing costs and providing incentives. Abolishing tuition fees and providing incentives such as free books, uniforms, school bags (in some states) and mid-day meals. Scholarships to children from 'unclean' castes/ financial assistance for children of indigent groups and attendance scholarships for girls.

[4] This section draws upon the following education policy documents: DoE 1986, DoE 1992, DPEP 1999, and GoI 2000.

● Recruitment of teachers from within these communities by relaxing qualifications if necessary.
● Providing non-formal and alternate/innovative programmes for children who are seen as unable to access formal schooling.

How serious have policy pronouncements been regarding educational provisioning as well as subsidizing private costs of schooling where Dalits are concerned? One indicator can be the actual resources set aside for the development of these communities. However, until the Sixth Plan barely 0.52 per cent of plan outlay was allocated as special central assistance (SCA) exclusively for the development of Dalits, tribes, and other backward classes. Subsequently, with the institution of the special component plan (SCP) at state level, the SCA for the development of these groups increased to 12.3 per cent in the Eighth Plan (see DoE 2000a, 12 and Planning Commission 2000).

According to the National Commission for Scheduled Castes and Scheduled Tribes, 'The most important cause for non-development of SC/STs is non-allocation of resources for their development on a priority.' Further the Commission states that though the SCA was 'conceived as supplement to the total development effort under general sectors of development, in practice these special programmes merely substituted the benefits available to SCs under normal development schemes. This resulted in much lower investment in their development than envisaged (see NCSC & ST 1998).

ACCESS TO SCHOOLS

By 1997 India had as many as 598,000 primary and 177,000 upper primary schools (see Planning Commission 1999). However, schooling within easy access has always been relatively poorer for the more vulnerable groups as compared to the population in general, especially in rural areas. As can be seen in Table 6.3, primary schooling (schools/sections) is available within a significantly smaller number of predominantly Dalit habitations (37.03 per cent) as compared to general rural habitations[5] (49.79 per cent). Where upper-primary schools are concerned, access within habitations is poor but this is definitely more in the case of Dalit habitations (only 6.51 per cent of which have upper-primary schools) as compared to general rural habitations (13.87 per cent) (see NCERT 1999). The official distance norm is that primary schools/sections are to be

[5] General rural habitations include predominantly Dalit and tribal habitations. If these habitations were excluded, the availability of schools within non-Dalit and tribal habitations would of course be much higher.

set up within a 1 km distance and upper-primary schools within 3 km distance of rural habitations with a population of 300 and above. In 1993, around 82 per cent of Dalit habitations had primary schooling within 1 km while 77.6 per cent had middle schools/sections within 3 km (see Table 6.3).

regarding school availability may be met for the majority (82 per cent) of Dalit habitations. However the fact that Dalit habitations are poorly provided when compared to general habitations implies that schools are mainly located in higher caste habitations within larger villages. Given the fact that norms of purity and pollution still

TABLE 6.3
Provision of Schools/Sections for Predominantly Dalit and all Areas in Rural India, 1986 and 1993

Distance at which available	All areas				Predominantly Dalit populated areas			
	% of habitations having schools/sections		% of population covered		% of habitations having schools/sections		% of population covered	
	1986	1993	1986	1993	1986	1993	1986	1993
Primary Schools/Sections								
Within habitation	51.16	49.79	80.38	77.81	37.67	37.03	66.31	64.27
<1 km	83.84	83.36	94.45	93.77	81.59	82.30	91.14	91.32
1.1–2km	10.81	10.72	4.06	4.24	12.97	12.19	6.58	6.21
>2km	5.35	5.92	1.49	2.00	5.44	5.51	2.28	2.46
Total	100	100	100	100	100	100	100	100
Upper-Primary Schools/Sections								
Within habitation	13.1	13.87	36.8	37.2	5.57	6.51	15.42	18.50
<3km	74.01	76.14	83.98	85.00	74.43	77.64	79.83	82.53
3.1–4km	9.51	8.05	6.55	5.52	10.31	8.22	8.74	6.55
4.1–5km	6.32	6.09	4.22	4.18	6.68	5.91	5.66	4.97
>5km	10.16	9.72	5.26	5.30	8.58	8.22	6.22	5.94
Total	100	100	100	100	100	100	100	100

Source: NCERT(1992, 1998), Fifth and Sixth All-India Educational Survey.

What is significant about the nature of educational access is that for each population slab, including those with more than 5000 persons, a relatively smaller proportion of Dalit habitations had primary schooling when compared to rural habitations in general. In 1993, there were as many as 53 per cent of predominantly Dalit habitations that had a population of less than 300 persons. Only 15.3 per cent of such habitations as compared to 21.4 per cent of general rural habitations within the same population slab had primary schools/ sections within them. It is interesting that though availability of schools to Dalits within their own habitations is relatively poor in comparison with general rural habitations, such disparities are less sharp if we look at school availability within a kilometre of rural habitations (see Table 6.4).

Dalit families usually live in spatially segregated clusters or habitations that are located at a distance from higher caste habitations within larger villages. This residential pattern has important implications for physical and social access to education, usually ignored in the larger concern with meeting quantitative targets vis-à-vis school expansion. In quantitative terms, distance norms

govern social relations in rural areas it becomes essential to understand whether schools are socially accessible for Dalit children even when they are located at officially prescribed distances.

There are very few references to social accessibility of schools. Aruna (1999, 1011–14) in her study of Tamil Nadu refers to 'qualitative dangers' to schools and says that 'in many habitations, the school is situated in the localities inhabited by upper castes who are hostile to students belonging to the lower castes and minority groups'. Ramaiah's observations of Akramesi village in Tamil Nadu where Dalits form a small minority has disturbing implications for social accessibility of schools.

> None of the Scheduled Castes were allowed even to walk through the residential areas of the dominant castes or through the village's main street running through the residential areas of the dominant castes. They had to walk a long way along the periphery of the village to reach their huts. [Ramaiah 2000, 5]

Putting the relationship between caste status and educational access into perspective Vasavi *et al.* observe that

> there are conditions in which the right to education for members of the socially marginal and low ranked *jati*

TABLE 6.4
Percentage of Habitations Served by Primary Schools/Sections

Population slab	No.of habitations		% of habitations served by primary schools/sections					
			Within the habitation		Within 1 km		Within 2 km	
	All	Dalit	All	Dalit	All	Dalit	All	Dalit
5000 & above	7119	231	96.26	92.21	99.20	98.70	99.72	99.57
2000–4999	52,928	2712	93.57	91.48	98.25	98.30	99.37	99.45
1000–1999	125,046	9287	88.31	83.54	97.20	96.46	99.13	99.00
1000 & above	185,093	12,230	90.12	85.46	97.58	96.91	99.22	99.11
500–999	213,059	21,752	74.34	66.49	93.70	92.42	98.19	97.98
300–499	182,438	22,487	54.84	44.06	87.65	86.89	96.25	96.37
100–299	319,397	42,389	27.82	19.92	76.40	78.72	92.12	93.90
Below 100	160,625	21,659	8.69	6.30	62.21	66.15	84.14	87.59
Below 300	480,022	64,048	21.42	15.31	71.65	74.47	89.45	91.77
Total	1,060,612	120,517	49.79	37.03	83.36	82.30	94.08	94.49

Source: NCERT (1999), Sixth All-India Educational Survey Main Report.

members remains contested. Members of the high-ranked *jati* groups and the dominant actors of the village often see education for the working and labouring caste and class groups as a waste and a threat. This denial is linked to the popular perception that low ranked *jati* members are incapable of being educated, and if educated, pose a threat to village hierarchies and power relations. [Vasavi *et al.* 1997, 3184]

WHO PROVIDES FOR SCHOOLING?

According to the Sixth All-India Educational Survey, NCERT (1998), Dalit communities mainly avail of government schooling. Of the Dalit children in primary schools, 91.3 per cent in rural areas and 64.6 per cent in urban areas were in schools managed by government and local bodies. At middle stage, a relatively larger proportion of Dalit children were enrolled in privately managed schools, though expectedly this is more so in urban areas (49.6 per cent) as compared to rural areas (32.9 per cent). A study of the increase in enrolment of Dalit children in elementary schools between 1986 and 1993 points to a significant trend. As much as 32 per cent of the increase in primary school enrolment among Dalit boys and 21 per cent among girls in urban areas was accounted for by private unaided (PUA) schools between 1986 and 1993.[6] In rural areas PUA schools accounted for a relatively smaller proportion of the increase in enrolments during this period, around 7 per cent for Dalit boys and 4 per cent for Dalit girls (see Tilak and Sudershan 2000). Official statistics on

enrolment in private schools do not include enrolment in private schools that are not granted official recognition by the government. These PUA unrecognized schools are mushrooming in cities and towns and in the larger villages. The NCERT survey (1993) estimates that there were around 38,000 such unrecognized primary schools in rural India pointing to a significant underestimating of the PUA sector in education even in rural India (see NCERT 1999). Tilak and Sudershan (2000) observe that the growth of private school enrolments at primary stage in India is a response to 'differentiated demand' for education, i.e. for education of 'good quality'. Studies suggest that this is true even for the poor and marginalized, among whom the decision to send a child to a private institution is usually a conscious one and is related to a demand for 'quality' education that is today popularly perceived as synonymous with that offered by the private sector (see Jain 1997).

There is very little research specifically on the demand for private education among Dalits. However, a study by Singh (1995) in four villages of Meerut district of Uttar Pradesh where 33–63 per cent of population is Dalit is revealing. The study documents the disillusionment of Dalit parents with the poor quality of teaching in the government school system leading to a search by them for 'alternate' private (presently unrecognized) schooling for their children. What is of concern is that Dalits who have made a shift to the private sector in search of good schooling may not necessarily be assured of quality education. Singh notes that teachers in unorganized private schools are poorly paid and likely to be untrained. On the basis of preliminary tests of achievement of children, Singh notes that performance of children in the PUA unrecognized schools did not differ much from that

[6] De *et al.* (2000) show that PUA schooling accounted for as much as 60 per cent of the general increase in enrolments at primary stage in urban areas and 18 per cent in rural areas between 1986 and 1993.

of children studying in the government schools. Further PUA unrecognized schools appear to have a fragile base and are often prey to local caste politics (see Singh 1995). Commenting on the quality of private schools that Dalit children in his sample from Mumbai city attended, Wankhede (1998, 47) notes that 'they were...of substandard nature without much reputation'.

The decade of the 1990s has witnessed a major shift in official policy to 'cost-effective', alternative and innovative schooling to meet the needs of the educationally deprived. These are schools that specially target Dalit and other educationally backward communities. The most well known of these programmes are the Education Guarantee Scheme (EGS) as well as Alternative Schooling (AS) of Madhya Pradesh now being seen as models for the rapid achievement of univerzalisation of primary education in the country at large. What is characteristic of schemes such as the EGS is that they are based on community demand for schooling and poorly qualified and trained local youth are employed as 'para teachers' who are paid lower salaries than regular teachers. Dalits and other educationally deprived communities have responded positively to the EGS and AS. For instance, in two districts of Madhya Pradesh it was found that the overwhelming majority of children (more than 98 per cent) enrolled in the EGS and AS belonged to educationally backward sections such as Dalits, tribes, and other backward castes (Government of MP 2000, 243). This is clearly indicative of the demand for schooling by hitherto educationally deprived groups. It also suggests that physical and social access (the EGS/ AS are established within habitations of Dalit, tribals, and backward castes) to schools is necessary to increase enrolment. However, the major criticism against these programmes has been that of the quality of education actually provided. A study of 'para' teacher schools (which included EGS and AS schools) notes that the quality of classroom transactions has been found to be poor. Para teachers are seen to lack the necessary training, professional development as well as ongoing academic support. In addition, 'para' teacher schools lacked 'appropriate physical infrastructure and a satisfactory school environment for carrying out effective and efficient teaching–learning' (see DPEP 1999).

DOES POVERTY CONSTRAIN SCHOOLING?

As mentioned at the outset, a large section of Dalit families are below the poverty line and agricultural and other wage labour is the primary occupation of the majority of households, especially in rural areas. Poverty is hence likely to continue to be a major deterrent to education despite growing aspiration for education among Dalit parents, which has been documented in a number of recent studies. NSSO data (1993–4) do show that the proportion of children who do not attend school sharply increases in lower monthly per capita expenditure (MPCE) classes. The proportion of non-attending (dropouts never attended school) rural children in the 5–14 year age group, which was less than 20 per cent in the MPCE of more than Rs 560, increases to around 40 per cent in the MPCE of Rs 190–210 (which includes the poverty line of around Rs 205 per month) and 60 per cent in the lowest MPCE of less than Rs 120 per month (see NSSO 1997b). Srivastava's recent study (1999, 437) of living conditions in villages in Uttar Pradesh and Bihar in 1997–8 (see Uttar Pradesh–Bihar survey) indicates that 'while almost half of the total SC children are out of school, 60 per cent of the poorest SC children are not in school but in Bihar, two-thirds of the poorest SC children are not in school'.

Among the poor, the extent to which households experience some security of livelihood is also likely to influence whether children are sent to school or not, how regularly they attend school, and how long they are able to continue their education. Irregular income, frequent migration in search of work, or the death or illness of a breadwinner is likely to place children from these households educationally at great risk. In his study of dropout among Dalits, Muralidharan (1997, 171) observes that 'schooling of the boys as well as girls came to a halt as soon as the head of the family was bedridden.... Every two out of 10 Harijan children were forced to leave their studies on the grounds of illness or death in the family'.

Costs of schooling and poor quality of education are seen as the most crucial factors that underlie educational deprivation (see Bhatty 1998). Using data from the NCAER survey conducted in 1993–4, Tilak (2000) shows that Dalit households, even in rural areas, incur sizeable expenditure on education of their children even at primary stage, on items such as books, stationery, and uniforms. On average, households spend around Rs 303 per student per annum at elementary stage in government schools. The expenditure per student is marginally higher in government aided schools (Rs 325) and significantly so in PUA schools (Rs 757), making such education out of reach for the majority of Dalits (see Tilak 2000). According to Muralidharan (1997, 171) the inability of Dalit parents to meet the 'educational needs' of their children in terms of books, notebooks, stationery, and so on is an important reason for discontinuation of children from school.

The role of public policy in providing incentives for education (textbooks, midday meals, etc.) and thereby reducing the direct costs of schooling has been seen as crucial in addressing educational deprivation. The mid-day meal programme in particular has been seen to encourage school enrolment and attendance and to raise the nutritional status of children as well. The PROBE report (1999, 95) notes that 'in areas where school meals are operational, most teachers take the view that they have boosted school attendance, and parents share this view'.

What is, however, quite clear from available data is that the actual coverage of incentives (other than free tuition) is extremely limited. For instance, textbooks and uniforms are a major component of school costs. However, in 1993 only 54.6 per cent of primary schools were covered by the scheme of free textbooks and barely 10 per cent of Dalit students were beneficiaries. While 29.3 per cent of schools received free uniforms, a negligible 4.6 per cent of Dalit students were covered under this scheme. Midday meals were reported to cover 13.9 per cent of schools, and barely 3.9 per cent of Dalits (see NCERT 1999). Further the programme itself has been diluted. Instead of hot meals being provided everyday to children and thereby seriously addressing the very real issues of hunger and nutrition that are major obstacles to learning among the poor, only dry rations are being given to families at specified intervals in most states. A study in remote villages of Udaipur district in Rajasthan also found that parents and teachers 'were strongly in favor of cooked mid-day meals being provided daily to children as they usually went hungry to school' (see Nambissan 2001, 500).

Studies have also emphasized that children do not receive incentives in time, and often do not receive them at all. Irregularities and delays in distributing textbooks and uniforms and other incentives as well as corruption, frequently reported, especially in relation to the midday meal scheme, are likely to make these incentives of little consequence to the majority of school children (see Jabbi and Rajyalakshmi 2001, 435; Nambissan 2001). On the other hand, these schemes give the general impression that Dalit and 'other weaker sections' are getting undue advantage.

One of the important survival strategies of the poor is the involvement of their children in work. According to NSSO (1993–4), around 8.1 per cent of Dalit children were categorized as workers. It is significant that though only around 2 per cent of children attending schools were working, a far greater proportion of Dalits (around 17 per cent) who dropped out of school were officially included under the category of workers. A fairly large number of Dalit children (30.8 per cent) were found helping in household chores in rural areas. While it is often felt that such activity does not constitute

regular work and can be combined with education, what this means for children in terms of time as well as energy and interest in schooling has not been seriously addressed.

The debate on children's work/child labour is usually polarized where education is concerned. On the one hand, compulsory, full-time formal education is seen as the most important instrument whereby child labour can be abolished and the child's right to education protected. On the other hand, there are those who feel that given the context of poverty, there is need to look for more flexible options where work can be combined with education such as that provided through non-formal schools. On the other hand, non-formal schooling has hitherto been a poor substitute for formal schooling. For the very young among the poor, the absence of schools that reach out to children in difficult circumstances has resulted in their entering the ranks of child workers by default. Whether education should be so provided that children can combine work and school, whether the transition from work to school should be an abrupt one or one that also addresses the process of this transition by providing children with the necessary supports to enable this change are controversial issues and need to be situated within the perspective of children's overall development in which meaningful schooling has a critical role to play.

What emerges from the forgoing discussion is that poverty and its bearing on costs incurred in schooling as well as children's work are likely to be serious constraints in the education of poor Dalit children. However, school participation varies among poor Dalit households and is likely to be influenced by factors such as the nature of livelihood, prevailing social norms, as well as the educational status of individual households. However, having said this, it is important that the dynamics of caste status in the education of Dalit communities is not ignored. This needs to be reiterated in the light of Srivastava's (1999, 437) finding that in all per capita consumption quintiles in his Bihar–Uttar Pradesh survey, Dalits had the lowest enrolment rates among 6–13 year olds of all caste groups. In fact, in the highest per capita consumption quintile, enrolment of SC/ST children in the 6–13 year age group was 65.1 per cent in comparison with more than 90 per cent for middle and upper caste groups. In the lowest consumption quintile, enrolment was significantly higher for upper castes (83.5 per cent) and middle castes (54.3 per cent) as compared to SCs/STs (40.7 per cent). The role of caste in relation to access to education of Dalit children has already been discussed. A look is now taken at 'schools themselves in order to understand whether discriminatory caste relations influence the experience of education for Dalit children and what this means for social justice in education.

SCHOOL PROCESSES AND EXPERIENCE OF EDUCATION

One of the most important indicators of educational outcomes is the achievement or performance of children in schools. What is available points to the relatively poorer achievement of Dalit children in competencies such as mathematics and language when compared to children in general. Assessment of children carried out during the DPEP baseline studies in 1993 show that

Scheduled caste students performed less well than all students in mathematics in five of eight states and language in six of eight states, with the difference greater than 25 per cent of a standard deviation for mathematics in Haryana, Karnataka and Kerala and for language in Karnataka, Kerala and Orissa'. [World Bank 1997, 134][7]

We do know that Dalit children come from homes that have been deprived of literacy and education for generations, in addition to which they bear the burden of poverty. Such children are likely to begin school less equipped with the language, social, and conceptual skills that schools demand as compared to children coming from relatively better educated homes.

The content of education and how it relates to group experiences is critical to social justice. Curriculum becomes important where Dalit communities are concerned in terms of how they are represented in the official curriculum, as well as their experience of the process of curriculum transaction, including the language of communication. The nature of social relations within which curriculum transaction occurs is equally pertinent.

The official curriculum is largely silent where Dalits and their experiences are concerned (see Kumar 1989). Recounting his own experiences of schooling, Ilaiah (1996) also reveals that Dalit and lower caste children are alienated from the language and content of education as both the content of education and the medium through which it is transacted do not relate to their own cultural experiences. Discrimination within the realm of social relations in the classroom is intangible and difficult to document. Though there is again very little documenta-tion of classroom processes, some insights are available from accounts of educated Dalits of their own school experiences. Nambissan (1996) puts together such experiences to highlight discriminatory school practices as well as the hidden curriculum of discrimination that

appears to pervade norms, values, and attitudes where Dalits are concerned. For instance, there are references to Dalits students being made to sit/eat separately, their copies/slates not being touched by higher caste teachers, and children themselves not being touched. Sainath reports that in Rajasthan children of the Balmiki (traditionally scavengers) caste, seen as the most polluting of castes, 'are made to sit on their own mats, often outside the room or at the door' (see Ramchandran 1999). Box 6.2 lists some of the discriminatory practices against Dalit children in schools in Uttar Pradesh.

BOX 6.2
Discrimination and Education

- Discrimination against SC settlements in the location of schools.
- Teachers refusing to touch SC children.
- Children from particular castes being special targets of verbal abuse and physical punishment by the teachers.
- Low caste children frequently being beaten by higher caste classmates.

Source: Dreze and Gazdar (1996, 85).

Studies also suggest that the formation of peer groups is influenced by caste status of children and friendships are formed mainly within the boundaries of caste membership (see Chitnis 1981). In one of the government schools that Kaul studied, children

complained that though prejudices and discrimination were not practised very openly in the classroom and the peer group appeared friendly in school, outside the school the attitudes changed. Children of upper castes did not invite the Kuruba or Dalit children home for playing and there was no social intermingling outside the school. [Kaul 2001, 158]

TEACHER ATTITUDES

One of the important recommendations of policy is that Dalits are recruited as teachers in proportion to their representation in the population. As far as the figures go, Dalits comprise only around 11 per cent of teachers at primary stage, 9 per cent at upper-primary stage, and 5–6 per cent at secondary and higher-secondary stages of education (NCERT 1999). This implies that non-Dalit teachers, usually higher castes, by and large teach Dalit children.[8]

[7] Nambissan suggests that the higher than average mean age of Dalits in each class may be due not only to late entry in school, but also to their 'relaitvely poorer progresses through school'. (Nambissan 2001, 484)

[8] Though non-Dalits comprise the majority of teachers at elementary stage, it is surprising that the ills of the school system and decline in standards is attributed to the recruitment of Dalits themselves through the policy of reservations. and what is popularly perceived as 'non-merit' criterion. Vasavi *et al.* in a study of villages in Gujarat comment that 'building on popular,

There are few studies that have actually explored teacher attitudes to Dalit children though the fact of social discrimination in classroom processes mentioned earlier suggests that teachers tend to reproduce discriminatory attitudes and practices that underlie caste relations in society. Anitha's study in Karnataka reports that Dalit pupils were called 'kadu-jana' (forest people) who would not learn without beating (see Anitha 2000, 94). The message that teachers appear to be giving to children is the inherently poor scholastic abilities of Dalit children, the lack of interest of parents, and the inevitability of their class (caste) status (see Anitha 2000). Srivastava in his study in Uttar Pradesh notes that 'children from the lower castes tended to be enrolled in schools that they felt were socially tolerant. These were schools that had teachers or management belonging to their own social groups and were not necessarily the ones geographically the closest to their homes' (see Srivastava 2001, 435). Jabbi and Rajyalakshmi's interviews with women and children from Dalit/tribal communities in their study in Bihar brought forth complaints about 'teachers' irregularity, absenteeism, negligence and utilizing services of children for their personal work, poor quality of teaching...and so on' (see Jabbi and Rajyalakshmi 2001, 448). In a similar study in Rajasthan, it was noted that 'fear of teachers as well as corporal punishment are factors that parents (mainly of SC children) cite as constraining regular attendance' (see Nambissan 2001, 485). On the other hand, Anitha (2000, 191) suggests that teachers who are sensitive to the difficult circumstances that Dalit children come from and who respond to their educational needs with a positive attitude do facilitate the education of children.

Decentralization of education and local-level participation of Dalits and other marginalized groups are increasingly being stressed in policy documents. Village-level committees that are being constituted are statutorily required to comprise a minimum number of members from the 'weaker sections.' However, caste relations that predominate at village level make the notion of 'community' itself problematic and this needs to be addressed. Commenting on village-level committees in her study in Karnataka, Kaul notes that

> the participation of Dalits was not easily acceptable to the dominant castes. Sometimes the representation of the SC groups was only on paper. The School Betterment Committees in urban areas also included Dalit representatives, but

very few of such members attended committee meetings because they felt they would not be in a position to make any difference to the school's functioning. [Kaul 2001, 159]

However, there can be no doubt, as Anitha (2000, 193) observes, of the 'positive impact' that a 'healthy schools-community relationship' can have on the effective functioning of primary schools and the role of the teacher in strengthening this relationship.

DISPARITIES AMONG DALITS

Disparities in the spread of education within Dalit communities, across states and among boys and girls, have already been referred to. Where girls are concerned, social norms and patriarchal values are likely to be compounded by caste status placing them educationally at greater disadvantage relative to boys in situations of poverty and discrimination. Pande in her study of Uttar Pradesh Himalyas notes that '...among the SC children a girl child is more likely to attend to young siblings and take care of old people than a boy child' (see Pande 2001, 102). In this context the fact that schools under the EGS/AS have shown relatively higher enrolment of Dalit girls relative to boys (60 per cent and 52 per cent respectively in districts studied in Madhya Pradesh) suggests that easy access to education located within their own habitations is important to increase the participation of Dalit girls in schools (see Government of MP, 2000).

The relatively large dropout of Dalit girls even within primary school needs serious attention. A study in villages of Orissa which included Dalit and tribal children indicates that financial difficulties are cited by parents/elders as the most important 'home related' factor for dropout of Dalit and tribal children in the surveyed households. Interestingly among school-related factors responsible for dropout of girls the two most important factors were 'poor performance/failure and inability to cope with studies' (see Debi 2001, 558–9). The burden of work that Dalit girls bear is likely to be among the factors that underlie their inability to cope with the exigencies of schooling. However studies do show that the presence of educated members within poor households, especially mothers who are literate and have some schooling, does increase the participation of children, particularly girls, in schools (see Vaidyanathan and Nair 2001).

Among the important factors that have been seen as responsible for the impressive gains in schooling among Dalits in states such as Kerala, Himachal Pradesh, or Tamil Nadu for that matter is effective state policy. In Kerala, state policy, which improved the living conditions of the Dalits in the post Independence decades,

---

but false, constructions of incapacity of teachers from low ranked castes, many community members, especially leaders from the dominant caste groups blame the decline of educational standards and the malfunctioning of village schools on the presence of such teachers'. [Vasavi et al. 1997, 3182]

provided impetus to the spread of education. The implementation of land reform, provision of health care and food security along with setting aside a major proportion of the state budget for education provided the larger political and institutional context in which Dalit aspirations for education have materialized to a far greater extent than anywhere else in the country (see Probe Team 1999, 12–13). Of course, it must be remembered that social movements of Dalit communities such as the Ezhavas and Pulayas played an equally critical role in confronting discriminatory caste structures and raising the demand for education of Dalits well before Independence. The Tamil Nadu government's midday meal scheme has been seen as particularly effective in bringing children, especially from marginalized groups such as Dalits, to school, increasing attendance, and providing institutional space where all children, regardless of caste, could eat together. The success of Himachal Pradesh has also been attributed to effective public policy in a society where class, caste, and gender hierarchies are less rigid, though the actual provisioning of schooling is relatively modest (see Probe Team 1999, 118). However, as mentioned earlier, the significant increase in the attendance rates in schools of Dalit girls merits research attention.

Educational disparities between Dalit castes have not received adequate attention. Some Dalit castes have been able to avail of opportunities for education and new occupations, and thereby, better their social conditions relative to other castes. Castes such as the Chamars/ Jatavs (in Uttar Pradesh), Mahars (in Maharashtra), and Malas (in Andhra Pradesh) are among those Dalits that have been able to improve their educational and economic situations, to a far greater extent than the Balmikis/ Bhangis, Mangs or Madigas in these states. Even within these castes a relatively small section has been able to avail of the benefits of policies and programmes of affirmative action directed at these communities. Pai (2001) speaks of 'new inequalities' that have been created by the present policies of affirmative action and the social conflict that results as the competition between Dalits for scarce resources heightens.

FUTURE CONCERNS

In the light of both educational policy and actual school participation, what are the major issues for the future where the education of Dalit children is concerned? As has already been discussed, policy interventions in education have been largely at the level of provisioning and providing incentives to encourage schooling. While provisioning is inadequate in terms of physical access even at primary stage, the issue of how socially accessible schools really are for Dalits has never been addressed. This is primarily because policy fails to acknowledge or confront the role of discriminatory caste relations that pervade the educational experiences of Dalit children. As is clear from the foregoing discussion, caste continues to obstruct the access of Dalit children to schooling as well as the quality of education they receive.

Poverty continues to be a major impediment in the education of Dalit children and costs of education, as well as children's contribution to work, remain serious issues to be considered. The present policy of providing incentives to children is unlikely to address the constraint of poverty in relation to education. Where children's work is concerned, the larger issue to be addressed is that of sustainable livelihoods of the poor. On the other hand if schools reach out to these communities with meaningful education that is attractive to young children, allow for flexibility in timings and schedules for children who work, and provide academic support that they invariably need, it is likely that very young children can be prevented from becoming workers by default, and the entry of older children into the workforce can be delayed.

Quality of education is an important issue and one that needs to be seriously addressed in the larger context of what is seen as the breakdown of the government system of 'free education' and the increasing privatization of education even at primary stage.

Dalit households aspire for education of good quality for their children and there are indications that they are looking towards the private sector for such education primarily because the publicly provided system of education has failed to perform. However, not only are the costs of private schooling relatively high, the quality of education provided by these institutions is of concern. Further, the shift of official policy towards alternate and innovative schools for Dalit and other educationally deprived communities merits serious attention. In the larger context of equity, and education without discrimination as a fundamental right of the child, it would be important to ensure that 'alternate', and 'innovative' schools do not become inferior systems of schooling for those who have hitherto been educationally deprived.

The foregoing discussion suggests that the actual educational experience of Dalit children must be factored in when the quality of schooling they receive is being considered. Here it is important to understand the manner in which caste relations influence the usually understood indicators of school quality such as facilities available for education, the nature of the official curriculum (the content of education) and pedagogy, as well the actual process of curriculum transaction in which social processes such as teacher attitudes and peer relations critically define the educational experience of Dalit children, their dignity, and sense of self-worth. It is here that policy documents, educational programmes, as well as research studies are largely silent. It is true that caste is one of the defining characteristics of the larger social structure and educational institutions are likely to reflect and reinforce these hierarchical social relations. However, a perspective of social justice in education requires that social discrimination is acknowledged and educational institutions intervene to address and confront it. A beginning needs to be made through sensitization of teachers to caste discrimination during training programmes, squarely addressing the issue of caste relations and human rights in curricula, evolving enabling pedagogies, and providing specific academic support to Dalit children. In addition, schools need to reach out to Dalit communities and strengthen school–community relations.

Disparities in education that are becoming increasingly visible among Dalits should also be a matter of concern. Attention needs to be directed to address the special needs of Dalit girls as well as the more deprived Dalit castes, particularly in educationally backward states.

Thus at the end of the 1990s, the gap between the constitutional commitment of education for all children up to the age of 14 years and the actual participation of Dalit children in schools remains large and is likely to continue. The role of effective state policy and political will is critical if the education of all children including Dalits is to be ensured, particularly in the context of the demands being made of education in the last few decades. The changing knowledge and skills package that will increasingly determine future life chances requires that EFA must mean more than basic, and indeed, school education. Education is thus of importance not only because of its critical linkages with human capabilities and empowerment, but also because in instrumental terms, in the globalizing world of today, lack of education will widen disparities between and within societies. The education of Dalit communities in India must hence be of serious concern.

REFERENCES

Anitha, B. K. (2000). *Village, Caste and Education*. Rawat Publications, Jaipur and New Delhi.

Aruna, R. (1999). 'Learn Thoroughly: Primary Schooling in Tamil Nadu'. *Economic and Political Weekly*. 1 May, 1011–14.

Bhatty, Kiran (1998). 'Educational Deprivation in India. A Survey of Field Investigations'. *Economic and Political Weekly*. 4 July, pp. 1731–40.

Chitnis, Suma (1981). *A Long Way to Go*. Allied Publishers, New Delhi.

De, Anuradha, Manabi Majumdar, Claire Noronha and Meera Samson (2000). *Role of Private Schools in Basic Education*. Ministry of Human Resource Development and National Institute of Educational Planning and Administration, New Delhi.

Debi, Sailabala (2001). 'Inequality of Access to Elementary Education in Orissa: An Inter-and Intra spatial Analysis'. In Vaidyanathan, A. and P. R. Gopinathan Nair (eds) *Elementary Education in Rural India: A Grassroots View*. Sage Publications.

Deliége Robert (1999). *The Untouchables of India*. Berg Publications. Oxford (English edition).

Department of Education (1986). *National Policy on Education 1986*. Ministry of Human Resource Development, Government of India, New Delhi.

————— (1992). *National Policy on Education 1992: Programme of Action 1992*. Ministry of Human Resource Development, Government of India, New Delhi.

————— (2000). *Spreading the Light of Education, Programme for Commemoration of 50th Anniversary of India's Independence*. Ministry of Human Resource Development, Government of India, New Delhi.

District Primary Education Programme (1999). *Every Child in School and Every Child Learning*. Ministry of Human Resource Development, Government of India, New Delhi.

————— (1999). *Reaching out Further. Para Teachers in Primary Education. An In-Depth Study of Selected Schemes*. Educational Consultants India Limited, New Delhi.

Dréze, Jean and Haris Gazdar (1996). 'Uttar Pradesh: The burden of Inertia'. In Dréze, Jean and Amartya Sen (eds) *Indian Development*. Oxford University Press, Delhi.

Francis, D. (2000). 'Dalit Rights as Human Rights' in Rao, Chandu Subba, D. Francis (eds), *Development of Weaker Sections*. Rawat Publications, Jaipur and New Delhi.

Government of India (1992). *Census of India 1991*.

————— (2000). *Sarva Shiksha Abhiyan A People's Movement for UEE of Satisfactory Quality*.

Government of Madhya Pradesh (2000). *From Your School to Our School*. EGS, Rajiv Gandhi Shiksha Mission, India.

Illaiah, Kancha (1996). *Why I am not a Hindu*. Samya Publications, Calcutta.

Illaiah, Kancha (2000). 'The State Oppressions and Weaker Sections' in Rao, Chandu Subba, D. Francis (eds), *Development of Weaker Sections*, Rawat Publications, Jaipur and New Delhi.

Jabbi, Mona and C. Rajyalakshmi (2001). 'Education of Marginalised Social Groups in Bihar'. In Vaidyanathan, A. and P. R. Gopinathan Nair (eds), *Elementary Education in Rural India: A Grassroots View*. Sage Publications.

Jain, S. C. (1997). 'Non-Official Initiatives to Cater to the

Human Resource Development Needs of the Urban Poor'. *Nagarlok*, vol. XXIX, April–June.

Kaul, Rekha (2001). 'Accessing Primary Education: Going Beyond the Classroom'. *Economic and Political Weekly*. 13–19 January, vol. 36, no. 2.

Kulkarni, P. M. (2000). 'Inter-State Variations in Human Development Differntials Among Social Groups in India.' National Council of Applied Economic Research, New Delhi. (Unpublished)

Kumar, Krishna (1989). *Social Character of Learning*. Sage Publications, New Delhi.

Muralidharan, V. (1997). *Educational Priorities and Dalit Society*. Kanishka Publishers, New Delhi.

Nambissan, Geetha B. (1996). 'Equity in Education: The Schooling of Dalit Children in India.' Studies on Human Development in India. Discussion Paper Series Number 15. Project of the UNDP.

Nambissan, Geetha B. (2001). 'Social Diversity and Regional Disparities in Schooling: A Study of Rural Rajasthan' in Vaidyanathan, A. and P. R. Gopinathan Nair (eds), *Elementary Education in Rural India: A Grassroots View*. Sage Publications, New Delhi.

National Council of Educational Research And Training (1992). *Fifth All-India Educational Survey*. New Delhi.

———— (1998). *Sixth All-India Educational Survey*. New Delhi.

———— (1999). *Sixth All-India Educational Survey Main Report*. New Delhi.

National Sample Survey Organisation (1990). *Employment Unemployment Situation of Scheduled Caste and Scheduled Tribe Population During late Eighties*. NSS 43rd Round, July 1987–June 1988. Department of Statistics, Government of India, New Delhi.

———— (1997). *Economic Activities and School Attendance by Children of India*. NSS 50th Round, Report No. 412. Fifth Quinquennial Survey. Department of Statistics, Government of India, New Delhi.

———— (1999). *Sarvekshana*. Journal of the National Sample Survey Organisation, vol. XXII, no. 4, 79th Issue. Department of Statistics, Ministry of Planning and Programme Implementation, Government of India, New Delhi.

NCSC&ST (1998). *National Commission for Scheduled Caste/Scheduled Tribe, 1998*. Fourth Report 1996–7 and 1997–8, vol. I. Government of India, New Delhi.

Oommen, T. K. (1984). 'Sources of Deprivation and Styles of Protest: The Case of Dalits in India'. *Contributions to Indian Sociology* (ns) 18, 1.

Pai, Sudha (2000). 'Changing Socio-Economic and Political Profile of Scheduled Castes in Uttar Pradesh'. *Journal of Indian School of Political Economy*, vol. 12, Number 3 and 4, pp. 405–22.

———— (2001). 'Affirmative Action, Group Rights and Democracy: The Mala-Madiga Conflict in Andhra Pradesh.' (Unpublished)

Pande, Anuradha (2001). 'Education of Rural Children in UP Himalayas' in Vaidyanathan, A. and P. R. Gopinathan Nair (eds) *Elementary Education in Rural India A Grassroots View*. Sage Publications.

Planning Commission (1999). *Ninth Five Year Plan, 1997–2002*, vol. II. *Thematic Issues and Sectoral Programmes*. Government of India, New Delhi.

———— (2000). *Mid Term Appraisal of Ninth Five Year Plan (1997–2002)*. Government of India, New Delhi.

PROBE (1999). *Public Report On Basic Education in India*. The PROBE team in Association with Centre for Development Economics. Oxford University Press, New Delhi.

Ramachandran, Vimala (1999). 'Community Participation and Empowerment in Primary Education Discussion of Experiences from Rajasthan.' Paper presented in the *National Seminar on Community Participation and Empowerment in Primary Education*. Organized by National Institute of Educational Planning and Administration held at India Habitat Centre, New Delhi. (Unpublished)

Ramaiah, A. (2000). 'Protective Measures Vs Oppressive Village system: The Case of Southern Tamil Villages'. *Report of National Seminar on Implementation and Impact of the SC/ST (Prevention of Atrocities) Act, 1989 on the Scheduled Castes*.

Seceda, Walter G. (1988). 'Educational Equity Versus Equality of Education: An Alternative Conception'. *Equity in Education*. The Falmer Press, New York.

Shariff, Abusaleh (1999). *India Human Development Report A profile of Indian States in the 1990s*. National Council of Applied Economic Research, United Nations. Oxford University Press, New Delhi.

Singh, Jagpal (1995). 'Political Economy of Unaided and Unrecognised Schools: A Study of Meerut District of Western Uttar Pradesh'. (Unpublished)

Srivastava, Ravi (1999). 'Inequality and Education Security'. *Indian Journal of Labour Economics*, vol. 42, no. 3.

———— (2001). 'Access to Basic Education in Rural Uttar Pradesh'. In Vaidyanathan, A. and P. R. Gopinathan Nair (eds) *Elementary Education in Rural India: A Grassroots View*. Sage Publications.

Thorat, Sukhadeo (1999). 'Social Security in Unorganized Sector in India: How Secure are the Scheduled Castes?'. *The Indian Journal of Labour Economics*, vol. 42, no. 3, pp. 451–70.

Tilak, Jandhyala B. G. (2000). 'Determinants of Household Expenditure on Education in Rural India: A Study Based on the National Council of Applied Economic Research Survey on Human Development in India.' National Council of Applied Economic Research, New Delhi. (Unpublished)

Tilak, Jandhyalaya B. G. and Ratna Sudarshan (2000).

'Private Schooling in Rural India.' National Council of Applied Economic Research, New Delhi. (Unpublished)

Vaidyanathan, A. and P. R. Gopinathan Nair (eds). *Elementary Education in Rural India: A Grassroots View*. Sage Publications.

Vasavi, A. R., P. G. Chand, Vijaya Sherry and R. Shailesh Shukla (1997). 'Blueprint for Rural Primary Education. How Viable?'. *Economic and Political Weekly*. 13 December.

Wankhede, G. G. (1998). 'Intracaste Educational Variations among the Scheduled Castes of Mumbai Metropolis.' Prepared for Board of Research Studies, Tata Institute of Social Sciences, Mumbai.

World Bank (1997). *Primary Education in India*. Allied Publishers, New Delhi.

7 Education Among Scheduled Tribes

K. Sujatha*

The Indian Constitution identifies for special consideration certain ethnic minority groups, traditionally referred to as tribes or tribals, as Scheduled Tribes (STs) who constitute around 8 per cent of the total population of the country. There are 573 STs living in different parts of the country. Most of the tribal communities have their own languages different from the language spoken in the state where they are located. There are more than 270 such languages. The tribal languages in India belong to all major language families among which the Austric, the Dravidian, Tibeto-Chinese, and Indo European families are the dominant ones.

One of the distinguishing features of STs is that the majority of them live in scattered habitations located in interior, remote, and inaccessible hilly and forest areas of the country. Nearly 22 per cent of tribal habitations have less than 100 population and more than 40 per cent have 100 to less than 300 people, while others have less than 500 people. Though tribals constitute only 8 per cent of Indian population, they constitute a majority in several states and union territories and sizeable population in others. In particular, they constitute an overwhelming majority in Mizoram (94.75 per cent), Lakshadweep (93.15 per cent), Nagaland (87.70 per cent), and Meghalaya (85.53 per cent). However, the states of Madhya Pradesh, Orissa, Bihar, Maharashtra, Gujarat, Rajasthan, Andhra Pradesh, and West Bengal account for 83 per cent of the total tribal population, even though non-tribals constitute the majority in these states.

POLICIES AND PROGRAMMES

Recognizing that the STs count among the most deprived

and marginalized sections of Indian society, a host of welfare and developmental measures have been initiated for their social and economic development. In this regard, particular reference has to be made to the tribal sub-plan approach which came into existence as the main strategy from the Fifth Five Year Plan. Along with core economic sectors, elementary education has been accorded priority in the tribal sub-Plan approach. Elementary education is considered important, not only because of constitutional obligation, but as a crucial input for total development of tribal communities, particularly to build confidence among the tribes to deal with outsiders on equal terms. Since primacy was accorded to elementary education, a broad policy frame for education was adopted in the tribal sub-Plans according equal importance to quantitative and qualitative aspects of education.

A second important development in the policy towards education of tribals came with recommendations of the National Policy on Education (NPE) in 1986 which specified, among other things, the following:

- Priority will be accorded to opening primary schools in tribal areas.
- There is need to develop curricula and devise instructional material in tribal language at the initial stages with arrangements for switchover to regional languages.
- Promising ST youths will be encouraged to take up teaching in tribal areas.
- *Ashram* schools/residential schools will be established on a large scale in tribal areas.
- Incentive schemes will be formulated for the STs, keeping in view their special needs and lifestyle.

The unique feature of the policy is its recognition of the heterogeneity and diversity of tribal areas. The policy also proposed the transformation of the structure of primary education with special emphasis on improving

* The author would like to appreciate and thank Mr M. Sreenivasa Rao, National Institute of Educational Planning and Administration for his help and assistance in data analysis and preparation of tables.

access in tribal areas. The policy has also underlined the importance of instruction through the mother tongue for effective teaching and encouraged incorporating locally relevant content and curriculum, besides emphasizing the localized production of textbooks in local dialects. Based on these considerations, the norms for establishing primary schools were relaxed to suit tribal areas in order to improve access to education. For instance, Andhra Pradesh has gone to the extent of establishing schools in habitations where there are even twenty school-age children; Madhya Pradesh has steadily decreased population size norms in order to open schools in habitations with 200 population. However, in spite of such relaxation of norms many tribal localities are still without school, as they do not meet even the relaxed criteria.

PROGRESS IN LITERACY

Literacy is an important and primary index of educational development. This section provides data on the actual position of literacy among the tribals in terms of decadal growth rates, gap between tribal and non-tribal population (see Figure 7.1), inter-tribal variations etc. It will also highlight inter-state, inter-group, and gender variations in tribal literacy.

falls well below the national average. In fact, data reveal that STs behind even SCs in educational progress.

It is found that the degree and level of educational development have been quite uneven among different states and among different segments of population within any given state. The data indicate that some of the states with higher tribal concentration in relation to their total population have done exceedingly well in terms of higher literacy rate. States in the north-eastern region of India like Mizoram, Nagaland, and Meghalaya fall in this category. But in the states of Madhya Pradesh, Orissa, Rajasthan, and Andhra Pradesh, which are inhabited by much larger numbers of tribals than the north-eastern states, tribal literacy continues to be very low. In 1971 tribal literacy in Madhya Pradesh was at 7.62 per cent, increasing marginally to 10.68 per cent by 1981 and standing at 21.54 per cent as per the 1991 census figures. The figures are similar for Bihar, Orissa, and Andhra Pradesh. In fact, Andhra Pradesh has the lowest tribal literacy rate in the country at 17.16 in 1991.

But what is important is the growth of the literacy rate between 1981 and 1991. The growth rate was steady between 1971 and 1981, but increased significantly during 1981–91. The trend is visible even in relatively backward states like Bihar and Madhya Pradesh. Another

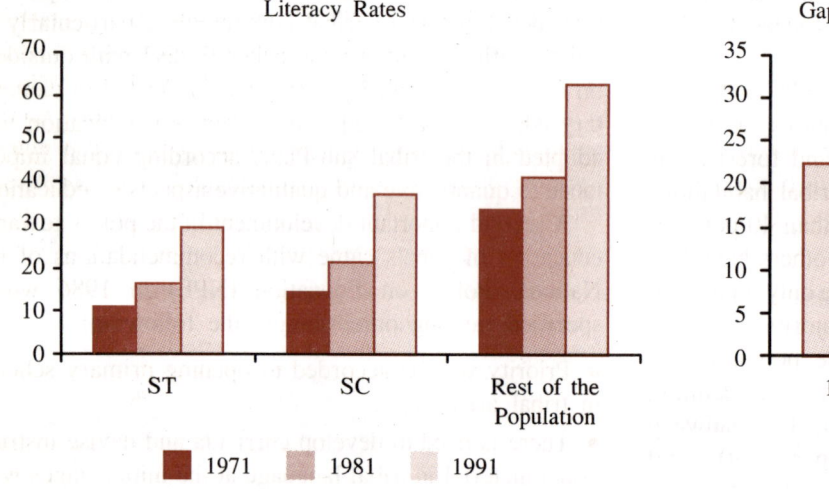

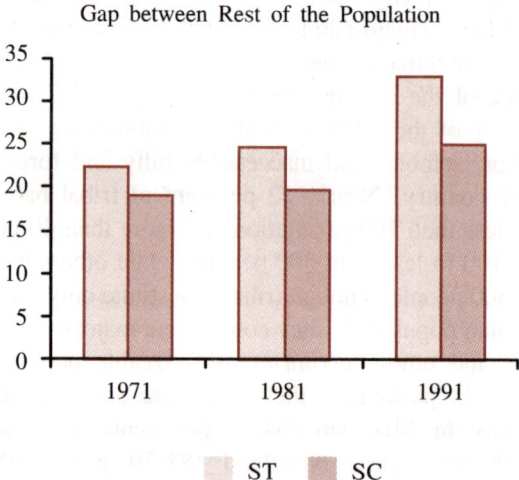

FIGURE 7.1: Gap between Tribals and the Rest of the Population

Source: Census 1971, 1981, 1991.

The data on literacy from 1971 to 1991 show that literacy rate for STs has gone up from a low of 11.30 in 1971 to 29.50 in 1991. But the increase in literacy rate does not express overall growth of educational standard. In fact, even though in absolute numbers the illiterates have increased over the years, the gap between ST and non-ST population has also increased from 22.50 to 33.05 between 1971 and 1991. Even today tribal literacy

factor that needs mention is that though educationally developed states like Kerala, Tamil Nadu, and Karnataka have higher general literacy rates, they are way behind the smaller and tribal-concentrated states in terms of tribal literacy rates. On the whole, disparity among various states in terms of tribal literacy rates is pretty high, ranging between 82.27 per cent in Mizoram and 17.16 per cent in Andhra Pradesh.

Further, states where literacy among tribes is lower than the national average tend to lag behind the national average even terms of the general literacy rate. The states of Bihar, Madhya Pradesh, and Rajasthan belong to this category. This shows that educational development of a state is possible only when its disadvantaged sections are properly taken care of.

Disparity in educational levels exists not only between states but also at district level. Out of a total 414 districts with tribal population, 13 have a tribal literacy rate of 0–10 per cent and in as many as 86 districts, tribal literacy is only 20–30 per cent. A substantial number of districts (240) have a tribal literacy rate of 10–40 per cent. Only three among all the districts of India have 90–100 per cent tribal literacy rate. Among the 45 districts in Madhya Pradesh tribal literacy rates vary between 2.14 per cent and 28.47 per cent.

Gender Disparity

In a highly stratified society like India, there are numerous layers of differentiation apart from caste and class. Gender is now recognized as a more pervasive and distinct category of social stratification. In the context of literacy, gender is an important aspect. The literacy rate among the tribals is not only low but also shows a high level of gender disparity. Data reveal that states which are low in general and tribal literacy are also states with higher gender disparity.

During 1971, female literacy among tribals was 4.85 per cent at all-India level and only 0.49 per cent in Rajasthan. By 1981 it had increased to 8.05 per cent at the all-India level and 1.20 per cent in Rajasthan. Despite massive efforts by government and non-government

agencies it was still 18.19 per cent at all-India level and 4.42 per cent in Rajasthan in 1991. The states of Andhra Pradesh with 8.68 per cent and Rajasthan with 4.42 per cent have remained at the bottom of the tribal female literacy table. On the other hand, states like Mizoram (78.74), Nagaland (54.51), Sikkim (50.37), and Kerala (51.07) have more than 50 per cent literacy among the tribal female population. It is significant that Andhra Pradesh, which has lower tribal literacy than Rajasthan, has higher literacy among the tribal female population.

PRIMARY EDUCATION: ACCESS AND PARTICIPATION

As mentioned earlier, tribal communities normally reside in interior, underdeveloped, and inaccessible areas. Demographically, tribal habitations are small in size, scattered, and are sparsely populated. Nearly 63.4 per cent of tribal habitations have less than 300 people covering one-fourth of total tribal population. While 22 per cent of tribal habitations have less than 100 inhabitants, the population covered by these habitations is only 3.82 per cent of the total tribal population. Because of this, most of these villages are bereft of basic infrastructural facilities like transport and communication. Formal education was also not available to these people and localities for a long time. A conscious effort to expand educational facilities began with the introduction of the tribal sub-Plan approach and got a major boost with the formulation of NPE. In this backdrop, this section attempts to examine the status of access to and availability of schools in tribal areas. Figure 7.2 graphically presents the availability of primary schools.

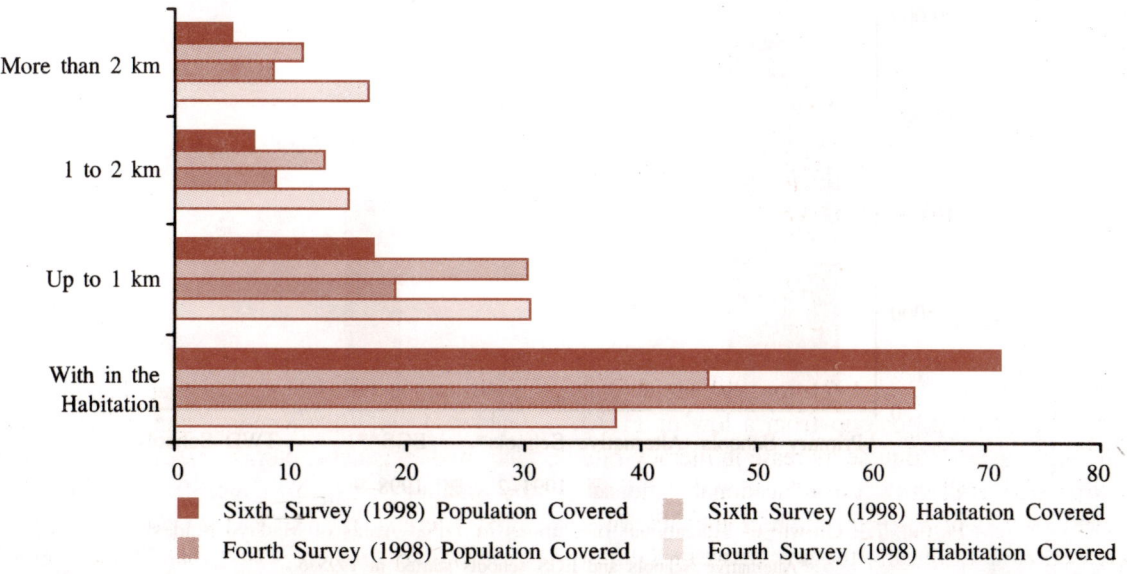

FIGURE 7.2: Rural Habitations with and without Primary Schools in Tribal Areas

Source: NCERT (1992, 1998).

Data from two surveys (fifth and sixth), 1986 and 1998 clearly show that the number of habitations having schools at a distance greater than 2 km is fast decreasing. In almost all the tribal-concentration states, the number of schools within 1 km of habitations has increased and higher percentage population coverage is achieved. The sixth All-India Educational Survey (1998) shows that 78 per cent of tribal population and 56 per cent of tribal habitations have been provided primary schools within the habitation. Another 11 per cent of tribal population and 20 per cent of tribal habitations have schools within a less than 1 km radius.

Comparing access conditions in tribal areas with those of rural habitations in general, one finds that the difference is only marginal. Around two-thirds of rural habitations, i.e. (64.80 per cent) covering 85.50 per cent of total rural population have primary schools within the habitation or within a distance of ½ km, as against 56.33 tribal habitations per cent and 78.73 tribal population, respectively.

In view of difficult terrain and geographical and ecological barriers in tribal areas, a distance of more than ½ km makes school attendance for young children a difficult proposition. In fact, a distance of 1 km or above between school and habitation practically means that such habitations and inhabitants lack access to primary schools, given the tribal context. Thus, a little more than one-fifth of total tribal population is constrained by this problem. Further, 10 per cent of tribal habitations have schools beyond a distance of 2 km.

The states of Mizoram and Gujarat have the highest percentage of population and habitations covered by primary schools within habitations. A huge 95 per cent of total tribal population and 85 to 90 per cent of tribal habitations of these states are provided with primary schools within the habitations. The state of Bihar occupies the lowest position in terms of population and habitation coverage with primary schools within habitations. In the states of Andhra Pradesh, Rajasthan, Orissa, and Madhya Pradesh the percentages of habitations and population served by primary schools within habitations are not only relatively low, but also a large number of habitations and population have schools only at a distance of more than 1 km.

Several innovative efforts have been made during the 1990s to increase access to schools of population living small habitations. For instance, in Madhya Pradesh, the number of formal primary schools has increased from 16,548 in 1990–1 to 18,716 in 1998–9 (see Figure 7.3). During the same period 1757 Alternative Schools, 10,626 EGS schools, and 1133 TWD schools have been established. These take the total number of schools from 19,295 in 1992–3 to 34,131 in 1998–9. Vishakhapatnam district in Andhra Pradesh, which has a large tribal concentration, has also witnessed a similar phenomenon with educational facilities having significantly increased in the last eight years through the establishment of alternative schools with active community partnership.

ENROLMENT

Enrolment is not an independent variable in the sense that it is dependent on factors such as availability of schools, their regular functioning, regularity of teachers, as well as on parental willingness, their perception of the value of education and their capacity. The participation of tribal

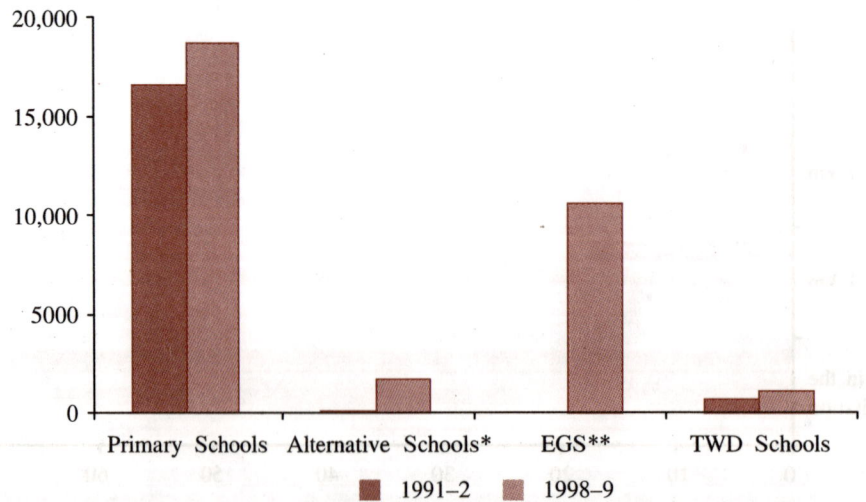

FIGURE 7.3: Growth of Educational Institutions in Tribal Areas of Madhya Pradesh

*Alternative Schools and EGS schools started in 1995–6.
**EGS: Schools under the Education Guarantee Scheme.
Source: Tribal Welfare Department of Madhya Pradesh.

children in education is very low in comparison to others. Enrolment of tribal children was about nine million in Classes I–V during the year 1997–8 (see Figure 7.4).

One observes a positive trend with respect to participation of girls in education among STs. For instance, the

RETENTION

Enrolment has no meaning unless students are retained in the system for the prescribed number of years to complete the primary level of education. However, in

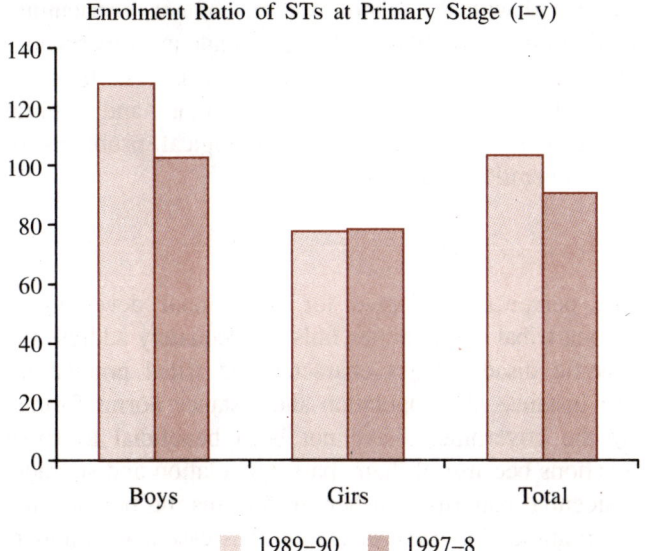

Enrolment Ratio of STs at Primary Stage (I–V)

1989–90   1997–8

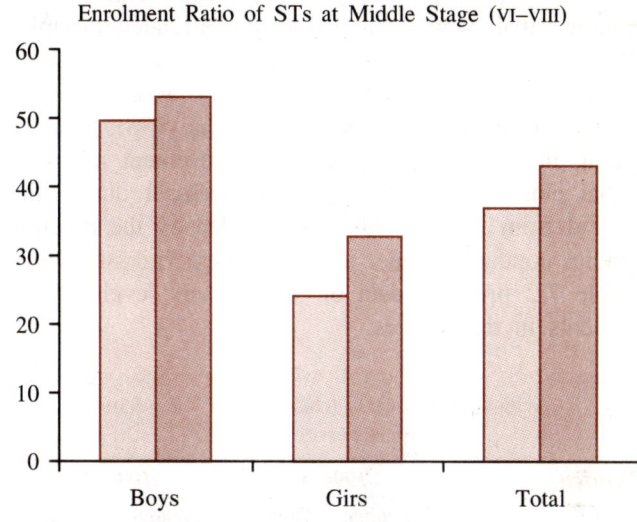

Enrolment Ratio of STs at Middle Stage (VI–VIII)

1989–90   1997–8

FIGURE 7.4: Enrolment Ratio of STs in Elementary Education
Source: Department of Education (relevant years).

proportion of girls has increased from 36.5 per cent in 1989–90 to 43 per cent in 1997–8 at all-India level. North-eastern states like Mizoram and Nagaland and West Bengal have more or less equal proportions of boys and girls among total enrolled tribal children at primary stage. Girls' enrolment shows positive growth in all tribal-concentrated states. Rajasthan shows the highest increase of 64 per cent in girls' enrolment during the 1990s. Their proportion to total enrolment has increased from a mere 23 per cent in 1989–90 to 35 per cent in the year 1997–8. A similar trend could be observed in the upper primary classes also.

Several innovative interventions such as appointment of local women as teachers in the Shiksha Karmi Project, micro-level planning and community mobilization under the Lok Jumbish project, and several NGO efforts at grassroots level seem to be the major reasons for significant improvement in girls' enrolment in Rajasthan. Some of the recent micro-level evidence shows that interventions and initiatives like the midday meal scheme, creation of self-help women's groups, environment-building programmes under different projects, appointment of local tribal teachers, and developing partnership between school and village communities in school management have helped tribals to realize the importance of education and adopt a positive attitude towards girls' education (see Sujatha 1998).

tribal areas, high levels of absenteeism, large-scale failure in year-end assessment, and alarming drop-out rates (see Table 7.1) contribute to slow progress of education.

TABLE 7.1
Dropout Rates of STs (class I–V) in Tribal States

State/Union Territory	1991–2		
	Boys	Girls	Total
01. Andhra Pradesh	66.65	71.95	68.64
02. Bihar	70.96	71.81	71.26
03. Gujarat	53.98	66.51	59.39
04. Madhya Pradesh	31.00	52.27	38.59
05. Maharashtra	56.24	63.88	59.48
06. Orissa	78.03	74.14	76.81
07. Rajasthan	73.01	84.20	75.92
08. West Bengal	62.47	69.68	65.07
09. Arunachal Pradesh	62.21	58.19	60.71
10. Assam	65.13	67.10	66.00
11. Meghalaya	68.00	67.95	67.99
12. Mizoram	57.91	58.37	58.13
13. Nagaland	45.83	49.23	47.42
14. Tripura	70.78	73.72	72.03

Source: Department of Education (1993).

LEARNER ACHIEVEMENT LEVELS

Almost all the studies on learner achievement levels in India have shown that tribal students in primary classes have lower achievement compared to non-tribals (see Govinda and Varghese, 1993, Varghese 1994, Sujatha 1998, Prakash *et al.* 1998). The low achievement levels among tribals were attributed to school-related variables as in the case of non-tribal students. However, tribal students had additional disadvantages arising out of social and locational factors (see Sujatha 1998). A silver lining in this regard is that the achievement levels of tribal children showed slight improvement during the period from 1993 to 1998 as revealed by the baseline studies conducted under the DPEP (see Prakash 1998). Table 7.2 provides data on achievement levels of ST students in three states.

TABLE 7.2
Achievement Levels (class I) of ST Students in Different States

Districts	1994–5		1997–8	
	Language	Mathematics	Language	Mathematics
MADHYA PRADESH				
Satna	3.65	1.58	5.58	3.72
Rewa	4.18	2.74	4.58	4.51
Sidhi	4.54	2.35	5.35	5.04
Tikamgarh	3.93	2.13	5.70	7.12
Chattarpur	3.39	2.16	5.15	5.29
Panna	2.37	1.45	4.60	5.24
MAHARASHTRA				
Aurangabad	5.21	3.24	7.24	6.35
Nanded	3.79	2.79	5.67	5.02
Parbhani	5.46	3.14	6.27	6.27
ASSAM				
Darrang			12.32	7.15
Dhubri			12.12	10.11
Karbi Anglong			NA	NA
Morigan			15.12	10.34

Source: NCERT (1996) and Prakash *et al.* (1998).

However, this marginal improvement is not sufficient to achieve educational parity in terms of levels of achievement between tribal and non-tribal students and it must be admitted that tribal students still have low achievement levels and fall a long way behind the expected levels. The tribal and non-tribal gap in achieving competency is very big, to say the least. This is a major concern and requires strategic intervention.

PROBLEMS OF TRIBAL EDUCATION

This review clearly underlines that in spite of constitutional guarantees and persistent efforts, tribal communities continue to lag behind the general population in education. The reasons for this can be categorized as external, internal, and socio-economic and psychological. The external constraints are related to problems and difficulties at levels of policy, planning, implementation, and administration. Internal constraints refer to problems associated with the school system, content, curriculum, medium of instruction, pedagogy, academic supervision, monitoring, and teacher-related problems. The third set of problems relates to social, economic, and cultural background of tribals and psychological problems of first-generation learners.

External Constraints

The perspective adopted for educational development among tribal communities fails to adequately address the specific disadvantages characterizing tribal population. For instance, the population and distance norms formed by the government have not been beneficial to tribal locations because of their sparse population and sporadic residential patterns. Further, in formulating policies and programmes for tribal education it is essential to understand the complex realities of tribal life and the expectation of tribals from the system, and this has never been done either by the tribal welfare department or by the education department. Consequently, no worthwhile policy for tribal education has been formed.

One of the major constraints of tribal education at planning level is the adoption of a dual system of administration. The tribal welfare department deals with tribal life and culture and administers development work at the local level, including education. But the tribal welfare department lacks expertise in educational planning and administration in general, and academic supervision and monitoring in particular. On the other hand, the education department is the sole authority for planning of educational development at state level. It formulates implementation guidelines and instructions regarding curriculum, textbooks, teacher recruitment, transfer policies, and so on. In this the department tends to formulate uniform policies for the entire state. The school calendar is a case in point, where vacations and holidays cater to the needs of the formal school set up in a non-tribal context, with little consideration for local context and tribals festivals. This lack of sensitivity to their problems and failure in understanding tribal social reality, coupled with faulty selection and appointment of teachers in tribal areas, have resulted in poor performance and teacher absenteeism in tribal schools.

Under the system of dual administration, absence of coordination and complimentarity as well as inadequate scope for reciprocal use of respective expertise and experiences between the two departments has invariably stunted educational development among tribals.

Internal Constraints

The internal problems of tribal education refer to the quality of school provision, suitable teachers, relevance of content and curriculum, medium of instruction, pedagogy, and special supervision. A majority of schools in tribal areas are without basic infrastructure facilities. Normally, school buildings in tribal areas have thatched roofs, dilapidated walls, and non-plastered floors. Research evidence shows that a large number of tribal schools do not have teaching–learning materials, or even blackboards. In tribal areas the opening of a school is equated with the posting of a teacher and same is the case with 'ashram' schools. It is found that in most of ashram schools which are residential in nature, there is no space for the children to sleep. Consequently, the classroom turns into the dormitory and vice versa. Due to lack of minimum sanitary provisions, it is not uncommon to find that many children studying in ashram schools are afflicted with contagious diseases like scabies and diarrhoea, leading to high drop-out rates. Schools in tribal areas just function with bare minimum facilities.

CONTENT AND CURRICULUM

Though the demand for changing the content and curriculum to suit the tribal context has been an old one, no serious effort has been made in this direction in any state, except for some sporadic pilot projects. The uniform structure and transaction of curriculum has put tribal children at a disadvantage. In respect of pedagogy, it has been found that the rigid systems of formal schooling, which emphasize discipline, routine norms, teacher-centred instruction, etc. have made the children wary of school. This goes against the culture of free interaction and absence of force as embedded in tribal ethos and culture prevalent at home. This has led to sharp division between home and school leading to lack of interest among the children towards school, and research findings have shown this as a major factor behind non-enrolment.

Another area is the inherent fear of tribal children towards the teacher, and their inability to establish a communication link with the teacher and this is reflected in low attendance and high dropout rates. This could be tackled to a great extent by using the regional language as the medium of instruction. The Constitution of India allows the use of tribal dialect (mother tongue) as the medium of instruction in case the population of the said tribe is more than one lakh. But this has not been adopted on the grounds of feasibility and viability of introducing and sustaining such a change. In recent years, some efforts have been made for preparing primers in tribal dialects but again they have been nullified in the context of inter-tribal rivalry, hierarchy, etc, and also, being on a very small scale, are incapable of influencing mainstream practices.

Socio-economic and Cultural Constraints

In a broad sense, these socio-economic and cultural factors can be outlined as poverty and poor economic conditions, social customs, cultural ethos, lack of awareness and understanding of the value of formal education, conflict and gap between the home and school, etc. Studies on educational deprivation of tribals have inevitably linked it to their poor economic condition and poverty. The main occupation of tribals is agriculture, practised either through shifting cultivation or terrace cultivation where productivity remains very low. Consequently, children play an important role, contributing directly or indirectly to family income by participating in the family occupation and household works like cattle grazing and fuel and fodder collection, etc.

Even though elementary education is deemed free and additional incentives are given to children, in practice, it is not free due to several reasons. First, the incentive schemes do not have full coverage, and thus, have limited value at community level. Second, many of the benefits do not reach the beneficiaries. Third, even though incentives like slates and uniforms are given, they are of poor quality and do not reach in time, thus nullifying the entire purpose. It should be noted that the impoverished economic status of tribals makes even the small amount of private expenditure involved in procuring writing material, clothing, etc a serious burden on the family. Under these circumstances, it is not surprising if education is not given priority. In an economy dominated by struggle for survival, options are limited. Since education does not provide any visible and immediate benefit and tribals do not see beyond their present state, the participation of tribal children in education also becomes limited. Another reason for low participation is the opportunity cost involved, as the majority of non-enrolled children are required to work in households or family occupations. Even if the economic contribution of children is indirect, they certainly facilitate the participation of parents in economic activity.

In recent years the efforts of the government have been directed towards improving economic conditions of tribes by introducing various developmental programmes and schemes, mostly related to agriculture, horticulture, and cattle rearing, backed by subsidies and monetary and non-monetary inputs. A critical analysis of development programmes and their effect on tribal households shows that till tribal households reach a threshold level of income and land size, the economic development programmes can come into conflict with other activities like education. In a way it can be said that these development programmes seem to be adversely affecting the education of tribal children (see Sujatha 1994).

Box 7.1 provides the specific example of conflict between education and short-term economics among tribals in Andhra Pradesh.

BOX 7.1
Development versus Education

In order to introduce permanent cultivation among shifting cultivators, the Government initiated orange and coffee plantation under the horticulture scheme in Andhra Pradesh. For this, the households were given two acres of forest land, and orange plants were supplied free of cost. For taking care of the plants, they were paid Rs 100 per month in the form of rice and other things. With some persuasion the tribals accepted the scheme as it had visible monetary benefit as well as getting some more land. But accepting a new scheme in addition to their traditional cultivation, means demand for more labour, which, in turn, brings change in the structure in the family labour. Work distribution pattern among the members of the household plays a crucial role in the success of the new scheme that they have accepted. This situation comes into conflict with the children's participation in education as their help in household work or in cultivation becomes essential. In another incident, a sheep rearing project was introduced and some of the tribal households were given a unit of sheep. Usually axe fell on education of children. For the household, direct benefit from sheep rearing is more attractive to improve their economic condition than the long-term benefits of education.

Source: Sujatha (1994).

Poor health is another major hindrance in the promotion and participation of tribal children in education. Contagious diseases like scabies, eye infection, malaria, and diarrhoea are common in tribal areas, and also affect children's attendance at school. Further, some tribal communities are seasonal migrants and this leads to absenteeism among their children and makes it difficult for them to effectively benefit from schooling.

PERSPECTIVES FOR THE FUTURE

Education of tribals cannot be left to short-term Plan strategies. It is important that planners take a long-term view which is embedded in a meaningful policy framework. Following are some important points emerging from the review here.

● Emphasis should be on quality and equity rather than quantity as has been the case in the past. The prime focus should be on provision of quality education that makes tribal communities economically effective and independent.

● In the tribal context, it is essential that the school schedule be prepared as per local requirement rather than following a directive from the state. It has been found that vacations and holidays are planned without taking into consideration local contexts, and thereby, unnecessarily antagonize tribal communities and keep them out of school.

● Though it has been highlighted time and again, no concrete step has been taken to provide locally relevant material to tribal students. Availability of locally relevant materials will not only facilitate faster learning but also help children develop a sense of affiliation to school.

● In order to make education effective and sustainable, building partnership between the community and the government is important. Results from pilot projects in Andhra Pradesh show that community partnership not only augments state expenditure on education but also guarantees supervision and monitoring, thus addressing an intractable problem for the state.

● Environment building is of immense importance in the context of educational development among tribal communities. Community awareness and community mobilization, which are its core elements, should receive adequate importance and attention.

● Decentralization of education management is another aspect that needs special consideration in the context of tribal areas. In fact, considering the geographical terrain and communication problems in tribal areas, it is crucial to restructure the existing system of educational management. Adaptation of structures such as school complexes and VECs to tribal areas needs careful consideration.

● Skill development, competency building, and teachers motivation also need to be strengthened for sustaining educational development. The teacher should be made the centre of educational transformation, and therefore, must remain the primary facilitator.

REFERENCES

Department of Education (1968). *National Policy on Education*. Ministry of Human Resource Development, Government of India, New Delhi.

———— (1986). *National Policy on Education*. Ministry of Human Resource Development, Government of India, New Delhi.

———— (relevant years). *Selected Educational Statistics*. Ministry of Human Resource Development, Government of India, New Delhi.

Government of India (1972). *Census of India 1971*. New Delhi.

———— (1982). *Census of India 1981*. New Delhi.

———— (1992). *Census of India 1991*. New Delhi.

Govinda, R. and N. V. Varghese (1993). *Quality of Primary Schooling in India: A Case Study of Madhya Pradesh*. International Institute of Educational Planning/UNESCO, Paris and National Institute of Educational Planning and Administration, New Delhi.

Ministry of Law (1967). *The Constitution of India*. Government of India, New Delhi.

National Council of Educational Research and Training (1982). *Fourth All-India Educational Survey*. New Delhi.

———— (1992). *Fifth All-India Educational Survey*. (*National Tables*, vols I–V). New Delhi.

———— (1994). *Baseline Assessment Study* on different States. New Delhi.

———— (1998). *Sixth All-India Educational Survey (National Tables*, vols I–V). New Delhi.

Planning Commission (1975). *Fifth Five Year Plan*. Government of India, New Delhi.

Prakash, Ved, S. K. Gautam, I. K. Bansal, and N. Bhalla (1998). *Mid-Term Assessment Survey, An appraisal of Student's Achievement*. District Primary Education Programme Core Group, National Council of Educational Research and Training, New Delhi.

Sujatha, K. (1994). *Educational Development Among Tribes: A Study of Sub-Plan Areas in Andhra Pradesh*. South Asian Publishers, New Delhi.

———— (1998). 'Evaluation of Quality Improvement Programmes in Education: A Study in Tribal Areas of Visakhapatnam, Andhra Pradesh'. National Institute of Educational Planning and Administration, New Delhi.

Varghese, N. V. (1994). 'School Quality and Students Learning: A Study of Primary Schooling in Kerala'. District Primary Education Programme Baseline Study, National Institute of Educational Planning and Administration, New Delhi.

8 Education of Children with Special Needs

Sudesh Mukhopadhyay and M. N. G. Mani

The 1989 UN convention on the Rights of the Child states that disabled children have the right to 'achieve participation in the community and their education should lead to the fullest possible social integration and educational development' (see Article 23). The World Conference on Education for All: Meeting Basic Learning Needs (see World Conference on EFA 1990) states that the learning needs of the disabled demand special attention. Steps need to be taken to provide equal access to education to every category of disabled persons as an integral part of the education system (see Article 5.5). Another UN initiative, The Standard Rules on the Equalization of Opportunities for Persons with Disabilities (1993) requires member states to provide education for persons with disabilities as an 'integral part' of the education system. The Salamanca Statement and Framework for Action on Special Needs Education (1994) stipulates that disabled children should attend neighbourhood schools. It declares that regular schools with this inclusive orientation are the most 'effective means of combating discriminatory attitudes, creating welcoming communities, building an inclusive society and achieving education for all. Moreover, they provide an effective education to the majority of children and improve the efficiency and ultimately the cost effectiveness of the entire education system'. India has been a signatory to all these declarations.

There has been no dearth of pledges and policy statements on the issue within the country. The National Policy on Education (NPE) (1986) recommended as a goal 'to integrate the handicapped with the general community at all levels as equal partners, to prepare them for normal growth and to enable them to face life with courage and confidence'. The Delhi Declaration on Education for All (1993) pledged that 'we will ensure a place for every child in a school or appropriate

education programme according to his or her capabilities' In the same spirit flowing from global affirmative action, India also passed the Persons with Disabilities (Equal Opportunities Protection of Rights and Full Participation) Act in 1995. Box 8.1 summarizes the national commitment on the issue.

Box 8.1

National Commitment to the Universalization of Primary Education

- The disabled have the same human rights as other citizens of a country.
- Increased autonomy of the disabled is a fundamental requirement if they are to obtain the same rights as their fellow citizens.
- Policy for the disabled should not be developed in isolation but should be an integral component of policies for society as a whole.
- Integration of the disabled into the education system cannot be regarded as an issue separate from the policies for society as a whole.
- The disabled are entitled to a comprehensive education which provides continuity of service from early detection and intervention through schooling, vocational preparation, independent living in the community, and lifelong education.

It is to be noted that issues of the disabled are becoming a part of the national education system and the planning and management of educational programmes is to be seen in the context of individual learners (disabled) from the viewpoint of access, survival, and success. However, demands of planning education for addressing the disabled are not necessarily identical to those for general education services. The requirements of the children with disabilities, even in terms of the number and location of services, cannot be projected in the manner in which they are for any usual planning exercise in education. The issue is further complicated when carrying out an exercise for specific disability. For example, education of the blind throws up challenges which are different from those of the hearing impaired or the orthopaedically handicapped.

These issues and challenges need to be addressed in a comprehensive manner cutting across education, health and social security, and welfare services. It is important that a child is identified as being in need of special services at the earliest possible. She/He can avail an educational facility as a means of serving some of the special needs and may also require support from other services to be able to benefit from an educational programme. Usually this whole range of processes would involve identification, assessment, placement for education and/or rehabilitation programme, support for success and confidence. The year 1981 was a benchmark year as

being the International Year for Disabled Persons (IYDP) but 1990 was the year when disabled children and persons were assured of rights and services at par with all other children and persons. All the related departments have independent schemes for serving this cause, but the challenge is to ensure that increased funding and expressed intentions translate into making a difference for disabled children.

As per the information brought out by Central Statistical Organisation per capita expenditure on education has doubled since 1989–90 and similar trend is observed for health and welfare services. But in the absence of data for the significant age groups and disabled children and persons, one really cannot comment with confidence that the assurances given are being fulfilled. This issue merits attention in view of the fact that magnitude of children requiring special education facilities is also an issue by itself (see Figure 8.1).

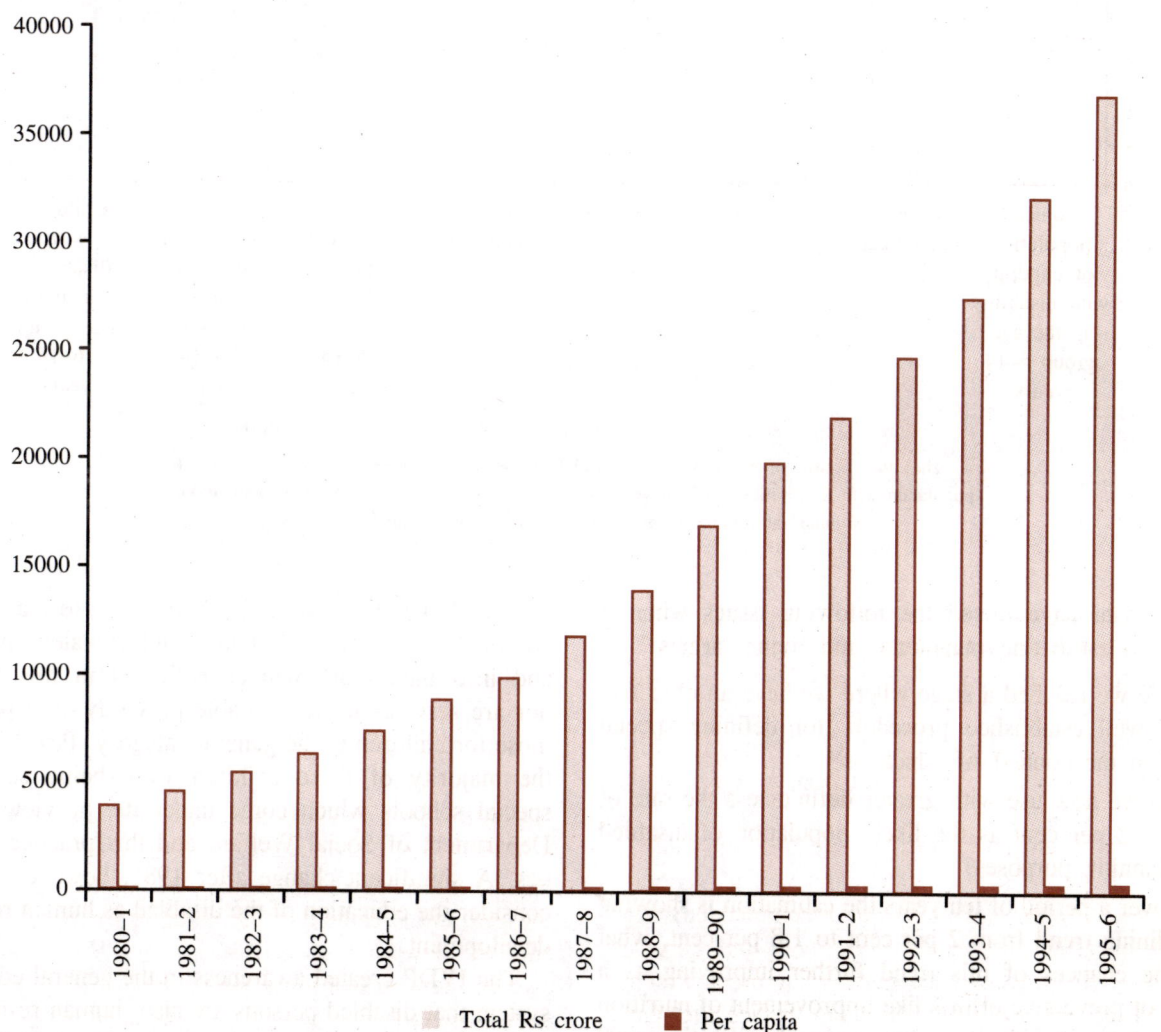

Figure 8.1: Expenditure Incurred on Education

Note: Population used is as on 1st October (estimates) for calculating the per capita expenditure.

Source: Central Statistical Organization Department of Statistics, 1999.

Magnitude and Targets

As in several other countries, India is still in the process of refining the procedures through which children with special needs can be identified. The first effort to really make some sort of estimation was done for the NPE and revised Programme of Action (POA) 1992 which estimated 12.59 million disabled children of school-going age for whom provision had to be made (see Figure 8.2). However, this estimation was guided to a great extent by the National Sample Survey (NSS) conducted in the year 1981. The process was revised in the year 1991 (see Table 8.1).

enough attention and coverage in terms of the efforts made for education for all (EFA). This hypothesis is being forwarded keeping in view the policy commitment made during the preceding decade.

PROGRESS TOWARDS INCLUSIVE EDUCATION

The direct and simple approach to the question of whether children with special needs are being adequately covered and have benefited from basic education programmes would be to match the number of children in the related age group with that of children enrolled

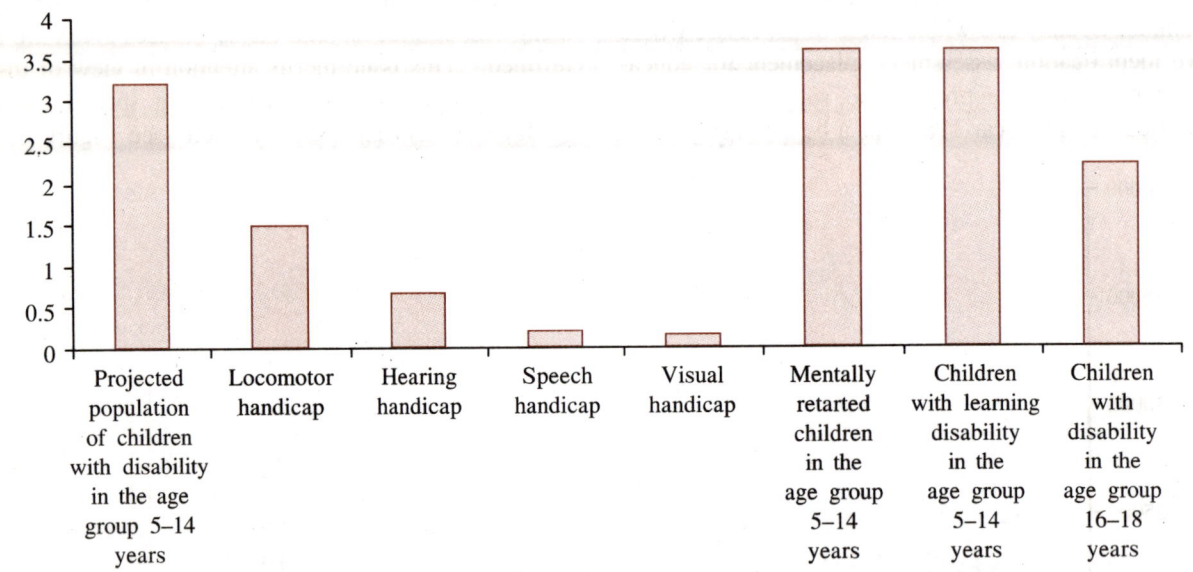

Figure 8.2: Projected Population of Children with Disability (in millions)

Note: The 1981 figures of the survey by NSSO have been extrapolated on the assumption that population with disabilities would have grown at the same rate as the general population. Estimated at 1 per cent of population in the age group 5–14 years.

Source: DoE (1992).

The data have raised the following issues when it comes to estimating magnitude and fixing targets:

- Have we reached a stage where we have an objective and a well established procedure for defining special needs in the context of education?
- Can we now use with greater definiteness the rate of 1.82 to 2 per cent as the likely population of disabled for planning purposes?
- If over a period of ten years the estimation is showing a declining trend from 2 per cent to 1.8 per cent, what are the chances of this trend further improving as a result of preventive efforts like improvement of nutrition status, better health provision, early identification, and better care for mother and child?

While this debate may continue, it is important to see whether the age groups 0–5 and 6–14 have received

in schools including special schools, non-formal centres and/or open learning systems. Unfortunately the data and information are neither collected in this manner nor are services made available presently on a par with those for children in the general category. Prior to 1974, the majority of these children were being served in special schools which come under the purview of the Department of Social Welfare and this practice continues. A significant change after 1981, however, was to consider the education of the disabled as human resource development.

The IYDP created awareness in the general education system that disabled persons are also 'human resources'. This shift in approach also resulted in the establishment of many premier institutes responsible for developing programmes for the education of children with special needs.

TABLE 8.1
Comparative Statement of Prevalence and Incidence (Disabilitywise) under NSS

(per 100,000 persons)

Sector	1981			1991		
	Male	Female	Personal	Male	Female	Personal
VISUAL DISABILITY						
Prevalence Rate						
Rural	444	670	553	471	548	525
Urban	294	425	356	263	346	302
Incidence Rate						
Rural	32	45	38	22	28	25
Urban	23	38	30	15	25	20
HEARING DISABILITY						
Prevalence Rate						
Rural	595	510	573	498	435	467
Urban	386	395	390	325	355	339
Incidence Rate						
Rural	20	18	19	16	14	15
Urban	14	15	15	11	14	12
SPEECH DISABILITY						
Prevalence Rate						
Rural	379	228	304	333	208	273
Urban	342	207	279	285	182	237
Incidence Rate						
Rural	6	2	4	6	4	5
Urban	7	3	5	5	4	5
LOCOMOTOR DISABILITY						
Prevalence Rate						
Rural	1047	597	828	1345	784	1047
Urban	800	544	679	1170	728	962
Incidence Rate						
Rural	64	42	53	64	42	53
Urban	61	47	54	64	39	52

Source: Pandey and Advani, (1995, 21–2).

In 1983, the National Council for Educational Research and Training (NCERT) included education of children with special needs as an area under its teacher education programme. Its first national workshop in March 1983 was an eye opener about the requirement to provide for education of children with special needs within the general education system. The first ever training programme for master trainers organized by the NCERT in June 1983 was a turning point in the special education teacher preparation programme in India. The NCERT also initiated special education teacher preparation courses through its Regional Institutes of Education (RIEs). The NCERT involved itself in research in education of children with special needs and innovative experiments towards providing access to all disabled children in the country. An Integrated Education for Disabled Children (IEDC) cell was established at the NCERT to focus attention and develop trained manpower. This intervention resulted in identification of children with disabilities within and outside the existing schools. It also resulted in networking across ministries (viz. Education, Health, Social Welfare, Labour) as well as institutions, government schools, and NGOs. Thus, for the first time an effort and need emerged to find a share for such children in all education programmes.

Enrolment Status

One of the direct indicators of progress towards EFA is the enrolment pattern in special schools and schools with integrated programmes.

SPECIAL SCHOOLS

Presently there are about 3000 special schools addressing persons with different disabilities. It is estimated that there are 900 schools for the hearing impaired, 400 schools for the visually impaired, 1000 for the mentally retarded, and 700 for physically disabled children (see UNISED 1999). The exact number of special schools is not fully known as there are many NGOs that run such schools that are not yet included in the lists available. The programmes vary from early childhood preparation to primary-level education with rehabilitation inputs, and in some cases, schools also cover secondary classes. These programmes have so far not been analysed for the 0–5 and 5–14 age groups in terms of enrolment, retention, and achievement trends. There are also concerns of curriculum, possibilities for continuing education, levels of achievement, management issues, and service conditions of these schools. The Rehabilitation Council of India is a statutory agency established in 1993 to look into some of these affairs.

Another aspect needing attention is the location of these schools and access to them. The largest number of special schools are in Mumbai, followed by Bangalore, Hyderabad, Chennai, Kolkatta, Delhi, and Ahmedabad. In terms of coverage of states/UTs, there are only significantly few with good coverage which are the same as those which, as such, are also doing better on literacy and gross enrolment ratio indicators. In terms of disabilities being covered, the pattern more or less matches with the estimated population in various disabilities. Hence, the concern is more serious when it comes to the rural–urban divide or poor urban locations. Needless to say, the coverage in terms of numbers is very meagre. The vision of the NPE and POA (1992) of one special school at each district headquarter remains a distant possibility.

INTEGRATED EDUCATION PROVISION

Integrated education emerged out of compulsion rather than choice. In the process of bringing more disabled children under the umbrella of educational services, integration emerged as the cost-effective approach and, therefore, the general education system started accepting special needs children in general schools. The implementation of the integrated education programme also addressed the needs of high-risk children who were suspected to be potential dropouts and, therefore, retention of such children improved. Integration of disabled children has actually reinforced better educational practices in the general school system. The centrally sponsored scheme of integrated education which was initiated in 1974 is being implemented in various states of the country. From data available with the Ministry of Human Resource and Development (see MHRD 1999), approximately 55,000 disabled children are benefited by this approach through 17,040 general schools in seventeen states/UTs. Details are available for fourteen states and UTs.

The Sixth All-India Educational Survey conducted by the NCERT (1998) has also tried to enumerate the children covered under integrated programmes at various stages of education.

• The share of disabled children in general schools which stands at 890,008 is much lower than the estimated total number of general children estimated at 10.32 million in the school going age group.

• Across disabilities, orthopaedically disabled children are better identified than those with other disabilities at all levels of education (26,388 for primary, 14,390 for upper primary, and 14,616 for secondary). This factor also needs attention as the identification and assessment procedures—even the definitions—are helpful in facilitating shift of focus towards actually deserving disabled children (see Table 8.2 and Figure 8.3).

TABLE 8.2
Details of Integrated Education for the Disabled Children (IEDC)

(as per State/UTs information)

S. no.	Name of the state/UT	No. of disabled children					No. of schools (IEDC)		No. of special teachers		No. of special schools		No. of districts
		VI	HH	MH	OH	Others	State	NGO	Trained	Untrained	State	NGO	
01	Andhra Pradesh	274	500	–	–	–	45	–	–	–	–	–	23
02	Arunachal Pradesh	–	–	60	–	–	–	1	9	–	–	1	–
03	Gujarat	1214	31	67	210	–	898	–	82	34	11	114	11
04	Haryana												
	IEDC	495	616	26	1197	98	–	–	27	–	5	4	4
	PIED	92	105	54	546	15	99	–	–	–	–	–	1
05	Karnataka												
	(Govt.)	1610	1446	1511	3305	210	1782	–	634	–	–	–	20
	(NGO's)	233	481	320	74	–	–	168	87	–	–	–	20
06	Kerala	4751	3849	3433	13723	–	6748	–	10	–	–	–	34
07	Madhya Pradesh	439	391	206	3783	93	2075	90	62	–	–	–	19
08	Manipur	94	158	163	267	–	269	–	39	–	2	3	5
09	Maharashtra												
	IEDC	241	570	102	62	–	39	–	65	–	17	–	11
	PIED	58	72	46	128	–	–	–	–	–	–	–	1
10	Nagaland	64	206	38	398	48	316	82	10	–	–	1	7
11	Orissa												
	(Govt.)	158	810	993	305	–	139	–	32	61	–	–	29
	(NGO's)	133	81	76	30	–	–	–	24	–	–	–	–
12	Rajasthan												
	IEDC	78	76	200	1101	146	41	–	66	12	3	19	24
	PIED	123	210	210	412	–	14	–	12	–	–	–	1
13	Tamil Nadu	422	235	60	836	–	681	–	61	–	–	–	6
14	Tripura	8	55	–	346	–	2	–	–	–	–	–	4
	Total	10,541	9892	7505	26,723	610	13,109	341	401	107	38	142	220

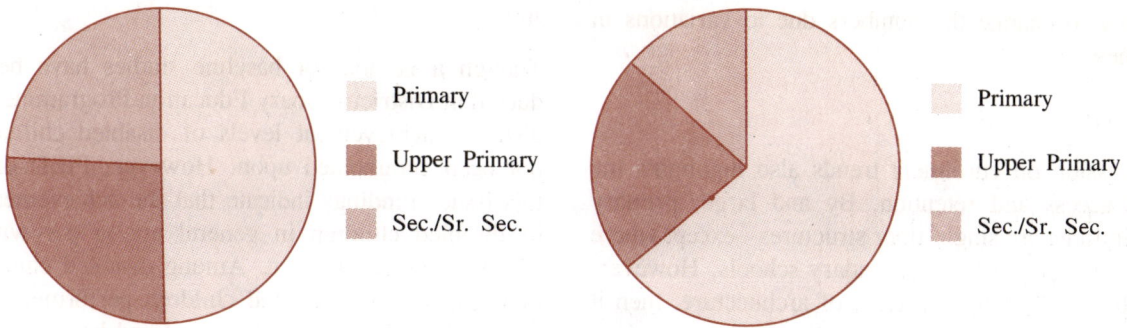

Figure 8.3: Enrolment of Disabled Children and General Enrolment
Source: NCERT, Sixth All-India Education Survey, 1998.

The data indicate that an effort has been initiated by national-level organizations to bring out information on children with special needs. However, it still lacks the emphasis needed for making a context-specific assessment of the situation and designing the appropriate interventions.

The NSSO data for urban and rural population of disabled persons (1991) has brought out certain attention-catching data (see Table 8.3). This survey has tried to give estimations of disabled children in the 0–4, 5–9 and 10–14 age groups across ST, SC, and others groups covering rural and urban locations. It indicates that more male children than female are disabled and more children (male and female) are located in urban areas. For the first time attention is also drawn to ST and SC children. The number of SC/ST disabled children is significant as it comes to about 1.3 to 1.8 per cent of population in the specific age groups.

This analysis of children in the school system (special and integrated) gives a picture which can be looked at positively only in the spirit of 'something is better than nothing'. For the first time these children are being referred to under the framework of EFA. No doubt the picture is dismal in terms of the total number of disabled children (approximately 10.39 million) in the 5–14 age group compared to their enrolment in schools. There is inconsistency in data from various sources (e.g. 55,000 according to the SSO 1999 and about 84,000 according to the NCERT survey 1998). But it needs to be appreciated that the definitions and coverage of disabilities can also bring in this difference. While things are better defined for the hearing and visually impaired, the issues of mentally retardated/intellectually challenged children and the possibilities of educating them up to appropriate levels, learning-disabled and even locomotor-handicapped children have

TABLE 8.3
Per 1000 Distribution of Disabled Persons (All-India) by Age Group for Each Social Group and Sex

	Urban									
	Male					*Female*				
Age group (years)	ST	SC	Others	nr	All	ST	SC	Others	nr	All
0–4	27	64	36	126	41	75	39	35	–	37
5–9	102	119	99	–	103	100	121	100	–	103
10–14	116	124	113	309	115	81	97	93	–	93
	Rural									
	Male					*Female*				
Age group (years)	ST	SC	Others	nr	All	ST	SC	Others	nr	All
0–4	28	40	35	–	36	23	41	35	101	35
5–9	113	105	103	241	105	105	94	90	–	93
10–14	96	94	101	–	99	76	84	78	208	80

nr: not recorded
Source: NSSO, 1991.

a tendency to change the numbers due to variations in approaches.

Access and Retention

The discussion on enrolment trends also highlights the issue of access and retention. By and large, primary schools in India are single-floor structures—except where these are sections in large secondary schools. However, if schools are 'friendly' in terms of architecture, then it is more because of prevailing conditions than concious effort. A recent survey of infrastructure in Delhi schools (see Mukhopadhyay and Bhatia 2000) has shown that no thought is given to this dimension. Though use of wheelchairs is not a common phenomenon with locomotor disabled persons including spastics, if it were to be so, practically all the schools would need modifications. This indicates that due to little thought to architectural barriers, access in this sense remains an issue.

Access in terms of location is also a concern which the IEDC Scheme tried to address by providing 'escort' allowance. Yet the meagre amount (Rs 50 per month per escort) allowed does not help in procuring the facility.

Retention data for disabled children has not been worked out except for the Project Integrated Education of the Disabled Children (see Mani 1994). The related findings on enrolment and retention of this project which was limited to ten states and ten blocks are now discussed.

ENROLMENT

• Though PIED was launched in 1988–9, enrolment started in the academic year of 1989.

• The project witnessed increased enrolment of disabled children (including SC/ST and girls) and also positively influenced the enrolment of non-disabled children; yet, some of the identified disabled children remained out-of-school.

• More orthopaedically handicapped children were enrolled than other categories.

• Enrolment of girls was lower than that of boys.

RETENTION

Disabled children enrolled under PIED very rarely dropped out from school. On an average, a 91 per cent retention rate was recorded, which is much higher than that for non-disabled children. Financial assistance appeared to be one of the most effective reasons for this retention pattern besides parental awareness and improved school climate. Absenteeism was also low among disabled children.

Achievement Patterns

Though a number of baseline studies have been conducted in District Primary Education Programme (DPEP) districts, achievement levels of disabled children have not been commented upon. However, PIED did touch this issue. Findings indicate that the achievement levels of disabled children in general are at par with those of non-disabled children. Among disabled children, orthopaedically handicapped children performed the best, followed by the visually impaired and hearing impaired. Mentally retarded children performed well below the average of other disabled children.

It can be inferred that efforts are in place for matching action with the intent of EFA. However, progress is relatively slow. The IEDC scheme has provision for early childhood education and support, aids and appliances for disabled children, escort allowance, teacher training impact, etc. One of the important features is the setting up of resource rooms for supporting and enriching integration along with resource teachers (school based/itinerant). According to the Sixth All-India Educational Survey, the largest number of such teachers are in primary schools (see Table 8.4). However, it is important to note that the share of NGO effort is remarkably high. In recent years, state governments have been reported to be discontinuing this provision, mainly because of the unclear policy position on the creation of a cadre. This is only one of the many examples that can be cited to explain the gap between action and intention.

TABLE 8.4
Schools Having IED Programme and Resource Teachers

	Schools with IED			IED with resource teachers		
	Govt	NG	Total	Govt	NG	Total
Primary						
Rural	6508	0478	6986	1504	327	1831
Urban	1198	0598	1796	0436	267	0703
Total	7706	1076	8782	1940	594	2534
Upper Primary						
Rural	2332	0356	2688	0928	239	1167
Urban	0801	0720	1521	0355	339	0694
Total	3133	1076	4209	1283	578	1861
Secondary and Higher Secondary						
Rural	1169	0569	1738	0697	439	1136
Urban	0743	0822	1565	0385	520	0905
Total	1912	1391	3303	1082	949	2141

Source: NCERT (1998 vol. IV).

Progress towards EFA during last decade indicates that the nation has come to realize that the inclusion of

12 million disabled children is very important in the realization of EFA's overall target and strategies. The education sector has initiated action which is reflected in the change of information collection and presentation formats. Parents have started giving information on their children who need special help. But it still needs to be seen whether this action can be accelerated to match the goals set for the first decade of the next millenium.

IS INDIA READY FOR ACCELERATED ACTION?

While the progress during last two decades must be appreciated, there is still need to look at the preparedness of the country to meet the challenge of EFA. Intentions have been expressed but have enabling conditions been created? Some signs of progress can be seen in terms of legislative actions.

Legislation

Two historic legislations enacted in the 1990s have given education of children with special needs in India a sound direction and solid footing.

The Rehabilitation Council of India Act 1992 (RCI) passed in Parliament, was created by the then Ministry of Welfare (presently known as the Ministry of Social Justice and Empowerment) to regulate manpower development programmes in the field of education of children with special needs. The major responsibilities of the RCI are to regulate training policies and programmes in the field of rehabilitation of people with disabilities; to bring about standardization of training courses for professionals dealing with people with disabilities; to prescribe minimum standards of education and training of various categories of professionals dealing with people with disabilities; to recognize institutions/universities running degree/diploma/certificate courses in the field of rehabilitation of the disabled and to regulate recognition wherever facilities are not satisfactory, and to maintain a Central Rehabilitation Register of institutions possessing the recognized rehabilitation qualification.

The RCI has so far developed or approved more than fifty courses dealing with special education and rehabilitation. The RCI has also recognized more than hundred institutions in India that offer these courses. Institutes working in the area of disability are encouraged to develop manpower development programmes in these categories, and recognition to the institutions is accorded when they comply with the norms prescribed by the RCI. The RCI has standardized BEd. and MEd. special education courses for the benefit of universities and colleges of education in India. The RCI has also taken up the gigantic task of offering bridge courses to nearly 20,000 personnel who are currently working in the field of education and rehabilitation without requisite qualifications.

The Persons With Disabilities (Equal Opportunities, Protection of Rights and Full Participation) Act was passed on 22 December 1995 in both Houses of Parliament, notified on 1 January 1996, and enforced with effect from 7 February 1996. The Act provides for preventive as well as promotional aspects of rehabilitation, like education, employment and vocational training, reservation, research and manpower development, creation of barrier free environment, rehabilitation for persons with disability, unemployment allowance for the disabled, special insurance scheme for disabled employees, and establishment of homes for persons with severe disability. The policies on education include girls, boys, men, and women with disabilities.

The Ministry of Social Justice and Empowerment has taken some measures towards its effective implementation. These are: (1) appointment of a chief commissioner for persons with disabilities; (2) setting up of five core groups of experts under relevant ministries to formulate appropriate schemes; (3) allocation of needed funds to the RCI; and (4) state-level mechanisms to redress the grievances of disabled persons. A National Advisory Council for the education of the disabled has been constituted under the Ministry of Education, and of course, now concern for the disabled is expressed under most basic education programmes like adult education, non-formal education (NFE), and Lok Jumbish.

Chapter v of the Act deals mainly with education. It asks the appropriate governments and local authorities to provide disabled children with free education; make schemes and programmes for their NFE; conduct research for designing and developing new assistive devices and teaching aids; set up Teachers' Training Institutions to develop trained manpower for schools for children with disabilities; prepare a comprehensive education scheme for providing transport facilities and books, etc; and provide amanuensis to students with visual handicap. Chapter IX emphasizes the promotion and sponsorship of research, and giving financial incentives to universities to enable them to undertake research.

A coordination committee has been appointed by the Government of India to monitor the work of Braille book production, and it was noted by the Conference of Managers of Braille Presses in January 1998 that Braille presses in India remained underutilized. Some new projects aiming to develop cost-effective assistive devices are supported by the Science and Technology in Mission Mode under the Ministry of Social Justice and Empowerment. The National Institute for the Hearing Handicapped and some NGOs in collaboration with the

Christoffel Blinden Mission are engaged in the development of an Indian sign language and a sign language interpretation course. Community-based Rehabilitation (CBR) programmes are used for early intervention services. The National Council for Teacher Education (NCTE) has recommended the inclusion of a component of special education in all pre-service teacher preparation courses. The NCERT is adapting instructional materials in teaching environmental studies to disabled children and has included mathematics and science in programmes for the blind.

Sectoral Schemes

Disabled children and persons require support from more than one sector in order to develop to their maximum potential. Any exercise in human resource development (HRD) of the disabled goes though the steps of early identification, assessment education, and rehabilitation to reach the maximum potential development. In India there have been specific schemes and projects for the disabled and there are certain general schemes which are equally applicable to all, disabled or otherwise. Some of these are briefly discussed to provide the context for the discussion on planning and management of education provision for the disabled.

THE INTEGRATED CHILD DEVELOPMENT SCHEME (ICDS)

ICDS of the Ministry of Woman and Child is designed both as a preventive as well as developmental measure in meeting the needs of the growing child. It extends beyond the existing health and education systems to reach children and their mothers in villages and slums and delivers to them an integrated package of services addressing children in the 0–6 age group in the form of:

• Non-formal preschool education
• Immunization
• Health check-ups
• Supplementary nutrition
• Medical referral services
• Nutrition and health education for women

The coverage under the ICDS when combined with other Early Childhood Care and Education (ECCE) facilities such as *Balwadis* run by voluntary agencies and pre-primary schools run by state governments, municipal corporations, and other agencies adds up to a total of about 86.46 lakh children. This coverage, though impressive in terms of absolute numbers, is minimal in percentage terms and covers about 15 per cent of the children requiring these services (see Muralidharan and Kaur).

Since the ICDS works in slums, and in tribal and rural areas, it is the most appropriate service to include disabled children who are primarily among the most vulnerable sections of the society. Yet, professionals associated with Early Childhood Care while designing manuals and curricula for training of para professionals in early learning have not included preschool disabled children in their purview. Policy makers too are aware of the critical 0–5 years and a large resource allocation has been made to the ICDS, yet, children with special needs are not a part of the social policy, concerning even basic needs such as health, nutrition, and preschool facilities. Thus, a major social policy in the country has left out disability, which should be one of the important agenda items. This aspect is important both for dealing with the onset of disability and for enabling children to use schooling facilities. This argument is being forwarded in the light of the empirically observed onset pattern of disabilities (see Table 8.5)

From the distribution of disabled persons of age 60 years and above by age at onset of disability it is revealed that physical disability is essentially an old age problem. The results also indicate that for visual, speech, and locomotor disability, the possibility of incidence is relatively higher in the early ages than in the middle ages of life. Here it is important that programmes like the ICDS have a focused input for prevention of disability as well as early identification and intervention to minimize the impact of impairments.

DISTRICT REHABILITATION CENTRE/SCHEME

The scheme was initiated in eleven districts on pilot basis by the Ministry of Welfare. The aims and objectives of the scheme encompass the issue of disability in its entirety—awareness, education, catering to each and every form of disability, encouraging voluntary effort in the cause of rehabilitation and establishing a comprehensive model of physical restorative services for the disabled within each district, medical intervention, education, vocational training, and employment. It includes delivery of a wide range of services, training of manpower and research, and the creation of awareness in the community about services available for the disabled. Counselling for the individual and the family is provided through the multipurpose rehabilitation workers and village rehabilitation workers in order to help the handicapped overcome disability through:

• the provision of appropriate aids and appliances like artificial limbs, calipers, hearing aids, and Braille kits.,

• dissemination and distribution of information to the rural community about the necessity of early intervention of appropriate medical care or surgery, including surgical

TABLE 8.5
All-India Per 1000 Distribution of Physically Disabled Persons of Age 60 Years and Above by Age at Onset of Disability for Each Type of Disability

Type of disability	Age at onset (years)										
	0–4	5–9	10–14	15–19	20–4	25–9	30–4	35–44	45–59	6o and above	Total (including NR)
Rural											
Visual	08	08	09	02	03	03	04	18	255	689	1000
Hearing	09	06	12	09	11	10	12	41	280	609	1000
Speech	42	23	24	0–	10	0–	12	25	262	594	1000
Locomotor	29	19	17	17	10	08	22	59	278	541	1000
Urban											
Visual	12	15	07	03	06	05	05	18	236	690	1000
Hearing	07	13	10	11	09	14	13	55	215	651	1000
Speech	35	39	09	0–	23	0–	07	27	287	572	1000
Locomotor	21	16	15	09	12	08	13	41	280	586	1000

Source: NSSO (1991).

corrections and therapeutical services in all fields of disability,

• provision of schooling for disabled children including the establishment of pre-primary schools, thereby facilitating the absorption of these individuals into the mainstream in later years,

• organization of voluntary training programmes for the adult disabled so that they can become productive members of society, either through self-employment in the informal sector or by providing them with jobs in the organized sector and

• the provision of services at primary health centre and village levels for maintenance and repair of appliances provided to the disabled.

RESTORATIVE AND REHABILITATION SERVICES

The Ministry of Labour runs special employment exchanges and Vocational Rehabilitation Centres. Seventeen Vocational Rehabilitation Centres for the Handicapped (VRC-H) are at present functioning. The ones at Ludhiana, Delhi, Kanpur, Jabalpur, Ahmedabad, Guwahati, Bombay, Bangalore, Trivandrum, Madras, Hyderabad, Calcutta, Bhubaneswar, Jaipur, Vadodra, and Patna have exclusively been assisting women handicapped in rehabilitation work. Vocational Rehabilitation Centres provide rehabilitation services to handicapped persons in accordance with physical and psychological capacities. The blind and orthopaedically handicapped have benefited from these scheme through shelter workshops.

Voluntary Organizations

The Ministry of Welfare funds NGOs to work for the education and rehabilitation of the disabled and for providing aids and applicances for the physically handicapped. It may be recorded here that voluntary organizations have played a major role in providing services for the disabled, at times greater than the governmental effort. Over the years, the number of such NGOs has been growing and they are becoming more organized, with their role extending to formulating policies, providing support to government efforts, and initiating action. A survey of organizations working for the disabled in the entire country was recently carried out by the government. There are more than 2456 voluntary organizations in the disability area and 1200 special schools, of which 450 receive grants from the government towards their operational costs. The majority of them are autonomous (see GoI 1995).

Some of the notable NGOs in the field are Sanjivini, Amar Jyoti Rehabilitation and Research Centre, the National Association for the Blind, the Blind Persons Association, the All India Federation of the Deaf, the Federation for the Welfare of the Mentally Retarted, the Spastic Society of India, and Tamanna. Besides national NGOs, many international NGOs in this area are also operating in India such as Christoffel Blindenmission, Sight Savers, and Action Aid.

However, one of the primary problems with the voluntary sector is the very limited and fast dwindling capacity to raise funds and their increasing dependence on grants-in-aid from the central and state governments.

As they obtain a major portion of their funding from the government, their main policy allegiance remains with the government, at times weakening their position to question governmental policy.

> NGOs and State are often locked in an institutional embrace, not simply the product of minimalist regulation by registration but more directly through finance and through capture and substitution. A society relying on NGOs as the mechanism for the delivery of social welfare, accepts their insecurity of funding and their social costliness. Such a society accepts the minimal regulations of NGOs' service provisions and their sometimes quirky allocation priorities. [White 1994][1]

The NGO sector has pioneered valuable services for the disabled, ensuring social integration into the community. However, with limited infrastructural services and limited funds, the voluntary sector can only serve at a micro level. For example, while some of the national-level NGOs have done remarkable work for the blind, an organization of the level of Royal National Institute of the Blind of England is yet to emerge in terms of comprehensiveness.

Role of Premier Institutes/Organizations

Most of the schemes and programmes in the area of special education have support from national-level institutes. At school stage, the NCERT has been playing a significant role since 1983 through advocacy (print media, face-to-face meetings, campaigns, and training and research). It has emerged as the apex institute for integrated education. The approach of National Institute of Educational Planning and Administration (NIEPA) has been diffused and limited. The University grants Commission (UGC) has also initiated a number of programmes since 1985, notable among which are 100 per cent assistance to university education departments for teacher preparation (1985 onwards) and teacher preparation in special education (1999 onwards).

A number of national institutes for the handicapped under the Ministry of Social Welfare have also significantly contributed to the cause viz. the National Institute for the Orthopeadically Handicapped, Kolkata; the Ali Yaver Jung National Institute for the Hearing Impaired, Mumbai; the National Institute for the Mentally Handicapped, Secunderabad; the National Institute for the Visually Impaired, Dehradun; the Institute for the Physically Handicapped, New Delhi; the National Institute for Rehabilitation, Training and Research, Cuttack.

---

[1] White, Harris, Oxford (1994) as quoted by Alur Mithu in Social Integration of Disabled People in India, Network Seminar on Integrated Education for Children with Special Education Needs, Mumbai, New Delhi, Jaipur, January–February 1997.

Such programmes under implementation, the role being played by voluntary organizations (national and international), and the technical support being provided by premier educational institutes reflect the overall intent of the authorities and the channels created for facing the tremendous challenge involved in covering the handicapped under EFA. However, much more is needed. One can only say that a beginning has been made through policies and programmes but implementation would need more concerted efforts.

CHALLENGES FOR THE FUTURE

The last decade of the century has seen the recognition of the fact that children with disabilities and special education needs constitute a significant group in the monitoring of EFA targets. A number of enabling provisions have been created by way of legislation, through the role of premier institutions as well as capacity building of the government and the NGO sector to provide inputs by way of manpower, learning materials, and others for upgrading the quality of education programmes, especially at preschool and elementary levels. However, there are still serious challenges which would require increased effort and decisions for ensuring expansion of educational facilities in all parts or pockets of the country. The focus has to be on the qualitative levels to be attained by the disabled through schooling and on sustaining the institutional and organizational structures for their educational development.

Expansion of Schooling Facilities

The vision itself needs to be expanded in order to provide opportunities and facilities for children with special education needs at par with those for any other child born in this country. Such disabled children who might have been placed in special schools would also need to be provided opportunities for being benefited from inclusive education programmes. A notification to this effect by the Ministry of Human Resource Development (MHRD) and state governments subsequently has to be issued to reflect this commitment to be achieved within a defined time-frame. To ensure political commitment, this vision needs to be shared with the political leadership in the backdrop of related legislation on compulsory education, as well as the Delhi Declaration and Persons with Disability Act. Any future debate or discussion on education policy, especially up to senior secondary level, would require the 'indicators of inclusion' to form an integral component. Special schools, presently with the Ministry of Social Welfare have to be reviewed and qualitatively supported, adopting the HRD approach rather than the welfare services approach.

Since the goal is to upscale to cover all disabled children, it is necessary that all modes of education—formal and alternative/open schooling are explored to the maximum to realize this target. Whenever a review of existing schemes is undertaken in the MHRD, it may be worthwhile to have a task force at the national level across bureaus and departments. This task force should have adequate representation of the Planning Commission, Finance Department, and other sector organizations so that proper coordination and linkages are established even at the stage of visioning. National and international NGOs and agencies' support can be enhanced through proper planning and supportive atmosphere, as this vision cannot be realized without proper support from all sectors. Thus, policy statement as well as the planning and management dimensions of provision for disabled children are the biggest challenge.

Capacity Building

Flowing from this type of consideration is the challenge of working with the mainstream education provisions and modes for making education an enjoyable as well as successful endeavour for such children. It has already been established through projects like PIED (Project Integrated Education for the Disabled) that when given a chance, these children can perform at par or better than their able-bodied peers. However, the role of well-planned educational inputs in terms of curriculum planning, transaction, teaching–learning materials, and timely availability of support cannot be undermined. It may also so happen that the general quality of schools would become better if they are persuaded to accept these children and to make them succeed. It is not enough to have an intent—it has to be translated into action. For example, the issue of resource teachers cannot be ignored. This is important for the success of the programme; if need be, a new cadre should be created and a long-term view on career development needs to be in place. Apex organizations like the NCERT and NIEPA as well as the national institutes for the handicapped need to come together and look at the provisions for children up to the age of 14 in a comprehensive manner while promoting a supportive role among one another. While programmes for teachers and other rehabilitation professions are being attended to, the sensitivity of administrators and planners is an issue still ignored. University departments have also not shown the required tenacity. Most of the special education initiatives in the Department of Education have either been closed or are performing poorly. They have to be reviewed and strengthened. The linkage and jurisdiction of teacher training among apex statutory organizations—the NCTE and the RCI—need to be properly looked out. They have implications for status, preparation, and recruitment of teachers for special education.

Reaching Out

Media has always played a significant role in advocating the cause of this group of persons. The new education channels like Gyan Darshan can focus on 'reach out' programmes for parents, teachers, and citizens to further strengthen and support the spirit of inclusive education. Information Technology avenues may also be expanded to cover this group of learners. Even in larger cities, parents feel frustrated due to lack of information on services and programmes. Internet facilities can overcome this requirement. The government can set up and fund websites under the IEDC scheme.

NGO–Government Partnership

While the government can today claim a significant role in the education of the disabled, it is important to acknowledge that NGOs initiated action in the field much before government support became available. A visible partnership between the two is emerging and NGOs are spread in rural and urban areas. However, there are still gaps in terms of coverage, location, and even mutual trust. A well-planned rather than ad hoc partnership may be the answer. National institutes can help articulate this vision and exercise. Some good lessons have been learnt in Kerala, Orissa, and Gujarat where NGOs have provided remarkable support for government schemes for disabled children.

Empowerment

Last but not the least is the challenge of empowerment of disabled children/persons and their immediate family members. The Act of 1995 has created hope. It is necessary that it be implemented in all seriousness. Besides, issues of the definitions and labelling need to be tackled. Should India continue to use the medical model of 40 per cent disability to get 'benefits'? If the human development approach is applied then even minimal impairment may create a special need. A debate is required to have a simplified approach for identifying 'limitations' imposed by disability conditions, leading to special needs in education. Perhaps cost-effective but wide-reaching approaches can then be worked out to provide opportunities for education to all and ensure their maximum utilization. Under the 1995 Act, disabled persons have already been provided a platform to participate in decision making and enhanced implementation. There is need for their greater visibility in other sectors and areas. Second, all other sub-Plans, for example, those for SC/ST and other focus groups also should encourage coverage of disabled men and women, boys and girls, and address the issue of rural–urban divide. It is important to note, realize, and advocate that a child with special needs is first of all a child, an individual, a citizen; hence, all such provisions and programmes must cover her/him as a general principle.

REFERENCES

Alur, Mithu (1997). *Social Integration of Disabled People in India*. The Spastics Society of India, Mumbai.

Central Statistical Organisation (1999). *Selected Socio-Economic Statistics, India*. Government of India, New Delhi.

Department of Education (1986). *National Policy on Education 1986*. Ministry of Human Resource Development, Government of India, New Delhi.

————— (1992). *Revised Policy Formulations on Education*. Ministry of Human Resource Development, Government of India, New Delhi.

Harris, White Oxford (1994). As quoted by Alur, Mithu in *Social Integration of Disabled People in India*. Network Seminar on *Integrated Education for Children with Special Education Needs*. Mumbai, New Delhi, Jaipur, January–February 1997.

Kundu, C. L. (ed.) (2000). *Status of Disability in India-2000*. Rehabilitation Council of India, New Delhi.

Legislative Department (1995). *Equal Opportunities, Protection of Rights and Full Participation*. Ministry of Law, Justice and Company Affairs, Government of India, New Delhi.

Mani, M. N. G. (1994). 'Project Integrated Education for the Disabled (PIED): Evaluation Study.' UNICEF, New Delhi. (Mimeo)

Ministry of Human Resource Development (1999). 'Official Data for Disabled.' (Unpublished)

Mukhopadhyay, Sudesh and Suman Bhatia (2000). 'Schools Where Children Learn: Investigation into Building Design and Infrastructure in Primary Schools of NCT of Delhi'. State Council of Educational Research and Training, New Delhi. (Mimeo)

Muralidharan, R. and B. Kaur (1984). *The Impact of Intervention Program on Language and Cognitive Development of Preschool Children from Urban Anganwadis*. National Council of Educational Research and Training, New Delhi.

National Council of Educational Research and Training (1998). *Sixth All-India Educational Survey: National Tables*, vol. IV (Enrolment in Schools). New Delhi.

National Sample Survey Organisation (1991). *A Report on Disabled Persons*. Report No. 393. 47th Round July–December 1991. Delhi.

Pandey, R. S. and Lal Advani (1995). *Perspectives in Disability and Rehabilitation*. Vikas Publishing, Delhi.

Rehabilitation Council of India (1996). *Report on Manpower Development*. Delhi.

The Delhi Declaration (1994). As a part of the *Report on Education for All Summit of Nine High—Population Countries: Final Report, New Delhi, 12–16 December 1993*. UNESCO, Paris.

UNESCO (1994). *Final Report: World Conference on Special Needs Education: Access and Quality*. Salamanca, 7–10 June. UNESCO, Paris.

UNISED (1999). As Quoted by Mani, M. N. G, UNESCO International Institute for Special Education (Mimeo) submitted to UNESCO and Government of India.

United Nations (1989). *UN Convention on the Rights of Child*.

University Grants Commission (1998). *Scheme for Teacher Preparation in Special Education (TEPSE) and Higher Education for Persons with Special Needs*. University Grants Commission, Delhi.

World Conference on Education for All (1990). *World Declaration on Education for All and Framework for Action to Meet Basic Learning Needs*. Inter-Agency Commission (UNDP, UNESCO, World Bank), New York.

II

Building Partnerships

Putting Community In-Charge for Universalizing Elementary Education

9 Decentralization of Education

Vinod Raina

If every habitation had its own school, education would be completely decentralized. But if providing free and compulsory elementary education is the duty of the state, as the Indian Constitution decrees, how can each habitation have its own school? Where would it find resources to run its school? It is the state that must provide schools, and since the state traditionally governs through bureaucracy, centralization is inherent in its functioning—except, of course, if the functioning of the state and the notion of development are different.

From its inception, the Indian state was confronted by two different visions of reconstruction: the Gandhian project of reviving the village economy as the basis of development and the Nehruvian plan of prosperity through rapid industrialization. Gandhi put his views together as early as 1909 in *Hind Swaraj*. Many years later, on the threshold of India's Independence (5 October 1945), Gandhi wrote to Nehru outlining his vision of free India.

> I believe that, if India is to achieve true freedom, and through India the world as well, then sooner or later we will have to live in villages—in huts not in palaces. A few billion people can never live happily and peaceably in cities and palaces.... My villages exist today in my imagination.... The villager in this imagined village will not be apathetic.... He will not lead his life like an animal in a squalid dark room. Men and women will live freely and be prepared to face the whole world. The village will not know cholera, plague or smallpox. No one will live indolently, nor luxuriously. After all this, I can think of many things, which will have to be produced on a large scale. Maybe there will be railways, so also post and telegraph. What it will have and what it will not, I do not know. Nor do I care. If I can maintain the essence, the rest will mean free facility to come and settle. And if I leave the essence, I leave everything.

One of the elements critical to realizing such a dream was Gandhi's notion of basic education (*nai talim*).

'God forbid that India should ever take to industrialization in the manner of the West,' he observed. 'The economic imperialism of a single tiny island kingdom (England) is today keeping the world in chains. If an entire nation of 300 million (nearly a billion today) took to similar economic exploitation, it would strip the world bare like locusts'. He had, earlier in 1940, already expressed his misgivings regarding centralization thus:

> Nehru wants industrialization because he thinks that if it were socialized, it would be free from the evils of capitalism. My own view is that the evils are inherent in industrializm and no amount of socialization can eradicate them.... I do visualise electricity, shipbuilding, ironworks, machine-making and the like existing side by side with village crafts. But...I do not share the socialist belief that centralization of production of the necessities of life will conduce to the common welfare.

The appeal of Gandhi lay in his programme of revitalizing village communities and craft production by employing simple technologies to provide jobs and a decent livelihood to a predominantly rural population. The liberation that Gandhi promised was not merely an economic independence; it was, most profoundly, an assurance that the cultural traditions of the Indian peasantry would reign supreme. Local culture and methods of production were at the heart of his vision of a supportive basic education. Decentralized development was therefore deeply integrated with a supportive school education system in Gandhi's approach.

Gandhi's vision held no appeal for Jawaharlal Nehru, who replied rather brusquely to Gandhi on 9 October 1945:

> It is many years since I read *Hind Swaraj* and I have only a vague picture in my mind. But even when I read it twenty or more years ago it seemed to me completely unreal.... A village, normally speaking, is backward intellectually and

culturally and no progress can be made from a backward environment.

Having dismissed Gandhi's plea thus, Nehru's own ambivalence was to surface only a few years later when he talked of the evils of centralized, gigantic, mega projects.

The idea here is not to pursue particular positions in what is a familiar historical debate regarding India's development, but to highlight the point that exploring the question of decentralization of education is superficial without delving into its political and developmental linkages. Descriptive accounts about various governmental initiatives regarding decentralization in education already exist (see Dhar 1997). Instead of repeating them, this chapter examines recent efforts at educational decentralization in India with reference to the tense relationship between state and market, which dominates the world today through the globalized neo-liberal economic regime. It is of particular interest because the decade of education for all (EFA), beginning in 1990, has coincided with such a regime in many countries of the world, including India.

During this decade, far-reaching changes in education have taken place in most countries. These changes have included shifts away from state control towards privatization and decentralization. However, these terms have different interpretations in different contexts, which necessitates locating them within a general framework involving state, market, and community. Following Dale (1997), it could be argued that for most of the countries the

> education system, like all state organizations, could not avoid addressing the three central problems confronting the state in capitalist societies: (i) supporting the capital accumulation process, (ii) guaranteeing a context for its continued expansion, and (iii) legitimating the capitalist mode of accumulation, including the state's own part in it, especially education.

These core problems set limits to state actions, though this does not mean that there would be no variations in the manner different states seek solutions. Applied to India, where education is a concurrent subject, the different ways each state government has sought solutions could be explored, restricted however by the general framework.

Education has been affected, both directly and indirectly, by the changes in the global economy in the recent past. The direct impact is clearly seen in developing countries whose education systems are increasingly being shaped by the lending policies of the World Bank and the demands of structural adjustment, particularly the shrinking of the public sector and the expansion of the private, on which organizations like the IMF make support conditional. More indirect effects are seen in advanced countries that have been coping with the decline of the welfare state to the point where public funding of services like education no longer seems feasible at previous levels.

In order to better understand the impact of these changes in a developing country like India, the reaction to them in advanced countries is relevant and a pointer to the future course of events. In advanced countries we may discern a loss of some activities of the state to supranational bodies as we go upwards in the education ladder, and a loss of others to sub-national or non-state bodies downwards towards elementary education. We therefore see similar moves towards various forms of privatization and decentralization of education in many countries of the world in recent years. It might therefore be said that while education remains a public issue, in common with many state activities, its coordination has ceased to be the sole preserve of the state or government. Instead, it has become coordinated through a range of forms of governance, among which decentralization and privatization figure prominently. Mass literacy campaigns (MLCs, also known as total literacy campaigns or TLCs) the District Primary Education Programme (DPEP), and the Lok Jumbish (LJ) Project provide examples of such newer forms of governance during the last decade, as shall presently be argued.

DECENTRALIZATION IN GOVERNANCE OF EDUCATION

In focusing on the governance of education, what it involves and how and by whom these activities are carried out must clearly be understood. It is generally believed that delivering education is a single-strand activity and that it is carried out by the state. Three distinct and separable activities that together constitute what is generally referred to as 'state intervention' (see Dale 1997) may however be discerned, i.e. its funding, delivery, and regulation or control. It may be argued that it is not necessary for the state to carry out all these activities while remaining in overall control.

These functions have to be coordinated and three major institutions of social coordination can be distinguished for the purpose. The state and market are two key institutions of social coordination. The third, the community, is always a residual category of the former two, and it is conceptualized differently according to the different conceptions of these two. It should be noted that the 'traditional' assumption has been that all the activities involved in the coordination of education used to be carried out by the state. However, a moment's reflection would suffice to show that the state has never done all these things alone; the market, and especially the community, have always been indispensable to the operation of education systems. The difference now is that their areas of involvement have greatly expanded and have been formalized as the area of direct state involvement has contracted. The governance of education can therefore be seen as a three by three table involving the state, market, and community on one side and funding, delivery, and regulation on the other. It then provides a framework to locate various activities and actors in education, in particular to make sense of various forms of decentralization and their relative merits.

The table demonstrates the inadequacy of a simple 'public-private/community' distinction and shows how confusing that distinction can be. Only if and when funding, regulation, and provision are all carried out by the state alone can we speak of a 'public' system. Only if and when they are carried out by 'non-state' bodies alone can we speak of a 'private/community' or decentralized system; even then 'private' would have to be interpreted as 'non-state'. The table, therefore, points to the complexity of the centralized/decentralized debate and the dangers of oversimplifications regarding 'decentralized', 'private', and 'community' forms of education. We have not only to ask what activities are being decentralized or handed over to the market or community, but also what this means. To do so, we need to look more closely at the complexities in the relationships between governance activities and coordinating institutions, in particular, at governance activities, for it is these which ultimately shape and invest the coordinating institutions with specific purposes.

Funding

Even though the state is responsible for 'free and compulsory education till age 14' as per the Constitution, a cursory glance at the funding mechanisms of schools would convince us that the actual situation is far more complex. In actual terms, funding can be made up of direct state funding, fee payments, community or parent-raised funds, international funds for education—whether 'public'(mediated through state/and or voluntary bodies) or 'private' provided by transnational sources or by international 'non-profit' organizations—or, of course, by any combination of these sources and types of funding. Thus, apart from the majority of state-controlled government schools in the country, we have the phenomenon of *panchayat* schools, unaided private schools, aided private schools, mission and convent schools, mostly church-funded, schools funded by other religious bodies like *madrassas* and RSS schools, and schools partially funded by corporate houses—in each case charging from moderate to heavy fees. The current regime of economic liberalization is shrouded in the ideology of 'public choice'

and as regards education too parents may be free to choose from an open market the best education for their children, and naturally, pay for it. This opens avenues for non-state funding of education, resulting in a 'decentralized' mode of functioning benefiting the middle classes, and in the process, widening caste and class disparities.

Regulation

It is the ultimate ability of the state to determine policy and sanctions through law that shapes the whole area of regulation. Together with funding, regulation provides the framework within which provision and delivery are made. Funding and regulation combine in different ways to create the context for educational policy, delivery, and practice. However as Prosser (1995) points out, the tendency towards greater marketization and privatization of education seems to be seen by policy makers as the resolution of technical issues of economic principle which are assumed to be similar in any market-oriented economy, so neglecting the particular constraints of legal and political culture. The tendency is to bracket out such cultural factors in favour of an 'acultural form of rational behaviour'. This emphasizes the crucial point that markets are in no sense 'natural' institutions, but are always shaped by patterns of state regulation. In looking at what might shape education markets, therefore, it is essential to pay close attention to the regulations that frame the attempted move towards them. This includes 'deregulation', the removal of existing regulations that are perceived to act as barriers to greater consumer choice of schools, and all that it is assumed will flow from it in the way of responsiveness, efficiency, and community participation. Such policies, seemingly promoting 'decentralization', typically seek to remove bureaucratic/democratic controls and minimize areas over which professionals have discretion.

Of interest here is another aspect of regulation concerning the use of law in structuring social, political, cultural, and economic life, which may be called juridification. The effect of juridification has been to remove particular, often politically contentious, issues from the political agenda, making them subject to legal and not political dispute. This applies in the field of education not only to issues like national curricula, but also to teachers' training, their conditions of service, and the bases on which schools are to run. Later such juridification shall be examined in relation to recent policies regarding Minimum Levels of Learning (MLLs), Education Guarantee Schemes, *shiksha karmis* (para-teachers), etc.

Delivery

Provision and delivery are undoubtedly shaped by changes in funding and regulation. A major factor here is the manner in which provision relates to the question of entitlement. Choice-based policies seek to make products and services available to consumers, even if that means they are not available to everyone, while entitlement-based policies place the emphasis on ensuring the widest possible distribution of a basic minimum, even if that means curtailing the choice for some. The distinction, when applied to education, concerns that between consumers and citizens. In a system of education designed for citizens, an attempt is made through the mechanisms of funding and regulation to ensure that everyone has access to a sound education—something missing in India as yet. For consumers the principle on which education is provided is that of ability to pay. For citizens education is provided as a universal entitlement—universalization entails treating all members of society on the same basis. In practice, however, as has been the experience in India and other countries, the definition of states of the population entitled to benefit from universally provided education does not include every child, but is typically based on caste, class, and gender. Consequently, in India at least, there has been greater stress in recent years on delivery mechanisms focused on the 'educationally deprived', but how decentralized these state initiatives have really been needs analysis.

EARLIER ATTEMPTS AT DECENTRALIZATION

Having abandoned the Gandhian approach to development in general and basic education in particular, the resurgent Republic of India, in 1950, however, acknowledged his vision through Article 40 of the Constitution of India which states that 'the State shall take steps to organise village panchayats and endow them with such powers and authority as may be necessary to enable them to function as units of self-government'. The launching of the Community Development Programme in 1952, which led to the creation of development blocks, was an attempt towards decentralized planning. But it soon became apparent that the programme was not working, mainly because of unabated bureaucratic control. This led to the setting up of the Balwant Rai Mehta Committee in 1957 to make recommendations on new structures to be created to involve local people in the development process. The committee recommended the 'establishment of an inter-connected three-tier organizational structure of democratic decentralisation at the village, block and district levels'. Many states enacted *Panchayati Raj* Acts in the 1950s, not all following the pattern suggested by the Mehta committee. However, interest and support for the *panchayats* declined in the sixties, with very little funds flowing into them and the reluctance of most states to hold *panchayat* elections on a regular basis.

Meanwhile, as a supportive measure to rapid industrialization, emphasis was placed on higher education, in particular on the setting up of elite Indian Institutes of Technology (IITs), and laboratories and institutions under the Centre for Scientific and Industrial Research (CSIR), Indian Council for Medical Research (ICMR), Indian Council for Agriculture Research (ICAR), etc. The school system did expand, as also children's enrolment, but not at a pace that would ensure universalization with quality by 1960, as the Constitution had decreed. The expansion of the school system went hand in hand with a bloating educational bureaucracy, controlled from the state capitals, which was mostly dealing with teacher appointments, transfers, and payment of their salaries that took up 95 per cent of their budgets. Expansion meant increasing centralization and greater distancing from ground realities. In many states, as has been the experience of some people, state education departments did not even have proper lists of the schools under them. Decentralization mostly meant adding further tiers in a bureaucratic chain of control, at district, block, and recently, cluster levels. As for the actual process of teaching–learning, which is why schools are set up in the first place, centralization went right up to national level. Most of the academic, pedagogic content and methodology norms continue to be determined at national level, the State Councils of Education Research and Training (SCERTs) and District Institutes of Educational Training (DIETs) acting as mere carriers of these norms in the form of school texts, teacher training, and other functions.

THE EFA DECADE 1990–2000

Consequently, at the time of the 1991 census, the nation was jolted to find that nearly half its population was illiterate and nearly half its 6–14 population was out of school, having never been enrolled or as dropouts, after nearly forty-five years of independence. The need for an alternative to centralized bureaucracy in school education had been articulated earlier in 1986 in the National Policy on Education (NPE) and was forcefully reiterated in the revised version of this Policy in 1992.

During the last decade, one finds fairly vigorous attention to the problem of management and control of education, both at policy and implementation levels, and greater advocacy for the need to involve communities in the process of school education through decentralization. This shall be outlined in some detail. There is, however, a disquieting aspect to such admittedly increased attention to the problem, which is the absence of relating the processes of management and control to the *purpose* of education, a major concern articulated, for example, by Gandhi. For many, therefore, any talk of decentralization without the purpose of education being the primary focus is some kind of techno-managerial issue, not an educational issue. At the same time, one can also not ignore the efforts that have been made in the past decade in this direction. It is only a critical appraisal of these efforts that can lead to a better policy and implementation perspective in the future.

Apart from the Revised Policy of Education, 1992, the other major events in the EFA decade that have a bearing on the question of decentralization are:

- The Central Advisory Board on Education (CABE) recommendations in light of the 73rd and 74th amendments of the Constitution;
- the MLCs;
- the DPEP;
- the LJ Project;
- People's Development Planning (PDP) process of Kerela;
- the EGS of MP;
- the joint UN–GoI Community Education Programme; and
- the efforts of some voluntary agencies.

CABE Recommendations on Decentralized Management of Education

The somewhat failed attempt at *panchayati raj* institutions (PRIs) during the 1960s was revived through the 73rd and 74th amendments of the Constitution in 1992 that made the setting up of local bodies at village, block, district, and municipal levels, through a process of elections, mandatory. This is arguably the most significant policy initiative for decentralized governance that India has formulated since Independence. The mandatory reservation of one-third of the elected posts for women, in particular, is a major step towards correcting the gender imbalance in the country's governance system. What is also heartening is that except for just one state, Bihar, all other states have gone through an election process to choose representatives to these local bodies. The powers of the PRIs extend to areas listed in the Eleventh Schedule of the Constitution, which also contains education, including primary and secondary schools.

The 73rd and 74th amendments provide an enabling framework for decentralization, but actual implementation requires positive action at executive level. That is where the pattern is uneven across the country. Empowering the PRIs to play a designated role clearly means a lesser role for the bureaucracy and political interests, requiring considerable will and efforts to overcome the consequent obstacles. In particular, proper flow of funds and other resource support mechanisms to PRIs are necessary in order for them to function meaningfully.

Taking cognizance of these amendments, CABE set up a special committee under the then Chief Minister of Karnataka, Veerappa Moily, in 1993 to formulate a framework for decentralized management of education under the PRI framework. Whereas the NPE 1986 had recommended the setting up of District Boards of Education, the Moily Committee took the process further in recommending the setting up of Village Education Committees and *Panchayat Samitis* on Education at block level, in addition to the District Board. The Committee reiterated the problem of flow of funds to the PRIs, and cautioned about the fragile nature of these bodies saying, 'These institutions may not grow immediately into their full potential and start performing.... They need to be nurtured, supported and encouraged in a positive manner.... The positive partnership between the PRI's [sic] and State governments will go a long [sic] way in confronting the multifaceted tasks of educational development'. Such tentativeness has marked the response to the PRIs from many quarters since they came into existence—'They are okay but can they deliver?' This is reminiscent of the British response to the concept of an independent India and Indians during the 1940s—'Can they govern themselves?'

As mentioned earlier, the involvement of the PRIs in education since 1994, when they were constituted, has been uneven across states. Kerela has moved seriously towards making them central to development planning, including education, Madhya Pradesh has shown a keen desire to give them a central place; while other states have shown varying responses. For example, in West Bengal, where the PRIs functioned even before the 1992 amendments, education has been organized under the nominated District Primary Education Councils for many years. Instead of constituting a body from elected representatives, the state government continues with the nominated Councils even now. Similar parallel systems, of village and other committees, exist under many other educational programmes and projects, sometimes producing a bewildering situation at the grassroots level.

Under the PDP process in Kerala, initiated by the Kerala Sastra Sahitya Parishad (KSSP) and later adopted by the government for statewide implementation, each *panchayat* has made its own ninth five-year plan. What is, however, unprecedented is the decision of the Kerala government to make available 40 per cent of the Ninth Plan funds directly to the *panchayats* for the implementation of these plans, which include education. Very often, state governments make policy statements regarding the powers of *panchayats*, but administrative rules and procedures that determine actual practice by the bureaucracy are left untouched. In Kerela, however, the Sen Committee has made an exhaustive study of the existing administrative laws that need to be changed or amended so that the rules and procedures allow *panchayats* to exercise their powers unambiguously and without conflict with other authorities. The Committee has identified over a thousand rules that require rectification!

Another state that has exhibited keenness to empower PRIs has been Madhya Pradesh. The process here is somewhat different. In the absence of a people's movement, or the reluctance of the state government to help one take shape, the means of empowering the PRIs are government announcements and promulgation. Announcements are made about the transfer of powers and responsibilities in various sectors from time to time, but a resource support mechanism that would help the PRIs meaningfully put their powers into practice seems to be absent, in either institutional form or through NGO collaboration. What is considered a significant step, however, is the highly publicized decision of the MP government, taken a few years ago, to provide access to education through an Education Guarantee Scheme. Under the scheme, if 40 parents in a locality (only 25 in a tribal area) seek an educational facility for their children, routed through the *Gram Panchayat*, the state government is committed to provide a low paid teacher's (*guruji*) salary for the purpose. The *Gram Panchayat* can appoint the guruji from within the community, and it also has to make arrangements for space where the guruji can organize the children into classes. Whether such rudimentary access can, in fact, provide even a minimum quality education to children is open to question. Since opening of new schools has been replaced by these EGS centres and instead of appointing regular teachers, the MP government has recruited about 70,000 less paid *shiksha karmis* in its regular schools through the *panchayats*, the danger is that such decentralized mechanisms in a state where the quality of education is already very low may be diluting the very concept of a school. School management and even the physical infrastructure of schools have, in fact, been transferred to *panchayats* in MP. But as Govinda (1999) points out,

Apart from the fact that the transfer of powers and functions to panchayati raj bodies has been effected only through a process of executive delegation, even the list does not signify true empowerment of the people in decision making. It is very clear that the list of transferred items mainly represent [sic] functions and responsibilities rather than power and authority. In fact most of the decision making areas are retained as the state government activities. There is

considerable vagueness and ambiguity in the items specified in the list.... No serious attempt has been made to restructure the management system operated by the Department of Education. Neither have the roles and functions of the existing functionaries been redefined nor has any systematic reorientation been given to them on the changed system of management.

The Lok Jumbish (LJ People's Movement) initiative in Rajasthan, though having somewhat lost its erstwhile lustre, is another significant example of an attempt to bring in community participation in school education during the EFA decade. Visualized as an autonomous project under the Lok Jumbish Parishad, created by the state government, the initiative departed from the tradition of keeping the district as the main level of planning and execution of primary education. Block-level bodies (popularly called KSPS from their Hindi acronym) were empowered to these tasks, through an executive order of the state government. Starting from a few blocks, the programme gradually spread to about 100 blocks of the state covering about 13 districts.

The attempt has been to create a system of management from below by laying great emphasis on the formation of village teams. A core team of the KSPS has functioned as a spearhead for the purpose, using participatory school mapping and other aspects of micro planning as a mobilizational method. It is the villagers themselves who carry out field surveys and prepare an educational map of the village indicating the status of every child in the village. Backed up by a strong emphasis on training at grassroots level, and the involvement of leading NGOs of the state and the country in developing teaching–learning material and teacher training, LJ provided a motivating atmosphere for others, including from other parts of the country. Sadly, many of its innovative aspects seem to be melting away now, since the state government decided to 'streamline' it and 'integrate' it with other initiatives, particularly the DPEP.

MLCs

A major effort during the EFA decade in India has been the MLCs or TLCs. Their visibility and impact have provoked strong sentiments, both for and against in recent years. Only the decentralization aspects of the campaigns will be examined here. As the name implies, these were conceived as people's campaigns, rather than as a usual government scheme or project. As is well known, the campaign form was used in many countries, notably China, Vietnam, and Nicaragua, for a rapid increase in literacy rates. In most of these successful examples, the literacy campaign was part of a political revolution, which gave it a people's character.

Historically, therefore, the campaign form is, by its very nature, a massive community programme, rather than a bureaucratic one.

It was the KSSP and the All India People's Science Network (AIPSN), both NGOs, that chose to experiment with the campaign form in a non-revolutionary setting in India. Choosing the district of Ernakulam for the experiment, the implementation structure was conceived as very broad-based, involving governmental and non-governmental agencies, as also political parties. The separately registered district committee so formed was later called the *Zilla Saksharta Samiti* (ZSS), which had units at block and right up to village level. The structure was not set up first; it evolved through a process of mobilization that was undertaken throughout the district. The mobilization was led by *kala-jatha* teams which used local cultural forms and travelled from village to village. Village- and block-level conventions soon followed where volunteers for the programme came forward, both for organizational work and for the actual teaching–learning process. An intensive household survey, conducted in festival form in a day in the entire district, helped identify both learners and volunteer teachers (VTs). A proper matching and batching of a volunteer with ten learners set the next phase of teaching and learning going, after a short training for the VTs. In Ernakulam about 25,000 VTs participated in the campaign lasting a total of about eighteen months. Except for organizational persons who worked full time for the duration of the programme and received modest honorariums, the entire campaign was run on voluntary basis, through community participation. The Government of India provided funds for teaching–learning material, given free to learners and for various trainings.

In the past ten years MLCs have taken place over nearly 500 districts of the country and have generated a great deal of debate about their efficacy, in both organizational and mobilizational terms, as also in terms of literacy outcomes. While the proponents of the programme see the MLCs as the biggest ever mobilization of the community for EFA in independent India, the opponents tend to see them as another highly publicized state-sponsored effort and a distraction from the real issues concerning Indian education. A critical view is therefore necessary while evaluating what has undoubtedly been a major effort in the last decade. The three-way table using the governance components of funding, regulation, and delivery on one side and state, market, and community on the other would be useful for such a critical review.

The MLCs were initiated through the Ernakulam experiment in 1989, nearly three years before the onset of the market-based economic liberalization programme in the country. Since the 'Ernakulam model' has subsequently become a topic of intense debate in Indian education, it would be worthwhile to dwell on it for a bit. The Ernakulam experiment was a non-governmental initiative conceived by a mass organisation, the KSSP. However, prepared under the title 'Lead Kindly Light' by KSSP, the campaign was conceived as a partnership between community groups, NGOs, *panchayats*, political parties, and government at district level. In order to ensure that all the participants felt equal, the KSSP deliberately proposed an independently registered set-up, the District Literacy Committee (later called Zila Saksharta Samiti), rather than house the programme under its own organizational banner or under the education department of the government. The motivation to launch a campaign using literacy was discussed by the KSSP in detail with the national federation of People's Science Groups, the AIPSN, on various occasions. The efficacy of the *kala-jatha* to mobilize people had been amply demonstrated by the Bharat Jan Vigyan Jatha (BJVJ) earlier in 1987, which was jointly organized by the groups who later formed the AIPSN as a consequence. Both the KSSP and AIPSN agreed that at that time in 1989 a call for literacy could mobilize the masses to work together for a common cause and act as an integrating agenda at a time when many divisive agendas were weakening community action. In that sense, the agenda of mass mobilization for literacy in a campaign form went beyond furthering reading and writing abilities amongst the masses. The initial initiative for the literacy campaigns, therefore, came from outside the government, very clearly motivated by a desire to mobilize a large number of people for community action in education, the impact of which might go beyond education.

The initiators of the campaign form were, however, clear from the very beginning that such a large-scale initiative could not be undertaken without involving the state. To begin with, the actual teaching–learning process would mostly involve learners from poor backgrounds who could not be expected to pay to get literate and that would require funding, which would have to come from the government. Also the delivery mechanism, though organized autonomously under the ZSS, could not expect to function at district level without the active support and cooperation of the district administration. At Ernakulam, given the particular personalities involved, the KSSP proposed that the then district collector head the ZSS by becoming its chairperson. The funds, however, were sought from the central government.

The major community contribution was conceived in the teaching–learning process, hitherto traditionally regulated by the state. This is what distinguishes, in my opinion, the MLCs from many other initiatives. State funding for the animators, the teachers, was sought to be replaced by volunteerism. In a sense, the entire mobilizational effort was focused on motivating the community to volunteer as teachers and/or organizers for a total of eighteen months. Since the teachers would no longer be employees paid by the government, the teaching–learning material was likewise conceived as not necessarily regulated by the adult education department or the state resource centre, as is traditionally the case. The ZSS was empowered to create its own primers and other books as also training for the voluntary teachers and other functionaries. Consequently, in Ernakulam, persons who were not directly connected with the adult education department or the state resource centre of the government devised the teaching–learning process.

The jump from the KSSP-initiated Ernakulam experiment to the nationwide programme is somewhat curious. Independently and around the same time as Ernakulam was being conceived, the Government of India set up five Technology Missions, one of which pertained to literacy. Though the objective was to initiate a rapid delivery mechanism that would integrate the functions of various government departments, the initial blueprint of the newly created National Literacy Mission (NLM) was no different from the centre-based model, involving paid animators. However, there was stress on involving mass media, particularly the AV media for awareness generation, and many front-ranking advertisement gurus of the country had been contacted by the NLM for the purpose. The rapid and successful culmination of the Ernakulam campaign in 1990 persuaded the NLM to adopt the Ernakulam approach for the entire country. Since the mobilizational aspect of the Ernakulam approach was based on person-to-person contact, spearheaded by the *kala-jatha*, the NLM requested the AIPSN to undertake such mobilization for the entire country. Subsequently, the people's science movement set up a separate organization, the Bharat Gyan Vigyan Samiti (BGVS) to undertake such a mobilizational exercise, the BGVJ, in 1990 across the entire country, setting up units in many states. In the meanwhile the Executive Committee of the NLM, comprising an equal number of non-government members, began processing proposals prepared at district level by the ZSSs for undertaking literacy campaigns.

There was no document or written norm that compelled the districts to exactly imitate the Ernakulam model. In fact, the adoption of local-specific approaches was stressed. However, district teams were exposed to some broad structural and organizational aspects of the campaign form. This included the need for an initial environment-building phase using local culture, music, songs, and theatre for person-to-person contact and the identification of potential organizers in the district through this process. The organizational structure of the ZSS was expected to evolve through such a mobilization exercise, rather than through initial nominations to various bodies of the ZSS. This was expected to be followed by a district-level one or two day house-to-house survey to identify each learner, as also the potential voluntary teacher, and that would become the basis for the campaign, rather than the statistics of the 1991 census. The survey itself, it was stressed, could act as a mobilization event if carried out in a festive manner that promoted empathy with the surveyed, rather than making them objects of a detached data-collection exercise. The identification of voluntary teachers and matching and batching each one of them with ten learners from their localities would be the next task. The ZSS was expected to set up a district academic team to create primers and other teaching–learning material, with help from the state resource centre. Only when all these initial tasks were satisfactorily completed, would the actual teaching–learning phase begin. The creation of a functional three-legged model, consisting of district administration, full-time ZSS functionaries, not necessarily government people, and the people's structures which included the voluntary teachers was emphasized, and each district was expected to flesh out its own proposal around such a skeleton. At no time was following the Ernakulam process in detail emphasized including, for example, who would be the ZSS chairperson. In West Bengal, for example, it was the *Zila Panchayat* president, the *Sabhadipati*, that headed the ZSS rather than the Collector.

Since these details are being examined here in the context of decentralization, it is necessary to point out that the decentralization of a variety of tasks to district level, that included planning, organization, curricula, training, and implementation, did not imply the absence of some centralized functions. Funds, for example, flowed right down from the central government, through the NLM, to the ZSSs, bypassing the state government or district administrative structures such as the district education office. Of the regulatory mechanisms, the one that was to cause a lot of distress and even damage to district efforts was the Improved Pace and Content Learning (IPCL) committee located within the NLM at the centre. The IPCL pedagogy had been adopted for the campaign in order to ensure that a new learner would become a neo-literate in about 200 hours of teaching. District academic teams were expected to work out their primers in conformity with the IPCL approach, and an IPCL committee was entrusted with the task of examining and certifying each of the primers before their being used. In practice, the committee became a bottleneck, with district academic teams being asked to travel to Delhi repeatedly for presentations and clarifications, resulting in long delays and frustration. Many districts, therefore, opted for the already certified primers of their state resource centres. However, the number of districts that did make and use their own primers was fairly large and a great deal of academic innovation is visible in them. In most of these cases, the presence of BGVS resource persons played a critical role in academic capacity building of district teams. Where such resource support was lacking, from any quarter, the tendency, expectedly, was to use the available academic material. For example, the primer of Darbhanga district of Bihar referred to the question of land relations, the focal point of Bihar's life and politics, explicitly. But it was the chapter in the primer of Nellore district that catalysed the women's anti-liquor movement in Andhra Pradesh. The state government initially acted on expected lines, decreeing that the district primers would have to be cleared by the state's home department! Because of the intervention of the EC of the NLM and also since the agitation forced the state government to finally bring in prohibition, the decree was withdrawn. This is an explicit example that illustrates why there is such resistance to decentralizing and weakening the states' role in regulating the teaching–learning process. One could say that the literacy campaigns, to a degree, managed such decentralization.

CONCLUSION

There is no doubt that during the past decade or so, a desire to decentralize primary education and literacy in the country has been noticeable. There may, however, be differences of opinion as to the motivation for such a desire. The most prominent motivation would be that the state has understood the limitation of its own bureaucratic structures universalizing elementary education and is therefore seeking the community's help in doing so. This is a process that can be traced from the Sixth Five Year Plan that raised the question about the ability of the state structures to deliver, in all areas of development. But as has been noted earlier, most of the attempts at decentralization have been confined mainly to administrative or management aspects, the delivery mechanisms. Voicing at times its inability to allocate adequate funds to universalize elementary education, mainly because of a lack of will to provide 6 per cent or more of GDP to education, the government has exhorted the community to contribute in cash and kind for various needs related to the schooling, even though the Constitution of the country squarely places such responsibility on the government. However, the limited attempts to involve communities have not really translated in the diminishing role of the state in controlling and regulating education. Even though privatization and community-based education are terms often used in education now, regulation and control are still unquestionably linked to the state. One may wonder, then, whether only responsibilities are meant to be decentralized and, if so, how can it be empowering?

In the state, market, community triad, marketization of education for greater public choice is also a form of decentralization, but it clearly lacks equity. A clear policy articulation that spells out the kind of decentralization the state and civil society ought to promote, keeping in view rampant caste, class, and gender disparities is necessary in India. But, above all, mere decentralization of the delivery mechanism completely ignores the major issue related to educational decentralization, that of the teaching–learning process itself. In a multi-cultural context, with traditional production systems rather than urban industry providing economic sustenance to a larger population, the linkage between the content, process, and pedagogy of education and the developmental and cultural aspects provides a more persuasive argument for educational decentralization rather than decentralized management. It is only in the MLCs that one notices a move in this direction, that too somewhat thwarted by a centralized regulatory mechanism in the form of the IPCL committee. Most of the special school programmes under the EFA have however worked under a more stringent centralized norm, the nationally prescribed MLLs, even while experimenting with limited forms of management decentralization.

Pedagogical questions regarding the production and diffusion of knowledge, linkage of social, cultural and natural environments with the teaching–learning process, and enhancement of the quality of education by making it relevant and interesting to the child are at the heart of the decentralization debate in education. There is, however, little evidence from state efforts in this direction. An approach whereby a programme begins with the decentralization of the teaching–learning process, evolving as it proceeds a facilitating administrative mechanism, as happened in the Hoshangabad Science Teaching Programme, is evident only in NGO efforts rather than through the efforts of the state.

It may be reasonable to conclude that the efforts of the previous decade, even if they have not significantly contributed to large-scale decentralization of education, have nevertheless provided vigour to explore and debate the question through an analysis of governance functions like funding, regulation and delivery on one hand, and the actors, state, market, and community, on the other, thus restoring the link between development, pedagogy and educational practice. And hopefully from such an analysis shall emerge a renewed policy perspective that goes beyond issues of management and administration and focuses on questions like equity, local and global knowledge systems and cultural plurism, and locates decentralization within these bounds.

REFERENCES

Dale, Roger (1997). 'The State and the Governance of Education' In Halsey, A. H., Hugh Lauder, Phillip Brown, Amy Stuart Wells (eds), *Education, Culture, Economy, Society*. Oxford University Press.

Dhar, T. N. (1997). 'Decentralized Management of Elementary Education: The Indian Experience'. In Govinda, R. (ed.), *Decentralisation of Educational Management: Experiences from South Asia*. International Institute of Educational Planning, Paris.

Govinda, R. (1999). 'Dynamics of Decentralized Management and Community Empowerment in Primary Education: A Comparative Analysis of Policy and Practice in Two States of India.' National Institute of Educational Planning and Administration, New Delhi.

Prosser, T. (1995). *The State, Constitutions and Implementing Economic Policy: Privatisation and Regulation in the UK, France and the USA*. Social and Legal Studies 4.

10 Role and Contribution of Non-Governmental Organizations in Basic Education*

Disha Nawani

CONTEXUALIZING NON-GOVERNMENTAL ORGANIZATIONS (NGOs) IN INDIA

NGOs today are widely acknowledged as the new, as well as important, political actors in the developing world (see Clarke 1998). The emergence of NGOs has been called the global 'associational revolution' that could prove to be as significant to the later twentieth century as the rise of the nation state was to the later nineteenth century (see Clarke 1998). NGOs in India have played a variety of complex roles and have collaborated with the state, its agencies, and officials in planning and implementing particular development programmes. However, they have as well, questioned the role of the state in perpetuating existing inequality and injustice, which tends to further marginalize the poor and the oppressed (see Tandon 1988, 37). The presence of NGOs is all-encompassing, from small grassroots groups working in small areas among the people to intermediary agencies operating at the global level. In accordance with their differing roles, NGOs have variously been called 'voluntary agencies', 'action groups', or 'activist groups'. The term NGO, therefore, does not denote a homogeneous category, even though it is used in a more or less uniform fashion. NGOs are complex and heterogeneous in nature and differ from each other in several respects.

Modern day NGOs in India have their predecessors in voluntary movements. For that matter, the idea of people's action is deeply rooted in India's history. Indian communities have, for centuries, found ways of joining hands at local level, to address shared concerns (see Chatterjee 1998, 282). The early years of the nineteenth century saw the beginning of reform movements which

were to exercise a great deal of influence on India's later history. Subsequently, the Societies Registration Act of 1860 was enacted which has regulated NGO activity ever since. It can then be said that this reflected the emergence of citizen's institutions in India (see Chatterjee 1998, 282). The most powerful example of early voluntary action was the Indian freedom movement, which Gandhi predicated on personal and community empowerment (see Chatterjee 1998, 288). While resources and help were sought from the business class, the essential strength came from thousands of dedicated workers and the support of the common man who felt that they were participating in the larger cause of national independence and reconstruction. Independence, in many ways, changed all this. The common citizen now expected the government to take care of all the problems (see Sethi 1988, 22–3).

The beginning of the 1990s saw a new trend in which voluntarism as an ideology came to be linked to liberalization as well as projected as an alternative. There are three reasons that point to this: first, the increasing preference shown by international financial institutions towards voluntarism; second, the increasing availability of funds to voluntary agencies through international financial agencies; and last, the projection of the primacy of development (see Mathias 1998, 61–2). Linked to liberalization has been the withdrawal of the state, which some feel should make way for the voluntary (viz. NGOs) on the one hand and free market forces on the other. In fact, the shift to NGOs has frequently been justified as an expression of the emphasis on popular participation or participatory development and has been much favoured by multilateral agencies (see Tandon 1996 as cited in Mathias 1998). Modern voluntarism is significantly different from conventional voluntarism in form, content, approach, role, and impact. Conventional voluntarism was primarily aimed at charity and relief, or

* This chapter is based on the research project, 'Role and Contribution of Non-Governmental Organisations in Basic Education in India', NIEPA–UNESCO (2000), New Delhi.

at best, social welfare and social reform. It sprang out of religiosity, generosity, and altruism. Idealism rather than ideology inspired it. While incorporating some elements of the conventional, modern voluntarism is based on ideology rather than mere idealism. Therefore, it aims at achieving development and social justice rather than relief and welfare. As a result, the tools, techniques, approaches, and objectives of modern voluntarism differ from those of the earlier version. Today's voluntarism strives to change the social, economic, and political positions of the poor, the deprived, the oppressed, and the weak. In the final analysis, therefore, it aims at redistribution of power, wealth, and status (see Bhatt 1995, 77).

It must be stated, however, that any discourse on voluntary agencies needs to take into account the character of the state and its relationship with voluntary agencies. In a democratic set up, the state plays an important role. The relationship between government and the voluntary sector in India is not new. As has already been stated, the relationship which a particular NGO shares with the existing government would also largely depend on the kind of activity it is engaged in. For example, NGOs which are either charity or welfare type may help in the implementation of concrete developmental programmes and enjoy the support of the government, but NGOs which concentrate on mobilizing marginalized sections around a specific issue which might challenge the distribution of power and resources in society or focus on 'empowerment' because of their political nature may sometimes lead to a clash of interests (see Rajasekhar 1999).

In the developing world, India has the second largest—more than 100,000—number of NGOs next to Brazil (see Clarke 1998, 36). The number of registered NGOs has grown enormously, particularly since the middle of the 1980s (see Tarkunde 1998, 18–19). It has been felt that the era of globalization and liberalization brought with it new NGO enthusiasts. Disillusionment with the public sector and India's own dismal record in providing quality social services to the poor prompted liberalization pundits, donor agencies, and banks to champion the cause of the private sector. For almost a decade now NGOs have been seen as the magic bullet that would cut through red-tapism, inefficiency, and corruption and reach much-needed health-care services, credit, education and so on to the poor. NGOs are seen as being more efficient and closer to the people (see Ramachandran 1996, 57). It has also been opined that people find in NGOs an effective alternative to implement programmes without middlemen, bureaucratic tangles, and red tapism. The approach had the charm of humanness (see Mukhopadhyay 1995, 57).

NGOs IN EDUCATION

There is no denying that over the years an essential link has come to be established between education and NGOs. With education being in the state it is in the country and the increasing reliance on NGOs' capacity and commitment to development work, the establishment of a bond between the two is not surprising. The manner in which to go about understanding this relationship and analysing the contribution of NGOs is quite challenging. What is the total number of NGOs working in this area? What is their proportion? What is the kind of work they are engaged in doing? What is their perception of education? Where does education fit in their scheme of things? Questions such as these need to be addressed and answered while analysing the contribution of NGOs to education.

How does one estimate the total number of NGOs active in the field of education? There is no comprehensive source or directory available which lists NGOs working specifically in the field of education, leave alone basic education. Though there are directories available that index NGOs in various categories, education being one of them, these categories are often overlapping or misleading. For instance, an NGO listed under the education category might have nothing to do with literacy or schooling or non-formal education (NFE), but may be interested in 'educating' or training people in AIDS awareness or wasteland development and is, therefore, listed under the subheading of education.

Further, aggregate numbers in different categories would perhaps be unable to provide a complete picture, as there are variations in their number across states as well. A list of NGOs published by Council for Advancement of People's Action and Rural Technology (CAPART) in 1990, for instance, showed that 470 NGOs were listed in West Bengal and 373 in Tamil Nadu as compared to 77 in Madhya Pradesh and 11 in Jammu and Kashmir. There are some states where there are many operating NGOs whereas there are others where they are scantily spread or virtually non-existent. There are within-state disparities as well. There could be several reasons for these disparities. For instance, the influence of missionary activity in an area, the supportive role of the government, the educational scenario in that state, and the presence of self-motivated people in an area.

It is important, therefore, that any statement about NGOs be qualified to avoid giving a false picture of reality. To reiterate, in a country as vast as India, with huge differences across its peoples and states, and NGOs characterized by a rich diversity of approaches, traditions, and activities, the task of generalization becomes truly problematic, if not impossible.

PROFILES OF NGOS IN BASIC EDUCATION

Though there are several NGOs working in the area of basic education, not all of them are equally focused on and committed to achieving the goals with regard to education. Analysis of the objectives and programmes of NGOs working in this area revealed that there were essentially three types of NGOs in basic education:

- Those for whom education is the central and the only concern and therefore, all their activities revolve around education.

- Those that pursue several objectives and consider education as one of the most integral. In their framework education has an important bearing on their overall developmental objectives.

- Those for whom education is one of several activities and not particularly a central or primary concern.

NGOs in the first category are totally devoted to education and develop no programmes besides education. For NGOs in the second category, education has an important role to play in improving the lives of the people they are trying to reach. The essential objective of these organizations is the development and empowerment of people to equip them to take on a stronger role in society. If education were not the central programme in their agendas, their larger objectives would remain incomplete without focusing on education. NGOs in the third category, inspite of working in the area of education, do not attach so much importance to it. It is simply one of the many programmes initiated or implemented by them. The aim of this typology is not to grade and place NGOs in different hierarchical categories but simply to understand that there may be a large number of organizations working in the area of basic education, but the importance they accord to education in their overall work agendas may greatly vary.

WHAT DO NGOS IN BASIC EDUCATION DO?

NGOs' Vision of Education and Objectives

NGOs have varying perspectives of education and attach different meanings to it. There are some NGOs that regard education as an important end in itself. In this case, their objectives are specific as well, like teaching literacy and numeracy skills to people, establishing educational structures like schools, or creating NFE centres. There are other NGOs for whom education is a means to an end, i.e. they emphasize the 'empowering' effects of education and enable people to develop a critical, questioning attitude, be it towards unequal distribution of resources in society, or towards existing gender or cultural stereotypes, or towards classroom processes and learning per se (see Box 10.1).

Education also assumes a different meaning when it is given to groups of people who have special needs, or when NGOs cater to people who are in a disadvantageous position in society, or reside in a particular area, which is either geographically isolated or poorly developed. The aim of some NGOs is not simply to enrol children in schools, but to see that the education they get in schools is something that makes sense to them, something to which they can relate and something which gives them joy. Therefore, there are NGOs that concentrate on redefining the school curriculum, redesigning textbooks, and also training teachers in progressive and child-centred pedagogy. It is important to study the meaning of education employed by different organizations, for that in turn shapes their goals, strategies, and activities.

Box 10.1

Education for Empowerment: Case of Nirantar and Agragamee

The focus of Nirantar is decisively on women. Gender issues permeate all its activities. Education for Nirantar, therefore, acquires a meaning that goes beyond imparting literacy and numeracy skills to women. Agragamee works with tribal communities in Orissa. 'Banda' and 'Kashipur' are the places where Nirantar and Agragamee work respectively. Banda is one of the most backward districts of UP. It is dacoit-ridden and is marked by extreme poverty, low literacy levels, and a high degree of violence against women. A significant proportion of its population belongs to the scheduled castes and tribes. Kashipur was deliberately and consciously chosen as an area of work by Agragamee as it had a population comprising 70 per cent tribals and 20 per cent Harijans. The area, at the time of Agragamee's setting up there, was underdeveloped in terms of infrastructure and communication facilities and other basic services. Literacy level was very low and the network of educational facilities very poor. Incidences of exploitation, bondage, and molestation were also quite high. Nirantar views education as a tool to empower women. Agragamee views education as a means to enhance the self-confidence and knowledge base of tribals. The essential aim of both these organizations is to enhance the status and self-esteem of the people it serves and enable them to critically view their socio-cultural environment.

Preferred Sectors of Work in Basic Education

Most NGOs work in a variety of sectors. This also means that they cater to the needs of different age groups at the same time. Among the sectors, preschool and NFE clearly emerged as preferred areas of work for a number of NGOs (see Table 10.1). NGOs also work for specific target groups from socio-economically disadvantaged sections of society (see Table 10.2). There are a few NGOs working with street children as well. Box 10.2 provides examples of two NGOs in the area of working children with their different perceptions of NFE. Children with special needs are, relatively speaking, still a neglected group. It is quite possible that there are several NGOs working for the general welfare of children with special needs, but they do not attach so much priority to educating them.

A large majority of NGOs were found to be working for children. A large number of them were also reaching out to the educational needs of girls and women. While there were also a number of organizations working for street children, adults, and socio-economically deprived

Box 10.2

Common Goal but Contrasting Strategies: The MV Foundation and the Indian Institute of Education (IIE)

Both the MV Foundation in Andhra Pradesh and the IIE in Maharashtra focus on the educational needs of working children but there is a stark contrast in their beliefs and manner of functioning. The IIE believes that NFE is a good substitute for formal school education for working children who find it difficult to attend school during their regular working hours. NFE in their case is carefully thought-out and a creatively and sensitively designed learning process so that it relates to children's lives and is of use to them. The MV Foundation on the other hand, is totally against the concept of NFE. According to them, NFE implies letting children remain child labourers. Even though children are given education, it is of a type which does not require them to leave their jobs, and, therefore, they continue to be child labourers. The IIE believes that NFE is not only a viable but also a desirable alternative for working children as there is nothing wrong in a child working and that context itself becomes a 'learning context', so there is no reason why a child should be weaned away from it.

TABLE 10.1
Sectorwise Ranking of NGOs (N=75)*

Sectors	Present	1	%	2	%	3	%	4	5
Pre-school	13	18	24	13	17.33	11	14.67	04	02
Formal primary schooling	12	09	12	10	13.33	13	17.33	09	06
NFE	10	23	30.6	13	17.33	09	12	04	02
Adult literacy	11	07	9.33	10	13.33	13	17.33	11	07
Post literacy	04	03	4	06	8	05	6	14	13

Note: * These five sectors were to be ranked by the respondents in terms of their work areas. However, some of the NGOs simply ticked right across them instead of ranking them. These responses were clubbed in the 'Present' category in the table. The numbers indicate the rank orders.

groups of people, there were few organizations working for tribals, and even fewer working for children with special needs.

TABLE 10.2
NGOs Catering to Specific Target Groups

Population	Number of NGOs (N#75)	Percentage
Children	63	84
Girls/women	57	76
Adults	50	66.7
Socio-economically deprived*	46	61.3
Street children	39	52
Tribals	32	42.7
Handicapped/special needs	25	33.3

Note: *Though it is assumed that most of the NGOs work for people from socio-economically deprived sections of society, it was included as a separate category which meant that this criterion was the crucial deciding factor for an NGO, irrespective of the age/gender composition of those people.

What could be the reason for a large majority of NGOs working with children? No doubt, children constitute the most important segment because they represent the future of society and neglecting their needs would, perhaps, be fatal to society. A majority of the NGOs were also working specifically with women because there is still huge gender disparity in this country in all spheres including education; therefore, there is a 'perceived need' to cater exclusively to them. Adults constitute another important section, though it is still not very clear whether these NGOs run literacy programmes for them or their education programmes are combined with an income-generating component.

Geographical Areas Reached

With three-fourths of India's population residing in villages, rural areas receive relatively more attention from the NGO sector as compared to urban slums and tribal and hilly areas. NGOs that base themselves deliberately in specific geographical areas try and mould their educational programme in accordance with the needs of local people, keeping in view the special characteristics of that region. This means that rather than following a uniform programme for everyone, NGOs design special and relevant programmes in consonance with the needs of the people and the world around them. This feature is unique to NGOs. They pick out areas for work which they feel are either neglected by the government or need special attention on account of their particular geographical locations. See Table 10.3 for a geographical distribution of NGOs.

TABLE 10.3
Area-wise (Geographical) Distribution of NGOs

Area	Number of NGOs (N#75)	Percentage
Rural	62	83
Urban slums	34	45
Tribal areas	34	45
Hilly regions	25	33

One finds a mixed distribution of NGOs in different geographical areas. Most of the NGOs studied were working in a number of areas—running similar, or probably different programmes in them. There were, however, a few NGOs which were working exclusively in one area (see Table 10.4).

TABLE 10.4
NGOs Working in One Specific Area

Area	Number of NGOs	Percentage
Rural	16 (N#62)	25.8
Urban slums	04 (N#34)	11.7
Tribal areas	02 (N#25)	08.0

Note: The 'N' in each case signifies the total number of organizations that claimed to work in these specific areas.

Thrust Areas in Basic Education

NGOs have several thrust areas (see Table 10.5 for numerical distribution in thrust areas). While issues such as improving the quality of education, training teachers in sound and creative pedagogy, and improving infrastructural facilities do figure in NGOs' priorities, issues such as community mobilization and literacy promotion still occupy a predominant place in their work. This, however, does not mean that the community does not perceive formal education to be an important need or requires any convincing about it. It could as well reflect either some constraints, financial or otherwise, on their part, or even a mismatch between the education provided by the system and its perceived relevance for the lives of the people. Literacy is also a major thrust area and in the light of the fact that almost half the country's

population is still illiterate, it is a need which cannot be underestimated. However, focus on literacy alone is unlikely to serve its purpose in the long run. There are NGOs concerned with improving the quality of education, training teachers, and evolving innovative curricula and teaching–learning material for learners, but their numbers are not large. Box 10.3 provides an example of one such.

TABLE 10.5
Focus Areas in Basic Education

Focus area	Number of NGOs (N#75)
Mobilizing community	60
Imparting literacy	54
Enhancing quality	49
Training teachers	34
Providing additional facilities	33
Providing teaching–learning material (TLM)	24

Enhancing the quality of education is still not a top priority for the majority of NGOs, as basic needs still remain to be fulfilled, but increasingly, there are a number of organizations for whom this has become one of the most important considerations guiding their work.

BOX 10.3
Eklavya: Pioneering Work in Curriculum Building

Eklavya maintains a strong link between the field reality and the world of academics. All its initiatives, be it in Science or Social Science at school level are academically sound, and yet, firmly rooted in field reality. The integrated model of teaching which it has evolved, combines in it a learner-centred curriculum and innovative textbooks with an open-book examination system. By means of a child-centred curriculum and pedagogically sound textbooks, children are taught several ways in which information can be used and interpreted. The teachers are also oriented and trained in this methodology. Eklavya's Hoshangabad Science Teaching Programme (HSTP) liberated science from the lifeless pages of textbooks and took it closer to children—their hands, minds, and hearts. Science was understood for its true worth—as an everyday experience to be lived with, to feel and enjoy, to question and discover, rather than something that was to be read, memorized for examinations, and subsequently forgotten.

Financial Issues

NGOs receive financial support for their activities from both government and private funding organizations. Government—both state and central, and funding agencies—both national and international, are often the main channels through which money for different activities flows. There are some NGOs that depend entirely on foreign funding, whereas there are others which depend on government funding and avoid taking grants from any foreign organization. While there are fewer bureaucratic hassles in getting money from international donors, there is also the fear of local needs getting submerged by international priorities. While there is a fear of loss of autonomy in receiving money from government sources, there is also the advantage of legitimizing its activities by receiving money from the government of the country in which they are based. There are a few organizations that generate their own resources as well. Charity constitutes a very important source of funds for many organizations. The decision to take money from either internal sources (could be the government or local funding organizations) or foreign funding agencies is determined both by the policies of that particular organization and practical considerations.

The annual budget for basic education in the seventy-five organisations studied during 1997–8 ranged from as low as Rs 2000 to as high as Rs 25 million. This huge gap indicates the vast variation in their scale of operation. This also shows that NGOs that claim to be working in education could be actually spending as little as Rs 2000 per annum on their basic education programmes. Where does one really place these organizations? Do they really merit being counted among organizations working in the area of education?

An important criterion of the extent to which NGOs work in education is the proportion of their total budget which is spent on education (see Table 10.6). It was found that only one-third of the organizations spent more than 50 per cent of their budgets on education. This shows their commitment to education. However, this is not the complete picture, as there were also organizations whose education budget was more than 50 per cent but who spent very little in actual terms on it, which means that their total budgets were very low. At the same time, there were organizations whose education budgets was not more than 50 per cent but who spent considerable amounts on it.

What does all this indicate? It has been seen that there are NGOs that spend more than 50 per cent of their budgets on education but because their budgets are small, they actually get to spend very little on education. Does it imply that these NGOs need to be supported if work in education is to be promoted? On the other hand, there are also NGOs for whom education is not a top priority area but who spend considerable amounts of money on education. Can their contribution be belittled? It is also possible that these NGOs adopt a holistic approach to development, and in that scheme, education is perceived as one of the integral constituents.

Another question that one needs to ponder is the extent to which money really reflects the earnestness with which a particular programme is being conducted. It could also be possible that an NGO actually facilitates the community in undertaking their own programmes or generating resources for them. There is also no guarantee that an NGO that spends a certain amount of money on education in a particular year may be able to spend the same amount the following year. Financial grants given to organizations are often time- or project-bound.

In-house Generation of Resources

Apart from funds from external sources like the government, funding organizations, and individuals, NGOs adopt a variety of other ways to generate resources for their activities and ongoing programmes. A large majority of NGOs said that they still relied on charity and public contributions for in-house generation of resources/funds. Membership fees and sale of material produced by NGOs were also stated to be important sources of revenue. Table 10.7 indicates that quite a large number of NGOs these days strive to create their own sources of financial grant rather than depending solely on external funding agencies which are generally not sustainable long-term sources, but charity and donations still constitute the bulk of the alternate source.

TABLE 10.6
Proportion of Budget Allocated by NGOs to Education in 1997–8

Share of budget allocated to education	Number of NGOs (N#66)*	Per cent
Less than 10%	05	6.7
Between 10 and 25%	24	32
Between 25 and 50%	14	18.7
Above 50%	23	30.7

Note: * 'N' indicates the number of NGOs that responded to this question.

TABLE 10.7
Sources of In-house Generation of Resources by NGOs

Methods	Number of NGOs (N#75)	Percentage
Charity and public contributions	62	83
Membership fees	40	53
Sale of material	31	41
Fees from parents	03	4
Agricultural produce	02	2.7
Training programmes	02	2.7
Consultancy fees	02	2.7
Loans	01	1.3

What is the Contribution of NGOs to Basic Education?

As stated in the previous section, if one refers to NGOs' reach and contribution in terms of numbers alone, it will perhaps be a little difficult to appreciate their contribution. The majority of them are small organizations, limited in their reach, with small budgets, either trying to implement government-sponsored schemes or working towards enhancing the quality of education and experimenting with new models of teaching and learning. Their aim is not to create structures parallel to those of the government but to supplement and strengthen government's initiatives in providing education to all its citizens.

NGOs have stepped in where there is a need, i.e. either some sections of society are being deprived of education or people of a particular geographical area are educationally backward. Literacy is provided where people lack even basic literacy skills. NFE is made available to children who work, at a time and place convenient to them.

Besides stepping in areas which need support, NGOs also create their own teaching–learning models, be it in the formal or the non-formal learning environment. In fact, NGOs' biggest strength perhaps lies in innovations they bring about in the education process. Eklavya's science and social science programme, Nirantar's attempt at empowering women through a relevant and meaningful curriculum, BGVS' strategy of putting literacy on the national agenda and linking it up with everyday livelihood problems, the IIE's integrated model for NFE and MV Foundation's effective mainstreaming of child labourers into formal government schools are just a few examples of successful interventions, amongst many others.

NGOs voice the concerns of people, particularly the oppressed. They form a part of the organized front of civil society but may not represent it across the board. For, it is well known that some of them follow implicitly different political ideologies and cater to different interest groups. Questions are often raised about the extent to which they can represent the voice of the people, being totally dependent on international funding agencies. It should, however, be noted that to draw monetary support from an international agency may not necessarily amount to compromising on one's goals. There could be a convergence of goals between local NGOs and the international agency funding them. On the other hand, NGOs which depend on the national government alone for finance may also have problems in acting independently. While it may be difficult to appreciate the role of NGOs as conscience keepers for all times to come, it cannot be denied that they do represent people's voices, concerns, and initiatives.

Emerging Issues

Dynamics Between Government and Non-government Agencies

NGOs in India have worked in collaboration with the government, both at state and national levels, and a large number of them receive funds from the government and even implement government-sponsored schemes. However, it is also true that NGOs have, at times, worked in opposition to the government, critiquing its programmes and offering alternative models of development. In terms of their relationship with the government NGOs can fall in one of three categories:

• NGOs that deliberately seek to work with the government to either seek legitimacy for their programmes or reach out to a larger number of people, rather than create separate niches for themselves.

• NGOs that have their own goals and pursue them independently of the government. Some such were founded even before the formation of the independent Indian government and continue working towards the fulfilment of their objectives without particularly bothering about the government's policy and programmes.

• NGOs that are critical of government machinery and encourage people to think about their position in society. They essentially work as conscience keepers of society and represent people's concerns through their actions.

The relationship between the Indian government and the non-governmental sector in the area of basic education is showing signs of an emerging partnership. This is because the government realizes and has reiterated in its official policy documents that the magnitude of the problem in the education sector is far too large to be resolved by a single delivery system, be it public or private. The non-governmental sector also realizes and believes that the final and ultimate responsibility of providing education to all its citizens rests on the Indian government, no matter how many profit or non-profit initiatives emerge in between. Education sector NGOs, even if they are critical of the efforts of the government, essentially perceive themselves in a partnership role with the government. Be it receiving funds from the government or implementing government-sponsored schemes or creating innovative and alternative learning models, they see themselves as supporting government initiatives in fulfilling the objective of providing education to all. However, this relationship may not always be smooth.

The NGOs studied here saw themselves in multiple roles (see Table 10.8). The majority of the NGOs did point out that their role was independent of that of the government as they wished to bring about innovations in education and carry out new experiments. Over half of them also felt that their focus was on areas neglected by the Government of India. However, an even larger majority saw their role as that of assisting the government in implementing its programmes. Whatever the case may be, the NGOs—at least a large majority of them—did see a complementarity in their work with that of the government. The idea was to essentially to reach out to people and to educate them. Whether the government was unable to fulfil its obligations towards the people, or lacked the political will to do so, NGOs largely saw themselves in a role which strengthened the government's efforts.

TABLE 10.8
Education Sector NGOs' Perception of Their Role vis-à-vis the Government

Perceived role	Number of NGOs (N#75)	Percentage
Assistance to government	47	62.7
Intervention	47	62.7
Innovation	42	56
Neglected areas	38	50.7

However, emergence of international funding organizations as major players in the field of education in India has influenced the nature of NGOs' investment and work in education. NGOs now need not depend on government resources alone. There has also been a spurt in NGO activity after their role has been recognized by these agencies and the financial grants have been greatly enhanced. The extent to which NGOs are guided by the terms and conditions set for funding by these international funding agencies remains to be explored. With the corporate sector wanting to invest in education, the dynamics between NGOs and conventional funding organizations might undergo further change.

Relationship between NGOs and Funding Sources

Many international funding organizations not only provide funds but also work jointly with local NGOs towards achieving the desired goals. Monetary support cannot be undermined as it determines and affects the scale of their operations. Research findings showed that there were some NGOs whose education budgets were more than 50 per cent of their total budgets, but who spent very little actual amount on education, as their total budgets were very small. These organizations accorded high priority to education in their scheme of things but were unable to contribute substantially because of the paucity of funds at their disposal.

NGOs have often complained of insufficient and irregular supply of money from government sources. Their projects are often time-bound and the grants stop once the project is over. Short–term grants lend ad hocism to their programmes and NGOs are constantly worried about finding the next donor organization for continuing their programmes.

By taking money from the international donors, does one run the risk of compromising on local needs and priorities? There are international organizations that generate resources from the governments of their own countries or private charitable trusts and are essentially formed for developmental purposes. Multinational organizations like the AKF (see Box 10.4), Action-Aid, and OXFAM have cross-cutting concerns. Is it not possible that local NGOs and international organizations have similar orientations and developmental objectives? Does receiving money from the government of one's own country have no strings attached? These are questions which defy unambiguous answers but need to be probed further.

Sustainability and Replicability

The efforts of NGOs are often criticized on account of their having little scope of replicability and long–term sustainability. The questions that need to be pondered in this context are many. Does the onus of initiating an innovation and then sustaining it for years to come and replicating it in larger contexts rest solely on NGOs or should the government take up the responsibility of ensuring the longevity of such programmes? What kind of support do NGOs need to ensure the long-term implications of these efforts? Is monetary support the only issue to be resolved? Should not the efforts of NGOs be appreciated and recognized for their worth and given due credit? How much space should NGOs be given by the government so that their creativity is not throttled? Should innovative endeavours of NGOs be confined to separate educational enclaves or should they be grounded in the larger social system? Would the institutionalization of innovations amount to their routinization as well? NGOs represent a plurality of voices, visions, and efforts; would replicating a successful programme from a certain socio-cultural milieu in another be as effective and meaningful? There are several such issues and dilemmas to be resolved which really need in-depth examination. At this juncture it is simply pertinent to raise questions that can give pointers to directions for research.

Box 10.4

Aga Khan Foundation (AKF): Educational Reform Through Partnership

The AKF is essentially an umbrella organization. It funds different organizations to carry out its various programmes. For its School Improvement Programme, it has four project partners—the Bodh Shiksha Samiti in Jaipur, the Aga Khan Education Service (India) [AKES(I)], Centre for Educational Management and Development in Delhi (CEMD), and the Narsee Monjee Institute of Management Studies (NMIMS) in Mumbai.

The AKES(I), which is a part of the Aga Khan Development Network works towards establishing quality schools. The aim is to promote access to education and create appropriate and joyful learning conditions so as to retain students. The CEMD carries out its project for 'Institutional Development' with a focus on enhancing the management inputs in schools in ten Delhi-based schools. These schools cater to the socio-economically and the historically disadvantaged communities. The CEMD adopts a 'systems approach' to study the entire system in order to understand the direct impact of any changes as well as other consequences on the quality of schools.

The NMIMS also believes that the quality of school education can be improved by strengthening the institution in terms of its management. It provides management inputs to nine schools in Mumbai and eight schools in Ahmedabad. It provides guidelines and direction to principals of the schools and trustees who are mutually responsible for fructifying the change and maintaining it. It follows an 'Organizational Development' approach, whereby the resources focused on management development are principals, 'core teams', and 'problem-focused activities'.

The Bodh Shiksha Samiti, the fourth partner of the AKF started its work in the mid 1980's as an initiative for providing primary school education to children of the urban poor in the slums of Jaipur. It was later expanded to seven slums. Approaches developed by the Bodh over the years reiterate the importance of community and parental participation in educating their children. Curriculum and pedagogic practices evolved by the Bodh seek to make education interesting and activity oriented.

The AKF is one of the premier organizations working in the area of basic education. All its partners have the same goal, i.e. improving the quality of education, though their perspectives and strategies to achieve them differ from each other. However, improving the quality of education in schools with the aim of trying out innovations, making the teaching–learning process joyful, interesting and a meaningful experience for both teachers and students, and maintaining the sustainability and replicability of such efforts is the thrust of all the project partners of the AKF.

With regard to sustainability and long-term implications of NGO activity, finance emerges as a major hurdle. NGOs often complain of inadequate and irregular supplies of funds. Many well-meaning programmes have had to be suspended due to financial constraints. Funding of NGOs by government and funding agencies is an issue which needs to be sorted out and a mechanism evolved so that NGOs doing good work do not get disheartened and leave midway on account of not being able to generate enough resources for their activities.

LOOKING AHEAD

It is now well recognized that there are many NGOs in the field of basic education working in their individual capacities towards realizing their objectives. Though their reach is limited, their budgets small, and their number few, their contribution is slowly being appreciated and recognized in India. On one hand, there are organizations that are repeatedly being written about, and on the other hand, there are those that anonymously do their work, some even deliberately avoiding any kind of publicity.

NGOs have not only managed to make many more people literate than what would have been possible through government structures alone, they have also tried to critically examine deeper questions of the 'type' and 'relevance' of education for learners. While some organizations have helped the government in replicating its programmes, others have even evolved alternative models of both non-formal and formal systems of education. Whatever be the diversity and complexity in the work of these organizations, there is no doubt about their contribution in taking India closer to the goal of EFA, be it in terms of a quantitative expansion or a qualitative change in the meaning and process of education.

The question that arises is how much space should NGOs be given in society to pursue their goals? NGOs represent a plurality of efforts, whereas the official education structure in India is essentially a uniform monolithic structure that finds it difficult to respond to differences which exists among people. It is the heterogeneous nature of Indian society and the democratic nature of its polity that makes the role of NGOs even more significant, for only small, local efforts of the NGOs kind, which the community closely identifies with, can make education a personal and enriching experience for everyone. There are two issues which emerge in this context.

• The government recognizes the contribution of NGOs and NGOs readily join hands with the government but ground reality shows that a large majority of NGOs simply replicate governmental schemes and programmes. What relevance does this kind of a partnership have for the future? Is the true potential of NGOs being recognized in this manner? A partnership which constrains NGOs to work in a limited direction, towards pre-determined goals leads to an underutilization of their potential and a negation of a meaningful partnership.

• The government in India is itself a major source of funds for NGOs, but it is observed that there is a relationship of 'control' and 'mistrust' between the two and not one of 'trust' and 'support'. The government, on its part, needs to recognize that its role is not simply to grant monetary support to NGOs so that they can implement its schemes but that it should promote new ideas and experiments as well. Being suspicious about NGO activities and monitoring the utilizations of grants should certainly not be its principal role. NGOs, on their part, also need to understand that simply implementing Government sponsored schemes is not a true expression of their potential. Working in isolation and shying away from forming meaningful partnerships with other NGOs will also limit their efforts. For a genuine partnership to emerge, both sides should be willing to cooperate with each other, keeping in view the larger social mission of EFA, thereby evolving new programmes, creating alternative models for teaching and learning, reaching the unreached, and abolishing all differences among people with regard to basic education.

Thus, the NGOs' role is neither to wipe out illiteracy nor to ensure that all children go to school, but essentially to play a catalytic role in mobilizing people and providing innovative thrusts in the education system.

REFERENCES

Bhatt, Anil (1995). 'Asian NGOs in Development: Their Role and Impact in Government-NGO Relations'. *Asia: Prospects and Challenges for People Centred Development*.

Chatterjee, Ashoke (1998). 'NGOs: An Alternative Democracy.' In Karlekar, Hiranmay (ed.). *Independent India: The First 50 Years*. Oxford University Press, New Delhi.

Clarke, Gerald (1998). 'Non-governmental Organizations (NGOs) and Politics in the Developing World'. *Political Studies*, XLVI.

Mathias, Edward (1998). 'The Emerging Confrontation Between PRIs and NGOs.' In Raj, S. J., L. Sebasti and Edward Mathias (eds) *People's Power and Panchayati Raj: Theory and Practice*. Indian Social Institute, New Delhi.

Mukhopadhyay, Alok (1995). 'Upscaling NGO Activity—Indian experience'. *IASSI Quarterly*, vol. 14, nos 1 and 2.

Rajasekhar, D. (ed.) (1999). *Decentralised Government and NGOs: Issues, Strategies and Ways Forward*. Concept, New Delhi.

Ramachandran, Vimala (1996). 'NGOs in the Time of Globalization'. *Seminar*, No. 447.

Sethi, Harsh (1988). 'Trends Within'. *Seminar*, No. 348, August.

Tandon, Rajesh (1988). 'Growing Stateism'. *Seminar*, No. 348, August.

Tarkunde, V. M. (1998). 'The Present Scenario: A Bird's eye-view'. In Raj, S. J., L. Sebasti and Edward Mathias (eds), *People's Power and Panchayati Raj: Theory and Practice*. Indian Social Institute, New Delhi.

11 Private Schools and Universal Elementary Education

Anuradha De, Manabi Majumdar, Meera Samson and Claire Noronha

This chapter looks at private sector involvement in school education with particular focus on UEE and with special reference to the education of disadvantaged sections of the population. The introductory section briefly touches on the various types of private initiatives present in the schooling sector and raises crucial issues regarding these types of schools. The second section is a statistical overview of the sector. It summarizes available evidence about size, locational distribution, growth, and social reach and its impact on universalization of elementary education. The third section takes a closer look at private schools, focusing on rural schools in four northern states, all crucial for UEE, and enables us to take advantage of qualitative and quantitative data. It also draws heavily from several micro studies on elementary schooling which have some bearing on privatization in this sector.

INTRODUCTION

The 1990s in India have seen growing disenchantment with the government's involvement in many fields, ranging from manufacturing steel and generating electricity to running schools and hospitals. Government is seen as a high cost provider of low quality goods and services, smothered in its own mammoth size, its rules and regulations, and its proneness to corruption. Its lack of progress in the field of literacy and basic school education is seen as yet another example of this. It is not surprising that the call for greater involvement of the private sector and for a reduced role of the government in providing goods and services is seen to apply to schooling as well. In this chapter we will examine how far this expectation is valid, i.e. how far the private sector is able and willing to shoulder the burden of providing education for all (EFA). In order to do that we have first to understand the nature of the private sector in education in India, especially in the context of EFA. This is a difficult task, owing to paucity of research on the private sector in school education as a whole. Barring a few notable exceptions (see Bashir 1994, Dreze and Gazdar 1996, Duraisamy et al. 1996, Govinda and Varghese 1993, Kingdon 1996(a), Majumdar and Vaidyanathan 1995, Mathew 1990, Shatrugna 1988, Tilak 1991), crucial issues about the involvement of the private sector in school education today, remain under-researched, despite the current preoccupation with privatization.

Private schools have a right to exist under the Constitution, irrespective of whether they are or are not recognized and aided by the state. In fact, diversity in educational provision has always been accepted and acknowledged in the country; educational efforts of individuals of vision, of community groups, of leaders of various social reform movements as well as of the government have worked in tandem; communities have operated schools alongside government schools, sometimes to offer education with particular ethnic, religious, political, or other orientation. Thus a pluralistic framework of education and a variety of delivery mechanisms within this have been in place for a long while. However, private educational initiatives have gained new prominence in recent years, though in a somewhat different way from the old—as substitutes for, not supplements to, government schools. There is now a popular perception that increased parental demand for education on the one hand and the declining quality of government schools on the other will inevitably lead to greater reliance on the private sector. Therefore, the question is not one of permitting private schooling but of its promotion or otherwise, and even, by extension, one of revival or retreat of the state-supported school system.

DIFFERENT TYPES OF PRIVATE SCHOOLS

As a starting point the several kinds of private schools and some important issues regarding them will briefly be delineated. This is important because of the sheer heterogeneity of the private sector in schooling, a heterogeneity which spans the entire range of socio-economic categories in India as well as diverse religious and ethnic groups, and which extends to the nature of funding in these schools.

Private Unaided (PUA) Schools

These schools are privately owned and funded, and rely, more or less, on user finance, unless they are schools which are run on philanthropic basis. Annual fees could range from Rs 180 to Rs 50,000 or more, thus showing that they cover the entire socio-economic spectrum. Not so long ago this used to be considered an elitist sector, catering to the upper classes and offering a very expensive brand of education (see Varghese 1993). Research in recent years contradicts these impressions (see Bashir, 1994; Kingdon 1996a).

This sector was also thought to have a negligible presence, particularly in rural areas. Drawing on some primary survey evidence and challenging the reliability of the official education statistics, Kingdon, among a handful of others, strongly contradicts the elitist picture of private schools. In broad outline, she suggests that official statistics, by excluding unrecognized schools from their enumeration, grossly underestimate the role of the private sector, especially that of self-financing schools in elementary education and that fee-charging education is extremely heterogeneous, 'drawing its clientele from across the social spectrum' (Kingdon 1996b, 3307). Neither is this phenomenon, she continues, confined to urban areas alone. If private schools vary so widely as to be accessible to the highly privileged as well as some of those far less privileged, it seems logical to assume that schools may also range from the 'luxury class' variant to the almost impoverished variant. The issue of user finance and quality of schooling acquires a sharper edge against the current background of private schooling. While it is often believed that disadvantaged sections can avail of schools charging low fees sponsored by philanthropists, the PROBE survey did not produce such heartening evidence (see PROBE Team 1999). Reputed NGOs who have been working with disadvantaged people over decades also say that the scale of their work can never hope to replace that of the government.

Private Aided (PA) Schools

These schools are funded almost wholly (90–95 per cent) by the government but management is private. In some states, the government sought the help of philanthropists to expand the educational system. In other states, philanthropists stepped in first and the government came in later. Basically, sponsors would provide the building and facilities while the government meets staff salaries and some of the other recurring costs. The schools would benefit from the flexibility and accountability of private management while fees could be kept low enough for the poorer sections because of the government subsidies: in effect, a way of enlisting community support and management and ensuring access to all income groups.

In the early decades after Independence such philanthropists/charitable trusts did open aided schools, though these were generally in urban areas. The schools did great service in education and many such schools still continue to do so. Interestingly, in some of the educationally more advanced states like Kerala and Tamil Nadu, the aided school system has a strong presence. The aided sector dominates school education in Kerala, managing nearly 60 per cent of total schools at elementary level and accounts for 60 per cent of expenditure by the state according to 1994–5 reports. In Tamil Nadu, too, aided schools accounted for about 20 per cent of elementary schools in 1993. The proportion is much higher for upper-primary schools.

Today, we need a clearer understanding of the aided school system, particularly since the health of the system varies greatly from state to state. If fiscal constraints are the reason that the government seeks collaboration with the private sector, then aided schools with their high quotient of government expenditure do not appear to be a solution. However, this may be balanced against the greater efficiency of these schools. In any case, since these schools also appear to have both coverage and equity, there is need for understanding the sector.

Religious, Caste, and Linguistic Schools

A great many schools set up in the decades immediately before and after Independence had the motive of providing educational facilities to particular caste, linguistic, or religious groups and fulfilled their promise with dedication. There were both aided and unaided schools with such orientation. Religious entrepreneurship has long been associated with private schooling and is trusted by adherents of that religion, and often even by members of the general public to propagate desired moral values/cultural orientation. Fifty years after Independence, schools run by Hindu missionary orders like the Ramakrishna Mission as well as Muslim and Christian schools are very much in evidence. There are also schools run by other religious groups.

Many of these schools are aided. Within this sector too there is great heterogeneity and its size and scope are perhaps not fully understood. Religious minorities enjoy certain privileges under the law and have thus been able to avoid the problems of centralized recruitment, etc. which have begun to worry private aided schools in many states. Again it is not clear how far these groups are willing to take up the cause of universal elementary education (UEE) on a large scale, or even willing to direct it.

A STATISTICAL OVERVIEW

As we have seen in the previous section, it is simplistic to talk of the private sector in schooling as if it were a homogeneous body which follows certain well-defined standards, or definite sources of funding and clientele. But differentiation within the private sector has not been the target of macro-level studies so far. It is still possible to get an idea of the range and influence of private schooling through official statistics, which generally refer to three categories of schools: government and local body schools, PA schools, and PUA schools.

Growth of Private Elementary Schooling

Culling data from various educational surveys conducted by the National Council of Educational Research and Training (NCERT), Figure 11.1 summarizes evidence on the relative size and growth of government (i.e. government and local body), PA, and PUA elementary (i.e. primary and upper-primary/middle) schools over a

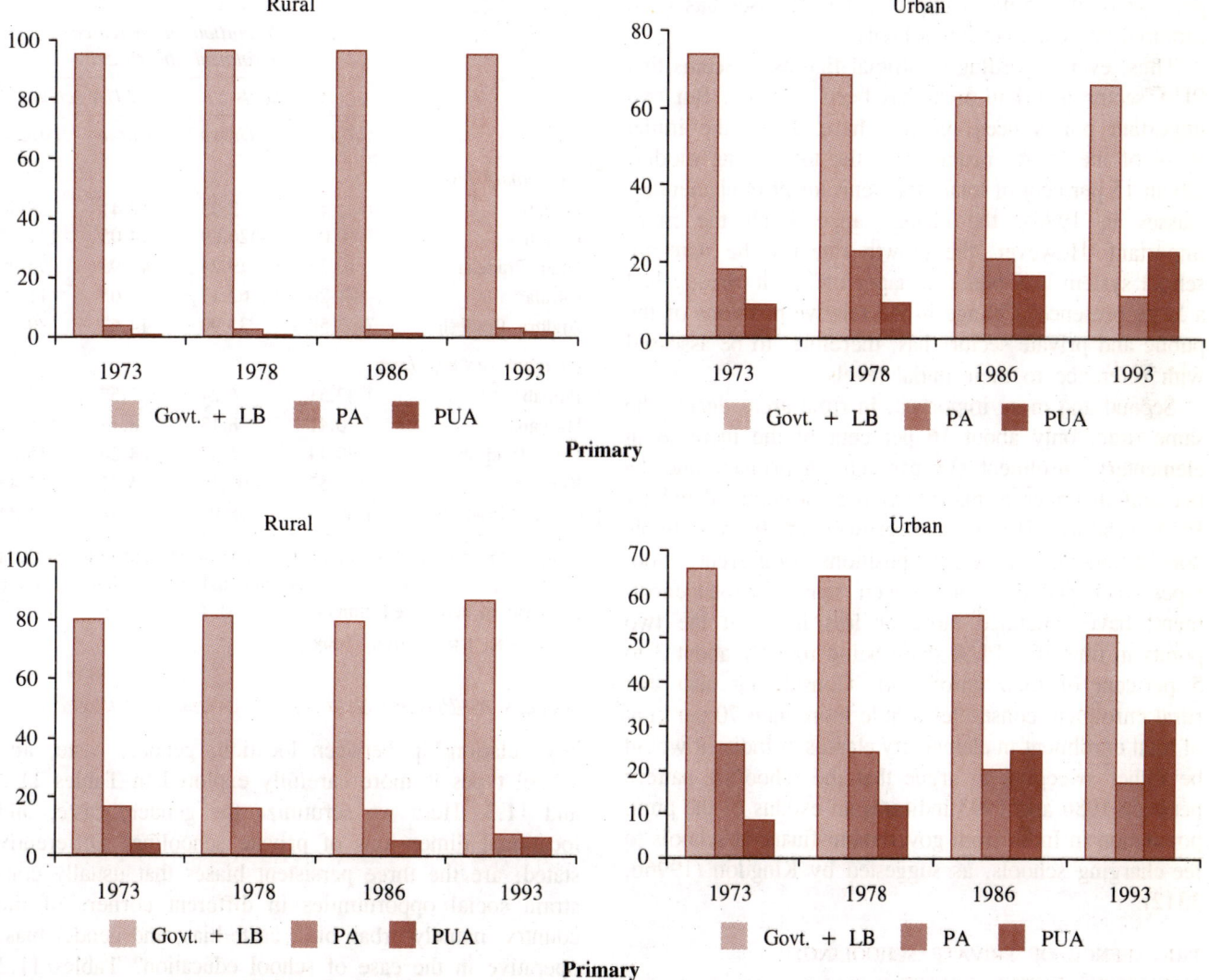

FIGURE 11.1: Recognized Elementary Schools under Different Managements
(in per cent)

period between 1973 and 1993. Clearly, in rural India the share of PUA schools as a per cent of all elementary schools is insignificant; PA schools too have only a limited presence. Hence rural India, according to these figures, still depends almost entirely on government schools. In urban areas, however, the size of the private sector, in particular of PUA schools, is far from negligible and has grown perceptibly over time.

When we compare the growth in enrolments in different school types over time, it appears that in urban India the growing demand for schooling has largely been catered to by the PUA schools. Coming to specifics, between 1986 and 1993 (the Fifth and Sixth Educational Survey reference years, respectively), in urban India nearly 51 per cent of the total increase in enrolment in elementary classes has been absorbed by the PUA school sector. Disaggregating further, 60 per cent of urban enrolment growth in primary classes and about 37 per cent of the same in upper-primary classes has been captured by fee-charging schools.

Thus, even according to official figures, it seems that PUA sector in urban areas has been growing. But two important points need mention here. First, the initial share of the PUA enrolment in the total being modest (about 15 per cent of total urban enrolment in elementary classes in 1986), the change appears all the more important. However, the growth rate for the state-run school system was bound to taper off, as it already had a large presence. Change in the relative positions of the public and private sectors has, therefore, to be assessed with reference to their initial levels.

Second and more important, in rural areas during the same time, only about 16 per cent of the increase in elementary enrolment (18 per cent in primary and 13 per cent in upper primary) has been accommodated by PUA schools. Hence, the growth of PUA schools notwithstanding, the relative positions of different school types (reckoned in terms of their shares in total enrolment) have remained more or less intact at the two points in time (the PUA share being roughly about 3 to 5 per cent of total enrolment). Considering also that rural enrolment constitutes a little more than 70 per cent of total enrolment in elementary classes in India, it would be rather sweeping to argue that the schooling pattern between 1986 and 1993 indicates an exodus of the pupil population in India from government-financed schools to fee-charging schools, as suggested by Kingdon (1996b, 3312).

PREVALENCE OF PRIVATE SCHOOLING: VARIATIONS WITHIN STATES

We now take a quick look at the extent of privatization in some of the major states.

A closer look at some of the states where privatization is rapidly increasing shows interesting patterns (see Table 11.1). In urban Haryana and UP, the migration from government to private schools is very evident, since enrolment in government schools is showing an absolute decrease. Out of the increase in enrolment in UP, 94 per cent is absorbed by PUAs and Haryana shows a similar trend. Punjab is different—uncontrolled privatiza-tion seems to be taking place in rural areas whereas there is only a moderate change in urban areas. In urban Andhra Pradesh on the other hand, there is increased pri-vatization but this is not so in rural areas. The privatization tendency is also observable in Kerala, where, against a backdrop of absolute decrease in enrolment, PUA enrolment shows a sharp increase. All these states would merit further attention.

TABLE 11.1
Comparative Growth in Enrolment in Private Schools

	Proportion of increased enrolment absorbed by			
	PA schools		PUA schools	
	Rural	Urban	Rural	Urban
At primary level				
Punjab	(–)1.47	2.33	12.41	28.86
Haryana	0.05	(–)26.09	14.05	111.17
Uttar Pradesh	10.25	19.24	41.95	93.95
Kerala*	(–)71.26	62.17	4.05	11.79
Andhra Pradesh	(–)3.58	33.90	14.63	79.90
At upper-primary level				
Punjab	(–)2.51	6.24	3.57	13.71
Haryana	0.41	8.13	8.13	106.25
Uttar Pradesh	49.44	55.47	54.26	15.83
Kerala*	110.57	102.19	5.31	(–)52.45
Andhra Pradesh	(–)0.50	38.91	1.38	61.34

Note: * The figures for Kerala should be interpreted in the context of decline in fertility rate in Kerala and the resultant absolute decrease in school enrolment.

Source: NCERT (1986, 1998).

Access to Private Schools: A Social Privilege?

The relationship between location, gender, caste, and school types is more carefully explored in Tables 11.2 and 11.3. Here we scrutinize the gender, caste, and locational dimensions of private schooling. Differently stated, are the three persistent biases that usually constrain social opportunities in different corners of the country, namely urban bias, caste bias, and gender bias, operative in the case of school education? Tables 11.2 and 11.3 summarize statistics on elementary school participation by location (rural/urban), gender, and caste, looking at enrolment shares of schools under different

TABLE 11.2
Percentage Distribution of Students in Classes I–V (1993)

	Management and location		Management and gender		Management and caste	
	Rural	Urban	Male	Female	'Others'	'SC/STs'
Govt & local body	90.5	52.2	81.0	80.5	78.4	86.9
PA	6.7	22.1	10.0	11.5	11.3	8.7
PUA	2.8	25.7	9.0	8.0	10.3	4.4
Total	100.0	100.0	100.0	100.0	100.0	100.0

Source: NCERT (1998).

TABLE 11.3
Percentage Distribution of Students in Classes VI–VIII (1993)

	Management and location		Management and gender		Management and caste	
	Rural	Urban	Male	Female	'Others'	'SC/STs'
Govt & local body	67.7	41.5	58.8	56.9	56.4	65.1
PA	25.8	39.7	29.7	32.8	31.8	27.9
PUA	6.5	18.8	11.5	10.3	11.8	8.0
Total	100.0	100.0	100.0	100.0	100.0	100.0

Source: NCERT (1998).

managements. Three clear conclusions can be drawn from the data. First, if we go by official statistics, the urban bias in private schooling once again becomes quite palpable, especially for PUA-type schools; only about 3 and 6 per cent of rural students go to unaided primary and middle schools, respectively. The corresponding figure for urban India is 26.19 per cent. Second, the caste bias is also recognizable, though less pronounced. Clearly, the degree of reliance on government schools is higher among Dalit children as compared to those from 'forward' castes. Third, interestingly, while urban and caste biases show some tendency to move together, no striking difference between boys and girls seems to emerge with respect to their choice of school types, a conclusion of interest in itself.

It is often feared that in a society as diverse and inequitable as ours, important socio-economic differences are 'washed out' in aggregate measures. In other words, averages obscure some important disparities of gender, space, and caste, and more crucially, the destructive synergy of these overlapping misfortunes. It is important to explore these differences as is done in Figure 11.2. When pupil population is divided (in primary and upper-primary classes separately) into eight

Percentage Distribution of Primary Students from Two Polar Groups (1993)

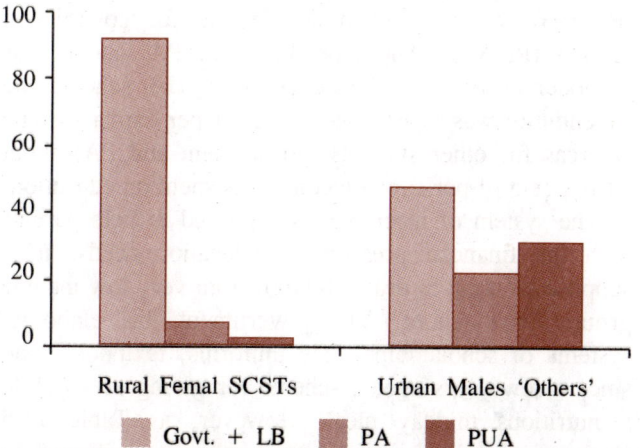

Percentage Distribution of Upper-Primary Students from Two Polar Groups (1993)

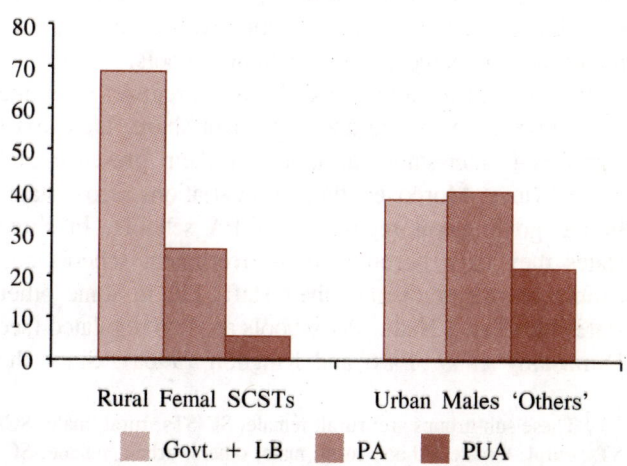

FIGURE 11.2: Segmentation in Schooling

distinct sub-groups, widely divergent realities are discovered to be coexisting within the 'same' educational system.[1] To take two extreme cases, a rural, female, SC/ST student of India and an urban, male, 'forward' caste student of the same country seem to inhabit two different 'worlds' of education. Only about 2 per cent (5 per cent) of the former category are taught in PUA primary (middle) schools, whereas about 31 per cent (22 per cent) of the latter sub-group are catered to by the fee-levying school sector.

It is possible that if private school enrolment is biased towards children from higher expenditure groups then the urban bias and the caste/class bias are stronger than the gender bias. We return to this issue later. But the same data tell a different story. A closer look at the growth in enrolment between the Fifth and Sixth All-India Educational Surveys (see NCERT 1986 and 1998) shows that 38 per cent of the growth in enrolment of boys is accounted for by PUA schools as against only 8 per cent of that of girls. There is a similar bias in the enrolment of backward castes, as well as in urban areas. Of the increase in enrolment of boys in urban areas 77 per cent is accounted for by PUAs as compared to only 46 per cent of that of girls.

Disaggregation by caste, region, and gender has, therefore, shown considerable biases in the clientele of private schools. Private schools are more for boys, for upper castes, and for urban areas than government schools. In other words, attending a PUA school is likely to be a mark of social privilege.

The Case of Aided Schools

A cursory look at the statistics presented here suggests that aided schools are no less equitable than government schools in terms of their coverage and the delivery of school-based incentive schemes, excepting that they are more expensive. They also appear to be more cost-effective in that they deliver more with similar investments as compared to government schools.

While at all-India level aided schools register a decline over time, both in size and enrolment share, there exist significant inter-state variations in their presence and performance. Moreover, there are variations across states in the government regulation of PA schools. In some states they have become quasi-government schools and cannot recruit or dismiss their staff. But in some other states like Tamil Nadu, PA schools are less regulated (see Duraisamy *et al.* 1996 and Kingdon 1996a). Since the

[1] These sub-groups are: rural, female, SC/STs; rural, male, SC/STs; rural, female, others; rural, male, others; urban, female, SC/STs; urban, male, SC/STs; urban, female, others; and urban, male, others.

government foots, in almost its entirety, the recurring expenditure bills of aided schools, research needs to focus on the implications of their being private in a managerial sense.

Costs of Private Schooling

Private schooling is very much more expensive than schooling in government schools according to data generated by NCERT surveys. Even PA schools, where fees are supposed to be kept at a nominal level by government decree, manage to get fairly high fees from their pupils (see Table 11.4).

TABLE 11.4
Average Annual Household Expenditure Per Student in Elementary Schools under Different Management 1995–6

	Primary			
	Rural		Urban	
	Male	Female	Male	Female
Government	219	219	509	470
Local body	223	223	714	621
PA	693	529	1652	1525
PUA	902	925	1975	1866
Total	305	286	1197	1092
Upper-primary				
Government	548	555	923	864
Local body	533	553	1148	995
PA	893	868	1884	1734
PUA	1240	1267	2933	2908
Total	640	641	1590	1456

Source: NSSO (1998).

However, the National Council of Applied Economic Research (NCAER) data (1994) show that aided schools are much closer to government schools in terms of cost. The average expenditure per student in PUA schools (Rs 893) was more than double that for government schools (Rs 346). The expenditure for PA schools was a moderate Rs 411. However, for PUA schools the expenditure was nearly one-fourth of per capita income whereas for other students (government and PA) about 14 per cent of per capita income was spent on education.

The system of incentives is supposed to help parents with the financial pressure of education needs. It is supposed to help to draw children from very low income groups into school. The government has elaborate systems of scholarships, free uniforms, textbooks, and since a few years ago, a scheme for giving every child a nutritious midday meal. However, as Table 11.5 shows, few children get the free textbooks, uniforms, or scholarships which could defray school expenses—not more than 13–15 per cent in government and PA schools. As for PUA schools, an almost negligible percentage of students in these schools receive incentives—these could either be philanthropic ventures or schools which charge higher fees but look after disadvantaged students. That the percentage is negligible is a telling comment on private schools. If the PUA sector is growing there is a probability, as Table 11.5 shows, that this is not really because of demand among the most disadvantaged groups of the population.

TABLE 11.5

A Comparative View of Government and Private Schools at Primary and Upper-Primary Level 1993

	Govt & LB	PA	PUA
1	2	3	4
PRIMARY			
Pupil Characterisitcs			
Proportion of female students	43.0	46.7	40.2
Proportion of SC/ST students	30.8	23.6	14.9
Proportion of rural students	83.6	47.3	24.0
Proportion of total enrolled students	80.8	10.6	08.6
School Characteristics			
Proportion of schools with drinking water facilities	41.4	66.0	87.1
Proportion with toilet facilities	07.6	31.5	64.9
Proportion of sections with adequate number of blackboards	62.8	85.1	95.6
Proportion with library	40.7	49.3	28.7
Proportion with adequate playground facilities	27.0	39.2	57.0
Proportion having pucca bulidings	65.0	54.4	75.8
Average number of rooms used for instructional Purposes	02.1	04.4	05.1
Proportion having noon-meal scheme	13.3	38.4	04.7
	(5.1)	(13.0)	(2.8)
Proportion having free uniform scheme	30.0	33.9	08.1
	(6.1)	(7.9)	(1.3)
Proportion having free textbooks scheme	56.0	60.8	15.5
	(13.1)	(15.2)	(3.2)
Teacher Characteristics			
Pupil–teacher ratio	40.9	39.8	31.0
Proportion of SC/STs among full-time teachers	20.5	13.3	08.4
Proportion female	27.5	57.4	51.9
Proportion trained	89.2	95.2	82.6
Proportion graduate and above	34.5	30.3	36.2
Proportion permanent	74.8	70.6	46.7
UPPER-PRIMARY			
Pupil Characterisics			
Proportion of female students	38.8	41.9	37.2
Proportion of SC/ST students	23.6	19.3	15.6
Proportion of rural students	73.5	52.6	37.0
Proportion of total enrolled students	58.0	30.9	11.0
School Characteristics			
Proportion of schools with drinking water facilities	57.5	82.5	89.9
Proportion with toilet facilities	21.3	56.1	69.1
Proportion of sections with adequate number of blackboards	79.6	91.6	98.2
Proportion with library	56.8	72.6	72.0

(Contd.)

Table 11.5 contd.

1	2	3	4
Proportion with adequate playground facilities	37.3	52.8	67.8
Proportion having pucca bulidings	67.8	62.4	78.8
Average number of rooms used for instructional purposes	04.6	07.7	06.7
Proportion having noon-meal scheme	20.0	28.0	02.1
	(8.9)	(12.8)	(1.3)
Proportion having free uniform scheme	33.8	19.6	07.3
	(8.6)	(6.1)	(1.4)
Proportion having free textbooks scheme	58.2	43.5	20.0
	(14.3)	(11.3)	(4.1)
Teacher Characteristics			
Pupil–teacher ratio	36.6	37.4	32.5
Proportion of SC/STs among full-time teachers	17.2	11.8	08.1
Proportion female	30.6	53.0	51.1
Proportion trained	88.8	90.1	71.6
Proportion graduate and above	44.5	49.9	71.8
Proportion permanent	76.2	75.9	55.5

Note: Figures in parentheses indicate the proportion of students benefiting.
Source: NCERT (1998).

Exclusion or Retreat

Further evidence comes from the NCAER survey, which puts population into different income strata while assessing various social and economic indicators. Table 11.6 shows the distribution of enrolment by school management and population groups. It shows that though the PUA sector includes low-cost private schools, their

TABLE 11 6
Distribution of Enrolled Students at Elementary Level by School Management and Population Groups

Population groups	Govt school	PA	PUA
HOUSEHOLD INCOME GROUPS (Rs)			
Up to 20,000	70.2	22.4	7.2
20,001–40,000	66.3	23.0	10.5
40,001–62,000	63.8	23.2	12.8
62,001–86,000	66.8	19.7	13.5
Above 86,000	66.0	14.8	19.1
SOCIAL GROUPS			
Caste			
STs	67.1	29.2	3.2
SCs	71.5	22.6	5.8
Religion			
Hindus	70.3	20.2	9.3
Muslims	49.4	37.3	13.3
Christians	42.9	47.5	9.6
Other minorities	80.4	6.6	12.3
All India	67.9	22.1	9.8

Source: NCAER (1994, Appendix A6.11).

presence/accessibility for low-income groups is limited. Similarly, backward castes have limited participation in PUA schools—perhaps the difference could be sharper for backward castes if the added incentives given in government schools are considered. PA schools play a larger role in the education of Muslim and Christian children as indicated by the higher enrolment figures for these groups, suggesting that these schools are minority schools.

In fact, not only is the participation of low-income groups in private schools lower than that for other groups, the ever enrolment rate (EER) defined as the percentage of children ever enrolled at any time in a school remains low for the underprivileged groups in many states. (see Table 11.7) Therefore, for these groups the actual participation in the PUA sector among the children in the 6–14 age group is even lower.

A priori, nothing definite can be said about the influence of private schools on the achievement of UEE. In Uttar Pradesh, among the lowest income group, a little more than half the children are ever enrolled, while about 25 per cent of them go to PUA schools. In Rajasthan, the EER rate is similar, while participation in PUA schools is much lower. In the same income group, Himachal Pradesh shows high EER and low PUA participation. Kerala has higher EER and higher participation rate in PUA schools. At most, it is possible to say that several states (Kerala, Himachal Pradesh, Tamil Nadu) have nearly achieved universal enrolment of the underprivileged section without depending on PUA schools.

TABLE 11.7
**Ever Enrolment Rates and PUA Participation at Elementary Level
Among the Underprivileged in Selected States**

	Income up to 20,000		Income 20,001–40,000		SC and ST	
	EER	PUA	EER	PUA	EER	PUA
Uttar Pradesh	54.7	24.6	67.7	27.0	53.4	17.9
Punjab	83.3	11.5	85.8	19.3	72.9	1.8
Haryana	69.2	7.1	78.5	11.4	68.5	5.8
Kerala	98.6	8.1	98.7	13.3	97.2	3.5
Andhra Pradesh	77.4	8.5	77.9	8.4	75.5	4.7
Karnataka	75.9	7.9	79.7	12.8	69.7	7.4
Bihar	49.8	4.6	66.5	10.8	44.7	4.4
Tamil Nadu	86.0	6.6	89.0	6.7	84.7	0.5
Himachal Pradesh	90.6	2.9	96.0	6.6	87.7	1.8
Orissa	65.2	2.4	81.6	5.5	52.6	2.0
Madhya Pradesh	54.6	2.0	67.7	4.6	51.4	2.5
Rajasthan	53.9	2.0	61.9	5.3	48.9	1.9
Gujarat	74.0	1.8	89.1	3.4	73.7	2.3
Maharastra	82.8	1.3	84.8	2.0	76.5	1.3
West Bengal	59.9	0.6	77.1	1.3	63.9	1.0
NE Region	78.3	0.1	80.1	0.1	88.5	0.4

Note: EER denotes the proportion of children in 6–14 age group who have ever been enrolled in school. PUA denotes the proportion of enrolled children in private unaided schools.
Source: NCAER (1994, Appendix A6.11).

Quality Indicators

One tempting hypothesis is that the PUA sector is growing rapidly because its quality is so superior. Certainly there is enough data at macro level to establish, for example, that more PUA schools have drinking water or toilet facilities than do government schools (see Table 11.5). However, the same source suggests that teachers in government and private schools are similar in qualification and training. Even the student–teacher ratios in the two types of schools are very comparable. It is also seen that PUA schools employ more teachers on a temporary basis, which could lead to higher teacher accountability. But in the absence of qualitative data to go with this information, it is difficult to say that the mere presence of a good student–teacher ratio on paper will guarantee a well-functioning school. Keeping this in mind this issue will be discussed when more qualitative data such as is available from micro studies can be presented. This is also important since our primary concern is really with the plight of the marginalized and poor and their problems concerning elementary schooling. The kind of schools which they can access are likely to be low quality fee-charging schools whose quality cannot be easily captured in aggregate statistics.

EVIDENCE FROM SMALLER STUDIES OF PRIVATE SCHOOLING

While the place of private schooling in the elementary sector is visible in its broader contours through macro-level official data, smaller studies which focus on particular regions are valuable. It is to be admitted, however, that this qualitative evidence is neither extensive nor elaborate as the general focus of the micro studies was on the schooling situation rather than on private schools, their nature, their origin, and their merits and demerits.[2]

Our major source for most of the findings in this section is the PROBE survey (see PROBE Team 1999), a survey which is somewhere between the macro studies which present data for the whole country and the micro-level studies which look at a number of villages in one district/state, or at urban and rural areas in a state. The PROBE survey, by looking at the four large Hindi-speaking states in northern India,[3] which are crucial to

[2] Only Jagpal Singh's (1995) study on Meerut district quotes parents about school quality in private schools.

[3] The PROBE states are the so-called BIMARU states, i.e. Bihar, Madhya Pradesh, Rajasthan, and Uttar Pradesh.

EFA since they contain the maximum number of out-of-school children, is a macro survey.

The PROBE survey looked at all schooling facilities available within a village and made a detailed study of facilities for primary level (classes I–V) education including schools under private management. There was also a household survey of about 1200 households, where at least 193 families were encountered who had at least one child studying in a private school, either within the village or outside.[4] A similar survey of forty eight villages was done in Himachal Pradesh as a contrast to the situation in the PROBE states. This contrast was extremely interesting from the point of view of attitudes to private schools as well.

Other studies which we have looked at for this chapter are useful in providing further glimpses of the schooling situation. Interestingly, many of the studies focus on schooling in the different districts of the state of Uttar Pradesh (Dreze and Gazdar 1996, Kingdon 1996a, Srivastava 1997, Pande 1997, Singh 1995) where privatization is very high according to macro-level data. There are also three studies of schooling in Tamil Nadu (Duraisamy 1996, Majumdar 1996, Bashir 1995), two from Rajasthan (Nambissan 1997, Majumdar 1997), two from Delhi (Aggarwal 1998, Noronha 1996b), two from Madhya Pradesh (Govinda and Varghese 1992, 1993), and one from Andhra Pradesh (Krishnaji 1996). There are two multistate surveys.[5] Much of what was seen by PROBE investigators is also reported by many of these studies. In addition, valuable inputs on cost-effectiveness and achievement come from two of these studies, one from Tamil Nadu by Bashir (1994) and the other by Kingdon (1996a). Kingdon's (1996b) study of Lucknow city is also important since it gives us a glimpse of schooling in urban areas as do Aggarwal (1998) and Noronha (1996) both of whom concentrate on Delhi. The PROBE survey did not focus on urban schooling or on cost-effectiveness or efficiency of public versus private schools.

Rising Demand and Fall in Quality of Government Schooling

Although micro studies cover varying areas and concentrate on different themes, from a reading of these studies it appears that certain factors dominate the current education scene: a rising demand for schooling, a decline in government school quality, and a growing number of private schools—even in rural areas. We begin by discussing the first two factors: rising demand for education and fall in quality of government schooling and possible reasons for the latter.

The PROBE survey found a massive surge in parental demand and a large-scale decline in the government schooling system. The surge in demand was confirmed by the drop in never-enrolled ratio found in the PROBE villages (20 per cent) from the level (50 per cent) recorded by the National Sample Survey Organization (NSSO) in the 42nd Round. A similar phenomenon is apparent in most of the micro studies (see Majumdar 1996, Bashir 1994, Sinha and Sinha 1995).

In the PROBE villages, although most villages had a government primary school, poor infrastructure, teacher shortage, and, even more importantly, teacher negligence was rampant. When PROBE investigators visited the government primary schools (without prior notice), 50 per cent of the schools had no teaching activity going on. Parents were disillusioned, cynical, hostile, and helpless about this state of affairs. Teachers were caught between the strain of coping with very dilapidated buildings, understaffing, and lack of teaching equipment and the demands posed by first-generation learners who were often irregular and whose parents could not support their learning needs.

Micro studies which have focused on education in Uttar Pradesh and Bihar also report inadequate infrastructure and lack of teacher accountability in government schools. The Tamil Nadu studies, however, make the same point about inadequate facilities in government schools in the face of rising demand, but stop well short of suggesting that the schooling system has collapsed. This does bring out the danger of generalizing across these micro studies as 'fall' in school quality could have very different implications.

Some of this demand was possibly fuelled by the incentive schemes of the government, notably the dry ration scheme, which teachers in the PROBE villages reported as having drawn in a large number of scheduled caste and very poor children. The PROBE villages also showed that increase in enrolment could also be correlated with whether a (TLC) had been undertaken in that area. The fall in school quality has commonly been ascribed to underfunding in the government school sector.

Growth of Private Schooling

Several factors appear to govern the growth of the private schooling sector according to these studies. Growth of private schools, more especially fee-paying

---

[4] There could be more families with children enrolled in private schools. Details about one child in each family were taken and that child was randomly chosen.

[5] Mehrotra (1995) surveys villages in UP, HP, and Kerala and Sinha and Sinha (1995) survey villages in the BIMARU (or PROBE) states.

ones, is itself, of course, a symptom of rising demand for education but it is the rising demand in the face of falling quality of government schools which appears most important. In the PROBE villages there were private schools in 4 of the 12 villages without a government primary school and such villages were therefore responding to a lack of schools, but all the rest of the villages had one or more government primary school. The major motivation for opening schools where a government primary school already existed did not appear to be a differentiated demand for innovative curriculum, or a community desire for a different linguistic or cultural orientation. Nor did it appear to be a social service type of orientation. The private schools were apparently responding to the unfulfilled demand for primary education since the government school system was largely dysfunctional. When asked whether they would put their child in a government school or a private school if the fees involved were the same, nearly all the parents asked they would choose the private school.

Kingdon (1994), for example, reports an exodus from the government school system in urban Lucknow into private schools and attributes this to a collapse of the government school system. Noronha (1996b) also reports a mushrooming of private schools in the context of a fall in government school quality in a low-income area of Delhi. Majumdar (1996) associates the stress on UEE and the consequent increase in enrolment with an increasing level of privatization. Bashir (1994) points out how state policies in Tamil Nadu relating to education have increased private-sector participation. She reports, among other things, that the private sector has grown rapidly because the state government encouraged the growth of PUA schools in order to ease the burden on the state by mobilizing resources from the private sector for educational expansion. It does not exercise any control on primary schools in terms of minimum norms. States like Rajasthan have greatly relaxed the norms for recognition of schools and this too has facilitated growth.

The UP government's policy of bringing PUA schools at upper-primary and secondary levels into the aided list to make them grant-in-aid schools has added to the rise in unrecognized primary schools. Many of the PA schools face an acute need for cash to cover at least the essential non-salary costs, since they get only salary payments from the state. They run unrecognized PUA primary sections to generate surpluses to subsidize the aided sections at the upper levels. Kingdon (1994) found that 8 out of 10 PA upper-primary and secondary schools in a survey of Lucknow city ran unrecognized PUA primary sections in 1991.

DIFFERENTIATED DEMAND

It is also important to recognize that there is possibly a spectrum of parental demand which ranges from pure excess demand to purely differentiated demand. In the PROBE villages it may well be the case that private schools were coming up because of the lack of a functional government school system. However, even here there were parents sending their children to private schools because they were delivering a certain good not available in the government domain, the teaching of English, for example. This is reported to be a major attraction in many studies (see, for example, Majumdar 1996, Aggarwal 1998, Nambissan 1997, Singh 1995).

Bashir (1994) underlines this by pointing out that educational and occupational aspirations of children from PUA schools who had an overwhelming preference for graduate courses and professional jobs. She makes a detailed study of such aspirations which included, for example:

• something which will help the child complete secondary education and get a job in the organized sector;

• knowledge of English which may help the child get admission into the English-medium government/aided schools at the next level;

• advanced Math/Science which is useful for professional courses;

• necessity of avoiding the poor quality of the government schools and having the child gain in intangibles such as learning how to study, growing in self-confidence and self-esteem, with plans to transfer to Tamil-medium government/aided schools later so as to secure state government jobs which require proficiency in Tamil and even give preference to Tamil-medium students.

The PROBE villages were not, on the whole, large-sized villages, ranging in size from a modest 600 to a medium size of 3000 inhabitants. Of the 188 villages some 35 had private schools, some having more than one private school. Most of these schools were primary schools and relatively new, suggesting that they were a recent phenomenon. Although there was a severe shortage of upper-primary schools in these villages (70 per cent of the villages had no upper-primary school) this had not resulted in a proliferation of private upper-primary schools.

Cost of Private Schooling

Private schooling in the PROBE villages demanded heavy expenditure in varying degrees from parents, disadvantaged as most of them were. Tables 11.8 and 11.9 show the cost of schooling in PA and PUA schools vis-à-vis the cost of schooling in government schools in these villages. They show that not only is the cost in the private sector substantially higher but also that there are no concessions like scholarships, etc. for disadvantaged children. This corroborates the macro-level statistics, and also suggests that costs in PA schools are considerably higher than costs in government schools, even though the government is doing substantial funding for these schools. However, aided schools do have somewhat better implementation of government incentive schemes, inadequate though the scope and coverage of these may be.

TABLE 11.8
Average Cost of Sending a Child to Primary School: Government versus Private

(Rs/year)

	Government	Private
Fees	16	296
Non-fee expenditure	302	644
Total	318	940

Source: PROBE Team (1999, parents' estimates).

TABLE 11.9
Average Cost of Sending a Child to Primary School: Private Aided versus Unaided

(Rs/year)

	Average annual cost of sending a child to primary school		
		PUA	
	PA	Recognized	Unrecognized
Class I	558	599	525
Class V	608	725	637

Source: PROBE Team (1999, teachers' estimates).

Table 11.10 demonstrates the same phenomenon—that the costs of private schooling are way beyond those of government schooling—observable from the other studies which provide such data. Estimates for the average cost of sending a child to private school vary between 4 and 8 times what it costs to send a child to government school. The implications of this scenario for parents, particularly marginalized parents who are the special target of UEE, are not clear. There are two major aspects to this: what sort of private facilities can be accessed by very poor parents and how effective are these facilities; and second, how do parents cope with the expenses?

It is important to recall at this point that both according to PROBE survey data (1999) and according to other micro studies even the cost of schooling in the government system was too heavy a burden for many parents (see Mehrotra 1995, Sinha and Sinha 1995, Dreze and Gazdar 1996, Pande 1996). Mehrotra's study (1995) (based on villages in Uttar Pradesh, Himachal Pradesh, and Kerala) showed that it is often inability to meet the direct costs of schooling which make parents withdraw their children from school. Pande (1996) reports from rural Uttarakhand that one-third of parents with non-enrolled children said that they could not afford the cost of books, uniforms, and other material required to send their children to school. It is possible that any scenario based on the fee-paying capacities of very poor parents would raise many questions.

One such question would be the sustainability and practicability of such an endeavour, even if parents did manage to put together the fees. Krishnaji (1996) found in rural Telengana district in Andhra Pradesh that a better-off family with a child in private school spends more than twice the amount on average per child than

TABLE 11.10
Comparative Costs of Schooling Borne by Parents for Sending a Child to School at Primary Level

Surveys conducted in	Costs in PUA schools (Rs/year)	Costs in government schools (Rs/year)	Col. 1/Col. 2
Rural Andhra Pradesh	710.40	197.52	3.60
Rural Rajasthan	1188.00	297.00	< 40
Rural Tamil Nadu	361.08	71.27	5.06
Rural Uttarakhand, UP	1458.30	404.50	3.60
Rural Rampur, UP	601.60	89.40	6.73
Rural Ballia, UP	678.00	82.46	8.22

Notes: 1. The figures in the last column give annual household expenditure on a child in a PUA school as a multiple of the amount spent on a child in a government school.
2. At upper-primary level the differential is much lower, except for Duraisamy's (1996) study, where it is roughly similar.

Source: Estimates have been taken from the following studies: AP: Krishnaji (1996), Rajasthan: Nambissan (1997); Tamil Nadu: Duraisamy (1996); Uttarakhand: Pande (1996), Rampur and Ballia: Srivastava (1997). All the studies were conducted in 1996.

a poor family also sending a child to private school. The average expenditure by a well-to-do family with a child in a private school is 5.3 times that which is incurred by a poor family on a child in a government school. Aggregating over type of school and family status, it was found that smaller amounts were spent on average on girls, partly because girls dropped out at higher levels of schooling which are the more expensive grades and partly because parents spent much more on boys on average, particularly on tuition and on travel.

There are other hidden costs to schooling: the cost of pre-primary education is one such cost, another important one is tuition. 'Private tuition is no longer an urban or elite class practice alone; it is the household's widely perceived solution to schooling inadequacies, even in rural Kanyakumari and among relatively poorer social groups,' reports Majumdar (1996) from Kanyakumari in Tamil Nadu. Bashir's (1994) study reports that the highest percentage of children taking tuition were found in PUA schools in rural areas (almost 60 per cent—few took tuition in government schools in rural areas). In urban areas the percentage of students taking tuition varied from 18 per cent in government schools to 50 per cent in PUA schools. Around 30 per ent of the PA school students also took tuition according to Bashir. Similar reports come from Kingdon (1996b) and Aggarwal (1998).

How much does the coaching cost? Majumdar (1996) reports that coaching expenses vary from Rs 15 to 50 in rural Tamil Nadu. Noronha's study finds wide variation in tuition fees. It seems apparent that just as all private schools are not equal, so also, coaching classes can be of varied quality. From the supply point of view, there are plenty of unemployed youth.

Clientele of Private Schools

Several suggestions seen in macro-level data are supported by evidence from smaller studies. As mentioned earlier, PROBE data also show wide variation in privatization in different states. Again, while macro-level data differentiate between rural and urban areas in terms of location of private schools, the data in the smaller studies refine this somewhat. Two major factors stand out from the micro studies:

• Private schools are biased towards more prosperous locations and at those locations, enrolment in private schools is greater for more privileged groups including those with higher asset status.
• Private school enrolment is biased towards males.

In the villages surveyed in the PROBE states, these two points become fairly clear if one reads 'privileged' in terms of caste and class, and gender as well.

The same bias towards upper caste and class in private and government school enrolment is seen in other studies also. Krishnaji's (1996) Andhra Pradesh study,[6] for example, shows that private schools in this educationally backward district are biased towards more privileged groups: less than 10 per cent of poor families have their children in private schools as against nearly 30 per cent of middle income families and 45 per cent of well-to-do families. Bashir's (1994) study of enrolment in private and government schools in rural and urban Tamil Nadu provides many insights:

• Pupils in PUA schools were from relatively more privileged backgrounds in both rural and urban areas. Less than 10 per cent were SCs. A negligible proportion were first-generation learners; 85 per cent had both parents educated. The father was employed in the organized sector in 60 per cent of the cases.

• In government schools, the proportion of SC pupils was 26 per cent in rural areas and 42 per cent in urban areas. In such schools 30 per cent of fathers and 60 per cent of mothers of students were illiterate. In rural areas, 35 per cent of pupils were from agricultural labour households, with no land or assets.

• PA schools had a clientele similar to government schools: large numbers of pupils whose parents were illiterate and from an SC background. But these schools were found to be biased against children of agricultural labourers. The proportion of these children in PA schools in rural areas was less than that in government schools.

As for the suggestion that private school enrolment is biased towards males, the evidence is more straightforward than that provided by macro-level data. Dreze and Gazdar (1996) report that school attendance in private schools in Uttar Pradesh is significantly male dominated: parents are more willing to pay for male children; also private schooling may involve the child going to a different village which parents are more willing to permit for a male child. Majumdar's (1997) study of three villages in Jhunjhunu district in Rajasthan also finds gender bias, both at primary and upper-primary levels. More research, however, needs to be done on this issue.

Quality Indicators

This is perhaps the crucial area if we are to look at private schools in terms of UEE. It is an area difficult to probe

---

[6] See also Srivastava (1997), and Aggarwal (1998). Aggarwal makes the interesting point that the proportion of SC children in the local municipal corporation schools was 26.5 per cent but it was 6 per cent in PUA schools and 5 per cent in Kendriya Vidyalayas, though the latter are also 'government schools'.

from macro-level statistical data, particularly at the elementary level.

INFRASTRUCTURE

As far as physical infrastructure is concerned, as the PROBE study indicates, private schools do appear to have an advantage over government schools, but not such as would warrant the overwhelmingly positive response from parents about education in private schools. It is also interesting that the unrecognized schools do not seem so very different, on the whole, from the recognized schools. In other words, private schools are not vastly superior to government schools in terms of teaching premises and equipment, nor are the recognized schools very superior to the unrecognized ones. Having said this, it must be admitted that the very worst private schools were unrecognized, had filthy, poky premises and compared very easily with the worst government schools which were in a state of collapse or without any building at all.

There is a possibility that macro-level data hide wide variations in quality between private schools in different areas and even between government schools in different areas. Govinda and Varghese (1992),[7] for example, find that most private schools are in urban localities and are able to provide the minimum infrastructure which they feel is required for school quality:

• a school building with a separate classroom for each grade;

• adequate number of trained teachers with minimum qualifications (preferably one per grade);

• proper student sitting places;

• blackboard in usable condition with chalk and duster in each classroom;

• all children having textbooks and writing material.

Deficiency in this area was common in government schools where there was no policy of free textbooks for children.

It is apparent that urban private schools are very different from private schools in the PROBE villages and that standards of infrastructure in the urban private schools are relatively high. Bashir's (1994) study of urban and rural Tamil Nadu provides another insight. In her study she finds that private schools spend nearly four times as much as government and PA schools on teaching material inputs. However, in her study two-thirds to three-quarters of children in all types of schools, whether private or government, had the right textbooks although both government and PA schools often had at least two classes with only a partition between them. In PROBE

villages, neither condition held true. In government schools it was common to find children without the right textbooks and in private schools this situation was not at all common. But government as well as private schools often functioned out of one or two rooms—and sometimes none at all.[8]

TEACHER–STUDENT RATIO AND TEACHER COMPETENCE

If we look at teacher–student ratio and teacher qualification, both aspects of quality in school infrastructure, the evidence is varied. According to PROBE data, private schools certainly had a better student–teacher ratio than government and aided primary schools. Even multigrade teaching, though common, was different. Since classes were smaller, it was obviously not as problematic. It was rare to find one teacher handling all five classes as we found in one-third of the government schools visited. Nor were teachers struggling with up to a 180 children. However, teaching skills for primary-level children were not superior to those found among government school teachers. Few teachers had professional pre-service training (20 per cent as compared to 70 per cent in government schools). It is here that unrecognized schools fared very badly. Teachers with the lowest qualifications and percentage of training were from these schools. As for in-service training, this was a rarity in these schools.

Bashir's (1994) Tamil Nadu study also reports that the pupil–teacher ratio in government and PA schools was about 45—about 1.8 times higher than that in PUA schools. However, she says that pupil–teacher ratio for government and PA schools is unreliable because names of many pupils who have dropped out or are irregular are still included. Her findings on teacher training in private schools were that PUA teachers were generally more qualified and better trained, with specialist teachers in Maths and Tamil. They were also younger and less experienced.

Govinda and Varghese (1992), studying urban private schools, report that teachers in private schools usually have a better educational background than government school teachers. They attribute this to manpower availability in urban areas. Aggarwal's (1998) study (in Delhi) found that teachers in PUA schools were generally younger and more qualified: 88 per cent had B.Eds. compared to 23 per cent in government (MCD) schools.

---

[7] They studied 59 schools in five localities (ranging from a very remote, underdeveloped region to a highly developed, urban zone) in Madhya Pradesh.

[8] Aggarwal's (1998) Delhi survey compares levels of schools without ancillary facilities. Government schools were the worst, but even 14 of the 40 PUA schools did not have toilets for girls. Bashir's (1994) study reports that 40 per cent of government schools had no source of drinking water available on the premises and few rural schools, private or government, had electricity.

Duraisamy (1996) differs from all the other studies in finding that the level of education of PUA school teachers was similar to that of teachers in government and aided schools, but the number of years of experience for the former was much less.

TEACHING METHODS AND CURRICULUM

Teachers in private schools were generally not found using innovative methods or making any changes in curriculum. Rote learning and recitation were rampant. Writing was the dominant activity. A favourite subject seemed to be English. Almost all schools were teaching their Class I pupils (to whom the survey paid particular attention) the English alphabet or English numbers. The quality of English was dubious, to say the least. But it is doubtful that parents would consider any of these points a problem in the school or realize the pedagogical unsuitability of a second language at a very early stage, and that too, poorly taught.

PUPIL ACHIEVEMENTS

One simple way of judging an effective school is the tangible mode of measuring learning achievement. Here too, there are differentials not immediately obvious. Govinda and Varghese (1992),[9] for example, found that after controlling for student background, performance of students in PUA schools was considerably higher than that of pupils in either PA or government schools. However, the kind of infrastructure in these private schools and in the type of correlates of achievement which they mention later makes it obvious that these private schools are not the low fee kind. Similarly, when Bashir (1994) talks of the functional literacy achieved in PUA schools, these PUA schools are different from the private schools seen in the PROBE villages.

Aggarwal (1998) compared average scores in language and maths for Class I students in his Delhi study: Kendriya Vidyalayas scored the highest; MCD schools the lowest; PA schools scored only a little lower than PUA schools and much better than government schools. For Class IV attainments in maths and Hindi, however, scores were highest in PUA schools. Underachievement was the highest in MCD schools.

Bashir (1994) found that 'although levels of mastery are grossly inadequate in all sectors, differentiation is more marked at lower levels of competence' (emphasis added). Children in PUA schools are at least functionally literate and able to answer a few questions involving simple comprehension skills. A large number of government school students have not attained even this degree of language development. This also applies in the area

of numeracy skills. Bashir concluded, 'PUA schools ensure that all pupils acquire a basic set of skills for continuing in school.'

PUA schools had the highest mean scores in all three tests, followed by PA schools. However, mean achievements of urban pupils were less than those of rural pupils. Overall performance of class IV children in maths and reading comprehension was extremely low. From mean scores, PUA pupil performance was not appreciably higher than that of government school pupils. But analysis of subscores in maths and reading comprehension revealed that more pupils in PUA schools had some knowledge of basic skills in these areas. A large number of government school students, especially in urban areas, had no knowledge even of competencies which should have been acquired in an earlier class. PUA schools were superior only in maths achievement in rural areas. Aided schools also showed superiority in maths achievement.

CORRELATES OF ACHIEVEMENT

Govinda and Varghese (1992) correlate higher achievement with several factors in these recognized PUA schools:

• Time spent on teaching–learning activities. Private schools have a pre-planned calendar of activities, and detailed teaching plans for teachers and external supervision to ensure these are followed. All this is missing in government schools.

• Regular homework.

• Possession of the right textbooks (government school children often did not have these).

Bashir found that multigrade teaching, unpartitioned classrooms, and the social composition of the class had the expected effects. But pupil–teacher ratio, teacher qualification, and teacher training were not significant predictors of achievement, whereas the teacher's subject competence was.

THE POPULARITY OF PRIVATE SCHOOLS AND PARENTAL SUPPORT

There is an interesting interrelationship between parental perception of private schools and their support for the schooling of their children which we shall also deal with in this section. Parents, on the whole, seemed clear that their children would benefit much more from private schooling. In PROBE study villages, at least, private schools certainly do somewhat better in teaching equipment and even in basic facilities like toilets and drinking water. They also look better (private schools are generally kept clean). But the major attraction of private schools in these villages seemed to be clear. Private schools had an atmosphere of active teaching. When investigators visited the schools, students and teachers were almost always at work. This was very different from the dysfunctional

---

[9] Based on their sample of 2159 pupils (in classes IV and V) in Madhya Pradesh.

scenario found in government schools in the PROBE villages. PUA schools had an 85 per cent attendance-enrolment ratio on the day of the survey and this figure was not faked. When the investigators counted the children, the figure corresponded closely to that recorded in the register (98 per cent). Government figures were often obviously unreliable.

Though parents can assess school in terms of active teaching, there are other parameters which are less obvious, especially to illiterate parents. One aspect would definitely be teacher competence and teacher experience. A second would be difficulty in assessing what exactly is happening in school. An interesting example is the teacher absentee data from the PROBE survey. Interestingly, it is not that all private school teachers were present in school on the day of the survey. On the contrary, the absence of teachers was in roughly similar proportion to that found in government schools. Either the schools had exaggerated the number of teachers appointed or absenteeism in government and private schools was on a similar scale. (However, 'duty-related' absence, or the coming-late/going-early syndrome was not there in private schools.) But in private schools teacher absence did not create an obvious problem since the teachers who were present saw to it that children in the affected class were quiet and effectively disciplined.

Judging by the 85 per cent attendance recorded in PROBE private school data, parents cooperate in sending children to school and regular attendance was, in fact, claimed by private schools. One-third of the schools even reported that parents had contributed to school needs. There was none of the helplessness and hostility against teachers associated with parents who had children in government schools in these villages. However, parents in these villages would find it difficult to judge the quality of teaching and could be taken in by appearances more easily. One puzzle is the sharp drop in enrolment after class I; it is not clear whether this is quality related or sustainability related. This pattern was also observed in private schools for low income pupils in Delhi (see Noronha 1996b) but was there associated with movement to government or other private schools on anecdotal evidence.

The experience of investigators in the PROBE states was strikingly different from that encountered in Himachal Pradesh. Interestingly, the attitude towards private schools was somewhat different. First, there were few private schools, though parental ability to pay is less in doubt in Himachal than in the PROBE states. Second, these private schools were even more impressive than the government schools and there were no dilapidated sheds functioning as private schools. Third, parents, on the whole, were very supportive of the government schools,

sent children regularly, helped with homework, and contributed to school needs.

Why do government schools in Himachal function better is, of course, an important question for UEE, especially in view of Himachal's achievement in school education, but just as important is the sense of possibility which it gives with regard to government schools. If schools deliver, parents are likely to support them, and if government schools are functional and of decent quality, then one can hope that private schools will not fall below a minimum benchmark. This could be an important signal when dealing with the problems of poor parents and quality of schooling.

MANAGEMENT ISSUES

One of the reasons for looking closely at the nature of privatization in schooling is to try to establish whether collaboration with this sector would hasten our achievement of UEE. This brings in a host of issues, ranging from the management costs of private and government schooling to the implications for marginalized parents, achievements of private versus government schools, and management advantages for private versus government schools. We shall deal with two of these issues here.

One preliminary issue is that of differing ways of looking at management costs in different studies. Most have focused on institutional recurring costs. Second, the available data usually has certain limitations. There is a downward bias in calculation of official costs of government schools since cost of management and supervision, in-service training of teachers, etc. are not included. In the case of aided schools, a part of the cost (maintenance and administration) is sometimes borne by the trust/institute which runs the school, and so, is excluded from expense accounts. For unaided schools the bias is not downwards but upwards because the reported expenditure on rent and on teacher salaries is usually inflated. In spite of these limitations, the general finding was that unit cost (i.e. institutional cost per enrolled student) of government schools and PA schools was far higher than that of PUA schools.

Apart from this higher running cost for government and PA schools, the government spends far less on infrastructure or teaching aids than private unaided schools do. This is because over 90 per cent of institutional costs consist of teachers' salaries as compared to about 60 per cent in the PUA sector (see Bashir 1994, Duraisamy 1996). There is little or no monetary provision in government schools for other educational expenditure.

Unit costs were lower in the PUA sector because of the much lower level of teachers' salaries. Recognized PUA school teachers earn between a third and a fourth of the salary paid to government school teachers. The average institutional cost for all three types of schools in urban areas is larger than that in rural areas. According to Sharma and Vinayak (2000) which studied Siddharth Nagar in Uttar Pradesh, in smaller private schools, both recognized and unrecognized, the unit cost is higher as compared to larger ones, i.e. economies of scale operate. It is possible that these schools are new, and so, relative expenditure is more.

The profitability of private schools and their lower running costs primarily depend on two factors if one looks across these micro studies: (i) the low teacher salaries and (ii) the much higher input from parents. Bashir (1994) feels that in the cost calculations the other direct costs on textbooks, stationery, etc. which critically influence the outcomes and are borne by parents, should also be included. In fact, if total direct cost per student is considered, the management in the government and PA sectors pays for the larger part, while in PUA schools parents pay the entire amount.

COST-EFFECTIVENESS

The cost–effectiveness ratio is supposed to indicate the comparative benefits received per unit expenditure. This has been calculated by Bashir (1994) by combining the relative cost and relative effectiveness of different types of schools. The main conclusion is that unaided schools are less cost-effective than government schools while aided schools are more cost-effective. That is, for imparting the same amount of learning in mathematics and reading comprehension, unaided schools cost more if all direct costs are included. Among the three sectors, PA schools are most cost-effective. Kingdon's (1996b) analysis, using only institutional costs, indicates that PA schools are slightly more cost-effective than government schools, while PUA schools have a huge advantage over government schools. The two results differ sharply because of the different definitions of unit cost. However, there seems to be another basic difference between the two results: the cost-effectiveness of PA schools. While costs of PA schools and PUA schools are similar, both according to Bashir (1994) and Kingdon (1996b), their effectiveness seems to differ greatly. It is possible that state-specific differences in education scenarios do not permit easy generalization.

Other factors, notably the role of the head teacher, are felt to be crucial in giving private schools an edge when it comes to management effectiveness. What the head teacher contributes first is timeless teaching activities so that he has more time for internal management and community building. (Govinda and Varghese (1992) contrast this to the indifference in government schools.) This is an important issue since it allows proper school management including making space for different activities in the school curriculum, and building up a rapport with staff and with community. Notice the correlates of achievement mentioned by Govinda and Varghese (1992) (see section on achievements earlier in this discussion). Second, he/she contributes qualifications and experience (most PUA head teachers, according to Bashir, (1994) had 9–14 years' experience and graduate-level teacher training, but government school head teachers were mainly class X pass, though they too had experience). In addition, private schools often have a managing committee and a watchful parent body who are aware of school activities. The head teacher liases with local bureaucracy as well.

Several studies comment on the flexibility of recruitment enjoyed by private school management. As Aggarwal (1998) points out, private schools can appoint head teachers and teachers on the basis of competencies and experience and are not obliged to follow guidelines such as SC/ST reservation or seniority. Teacher selection is also immediate; for government school teachers a long selection procedure is involved. Unfortunately, the benefits of the head teacher's role and school autonomy in recruitment of staff have been severely compromised by the aided school system in states like UP.

Based on an inter-district study in Tamil Nadu, Duraisamy et al. (1996) argue that aided schools have an advantage in utilizing the services of their teachers. They have a right to find substitute teachers and fill vacancies expeditiously, sometimes at a small fraction of the regular pay scales of government-paid teachers. And they show that due to greater availability of teacher input, PA schools have an achievement advantage in that they have better examination results than government schools.

This is an important issue to consider when the incidence of teacher absenteeism, vacant teaching posts, and slowness to fill vacancies are high and when, as a result of all this, pupil–teacher ratio is rising and found to be higher in publicly than privately managed schools. However, hiring additional teachers through the private market at a low pay scale has its own problems. Also, as the Report of the Kerala Education Commission candidly states, many aided schools have used the right to hire teachers to provide employment opportunities to 'their own' people, often ignoring academic standards. This managerial autonomy has been converted, in several cases, into an opportunity to make money or consolidate power. In the light of these practices, future research should direct its attention to both the potential and perversions of aided schools.

UNRECOGNIZED SCHOOLS

Little information is available on quality of unrecognized schools. From the glimpses of the sector available one can surmise that this is also a heterogeneous sector. For example, an aided recognized school in UP which is subsidizing itself through a fee-paying unrecognized primary section will ensure the popularity of the school by paying careful attention to quality. Quality of student intake from the primary section will be another factor in this.

No definite statement can be made about infrastructure. Usually the infrastructure is reported to be worse than that in government schools, but the standard of teaching is reported to be better. Majumdar (1997) gives an interesting example of an area of clean government schools with better infrastructure (in Keharpur Kelan, Jhunjhunu district, Rajasthan) than private schools. But only the private school had desks and chairs for upper-primary level. The number of working days for this lone PUA school was almost twice that of the government schools. Evidence on teacher qualification is also varied with some examples of less, even poorly qualified teachers than in government schools and others reporting more qualified teachers. But teacher salary is invariably reported as the lowest in the whole sector.

CONCLUDING OBSERVATIONS

Available evidence indicates that private schools have been expanding rapidly in recent years. They now include a large number of primary schools which charge low fees and have also apparently spread to rural areas according to both macro-level and micro-level data. It is most debatable, however, that they can be relied upon to achieve the goal of UEE while the government allows its own system to deteriorate further. In this connection, a brief mention may be made of the scale of operation required for achieving UEE, as delineated by the Majumdar Committee Report.[10] As per the estimates of the Expert Group, we require additionally Rs 137,000 crore over the next ten years for UEE.[11] The Report categorically asserts that to find financial resources of this magnitude the state will have to play a pivotal role.

The sheer heterogeneity of the private sector makes it important for us to understand the contributions of the different components of the private sector to schooling. One important problem is that the category which is at

[10] A group of experts was appointed by the Ministry of Human Resource Development (MHRD) under the chairmanship of Tapas Majumdar to assess the total financial requirement for operationalizing the Right to Free and Compulsory Education up to the age of 14 as a justiciable Fundamental Right. The Committee submitted its report in January 1999.

[11] To get an idea of the size of the task of UEE, by the year 2001, as per the projections made by the Registrar General of India, Census, the elementary education sector would have to cater to a little more than 200 million children who join classes I–VIII.

risk for non-enrolment/non-achievement/dropping out is in the low income category. As the National Council of Applied Economic Research (NCAER) survey points out, ever enrolment rates show a distinct relationship with household income in different states in the survey. Numbers involved are also very large. The two lowest income categories (below 20,000 rupees and between 20,000 to 40,000 rupees) cover 82 per cent of households and approximately the same proportion of children come from these income classes. This report says that 'resource constraint' is the most important reason for dropping out. It is children from these families who have little easy access to electricity, potable water, adequate food, health care. Such problems affect their enrolment/school attendance in government schools in spite of the incentives offered.

It is the massive government school system on which the poor still rely and the costs of schooling even here are often too much to sustain. The system has expanded to include lower socio-economic groups but without sufficient funds to retain desired levels of facilities and teacher strength. In some states the decline has progressed to the point of making the system dysfunctional. Though the demand for schooling is high, it is still varied. Considering that the government school system provides unrestricted entry to all children, have-enough or have-little, mediocre or meritorious, it is imperative to carefully examine whether we need to revitalize rather than just abandon such a system. From a practical point of view, the quality of government schooling will also suffer if the more prosperous are encouraged to leave the system. At the same time, their exit from the system is unlikely to generate a healthy, efficiency-enhancing competition between private and government schools.

Enrolment in aided schools has fallen somewhat and cost of schooling in such schools, contrary to what one would expect, is somewhat higher than in government schools. However, reliance on PA schools is far higher than reliance on PUA schools for the low-income groups. It is also a more cost-effective sector according to some studies. Many state governments, however, find the sector problematic. It is a sector which needs state-specific research for effective models if it is to help in UEE.

Private education is also a costly business, as both macro- and micro-level data indicate. Not only are incentive schemes not in evidence but fees, books, etc. are hugely expensive. Even if poor families are game to put one child in a private school, that child is likely to get far less inputs to support his learning than a richer child. Also, we need to closely scrutinize whether the poor parents' so-called 'willingness' to pay for expensive private schooling can be taken, in a straightforward way, to be an indicator of their 'ability' to pay, as many of them have to sacrifice in other essential areas of spending.

Little can be said about the correlation between enrolment and privatization at the macro level, if one looks at state-level figures, but one important conclusion drawn by the NCAER is that increasing privatization will only increase the already strong gender bias in schooling. Another important issue is the cross movements between the government and private systems—the degree, the reasons, and the repercussions of this situation. A third is the achievement of those who expend scarce family resources to avail of private schooling (at whatever cost to their families). Their numbers will increase if the government system is allowed to deteriorate further. Presuming that these can afford poor quality private schools and haven't adequate home support, could this lead to frustration and non-enrolment as has already happened in government schools?

It is thought that private schools have the advantages of operational efficiency, lower running costs, and higher achievement as the data bring out. However, more research is needed to explore the validity of these claims. Even were they true, it is not clear how these advantages of the private sector can be wedded with the more egalitarian amplitude of the government school system.

REFERENCES

Aggarwal, Yash (1998). 'Primary Education in Delhi: How Much do the Children Learn'. National Institute of Educational Planning and Administration, New Delhi.

Bashir, Sajitha (1994). 'Public versus Private in Primary Education: Comparisons of School Effectiveness and Costs in Tamil Nadu'. Unpublished Ph.D. Dissertation, University of London, London School of Economics, London.

————— (1995). 'Analysis of the Determinants of Learning Achievement: How Useful for Policy and Planning?' NIEPA seminar on *School Quality in India*. 14–15 November 1995, New Delhi.

Dréze, Jean and Haris Gazdar (1996). 'Uttar Pradesh: The burden of Inertia'. In Jean Dréze and Amartya Sen (eds) *Indian Development*. Oxford University Press, Delhi.

Duraisamy, Malathy (1996). 'Demand for and Access to Child Schooling in Tamil Nadu'. UNDP Studies on Human Development.

Duraisamy, P., Estelle James, Julia Lane and Jee-Peng Tan (1996). *Is There a Quantity—Quality Trade-off as Enrollments Increase? Evidence from Tamil Nadu, India*. The World Bank, Washington, D.C.

Govinda, R. and N. V. Varghese (1992). 'Quality of Primary Education: An Empirical Study'. *Journal of Educational Planning and Administration*, vol. 6, no. 1, January.

————— (1993). *Quality of Primary Schooling in India: A Case Study of Madhya Pradesh*. International Institute for Educational Planning, Paris and National Institute of Educational Planning and Administration, New Delhi.

Kingdon, Geeta G. (1994). 'An Economic Evaluation of School Management—Types in Urban India: A Case Study of Uttar Pradesh'. Unpublished D. Phil Thesis, University of Oxford, London.

————— (1996a). 'The Quality and Efficiency of Private and Public Education: A Case Study of Urban India.' *Oxford Bulletin of Economics and Statistics*, vol. 58, no. 1.

————— (1996b). 'Private Schooling in India: Size, Nature and Equity-effects'. DEP no. 72, LSE.

Krishnaji, N. (1996). 'Poverty, Gender and Schooling: A study of Mahboobnagar and Adilabad Districts'. UNDP Studies on Human Development.

Majumdar, Manabi (1996). 'Kanyakumari: The Leading Edge of Education in Tamilnadu.' UNDP Studies on Human Development.

Majumdar, Manabi (1997). 'Educational Changes in Rajasthan: Despair and Hope'. UNDP Studies on Human Development.

Majumdar, Manabi and A. Vaidyanathan (1995). 'The Role of the Private Sector in Education in India: Current Trends and New Priorities'. UNDP Studies on Human Development in India, DP no. 10.

Mathew, E. T. (1990). 'Financing College Education in the Private Sector in India'. *Economic and Political Weekly*, vol. 25, no. 17.

Mehrotra, Nidhi (1995). 'Why Poor Children Do Not Attend School: The Case of Rural India'. University of Chicago. (Unpublished)

Muzammil, Mohd. and Geeta Kingdon (1997). 'Political Economy in Uttar Pradesh, India'. Department of Economics, Lucknow and Institute of Economics and Statistics, Oxford.

Nambissan, Geetha B. (1997). 'Schooling of Children in Rural Rajasthan: A Study of Jhadol and Alwar Tehsil'. UNDP Studies on Human Development.

National Council of Applied Economic Research (1994). 'Non-Enrolment, Drop Out and Private Expenditure on Elementary Education: A Comparison across States and Population Groups.' New Delhi. (Mimeo)

National Council of Educational Research and Training (1982). *Fourth All-India Educational Survey*. New Delhi.

————— (1992). *Fifth All-India Educational Survey*. New Delhi.

————— (1998). *Sixth All-India Educational Survey*. New Delhi.

National Sample Survey Organisation (1998). *Attending an Educational Institution in India: Its Level, Nature and Cost 1995–96*. NSS 52nd round (1996–7) Report

No. 439. Department of Statistics, Government of India, New Delhi.

————— (1993). Results of Participation in Education for Major States, NSS 42nd Round (July 1986–June 1987) *Sarvekshana*, 56th Issue 17(1), Department of Statistics, Ministry of Planning, New Delhi.

Noronha, Claire (1996). *Private Schools for the Low Income Group: A Case Study of a Low Income Area in Delhi.* Probe Background Papers.

Pande, Anuradha (1997). *Educational Survival of Rural Children in the UP Himalayas: Uttarakhand.* Project on Strategies and Financing for Human Development, UNDP, New Delhi. (Mimeo)

PROBE (1999). *Public Report On Basic Education in India.* The PROBE team in Association with Centre for Development Economics. Oxford University Press, New Delhi.

Sharma, P. N. and Vani Vinayak (2000). 'Role of Private Schools in Expanding Primary Education: Siddharth Nagar Experience.' Study sponsored by State Institute of Educational Management and Training, Allahabad.

Shatrugna, M. (1988). 'Privatising Higher Education'. *Economic and Political Weekly*, vol. 23, no. 51.

Singh, Jagpal (1995). *Political Economy of Unaided and Unrecognised Schools: A Study of Meerut District of Western Uttar Pradesh.* National Institute of Educational Planning and Administration and Indira Gandhi National Open University, Regional Centre for Haryana, Punjab, Chandigarh and Jammu and Kashmir, Karnal.

Sinha, Amarjeet and Ajay Sinha (1995). *Primary Schooling in North India: A Field Investigation.* Centre for Sustainable Development, Lal Bahadur Shastri National Academy of Administration, Mussoorie.

Srivastava, Ravi (1997). 'Access to Basic Education in Uttar Pradesh: Results from Field Survey'. UNDP Studies on Human Development.

Tilak, J. B. G. (1991). 'Privatization of Higher Education'. *Prospects*, 21(2).

Varghese, N. V. (1993) 'Private Schools in India: Perceptions and Provisions.' In R. P. Singh (ed.), *Private Initiatives and Public Policy in Education.* Federation of Management of Educational Institutions, New Delhi.

III

Meeting Quality Concerns in Elementary Education

12

Texts in Context
Development of Curricula, Textbooks, and Teaching Learning Materials

Anita Rampal

INTRODUCTION

Redefining learning in an empowering context, and changing curricula and texts to address the life concerns of the disadvantaged has been an unachieved task in other countries too. It shall be discussed how this is also our weakest area, and though we might ultimately be on a better track as far as 'joyful' texts are concerned, issues of 'relevance' are indeed most difficult to approach and continue to face great resistance. In shying away from presenting reality as it exists and encouraging learners to critically question it, textbooks tend to paint a distorted and false picture of the lives of the disadvantaged and the poor. In addition, the centralized pattern of developing curricula and textbooks and conducting examinations never allows the distance to be truly bridged. There are, however, many lessons to be learnt from initiatives taken by innovative experiments, normally outside the larger formal system.

In 1986 the National Policy on Education (NPE) put forth an honest evaluation of the state of education in the country and posited some radical recommendations to restructure the system. It looked at education within a broad framework, with special attention to those outside the formal system—for instance, working children, youth as well as non-literate adults. An entire chapter in its Programme of Action was devoted to the 'Content and Process of School Education', which looked at the policy implications for change, the interventions and strategies to be adopted, and the immediate tasks to be undertaken. It categorically stated that: 'one of the major weaknesses of the attempts to bring about curricular reform in the past has been the lack of a comprehensive plan to link curricular changes with the processes

of teaching, learning, teacher training and examination reform'. This recognition of the need for a comprehensive link between curricular change and processes of teaching and learning is crucial.

The NPE went on to state that several earlier reviews of textbooks had revealed some shortcomings that needed to be looked at carefully and acknowledged that 'without making room for the introduction of new ideas into the system, through deliberate promotion of its linkages with existing innovative projects (run by other governmental and non-governmental agencies), the present system on its own may act as a self-propelling one'. This issue needs to be carefully reviewed, to understand how far we have succeeded in bringing in fresh ideas from outside the system, and if we have managed to mainstream the innovations and strategies tried out in field situations.

The NPE envisaged adult education as a means to reducing economic, social, and gender disparities, through the creation of effective mechanisms to help deprived and disadvantaged people access programmes of development. It stated that 'continuing education is an indispensable aspect of the strategy of human resource development and of the goal of creating a learning society'. Invoking 'momentous scientific, technological and pedagogical' achievements it proposed a Technical and Societal Mission for the National Adult Education Programme.

UNBURDENING TEXTS, UNDERSCORING LEARNING[1]

The Yashpal Committee Report

One of the most comprehensive studies on issues related to school curriculum and textbooks in India was conducted

[1] This and the following section draw upon chapters written

by the Yashpal Committee (see GoI 1993). The Ministry of Human Resource Development appointed the National Advisory Committee chaired by Professor Yashpal, in response to a debate in the Rajya Sabha on the issue of the 'load of the school bag'. It was meant to advise on how to 'reduce the burden on school students, while improving the quality of learning, including capability for lifelong self-learning and skill formation'. Professor Yashpal, in his Preface, reflectively states that

> after this study I and my colleagues on the Committee are convinced that the more pernicious burden is that of non-comprehension. In fact, *a significant fraction of children who drop out may be those who refuse to compromise with non-comprehension—they are potentially superior to those who just memorise and do well in examinations, without comprehending very much!* [Yashpal Committee Report, DoE 1993, Preface] [Emphasis added]

The Committee was critical of the overarching trend in curriculum and textbook preparation to package as much information as possible in a 'highly compressed and abstruse manner'. It noted that:

> Barring exceptions, our textbooks appear to have been written primarily to convey information or 'facts', rather than to make children think and explore. The common style used in textbooks is exemplified by the following passages:
>
> *The term pH is defined as the negative logarithm to the base 10 of the hydrogen ion concentration expressed in gramions per litre or moles per litre. (class X)*
> *We find that while dividing a decimal by a multiple of 10,000 or 1000 we first move the decimal point to the left as many places as there are zeroes in the number and then divide the resulting decimal by the second factor of the divisor. (class V)*
>
> The distance between the child's everyday life and the content of the textbook further accentuates the transformation of knowledge into a load. Neither the mode of communication, nor the selection of objects depicted, nor the language conveys the centrality of the child in the world constructed by the text. Not just books used for the teaching of the natural and social sciences, but even those used for the teaching of the mother tongue are written in such stylised diction that children cannot be expected to see the language as their own. Words, expressions and nuances commonly used by children in their milieu are absent. So is humour. An artificial, sophisticated style dominates, reinforcing the tradition of distancing knowledge from life. The language used in textbooks thus deepens the sense of 'burden' attached to all school-related knowledge.

Readability of Textbooks

The incomprehensible language of textbooks has continued to remain a major cause of concern. A detailed study

by the author for the Public Report on Basic Education, (see PROBE 1999) and the Madhya Pradesh Human Development Report (MPHDR), 1995.

(see Kaul *et al.* 1995) of the readability of class III textbooks, conducted by the National Council of Educational Research and Training (NCERT) and the Central Institute of Indian Languages in six states of the country, confirmed that the vocabulary and sentence structure was too difficult for children at primary level. Average student comprehension in both language and mathematics texts was found to be higher in Tamil Nadu and Maharashtra than in the other states. A linguistic analysis indicated that a lower percentage of compound sentences, higher number of verbs, and the presence of shorter, simpler sentences were positively related to higher comprehension results. The environmental science texts were found to be highly technical and less comprehensible, and teachers said they normally had to explain the given concepts in their own words. In fact, the mathematics books were low in readability and teachers said those were used only as teachers' guides rather than as textbooks. Reading and writing tests based on the ten most frequently used words in the texts showed that students had difficulty writing words that were not part of their vocabulary. The need to systematically compile children's natural vocabulary for different regions and states, to be used while developing textbooks, was strongly felt. This also leads to the issue of decentralized curricula and preparation of textbooks.

MATHEMATICS TEXTS

A detailed study of mathematics textbooks and teachers' manuals was undertaken by Mary Harris (on behalf of the Commonwealth Secretariat) last year, to identify the extent to which gender bias was apparent in the NCERT texts. She points out that the language of the Class I book *Let's Learn Mathematics* is already too formal and runs the risk of alienating girls right from the beginning.

> Girls find co-operative and generative ways of working a better way of understanding mathematics than the more definitional, hierarchical ways used in this text and indeed throughout the series. For 5 year-olds, whose first language may not be English, the sentences: *A numeral is a symbol representing the number of things in a collection. The term 'numeral' is used while referring to the written symbol of the number, otherwise the word number is used* are very hard to understand. Although teachers are asked in the Manual to 'make children recognise' what some of these complex sentences mean, the instruction to follow the formal procedures of mathematical definition remains. When (learning) outcomes are expected to include complex language under discussion, children may have no choice but to commit what they see a rigmarole to memory,...a habit that is known to lead to great difficulties with mathematical understanding. (Harris 1999)

Redressing gender imbalance in textbooks, moreover, is not simply a matter of introducing more examples with women, but of understanding that women have continued to play an important role in accumulating and refining traditional knowledge in various spheres of activity. She refers to the book *Numeracy Counts*! (see Rampal *et al.* 1999), that highlights how women continue to actively and remarkably engage with complicated concepts of everyday mathematics as part of their daily work. She urges curriculum makers and textbook writers to appreciate and also highlight in textbooks 'that a woman carrying milk knows precisely, if informally, its volume, its value and how many mouths it can feed'.

INFORMATION INVASION

Textbook writers and curriculum makers have been beset with the notion of a global 'information explosion', and believe that a backward country like India has to quickly 'catch up' with the developed world, where knowledge is fast expanding. There is a major pedagogical problem in this notion, which seems to treat knowledge as synonymous with information. The crucial component of children's education should be to promote concept formation and enhance their capacity for theory building. All children are natural theory makers, and from much before they go to school they begin to construct their own theories and explanations for the world they observe. Learning in childhood is not a process of accumulating or storing information about different topics, but the ability to apply the understanding of one phenomenon to others. Observation, categorization, and generalization are natural skills with which a baby first responds to her/his environment and then learns to communicate through language. Moreover, current research has shown that children often form consistent 'alternative frameworks' or 'naive theories' that may even be contradictory to established knowledge. Therefore, textbooks also need to consciously elicit and address children's intuitive ideas before presenting new ideas or information.

Another problem is that our textbooks normally follow a strictly linear pattern of imparting information. For instance, we first teach 1–10, then 20–30, and so on. Or say, 'Our Locality' in class I, 'Our District' in class III, 'Our State' in class IV, and 'Our Country and the World' in class V. However, children do not necessarily understand the concept of 'district' or 'state' at that age, while they may be familiar with the idea of the country somewhat earlier. In addition, knowledge is treated as disjointed fragments of information that can simplistically be slotted in the syllabus, e.g. teaching 'parts and properties of plants' in class II, 'the function of leaves and photosynthesis' in class III, and in class IV the 'seed–flower–fruit cycle', etc. On the contrary, the learning process in children is far from linear, and the

way they process information about the world they live in is far more holistic and integrated.

Since the very notion of teaching in our education system is generally reduced to 'giving information', the teacher is conditioned and often constrained to perform accordingly. Teaching is usually limited to a set of actions which include asking children to read on their own, making one child read out aloud, writing a few words on the board, or dictating 'correct' answers to questions given in the book. In this scenario the textbook becomes the Bible, and the nature of the information it contains shapes the pattern of the transaction in class. Textbooks may pretend to be activity based but actually discourage any exploration or activity. Children are asked to observe the 'picture' of an object, rather than go out and look at the 'real' thing, be it a common sparrow or the leaf of a plant. As mentioned in *Learning Without Burden* (see Yashpal Committee Report 1993) 'Over the recent years, some textbooks have adopted the vocabulary of observation and exploration,...but even here virtually all commands for observation conclude with statements about what will be seen,' thereby making it unnecessary to actually perform any activity.

FALSE EXPLANATIONS

A passage on 'Weather' from the class III textbook *Exploring Environment* shows how far it is from a truly exploratory approach. In this the density of the text and also the use of statements that do not really explain anything may be noticed:

> When water evaporates it changes from liquid into water vapour. Water vapour is the gaseous form of water. Wet things dry when the water in them becomes water vapour and moves into the atmosphere. You cannot see water evaporating into water vapour. Water vapour exists in the form of very tiny particles.

Most of these sentences do not offer any real explanations, which for this particular concept are actually not possible for children of this age. They are only statements that go round in circles, as tautologies. If a child asks, 'But what *is* water vapour?' she/he gets the answer, 'Water vapour is the gaseous form of water'! Naturally the child stops trying to make sense of what is being 'taught', and falls in line with what is expected—to unthinkingly repeat what has been told. At the time of examinations, she/he is hailed as a 'good student' only if she/he manages to faithfully reproduce these *mantras*, when asked.

THE EXAMINATION TRAP

The present pattern of evaluation sets the tone for most problems related to the quality of learning. It also serves as a major stumbling block in trying to change textbooks or methods. If examination questions expect children to memorize information and give answers in fixed predetermined phrases, irrespective of whether they understand them or not, there is little hope of changing the learning environment. In fact, in a significantly large number of schools, teachers no longer insist on textbooks, but resort only to *kunjis* or guidebooks.

Teachers and textbook writers do not know how to assess children's 'understanding', and have never been trained to think in this manner. In fact, to think, understand, express in one's own words, to explore or to experiment, to use logical reasoning, to observe carefully, etc. are given no value or place in the school, because ultimately they are not evaluated in any way. More significantly, crucial aspects of the non-cognitive or affective domain of a child's personality are never accorded a place in the curriculum since these are not easily quantifiable, and therefore, not assessable in the traditional pattern. In the present system, all accountability is vested in the examination, since teachers teach and children 'learn' with the sole purpose of facing the ultimate test. It thus becomes imperative to simultaneously change the pattern of examinations if any meaningful change is to be expected in the way 'learning' is transacted through textbooks and classrooms.

CHILDREN'S PERCEPTIONS

There has been no systematic attempt to get a feedback from children and to elicit their perceptions about their textbooks. Most people who have looked at children's responses have pointed towards school learning and textbooks being considered 'boring' or 'difficult'. It is generally believed that if they fail to learn in school or from their books there must be something wrong with the children, for which they need all kinds of additional inputs, from special tuition to tonics.

Not many children would react like 11-year-old Gargi who, when asked to critically analyse her textbook, actually dared to question the suitability of what was being taught. She chose one section from the chapter on 'Air' and sent her expressive comments with a drawing, appended with two pages of her textbook: 'The section on Priestley's experiment was most confusing. Mercury, red powder, heating, re-heating...Add to this Preistley, Lavoisier, glowing splinter, oxygen....Garbage! It went zoom over my head.'

Those two pages of her textbook contain a host of unfamiliar terms and concepts, such as crucible, mass, dessicator, clay pipe triangle, magnesium, apparatus, and mercuric oxide. In addition, it is shocking to see how the book thoughtlessly goes into elaborate instructions for doing an experiment normally given to high school students—to find the difference in the 'mass' of magnesium after burning it in air! (This, incidentally, is supposed to be among the better textbooks used by well-known schools and published by a private concern.)

Amongst the millions of our schoolchildren, as well as teachers, very few would place the blame squarely on their textbooks, and even dare to call them 'garbage'! Unfortunately, most have been conditioned to accept it as it is, and have long given up trying to make sense of it.

QUESTIONS OF RELEVANCE AND LIFE ORIENTATION

The most crucial issues about 'relevance' and 'life orientation' of curricula and text material are also the ones most difficult to address, given the dominant influence of the urban middle classes on the present educational systems. Relevance goes much deeper than merely providing a 'familiar' village scenario, or doling out ostensibly 'useful' information. Ironically, in the name of 'relevance' textbooks tend to get moralistic, oversimplified, and even contrived.

The lesson 'Aao Sikhen' (Come Let's Learn) of the class III book *Bhaashaa Bharti* (SCERT, MP 1996) states:

'*Vaahan chalaate samay mudne se pehle haath se isharaa karen*'. [While driving a vehicle indicate with your hand before turning]
'*Ambulance, police ya fire brigade ki gaadi ko pehle jaane den*'. [Allow the ambulance, police or fire brigade to proceed first]
'*Bacche, boorhe avam apaahij ko raastaa paar karne men madad karen*'. [Children, help the old and the handicapped to cross the road]

This last sentence epitomizes how easily textbook writers forget the age, capacities, interests, and concerns of the learners. Text clearly meant for adult drivers has been imposed on young children (most of them living in rural areas with no roads, hospitals, or fire brigades!), ostensibly in response to a central norm (MLL 1.3.4) that traffic rules must be 'taught' in class III. In the same unthinking manner, these children will be made to regurgitate these rules in examinations.

This particular lesson may be an extreme example of 'irrelevance' but there are many others that continue to waste time in trivial preaching. Thus, we find either highly prescriptive and moralistic lessons (about hygiene, cleanliness, hard work, etc.) or rather simplistic generalizations about the perceived needs of the rural poor.

The class III textbook *Bhaashaa Bharti* mentioned earlier contains separate chapters to describe each of the following:

• An equipped village primary health centre, with a doctor, a nurse, and a compounder.

• A village *panchayat* (local self-government) which discusses development plans for the '*gramin rozgaar kaaryakram*' (rural employment programme) and proposes to open a crèche for women agricultural workers.

• A woman who takes her child to the hospital for a vaccination and convinces her neighbour to follow suit.

Similar overidealized and almost surrealistic situations abound in other school textbooks—of truly democratic *panchayats*, benevolent employers, and effective government schemes. These are routinely doled out as facts of 'social studies'. Ironically, rural children, unlike those from protected urban homes, are much more conscious of the conflicts and complexities of life, which form a part of their reality. They know very well that these lessons are contrived, but have no chance to question the platitudes they must passively accept.

WHICH KNOWLEDGE COUNTS?

The village child is also far more knowledgeable about the natural world, and does not need to look at 'pictures' to count the legs of a spider, or to identify the eggs of a frog and leaves of a neem tree. Ironically, a tribal child may learn from her/his community details about metal casting, about identifying medicinal herbs, and the rich bio-diversity of her/his forests that foreign companies might vie to patent, but schools would not acknowledge as being 'valuable' knowledge. The way school curricula and texts are structured, the rural child is offered unrealistic platitudes in the name of 'relevance' and, even in matters she/he knows better, is never allowed an edge over her/his 'privileged' urban counterparts.

Science texts (both for children and also for adult learners) often contain information about personal hygiene and cleanliness presented in a didactic manner. However, real life stories about children's everyday problems, such as, lice or scabies, and safe practical ways to deal with them are never included. Lice are very common in young children and it was found that poor mothers sometimes use cheap insecticides on children's heads. However, the urgency of this problem and the need to tackle it sensitively and creatively in the classroom does not get reflected in textbook writing. There is often a topic on 'types of houses'. A 'good' house is always one with a kitchen, toilets, windows, electricity, etc. and millions of children who live in conditions that do not conform to these norms are immediately alienated, and signalled that their lifestyle is 'bad'.

In the case of tribal children the sense of alienation is severe, since their very existence and identity are portrayed problematically in textbooks. Moreover, teachers themselves are deeply conditioned by social biases against those belonging to Scheduled Castes and Scheduled Tribes (SCs and STs), and they reinforce these in the classroom. In a textbook for class VI, questions about 'where in the state are tigers found?' were framed in exactly the same way as 'where are tribals found?' ('*Aadivaasi kahaan paaye jaate hain?*'). No effort was made even to semantically differentiate between 'where people are *found*' and 'where people *live*'. No tribal characters and no tribal names normally appear in school textbooks. One textbook contains a chapter on 'Our State' ('*hamara pradesh*') with the statement 'tribal and backward persons (*pichhade log*) inhabit our State in large numbers'. One can only imagine what this does to the self-image of the large numbers of tribal and so-called 'backward' children, and what message it gives to others.

LANGUAGE TEACHING

The foundation of all school learning depends on the way language is taught, and this has been found to be critically problematic. Language teaching in the earliest classes tends to focus on alphabets, and the words chosen are often not from any living context for the child. Language teaching makes no effort to include colloquial forms from different dialects and assumes that children will learn to communicate only through repetition or rote memorization. This is certainly not how children learn a language, and unless they are made to actively engage with words and meanings, to play with them, they remain diffident about coping with any further demands of the curriculum.

Moreover, there is an obsession with 'correcting' each 'mistake' they make, so that exploratory and fearless use of language is not allowed a chance. Indeed, this is also why children who are amazingly proficient in speaking and expressing themselves, with a high level of language sophistication in their own mother tongues, cannot read or write simple sentences in it, even after four to five years of regular schooling. Encouraging children to write creatively, expressing their own thoughts and views, should be the basis of all textbooks and materials, not just those used for language teaching.

The issue of textbooks in minority and tribal languages is quite complicated. While language is central to the very identity of a person, and most tribal communities would want to preserve their own languages as part of their culture, they are also acutely aware of the 'market' value of the dominant language. Moreover, tribals who regularly transact with non-tribals are often bilingual. Therefore, education must begin with the mother tongue, even if it is a tribal dialect written in Devnagari script (or the prevalent script of that region). The child can continue to learn bilingually, and gradually switch to Hindi (or the dominant regional language) taught in a more conversational form. Indeed, such textbooks need to be developed with care and greater sensitivity towards minority or tribal culture.

In most so-called 'English-medium' schools children are burdened with an even more alien language, which is not taught as it should be, namely as a 'second language', but which is the medium for all the content they must grapple with. Normally young children can quite easily learn to speak many languages at the same time, if they are provided with a stimulating environment to use these naturally and fearlessly. However, for most of our children there are very few natural 'learning environments' to listen to or speak in English, either at home or outside. Teaching materials in English, therefore, need to be developed much more carefully, with professional insights about children's strategies for learning a foreign language.

CENTRALIZED NORMS OF LEARNING

The Yashpal Committee was critical of the highly centralized character of the system, which justifies the use of national norms for achievement and testing, on account of a confusion between 'content' and 'learning'. The formulation of minimum levels of learning (MLLs) as national criteria to evaluate achievement outcomes was one such move that created several problems. The slogan of 'competency-based learning', which only followed the MLL list of 'facts', barely disguised as 'competencies', did not make much difference to the textbooks. There are, indeed, many contentious issues regarding the philosophy of framing such national norms, which do not take account of diversities, but here the 'minimum learning' expectations from children and their impact on textbooks will be reviewed.

In their zeal for adhering to the national criteria, some textbook committees had actually assigned chapters to be written on given MLL codes. For instance, one person was asked to write a chapter on '1.5.8', which is the 'competency' statement (for class V) 'Calculates Lowest Common Multiple of 2 or 3 numbers each of which do not exceed 10'. In fact, in some textbooks a chapter was either given the same heading or boldly indicated the MLL for which it was written. This approach to textbook writing was fundamentally flawed. Instead of trying to create chapters around interesting 'themes' for children, that allow for many different competencies and skills to be holistically and creatively enhanced, this approach prompted a deeper slide into a reductionist framework.

For instance, let us look at the MLL statement 1.5.2: 'Writes number names up to 10,000,000 (one crore)'. Not only do such statements mislead teachers about what and how arithmetic must be taught, but also encourage them to inflict impractical and tortuous tasks on children. The MLLs for environmental studies were particularly unrealistic. Not really framed in terms of 'competencies', the list essentially constituted 'topics', such as:

1.1—'Our body and its cleanliness'; 10.3.1—'Earth–sun relation and consequences'; 5.4—'Progress of Man from Early Times to the Present Age'; 7.4—'Nutrition, pollution and cleanliness'; 10.4.1—'Heavenly bodies'; 10.4.5—'Weather phenomena'; 9.4.1—'Knows the three states of matter'; 8.5.3—'Knows the present schemes to increase and improve forest cover, cleaning of rivers, tanks and such others, e.g. the Ganga.'. Even a large majority of adult population would probably not be able to contend with the following MLLs for Class V: 6.5.5—'Finds out increase in population according to each census since Independence and understands its implications'; 10.5.1—'Knows about dangers from misuse of scientific knowledge, e.g. in war'.

The problem with national criteria such as the MLLs is that once these have been enumerated by an apex body they become sacrosanct, and no amount of clarification about these being 'suggestive' guidelines, can dilute the authority of these norms. In their national evaluation of the implementation of the MLL programme, Jangira *et al.* (1997) remarked that 'the MLL approach reflects essentially a behaviouristic model which focuses on specific competencies and attainments at "mastery" level'. In a refreshingly reflective fashion the report recommended that the MLLs would need to be reconceptualized in line with a humanistic, child-centred approach. The team had visited four states and found that the evaluation of children's learning was the weakest component of the programme. Commenting on the textbooks, the report said, 'A great deal of effort has been expended on development of "competency based textbooks" without a clear understanding of the direction in which the changes are required,' and in some cases the new books were not very different from the earlier ones. Textbooks 'should be prepared not sequentially on each competency separately, but on clusters of competencies, thus providing for a more holistic learning experience'. The need for detailed teacher handbooks was also highlighted.

In 1998 the NCERT responded to the concerns expressed in the field, and attempted to redress the problems in the MLL approach by reinterpreting those as 'Expected Learning Outcomes'. The document 'The Curricular Framework' suggested reorganization of curricular areas, with separate focus on Arts Education, and also departed from the finely codified 'levels' to broad 'indicators'. It has yet to be seen how far this rethinking at national level would percolate to the states and influence textbooks and curricula at that level.

PARTICIPATORY DEVELOPMENT OF TEXT MATERIALS

A serious lacuna of our system has been that our textbook writers, however eminent in their own disciplines, have had little experience of actually working with children or schoolteachers. In fact, teachers are normally not involved in the preparation of textbooks, and only a few may be included in committees to register their token presence. According to one report, 'the failure to involve teachers in textbook development in India may be one of the most important reasons for the poor quality of textbooks' (see World Bank 1997). As recommended by the Yashpal Committee, close interaction with children in the classroom situation 'might enable experts to develop a certain amount of sensitivity towards the living and versatile approaches used by them. They might then also perceive the need to equip themselves with knowledge of children's psychology, particularly the psychology of learning, before venturing out on the task of textbook preparation'.

There have been many new initiatives in different states as part of school education programmes, such as the Distict Primary Education Programme (DPEP) in Karnataka, Madhya Pradesh, and Kerala, the Lok Jumbish (LJ) in Rajasthan, and the Bihar Education Project. In addition, many voluntary groups have been developing text materials for both, the formal and the non-formal systems of education. Eklavya has designed curricula for the formal primary and middle schools of Madhya Pradesh within its project areas, and has also contributed to the state textbooks under the DPEP. Similarly, Digantar and Sandhan have contributed towards this task in Rajasthan, and Digantar has also helped develop materials for the alternative and non-formal schools of Madhya Pradesh. The Kerala Shastra Sahitya Parishad (KSSP) has actively participated in curricular and textbook reform efforts of the state, and in 1996 had also set up its own Education Commission (see KSSP 1999) to comprehensively review the status of education. The following section presents two case studies of efforts made towards participatory development of text materials, and the issues that emerge from these exercises.

THE KERALA EXAMPLE—CONTINUOUS MOBILIZATION

One striking example of a participatory approach to textbook development for formal schools was the one adopted by the state of Kerala. Though this state has achieved almost universal enrolment in primary schools, which function efficiently with teachers taking classes regularly, there has been concern regarding the poor learning achievements of children and the growing parallel network of commercial institutions. In November 1995 the KSSP organized a *Vidyabhyasa Jatha*, which toured the entire state and engaged with the problems of the education system. Subsequently, a People's Education Commission, comprising eminent educationists, was set up to analyse the situation and recommend measures to improve the system. Curriculum renewal and textbook revision were sought in the light of such concerns.

A DPEP discussion paper entitled 'Textbooks, Why and for Whom?' was circulated widely in 1996, amongst the Zila Parishads and other public forums, where it was debated and suggestions for curricular reforms were sought. Teachers invited from all the districts were screened during a two-day workshop, and those selected were subsequently given a ten-day orientation on child-centred classroom processes. These teachers, along with the State Resource Group, drawn from among the faculty of various institutes, academicians, illustrators, subject experts, etc. then constituted a team for textbook development.

The curricular framework was developed through a series of interactive workshops, and through detailed discussion on approach papers about different aspects of the curriculum, including the underlying 'beliefs and assumptions'. The MLLs were critically reviewed and redefined, with a focus on the 'basic experiences' to be provided to children. The basic outlines, lesson frames, and guidelines were written and the textbook prepared through a series of workshops. Teachers who were also the writers systematically field-tested the lessons in different types of schools, to revise those for the textbook and the teachers' handbooks.

One significant achievement of this approach was the consciously sought participation of the community. Since there has been apprehension and resistance from the public regarding the changed curriculum, the programme attempts to reach out through the active parent–teacher associations. However, as noted by the NCERT study (see Kaul *et al.* 1998), little attempt was made to involve the private school system, which in Kerala wields substantial influence on the curricular and classroom practices adopted. Another lacuna was the absence of curricular reform at pre-primary stage—a large number of children in Kerala attend pre-primary schools, where they are generally burdened with a heavy content taught in conventional style. The NCERT study (see Kaul *et al.* 1998) notes with appreciation that 'it was very unusual to find children saying that they enjoyed mathematics and liked the book because it has so many games in it!' However, the study suggests that the textbooks for Class IV seem to be heavy in terms of content load, while those on environmental science devote less attention to social issues.

THE MADHYA PRADESH EXPERIENCE— UNFULFILLED PROMISES

Madhya Pradesh is the only state that has for over twenty five years made it possible for a voluntary agency (Eklavya) to develop curricula and text materials for some of its formal schools. As part of the DPEP initiative, the Madhya Pradesh government began in a participatory mode, by collaborating with a number of individuals and organizations working at field level. As part of the curricular renewal exercise, it was decided to undertake intensive field trials over five years, of multiple 'packages' of processes, not just new textbooks.

As a commendable step towards promoting academic decentralization, a large number of agencies from within and outside the state were invited to present proposals on curriculum development, through field trial among selected schools in any one block. In addition to the agencies formally invited, which included the State Council of Educational Research and Training (SCERT), the Department of Education at Indore, some voluntary agencies, and a few active Zilla Saksharta Samitis, there was also an open invitation to any group that wished to take up this task. It was hoped that such varied agencies would bring in different kinds of expertise and experience, and would introduce the desired degree of plurality in the exercise. It was also hoped that groups working amongst different communities, in different regions of the state, would provide essential insights into their varied concerns. However, owing to the pressures of time, only the SCERT and Eklavya took up this task initially (in 1994–5), and were later joined by the *Shikshak Samakhya* programme team. For the field trial the SCERT chose 25–30 schools in one block in five different districts, while Eklavya took all 125 schools in one block. Both agencies developed teaching learning materials and trained teachers for the purpose. The primary challenge was to combine the trial efforts of the SCERT, Eklavya and the Shikshak Samakhya programme, to produce an amalgamated common package, despite the different premises on which they were based. The new curricular package, called '*Seekhna Sikhana*', was based on an integrated approach, which combined language with environmental studies and presented mathematics in a separate section of the same textbook.

The first four years of this curriculum renewal process were educative and participatory, with teachers and resource persons from the three programmes and from District Institutes of Educational Training (DIETs) and Block Research Councils (BRCs), working collaboratively to produce new material. Textbooks were prepared through a series of workshops, with much creative effort put in to develop each chapter, in line with holistic themes suitable for a child-centred approach. It was clear that none of the trial textbooks was fully satisfactory, especially in light of the larger objectives of addressing issues of relevance and life orientation. The Eklavya programme had been engaged with a child-centred curriculum developed participatively with teachers, though on a much

smaller, and therefore, more controlled scale, while the Shikshak Samakhya had extensively trained teachers to adopt joyful methods in the classroom. Whenever it was found that a given trial textbook had tried a useful theme even partially, it was taken up for further development through intensive collective brainstorming.

An attempt, however nascent, was made to critically address issues related to the lives of those normally marginalized by the curriculum. For instance, it was found that the trial book contained a usual poem on the festival of 'Diwali', which portrayed typical urban middle class concerns—about buying new clothes, sweets, and crackers. After some discussion one teacher from a tribal district was encouraged to describe the way his people celebrate Diwali, and it became evident that the festival had a much deeper cultural significance for a majority of those living in rural or tribal areas of the state. It not only involved the community in a larger social process, through elaborate articulations of folk art, dance, and music, but also revealed deeper bonds of people with their animals, which were also artistically embellished on this occasion. It was therefore decided to include this rich description of Diwali too, as being told by a child who has just returned from her/his village after participating in one such celebration lasting a fortnight.

There were, however, many difficulties and tremendous resistance on this account. As mentioned earlier, in the section on 'relevance and life orientation', it was often the conventional experts who felt insecure when 'different' content was to be included. Incidentally, such resistance was also witnessed in Kerala, where people happen to be more politically conscious, but there the programme managers continued to mobilize public opinion and respond to the community much more effectively. Unfortunately, despite having started with an ostensibly autonomous 'mission', the Madhya Pradesh government could not carry forth its stated objectives, and allowed the process to regress.

It has been seen that such externally funded programmes as the Madhya Pradesh DPEP or LJ have tended to retract, owing to increased bureaucratic and political control. Managers of such programmes, by virtue of the financial and political clout they wield, often ignore existing systems and long-term objectives in order to show quick results to their donors. Innovative materials or agencies are used as resources only as long as it is essential to project that some 'innovation' has taken place.

ACADEMIC DECENTRALIZATION AND A NEW ROLE FOR NATIONAL AGENCIES

The proposal for academic decentralization of the curriculum, textbooks, examinations, etc. has generally tended to raise a plethora of doubts, apprehensions, and even resistance. How can it be effected? How far 'down' can we take the process of decentralization? Does it mean further polarization, in terms of having separate curricula for the urban and the rural, the tribal and the non-tribal? How can we ensure 'equivalence', and what does equivalence really imply? What will happen to examinations, and would school boards need to be reconstituted? All these may be valid questions to discuss. However, it needs to be stressed that a suitable model for academic decentralization, that takes us beyond the macro level of the state, often a large and diverse one, to a more convenient unit that offers greater proximity, can indeed be worked out. A convenient unit would ultimately be the district, and ideally materials and textbooks must be developed by each DIET, in conformity with a skeletal 'core curriculum', and in close collaboration with a resource group of schoolteachers and other academics.

At present DIETs are academically inadequate, but a hands-on programme to upgrade their capacities and train their personnel can be taken up gradually. Such capacity building and facilitation of decentralization should be the major task of state- or national-level institutions. This should imply radically restructuring the NCERT, the SCERTs, the Textbook Corporations, the State Institutes of Education, etc., not only academically, but functionally, managerially, financially as well. The new role of national bodies such as the NCERT would be to provide forums for experience sharing and facilitate exposure to the experiences of various voluntary groups and state projects, through a close analysis of the materials developed.

It has often been pointed out that, in keeping with the spirit of academic decentralization, the NCERT must desist from producing textbooks of its own. At present the NCERT brings out textbooks for the network of Kendriya Vidyalayas, which exist all over the country. By doing so it only legitimizes the notion that for the dominant class of students studying in these national schools, 'culture free' textbooks are desirable, whereas it is for the ordinary child that 'relevant' books are prescribed. If text materials in conformity with local language, culture, and environment are indeed pedagogically important, then the NCERT must pursue this philosophy in its own work too.

LITERACY AND POST LITERACY MATERIALS

The next three sections look at issues specific to adult education, in the particular context of literacy campaigns. This is at present of crucial importance, since most of the district literacy campaigns are either over or have lost momentum and there is need to look ahead and plan for meaningful continuing education programmes. If a continuously learning society is to be established it is essential to understand the diverse literacies of our people and promote development of materials which can reflect their needs and interests.

Decentralized Production, Centralized Norms

One of the distinctive features of the mass literacy campaigns was that, for the first time in the country, and contrary to the case of school textbooks, the development of literacy primers actually got decentralized. District academic teams, consisting of local persons voluntarily participating in the effort, were asked to design their own primers in the language they thought appropriate. Despite tremendous pressures of time, many district teams did try to take up this challenge. However, the national committee meant to support such primers did not always help in encouraging diversity and the much needed flexibility in this process.

While it is true that primers for adult learners have to keep in mind their initial limitations, yet the language is often overly simplified and unnaturally truncated. The Improved Pace and Content of Learning (IPCL) norms, initially meant to indicate to textbook writers that language learning among adults was different from that in children, now tend to be invoked mechanically and rigidly, and limit the creativity of materials. It is now acknowledged that lack of experience or unfamiliarity with the context pose a greater barrier than mere vocabulary or the length of sentences used. However, IPCL norms continue to impose often unrealistic constraints regarding sentence length and vocabulary, even for post literacy materials.

A large proportion of the books meant for neo-literates bear a patronizing and condescending stance towards their readers, while carrying material considered to be 'informative' and 'instructive'. This distances the readers and also constrains their ability to read. There is little in such books that can excite or fascinate a reader. Neo-literates are adults who have knowledge and experience of their own, and writing for them has to be distinctly different from writing for children. Moving into the cognitive domain of neo-literates requires a conscious lateral shift, and is not simply 'going down to their level', as is commonly assumed.

Of Tastes and Contexts

It is commonly assumed that the act of reading is a mechanical and continuous process of scanning each word in a line and making sense of its meaning as we go along. We tend to believe that our eyes move smoothly from left to right as we traverse each line. However, reading is a much more complicated process. The reader constructs her/his own meanings through an entangled method—of making sense through social conventions, personal experiences, previous readings, and private tastes. The personal taste of a reader seems a factor not normally taken into account while preparing reading materials for neo-literates. A reader's taste is shaped by, and also shapes, the literate skills of an individual. How can one define a good book? As Francis Bacon had succinctly put it, 'Some books are to be tasted, others to be swallowed and some few to be chewed and digested.' The gastronomic metaphor has more to suggest about why and how someone reads a particular book, and helps us move towards understanding what forms 'attractive' reading material for a given set of readers.

Use of Oral Traditions in Written Language

In the context of writing for neo-literates, it becomes crucial to recognize that the language style of oral communication is much more expressive and personal, and draws upon rich traditions of narrative, through the imagery of metaphors and analogies. Written language which is formal, impersonal, and terse in comparison can seem alien and distanced for readers, and may often fail to engage their interest. Moreover, since adult learners need to make an additional effort to effectively use their as yet fragile literacy, it can also discourage them. Writing that creatively draws upon the strengths of oral traditions, is simple yet not simplistic, and is equally sophisticated in its literary content, needs to be promoted. It is interesting to note that historically the use of ballads had played a significant role in the spread of literacy in England, much before institutionalized schools had begun. They too dealt with a range of subjects—history, folk tales, retellings of classical myths, tales of crimes and criminals, prophecies, etc.

Dissemination and 'Flooding' of Literacy Materials

It is now well accepted that for neo-literates to be able to attain fluency in reading they need to be 'flooded' by attractive and affordable materials. For this, it is crucial to go into the nature of the agencies/organizations engaged in the publication of material for neo-literates and to analyse the distribution system used by them. This influences the accessibility, cost, and quality of such materials. At present there are a plethora of agencies bringing out books for neo-literates, and there are indications that more are poised to jump into the fray for purely commercial reasons. Are these agencies really addressing the demands of the readers? Are these books at all affordable for individual readers or are they distributed only to centres/libraries? What is the nature

of the language used? These are some of the issues that each state needs to review carefully.

Materials in Different Dialects

There are at present hardly any reading materials in different dialects, and this is an area that needs immediate attention. Though a few districts have tried to develop primers in tribal dialects (such as the ones made by the State Resource Centre at Jaipur, or those in Vagri by the Banswara literacy campaign), there do not exist adequate books and materials in the spoken languages of neo-literates. In Dumka district of Bihar, for instance, it was found that the health primer in Santhali was very popular as compared to the same book in Hindi. The National Book Trust (NBT) has produced only three or four booklets in Santhali, and those too are translations of books meant for children which does not always bring out the nuances and richness of the original idiom. The NBT needs to devote more serious attention to this area of work, and to forge closer links with the local people in such districts, while encouraging them to write (and draw) for themselves.

Visual language is also an important medium of communication and is deeply embedded in cultural traditions and social symbolic conventions. Most of the literacy material is inadequately or poorly visualized and it is clear that this aspect is generally not taken seriously. Notable exceptions are some books prepared by the NBT, which make conscious use of visuals designed by creative artists and illustrators. It is, therefore, necessary to include folk and rural artists in production teams, and some groups such as Eklavya, Katha, and Nirantar have managed to enlarge the repertoire of visual design in learning materials, through such consistent efforts.

Learners as Writers and Designers

A rich body of oral material has been generated through the literacy campaigns in many districts, in the form of songs, poems, slogans, anecdotes, and biographical stories. These have to be brought out as suitable written booklets, with the close involvement of learners and volunteers themselves. Some attempts have been made in this direction but have not been sustained for long. One exemplary effort that has sustained over the last few years is that of the *Mahila Dakiya* (Women's Post), which is brought out every month by the women's group at Banda (UP). Started in response to the literacy needs of village women trained as hand-pump mechanics, it has developed into a regular feature managed by them. A combination of different types of texts is used—direct text, short blurbs, poems, songs, picture stories—and the illustrations too are made by the learners themselves. The contributory cost is kept at Re 1 per copy and a thousand copies are normally printed.

Materials for Public Reading

The art of reading aloud has had a significant place in the history of literacy and in many countries it played an important social function. Several literacy campaigns made conscious use of public reading to mobilize learners, and it would be useful for us to understand the different methods and materials employed. In fact, for neo-literates working for long hours in sedentary occupations, it has been found enriching and motivating to have someone read out to them. A *beedi* factory in Kerala continues to have one worker, whose salary is paid by the workers' collective, to read out the newspaper to them while they work.

Interestingly, over a century ago this tradition of public reading in factories was established in Cuba, as part of its cigar making industry. In 1865 a poet turned cigar-maker had conceived of publishing a newspaper called *La Aurora* for industry workers, which would contain political features, articles on science, literature, poetry, etc. But lack of literacy was a major stumbling block. In order to make the paper accessible to all workers, the publisher hit upon the idea of a public reader. One worker served as the official 'lector' while the others paid for his efforts from their own pockets. Among the books read aloud were collections of poetry, historical compendiums, novels, and also manuals of political economy.

In our country it has been recognized that only setting up rural libraries is not enough to get neo-literates to read. A massive effort to mobilize readers, through folk media and *jathas*, has proved to be effective in popularizing material produced for neo-literates. The Bharat Gyan Vigyan Samiti (BGVS) had undertaken the 'Jan Vachan Andolan' and prepared numerous small booklets for this purpose. Indeed such reading aloud was found to trigger people's interest in the books read, and gave them confidence to buy those for themselves.

The Themes and the Content of Literacy Materials

Among the existing learning materials, areas such as history and science are particularly marked by uninteresting themes and inappropriate language and treatment. Indeed, even in regions that have a rich tradition of oral history, of legendary persons and memorable events, there is no attempt made to capture such themes in the form of readable booklets. There is also a need to prepare books for adult learners based on good literature and well-known classics. In Hindi this is being attempted by some groups such as Nirantar, Katha, and BGVS which have published small booklets, especially as adapted versions of famous classics. Good writers could be encouraged to adapt such literature for neo-literates, while maintaining the essence and flavour of the original work.

One crucial area of work that has not been explored by most agencies has been that of folklore, riddles, games, and folk stories. The Virudunagar district in Tamil Nadu had made an attempt to bring out booklets based on such folk knowledge. In fact, one booklet based on the oral legend of 'Naalatunga' became so popular that thousands of copies were sold out immediately. Encouraged by this interest in folk stories and people's ability to buy low-priced books (at Rs 1–2 each), the BGVS Resource Centre at Madurai developed over a hundred titles for neo-literates, based on a variety of themes. This shows that readers are keen to buy books if only such books are interesting and, more importantly, affordable for them.

The need to challenge readers and provoke them to think and articulate their views has repeatedly been stressed by Paulo Friere and other educationists. It is worth mentioning here that a series of discussion-based workbooks, entitled *Oru Mudivu Eduppom* or *Let Us Decide*, were widely used during the post-literacy phase of the *Arivoli Iyakkam* campaign in Virudunagar. Real life problems and dilemmas were posed to the readers and they were provoked to discuss their own responses, which often resulted in absorbing sessions of introspection and debate.

Numeracy

It has been found that numeracy is a very weak area and most learners feel frustrated at not being able to cope with the curriculum designed for them in their primers, though they do acutely feel the need for such written skills in their lives. Adults are treated as children, and are taught slowly and often painfully linearly, in a misguided manner adopted even in our schools. Adults are often adept at mental arithmetic as part of their daily transactions, and use effective algorithms and strategies to get results that are normally more accurate than when they use written algorithms. Traditional methods of estimation, sorting, and measurement still used in villages provide more familiarity, and are also more meaningfully related to their real-life contexts. These issues were highlighted in a resource book entitled *Numeracy Counts!* (see Rampal *et al.* 1999), which suggested ways to creatively incorporate folk and street mathematics in various teaching–learning situations.

Gender Roles and Stereotyping

One striking feature of most of the material reviewed was the lack of themes dealing with gender issues, especially those that could help inspire women to dare to think differently or to change their own lives. Most materials, including primers, tend to portray women in stereotyped roles, which only reinforces the dominant traditional patriarchal relationships in society. Exceptions were to be found, for instance, in some issues of *Pitara* and *Subah* and in a few books by the State Resource Centres. The story of Kamla (from the *Pitara* issue '*Banda ki Batiyan*') is very interesting and describes how two women from the literacy circle of Banda had documented the oral narrative of 85 year old Kamla. It presents a true heroic story of the way women have participated in many struggles in the past, and are still doing so today. More importantly, it shows that a lot of material can be based on oral history, documented by the literacy activists or the learners themselves.

Local Histories and Biographies of Learners

Much material can be published based on oral accounts of living persons about important national events such as the freedom movement. Similarly, innumerable accounts of local history need to be documented. It is indeed surprising that there are no inspiring biographies of ordinary men and women, from marginalized backgrounds, who have participated in overwhelming numbers in the literacy campaigns. There are thousands of women who have assumed an enhanced self-image and encouraged many others to challenge the stereotypical role they have been expected to play. In fact, it was often this sense of empowerment that motivated women to continue with literacy classes.

Scientific and Technological Literacy

As part of a conscious drive to address the issue of scientific literacy there is need to be sensitive to people's deep social beliefs while providing them alternative 'scientific' explanations. For instance, we can speak of eclipses, but must link the description to what is observed by them, and also to their existing legends about such cosmological phenomena. Dismissing their beliefs cursorily, without addressing how past civilizations have sought various explanations for such natural occurrences, can be alienating. It also gives the unnecessary impression that science is too 'impersonal' and opposed to all that they hold dear or sacred. Inculcation of scientific temper is a slow and complex process, and remains embedded within the various layers of social cognition—between myths, beliefs, folklore, superstitions, and taboos—that have influenced people's thinking for centuries.

In this context, one example of an attempt to sensitively address such issues is from the book *Brahmaanda*

Yaatra or *Cosmic Voyage* (see BGVS, Delhi). The poems and plays in this book indicate how to use methods of communication that incorporate people's own beliefs and legends, while presenting new knowledge. For instance, the poem *Bahut Sundar Lagega Surya* by Arun Kamal describes the amazing beauty of the sun during the total eclipse, and provokes people to observe the fascinating phenomenon. The play *Grahan men bhi Surya Sundar* (*The Sun is Beautiful During Eclipse Too*) effectively uses folk humour and satire to portray people's beliefs and rituals related to the eclipse, while also trying to motivate them to see the spectacular event. Similarly, Eklavya has published material that looked at both the modern theories about astronomy and simultaneously at what tribal societies have conjectured through their own observations.

In the context of scientific and technological literacy it is also felt that more material should be made on 'artisanal science'. It is important to write on issues people may deal with as part of their vocations, on the techniques they have learnt through empirical observations and yet which may not be considered 'science'. For instance, the techniques and knowledge people have refined over the centuries about natural dyes used in block printing, and the indigenous methods of metal casting or of baking and firing in furnaces meant for different types of ceramics and terracotta.

'Real' Literacy Materials for Reading and Writing

It is imperative to think of literacy in terms of different real-life materials, if one has to create a truly literate environment. Moreover, users of 'real' texts do not just read them, they engage with them. Different users will engage with texts according to their differing experiences and purposes (see Rogers *et al.* 1999). There have been some attempts to help this engagement with 'real' materials, both in terms of writing and reading by neo-literates. For instance, in some districts the making of village resource maps by neo-literates was undertaken in the context of school mapping or watershed management exercises. Such activities also provide opportunities to learners for improving their own technical knowledge and skills.

In some districts the campaign for the right to information was taken up as part of the post literacy work. Neo-literates were encouraged to personally check muster rolls or records of the public distribution system, to ensure proper utilization of funds and food rations, and to unravel frequent malpractices. This provided an added motivation, to read lists and records and look for false entries made in their names. It is clear that the use of real materials, through such activities, will not only promote participatory management but also provide opportunities for the reinforcement of people's newly acquired literacy skills.

In concluding this section it is worth reiterating that adults use various kinds of literacies in widely differing contexts. However, most persons engaged in developing literacy primers or materials do not necessarily appreciate this diversity, and often conform to a uniform pattern. Much mobilization is required, both at national and regional levels, to orient resource persons in this regard. Much effort is also needed to motivate learners to sustain their reading and writing skills, through different life-related literacy practices, while also ensuring that they are indeed surrounded or flooded by truly attractive and affordable materials.

Public awareness, acceptance of new ideas, and collective action for change are significant indicators of a truly literate society. It must be acknowledged that scientific and technological literacy is not simply achieved through publishing or reading of scientific materials alone, but is a more complex and gradual process of reviewing our own belief systems. Linking literacy with various other programmes and campaigns, involving participatory resource management and greater political participation at village level, can help generate 'real' learning materials and place a premium on literacy skills.

POSTSCRIPT

There have been some major developments in the last decade, though much still remains to be done. For one, there has been a perceptible shift from a monolithic mechanism of curriculum design, through an apex centralized body, to many more agencies involved in the exercise. In the formal school system this has happened, to a large extent, under externally funded projects such as the DPEP in Karnataka, Kerala, Madhya Pradesh, etc., the LJ in Rajasthan, the Bihar Education Programme, and the Andhra Pradesh Education Project. Some states, such as Kerala and Karnataka, have actually managed to make primary school teachers active participants in curriculum design, a practice considered unacceptable in the past. The hierarchical structure of the system, with secondary school or college teachers acting as the experts in all educational processes, including textbook writing, teacher training, and evaluation, is slowly, though not extensively enough, being forced to give way to a more participatory procedure. As an example of this we could look at the Nali Kali programme, being run in over 4000 government schools, as part of the DPEP in Karnataka. Primary teachers are the protagonists, and have been instrumental in working out the entire scheme of transacting the curriculum, with the help of block officials and some resource persons.

One significant issue emerging from the Nali Kali programme (first initiated in the H. D. Kote block of Mysore district), as well as from the other innovative experiments mentioned earlier, is that upscaling this effort cannot imply simple replication in other geographical areas.

Curriculum development and textbook preparation must remain an important ongoing and creative activity, which involves most teachers in some way or the other, in order to ensure their motivation in the process of teaching and their sense of ownership. This brings us to the question of academic decentralization, from the present state level to at least district level. Curricular renewal would have to be further decentralized, so that it allows teachers to engage with the process, to own it, and also to locate it within the local social and cultural context of their children. As was attempted in the mass literacy campaigns, where curriculum planning and textbook preparation were meant to be done at district level, the school system would also need to be freed from the hegemony of centralized bodies which seem to offer the greatest resistance to change. This could, and is, often thwarted by those who view decentralization as a threat to their control, and as an obstacle to what they might define as 'national integration'. However, promoting local, ethnic, and heterogeneous cultural identities and giving voice to the marginalized is the only way towards shaping 'national identities', and addressing issues of equity in human development.

One disturbing observation regarding various curriculum and textbook renewal attempts has been that the state projects have remained isolated to some extent as they have either not been able to involve the existing structures and institutions of the system or have chosen to work in parallel. This has serious implications for the future, especially regarding the spread and sustainability of these efforts. It also raises questions regarding the feasibility of building capacities and changing the mindsets of persons who have been part of the system, especially in positions of authority.

The NPE acknowledged that the formal system would have to make room for creative ideas to flow in, through the promotion of its linkages with innovative projects run by other agencies. The reference was to the role of voluntary and non-government groups engaged in developing models for 'meaningful' education for the disadvantaged. However, the space for this has remained limited, and such agencies have been invited to participate in some state projects, with very little influence on the system itself. Linkages of such agencies with the formal system are therefore, only tenuous, and have tended to snap at the smallest pressure or jolt, as was seen in Rajasthan and Madhya Pradesh.

Though there have been substantial efforts to make learning joyful and activity based, issues of 'relevance and life orientation' have not really been addressed. Recognition of local and indigenous knowledge systems, with emphasis on learning in a contextual manner, through the work of most people, engaged in agriculture or artisanal trades, has still not been accepted as a legitimate focus of the curriculum. In fact, most opposition to the new curriculum or textbooks has come from the urban middle classes, who see it as a threat to their control over the system and the benefits it seems to offer exclusively to them. There have been angry reports and demonstrations against the 'dilution of standards', the 'corruption of literary language' and the 'song and dance' introduced as part of these curricular efforts. On the other hand, political opposition has been double-pronged, and has also taken recourse to declaring that these 'experiments with the children of the poor', who study in government schools, ruin their future chances. As mentioned earlier, such criticisms and opposition have been faced by many other countries while initiating radical reforms. But it is important to realize that it is only when the excluded majority sees its children learning and performing better in schools and in life that such criticism can be countered. And this is beginning to happen. One has to ensure that this effort is sustained and expanded, in accordance with the expanded vision of education for all.

REFERENCES

Department of Education (1993). *Learning Without Burden*. Report of the National Advisory Committee appointed by the Ministry of Human Resource Development, Government of India, New Delhi.

Harris, Mary (1999). *Gender Sensitivity in Primary School Mathematics In India*. Commonwealth Secretariat, London.

Jangira, N. K., Venita Kaul, and M. B. Menon (1997). *Implementation of the MLL Program: An Evaluation*. (Mimeo)

Kaul, V., D. Gupta, V. P. Gupta, S. Varma, and Neeru Bala (1998). *Textbooks With a Difference*. Department of Pre-School and Elementary Education, National Council of Educational Research and Training, New Delhi. (Mimeo)

Kaul, Venita, Daljit Gupta, Neeru Bala, A. R. Barbhuiya, K. V. V. L. Narasimha Rao, and B. Mallikarjun (1995). *Readability of Primary Level Textbooks*. Department of Pre-School and Elementary Education, National Council of Educational Research and Training, New Delhi. (Mimeo)

Kerala Shastra Sahitya Parishad (1999). *Report of the Kerala Education Commission*. KSSP, Trivandrum.

Madhya Pradesh Human Development Report (1995). Madhya Pradesh Government, Bhopal.

PROBE (1999). *Public Report On Basic Education in India*. The PROBE team in Association with Centre for Development Economics. Oxford University Press, New Delhi.

Rampal, Anita, R. Ramanujam and L. S. Saraswathi (1999). *Numeracy Counts!* National Literacy Resource Centre, LBS National Academy of Administration, Mussoorie.

Rogers, A., B. Maddox, J. Millican, N. Jones, U. Papen, and A. Robinson-Pant (1999). 'Redefining Post-literacy in a Changing World'. Education Research Papers, serial no. 29, Department for International Development, London.

World Bank (1997). *Primary Education in India*. Allied Publishers, New Delhi.

13 Learning Conditions and Learner Achievement in Primary School

A Review

M. S. Yadav, Meenakshi Bhardwaj
with Mona Sedwal and Neeti Gaur

The National Policy on Education (NPE) (1986) took serious note of conditions related to basic facilities and other support systems in schools, emphasizing the need to improve the quality of publicly funded schools so that irrespective of socio-economic background, every child has access to basic education of comparable quality. It is in this context that learning conditions related to primary schooling have been examined in this chapter. Specifically, the review focuses on four basic dimensions that relate to the learning environment in the school and consequent learning levels among children, namely school building and other physical facilities, teachers in primary schools, teaching–learning material, and learner achievement levels.[1] It should be recognized that availability of facilities by itself does not represent supportive learning conditions. Actual utilization of facilities is the real indicator of the qualitative aspect of schooling. However, for such assessment, more process-oriented studies have to be conducted, which are not easy to come across.

[1] Empirical information for the present review has mainly been drawn from six major survey studies conducted in recent years, namely the Fifth All-India Educational Survey (NCERT 1986); the Sixth All-India Educational Survey (NCERT 1998); Baseline Assessment Studies (NCERT 1994); Mid-term Assessment Studies (NCERT 1997a); Learning Achievement in Primary Schools (Jacob Aikara 1997); Baseline Assessment Studies (NCERT 1997b). Of these, the Fifth and the Sixth All-India Educational Surveys conducted by the NCERT were on complete enumeration basis. The data of other studies cited, however, are based on sample surveys. It may also be mentioned that the Baseline and Mid-term Assessment studies refer to surveys conducted in the DPEP districts.

LEARNING CONDITIONS IN PRIMARY SCHOOLS

Physical Infrastructure

The Fifth All-India Educational Survey of 1986 showed that nearly 95 per cent of population was served by a primary school within a 1 km radius. However, the large-scale expansion of schooling resulted in the creation of educational facilities with widely varying quality in terms of institutional infrastructure, teaching–learning processes, as well as the quality of students passing out of these institutions. It is against this backdrop that the NPE (1986) called for paying immediate attention to:

• improving the unattractive school environment, the unsatisfactory condition of buildings, and the inadequacy of instructional materials; and

• laying down minimum levels of learning (MLLs) that all children completing different stages of education should achieve.

It is this emphasis on qualitative improvement in conditions of primary schooling that characterizes several programmes of educational development launched during the 1990s. The entire spectrum of factors related to primary schooling such as curricular structure, textbooks, teaching–learning materials, teacher competence and performance, and all other supportive inputs were to be viewed in terms of their contribution towards improvement of quality of schooling. Thus, reviewing learning conditions in primary schools in terms of 'quality schooling' that would yield anticipated 'learning achievement' represented the paradigm for educational development during the present decade.

SCHOOL BUILDING

A cursory glance at the data on the type of buildings in primary schools as in 1986 and 1993 suggests two trends (see Figure 13.1). One, the number of *pucca* and partly *pucca* buildings of 1986 shows considerable increase in 1993. Two, the number of *kachcha* buildings, thatched huts, tents, and primary schools in open space in 1986 substantially decreased in 1993.

However, there is a large variation among different states/UTs with respect to *pucca* buildings for primary schools, ranging from 2.21 per cent in Manipur to 88.21 per cent in Gujarat in 1986. The corresponding range

in 1993 is from 4 per cent in Nagaland to 96.60 per cent in Goa. A large number of primary schools in India (7.42 per cent) functioned in open space in 1986. This percentage got reduced to 3.83 in 1993.

INSTRUCTIONAL ROOMS

Another aspect of building component in primary schools is the number of instructional rooms available. This is pertinent, as Operation Blackboard (OB) is, perhaps, the largest project initiated on all-India basis for improving school infrastructure. The most important feature of the OB scheme was its specification of basic norms of school facilities at national level (see Box 13.1). This, in fact, continues to be the guiding framework for school provisions in many states.

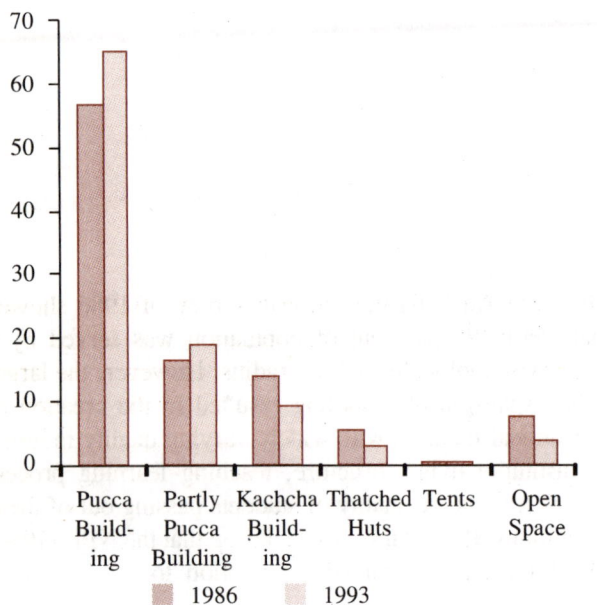

Schools according to Types of Buildings

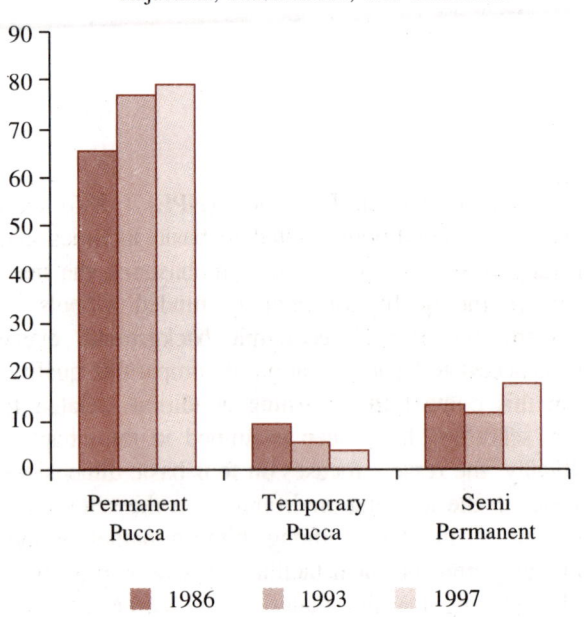

Schools according to Types of Building in four States, Bihar, Rajasthan, Maharashtra, and Karnataka

FIGURE 13.1: Schools according to Types of Buildings (per cent)
Source: NCERT (1992 and 1998).

BOX 13.1
Essential Facilities for Primary School: OB

- Provision of at least two reasonably large rooms that are usable in all weather, with a verandah along with separate toilet facilities for boys and girls (Building Component).
    - For the construction of buildings, the state governments were expected to utilize resources available under the ongoing rural employment programmes, provided by the Finance Commission or any other source. In 1990, it was decided that the central assistance under the rural employment scheme, Jawahar Rozgar Yojana (JRY) would supplement the state resources on a matching basis for construction of buildings. In 1993, school-building construction was made a high priority item under the newly introduced Employment Assurance Scheme (EAS) in selected blocks and in 120 backward districts identified under the JRY. These funds were in addition to the existing funds made available by the Ministry of Rural Areas and Employment. Separate district-specific projects had to be formulated for the purpose.
- Provision of at least two teachers, one of them a woman as far as possible, in every primary school (Teacher Component).
- Provision for essential teaching–learning material including blackboards, maps, charts, a small laboratory, and some equipment for work experience (Equipment Component).

Of the classrooms planned to be constructed (263,616) under OB, 176,703 rooms had been completed by June 1998. Bihar, Andhra Pradesh, and Uttar Pradesh have the maximum number of classrooms planned, out of which UP has already completed the construction of all additional classrooms. Assam and Orissa are lagging in this respect. This massive construction of classrooms has substantially changed the scenario of physical facilities in primary schools in the country. However, evaluation studies indicate that some of the buildings constructed under OB, in the absence of appropriate maintenance, have started leaking and the floors have cracked. A comprehensive review regarding maintenance of school buildings and the procedure followed for release of such grants is required.

The percentage of primary schools with zero or 1 instructional room shows a decreasing trend through the decade 1986 to 1997, whereas the percentage of primary schools with 2 or more instructional rooms clearly show an increasing trend over the years in 1990s. Both these trends are clear indicators of improvement in infrastructural facilities in primary schools in the country. Figure 13.2 shows the position of instructional rooms in primary schools from 1986 to 1997.

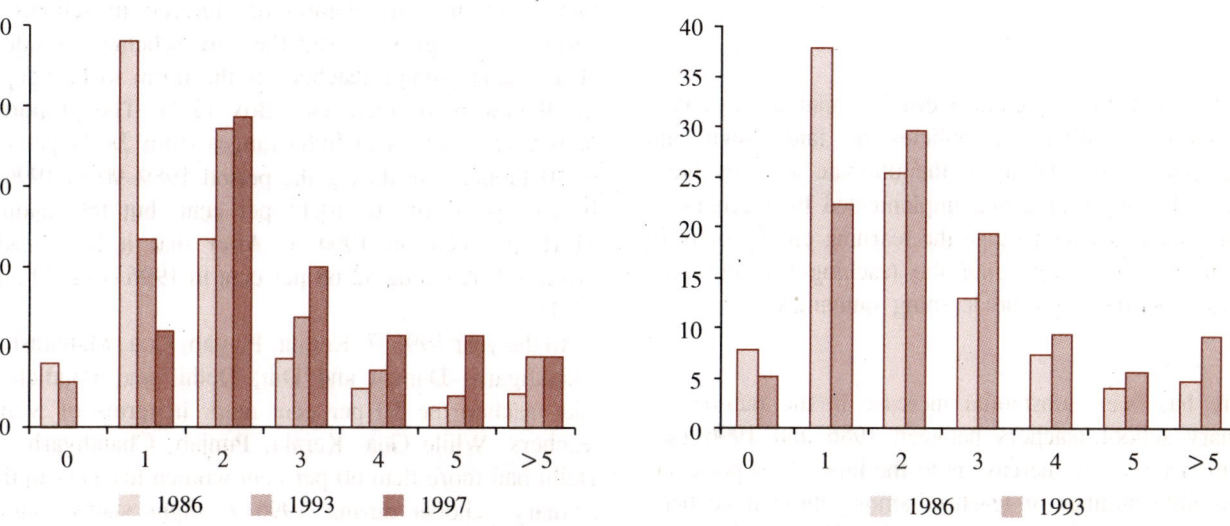

Schools according to number of Instructional Rooms in Four States—Bihar, Rajasthan, Maharashtra, and Karnataka

Overall Position of Instructional Rooms in Primary Schools (%)

Source: NCERT (1992); NCERT (1998, vol. II); Jacob Aikara (1997).

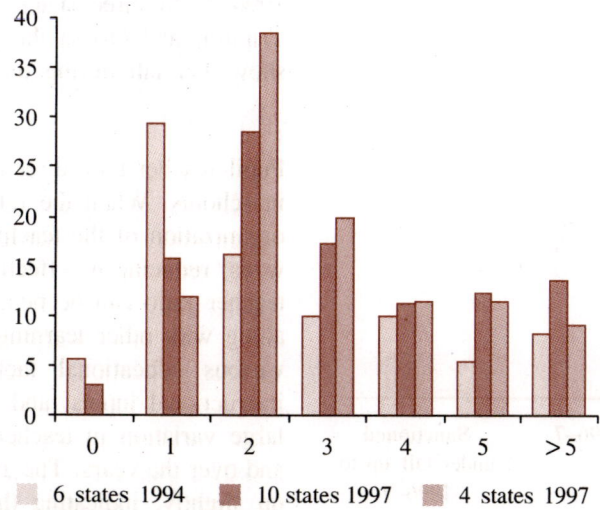

Overall Position of Instructional Rooms in Primary Schools (%)

FIGURE 13.2: Schools according to Number of Instructional Rooms
Source: NCERT (1994); NCERT (1997b); Aikara (1997).

In some states such as Andhra Pradesh, community participation in the creation of physical facilities has been forthcoming in a big way. The community has contributed upto Rs 30,000 per school. There have been instances of villagers contributing through *Shramdan* (voluntary labour) by working at the school site. These are very encouraging developments.

There is no denying the fact that physical facilities, namely buildings and instructional rooms are essential to create a learning environment for effective primary schooling, though mere availability of facilities is not a sufficient condition to create an enriched learning environment. However, there is not much research evidence directly available on this aspect of utilization of physical facilities.

Teachers

Teachers constitute the most crucial input at any stage of schooling. Whatever policies be laid down and programmes formulated, in the ultimate analysis these have to be interpreted and implemented by teachers. It is their actions which shape the learning environment in the institutions, influencing the teaching–learning processes, and thereby, the learning outcomes.

AVAILABILITY OF TEACHERS

There has been substantial increase in the number of primary school teachers between 1986 and 1996 (see Figure 13.3). The increase is to the tune of 20 per cent. A sizeable number of teachers among these have been appointed under the OB scheme. Specifically, the number of teacher posts sanctioned under OB constituted more than 10 per cent of total number of teachers in

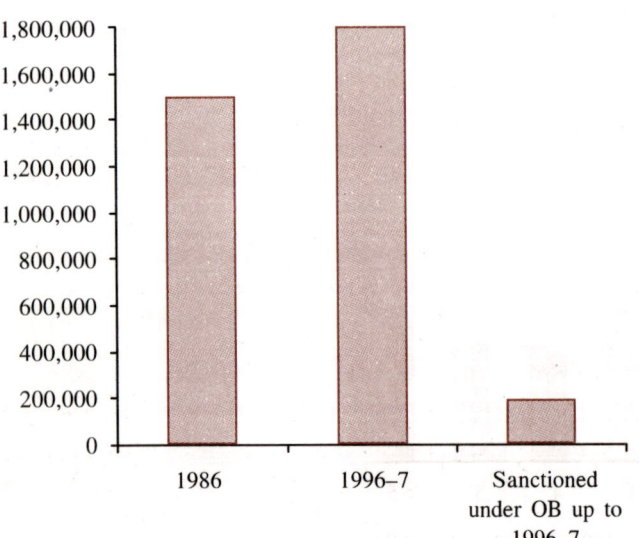

FIGURE 13.3: Number of Primary School Teachers
Source: Department of Education, MHRD.

primary schools in 1996–7. Andhra Pradesh, Orissa, Karnataka, and Rajasthan account for the largest number of sanctioned posts. In fact, the number has further increased in recent years.

Of the additional posts sanctioned for primary school teachers in various states 149,000 were in single-teacher schools. During the Eighth Plan and in the year 1997–8, 55,951 third-teacher posts were created in primary schools, with enrolment exceeding 100 and additional posts of 45,091 teachers were created in upper-primary schools spread over twelve states.

WOMEN TEACHERS

As has been noted earlier, government views appointment of women teachers as a positive measure for improving the participation of children in schools, in particular of girls. Also, the OB scheme considered 50 per cent women teachers as the norm to be adopted in all new recruitment (see Box 13.1). The proportion of women teachers in India ranges from 28.74 per cent to 40.11 per cent during the period 1989–90 to 1996–7. In 1993–4 it rose to 40.11 per cent, but fell again to 31.10 per cent in 1994–5. After that it has steadily increased, reaching 32.68 per cent in 1996–7 (see Figure 13.4).

In the year 1996–7, Kerala, Punjab, Goa, Maharashtra, Chandigarh, Daman and Diu, Delhi, and Pondicherry had reached the 50 per cent mark in terms of women teachers. While Goa, Kerala, Punjab, Chandigarh, and Delhi had more than 60 per cent women teachers in their primary schools during 1996–7, eight states, namely Arunachal Pradesh, Assam, Bihar, Madhya Pradesh, Orissa, Rajasthan, UP, and West Bengal had less than 30 per cent women teachers; UP, in fact, had less than 20 per cent women teachers in its primary schools in 1996–7. In three states, namely Jammu and Kashmir, Tripura, and Orissa the percentage of women teachers showed a fall during the period 1989–90 to 1996–7.

TEACHER–PUPIL RATIO

Pupil–teacher ratio directly affects the learning condition in schools. When the ratio is high, it impinges on the organization of the teaching–learning process in several ways, reducing its effectiveness. Yet, the role of pupil–teacher ratio can be better understood when considered along with other learning conditions like availability of various educational facilities, utilization of relevant instructional inputs, and multi-grade teaching. There is large variation in teacher–pupil ratio across states/UTs and over the years. The average for the country has gone up slightly, indicating that the strength of the teacher force has not kept pace with increasing enrolment of children in primary classes (see Figure 13.5).

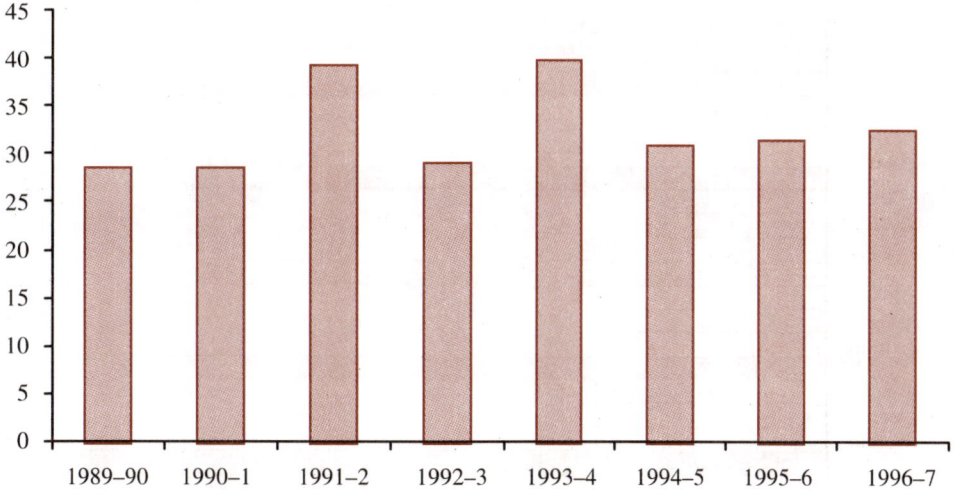

FIGURE 13.4: Percentage of Women Teachers from 1989–90 to 1996–7
Source: DoE (1989–97).

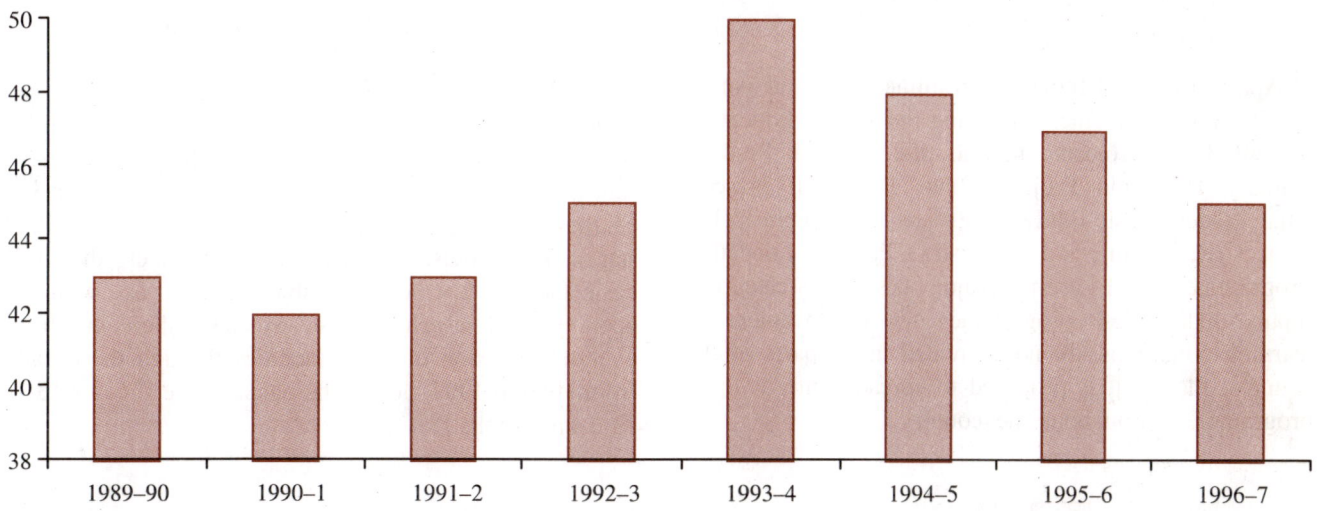

FIGURE 13.5: Teacher–Pupil Ratio
Source: DoE (1989–97).

For states where literacy rates are comparatively high, teacher–pupil ratios have got stabilized over the decade. These ratios are moderate and well within the norm of the class-size of 40 laid down by the Education Commission (1966) and emphasized in later policy documents. A perusal of these ratios in respect of states like Kerala, Mizoram, Goa, Delhi, and Lakshadweep will substantiate this (see Figure 13.6).

In five other major states, namely Bihar, Uttar Pradesh, Rajasthan, Madhya Pradesh, and Andhra Pradesh, which have lower-than-national-average literacy rates, access to primary schooling has been a serious challenge during the present decade. In all these states, the incidence of large classes is very high and the pupil–teacher ratio has been, on average, more than 40. For UP and Bihar, the average ratio has been more than 50 during the last five years.

West Bengal is another major state for which, though the literacy rate is greater than the national average (57.7 per cent as against 52.1 in 1991), the teacher–pupil ratio is very high. It has exceeded 50 and continues to be 57 since 1992. In Chandigarh also, there has been a marked increase in the ratio from 27 to 51.

There are fourteen states/UTs in which the ratio has been less than 40 throughout the period from 1989–90 to 1996–7. These states/union territories (UTs) are Arunachal Pradesh, Assam, Goa, Kerala, Manipur, Mizoram, Nagaland, Sikkim, Tripura, Orissa, Andaman and Nicobar Islands, Delhi, Lakshadweep, and Pondicherry. The average teacher–pupil ratio, which can be considered as a rough indicator to describe the all-India scenario, was greater than 40 throughout the period. Since 1993, it has crossed 45.

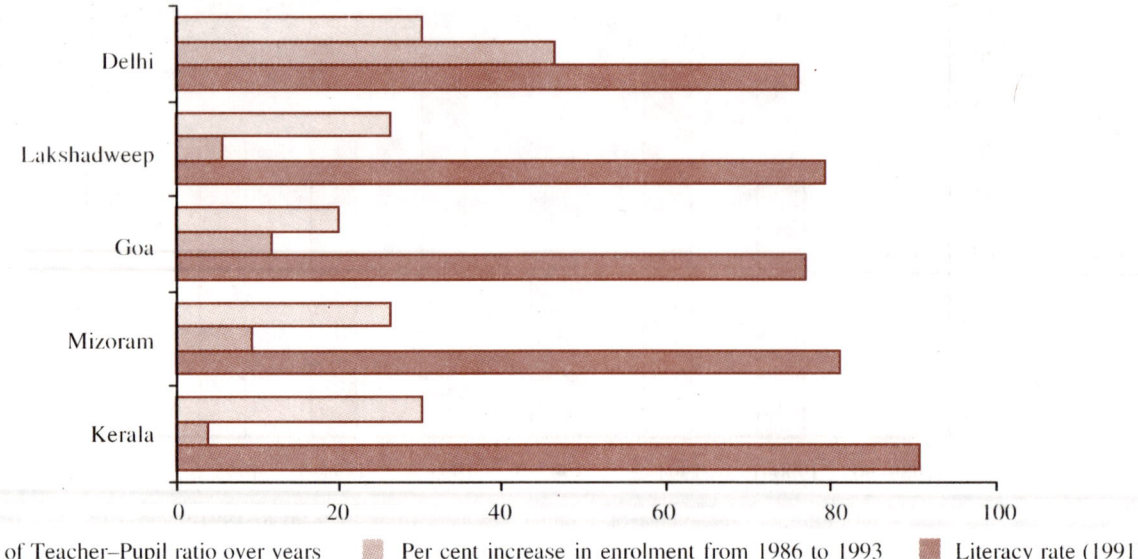

Range of Teacher–Pupil ratio over years | Per cent increase in enrolment from 1986 to 1993 | Literacy rate (1991)

FIGURE 13.6: Literacy Rate, Per cent Increase in Enrolment, and Teacher–Pupil Ratio Over the Years in Selected States/UTs

Source: Literacy rate; National Institute of Adult Education (NIAE) (1992); increase in enrolment (Educational Surveys 1986– 1998).

Apart from all-India programmes, several state-specific initiatives emerged during the 1990s. Education for all EFA projects such as the Andhra Pradesh Primary Education Project, Bihar Education Project, Uttar Pradesh Basic Education Project, Lok Jumbish (LJ) Project (Rajasthan), and the District Primary Education Programme (DPEP) are the major ones in this category. Inputs under these programmes for improvement of learning conditions are not provided in all parts of the country, though it is proposed to spread some of these programmes throughout the country.

Basic Facilities in Schools

There is wide variation in the availability of basic facilities such as drinking water and toilets in schools in different states. There is noticeable difference in the expansion of these facilities between the DPEP and non-DPEP states. The provision of safe drinking water, the most basic facility, has not been able to keep pace with the opening of new schools. Nevertheless, there has been overall expansion of these facilities through the decade from 1986 to 1997, across the country (see Figures 13.7, 13.8 and Table 13.1).

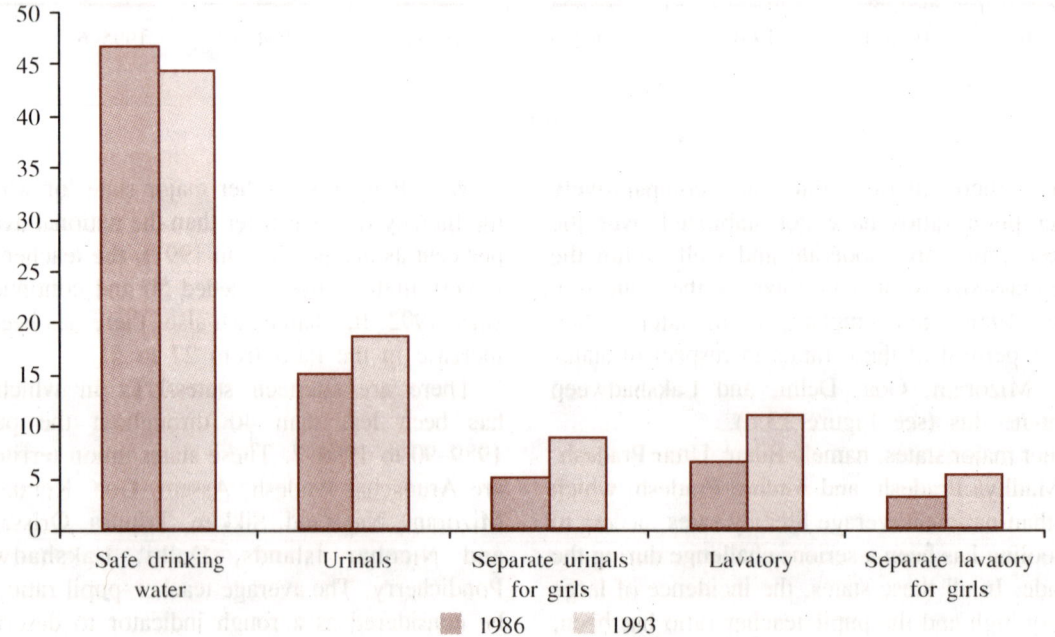

1986 | 1993

FIGURE 13.7: Schools Having Basic Facilities (per cent)

Source: NCERT (1992 and 1998).

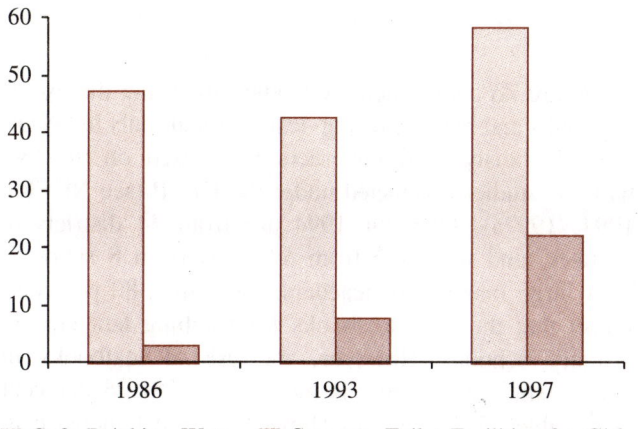

Safe Drinking Water ■ Separate Toilet Facilities for Girls

FIGURE 13.8: Schools with Essential Facilities in Four States—Bihar, Rajasthan, Maharashtra, and Karnataka

Sources: NCERT (1992, 1998); Aikara (1997).

In DPEP districts a special Innovation Fund has been created to encourage implementation of civil works in an innovative fashion. The fund is to be utilized for activities such as:

• Studying available building materials and technologies.

• Evolving cost-effective designs.

• Orienting engineers and Village Education Committees (VECs) on such constructions.

• Designing renewal activities.

Teaching–Learning Materials

During the 1990s, as part of the overall effort to improve learning conditions in primary schools, a variety of teaching–learning materials have been supplied to elementary schools under different government-sponsored schemes and programmes.

TABLE 13.1
Overall Position of Basic Facilities in Primary Schools (1986–97)

(per cent)

State	Year	Safe drinking water	Schools with urinals	Separate urinals for girls	Lavatory	Separate lavatory for girls	Electric connection
All India[a]	1986	46.59	15.00	4.86	06.37	2.90	–
All India[b]	1993	44.23	18.93	8.66	10.86	5.12	–
7 States[c]	1994	41.73	20.64	12.83	–	–	19.16
9 States[d]	1997	48.84	12.77	14.48	–	–	16.30
5 States[e]	1997	56.14	39.49	31.20	–	–	34.36
4 States[f]	1997	58.60	–	22.40	–	–	–

Sources: [a]NCERT (1992); [b]NCERT (1998, vol. II); [c]NCERT (1994); [d]NCERT (1997b); [e]NCERT (1997a); [f]Aikara (1997).

BOX 13.2

Prashika of Eklavya

Prashika is the primary school programme being run in several schools of Madhya Pradesh by a voluntary group called Eklavya formed in 1982. Prashika is coined as a short form of *prathmik shiksha*, which means primary education.

Eklavya believes:

• That education should first be centred around the needs and thought processes of the child, and only later address the needs of the concerned disciplines.

• The teacher's role is crucial, not only in the process of teaching, but in the evolution of educational innovations. The teaching community should be given its due in all matters pertaining to education.

• The process of education should be one of constant change and evolution in terms of content and methodology.

• Education equips children with motor and mental skills, as well as methods for analysing the physical and intellectual world. It helps develop problem-solving skills, the spirit of inquiry, and a scientific temper.

• Education cannot be looked at in isolation from the society and environment in which it is situated. It is, in fact, a means to motivate people to reflect on and improve the conditions in which they live.

AVAILABILITY OF TEACHING AIDS

The issues of availability of teaching aids in primary schools and their utilization by teachers and students constitute an important set of learning conditions which influence teaching–learning processes, and thus, contribute to the learning achievement of students. Availability of ten teaching aids, as reported by teachers of primary schools, has been studied in this section (see Figure 13.9). These aids are teacher guides, dictionaries, maps, globes, charts, flash cards, science kits, mathematics kits, books other than textbooks, and others (miscellaneous). Data in respect of these teaching aids have been taken from the baseline and mid-term assessment studies conducted under the DPEP (see NCERT 1994, 1997a, 1997b). The data are available from thirteen states in all, for a varying number of districts in each state. As the data are for DPEP districts, they represent the situation in relatively backward districts of the respective states. The data should therefore be treated as indicating a rough estimate of the availability of the teaching aids in primary schools located in geographical areas covered under the three studies.

One could broadly conclude that the availability of teaching–learning materials has considerably improved in all project districts under the DPEP between 1994 and 1997. To some extent, this is obvious as special attention was given under the project to equip the schools with basic teaching–learning material.

UTILIZATION OF TEXTBOOKS AND OTHER TEACHING MATERIALS BY TEACHERS

There are no comprehensive studies analysing the use of textbooks and basic teaching–learning materials by teachers. The analysis in this section is based on the two baseline studies conducted under the DPEP (see NCERT 1994, 1997a). Data for 1994 are from 34 districts in 6 states, and for 1997 from 54 districts in 8 states.

A large majority of teachers, more than 80 per cent, report that they use textbooks for teaching language in primary schools. However, the use of textbooks in mathematics by teachers is much less at 51.38 per cent (see Table 13.2). Figures show a marginal increase in textbook use between 1994 and 1997 (comparing overall figures in tables 13.2 and 13.3).

Data show that 'specially prepared materials' in mathematics are used by teachers in primary schools in much larger numbers than in language. One also finds a slight increase in usage between 1994 and 1997 in all the project states.

Under the DPEP, special efforts have been made to provide teaching aids in primary schools, namely teacher guides, dictionaries, maps, globes, charts, flash cards, science kits, mathematics kits, and books other than textbooks. Wide variations were found among states with regard to the availability of teaching aids and improvement in their availability over the years during the 1990s. However, the overall picture depicted by these studies

---

BOX 13.3

Rishi Valley Education Centre (RVEC)

The Rishi Valley Education Centre located in Chittoor district in Andhra Pradesh prepares students up to class VII of the Andhra Education Board. It is a day school and provides free midday meals, free healthcare, and two sets of clothes to children. A rich programme of crafts, music, athletics, puppetry, and organic methods of farming supplements academic training. The centre has a network of sixteen satellite schools within a distance of a few kilometres. Most of these are one-room schools and are located on land held in common by villagers or donated by individual villagers. Each school has around thirty children and in the evening these are the adult education or non-formal supplementary centres. Over the years, the Centre has developed an innovative educational kit consisting of 1500 graded cards, 500 cards on each subject, namely language, mathematics, and environmental science for classes I to V. The staff at Rishivanam maintain an active training programme for youth who may have minimal qualifications such as school-leaving certificates. Young men and women are prepared as teachers in basic elementary education.

Objectives of RVEC:

- To extend the educational resources of the Rishi Valley School into the neitghbouring countryside of Chittoor district.

- To regenerate the surrounding drought-affected region and that of degraded forests.

- To develop an integrated curriculum that is relevant to the needs of the people.

- To provide opportunities for teachers and children of Rishi valley school for meaningful interaction with village children.

- To ultimately promote a village-based educational system with the hope that in due course these satellite schools would not only provide quality education but also become a nucleus for reviving village commons abounding in natural flora.

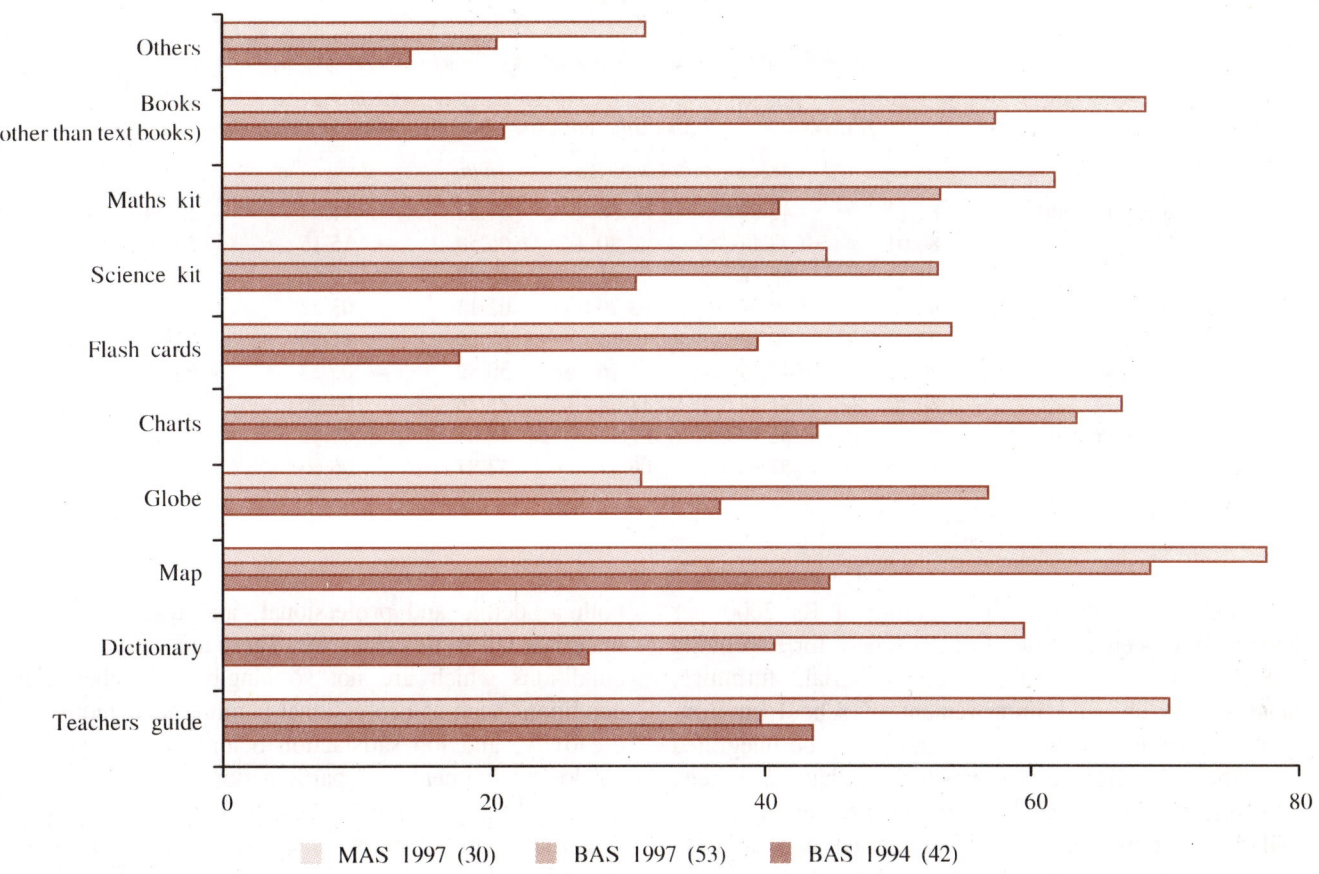

FIGURE 13.9: Teachers Reporting on Availability of Teaching Aids (per cent)
Source: NCERT (1994, 1997a, 1997b).

TABLE 13.2
Use of Textbooks and Teaching Materials by Teachers* (1994)

(per cent)

States	Textbooks		Specially prepared material		Do not teach these subjects	
	Language	*Maths*	*Language*	*Maths*	*Language*	*Maths*
Assam	91.50	87.98	0.16	01.93	8.16	10.05
Haryana	90.83	82.13	8.88	17.75	0	00
Karnataka	95.20	33.50	3.60	63.30	1.10	03.20
Kerala	88.90	13.27	11.10	86.73	–	0–
Madhya Pradesh	81.70	51.53	04.06	31.29	4.91	05.93
Maharashtra	85.85	32.82	05.99	58.14	5.39	06.26
Total	81.02	51.38	08.03	39.40	3.70	03.57

Note: * Percentage of responses of teachers about the use of textbooks and specially prepared materials are computed by taking the total number of teachers in the sampled schools. Some teachers do not teach the subjects of language and mathematics, therefore the percentage of teachers who reported about the use of 'textbooks' and specially prepared material are actually underestimates of the usage.

Source: NCERT (1994).

about availability of teaching aids and their use indicates a consistent trend of improvement over the years.

Teacher grants and school grants are project components within the DPEP through which funding is provided for preparing teaching–learning materials and improving the overall environment of schools. Teacher grants of Rs 500 per teacher per annum have been provided for preparing and purchasing teaching–learning

TABLE 13.3
Use of Textbooks and Teaching Materials by Teachers (1997)

(per cent)

States	Textbooks		Specially prepared material		Do not teach these subjects	
	Language	Maths	Language	Maths	Language	Maths
Andhra Pradesh*	82.12	42.82	06.38	41.50	11.54	15.54
Bihar*	80.01	73.14	04.80	06.50	15.15	20.36
Gujarat*	92.33	58.75	07.01	40.57	00.66	00.66
Himachal Pradesh*	93.08	89.45	03.70	02.18	03.22	03.37
Kerala	77.90	30.03	10.33	57.20	11.73	12.80
Maharashtra	90.70	42.19	03.66	50.82	05.23	06.50
Orissa	80.10	71.12	11.24	25.78	00.66	01.10
Uttar Pradesh	85.87	55.77	07.42	38.24	04.61	05.37
Total	85.26	57.90	06.81	32.84	06.60	08.21

Note: * Baseline conducted in 1995–6.
Source: NCERT (1997b).

aids and consumables. School grants of Rs 2000 per annum have been provided to each school for improving school facilities such as reading material, furniture, health check-up, and improvement of school environment. Utilization of the teacher grant is to be integrated with the new ideas and competencies that have been developed through teacher training programmes, and pedagogic approaches like child-centred and activity-centred teaching–learning. The school grant provides an opportunity for school authorities and community members to play a proactive role in school development.

Evaluation of this scheme of giving teacher and school grants has shown that, by and large, these grants are distributed and fully utilized by the recipients. The teacher grant has helped in reinforcing the confidence of the teaching community to improve the educational standards prevalent in primary schools. The changes in school and classroom environment through the utilization of school grants have made the school more attractive to the child. At the same time, it has made teachers' workplace more supportive of their performance of professional tasks. While the evaluation study revealed the gains that accrued from the utilization of the two grants in terms of capacity building of teachers, it has also made concrete suggestions to evolve more effective ways of implementing the scheme (see DPEP 1997).

Conclusion

Conditions of learning in schools have to be viewed within the complex context involving a variety of factors within and outside the education system. For some of these conditions 'hard data' can be collected and relevant indicators developed for assessing their adequacy and appropriateness. School building and its design, classrooms, other physical facilities, teachers' qualifications

both academic and professional, and teaching–learning materials fall in this category. There are, however, other conditions which are not so tangible. Teacher-related conditions such as professional commitment, motivation, creativity, and job satisfaction belong to this category; so do involvement and participation of the community in schooling processes. These conditions are no less important than the measurable ones, and present greater challenges for measurement and assessment.

However, isolating the 'effect' of learning conditions individually or collectivity towards the effectiveness of the learning environment in primary schools presents a real challenge. It is in such a context that the findings of the studies reviewed in this chapter are to be considered and assessed for arriving at meaningful conclusions.

Further, despite the positive trends, the general perception about primary schooling is that learning conditions leave much to be desired. Learning achievement, as brought out by many studies, is a pointer to this. Many of the activities undertaken under various programmes aimed at improving schooling have initiated actions to improve learning conditions with teachers' involvement. Experience gained by them—successful and rewarding, difficulties and challenges—is of immense relevance to understanding schooling processes and improving them further.

Aggregated facts at national, state, or even district level seem to conceal more than they reveal about actual happenings in primary schooling. Therefore, large-scale surveys or studies need to be conducted to ensure the availability of learning conditions and inputs, as they are essential for effective classroom transaction. Further, such studies should gather relevant and more complete information and facts about primary schooling. This could be a part of a periodical data generation exercise, i.e. annual, three- or five-yearly surveys. But these have to be coupled with qualitative studies that make in-depth analyses of school settings in a contextualized manner. By relating such data, both quantitative and qualitative, and triangulating them, incorporating corroborative evidence, attempts need to be made to arrive at a meaningful picture of the total learning environment in a school situation. Studies of this kind need to be sponsored and encouraged to give a professional orientation to the process of schooling.

LEARNER ACHIEVEMENT IN PRIMARY SCHOOLS

Inreased focus on educational achievement in India began around 1980 with the preparation of the document called 'Minimum Levels of Learning' (MLL) by the National Council of Educational Research and Training (NCERT) as a framework for preparing local-specific learning packages. Following this, a battery of criterion-referenced achievement tests were prepared to measure learning achievements of pupils in language, mathematics, and environmental studies for Classes I–IV. A large-scale national survey of learning levels was also conducted.

The idea of MLLs was further restated by an Experts Committee appointed by the Government of India in 1991 (see NCERT 1991). The MLL as a strategy for improving quality of elementary education was incorporated in policy documents as an attempt to combine equity with quality (see MHRD 1992). It laid down learning outcomes in the form of competencies or levels of learning for each stage and grade of elementary education. The strategy also outlined the adoption of measures that would ensure achievement of these levels by children in both formal schools and non-formal education (NFE) centres. Almost all major states have now adopted/adapted the MLLs, translated these into regional languages, and developed, or are in the process of developing textbooks, teacher guides, and teacher training material.

Evaluation studies on the MLL programme have revealed some noticeable gains from its implementation (see Jangira *et al.* 1997) which include:

• Awareness about MLL among teachers and other personnel in education.

• Focus on teaching shifting from 'syllabus based' to 'learning by all children'.

• New textbooks being developed by the states which contain activities required as per MLL competencies and which have provision for self-learning or drill.

• Competency-based student progress profiles being developed in some states like Gujarat, Tamil Nadu and Karnataka.

• Large number of primary school teachers who otherwise rarely had an opportunity of receiving in-service training with MLL as one of its components.

• During in-service training, teachers developing teaching aids.

• Experienced primary school teachers acting as resource persons for training; in Bihar, this practice was found very commendable.

A closer scrutiny of documents related to conceptualization, implementation details, and evidence from evaluation studies points to a few concerns which deserve attention:

• Operational and clearly visible activities got greater focus, namely revision and re-revision of 'competency-based text books' and training. Other aspects of classroom teaching such as developing competency-based skills in teachers, internalization of skills by them, and utilizing skills professionally through independent practise, synchronizing their use with textual and other inputs seem to have received inadequate attention.

• Measures like remedial teaching which are intended to improve learning conditions of schools do not seem to have been adequately operationalized and practised (see Jangira *et al.* 1997).

• There is need to view the school as the entire unit and adopt a holistic approach, as is evident from the findings of various studies.

One can state that, notwithstanding the critical observations of the MLL programme, the initiative played a major role in focusing the attention of planners and policymakers as well as administrators and practitioners all over the country on the issue of learner achievement.

Analysis of Empirical Evidence on Learner Achievement

During the decade 1990–9, there have been considerable efforts to bring learning achievement under systematic investigation. Several studies involving achievement testing have been conducted by the NCERT and other organizations during this period. All these studies had a common objective, i.e. to assess the level of achievement of primary school children from different classes/grades in different subjects. However, none of them have been on an all-India basis. They have been conducted in different parts of the country independently at different points of time. Keeping in view this fact, the present review describes them independently and not in any chronological order; no attempt is made to combine the findings of these investigations and draw generalizations.

The NCERT had conducted four studies in different states of the country during the period 1989–97. The first Achievement Study was conducted in 1989 in twenty-two states and one UT. This was done to assess the level of achievement of children at the end of primary schooling in language (mother tongue) and mathematics. The next Baseline Assessment Survey (BAS) was undertaken as a part of the DPEP project, launched in 42 districts (7 states) under Phase I in the year 1994 and in 140 districts (15 states) under Phases II and III in 1997. Another study conducted by the NCERT was the Mid-Term Assessment Survey (MAS) in the year 1997 for all the forty-two districts of DPEP Phase I. The MAS measured students' achievement in language and mathematics at the end of class I and at the end of class IV. A comparative study was also undertaken by the NCERT in the year 1997, in DPEP Phase I districts. The study mainly dealt with the comparison in achievement levels of children in mathematics and language as measured by the two sets of tests (1994 and 1997).

Jacob Aikara conducted a study in the year 1997 in four states, which tried to assess the level of learning achievement in primary schools in language, mathematics, and environmental studies. Two achievement surveys were conducted under the LJ project in Rajasthan in the period 1992 to 1997. The first one was between the years 1992 and 1995 in 25 blocks and the second in 15 blocks in 1996.

BAS 1989

This was one of the earliest studies conducted on a large scale by the NCERT (1989). The main purpose of the study was to assess the levels of achievement of children at the completion of primary school in mother tongue and mathemetics. As the study was limited to basic skills, and that too at the primary stage, a great deal of commonality was expected in both the subject areas. The reported results on achievement are based on the analysis of data obtained from 65,861 pupils, drawn randomly from 4700 schools according to a sampling design. The test in mathematics consisted of forty items. National average of achievement in mathemetics was 41 per cent. Four forms of the test were prepared in Hindi and three other regional languages.

The national average of the pupils of Class IV on the battery of tests was 45 per cent. Average scores in different states varied from 32 per cent to 69 per cent. On the whole, there was no difference between the achievements of children from urban areas and children from rural areas. However, there was a general tendency for the achievement of children in the capital cities to be higher than that of those in other parts of the states. For the entire country, the Backward Classes and Others

as a group did better than Scheduled Caste (SC) and Scheduled Tribe (ST) pupils but there was a strong tendency for the majority group in the state to have the highest score as well.

A STUDY OF LEARNER ACHIEVEMENT IN PRIMARY SCHOOLS BY JACOB AIKARA 1997

Jacob Aikara (1997) conducted a study *Learner Achievement in Primary School* covering 3719 Class IV and 1662 Class V students of 237 schools from 8 districts in 4 states—Bihar, Karnataka, Maharashtra, and Rajasthan. A multi-stage sampling design was adopted for selecting states, districts, and *talukas*/blocks by applying the criterion of the female literacy rate. Finally, from each taluka/block fifteen primary schools were selected by using the simple random method. Thus the sample consisted of 4 states, 8 districts, 16 talukas/blocks, and 237 primary schools in all.

The study sought to test the learning achievement of students of Class IV, which is the final year of primary schooling in Karnataka and Maharashtra keeping the specification of competencies under the MLL framework in mind. However, in Bihar and Rajasthan, where primary schooling is up to Class V, the sample included students of both Classes IV and V. The study was restricted to students of primary schools run in the vernacular medium by both government/local bodies and private agencies. However, a few English medium schools from Karnataka, Maharashtra, and Rajasthan were also included in the sample for illustrating the differences in the performance of students. No sampling method was used for selecting the English medium schools (see Table 13.4).

The study has utilized MLL specifications as the basic framework and focused on measuring the competencies specified therein. Therefore, an attempt was made to depict learning achievement expressed as the percentage of students who attained various levels of achievement (see Table 13.5).

Students from Bihar and Rajasthan performed significantly better than those from the other two states on all the three tests. A study of the NCERT (see Shukla *et al.* 1994) came out with more or less the same findings as regards the rank order of the states in student achievement.

It was observed that students performed better in language as compared to the other two subjects. The study further showed that there was marginal difference in the performance of boys and girls in language and environmental studies. But in mathematics, boys had a higher mean score than girls. Students belonging to the general category and Other Backward Classes performed better than those belonging to the SCs and STs in all

TABLE 13.4
Distribution of Mean Scores of Students in the Four States in Language, Mathematics and Environmental Studies

(per cent)

Test score	Language				Mathematics				Environmental studies			
	Bihar	Karnataka	Maharashtra	Rajasthan	Bihar	Karnataka	Maharashtra	Rajasthan	Bihar	Karnataka	Maharashtra	Rajastan
0	0.3	0.9	6.0	1.4	2.3	3.0	8.4	1.4	1.5	4.4	9.1	1.0
1–10	6.0	18.2	24.8	4.5	8.1	17.3	24.0	5.9	6.0	14.6	17.7	6.7
11–20	8.0	12.6	13.4	5.8	14.3	19.1	16.9	8.8	9.6	10.8	9.4	6.7
21–30	12.0	16.4	11.1	11.3	12.3	20.3	15.8	11.0	9.7	14.0	10.0	8.4
31–40	11.9	12.7	8.8	9.5	11.2	15.1	10.3	11.5	9.1	11.7	9.5	8.6
41–50	8.1	12.2	8.6	11.4	12.5	11.6	10.0	14.7	10.1	15.3	12.5	14.1
51–60	7.6	10.4	7.1	14.7	9.9	5.9	5.6	12.3	10.2	11.1	10.6	13.6
61–70	13.0	7.4	7.7	12.4	9.7	4.6	4.4	14.2	11.2	9.5	11.9	16.4
71–80	13.8	6.2	7.4	14.4	9.3	2.2	2.6	11.7	9.4	5.5	5.9	9.7
81–90	10.7	2.3	4.3	8.6	4.7	0.9	1.6	7.6	14.1	2.6	3.3	10.3
91–100	8.6	0.7	0.8	6.0	5.7	0.0	0.4	0.9	9.1	0.5	0.1	4.5
Total	100	100	100	100	100	100	100	100	100	100	100	100
N	616	769	1554	780	616	769	1554	780	616	769	1554	780
Mean*	53.8	35.7	32.6	53.3	44.5	29.2	26.5	48.2	53.5	36.8	35.2	52.2

Note: *Calculated from the original scores.
Source: Aikara (1997).

179

TABLE 13.5
Per cent of Students with Different Levels of Achievement

Achievement level	Language	Mathematics	Environmental studies
50% or more	40.2	27.1	41.5
75% or more	14.7	o7.6	13.5
80% or more	10.8	o5.6	10.1
Mean achievement	41.2	34.7	42.2

Source: Aikara (1997).

the three tests. Students from private unaided (PUA) schools had a higher level of achievement than those from government schools.

The number of classrooms and the number of teachers were found to be positively correlated with performance of students in all the three tests. However, the community factor of certain development-oriented activities such as the experience of total literacy campaigns (TLCs), experience of women's groups and existence of *balwadis* or the Integrated Child Development Services (ICDS) did not show any positive relationship with the performance of the students in learning.

Students of English medium schools performed better than those of vernacular medium schools. The differences observed in achievement levels of students in various samples from the four states seem to be explained by the characteristics of student population and learning environment.

BAS 1994 AND 1997

The DPEP was launched in 1994 in 42 districts across 7 states under Phase I and subsequently in another 140 districts spanning 15 states under Phases II and III. The criteria for selection of districts were: (i) backward districts with female literacy below the national average, (ii) districts where TLCs had generated a demand for elementary education. Baseline Assessment Studies were conducted in all the selected districts (see NCERT 1994 and 1997b). The design of the study and the instruments at the national level were provided by the NCERT. Two tests of language and mathematics used in the survey focused on the measurement of basic competencies as identified for primary schooling. The tests were administered to student groups which had completed class I and class IV of primary schooling (see Table 13.6 for 1994 data).

The students of Madhya Pradesh performed significantly better in language and those of Karnataka in mathematics compared to other states. The results revealed that:

• only one state (Assam) falls below the 40 per cent mark in both language and mathematics—class I/II.

• three states (Haryana, Madhya Pradesh, and Tamil Nadu) in language and one (Karnataka) in mathematics have crossed 40 per cent achievement level—class IV/V.

The data were collated to summarize the position of children who were below the MLL (i.e. less than 40 per cent) and those who were nearing mastery (i.e. 60 per cent and above). Table 13.7 depicts the distribution of children 'below MLL' or 'nearing mastery' in both language and mathematics in 1994.

TABLE 13.6
Mean Achievement of Students of Class I/II and Class IV/V in Language and Mathematics (BAS 1994)

State	Class	Language		Mathematics	
		Mean	Mean %	Mean	Mean %
Assam	Class I/II	5.75	38.12	4.78	33.87
(4)	Class IV/V	10.45	36.30	19.72	28.08
Haryana	Class I/II	05.31	53.16	03.36	50.56
(4)	Class IV/V	18.46	43.97	15.14	37.87
Karnataka	Class I/II	NA	41.46	NA	70.50
(4)	Class IV/V	–	23.74	–	48.56
Kerala	Class I/II	13.4	55.38	08.30	49.88
(3)	Class IV/V	20.7	39.12	14.90	35.20
Madhya Pradesh	Class I/II	06.41	66.83	2.95	59.86
(19)	Class IV/V	13.98	47.00	11.20	37.20
Maharashtra	Class I/II	06.94	48.26	06.50	42.53
(5)	Class IV/V	07.47	32.73	10.91	28.35
Tamil Nadu	Class I/II	03.73	49.49	03.16	43.59
(3)	Class IV/V	15.26	46.68	11.31	34.97

Note: **Number of districts in brackets.**
Source: **NCERT (1994).**

TABLE 13.7
Percentage Distribution of Students of Class I/II and Class IV/V at Different Levels of Achievement (BAS 1994)

State	Class	Language		Mathematics	
		Not achieved MLL	Near mastery	Not achieved MLL	Near mastery
Assam	Class I/II	17.70	26.01	14.08	25.85
(4)	Class IV/V	38.15	15.75	40.50	13.01
Haryana	Class I/II	16.20	24.96	17.91	19.58
(4)	Class IV/V	36.60	09.70	00.36	03.57
Karnataka	Class I/II	NA	NA	NA	NA
(4)	Class IV/V	–	–	–	–
Kerala	Class I/II	NA	NA	NA	NA
(3)	Class IV/V	–	–	–	–
Madhya Pradesh	Class I/II	15.48	24.39	19.39	14.30
(19)	Class IV/V	48.42	06.00	83.72	01.03
Maharashtra	Class I/II	10.67	23.19	24.68	15.26
(5)	Class IV/V	49.68	07.52	76.64	01.53
Tamil Nadu	Class I/II	NA	NA	NA	NA
(3)	Class IV/V	–	–	–	–

Note: Not achieved MLL= Below 40%; near mastery = 60% and above. Number of districts in brackets.
Source: NCERT (1994).

It is found that the achievement levels in mathematics are clearly lower than those in language for both classes I/II and IV/V. The percentage of students who did not achieve the prescribed MLL level in language for class I/II, i.e. those who failed to score more than 40 per cent marks in the achievement test, ranges in language from 17.70 per cent (in Assam) to 10.67 per cent (in Maharashtra) and in mathematics from 24.68 per cent (in Maharashtra) to 14.08 per cent (in Assam). While the percentage of students 'near mastery' in language ranges from 23.19 per cent (in Maharashtra) to 26.01 per cent (in Assam), whereas for mathematics it ranges from 14.30 per cent (in Madhya Pradesh) to 25.85 per cent (in Assam).

The percentage of students for Class IV/V who did not achieve the prescribed MLL in language ranges from 49.68 per cent (in Maharashtra) to 36.60 per cent (in Haryana) and in mathematics from 83.72 per cent (in Madhya Pradesh) to 0.36 per cent (in Haryana). While the percentage of students 'near mastery' in language ranges from 6.00 per cent (in Madhya Pradesh) to 15.75 per cent (in Assam) and for mathematics it ranges from 1.03 per cent (in Madhya Pradesh) to 13.01 per cent (in Assam).

As for the findings of the 1997 study, Table 13.8 depicts the mean achievement language and mathematics for students from Class I/II and Class IV/V.

The data in Table 13.8 show that:

• Except two states (Madhya Pradesh and Uttar Pradesh)

in mathematics, all others have crossed the 35 per cent achievement level in both the subjects—Class II.

• Two states (Himachal Pradesh and Kerala) have crossed 70 per cent level of achievement in language and 60 per cent in mathematics—Class II.

• While all the states except one (Madhya Pradesh) have crossed the 35 per cent achievement level in language, four states (Andhra Pradesh, Haryana, Karnataka, and Uttar Pradesh) fall below this mark in mathematics—Class IV/V.

• Of all the states, the state of Kerala showed the best performance than its counterparts in both the subjects—Class IV/V.

Table 13.9 depicts the distribution of children 'below MLL' or 'near mastery' in 1997 for both language and mathematics.

Achievement levels in mathematics are clearly lower than those in language for most states. The percentage of students for Class II who did not achieve the prescribed MLL in language (i.e. they failed to score more than 40 per cent marks in the achievement test) ranges from 58.50 per cent (in Gujarat) to 20.22 per cent (in Himachal Pradesh) and in mathematics from 60.25 per cent (in Gujarat) to 33.13 per cent (in Himachal Pradesh). While the percentage of students 'near mastery' in language ranges from 31.30 per cent (in Bihar) to 68.71 per cent (in Himachal Pradesh), for mathematics it ranges from 23.66 per cent (in Gujarat) to 55.11 per cent (in Orissa).

TABLE 13.8
Mean Achievement of Students of Class II and Class IV/V in
Language and Mathematics (BAS 1994)

State	Class	Language		Mathematics	
		Mean	Mean %	Mean	Mean %
*Andhra Pradesh	Class II	9.48	47.40	6.70	47.76
(5)	Class IV/V	33.59	39.99	11.38	28.00
Bihar	Class II	7.94	39.69	5.90	43.20
(10)	Class IV/V	31.42	37.25	14.26	35.65
*Gujarat	Class II	11.55	57.75	8.15	58.21
(3)	Class IV/V	20.38	46.31	17.84	44.61
Haryana	Class II	8.93	44.67	3.32	39.71
(3)	Class IV/V	30.90	36.78	12.84	32.10
*Himachal Pradesh	Class II	7.04	70.76	4.58	66.92
(4)	Class IV/V	19.15	45.97	–	39.23
Karnataka	Class II	8.35	41.78	5.61	40.07
(5)	Class IV/V	18.00	40.92	11.07	27.68
Kerala	Class II	14.71	73.56	6.40	60.00
(3)	Class IV/V	14.71	73.55	6.40	60.00
Madhya Pradesh	Class II	3.50	35.00	2.41	17.25
(1)	Class IV/V	13.45	15.98	14.27	35.68
Maharashtra	Class II	10.73	53.62	3.72	36.23
(4)	Class IV/V	9.29	–	13.33	–
*Orissa	Class II	12.14	59.80	7.95	39.79
(5)	Class IV/V	35.14	41.83	15.12	37.80
Tamil Nadu	Class II	–	54.71	–	52.91
(3)	Class IV/V	–	45.16	–	38.80
Uttar Pradesh	Class II	9.21	46.03	3.44	24.60
(18)	Class IV/V	35.05	42.23	12.88	32.20

Notes: Number of districts within brackets.
* BAS conducted in 1995-6.
Source: NCERT (1997b).

Achievement levels of Class IV in mathematics are lower than those in language, with the exception of Madhya Pradesh. The percentage of students not achieving the prescribed MLL in language ranges from 76.47 per cent (in Gujarat) to 41.04 per cent (in Himachal Pradesh) and in mathematics from 90.50 per cent (in Gujarat) to 53.30 per cent (in Himachal Pradesh). The percentage of students 'near mastery' in language ranges from 5.6 per cent (in Haryana and Kerala) to 17.35 per cent (in Orissa) and in mathematics from 2 per cent (in Uttar Pradesh, Haryana, and Kerala) to 12.87 per cent (in Himachal Pradesh).

BASELINE STUDIES OF RAJASTHAN 1997

The DPEP was launched in ten districts of Rajasthan during 1998. Before implementation, the BAS was conducted in Rajasthan by the State Institute of Education Research and Training (SIERT) in 1997. The design suggested under the DPEP for baseline assessment was followed in conducting BAS in Rajasthan. The study was

conducted on 13,625 students of 500 schools in ten districts. The main objective of the BAS was (i) to assess performance of students on the competency-based achievement tests in language and mathematics at the end of class I and at the end of penultimate class IV of primary schooling, (ii) to compare performance of general students' achievement on the BAS tests with that of achievement of students of *shiksha karmi* schools (SKS) on the same tests, and (iii) to assess learning achievement in relation to certain variables, namely area, gender, and social groups. Table 13.10 gives the mean achievement of students across districts.

The performance of students of class IV on mathematics has been quite low; for none of the districts is the achievement more than 45 per cent. Students of urban areas have done better than their counterparts from rural areas. Also students of general category have performed better as compared to SC/ST category students in both types of schools, namely general and *shiksha karmi*. In most of the districts the performance of students from

TABLE 13.9

Percentage Distribution of Students of Class II and Class IV/V at Different Levels of Achievement (BAS 1994)

State	Class	Language		Mathematics	
		Not achieved MLL	Near mastery	Not achieved MLL	Near mastery
*Andhra Pradesh	Class II	NA	NA	NA	NA
(5)	Class IV/V	–	–	–	–
Bihar	Class II	55.80	31.30	50.60	38.40
(10)	Class IV/V	53.02	14.31	66.90	09.80
*Gujarat	Class II	58.50	33.75	60.25	23.66
(3)	Class IV/V	76.47	10.44	90.50	–
Haryana	Class II	49.50	33.00	56.10	27.90
(3)	Class IV/V	59.00	05.60	76.50	02.40
*Himachal Pradesh	Class II	20.22	68.71	33.13	48.92
(4)	Class IV/V	41.04	26.86	53.30	12.87
Karnataka	Class II	32.94	43.84	41.44	39.88
(5)	Class IV/V	49.19	15.89	70.62	06.84
Kerala	Class II	49.50	33.00	56.10	27.60
(3)	Class IV/V	58.60	05.60	78.50	02.40
Madhya Pradesh	Class II	34.66	45.34	40.84	45.87
(1)	Class IV/V	69.07	11.39	56.98	11.54
Maharashtra	Class II	40.34	47.91	40.35	47.91
(4)	Class IV/V	–	–	69.96	03.98
*Orissa	Class II	39.56	54.54	45.80	55.11
(5)	Class IV/V	63.56	17.35	81.78	08.46
Uttar Pradesh	Class II	47.24	34.39	51.75	30.02
(18)	Class IV/V	48.03	05.67	83.48	02.20

Number of districts in brackets.

Notes: * BAS conducted in 1995–6.

Not achieved MLL = below 40%; near mastery = 60% and above

Source: NCERT (1997b).

TABLE 13.10

Mean Achievement of Students of Classes I and IV Across Districts in Language and Mathematics

Class	Subject	Mean achievement (%) varies across districts	
		From	To
Class I	Language	39.00	68.80
	Mathematics	48.55	71.70
Class IV	Language	48.51	61.37
	Mathematics	26.65	43.42

Source: Srivastava (1998).

shiksha karmi schools is better than that of general school students. This applies to both gender groups and for both the classes in language and mathematics.

It was found that students whose mother tongue was the same as the medium of instruction, were in an advantageous position with regard to achievement in language and mathematics. This conclusion holds good for most of the districts in which significant difference has been found in the achievement of the two groups.

COMPARISON OF ACHIEVEMENT LEVELS IN VARIOUS STUDIES BETWEEN 1990 AND 1997

The findings of different studies are not directly comparable as they have been conducted with different set of parameters and sample students. However, placing the overall figures of the different test together could help us identify certain broad trends as attempted in Table 13.11.

Mean per cent achievement of students of class IV/V in language, mathematics, and environmental studies in various states is based on students' performance on tests of basic competencies administered at different times; yet, since they are tests of basic competencies, they provide a basis of some meaningful comparison. Inspection of mean per cent achievement figures and their comparison across states and also across time may help to form meaningful perceptions about the scenario of achievement levels attained by children at the end of primary schooling. It is with this purpose the results of various studies presented earlier in this section are presented in a consolidated table (see Table 13.11). A

TABLE 13.11

Mean Achievement of Class IV/V Students in Different States/UTs as Found in Various Studies between 1990 and 1997

(per cent)

State/UT	Study I		Study II		Study III		Study IV			Study V	
	Language	Maths	Language	Maths	Language	Maths	Language	Maths	ES	Language	Maths
Andhra Pradesh	46.97	058.5			39.99*	28.00*					
Arunachal Pradesh	40.10	038.5									
Assam	52.81	46.00	23.74	48.56							
Bihar	69.85	69.50			37.25	35.65	53.80	44.50	53.50		
Gujarat	55.43	49.50			46.31*	44.61*					
Haryana	52.12	48.50	43.97	37.87	36.78	32.10				41.36	41.17
Himachal Pradesh					45.97*	39.23*					
Jammu & Kashmir	42.49	44.70									
Karnataka	33.77	27.50	39.12	35.20	40.92	27.68	35.70	29.20	36.80		
Kerala	42.92	35.20	47.00	37.20	73.55	60					
Madhya Pradesh	38.98	32.50	32.73	28.35	15.98	35.68				37.75	29.16
Maharashtra	31.63	37.70	46.68	34.97	42.98	33.64	35.70	26.50	35.20		
Meghalaya	47.94	49.20									
Mizoram	60.80	51.50									
Nagaland	34.98	35.80									
Orissa	47.94	42.50	35.13	15.05	41.83*	37.80*					
Punjab	52.62	53.70									
Rajasthan	51.76	48.20			54.94	35.03	53.30	48.20	52.20		
Sikkim	52.10	36.70									
Tamil Nadu	44.03	41.20	36.30	28.08	45.16	38.80				49.70	41.81
Tripura	37.99	30.20									
Uttar Pradesh	51.52	45.70			42.23	32.20					
West Bengal	39.75	41.00									
Delhi	44.85	35.70									
All India	46.66	41.20									

Note: Study I—Shukla *et al*. (1994); Study II—NCERT (1994); Study III—NCERT (1997b), * BAS 1995–6; Study IV—Aikara (1997); Study V—NCERT (1997a). ES: Environmental Studies.

cursory glance at the mean per cent achievement figures shows that:

• most mean per cent achievement levels are above 40 per cent;

• in some cases the achievement levels are less than 35 per cent;

• in two cases achievement levels are more than 70 per cent;

• in respect of two states, achievement levels are less than 20 per cent.

COMPARATIVE STUDY OF ACHIEVEMENT OF PRIMARY SCHOOL CHILDREN IN LANGUAGE AND MATHEMATICS IN DPEP DISTRICTS (BAS 1994 AND MAS 1997)

As already mentioned, BASs (see NCERT 1994) were conducted in 1994 to provide the benchmark for learning achievement. Two tests of language and mathematics used in the survey focused on the measurement of basic competencies in all the forty-two districts of DPEP-I. In order to assess the level of success of three years of DPEP interventions, a subsequent study, an MAS (see NCERT 1997a) was conducted in all the DPEP-I districts in 1997. The same tests that were used in BAS 1994 were administered to children of the same class in all the forty-two districts. The results revealed the following trends:

• The average performance in 25 districts in language and 24 in mathematics crossed the 60 per cent level.

• Except two districts in language and four in mathematics in the state of Madhya Pradesh, all other districts have crossed the 55 per cent level of achievement in the two subjects.

• Two districts (Belgaum in Karnataka and Malappuram in Kerala) in language and three (Kaithal and Sirsa in Haryana and Belgaum in Karnataka) in mathematics have crossed the 80 per cent level of achievement.

• Only one district (Guna in Madhya Pradesh) in mathematics falls below the mark of 40 per cent achievement.

• Of all the states, the students of Assam and Kerala displayed better performance in both the subjects than their counterparts. However, the students of Karnataka and Haryana tended to approximate their performance with Assam and Kerala followed by Maharashtra, Tamil Nadu, and Madhya Pradesh.

• While no district crossed the 60 per cent level of achievement in language, one district (Dhubri of Assam) has crossed this mark in mathematics.

• Six districts in language and five in mathematics have crossed the level of 50 per cent achievement.

• Three districts (one from Karnataka and 2 from Maharashtra) in language and nine (one from Karnataka and all the eight districts from Kerala (3) and Maharashtra (5)) in mathematics have attained less than 40 per cent level of achievement.

• While all districts have crossed the 35 per cent level of achievement in language, five districts (one from Karnataka and four from Maharashtra) did not reach this level of achievement in mathematics.

• Of the four states, the state of Assam showed better performance than its counterparts. It may be remarked here that even in class I performance, Assam had outscored other states. The students of Karnataka and Kerala tended to approximate their performance with students of Assam only in language but not in mathematics. In Maharashtra, while three districts crossed the 40 per cent level of achievement and one even crossed 46 per cent in language, no district could cross 40 per cent mark of achievement in mathematics.

A few other significant trends that emerged from the analysed data are as follows:

• Except six districts (all in Madhya Pradesh), all others have reached mean achievement in language higher than 35 per cent.

• Of the 27 districts, only 10 districts (all the 4 of Haryana, 3 of Madhya Pradesh, and 3 of Tamil Nadu) have crossed the 35 per cent level of achievement in mathematics.

• Only 2 districts have shown mean achievement greater than 50 per cent in mathematics, 1 of these (Sirsa in Haryana) has registered achievement greater than 60 per cent in mathematics.

• Only two districts (both in Tamil Nadu) have demonstrated achievement level in language, which is greater than 50 per cent.

The comparative analysis of mean achievement of students of two surveys—BAS 1994 and MAS 1997—is intended to study the gains with respect to students' achievements in the two subject areas (see Table 13.12). For these comparisons, however, it may be remembered that the two samples of BAS 1994 and MAS 1997 differ substantially in terms of size and also the time dimension.

Results show that the average achievement level has risen as compared to benchmark achievement level of 1994. The range of this rise is from 10 per cent to 44 per cent in language. For 6 districts the improvement is more than 25 per cent, while the rise with respect to 12 districts is less than 10 per cent. Thus, in all, 28 districts of 42, show an improvement over the achievement level of 1994. The remaining 14 districts show a downward trend. Average achievement in these districts has declined and ranges from 1 per cent to 18 per cent.

Clearly the improvement in average achievement in mathematics is greater than that in language. In all, thirty-three districts show an improvement in their average achievement. Of these districts, 9 are such where the rise is in the range of 25 per cent to 44 per cent; the improvement in 18 districts ranges from 10 per cent

TABLE 13.12
Comparative Profile of Class I, III, and IV Students in Mathematics (BAS 1994 and MAS 1997)

State	Number of districts			Districts showing positive trend			Districts showing negative trend			Number of districts showing significant decline		
Class	I	III	IV	I	III	IV	I	III	IV	I	III	IV
Assam	3	3	–	2	1	–	1	2	–	0	2	–
Haryana	4	–	4	4	–	3	0	–	1	0	–	1
Karnataka	4	4	–	4	4	–	0	0	–	0	–	–
Kerala	3	3	–	2	2	–	1	1	–	1	1	–
Madhya Pradesh	19	–	19	13	–	11	6	–	8	6	–	6
Maharashtra	5	5	–	4	4	–	1	1	–	0	–	–
Tamil Nadu	4	–	4	4	–	4	0	–	–	0	–	–
Total	42	15	27	33	11	18	9	4	9	7	3	7

Source: Based on Prakash *et al.* (1998).

to 25 per cent. The number of districts which show a downward trend in average achievement are nine, and the deterioration ranges from 1 per cent to 17 per cent in these districts.

A comparative analysis of students' achievement in class III on BAS tests administered during the initial survey in 1994 and re-administered during mid-term survey in 1997 was calculated. It was found that 13 districts in 4 states—Assam, Karnataka, Kerala, and Maharashtra—have demonstrated an improvement upon the benchmark achievement of 1994 in language. The range of this improvement is from ·10 per cent to 38 per cent. With respect to 2 districts, the rise in achievement is more than 25 per cent, while 4 districts have registered improvement which is less than 10 per cent. The remaining two districts have shown a decline in the mean achievement, from 1 per cent to 2 per cent.

A comparative assessment reveals that 11 of 15 districts have shown an upward change in their mean achievement in mathematics, whereas the remaining 4 districts have indicated a reverse trend. Of the 11 districts with positive trend, only 1 showed an improvement of more than 25 per cent in its mean achievement. The range of decrease in mean achievement in respect of the four districts is from 1 per cent to 9 per cent.

It may be mentioned that the degree of improvement in mean achievement of MAS 1997 for class III children over BAS 1994 in language is greater than that in mathematics. Variations among the different districts in the assessment made in 1996–7 supports this trend.

Following the same pattern as was done for class I and class III, a comparative picture of mean achievement of class IV students in language and mathematics on the basis of BAS 1994 and MAS 1997 is also calculated.

Out of 27 districts, 18 have shown a gain in their mean achievement in language for class IV children. The gain ranges from 1 per cent to 22 per cent. Nine districts have, however, shown a decline in their mean achievement, which ranges from 1 per cent to 9 per cent. In mathematics 18 out of 27 districts showed a rise in their mean achievement, ranging from 1 per cent to 24 per cent. In nine districts there is a decline in mean achievement which ranges from 2 per cent to 13 per cent. None of the districts showed an improvement beyond 25 per cent, both in language and mathematics for children of class IV in the three states for which comparisons were made.

The major finding of this comparative study is about the degree of improvement in mean achievement in language and mathematics across classes I, III, and IV in 1997. The gain in achievement in both subjects noticed in class I tapers off as one proceeds to classes III and

IV. This is a pointer to the differential effectiveness of pedagogical renewal processes introduced in DPEP districts in successive classes. It may be mentioned in this connection that the DPEP has set the goal of raising average achievement by 25 per cent, in phases. Applying that as a criterion, it is found that at the end of three years of implementation of the DPEP programme, nine districts achieved the goal in mathematics for class I, only one district for class III, and none for class IV. Similarly for language, at the end of three years of implementation of the DPEP programme, the enhancement of average achievement beyond 25 per cent is found in 6 districts for class I, two districts for class III, and for none for class IV. One cannot take these differences decreasing or increasing as decisive indicators of the magnitude of change and impact considering the methodological problems involved in any such comparison.

Such aggregated findings can only focus the problem of examining pedagogical renewal processes more specifically. For a fuller understanding of these process-related problems, intensive studies in select areas over longer periods of time are needed. In such investigations varied data through testing and observational techniques may have to be collected and related to class-specific and student-specific variables as they operate within the context of school and outside environment. Such investigations would, perhaps, be small-scale studies that will bring under observation a larger number of variables and the processes generated through them. The outcomes from such pieces of research carried out in several states with varied conditions will not only lead to better understanding of pedagogical processes, but also suggest more direct ways for utilizing educational inputs to enrich the learning environment in primary schools. Also, 'process studies' will bring out useful experiences of pedagogical processes that can be utilized as training inputs for teacher development programmes.

Main Observations

This review of 'learning achievement' is, however, restricted to achievement by children through schooling in primary schools of the formal system run by government/local bodies, which cover a vast segment of schooling in the vernacular medium in the country.

• The review has included relatively large-scale studies. Though these have been conducted under different projects with different methodological framework, certain common elements can be discerned. They:

– provide benchmarks about levels of achievement in different states. The indices of achievement levels are mainly in per cent form of mean performance of students—aggregated at state and district levels.

– make comparisons of achievement of students, with a view to subsequently assess the contribution of instructional and other inputs towards enhancing student performance.

– diagnose the weaker areas in learning achievement for which specific remedial measures are needed to improve effectiveness of teaching–learning processes for all groups of learners.

• A review of the mean achievement scores shows that:

– most mean achievement levels are above 40 per cent;

– only in a few cases are achievement levels less than 35 per cent;

– in two cases achievement levels are more than 70 per cent;

– with respect to two states achievement levels are less than 20 per cent.

These achievement figures, when examined against the reasonably high standards set by MLLs, suggest that the quality of learning remains a matter of serious concern in government-supported schools across the country. Moreover, a perusal of mean achievement percentages leads to a rather difficult situation for drawing any meaningful conclusion. States like Bihar and Rajasthan seem to show a higher mean achievement among primary school children than certain other states like Maharashtra, Karnataka, and Kerala, though the latter states are considered comparatively better developed educationally. Also, other indices of social and economic development, which are conducive to educational development, are favourable in the latter set of states.

• This difficulty of comprehending the results of learning achievement increases further due to inconsistency noticed in the trends that emerge from various studies presented in the chapter. For example, results with respect to states like Kerala, Uttar Pradesh, and Andhra Pradesh from different studies are rather inconsistent; they are not indicative of any consistent trend.

• A close scrutiny of results about learning achievement leads to the following trends:

– Mean achievement in respect of different states as found under different studies could be interpreted in different ways depending upon the criterion one uses for assessing the level of achievement.

– If one considers 35 per cent marks in a test as a measure of 'pass marks' as is done in usual examination situation, per cent achievement means

in most states appear to be satisfactory and do not seem to present any alarm.

– The mean achievement levels reported under different studies would appear rather poor if the criterion of MLL were applied for assessing the achievement. In fact, standards of learning achievement had been defined in terms of MLL in 1991 and the same were included in policy documents on education (see NPE and POA 1986—Revised 1992). Also, these standards have been pursued through various programmes of educational development to ensure universalization of 'access' and 'achievement' in education in the country.

– The MLL pedagogically relates to 'a statement or a set of identified competencies which are considered as essential for all children to acquire at the level of mastery at the primary stage'. Further 'mastery' refers to the level at which MLL is to be acquired. The programme goals specify that mastery will be attained only when a child acquires 80 per cent of the specified competencies and at least 80 per cent of the class is able to achieve these at specified level. These are 'essential' learning for all children as termed by national policy documents. Viewed against this policy perspective about learning achievement it can be easily and clearly seen that the levels of mean achievement found in different studies present a very dismal picture. These learning achievements found for all classes and in all states/UTs are indicators of the poor quality of education being imparted through primary schooling in the country. Further, it may be remarked here that seeking solace in the criterion of 35 per cent marks as 'pass marks', as mentioned earlier, has no place if one accepts the principles of measurement emphasized by the specification of MLLs.

– Yet another criterion to assess the achievement levels could be to examine them against the 'expected rise' over a certain time period. For example, under the DPEP the learning achievement was expected to rise by 25 per cent in course of its implementation. When this criterion was applied to results of learning achievement by students of class I in 42 districts of 7 states, after 3 years of implementation, it was found that the achievement in language and mathematics improved by more than 25 per cent in 6 and 9 districts respectively. The number of districts showing this degree of improvement, however, decreased for subsequent classes, and got reduced to none for class IV (see Prakash et al. 1998). Also, in respect of some districts the learning achievement in language and mathematics in successive classes showed a declining trend in 1997, as compared to the mean achievement in 1994.

• As mentioned earlier, MLL-based schooling was adopted as a policy to combine quality and equity. Towards this, the MLL Committee had delineated MLL for primary schooling in the areas of language, mathematics and environmental studies. The Committee had, however, taken a more comprehensive view of the curriculum at that stage and highlighted the need for delineating MLLs for other areas also, such as physical education, work experience, and music and art education. However, the studies reviewed in the document covered mostly two areas, namely language and mathematics. In only one study has environment studies been included. Other areas have remained altogether uncovered. 'Non-cognitive' learning achievement involving attitudinal make-up and value orientation on the part of learners was also given importance by the MLL Committee. This component of learning achievement is also highlighted in the NPE 1986. The studies reviewed did not cover these aspects of learning achievement.

Some Implications

• The majority of children who are studying in primary schools run by government/local bodies with the mother tongue or local language as the medium of instruction are from families wherein the environment is, very often, not conducive to learning. This is primarily because of parents' economic and educational conditions. Available evidence also shows that learning achievement varies according to the background of the child and it varies across schools and states. Therefore, any attempt to improve learning achievement will have to be through overall efforts to enhance effectiveness of those schools where children of poor families and educational background receive primary schooling.

• The study by Srivastava (1997) of the LJ project in Rajasthan highlights the need for remedial work with the weak children. Also recommended in the study is a review of the various activities under the MLL programme, identifying the weak spots in its implementation and providing additional inputs of learning materials and teacher training where required.

• There is need for conducting small-scale but intensive studies using qualitative methods of analysis with a view to relating learner development to learning inputs and operational aspects. This would help in understanding how children with varied backgrounds learn under different conditions, how much they learn, and how the quantum of learning can be increased through the use of various pedagogical inputs. These studies need to be conducted as independent studies in large numbers covering varied situations. The basic idea is to capture the complexities of teaching–learning and draw out research-cum-experience-based pedagogical and organizational insights. It may not be possible to generalize the knowledge gained through such studies. But the insights gained would contribute to the core of professional knowledge about teaching–learning, its conduct and management, teacher's role, family support, community support, etc. The outcomes of such studies could also become useful inputs for teacher training and other orientation programmes.

• Finally, it may be noted that during 1990s, special efforts have been made through several programmes to improve the quality of primary schooling. In this endeavour, partnership between government and non-government agencies, as well as community and other social groups has become more visible. The purpose of such collaborative effort has been to make the whole endeavour of primary schooling more contextual, relevant, and responsive to individual learner needs and social demands. In order to operationalize such a perspective, it is imperative that a broader view of learning achievement is taken and the same gets reflected in schooling and also in its assessment. There is also a need to encourage institutions to undertake developmental activities that view learning achievement in broader terms, develop appropriate schooling inputs to achieve them, and also assess them in a regular fashion under actual school conditions.

REFERENCES

Aikara, Jacob (1997). *Learner Achievement in Primary School.* Unit for Research in the Sociology of Education, Tata Institute of Social Sciences, Mumbai.

Department of Education (1968 and 1986). *National Policy on Education.* Ministry of Human Resource Development, Government of India, New Delhi.

——— (1990-7). *Selected Educational Statistics.* Ministry of Human Resource Development, Government of India, New Delhi.

——— (1992). *Programme of Action.* Ministry of Human Resource Development, Government of India, New Delhi.

——— (1993). *Education for All: The Indian Scene, Widening Horizons.* Ministry of Human Resource Development, Government of India, New Delhi.

District Primary Education Programme (1997). *Utilisation and Effectiveness of Teacher Grant and School Grant— A Synthesis Report.* Educational Consultants India Limited, New Delhi.

Jangria, N., Venita Kaul, and N. Menon (1997). *Implementation of MLL Programme A Report, An Evaluation.*

National Council of Educational Research and Training (1988). *National Curriculum for Elementary and Secondary Education—A framework.* New Delhi.

————— (1991) *MLL Document at Primary Stage.* Report of the Committee set up by the Ministry of Human Resource Development, Department of Education, Government of India, New Delhi.

————— (1992). *Fifth All-India Educational Survey (National Tables, vols I–V).* New Delhi.

————— (1994). *Baseline Assessment Study* on different States from 1994 onwards.

————— (1997a). *Mid-term Assessment Study* on different States from 1997 onwards.

————— (1997b). *Baseline Assessment Study* on different States from 1994 onwards.

————— (1998). *Sixth All-India Educational Survey (National Tables, vols I–V).* New Delhi.

National Institute of Adult Education (1992). *Literacy Rates.* Government of India, New Delhi.

Prakash, Ved, S. K. Gautam, I. K. Bansal, and N. Bhalla (1998). *Mid-Term Assessment Survey, An Appraisal of Student's Achievement* District Primary Education Programme Core Group, National Council of Educational Research and Training, New Delhi.

Shukla, Snehlata, V. P. Garg, V. K. Jain, Sarla Rajput, and O. P. Arora (1994). *Attainments of Primary School Children in Various States.* National Council of Educational Research and Training, New Delhi.

Srivastava, A. B. L. (1997). *Report of Post Test Achievement Survey (1996) in Hindi & Mathematics (classes I and II) in fifteen Blocks of Phase I.* Society for Applied Research in Education and Development.

14 Status of Elementary Teachers in India
A Review

A. S. Seetharamu

INTRODUCTION

Efforts for provision of elementary education since Independence have been steady and gathering strength over the years. However, community response to state efforts in the expansion of elementary education has been below expected levels. Response to literacy campaigns and non-formal education (NFE) to realize the goal of education for all (EFA) has been half-hearted. Teacher status is an important ingredient of efforts and progress towards EFA.

The Fifth All-India Educational Survey conducted in 1987 reported for the first time that a school was available in almost every one of the 587,000 villages of the country. But in around 40 per cent of the cases, a school represented a teacher teaching in classes I–IV or V in one instructional room. It is only after the adoption of the National Policy on Education (NPE) in 1986 that teacher strength began to grow under the auspices of the Operation Blackboard (OB) strategies. OB comprised three strategies, one of which was to provide an additional teacher, preferably a woman, to every single-teacher school.

Since Independence, and specifically after the NPE, the social composition and status of teachers has been significantly changing. Nine significant factors have contributed to the changing social profile and status of teachers in independent India. They are:

• a commitment to mass education and a concomitant expansion of schooling;

• unprecedented growth of population and accompanying growth in demand for schooling;

• state policy of reservation in education and employment for Scheduled Castes, Scheduled Tribes (SCs/STs) and Other Backward Castes (OBCs) in order to promote justice and equality;

• efforts towards raising the status of women in India symbolized in the first-ever publication of a national status report titled *Towards Equality* in 1974;

• social movements such as the Dalit movement in Maharashtra and Karnataka and Backward Classes Movement in north India;

• efforts towards abolition of child labour and initiatives from non-governmental organizations (NGOs) therein;

• a movement for promotion and realization of human rights;

• international pressures symbolized in the observance of the 'International Decade for Women' and 'International year of the Girl Child'; and

• finally, the international movement for EFA symbolized in the resolve by 155 nations at the conference at Jomtien, Thailand, during March 1990, to which India was a signatory.

In the context of elementary school teachers, the number of years of schooling, certification obtained for teaching, salary received at the point of entry and over time, welfare benefits, maternity benefits, retirement benefits, career advancement opportunities, are considered indicators of status. They are compared with similar endowments, benefits, and opportunities of teachers in other regions or with the requirements of a decent living. Such comparisons are indicative of the status of teachers in comparative or absolute terms. Teacher status in this chapter will be discussed using many of these parameters/indicators.

Discussion of teacher status should not be confined to material incentives or rewards or opportunities. There are many other determinants relating to autonomy, professionalism, and ownership (of the school system) which contribute to it. These determinants will be taken up for discussion in the concluding section.

ELEMENTARY SCHOOL TEACHERS IN INDIA

The year 1991 is a landmark in the reckoning of educational progress in India, for several reasons. It is the year in which a new economic policy of liberalization, privatization, globalization, decentralization, and marketization of Indian economy was adopted. The new economic policy met with heavy criticism within the first two years on account of lack of concern for the social sectors as reflected in downward allocations for these sectors. Immediately a National Renewal Fund (NRF) was created out of the massive international assistance received in 1991 (essentially the World Bank Loan). A Social Safety Net (SSN) was proposed out of the NRF to promote basic education and basic health services. Basic education got a boost from this measure.[1] The OB provided for additional teachers to teacher-starved schools, beginning from 1988.

Size of Teacher Force

The year 1986 is the year of reference of the Fifth All-India Education Survey as well as that of the adoption of the NPE. There has been a steady increase in the supply of teachers in India after Independence. The thirteen years between 1986 and 1999 are the years of consolidation, wherein single-teacher schools at lower-primary stage were supplied with an additional teacher and two- or three-teacher schools at higher primary stage were also supplied with additional teachers (see Figure 14.1).

Gender Composition of Teachers

The OB scheme of 1988 provided for increased participation of women in the teaching force. Every alternate teacher to be appointed after 1988 had to be a woman. Because of these developments one would have expected a phenomenal change in the gender composition of teachers. Figure 14.2 depicts the increase in female teachers from 1978 to 1999.

Caste Composition of Teachers

The SCs and STs constitute 15.75 and 7.76 per cent respectively of the total population of India. There is underrepresentation of primary school teachers from these groups (see Figure 14.3). It is more so at higher-primary stage than at lower-primary. The gap will be more in case of SCs as caste Hindus would not hesitate to and might even be rather eager to serve in villages where the SCs also live. In contrast, they may not like

[1] Seetharamu, A. S: 'Reforms and Education', *Business Line*, 9.3.1995 'Forming the Social Safety Net' 10.3.1995 'Scouting for Resources' 11.3.1995 'How to Exploit the Interface'.

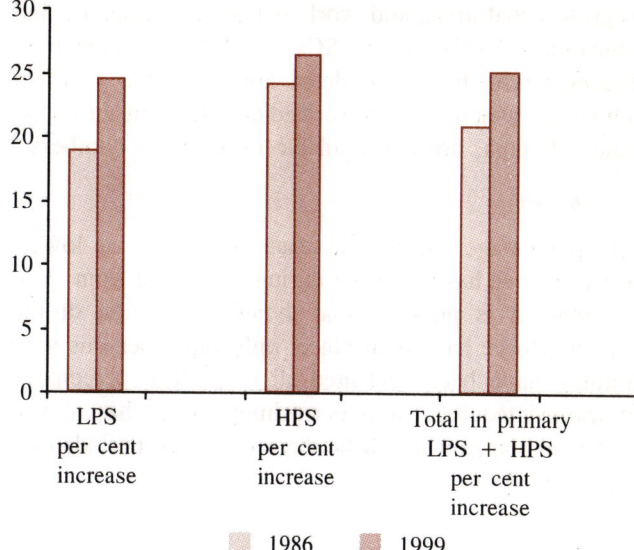

FIGURE 14.1: Increase in Number of Teachers (%)

Note: LPS means lower primary or classes I–V standards. HPS means higher-primary or classes VI to VIII. This note is applicable from Figures 14.1 to 14.5 and Table 14.1.

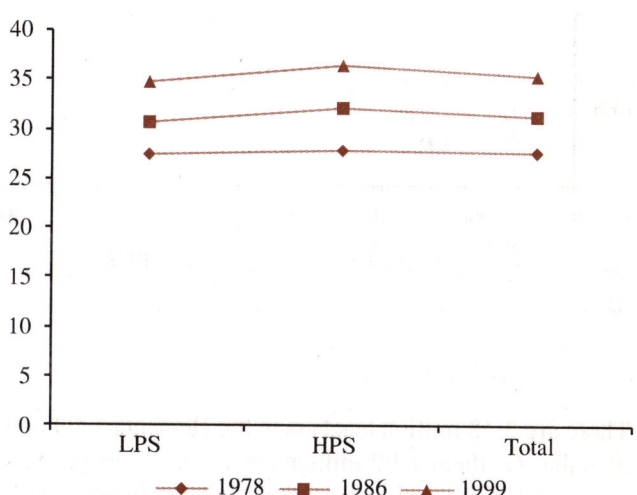

FIGURE 14.2: Female Teachers in Primary Schools (%)

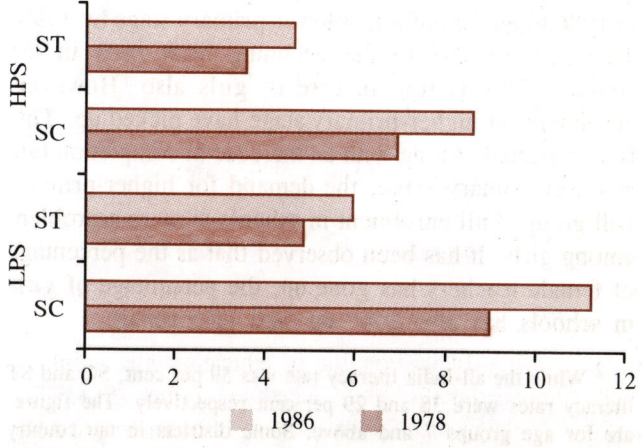

FIGURE 14.3: SC and ST Teachers (%)

to go to tribal areas and work as teachers. Literacy and educational levels among SCs and STs are quite low. Teachers who have completed ten or twelve years of schooling, which is the prescribed qualification across the states of India, are not available in adequate numbers.[2]

Teachers by Training

The percentage of trained teachers serving at lower-primary stage has increased during the period from 1986 to 1999. It is possible that though expansion of the teaching force has taken place, only those persons with training have been recruited all over. The percentage of trained teachers at upper-primary stage has almost remained stagnant in all the three reference periods (see Figure 14.4).

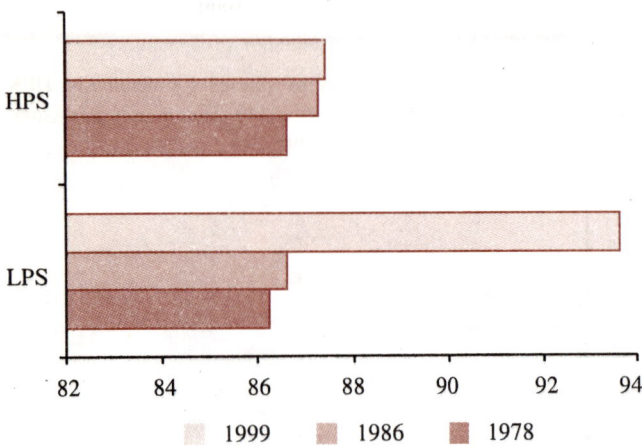

FIGURE 14.4: Trained Teachers (%)

Teachers and Their Pupils

There are 3.18 million teachers in the elementary schools of India. Of them 1.90 million are at the lower-primary stage and 1.28 million at the higher-primary stage. Between 1978 and 1986 there was an increase in enrolment of students. But it dropped from 86.68 million in 1986 to 80.26 million at lower-primary stage by 1999. This may be due to the declining birth rates in the country. This is true in case of girls also. However, enrolments at higher-primary stage have picked up. This is as expected. Along with an increase in completion rate at lower-primary stage, the demand for higher-primary will go up. Full enrolment in schools is more a problem among girls. It has been observed that as the percentage of female teachers has gone up, the percentage of girls in schools has also gone up (and vice versa).

[2] While the all-India literacy rate was 59 per cent, SC and ST literacy rates were 38 and 29 per cent respectively. The figures are for age groups 7 and above. Some districts in the country showed less than 10 per cent SC female literacy rate in 1991.

Pupil–teacher ratios are in the range of 41 to 44 during 1978 to 1999 at the lower-primary stage. However, at the higher-primary level the range has been between 25 and 37 and has increased significantly (see Figure 14.5). teacher–Pupil ratio based on enrolments will be misleading as it will not take into account the effective enrolment, that is enrolments net of dropouts. Even if effective enrolments are considered, the ratios will be higher for two reasons: (a) multigrade teaching because of unviable schools (the size of the villages in many parts of India is so small that it is difficult to get a minimum of thirty children for each standard); (b) the prevailing ratios in advanced countries are comparatively quite low. They calibrate around 25 to 27 students per teacher without multigrade teaching compulsions.

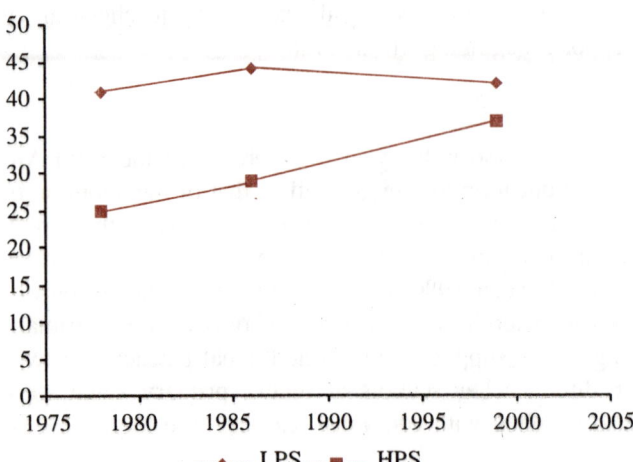

FIGURE 14.5: Teachers–Pupil Ratio

Inter-state Variations

As per the Sixth All-India Educational Survey (1993), 93.76 per cent of total rural habitations have a primary school (lower primary) within a distance of 1 km. There are 586,465 rural habitations spread across 26 states and 6 union territories (UTs) in the Indian federation. Access is poor only in Arunachal Pradesh, Himachal Pradesh, Sikkim, and Andaman & Nicobar Islands at the lower-primary stage.

Around 57 per cent of the population has a higher-primary school within a distance of 1 km and 85 per cent have one within a distance of 3 km. Himachal Pradesh, Arunachal Pradesh, Assam, Madhya Pradesh, Meghalaya, Sikkim, Uttar Pradesh, and Dadra and Nagar Haveli have not been able to provide a higher-primary school for 50 per cent of the age group population within a distance of 1 km.

It is obvious that the performance of states with regard to universal elementary education (UEE) goals is not uniform. Provision of access, facilities, and teachers is also not uniform. Bihar, Madhya Pradesh, Rajasthan, and Uttar Pradesh have lagged behind in universalization of primary education. Differentials in provision of facilities might have contributed to corresponding variations in performance. The profile of inter-state differentials in the position vis-à-vis teachers in Table 14.1 may provide some insights.

Indian states/UTs fall under three categories with regard to trained teachers in position in elementary schools. (a) Both at lower-primary and higher-primary stages above 85 per cent teachers are trained. Andhra Pradesh, Bihar, Goa, Gujarat, Haryana, Himachal Pradesh, Karnataka, Kerala, Maharashtra, Orissa, Punjab, Rajasthan, Tamil Nadu, Uttar Pradesh, Andaman and Nicobar Islands, Chandigarh, Dadra and Nagar Haveli, Daman & Diu, Delhi, Lakshadweep, and Pondicherry fall under this category. They constitute 15 states and

6 UTs out of a total of 26 states and 6 UTs. (b) States which are visible in poor light, that is 50 or less than 50 per cent teachers at both lower-primary and higher-primary stages. There are six states that fall under this category: Arunachal Pradesh, Sikkim, Manipur, Meghalaya, Nagaland, and Tripura. All of them are in the Himalayan region, the north-eastern frontier states. The terrain is hilly and uneven. Schooling here is a post-Independence phenomenon. Even qualified (not to speak of trained) teachers are a rare commodity. The problem of supply of trained teachers is challenging while the scale of the problem is low. (c) There are four more states where training of teachers has crossed 51 per cent at least at lower-primary stage. They are Assam, Jammu & Kashmir, Madhya Pradesh, and West Bengal. Both Assam and Jammu & Kashmir are states with problems of persisting militancy. Madhya Pradesh is a state with

TABLE 14.1
Teachers across States/UTs of India 1998–9

	LPS (1999)			HPS (1999)		
	No. of teachers	% trained	1986	No. of teachers	% trained	1986
Andhra Pradesh	135,690	97	97	62,845	88	96
Arunachal Pradesh	2949	47	43	2338	45	37
Assam	86,934	68	63	59,145	36	29
Bihar	115,486	92	93	99,181	92	95
Goa	2820	96	80	748	97	87
Gujarat	35,040	98	99	142,200	94	98
Haryana	45,956	96	99	7963	91	99
Himachal Pradesh	23,173	88	97	5620	100	98
Jammu & Kashmir	22,113	61	78	23,362	59	72
Karnataka	60,540	100	91	142,580	100	94
Kerala	45,226	98	94	48,651	95	92
Madhya Pradesh	231,564	66	69	108,279	67	71
Maharashtra	176,127	95	90	179,091	95	99
Manipur	9660	47	56	6722	30	36
Meghalaya	10,966	45	50	4558	37	30
Mizoram	4818	73	58	4918	76	49
Nagaland	6847	36	45	4881	42	36
Orissa	111,040	100	88	38,914	400	75
Punjab	45,524	99	99	18,349	99	98
Rajasthan	101,064	86	84	109,136	91	89
Sikkim	3482	50	50	1701	42	29
Tamil Nadu	115,739	100	100	61,719	100	100
Tripura	10582	30	40	8827	29	42
Uttar Pradesh	312,669	98	95	103,943	95	89
West Bengal	149,071	65	64	23,029	80	71
A & N Islands	844	93	96	715	96	94
Chandigarh	416	100	100	558	100	100
Dadra & Nagar Haveli	217	100	97	447	100	85
Daman & Diu	347	100	83	181	100	88
Delhi	34,056	100	99	8710	100	97
Lakshadweep	290	95	90	110	100	93
Pondicherry	2289	91	99	1474	96	100
India	19,03,539	2610	87	12,80,895	2872	87

large tribal concentration and there are difficulties in organizing training institutes and getting trained teachers. The only enigmatic state in the country is West Bengal, where only two-thirds of the teachers at lower-primary stage are trained. It is interesting to note that trained teachers at higher-primary stage constitute 80 per cent of total teachers at that stage in West Bengal.

Thus the status of elementary education with regard to trained teachers in position is not a serious problem in mainland India with exception of four states, as discussed.

Trained Teachers: 1986 and 1999

There was stability in the pattern of recruitment of teachers in the majority of Indian states. Trained teachers were recruited in 1999 to the extent that they were in 1986. However, the proportion of trained teachers declined at both lower-primary and higher-primary stages in Jammu and Kashmir, Madhya Pradesh, Manipur, Nagaland, and Tripura and at lower-primary stage in Himachal Pradesh and Meghalaya. This was a cause for concern. It is possible that teaching jobs may not attract the educated youth of the region. Another possibility is that the supply of trained teachers may not meet the demand for the same. Alternative channels for training of teachers through the use of distance education technology, coupled with limited contacts may also be difficult to try out in these regions.

Teachers and Their Qualifications

There is variety in the standards of recruitment of teachers across the country. The qualifications prescribed for teachers is one of the sources of this variation. A study for the District Primary Education Programme (DPEP) by N. K. Jangira and others (1995) revealed that Haryana, Karnataka, Madhya Pradesh, Maharashtra, and Tamil Nadu prescribe twelve years of schooling and a two-year course of diploma in elementary education (training) while Kerala and Orissa are satisfied with ten years of schooling with a diploma in teaching. Assam is happy with ten years of schooling, and does not insist on training.

In this context it is to be noted that the Central Advisory Board of Education (CABE) and Parliament envisaged the raising of the general education level of teachers to twelve years of schooling. In a personal communication to the World Bank in 1996, the Secretary, Ministry of Human Resources Development (MHRD), informed them that 10 of the 15 major states, viz. Andhra Pradesh, Gujarat, Haryana, Karnataka, Mahdya Pradesh, Maharashtra, Punjab, Rajasthan, Tamil Nadu and Uttar Pradesh have already raised the minimum qualifications to twelve years. (The states left out are Assam, Bihar, Kerala, Orissa, and West Bengal) (World Bank 1997).

The observation of the World Bank report in this regard needs to be quoted: 'This places India ahead of other countries with comparable education indicators and on a par with some OECD countries. For example China required nine years of general education for Primary teachers, and Pakistan ten years.'

There are other problems with regard to educational-qualification requirements of teachers and their teaching work in primary schools. The pattern of education structure adopted in India can broadly be described as consisting of 10+2+3 years.

TEACHER–PUPIL RATIOS AT ELEMENTARY STAGE

Pupil–teacher ratios at all-India level at two points in time 1986 and 1999 have already been discussed. The states/UTs of India can be classified under eight categories as follows:

- States/UTs where teacher–pupil ratios have come down both at lower-primary and higher-primary: Goa, Haryana, Himachal Pradesh, Tripura, Andaman and Nicobar Islands and Pondicherry.
- States/UTs where the ratios have remained almost the same at both lower-primary and higher-primary stages (variation of 2 to 3 at lower-primary and 4 at higher-primary): Jammu and Kashmir, Manipur, Meghalaya, Mizoram, Nagaland, Orissa, Sikkim, Lakshadweep.
- States/UTs where the ratios have gone up both at lower-primary and higher-primary stages: Arunachal Pradesh, Bihar, and Dadra and Nagar Haveli.
- States/UTs where the ratios have come down at lower-primary stage but remained stationery at higher-primary stage: Kerala, Maharashtra, and Tamil Nadu.
- States/UTs where the ratios have come down at lower-primay stage but gone up at higher-primary stage: Karnataka, Rajasthan, and Gujarat.
- States/UTs where the ratios are stationery at lower-primary stage but have come down at higher-primary stage: Assam, Punjab, Uttar Pradesh, and Chandigarh.
- States/UTs where the ratios are stationery at lower-primary stage but have gone up at higher-primary stage: Andhra Pradesh.
- States/UTs where the ratios have gone up at lower-primary stage but remained stationery at higher-primary stage: Madhya Pradesh, Daman and Diu, and Delhi.
- There is no state/UT where the ratios have gone up at lower-primary stage but come down at higher-primary stage.

States/UTs which cause concern are Arunachal Pradesh, Bihar, Dadra and Nagar Haveli where ratios have gone up both at LPS and HPS stages. In Karnataka, Rajasthan,

Andhra Pradesh, and Gujarat, the higher-primary stage where the ratios have gone up is a cause for concern. Madhya Pradesh, Delhi, Daman and Diu have recorded increases in the ratio at lower-primary stage.

Pupil–teacher ratios are only crude indicators of the health of a school system. They should be read along with several other variables such as classroom organization, effective enrolment rates, increasing/declining population growth rates (demand for schooling), community involvement, and task analysis of teachers.

Salary Scales of Elementary Teachers

Teachers are lowly paid in developing countries. It is true of India also. The Kothari Commission had recommended a uniform national scale of pay for elementary teachers in India. This has not been possible to implement because of various reasons including differentials in supply of qualified, trained teachers belonging to both general and reserved categories. The World Bank Report on Primary Education (1997) gave an update on the entry-level salaries of teachers and other government employees with comparable education. In many parts of the country, teachers receive lower salaries than upper division clerks, revenue inspectors, trained nurses, and pharmacists. They are better placed than police constables and in some places better placed than lower division clerks.

Salaries of teachers are revised periodically (every ten years) along with those of other state government employees. Such revisions are generally preceded by revisions of salary scales of central government employees. The latest revision took place in 1997 (see Table 14.2). Variations in salary scales between teachers whose qualification to teach in primary schools is either tenth or twelfth standard and those who are trained teachers is understandable. But if teachers in one state who have completed class XII and also two years of diploma in teaching at primary level are paid much lower than teachers in a neighbouring state with similar qualification and training, then it is felt to be unjust.

It is on this count that The Karnataka State Primary School Teachers' Association sent a memorandum to the President of India as recently as 15 March 2000.

It is pertinent to note that the salary of elementary teachers in Karnataka is much lower than that in Kerala state whereas the entry qualification for teachers in Karnataka is twelve years as it is in Maharashtra and Tamil Nadu, while it is just ten years in Kerala state. In the case of headteachers also such inter-state anomalies exist.

Promotion Opportunities

The promotion opportunities of teachers are very limited. There is no separate cadre and recruitment provision for primary teachers. Some of the teachers may hope to become headteachers of primary schools on the basis of seniority and experience. The lucky ones may get promotion as inspectors of schools. But these positions are limited in number. There were around 400 inspectors of schools in 1995 for a 200,000 strong primary teaching force. In some states, posts of educational assistants to assist block-level education officers have been created and teachers at these posts are paid salaries higher than that of a headteachers of a primary school. But the posts are again quite limited in number (385 posts in Karnataka state). At any point in time, promotional opportunities for elementary teachers may be limited to 25 per cent of the teachers who enter the profession. In 75 per cent of cases, teachers retire with the same status with which they had joined but with higher salaries as commensurate with their length of service in the profession. The majority of teachers surveyed by N. K. Jangira and others perceived their economic status to be low which is a fact.

Welfare Benefits for Primary Teachers

A National Foundation for Teachers' Welfare (NFTW) located at New Delhi was set up in 1962, under the Charitable Endowments Act 1890. The objective of the

TABLE 14.2
Salary Scales of Elementary Teachers

(Rs)

	Primary teachers		Head teacher	
	Pre-revised	Revised 1997	Pre-revised	Revised 1997
Central govt	1200–2040	4500–7000	1400–2600	6500–10,500
Tamil Nadu govt	1200–2040	4500–7000	1400–2600	05900–9900
Maharashtra govt	1200–2040	4500–7000	2000–3500	7500–12,000
Goa govt	1200–1800	4000–6000	1400–2600	05000–8000
Kerala govt	1125–1725	4000–6090	1640–2900	05500–9075
Karnataka govt	1130–2100	3300–6300	1400–2675	04150–7800

NFTW is to provide relief to teachers who are in indigent circumstances. Every year 5 September is celebrated in India as 'Teachers' Day' in memory of Sarvepalli Radhakrishnan who rose to the position of President of India from a university teacher during his early life. The NFTW collects donations for Teachers' Day through the sale of a 1 inch colourful flag. The Central Social Welfare Board of India, the All India Women's Conference, the National Council for Women's Education, universities, colleges, schools, and other organizations and prominent citizens help the NFTW collect donations in this way. The NFTW allows states/UTs to retain 80 per cent of the collections with them and the remaining 20 per cent is transferred to the corpus fund of the NFTW. The Memorandum of Association and the Rules and Regulations for the Administration of the NFTW are issued by the MHRD, as incorporated in a twenty-two page monograph.

Some states of India are quite vibrant and involved in the facilitation of the welfare to teachers. The case of Karnataka in the form of a case study is insightful.

Welfare of Teachers: The Case of Karnataka

The Karnataka State Teachers' Benefit Fund (KSTBF) is affiliated to the NFTW. Nearly two-thirds of the 240,000 elementary teachers of the state in 1998 were members of the KSTBF. Collection of funds through sale of flags is in addition to the life-membership fee which is collected from teachers in a routine fashion. In 1998, 6,000,000 children (out of 7,600,000 children) paid Re 1 each for the flag. The majority of these children are from elementary schools. The accumulated fund under the flag sale account, up to March 1999, was Rs 11.90 million. The KSTBF transfers only ten per cent of its collections to the NFTW. Membership of teachers, though voluntary in principle, is done through the Block Education Officers.

The following welfare benefits are given to teachers by the state government: pension for life; commutation of pension; family pension; gratuity; group insurance benefit; encashment of earned leave; and maternity leave. In addition, the KSTBF gives the following benefits: medical reimbursement; medical relief for hospitalization, maternity benefit for women teachers; scholarship for meritorious children of teachers who are in-service or retired; construction of guest hostels for teachers at block, district, and state headquarters; awards for teachers (there are district- and state-level awards for elementary teachers as well as awards for innovative teachers on a competitive basis); and death-relief assistance.

Are these benefits only on paper or do some translate into reality? It is observed that the KSTBF is quite popular among teachers. At an annual function coin-ciding with 5 September every year, twenty primary teachers are given Rs 10,000 as state awards in the form of National Savings Certificates (NSCs). Again nine primary teachers are given national awards of Rs 25,000 every year in the form of NSCs. The national awards also carry Rs 10,000 paid in cash from the NFTW. Medical reimbursement and medical assistance for hopitalization are two major items of expenditure for the KSTBF. The Funds of the KSTBF are quite impressive (see Table 14.3).

TABLE 14.3
Status of Funds of the KSTBF
(as on 15.3.2000/million Rs)

Funds	Fixed deposits	Savings bank a/c	Total
KSTBF	99.05	15.20	114.25
KSSWF	113.90	7.04	120.94
NFTW	10.15	3.16	12.31
Total			248.50

Note: KSSWF is the Karnataka State Student Welfare Fund.

PARA-TEACHERS OF ELEMENTARY SCHOOLS

Qualified persons are not available in adequate numbers to teach in elementary schools in different parts of the country. Facilities for training teachers are also not uniform. Even when qualified and trained teachers are available, the state government may not have the resources or compulsion to spend on an adequate supply of teachers for primary education. For all these reasons, several state/UT governments have resorted to employing unemployed educated youth as teachers at elementary level to assist the regular/salaried teachers. They are called by various titles such as 'para-teachers', *shiksha karmis*, 'contract teachers', and *vidya upasaks*. Information about these teachers is very limited. They are paid consolidated salaries which vary between one-tenth and one-fifth the salary of a regular elementary school-teacher, across different regions of India.

Para-teachers perform several functions: keeping school open when the regular teacher goes on leave, following up those students to their homes who are long absentees from school, assisting teachers in enrolment drives, assisting students in their home assignments, assisting slow learners, assisting teachers in maintaining school records, assisting teachers in organizing school functions, etc. There are certain remote rural habitations where para-teachers function as regular teachers, whether they are qualified and trained or not. For instance, in Madhya Pradesh there is a scheme known as Educational Guarantee Scheme (EGS), which provides a school on demand to any *panchayat* school-less village/habitation with 25–40 children, engaging para-teachers on limited honorarium.

Some non-governmental organizations working in the field of education also engage para-teachers. SAMOOHA is an illustration of such an organization that has educational projects in backward regions of Karnataka, Andhra Pradesh, and Tamil Nadu. They are financially supported by ACTION AID.

Several issues of teacher status are associated with the system of employment of para-teachers. Some of them are discussed herein. One of the allegations against the system of para-teachers/*shiksha karmis* employed in Rajasthan was that because of them, laxity among regular teachers had set in. Besides, the educational bureaucracy has found it convenient to work with para-teachers. They carry an 'unemployed educated youth' tag. They accept low payments and are unorganized. The state does not need to spend on welfare benefits and give pension under the para-teachers system.

NFE TEACHERS

Research during the 1960s on progress and problems of primary education highlighted the problems of non-enrolment and dropout. Poverty, engagement in paid and unpaid child labour, inaccessibility of schools, household responsibilities of girl children were some of the prominent reasons. In response to these, a nationwide drive for providing sandwich forms of education to

children in the 9–14 years age group was launched during the Fifth Five Year Plan (1974–9). Engaging educated unemployed youth of villages/slums to organize and conduct evening classes for non-enrolled children and dropouts on token honorariums was the strategy herein. (Incidentally, it needs to be recalled that for the first time such a strategy had been adopted though on a limited scale, by M. V. Parulekar as early as 1929). Table 14.4 provides numerical data on NFE centres in 1993.

TABLE 14.4
NFE Centres in India 1993

	Rural	Urban	Total
Primary level	106,294	5671	111,965
Government	100,073	5519	105,592
Upper-primary	5020	653	5673
Government	4538	626	5164
Both primary & upper-primary	2628	278	2906
Government	2315	163	2478
All total	113,942	6602	120,544
Government	106,926	6308	113,234
Voluntary organizations			7310

Source: Sixth All-India Educational Survey, NCERT.

Reliances on NFE, however, is not uniform across the country. The NFE umbrella does not cover the whole of India. NFE is visible in only six major states, which carry 95 per cent of the total centres (see Figure 14.6).

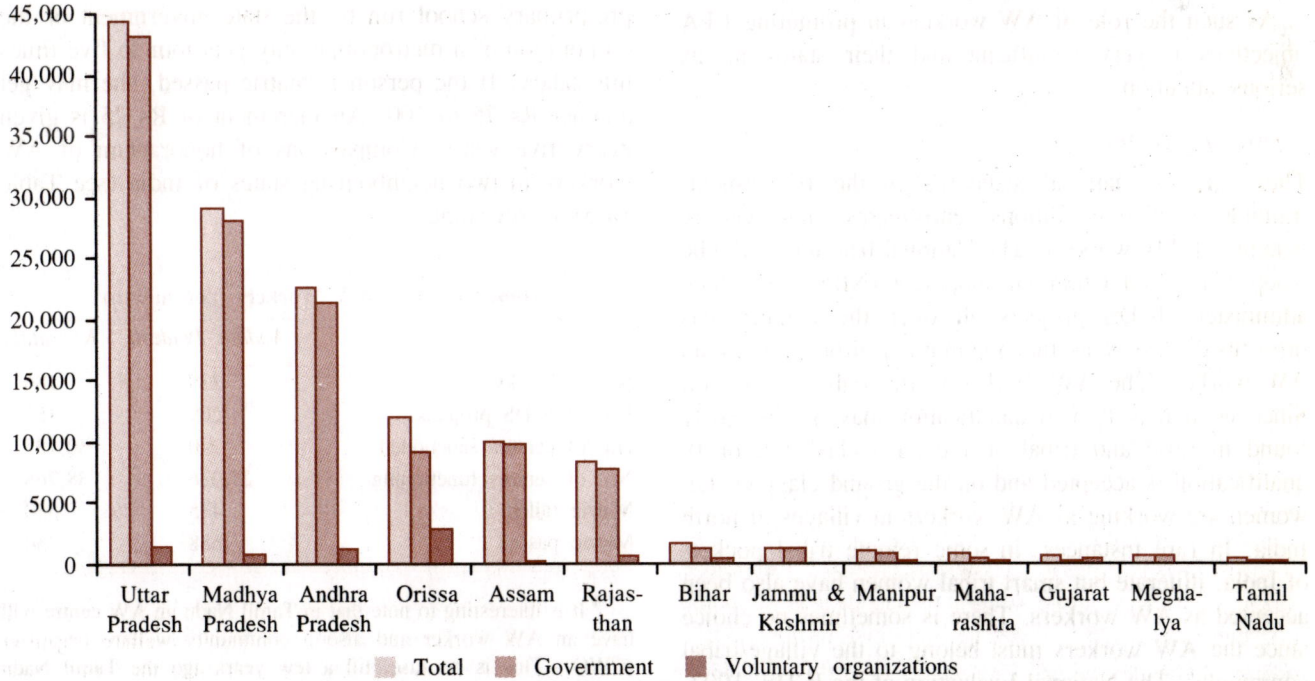

FIGURE 14.6: Statewise Number of Instructors of NFE Centres (1993)

Note: The rest of the country, that is Arunachal Pradesh (44), Goa (5), Himachal Pradesh (104, Haryana (6), Kerala (118), Mizoram (121), Andaman & Nicobar Islands (9), Chandigarh (104), and Delhi (84), have 595 instructors.

ANGANWADI (AW) TEACHERS

A supportive hand for basic education in India is the Integrated Child Development Services (ICDS) Programme which employs AW workers. Health, nutrition, and education are through the ICDS programme integrated at the point of delivery to children below 6 years of age.

By March 1996, 5614 projects under the ICDS had been sanctioned in the country. The break-up for rural, urban, and tribal areas was: 4571, 733, and 310 respectively. By March 1996, 3926 projects were operational and served 22.2 million beneficiaries. It meant roughly 392,600 centres and as many AW workers in the country. Assuming that all the 5671 projects sanctioned by March 1996 were operational by 2000, there should be a minimum of 567,100 AW workers in the country. In terms of ratio, there are three AW workers per ten lower-primary school teacher in the country (567,100 as against 1,903,539 in absolute numbers). The outreach of ICDS/AW centres is very large. The major states of India have been almost completely covered.

An AW centre is expected to promote the objectives of EFA in another way. Research studies in the country discovered that one of the reasons for girls withdrawing from schools is younger sibling care. A 7–8 year-old girl may be required at home to look after a younger brother or sister of three, four or five years. The AW centre relieves the girl child of her responsibility/burden and facilitates her attendance at school.

As such the role of AW workers in promoting EFA objectives is very significant and their status merits serious attention.

Status of AW Workers

There are no national standards in the recruitment, training, service conditions, enrolments, and welfare benefits of AW workers. The National Institute of Public Cooperation and Child Development (NIPCCD) which administers ICDS projects all over the country has prescribed class X as the minimum qualification for an AW worker. The AW worker is invariably a woman. Since women with such qualification may not be easily found in rural and tribal area even a class VIII or IX qualification is accepted and on the ground class VII fail women are working as AW workers in villages of north India. In rare instances, in some remote tribal pockets of India, illiterate but smart tribal women have also been accepted as AW workers. There is sometimes no choice since the AW workers must belong to the village/tribal community. The National Evaluation of the ICDS, 1992, collected information from sub-samples of 698 AW workers about their qualifications and it was observed that the proportion of underqualified AW workers was

as high as 52.9 per cent in tribal areas. At national level underqualified AW workers constitute 29.7 per cent of the total sample (Figure 14.7).

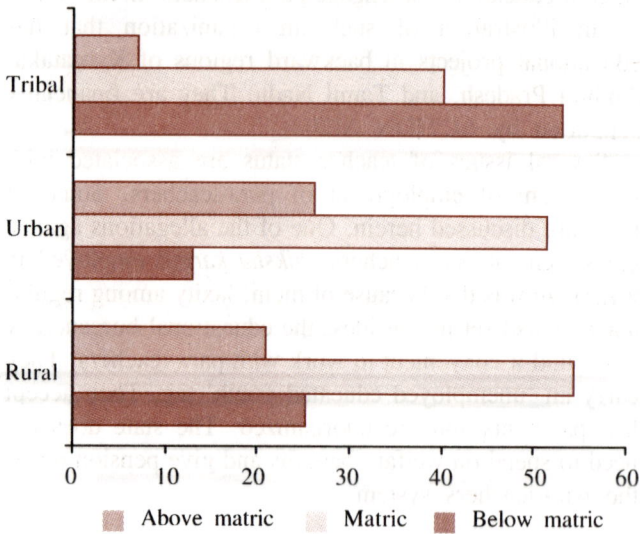

FIGURE 14.7: Educational Qualifications of AW Workers

By and large, with exceptions in tribal areas, all the AW workers are given job training for three months under a scheme called UDISHA. Training is organized by the Child Development Project Officers (CDPOs) in cooperation with other block-level agencies.

The salary of AW workers ranges from Rs 500 to Rs 800 per month. A pre-primary school teacher in a pre-primary school run by the state government or the corporation of a metropolitan city gets four to five times this salary. If the person is matric passed, she may get another Rs 75 to 100. An increment of Rs 25 is given every five years. Comparisons of honorarium of AW workers in two neighbouring states of India (see Table 14.5) is revealing.

TABLE 14.5
Honorarium of AW Workers (per month)[3]

	Andhra Pradesh	Karnataka
No. of blocks	338	186
No. of ICDS projects	209	185
No. of centres sanctioned	–0	40,155
No. of centres functioning	29,086	38,768
Matric failed	475	550
Matric passed	688	750

[3] It is interesting to note that in Tamil Nadu an AW centre will have an AW worker and also a community welfare organizer (CWO). This is because, till a few years ago the Tamil Nadu government was operating a Tamil Nadu Integrated Nutrition Project (TINP) along with the centrally sponsored ICDS AW centre, project. It posted a community nutrition worker (CWW) at the AW centre for managing the TINP. Later the TINP was

Demonstrations by AW workers demanding a rise in emoluments are common sights in state capitals, but they haven't had much success so far.

ISSUES AND PROBLEMS

The dynamics of status is both subtle and complex. It is inherent in the valuation of an individual, an institution, an occupation, a profession, a custom, or any similar element or phenomenon or process of a group by the group. This is true of elementary teachers also. The status of a teacher is the value attributed by the society to her/him. How does the valuation take place? How can the status/valuation of elementary teachers be appreciated/raised? What, after all, is value?

The value of a person or her/his activity/occupation/ profession is unconsciously measured by a society on the basis of the perceptions a society has of the contribution the person makes to the furtherance of its goals. What is the contribution that elementary teachers make to society? Do they add value to the lives of the people around them? The answer to these questions depends upon the answer to another question. What do people value in life? People value something which gives satisfaction to them. In this sense, there is a hierarchy of satisfaction/values in life. Physical and physiological needs form the base of this hierarchy. Pursuit of education and culture, preservation and promotion of democratic values, citizenship, global concerns, and the like become leisure-time pursuits which get attention only after the satisfaction of the physical needs of life. In a country like India, where, as per official figures, one-third of the people are not completely free from starvation, poverty and food insecurity haunt the people. Elementary education is a higher value of life, higher than food needs and social security. The main challenge is to create a demand for elementary education in a society that is besieged by a variety of problems.

Are teachers conscious of the need to prove their value to the community in which they function? Teachers are not chosen by the community to serve them. They are appointed by the government. A primary school teacher is looked upon as a 'government employee' and for some teachers 'teaching' is just a 'job'. It is one of the many 'jobs' that they would have been happy to get. In contrast, those teachers who have been taking interest in the attendance and learning of their students get recognition over a period of time and thus earn respect and love from their community. How can all teachers be made to involve themselves in the schooling process and earn 'status' from the community?

Teachers are rarely aware of the value of their work in day-to-day contexts with the overall goals and values of EFA. EFA is not integral to their thought process. When such a thought process sets in, they shall take a proactive role in enrolment and retention drives. They shall organize remedial teaching for slow learners and ensure that all children realize expected attainment levels. They need to be oriented to 'EFA goals' though such orientation by itself will not metamorphose a tradition-bound society. Along with it, there is need to build ethos and traditions which sustain the school system.

As of now, along with teachers, everything else in the school system is imposed by an 'invisible force' called the government. The curriculum, syllabus, examination, records to be maintained, working days and working hours, holidays in the year, monitoring system, textbooks, incentives and facilities, school equipment are all 'given' to the community. There is no autonomy at grassroots level in the system. How can there be accountability without autonomy?

Autonomy given to a community to organize and manage the education of its children automatically generates a sense of ownership. Ownership leads to possessiveness and responsibility. Non-performing teachers are taken to task. Performing teachers are rewarded. A market for good teachers is set in place. The village *panchayat* should be given the responsibility for education of children of the community.[4]

Several arguments object to the transfer of the management of education to *panchayats*. It is observed that 'you can delegate authority to an agency, but not responsibility. It has to come from within'. '*Panchayats* are not competent to manage education.' Basically, the well-entrenched bureaucracy in education which has evolved over a 150 years is not in favour of such transfer of authority. Elementary teachers also find it more convenient to function in relation to an educational bureaucracy that is at a distance rather than with the immediate community represented by *panchayats* many of whose members are looked down upon by the teachers as inferior to themselves in caste status, educational attainments, and exposure to the world outside. The 73rd and 74th amendments to the Indian Constitution have democratized Indian polity and provided for decentralization of powers and functions. Right opportunities have been created and the climate is favourable. But Indian society is still inegalitarian in its structures and functioning. It is also male dominated. The distance between the system of education and the grassroots communities

---

closed down. The CWW was accommodated as a CWO. The CWO gets lower emoluments than the AW centre.

4 In the United States and the United Kingdom, education of children is the privilege of the Local Education Authority. Teachers are hired for the job. Salary scales differ from country to country. Well-performing teachers find better markets for themselves.

needs to be bridged. Teachers' social status will go up if they cooperate with this process.

The foregoing arguments about teacher status in the context of EFA goals and community ownership may not find immediate acceptance within the teaching community. Teachers are more concerned with the anomalies in the country. For similar levels of qualifications, certification, and performance teachers are paid different salaries. At times, they are paid lower salary in one state (Karnataka) which prescribes higher qualifications (class XII) than in another state (Kerala) which is satisfied with lower qualifications (class X) for elementary teachers.

There is no harmony in the salary scales of elementary teachers across the country. This is the problem of a federal polity. It has led to militancy among teachers and it is difficult to sell EFA philosophy to agitated teachers.

Teacher militancy at elementary level of schooling is not strong in India. Elementary school teachers do not constitute a force to be reckoned with. They cannot hold up public examinations (unlike college/university teachers) as there are no such examinations at elementary level. When elementary education itself is not valued by the people (village India), where is the question of valuing teacher militancy at this level. While there is an All India Association of Primary School Teachers which is a registered body and State Associations affiliated to it, they are not very strong. In some states, the president of the State Association or his nominee (office-bearer) is involved by the state government in selection of teachers for state/national awards. The State Association has a limited role. District Associations hold district-level annual conferences. These associations are not professional bodies and academic matters are hardly discussed at these conferences.

Formerly, teacher transfer was a big issue among teachers. Now some states of India, as in Karnataka, the transfer of teachers is computerized. There is transparency in the transfers. Ground rules are laid down and not violated. Incidentally not only transfer of teachers, even their recruitment (at district-level) and selections for teacher training courses are computerized in several parts of the country. Transparency and systemic logic have reduced resentment, tensions, and militancy among teachers. It is only with respect to salaries, promotion opportunities, and service conditions that there is agitation among teachers.

State investment in elementary education is an important determinant of teacher status. Specifically, the non-Plan expenditure of the state is a variable in salary scales awarded to teachers. It may be observed that the total expenditure on education in India went up from Rs 172,139 million in 1990–1 to Rs 323,333 million in 1995–6, an increase of 88 per cent from 1990–1, at current prices. Of the total expenditure 99.2 per cent is on revenue account. Of the total revenue expenditure on education in 1995–6, that on elementary education was Rs 155,548 million, almost double the expenditure of the base figure for 1990–1, in current prices. Non-Plan expenditure in 1995–6, which mostly goes to teachers' salaries (general administration and salaries of educational officers), was around 80 per cent of total expenditure. It has come down from 88 per cent in 1990–1, perhaps because of expenditure under the DPEP. Non-Plan expenditure on elementary education as per cent of total educational expenditure in India was 39 per cent in 1995–6. Hence, as a proportion of total expenditure, not much is spent on elementary school teachers' salaries in India.

Per pupil expenditures across Indian states in 1995–6 (at 1980–1 prices) reveal interesting insights although it must be cautioned that inflation rates vary from state to state and the expenditures are not strictly comparable. While Kerala, Himachal Pradesh, and Haryana record high levels of per pupil expenditure, states like Karnataka, Orissa, Andhra Pradesh, Madhya Pradesh, Uttar Pradesh, and West Bengal spend very little on elementary education.

While more meaningful analysis would perhaps have been an inter-state comparison of expenditure on salary and other benefits to elementary teachers in relation to enrolment, retention, and attainment levels, data are not available for such an analysis.

PROFESSIONALIZATION OF TEACHING AND TEACHER STATUS

Teacher status will improve when teaching is transformed into a profession (Stinnet 1965, Corwin 1975, and Singh 1969.[5] A profession renders an essential, definite, and specialized service to society. When the knowledge base of the teachers, their standards and quality of certification, are enriched, teachers will get better status. This also relates to non-bookish knowledge, especially that concerning the community in which a teacher is serving.

Teachers should develop a professional approach. Teacher centres for a cluster of villages/urban areas are required. Teachers should meet there regularly and discuss problems of school management, children's

[5] There is a National Union of Teachers in England and National Educational Association in the United States. They are quite professional in their work. There is a vacuum in India in this regard. The present All India Federation of Teachers' Association has not made a mark.

behaviour, subject curriculum, and evaluation procedures. They should share findings/insights of action research that they may have conducted during the year. In this way, they can break isolation among themselves and get rid of the 'government servant' tag. The centre can maintain a small library and subscribe to useful magazines/journals. In this way, primary education can become vibrant at the grassroots in an otherwise dormant school culture.

There is also a need to formulate, adopt, and get committed to a professional code of ethics. Teachers should become more and more self-disciplined and autonomous in their functioning. The level of autonomy enjoyed by a person in her/his work is an index of her/his professional status.

TEACHER STATUS AND CIVIL SOCIETY

Teachers are employed by the state/government for the benefit of society. The state, however, is a creation of civil society. Neither teachers nor civil society appear to be conscious of this basic fact of civic life. Teachers' identity is confined to the government/corporation. A teacher is hardly conscious that she/he is an Indian teacher, promoting the goals of national life in India— He is a teacher in the classroom, at the same time a role model for students. Democracy in India will succeed and prosper if the proverbial 'man-on-the street' can question authority with information, frankness, and fearlessness. Teachers have to develop a questioning attitude of mind themselves and encourage their students to develop such attitudes, respect the dignity and individual worth of every student and promote a dialogical culture in the school. They should become knowledgeable not only about their subjects but also about current affairs and issues of common interest to civil society. This way they can enhance their self-regard. Ultimately, it is teachers themselves who hold the key to status in their own hands through their character, temperament, personality, scholarship, and services.

REFERENCES

Corwin, R. G. (1975). 'The New Teaching Profession'. *Teacher Education*. 74th Yearbook of the NSSE.

Janigra, N. K., Ajit Singh, and S. K. Yadav (1995). 'Teacher Policy, Training Needs and Percieved Status of Teachers'. *Indian Educational Review*, vol. 30, no. 1.

Seetharamu, A. S. (1995a). 'Reforms and Education' 'Forming the Social Safety Net'. *Business Line*. (9.3.1995)

———— (1995b). 'Reforms and Education' 'How to Exploit the Interface'. *Business Line*. (11.3.1995)

———— (1995c). 'Reforms and Education' 'Scouting for Resources'. *Business Line*. (10.3.1995)

Singh, R. P. (1969). *The Indian Teacher*. National Publishing House, New Delhi.

Stinnet, T. M. (1965). *The Profession of Teaching*. Prentice Hall.

World Bank (1997). *India: Primary Education. Achievements and Challenges*. A World Bank Report No.15756-IN.

15 Educating the Educators
Review of Primary Teacher Training

C. Seshadri

POLICIES AND PROGRAMMES

The decade 1990–2000 witnessed unprecedented developments in primary teacher training[1] on most fronts. Structures that had come into existence under the Government of India sponsored Scheme of Teacher Education like the District Institutes of Education and Training (DIETs) received a boost leading to the implementation of the scheme on a much wider scale. The Programme of Mass Orientation of School Teachers (PMOST) also got fine tuned with the introduction of distance learning mode and application of interactive video technology. The middle of the decade (1995) also saw the establishment of the National Council for Teacher Education (NCTE) as a statutory authority to regulate growth and development of teacher education. The establishment of Block Resource Centres and Cluster Resource Centres (BRCs and CRCs) under the District Primary Education Programme (DPEP) advanced the cause of decentralization of training and its eventual institutionalization. A spin-off of this entire upsurge in in-service training was that it led to an examination of the content and processes of initial teacher training and the appreciation of the need to impart to it a similar thrust. In sum, primary teacher training during the 1990s, especially of the in-service variety, grew and developed in all directions—expansion of institutions, evolution of new models and designs, review and reform of training content and processes, production of new generation training materials, application of modern technology in materials preparation and training methods, and creation of training structures at sub-district level.

[1] The terms 'primary' and 'elementary' are used interchangeably here. The reference is to elementary teacher education (covering the first seven or eight years of compulsory schooling).

Policy Initiatives

But what is perhaps the most significant contribution to primary education thinking, especially on curriculum and teacher training, came from the report of the National Advisory Committee on Curriculum Load entitled, *Learning Without Burden* (See DoE 1993). Set up in the context of the growing tendency of overloading young children with 'academic burden', the Committee drew attention to the 'more pernicious burden of non-comprehension' in primary schools. The major outcome of the report has been the appreciation of the need for the involvement of teachers in curriculum and textbook preparation and training teachers in fostering learning through activity, discovery, exploration, observation, and understanding without making school learning a wearisome burden.

The Committee pointed out that teachers perceive the content of the textbook as a rigid boundary or definer of their work in the classroom, and their role as 'teaching the text'. This perception that a teacher can do little in the classroom outside of the textbook must be changed through teacher training. In the context of constructing a new self-image of the teacher, the Committee admitted preservice training 'as a key but an elusive area of reform'.

MAJOR SCHEMES, PROGRAMMES, AND PROJECTS—DIETs

The District Institutes for Educational Training (DIETs), established as a follow-up of the National Policy on Education (NPE), 1986, are the main supply institutions for the initial training of elementary teachers in most states. In most cases, these were developed by upgrading existing teacher training institutes. The broad mandate implied that DIETs function in multiple areas—teaching, training, curriculum and materials development, research and extension, planning, and management. There are more than 400 DIETs in the country today. Of them, 337 are said to be 'operational' (see DoE 1998). Even those that are operational are not adequately staffed. The staff are mainly drawn from school- and field-based cadres, and most of them have little experience of working in teacher training or research and development institutions. The government finds it a challenge to make all the DIETs fully functional and to open new DIETs in the remaining districts during the Ninth Plan (see DoE 1998). An assessment of the technical and infrastructure capacity of DIETs is under way. The object of the exercise is to assess the quality of functions being carried out by DIETs and to make recommendations to improve their capacity.

NCTE and Quality Control in Teacher Education

The NCTE was established in August 1995 as a statutory authority for 'achieving planned and coordinated development of the teacher education system throughout the country, the regulation and proper maintenance of norms and standards in the teacher education system, and for matters connected therewith' (The Parliament Act No. 73 of 1993). The Council is vested with both regulatory and academic functions of providing resource support for the qualitative improvement of teacher education programmes. Under the statute it is now mandatory for teacher education institutions to seek the recognition of the NCTE. All institutions of teacher education—preschool, elementary, secondary, higher secondary, NFE, institutions preparing teachers for physical education, education of the disabled, adult education—are brought under the authority of the NCTE. During its five years of existence, the NCTE, acting on its wide brief, has laid down norms and standards, submitted them to periodic review on the basis of feedback from the field, and accorded recognition to institutions fulfilling the norms. An important activity of the NCTE in terms of its potential to transform teacher education content and processes throughout the country is the development of a curriculum framework for teacher education programmes for different levels of schooling. For the elementary stage, multiple models are recommended in view of diverse practices relating to training of teachers at primary, upper-primary, and elementary levels.

DPEP Teacher Training: Decentralized Structures and Participatory Approaches

The advent of the DPEP in the middle of the decade drew public attention to the dismal state of primary education in the country, especially with reference to learning levels in the basic skills of language and arithmetic. Of special significance is the freshness of thinking it has

generated on matters concerned with the content and processes of teacher training. Attention has also been drawn to the training mode with the increasing adoption of modular approaches and on-site training. Teacher education structures have been decentralized down to the block and school cluster levels with the creation of BRCs and CRCs. The BRCs and CRCs are decentralized academic support institutions to provide on-site support to teachers in terms of school visits, demonstrations, feedback, teacher training, material preparation, and discussion of special problems at monthly meetings.

While there was no direct intervention into initial teacher training structures and processes, developments in the DPEP have spurred national and state-level efforts to examine initial teacher training programmes critically with reference to universalization of elementary education (UEE) needs.

A significant contribution in this context is the development of a curriculum framework for the primary stage by the NCERT, *The Primary Years—A Curriculum Framework* (1997) which is based on the appreciation of the uniqueness of the primary stage. It is not education for passing on to higher stages but an education that lays the foundation for life and the centrality of the child in the learning process.

Advent of Educational Technology (ET): Interactive Television and Distance Learning

Another development that had great influence on in-service teacher education modes and methods, but so far has failed to impact initial teacher training is ET. The application of ET in teacher training had begun as early as the 1980s. The National Council of Educational Research and Training (NCERT) through its Central Institute of Education and Training (CIET) had produced audio/video programmes on a wide range of subjects related to teacher education. These were telecast on the national TV channel, namely Doordarshan, for teachers in several states. But the real breakthrough in moving away from the centre-based teacher training strategy and its cascade mode known for its transmission loss was achieved with the launching of the Tele SOPT programme of training teachers through interactive video technology. The programme, initially tried out in the states of Karnataka and Madhya Pradesh, provides in-service education to teachers through teleconferencing (one-way video and two-way audio) mode.

Distance education has come a long way from broadcast television and radio, through video and audio cassettes to computer and satellite. It is now claimed that the learning experience is strongly in the grip of an 'interaction paradigm' and technologies which offer some form of interaction are the ones in demand. Future teacher education programmes, especially the ones with large target coverage in the shortest possible time are being conceived and planned primarily in the distance learning mode.

In contrast to these exciting developments in in-service education, initial teacher education remains unconcerned and unaffected with the possibilities and potential of ET, except for including them—in the best case scenario—as 'topics' to be studied to make trainees aware of these developments. Hardly are there any significant attempts to apply the technology to improve the curriculum transaction in teacher education programmes, not to speak of training teachers in the skill of using the technology.

CURRENT STATUS OF PRIMARY TEACHER TRAINING

Overall Country Scenario

At the turn of the century India has one of the largest teacher training systems in the world with nearly 30,000 teacher educators engaged in the task of teacher training at preschool, elementary, secondary, and higher levels of schooling. There are more than 1200 teacher training schools and 700 colleges of education and university departments of education supporting an expanding school system employing 4.52 million teachers, of which primary teachers alone account for 3 million. There are also institutions for training teachers in preschool education, special education, physical education, adult education, and non-formal education (NFE). The continued pursuit of the goal of UEE would mean a further expansion of schools and teachers in coming years. At the rate of 11.27 per cent growth registered during the period 1986–93 (1.61 per cent annually), the number of primary teachers that would be added at the end of Ninth and Tenth Five Year Plans is estimated to be 2.12 million and 2.30 million, respectively. Correspondingly, the teacher education system finds itself poised for further expansion.

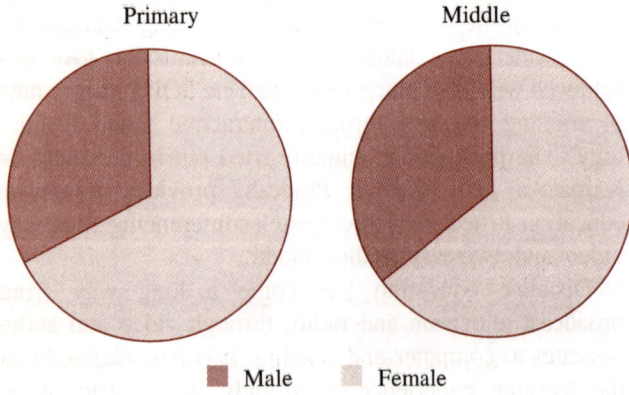

FIGURE 15.1: Male and Female Teachers in Primary and Middle Schools

According to official statistics, the number of untrained teachers is not high in most states. However, in the eastern and north-eastern regions it is quite high—in some cases as high as 60 to 70 per cent.

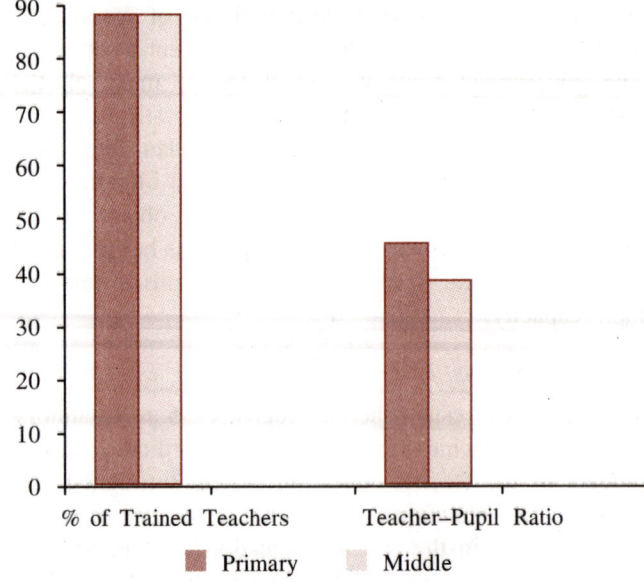

FIGURE 15.2: Trained Teachers and Teacher–Pupil Ratio in Primary and Middle Schools

The more serious problem with primary teacher training is the non-observance of standards and norms with respect to entry-level qualifications, duration of training, certification requirement for recruitment of teachers, and infrastructure and physical facilities. The NCTE has also laid down norms for physical infrastructure, human resources, academic inputs, and financial resources. With respect to all these, practices vary across states. The NCTE's goal of bringing all training institutions into its fold has largely been achieved with 2127 institutions out of 2570 applying for recognition by the end of March 1998. Of the total number of 1158 elementary teacher education institutions, 955 had applied for recognition: 89 were granted recognition and 457 provisional recognition, 15 were refused recognition. Besides, 469 new institutions also sought recognition, of which 4 were granted recognition, 21 were provisionally recognized, and 61 refused recognition. There are still a large number of institutions which have not applied for recognition.

Primary teacher training continues to remain an undergraduate certificate/diploma programme offered at exclusive training establishments which could, at best, be described as modest in respect of infrastructure, facilities, and staff. These institutions go by various names—elementary teacher training institutions, teacher's training institutes, basic training institutes, and so on. DIETs in most states are the main institutions that prepare elementary teachers. The programmes that are offered in these institutions also carry a welter of nomenclatures like, TCH, D.Ed., JBT, PTC, TTC, and ETT standing for Teacher's Certificate (Higher), Diploma in Education, Junior Basic Training, and so on. No fresh initiatives have been launched or interest evinced to upgrade primary teacher training to a degree-level programme by the universities. The exception is provided by a few institutions like Delhi University which has started an integrated B.El.Ed. Degree programme in elementary education. The national norms prescribe an academic education of twelve years and a two-year programme of professional training for teachers. But the entry qualification for primary teacher training remains in the range of ten to twelve years of academic education and the duration of training in the range of one to two years (see Table 15.1).

TEACHER EDUCATION IN THE STATES: AN OVERVIEW

The NCTE initiated a series of state-specific studies to assess the status of teacher education in the country. These state-specific studies (NCTE 1998e and 1998j) have drawn attention to the following aspects which need to be addressed towards quality improvement of teacher education:

• Absence of compulsory requirement of pre-service teacher training for appointment of teachers and continued appointment of untrained teachers in some states. e.g. West Bengal, Arunachal Pradesh, Tripura.

• Non-observance of the NCTE norm of 50 per cent marks for minimum eligibility to the training course and the criticism of the norm itself as being too low for preparation of teachers to the elementary schools with classes from I to VIII. e.g. Rajasthan, Madhya Pradesh.

• Non-observance of norms with regard to minimum academic qualification for entry into training and the duration of training. In some states these are class X pass and one year respectively, e.g. West Bengal, Arunachal Pradesh, Tripura, and Himachal Pradesh.

• The admission test for training institutions is not satisfactory with respect to what it tests, which does not ensure entrance of those with the right ability and aptitude for teaching.

• Institutional capacity for teacher training is largely unutilized in some states like West Bengal and is in inadequate supply in others like Arunachal Pradesh.

• The ability in content of most entrants to the training institutions leaves much to be desired and needs to be upgraded.

PRIMARY TEACHER TRAINING DURING THE EFA DECADE: A CRITICAL REVIEW

An Overall Appraisal

At the threshold of the new millennium the picture that one has of primary teacher training is one of notable achievements as well as tasks yet to be addressed. As to the gains, the system has responded gamely to the demands arising from expansion in the school education sector in terms of substantial increase in number and variety of teacher training and support institutions. Teacher support actions exhibit a range and variety. There are more funds for training activities and more programmes for teachers. There is greater availability of a variety of materials—workbooks, guide books, training manuals, self-learning materials. Grants are available for teachers to fabricate their own teaching aids.

Much of the upsurge of post-NPE activity, however, has been number driven. The implementation of the centrally sponsored programme for strengthening teacher education, unfortunately, was not accompanied by concurrent concern and reflection on issues relating to the capacity of the teacher education establishment to assimilate and respond in terms of appropriate programmes and projects. In the case of the much hyped DIETs, the capacity of the institutions to carry out their omnibus terms of reference was not considered in-depth. Granting that teacher education alone cannot be the sole determinant of teacher behaviour, one cannot help feeling that the system has been found wanting in its 'readiness' to creatively respond to state-sponsored initiatives by way of innovative programmes and projects of teacher performance improvement as there are no matching human resources to assimilate and sustain them.

The steady increase in the demand for teachers and the requirement of professional certification for appointment as teachers has enhanced the market value of teacher education, if not the status of the teaching profession. Issues relating to teacher training have been brought to the centre stage of the educational debate. Primary education is also slowly getting accepted as a 'respectable' sphere of study and research by academics, overcoming the disdain with which it was treated earlier. Some indicators of this development are the increasing involvement of university academics in primary education projects, the availability of increased funding for primary education research under different schemes, and the starting of innovative teacher education programmes like B.El.Ed by Delhi University. That the teacher is the key actor in educational reform is not passed off as a various truism anymore, but has issued forth in deliberate teacher development policies and programmes. All this augurs well for the future development of teacher training.

TABLE 15.1

**Primary/Elementary Teacher Education Programmes and
Recruitment Qualifications for Primary Teachers**

States/UTs	Course	Duration (years)	Eligibility for admission	Recruitment qualifications	
				Academic	Professional
Andhra Pradesh	TTC	2	10+2	10+2	TTC
Arunachal Pradesh	DPTT	1	10+2 (Tribals) Grad.(Others)	10+2 (Tribals) Grad.(Others)	Nil
Assam	JBT	1	10 (LP) 10+2 (UP)	10 (LP) 10+2 (UP)	Nil
Bihar	PTT	2	10	10	Nil
Goa	D.Ed	2	10+2	10+2	D.Ed
Gujarat	PTC	2	10+2	10+2	PTC
Haryana	JBT & ETT	2	10+2	SSC (10+2)	TTC
Himachal Pradesh	JBT & ETT	2	10+2	SSC (10+2)	TTC
Jammu and Kashmir					
Karnataka	TCH	2	10+2	10+2	TCH
Kerala	TTC	2	10+2	10+2	TTC
Madhya Pradesh	D.Ed	2	10+2	10+2	D.Ed
Maharashtra	D.Ed	2	10+2	10+2	D.Ed
Manipur	Dip. in ETE	2	10	10 for Primary Grad. For UP	
Meghalaya	JBT,	1	10	10 (+ 2 Prop)	
	Sr. TT	2	10	10 (+ 2 Prop)	
Mizoram	Dip. in ETE	1	10+2	10+2	
Nagaland	Jr.TT,	1	8	8	TTC
	UGTTr	2	10	10	
Orissa	Tr.Tg.Certificate	2	10	10	Nil
Punjab	JBT, ETT	2	10+2	10+2	Nil
Rajasthan	STC	2	10+2	Sr. High (10+2)	Nil
Sikkim	Pr.Tr. Certificate	1	10	10	TTC
Tamil Nadu	DTE	2	10+2	10+2	Nil
Tripura	JBT	1	10	10	BTC
Uttar Pradesh	JBT	2	10+2	10+2	Nil
West Bengal	Pr. Tr. Certificate	1	10	10	JBT
Andaman & Nicobar	JBT	2	10+2	10+2	JBT
Chandigarh	JBT	2	10+2	10+2	D.Ed
Dadra and Nagar Haveli				10+2	D.Ed
Daman	Maharashtra Pattern			10+2	D.Ed
Delhi	ETT	2	10+2	10+2	ETT
Lakshadweep	DTE	2	10+2	10+2	DTE
Pondicherry	DTE	2	10+2	10+2	DTE

Source: NCTE (Provisional).

Note: The figures in the table represent the general picture in the states. There are variations in states with regard to specific details about recruitment qualifications. Under the Shiksha Karmi Yojna in Rajasthan, for example, recruitment qualifications are class VIII for men teachers and class VI for women teachers with no training. Such variations have come up of late in Madhya Pradesh and other states as well.

At the same time, it is disquieting that a climate has not been created in the country during all these years for the emergence of context-specific initiatives at state and sub-state levels towards the reform of teacher training structures and processes. Even the 'district-specific' DPEP has not done much in this area. Reform actions in primary teacher education carried out so far have been pan-Indian, emanating from the centre, proposing standard, across-the-board solutions at the national level. The trend is in favour of grand designs and strategies. Far from enabling local initiatives to emerge, the all-India plans and programmes seem to have created a dependency syndrome. The SCERTs at state level and the DIETs at district level have yet to emerge as the fully empowered institutions that one would wish.

The mood of in-service training is upbeat and it exudes a robustness that raises hopes for the future of initial teacher training. It has shed its ad hocism and is getting institutionalized, aided by the new structures like the Teacher Centres, BRCs/CRCs, and the plethora of training cascades launched by states as well as the centre. The support base for teachers has widened. The approach to planning and management of training is becoming increasingly professional, as evidenced in the sophistication that characterizes designing, delivery, and evaluation of training programmes. Also evident is the scientific approach to the development and production of training packages and monitoring and evaluation of programmes.

Teacher training has also gradually ceased to be the preserve of formally trained professionals. The field experiences of many NGOs have provided useful inputs towards demystification of teacher training and evolution of innovative training methods. For example, the Shiksha Karmi project which arose out of the need to deal with the problem of teacher absenteeism, is built on the deployment of ordinary people with enthusiasm and desire to teach but with no formal education to do so. Lok Jumbish (LJ), another major education for all (EFA) initiative has set up vibrant block and cluster resource groups for providing academic supervision and regular training of teachers. Eklavya's teacher training programme adopts methods that rid teachers of their inhibitions in dealing with children at children's own level. There is also increased direct involvement of NGO activists and the general community in training activities, much to the benefit of teacher education. Aided by the legislation empowering *panchayati raj* institutions with respect to education, the sectoral approach to primary education is slowly making way for treating primary education as an integral aspect of overall development strategy. In other words, primary teacher training has come to assert its interdisciplinarity, as it should have done long ago.

All this, however, has happened in connection with the training of in-service teachers under different schemes. In contrast, initial teacher training has remained untouched by these happenings. Its profile continues to remain low. Benign neglect characterizes the way it is treated by those who control it. Although certification is essential for entry into the teaching profession, it is still not so in several states and UTs. There is improvement in pupil–teacher ratio at all-India level but in several states it is still very high. More serious is the problem of the poor quality of the human capital that is presently engaged in teaching.

Issues relating to quality reform of pre-service teacher education content and processes have not, however, received adequate attention. In the early 1980s the CAPE (Comprehensive Access to Primary Education) project introduced into the curriculum of elementary teacher education a training-cum-production mode for providing experience to trainees in developing local-specific curricular materials and learning episodes. This was a major breakthrough in the reform of teacher education curriculum. But the innovation was not sustained. Today, formal, institutional initial teacher training continues to function basically as an academic activity. Efforts made for training *shiksha karmis* in Rajasthan, Madhya Pradesh, and elsewhere, no doubt, present encouraging exceptions. It is also true that states have, from time to time, reviewed the curriculum of pre-service teacher education. But these reviews have not been able to bring about any significant change in the basic character of the system as such.

Situating Initial primary Teacher Education in the EFA Context

Initial teacher education, as already noted, is run primarily as an academic programme and its performance is judged by criteria internal to the programme. It is concerned with the goals and strategies of UEE only incidentally. It is now time to bring initial teacher education into the 'firing line' as a deliberate strategy to deal with the unfinished tasks of UEE. And these tasks remain as daunting as ever. Although India has now acquired the status of a 'medium human development' country, it still has a long way to go in the crucial indicators of literacy and education. It is clear that human development in India is flawed in that it has not touched the lives of millions of Indians, especially those who live in rural areas or happen to be female. This is so, despite the declaration of primary education as a fundamental, legally enforceable human right.

Situating initial teacher education in the context of UEE would mean treating it as a national programme of action towards achievement of UEE goals and not as a cloistered academic activity. It also means shaping it as an effective instrument to tackle the various UEE tasks, most important of all, the quality and thrusts of the training programme.

There are more than 1200 primary teacher education institutions in the country, with more than 120,000 students enrolled in them (see DoE 1996). If properly trained through focused programmes, this would constitute a powerful teacher force to handle the UEE tasks. This may have to be augmented in the coming years, taking note of the increase in child population, the number of children out of school and the increase in the enrolment, apart from the total number of teachers in position, further teachers required and the pupil–teacher ratio that can be sustained. It also has to take note of the increase in the number of schools and the number of single-teacher schools. The Ninth Plan target for primary education includes bringing down the dropout rate from 36.3 per cent to 20 per cent for classes I–V and from 56.5 per cent to 40 per cent for classes VI–VIII (see DoE 1998). According to the *Sixth All-India Educational Survey* (see NCERT 1998) the total number of teachers in the primary and upper-primary schools was 2.013 million and 1.036 million, respectively. In 1996–7, there were 36.3 million children in the 6–14 age group who were out of school. For taking care of these children, at the rate of 1:40, 907,000 teachers would be required. Also, if the pupil–teacher ratio is to be 1:40, for the 151.4 million children attending school, an additional 735,000 teachers would be required. Thus, 1.642 million new teachers would be required for keeping all children of schoolgoing age in schools. This calculation is based on the projected child population in 1996 being 187,704,000 (see DoE 1998). With the population increasing further, the demands on the system for teacher supply would escalate even further.

In the light of the findings of the state studies quoted earlier, this would mean that states have to reassess the capacities of their training institutions to match them with the teacher supply position. Regional imbalances in the availability of institutional facilities also need to be removed. Also important in this connection are the pupil–teacher ratio and the percentage of female teachers. Enrolment and retention of girls in school would demand gender-fair approaches to the distribution of places in teacher education institutions and recruitment of teachers. States like West Bengal and generally the north-east region are low on this indicator and planning of teacher education has to accommodate these concerns.

Even more crucial is the quality of human capital involved in teaching and the country's commitment to invest in its improvement. It is well known that the quality and extent of learner achievement are determined primarily by teacher competence and teacher motivation. The length of academic preparation, the level of subject matter knowledge and the repertoire of pedagogical skills teachers possess to meet the needs of diverse learning situations, the degree of commitment to the profession and the level of motivation significantly influence the quality of curriculum transaction in classrooms, and thereby, pupil learning. To ensure quality in teacher education, national norms have been stipulated: twelfth class pass for entry into the training course, minimum eligibility of 50 per cent marks in the qualifying examination and a two-year training for certification. But on the ground these are not fulfilled in a number of states. A large number of underqualified and undertrained teachers are still in the system and their number may increase if the extant policies governing teacher certification and recruitment continue. It is a fact of life that primary teaching as a career does not attract the academically bright in view of its low status and absence of career prospects. Teacher education has to function within the confines of these ground conditions and gear itself to address its mandate.

Upgrading Primary Teacher Education

Primary teacher training in India has had its roots in the Normal Schools which were set up to prepare teachers for schools which the masses went to, the so-called 'vernacular schools'. This colonial hangover continues to weigh on primary teacher training which still is struggling to establish its importance. Colleges of Education which are of much later origin are more visible than primary teacher training institutes, even at a time when primary teacher education has become a priority national concern. There is a hierarchy among institutions, with institutions catering to 'higher' levels occupying higher status. Due to this historical reason, in discussions on reform of teacher education, it is the BEd. which provides the frame of reference and not the diploma or certificate of primary or elementary teacher training.

There is rarely any participation of primary teachers or teacher educators in these discussions. It is only recently that primary teacher education has staked its claim to special identity. Even the professional associations of teacher educators, for example the Indian Association of Teacher Educators (IATE), are predominantly controlled by the university academics and secondary teacher education faculty. The representation and participation of primary teacher educators is only notional.

A situation like the above is the result of several factors. Study in a college and a university degree carries higher prestige than other pursuits at lower levels. Unlike secondary teacher training, a degree programme which comes under the purview of the universities' primary teacher training, continues to be the responsibility of the State Boards or Departments of Education or the State Councils of Educational Research and Training (SCERTs). Primary teacher education is also in dire need of qualified and competent professionals to effectively articulate its concerns and provide leadership in organizing it as an undertaking of national importance.

The reluctance of the establishment to upgrade primary teacher education by enhancing its duration or elevating its status to a degree programme has made things more difficult. More than two decades ago, the Education Commission (1964–6) and NCTE (1978) made efforts to bring all types and stages of training under one umbrella, a comprehensive college of education which offered teacher preparation programmes for preschool, elementary, secondary, and higher secondary stages under one roof with provision for flexibility of vertical and horizontal movement for both staff and students. But the recommendation did not evoke enthusiastic response, nor have attempts to sell integrated long-duration training courses leading to a university degree. It appears that there are boundaries set within which quality improvement of primary teacher training has to be conceived.

The isolation of primary teacher education and its low academic status is of three kinds—isolation from schools, from the community, and from training institutions at higher levels. The DIETs were expected to achieve a breakthrough in this area with their physical and human resources and programmes but on the ground this has not happened. The DPEP has to some extent made inroads to break this isolation. Commendable as this is, it is sad that the DPEP did not show interest in initial teacher education and bypassed it. However, it is the third kind of isolation that largely accounts for the low image of primary teacher education. And here there are no quick-fix remedies. Actions required are of a nature that need political will and courage to invest in human capital development. In a situation where investment priorities do not favour enterprises which do not assure a quick pay-off, this seems most unlikely. In the meanwhile, one has to keep the fight alive. One of the NCTE initiatives in this regard is its project, Networks for Institutional Capacity Enhancement. The project seeks to bring together educational research institutions like SCERTs, university departments of education, and elementary teacher education institutions in a symbiotic relationship for improving teacher education at the elementary level.

On a more practical plane, upgrading primary teacher education calls for improvement in the status of primary teachers, enhancing the entry qualification and duration of training to make it equivalent to a degree programme, and vesting the management and control of primary teacher education in a body that enjoys a status equal to a university faculty. The issues are interlinked. For the immediate present, a promising avenue is to shape the Institutes of Advanced Studies in Education (IASEs) into Comprehensive Colleges of Education. Presently the IASEs, with a few exceptions, do not interest themselves in elementary education issues. A second action to take is to step up efforts to develop integrated programmes of teacher education leading to a degree. In the past such efforts have floundered for want of support from the establishment by way of supportive recruitment policies and increased status for primary teachers with comparable wages. Even now, several states give incentives in the form of promotion and wage increase to teachers who acquire a degree while in service. The costs involved in this practice and elevating the status of primary teacher training to a degree could be compared and the trade-off, if any, has to be in favour of long-term gains.

Lessons from in-service Teacher Training

The UEE concerns triggered a number of changes in the format, substance, delivery, and management of in-service teacher training. This has been facilitated mainly through the application of educational and information technology and management principles to the training enterprise. It was hoped that the advent of ET and IT would lead to a similar review of concepts and practices that drive mainstream, initial teacher education programmes. This has not happened and initial teacher education blissfully continues with its traditional academic style of functioning in splendid isolation. Initial teacher education will soon find itself caught in a time warp if it does not respond to educational technology.

Even the terms of debate on curricular reform differ in the two training modes. The initial teacher education discourse revolves around such theoretical issues as the epistemological status of its knowledge base or general academic and organizational matters. The NCTE publication *Policy Perspectives in Teacher Education—Critique and Documentation* (1998c) under 'conclusions' highlights issues like organizational structure, system's inability to sustain innovations, quality of trainees and teacher educators, duration, commercialization, competencies in IT, research, and its usability, in-service-pre-service link, theoretical perspectives, knowledge base, school–training institution coordination, teacher-community link. The tone of discussion is scholarly and academic but bereft of an aggressive social stance. The more substantive issues of primary education like access, dropout, participation, achievement, gender, teaching in difficult contexts, when they are mentioned at all, appear as academic points to be reckoned. The debate is not driven by the UEE agenda. What is even more disconcerting is that teacher education is discussed as a general category. The concerns of the first level of education are either not treated at all or subsumed under general problems. The discussion does not reflect the special importance of the primary stage, the orientation which should be given to it, the tasks for which teachers are to be prepared, the training strategies that need to be adopted to enable teachers to address the tasks, and the challenge involved in the whole exercise. Even the NCTE *Curriculum Framework for Quality Teacher Education* (1998b) does not forcefully emphasize the very special concerns of primary education and primary teacher education.

The concerns of in-service teacher education, on the other hand, are systematic planning, imparting skill specificity, professional approach to development of training materials and strategies, and cost-effective management. In-service training is concerned with such questions as what training should focus on. How are the training materials to be planned and developed? What different ways of organizing training would result in maximizing the returns—training individual teachers or whole schools? Would training conducted in school or on-site yield more returns than if it were conducted elsewhere? Would training the head teacher first be more effective? For instance, under the DPEP, in the planning and designing of training modules and their transaction, a cross-section of national- and state-level experts including NGOs, teacher educators, and teachers were involved to make the training exercise more responsive to the field realities. A similar focus, programmatic thrust, and concern for output efficiency is singularly lacking in initial teacher education, even allowing for the obvious differences between the two modes. The State Studies on Teacher Education have reported that there is no adequate treatment of minimum levels of learning, gender and environmental issues, dropouts, enrolment, multi-grade teaching, and teaching in difficult contexts in pre-service teacher education curricula.

In view of the lethargy of the initial teacher education system, reforms are being pushed through ad hoc in-service programmes. But in-service education cannot be a substitute for initial training. While in-service can help incumbent teachers, it is also necessary to simultaneously change the form and substance of institutional pre-service programmes and ensure a regular supply of properly trained new teachers, reduce pressure on in-service training, and avoid duplication of efforts. The fact that current forms of initial teacher training are not adequate is no reason to deny the contribution of educational science and to fall back exclusively on in-service training. What is important is to impart the programmatic nature of in-service training to pre-service training also. Only then can the required synergy be generated to deal with the UEE tasks.

The Cutting Edge of Teacher Education—Curricular Reforms

The important question before teacher education is what value it adds to the teachers' academic learning vis-à-vis the actual problems of classroom teaching and learning. In order to identify the contours of curriculum renewal to direct initial teacher education towards the UEE goals, one has to reassess the basics of initial training and relevance of current methods and objectives against the actual needs of the school system. These concerns in the Indian context may be teaching large-sized classes of 50 and above, teaching in difficult contexts like multi-grade classrooms, teaching first-generation school-goers, classroom management, working with parents, enlisting community support, implementing incentive schemes, and so on.

What is missing in ongoing efforts at reform of teacher education curriculum is the thrust to make its content and methodology more relevant to the problems of the primary classroom, taking into account the priority needs and demands of compulsory schooling in India. The heart of teacher training is skills related to performance of classroom tasks. The pedagogical skills involved in performing these tasks include critical analysis of material, capacity to exploit analogies and examples to convey the information, ability to adapt materials to students' interests and abilities, ability to organize, and manage classrooms to evaluate, discipline and encourage students to promote their learning. Apart from these, special training needs of those who have to teach children from disadvantaged groups and in difficult contexts like large-sized classes, multi-grade teaching, bilingual and multilingual settings, remote areas are to be identified. It would be worthwhile in this context to revisit the concepts of 'core' and 'special training programme packages' suggested in the 1978 curriculum framework of the NCTE.

The elementary teacher education curriculum presently is a scaled down version of the B.Ed. curriculum. The curriculum is divided into two parts, theory and practical, with courses in Principles of Education, Educational Psychology, Education in India, Special/Additional papers and Methods of Teaching in Mother Tongue, Arithmetic, Environmental Studies, Health and Physical Education, and Work Experience. Theory dominates the teacher education programme. In Haryana the D.Ed. sets apart 58 per cent marks for theory, 29 per cent for practical, and only 13 per cent for teaching practice. A similar picture prevails in the other states also. Sometimes the two-year course is divided into a year each for teaching classes I to IV and V to VIII. Neither in its design nor in content does it reflect the stage-specific concerns of elementary education.

It is clear that the primary teacher education curriculum should have as its basic frame of reference the primary school curriculum itself. To the extent it seeks to fulfil the expectations and requirements of the primary curriculum, it retains its relevance. Often the teacher education curriculum has lost its relevance, either because the primary curriculum itself was not found relevant or the teacher education curriculum did not adequately respond to the thrusts of the school curriculum. In the context of UEE, it is imperative that the content, teaching, and evaluation processes of primary schooling strongly pursue the basic education objectives and goals. But such a development-orientation of basic education is not adequately reflected in the primary education curricula of most states. For the most part, primary education continues to be treated as the feeder for higher levels of schooling. A welcome development is the NCERT's new initiative *The Primary Years—A Curriculum Framework* (1997) to which reference has already been made. What is special about the work is its bold acknowledgment of the self-contained and self-sustaining nature of primary schooling and the centrality of the child in the learning process. It outlines the expected profile of the child at the end of primary schooling, clarifies certain misconceptions, focuses on child-centred and activity-based teaching and learning, highlights favourable learning conditions necessary for 'access with success', and identifies ways in which teachers can be helped to realize the objectives of the curriculum. A curriculum of this kind provides a good frame of reference for quality improvement of primary teacher education.

The issue of directing the thrusts of initial teacher education towards UEE cannot be treated as a simple matter of reform of training methodology within existing structures and parameters. It is one of transforming the basic orientation of training towards the UEE goals and preparing teachers to carry out actions towards the achievement of these goals. In the designing of such a curriculum for primary as well as primary teacher education there is a great deal to learn from the experience of the NGOs like Shiksha Karmi, LJ, and Eklavya to cite only a few. Presently the responsibility for developing primary teacher education curriculum vests with the SCERTs or the concerned department of education in the states. This arrangement should make way for a wider and more participative arrangement involving different stakeholders—teachers, teacher educators, educationists, educational planners, NGOs with a good track record in basic education, educational administrators, and the community. Second, the current bifurcation of teacher education curriculum into two compartments—theory and practicals—with 'theory' covering educational courses and 'practice' covering school teaching and practicum, is pedagogically and from the practical point of view unsound. The entire curriculum should be treated as one whole integrating theory with practice and set down in terms of identified specific teacher performances and tasks. A modular organization of the curriculum would answer the demands of a programmatic teacher education curriculum better. Third, there has to be more curriculum time for skill practice. And last, like in-service training, initial training also should adopt the professional approach to the preparation of training materials, designing of training methods, application of educational technology, and monitoring and evaluation of the training programme.

Institutional Development of DIETs

The target of establishing DIETs in each district has almost been achieved but not the task of making them deliver. These institutions across the country exhibit wide variations in the degree and extent to which they have addressed their mandate and in the quality of performance. Judging by the yardstick of technical proficiency and quality of performance in its different programme areas, one may feel that even a DIET identified as 'good' still has a long way to traverse. From the point of view of vision and overall planning, relevance of programmes to field realities, the implementation of the lab area concept, and the extent and quality of field interaction the performance of the typical DIET leaves a lot to be desired.

The establishment of DIETs has not been accompanied by sustained efforts towards capacity building of functionaries. Most of the faculty are on promotion from their earlier postings within the department and have no formal training in the special skills needed to carry out their tasks. There has been no concerted effort to address the problem. After the initial round of capacity-building ventures by the national resource organizations the responsibility was handed over to the states. With DIET faculty being constantly on the move due to transfers and promotions, a more enduring arrangement for the training of faculty is needed and this is not in place yet in most states.

The problems which the DIETs are facing in pursuing their objectives, as have been pointed out time and again, mainly relate to personnel policies as well as administrative and financial procedures. DIETs lack functional autonomy. Decentralization and functional autonomy remain buzz words. DIETs also remain marginalized from mainstream project activities such as the DPEP affecting their institutional profile. Existing practices related to faculty posting, recruitment, and transfer are not helpful in staffing DIETs with motivated and competent persons. The DIET Guidelines mention the basic objectives of its personnel policy as to ensure that DIET faculty are allowed a stable tenure in the teacher education/educational research stream; their emoluments and service conditions are attractive enough for them to want to make a career out of teacher education/educational research; to make arrangements for their continuous professional development. These guidelines are, however, yet to be acted upon and appropriate policies formulated for the encadrement of the DIET faculty.

The immediate issues to be addressed towards the improvement of functioning of DIETs have been identified as creation of a separate cadre of teacher educators to ensure quality of personnel, orientation and exposure of DIET personnel in different areas of concern, institutional development strategy with a vision of the role of DIET in UEE, strengthening linkages with SCERT and BRC/CRC. The problem has been diagnosed but action has been slow to emerge. However, there are positive indications of things happening.

The Profile, Training, and Status of Teacher Educators

If high quality teachers are needed for enhancing learning in schools, high quality teacher educators are needed to produce such teachers. But the profile of the typical 'teacher of teachers' is certainly not edifying. And with the large-scale expansion of the field, it has further suffered. It has been observed that teacher training institutions and teacher educators enjoy no political visibility unlike schools; there is no well-formulated and planned policy for the recruitment of teacher educators in India; the field generally attracts mediocre individuals who have drifted into it without specific motivation or preparation; their professional productivity and research capabilities are very limited; their academic life is almost bankrupt and they show tremendous resistance to change. Strong words indeed, but none can deny the ring of truth they carry.

It is generally the case that those who function as teacher educators in elementary teacher education institutions do not possess appropriate stage-specific professional training or experience. Primary teacher training institutions are generally staffed by persons with a college degree and BEd., which is basically a course for preparing secondary school teachers. The paradox is that although the teachers are trained for specific levels of schooling, teacher trainers are not. There are no sure-fire remedies for the situation. But certain enabling actions can be initiated. First, greater rigour needs to be imparted to the preparation of the teacher educator. Alongside there are actions to be taken to remove the irrational disparities in the career path, remuneration package, service conditions, and conditions at the workplace.

There are inherent difficulties in the way of imparting professional rigour to programmes that prepare teacher educators. Following the distinction suggested by the analytical philosophers, teacher education which is essentially concerned with 'teaching how to teach' can be considered as a second order activity as against teaching per se, which is a first order activity. However, it is problematic that teacher education, as it is practised, rests on a firm knowledge base, that its content, modes, and processes are duly shaped by reflective practice, and that teacher educators as a body of professionals possess and deliver definitive knowledge as would lead to improved school and classroom practices. Given the epistemological status of the social and behavioural sciences that constitute the foundation of educational theory, one would not expect such knowledge to be available in a ready-to-use form for teacher education to carry out its mandate.

This difficulty of not having a secure knowledge base is not something peculiar to teacher education. It is characteristic of most modern professions which are interdisciplinary. Unfortunately, in the case of teacher education, this inherent difficulty is compounded by the system's lack of initiative to institute enabling measures to encourage good practices and corrective actions to eliminate the bad ones. For example, in the past, teacher educators came from the ranks of experienced schoolteachers. In fact, it was considered a crowning glory for a career teacher to become a teacher educator. And this high point was reached only after years of schoolteaching experience was tempered with formal learning and understanding of educational theory from the interdisciplinary perspectives of philosophy, history, sociology, and psychology. Later, at least three to five years of teaching experience in a school was prescribed as a requirement for entering the profession, apart from the possession of a post graduate degree in education. With the mushrooming of teacher education institutions all over the country and the consequent demand for trained manpower to run them, these conventions were cast aside. Teacher education has, thus, singularly failed to create a reliable and vibrant system for supplying competent human resources to run the thousands of teacher education institutions in the country.

The NCTE's efforts to redress the situation through restructuring of the programmes for the preparation of teacher educators are welcome. The curriculum framework it has presented highlights several new concerns—the imperatives of the emerging social context, the demands of IT and the new pedagogy, continuing and lifelong learning, the interdisciplinary nature of teacher education, and teacher education–development interface. But the curriculum guidelines suggested in this regard are too general and do not address the stage-specific training needs of elementary teacher educators. Teacher education is a reflective undertaking that also issues forth in pedagogical prescriptions for carrying out teaching at the ground level. Being a meta-activity it deals in showing how things are done at school and classroom levels, explaining the 'reason why' of things and the basic theory and principles behind classroom practices. These call for skills and understanding of a different kind, in addition to the skills required for actual school-teaching. It is a truism that one cannot teach how to teach unless one is a good teacher oneself. What, in the final analysis, distinguishes teacher educators from teachers is their concern for identifying usable second-order knowledge—theories, principles, generalizations—from first-order practice and communicating it to their charges. What is needed to prepare such teacher educators is a programme at post graduate level which is focused on the knowledge, skills, and competencies leading to a deeper understanding of the philosophy, programmes and processes of primary/elementary education and development of professional skills for training teachers.

As to service conditions, promotional opportunities, and the remuneration package, teacher educators face an identity crisis. This has its echo in the absence of a separate service cadre for teacher educators. A teacher educator has virtually no opportunity of career advancement. In government institutions, a kind of lateral movement occasionally takes place but within the training cadre the movement is virtually non-existent. This is so because historically trainers came from field-based cadres and went back to them after a tenure of training teachers. The issue here is the encadrement of teacher educators. Unless teacher educators are accorded a separate status with benefits appropriate to their job, it will fail to attract the right kind of persons. One good outcome of the establishment of DIETs is that it has focused national attention on personnel policy with respect to elementary teacher training institutions.

Accreditation of Teacher Education Institutions

The NCTE is presently concerned with adherence by the teacher education institutions to the essential norms and standards stipulated by it although the desirable ones are also specified. Extending and elaborating this idea, it is desirable for the NCTE to set before itself the goal of

evolving a system of accreditation of teacher education institutions in the country and setting up a mechanism for carrying out the task. Such an arrangement is already in existence in respect of colleges and universities in the form of the National Assessment and Accreditation Council set up by the University Grants Commission (UGC). There are also the National Board of Accreditation and the All India Council for Technical Education for disciplines like engineering, management, and pharmacy. Setting up an accreditation mechanism for teacher education fits in with the NCTE function related to the evolution of suitable performance appraisal systems, norms, and mechanisms for enforcing accountability.

The institution of an accreditation system for institutions of learning derives from the concern for promotion of quality and pursuit of excellence in education in the context of large-scale expansion of educational opportunities and institutions at all levels. For institutions desirous of striving to achieve high standards and pursue excellence, there exist no standards or criteria (apart from the minimum stipulated by the NCTE) with which they can compare themselves with their peers. Examination results do not provide a comprehensive picture of the institutional profile. An objective and comprehensive picture of institutions constructed from factual information pertaining to the institution and the institutional goals and objectives pursued by it would serve as a framework of comparison for institutions to learn from each other, set their own standards of institutional performance, and pursue them with zeal and evaluate their performance to their satisfaction. The eventual purpose of the mechanism would be to promote the culture of pursuit of standards of excellence set by the institutions themselves and self-appraisal and self-evaluation and mutual sharing of institutional experiences. Details regarding the organizational set-up and functioning of the proposed mechanism will have to be worked out after study of the mechanisms already in place in respect of higher education institutions (liberal arts and the sciences) and technical education institutions. A happy development is that the NCTE has accepted the idea in principle and initiated preliminary action to pursue it further.

A Promising Future for the Pursuit of Quality

The academic level of the entrant, duration of training, quality of training inputs, institutional infrastructure, and academic profile of staff are key determinants of the quality of teacher education. With respect to all these the NCTE has stipulated norms and standards which institutions must fulfil before they are granted recognition. All teacher education institutions are now required by law to get NCTE recognition. Although the majority of institutions have applied to the NCTE for recognition, a large number are still functioning without NCTE approval. Further, attempts have been made to checkmate the NCTE function of enforcing standards and norms by vested interests. Happily the courts have not only upheld the authority of the NCTE but also chastized those who undermine quality considerations in the preparation of teachers. It feels good to end this review on an optimistic note with the following excerpts from the recent landmark pronouncements of the Supreme Court:

(Supreme Court judgement in Civil Appeal No. 2914–16 of 1993–15.6.93 arising out of SLP (Civil) No. 6720–2 of 1993).

> The Teachers Training Institutes are meant to teach children of impressionable age and we cannot let loose on the innocent and unwary children, teachers who have not received proper and adequate training. True they will be required to pass the examination but that may not be enough. Training for certain minimum period in a properly organised and equipped Training Institute is probably essential before a teacher may be duly launched.
>
> It is therefore, needless to state that teachers should be subjected to rigorous training with rigid scrutiny of efficiency. It has greater relevance to the needs of the day. The ill trained or substandard teachers would be detrimental to our educational system; if not a punishment on our children. The Government and the university must therefore, take care to see that inadequacy in the training of teachers is not compounded by extraneous consideration.
>
> The qualitative training in the training colleges or schools would inspire and motivate them into action to the benefit of students. For equipping such trainee students in a school or college all facilities and equipment are absolutely necessary and institutions bereft thereof have no place to exist nor entitled to recognition. In that behalf compliance of the statutory requirement is insisted upon. Slackening the standard and judicial fiat to control the mode of education and examining system are detrimental to the efficient management of education.
>
> . . . training in a properly organised and equipped training institute is essential before a candidate becomes qualified to receive teachers training certificate. Simply passing the examination is not enough. The future teachers of the country must pass through the institutions which have maintained standards of the excellence at all levels.

Actualizing the Vision

The vision that is presented of primary teacher education in the preceding pages is anchored in its contextuality and local specificity. Primary education is local-specific and so is primary teacher education. Alternative scenarios can be visualized to move towards such a goal. Drawing from the DPEP experience one may visualize a 'district-specific' teacher education programme (conceived as a geographical, cultural entity). This could either mean the contextualization of the state-prescribed curriculum to fit the specific needs of the district or an exclusive district-specific curriculum developed locally involving all stakeholders. For either of the options, we need resources in the form of competent local professionals, resource institutions, and other resource facilities to conceptualize, develop, and implement the plan. The question is whether such resources are actually available locally and, if available, how feasible it would be to generate, activate, and mobilize these initiatives. One possibility is to link the vision to the implementation of the DPEP if it is a DPEP district. In that case the relevant DPEP activities and strategies could inform and even give shape to the teacher education curriculum. The existence of DIETs in each district opens up another promising avenue for actualizing the vision. DIETs can be empowered to function as the really district-specific teacher training institutions which they were originally supposed to be. The training-cum-production (of local-specific learning episodes) mode of project CAPE could then be adopted in the training of teachers in the DIETs. Lessons could also be drawn from the LJ experience on local specific curriculum planning involving the community as partners in the exercise. The Eklavya experience of designing local-specific curriculum and teacher training provides another rich resource. To move in the direction of imparting contextual relevance to teacher education the 'climate' has never been so conducive as now. *Panchayati raj* institutions have come into being and they are being empowered to 'deliver the goods'. Recruitment and posting of primary teachers is decentralized at district level. Accumulated experience of a variety of projects carried out in the past and of enterprising NGOs is available in good measure to guide the way. What is now needed is the determination to act.

CONCLUSIONS

• Primary teacher education has made remarkable progress in terms of increase in enrolment, number and variety of training and support institutions, establishment of DIETs, strengthening of state-level resource institutions, greater access to programmes and materials, and increased funding for training activities. Its national visibility has increased and it has also gained acceptance of academics as an important area of study and research.

• Primary teacher education reform actions carried out so far have been in the form of grand, pan-Indian programmes and schemes emanating from the centre. It is disquieting that a climate has not been created for the emergence of context-specific initiatives at state and sub-state levels towards the reform of teacher training structures and processes. The dependency syndrome that is beginning to be felt has to be fought by resurrecting local initiatives. Primary education is local-specific if it is anything, and solutions to its varied problems including teacher training should come out of contextual realities. There can be no across-the-board and a priori solutions to the problems of primary education.

• Even with the creation of new structures and the availability of state-sponsored initiatives, the teacher education system has to contend with a situation where there are no matching human resources of high quality to effectively respond to these initiatives in terms of teacher performance improvement programmes and strategies.

• The establishment of the NCTE as a statutory body has effectively controlled commercialization of teacher education by enforcing norms and standards with respect to physical infrastructure, faculty profile, certification and academic requirements like entry qualifications, duration of training, teacher–student ratio, and training inputs. Although the national norms are not followed in a few pockets, the NCTE has, by and large, succeeded in creating a conducive climate for the pursuit of quality in primary teacher education.

• As one more initiative towards quality reform the NCTE has initiated work towards exploring the possibility of an assessment and accreditation arrangement for teacher education institutions. The eventual purpose of the arrangement would be to promote the culture of self-appraisal and self-evaluation by institutions, pursuit of standards of excellence set by themselves, and mutual sharing of institutional experiences.

• The plethora of teacher-capacity-building activities launched under different schemes has targeted in-service teachers. They are focused on skill development in identified UEE tasks through cost-effective training and management strategies and application of distance education technology including ITV. In the process, in-service training has undergone major reforms in its format, substance, delivery, and management. It has shed its ad hocism and is getting institutionalized, aided by new structures and the training cascades.

• Initial training suffers from isolation, a low profile, and poor visibility in view of its being a non-degree programme administered by a government department as one among its other concerns. In professional discussions, teacher education is viewed as a unitary, undifferentiated category, with BEd providing the frame of reference. The special significance of initial primary teacher education is overlooked and its concerns are subsumed under general problems.

• Upgrading initial teacher education calls for enhancing the entry qualification and duration of training to make it equivalent to a degree programme, improvement in the status of primary teachers, and vesting of management and control of primary teacher education in a professional body of university faculty status. Experimentation in elementary teacher education structures and programmes needs to be encouraged to evolve innovative designs like integrated programmes of teacher education leading to a degree in elementary education. To break the isolation, the teacher education programmes for different stages could be offered under a comprehensive college of education arrangement and organized in a flexible manner that provides for vertical and horizontal mobility.

• Initial teacher education has remained isolated from the front-line concerns of national education, although the DIETs were started to provide support to UEE at district level. It is not treated as a UEE strategy. It is run primarily as an academic programme and its performance judged with reference to academic criteria internal to the programme.

• It is now time to integrate initial teacher education as a deliberate strategy to deal with the unfinished UEE agenda. This implies action on two fronts. First, further growth of initial teacher education has to be regulated with reference to the demand and supply position of teachers, required institutional capacity for initial teacher training, the desired pupil–teacher ratio, and percentage of female teachers. Second, and more importantly, actions are to be initiated to direct the thrusts of the programme towards specific UEE tasks by adopting a proactive curriculum policy.

• Mismatch between institutional capacity and teacher supply in some regions, especially the north-east, needs to be removed through proper planning. The number of underqualified, untrained, and undertrained teachers in the system is sizeable. The efforts that are being made to clear this backlog through appropriate training arrangements are commendable. At the same time, the system should develop safeguards to prevent further addition to this backlog through necessary policy changes in teacher recruitment rules, entry qualifications, duration of training, and other aspects as per national norms.

• The issue of directing the thrust of initial teacher education towards the UEE goals is not a simple matter of reform of training content and methodology with a few add ons. It is one of transforming the basic orientation of training towards the UEE goals relating to access, dropout, participation, achievement, gender, teaching in difficult contexts, and preparing teachers in carrying out actions towards their achievement.

• This calls for participatory curriculum planning involving all stakeholders, modular organization of curriculum in terms of tasks integrating relevant theory, de-emphasizing theory for its own sake, greater curriculum time for skill learning and practice, a professional approach to training strategies and development of materials, and application of appropriate educational technology in training processes. The curriculum is to be seen not as so many subjects to be studied but as so many learning experiences provided in preparing teachers to help children fulfil their basic learning needs.

• Primary schooling is the single most important delivery channel of basic education and its goal, the fulfilment of children's basic learning needs. Primary teacher training is essentially the process of developing the capability in teachers to translate these needs into appropriate teaching–learning experiences. This would mean training teachers in such professional tasks as helping children to learn to read, write, communicate, and carry out simple mathematical operations and understand basic facts and develop skills with respect to health, hygiene, nutrition, housing, and sanitation. It would also mean training teachers in helping children to participate in production processes and developing skills of problem solving, discussion, and working together.

• In light of this philosophy, the teacher education curriculum and its transaction should be made relevant to the realities and demands of teaching in difficult contexts like large-sized classes, multi-grade teaching, bi- and multilingual settings, and remote areas. The curriculum should focus on pedagogical skills relevant to the performance of classroom tasks. Some of these skills are critical analysis of material, capacity to exploit analogies and examples to convey information, ability to adapt materials to children's interests and abilities, ability to organize and manage classrooms, ability to evaluate student learning and encourage them towards higher levels of achievement.

• The objectives of primary education and the professional tasks of teachers point to the essentially interdisciplinary character of the teacher education curriculum. They also underscore the cardinal need to contextualize the curriculum and integrate theoretical learning with practical experience instead of bifurcating the two. Theoretical insights deriving from psychological and socio-cultural study of how children learn and grow, for example, should feed into the development of pedagogical practices or professional competencies through solid field training. Teacher trainees should be given every opportunity to experience real schools, real classrooms, 'real' children, try alternate ways of using pedagogical skills and developing their professional capability. The knowledge base of pedagogy is built through such reflective practices.

• A decade of DIET experience has shown that the functioning of DIETs has been adversely affected due to faulty practices of staff recruitment, posting and transfer, and want of functional autonomy. A rational personnel policy for DIETs that would ensure posting of qualified, competent, and motivated staff, however, is yet to be implemented on the ground in most states. The SCERTs and DIETs have a long way to cover to emerge as the fully empowered resource institutions that they were envisaged as.

• Primary teacher educators do not possess special qualifications and professional training to train primary teachers. Their academic profiles and career prospects are low. They usually hold a college degree with BEd, which basically is a course for preparing secondary school teachers or MEd, which is poorly focused as a professional preparation for training teachers. There are no suitable programmes for training primary teacher educators. The situation needs to be redressed by imparting greater rigour into the preparation of the teacher educator.

• With the judiciary upholding the quality improvement measures of the NCTE with respect to enforcement of norms and standards on teacher education institutions, the pursuit of quality in teacher education has received a shot in the arm. The court judgements have strengthened the morale of all who believe that the job of teaching must be in the hands of those who are competent and capable and that a teacher education institution should strive to produce such teachers by not compromising on quality requirements.

REFERENCES

Department of Education (1993). *Learning Without Burden.* Report of the National Advisory Committee appointed by the Ministry of Human Resource Development, Government of India, New Delhi.

———— (1996). *Selected Educational Statistics.* Ministry of Human Resource Development, Government of India, New Delhi.

———— (1998). *Annual Report 1997–98.* Ministry of Human Resource Development, Government of India, New Delhi.

District Primary Education Programme (1997). *Study on Institutional Development of SCERTs & DIETs in Assam, Haryana, Kerala and Tamil Nadu.* Educational Consultants India Limited.

National Council for Teacher Education (1978). *Teacher Education Curriculum: A Framework.* New Delhi.

———— (1997). *Teacher Education in Madhya Pradesh.* New Delhi.

———— (1998a). *Annual Report 1997–98.* New Delhi.

———— (1998b). *Curriculum Framework for Quality Teacher Education.* New Delhi.

———— (1998c). *Policy Perspectives in Teacher Education.* New Delhi.

————— (1998d). *Teacher Education in Arunachal Pradesh.* New Delhi.

————— (1998f). *Teacher Education in Haryana.* New Delhi.

————— (1998g). *Teacher Education in Himachal Pradesh.* New Delhi.

————— (1998h). *Teacher Education in Rajasthan.* New Delhi.

————— (1998i). *Teacher Education in Tripura.* New Delhi.

————— (1998j). *Teacher Education in West Bengal.* New Delhi.

————— (1999a). *Teacher Education in Karnataka.* New Delhi.

————— (1999b). *Teacher Education in Uttar Pradesh.* New Delhi.

————— (August 1995). The Parliament Act No. 73 of 1993.

————— (1998e). *Teacher Education in Delhi.* New Delhi.

National Council of Educational Research and Training (1997). *The Primary Years: A Curriculum Framework.* New Delhi.

————— (1998). *Sixth All-India Educational Survey.* New Delhi.

IV

Education for
Empowering the Adult

16

Indian Engagement with Adult Education and Literacy

A. Mathew

INTRODUCTION

Universalization of elementary education (UEE) and adult literacy always had an emotive tinge in national discourse and policy deliberations. These were perceived as the basic entitlement of citizens, the minimum that the state owed its people and something which had a critical role in the nation's socio-cultural and economic development and the well-being of India's democracy. Time and again, this issue of the state's basic obligation—UEE and adult education—would come up and witness new resolves, policy intents, fresh programme packages and deadlines for target achievement. It is in this background that any review of the adult literacy programme in the country has to be carried out. This chapter traces the National Literacy Missions's (NLM) journey through an anxious search and frantic efforts to lend a much needed mass character to the literacy efforts to the sense of relief when a genuinely mass movement oriented total literacy campaign (TLC) approach as adopted in Ernakulam, came to be accepted and adopted by the NLM.

Soon after the launching of the National Policy on Education (NPE) 1986, a thorough review of the strengths and weaknesses of past programmes of adult education was undertaken and wide-ranging consultations organized. As a result, the government initiated a move to start a number of 'missions', most of them for application of modern science and technology to developmental issues concerning the disadvantaged social groups. The NLM started in 1988 was one such mission with the aim of imparting functional literacy to 80 million adults, aged 15–35 years, by 1995 (see Bordia and Kaul 1992). Different from other Technology Missions, the NLM was conceived as a 'societal mission' to demonstrate that 'there is a political will at all levels for the achievement of Mission goals...a national consensus... for mobilization of social forces, and mechanisms...

for active participation of the people' (see DoE 1988).

The key reasons for the success of the NLM, based on strengths and weakness of earlier programmes, were identified as national commitment, motivation of learners and instructors, creation of a positive environment, mass mobilization, people's involvement including voluntary agencies, techno-pedagogic inputs, and efficient monitoring and management. The most momentous of these experiments in mass campaigns for total literacy was the one undertaken in Kottayam city of Kerala in April 1989. The District Collector of Kottayam district mobilized some 200 university student volunteers who made literate the 2000 illiterates, within 100 days (see Mishra 1992).

What started as a time-bound one-shot affair on a modest scale in Kottayam soon grew into a massive movement, first in the Ernakulam district, then the entire state of Kerala and many other states. The TLC model, which became the dominant strategy and approach of the government for adult literacy from the Eighth Five Year Plan (see DoE 1992), grew out of the Ernakulam TLC.

KEY PREMISES AND ELEMENTS OF THE TLC

In formulating the perspective and approach, the NLM document articulated some of the basic premises implicit in the programme. The idea behind bringing literacy under one of the five Technology Missions was to indicate a new sense of urgency and seriousness, a definite time-frame, people's involvement and result orientation, an area-specific approach, and cost-effectiveness. The essence, as premised by the Mission was that literacy, a basic human need, enables access to the world of information, and when it goes beyond alphabetical literacy to functional literacy, it enhances skills of communication, survival, and occupation. Literacy has to be demand driven and the need perception and demand have to be consciously aroused. This can be done through a campaign of environment building when the transformational role of literacy is conveyed through a variety of communication forms. The community with its reservoir of innate wisdom, idealism, and voluntarism should be allowed adequate space in owning and supporting the programme.

In any discussion of literacy campaigns in India and of how the TLC approach became the NLM's dominant approach to literacy, the role of the Bharat Gyan Vigyan Samiti (BGVS) occupies an important place. Creating a need for literacy among people was the major issue facing the NLM when it set out in 1988 on the task of making 80 million people literate. The NLM's strategy of creating a mass upsurge of need and demand for literacy owed partly to the impact of the BGVS (1987) launched by people's science organizations (the All India People's Science Network—AISPN, as it was later known), led by the Kerala Shastra Sahitya Parishad (KSSP).

ERNAKULAM MODEL BECOMES THE NLM LITERACY APPROACH

The NLM brought out guidelines on different aspects of TLC processes and strategies that were closely aligned to the principles and processes adopted in the Ernakulam model. Call it the heady days or the formative period when the NLM was anxiously and zealously wanting to establish the TLC approach as the dominant and national approach: any doubts about the TLC approach or criticisms of the distortions inherent and apparent in the implementation process were seen as being inimical to the cause of the literacy movement. Such criticisms were viewed in NLM circles as being cynical and anti-literacy when the NLM was clearly orchestrating a strategy of using the media and other means to deliberately play up the movement's success (see Mishra 1998, 2809).

NLM BETWEEN 1990 AND 1998: PROGRAMME GROWTH AND ANALYTICAL OVERVIEW OF ACHIEVEMENTS

From 1989 to 1992, even before the Eighth Five Year Plan was launched, there were already 22 TLCs, and within barely five months, the number went up to 156. The Eighth Plan proposed to cover another 345 districts—nearly 75 per cent of the districts in India, under TLCs (see Shah 1999, 15). The progress of the NLM exceeded its target. As regards the trend, the jump from 1992 to 1993 is evident. With the focus shifting to Hindi-belt states from 1992, the acceleration of TLCs has been greater. States with high rates of transition from TLCs to post literacy campaigns (PLCs) over the 1990–5 period were Andhra Pradesh, Karnataka, and West Bengal, and those with low rates were Assam, Meghalaya,

Uttar Pradesh, and Bihar. The middle category states with around half of their TLCs in the PLC stage were Rajasthan, Orissa, and Maharashtra, among others.

Targets and Achievements

When the NLM began, the target was to cover 80 million non-literate adults in the 15–35 age group—30 million by 1990 and another 50 million by 1995. It was subsequently revised and reset at 100 million, and the deadline was extended to 1997. The Ninth Plan again reset the deadline. The position now is—total literacy (15–35 age group) by 2000. The shift of target deadline, perhaps, is influenced by the NLM's achievement levels.

The basis of the NLM's achievement figures, meaning the number of non-literates being made literate, are the figures supplied by the TLC/PLC districts. 'Achievement level in these projects', says the NLM's Status Report (see DAE 1993a), 'is the focus of monitoring at a national level', as reported in the monthly progress reports of the districts and the consolidated reports of the state/UT Directorates of Adult Education based on their assessment of learners completing (passing in) Primer III. However, the NLM adopted differing methods of collating and arriving at the achievement figures at a national level. Till 1994, the achievement reported by TLCs about Primer III completion was assorted under four categories, viz. districts reporting achievement levels of: (i) less than 20 per cent; (ii) 20 to 30 per cent; (iii) 35 to 50 per cent; and (iv) above 50 per cent. These were shown against the total number of TLCs and PLCs. But as the number of TLCs increased, the categories were reduced to three, and details of survey and enrolment were included. However, instead of showing achievement under the three categories against the total number of TLCs and PLCs, it was shown statewise, which makes it difficult to get an idea at a glance about target, enrolment, and achievements. This could be illustrated with two examples at two different points in time—1993 and 1997–8.

The coverage was for all programmes of the NLM, not TLCs alone. Even so, the overall achievement against the target has been 41.53 per cent (see DAE 1993a, 23). Tables 16.1 and 16.2 provide figures on NLM achievement according to internal and external assessment.

TABLE 16.1
NLM Literacy Achievement, September 1993

Total TLCs	187
TLCs with above 50% achievement	41
TLCs with 35–50%	10
TLCs with 20–35%	7
TLCs with less than 20%	30
No. of PL projects sanctioned	52

TABLE 16.2
NLM Achievement: The 1997–8 Situation: Internal Reports and External Evaluations

(in thousands)

State/district	Target survey	Effective enrolment	Achievement % with respect to Primer III	Achievement % external evaluation
Andhra Pradesh				
Karimnagar	708,952	669,041	71.63	92.30
Kurnool	588,752	584,027	43.10	20.00
Nellore	476,974	408,610	37.34	57.08
Srikakulam	654,298	559,498	68.28	82.05
Visakhapatnam	668,245	501,062	48.86	92.27
Vizianagaram	536,228	464,845	69.26	39.10
Warangal	700,954	636,205	51.49	13.00
Bihar				
Dumka	384,368	384,368	81.23	49.00
Haryana				
Panipat	161,000	154,617	43.40	9.20
Yamunanagar	103,323	98,926	70.10	49.60
Himachal Pradesh				
Bilaspur	32,024	27,360	83.42	59.28
Kangra	80,921	72,580	63.14	45.60
Maharashtra				
Aurangabad	340,124	335,214	9.21	78.21
Jalna	242,261	242,261	100.00	75.97
Nanded	662,487	542,581	64.29	38.80
Sindhudurg	27,830	27,830	100.00	34.40
Rajasthan				
Alwar	401,502	352,933	24.86	46.18
Banswara	359,788	359,788	14.04	36.00
Bharatpur	301,072	301,072	80.96	64.00
Jhunjhunu	234,409	205,245	61.34	66.90
Tonk	256,595	193,530	63.40	25.40
Uttar Pradesh				
Agra	421,760	393,577	92.72	70.06
Barelli	433,042	148,206	31.17	59.00
Moradabad	457,724	264,000	57.02	62.80
West Bengal				
Birbhum	877,372	657,655	68.89	93.09
Burdwan	1,200,143	1,181,527	90.72	90.30
Howrah	464,188	204,247	34.30	87.00
N. 24 Parganas	1,000,000	105,000	80.60	82.01
S. 24 Parganas	1,248,337	1,006,546	60.41	90.48

Source: DAE (1999b).

One finds three types of situations: (i) where external evaluation showed achievements higher than internal reports; (ii) cases where both internal and external assessments proved similar; and (iii) cases where external evaluation results were much below what the TLCs claimed in their internal assessment. If one looks at the performance of the literacy projects—internal reports and external evaluations, and the backlog—the NLM's assessments about targets, target deadlines, and achievements leave an uneasy feeling. A look at the performance of TLCs across different states makes this clear (see Table 16.3).

Two trends emerging from the data in Table 16.2 are worth noting. One, in states like Karnataka, Maharashtra, and West Bengal more than half the districts were already covered by the TLC in 1995, and all their districts by PLC by 1998. The Hindi-belt states like Bihar and UP were, however, really lagging in both TLC and PLC could be seen. The second point worth noting is not so much the transition rate between TLC and PLC but

TABLE 16.3
NLM Achievement: The Regional Pattern

(in thousands)

State	TLC–PLC transition trend (no. of districts)			TLC achievement profile		
	1995	1998	PLC	Target	Achievement	Backlog
Assam	12	20	2	3296	396	2900
Bihar	20	42	11	9853	2259	7594
Haryana	13	16	4	2206	327	1879
MP	52	45	19	12,589	4238	8351
Maharashtra	22	30	15	6408	3807	2601
Orissa	17	25	13	5493	2096	3396
Rajasthan	20	31	18	9117	2862	6255
UP	50	68	11	18,915	4626	14,289
Karnataka	20	0	18	7345	3827	3518
Meghalaya	–	3	–	138	12	126
Punjab	5	15	4	1981	275	106
Andhra Pradesh	23	24	23	14,162	7290	6872
West Bengal	17	15	14	14,292	8253	6039

Source: DAE (1999a); DAE, Literacy Rates (n.d.c., 15).

actually the TLC achievement and the backlog. In states like Andhra Pradesh, Karnataka, Maharashtra, and West Bengal, the achievement was more than 50 per cent of the target, whereas in Bihar, Madhya Pradesh, Rajasthan, and UP it ranges between one-fourth and one-third of the target. This position becomes clear when we look at the NLM's threefold classification of states according to their performance, both with respect to TLC and PLC.

As per DAE (1999a), the number of TLCs sanctioned so far is 450, of which 250 have moved into the post literacy phase, but it does not give details of target, as per survey, enrolment, and achievement.

NLM Achievement and Future Scenario

If one looks at the backlog of illiterates in the threefold achievement category of states, it is evident that: (i) even in the 9 states with 50 per cent and above results, the backlog is 26.048 million; (ii) it is 18.05 million in the 4 medium achievement states (Madhya Pradesh and Rajasthan accounting for the lion's share); and (iii) 29.11 million in the 7 low achievement states (although their total target is less, their backlog is higher than that of the 9 high achievement States—29.11 as compared to 26.48 million).

In 434 TLCs (March 1998), the total target, as per survey figures, was 126.32 million and enrolment was 96.57 million, representing 76.45 per cent success rate. The number of learners who completed Primer III was 52.47 million, which is 41.53 per cent of the target. Similarly, in 250 PLCs, against a total target of 42.42

million, enrolment was 30.14 millions (71.06 per cent) and PL-I (Post Literacy Phase I) completion was 16.98 million which is 40.02 per cent against the target.

With Madhya Pradesh and Rajasthan showing an achievement between 31 and 38 per cent, and UP and Bihar with less than 25 per cent achievement, roughly 60–75 per cent of adults still remain non-literates, even after all the districts (except Bihar) have been covered under TLCs and PLCs. Considering that external evaluations show results much lower than internal reports in many cases, there does not seem much basis to share the NLM optimism of total literacy by 2000 and universal literacy by 2005. The fact is that in many states, and especially in the Hindi-belt, nearly 60–75 per cent of adults still remain illiterate.

Completion of PL-I is considered the self-reliant level of literacy. And if we reckon the NLM's norm of PL-I pass as a non-relapsable level of literacy achievement, then it is 16.98 million literates out of a population of 126.32 million, which represents 13.43 per cent, and the backlog as 109.38 million! Thus, even after the NLM's decade-old adult education efforts, the illiterates would seem to be far in excess of what is generally presented. In this kind of literacy achievement scenario, is it realistic to project that the main future concern of the NLM will be continuing education (CE) and not basic literacy? What happens to the vast number of adults who still continue as illiterates? Are we done with the literacy campaign phase or do we have to repeat it, not just to cover the left-outs but even to retain the literacy of those who have become literate?

SOME SIGNIFICANT QUALITATIVE GAINS

Though the literacy achievement does not by itself seem impressive, studies have revealed that there were some important social gains that sustained the morale of organizers and aspirations of the learners. In the balance sheet of the NLM's achievement, these social gains are as noteworthy as the literacy achievement and deserve notice.

The qualitative impact of the NLM's decade-long endeavours was represented in some of the more illustrious TLCs and PLCs. Qualitative gains, as abstracted here, are cumulative. Disaggregation would be difficult, as even illustrious TLCs and PLCs varied, not only in facets, but also in breadth and intensity: if one TLC was known for women's empowerment, another was known for creation of grassroots networks for sustainability, and so on. Even so, some of edifying features of the literacy movement are worthy of mention.

One of the initial advantages with which the NLM started and which helped the programme to strike a radical departure from the earlier approach to literacy was the Mission structure, empowered to decide policy, direction, and perspective with a great deal of flexibility despite being located within the government framework. Another was the creation of the District Literacy Society [*Zilla Saksharta Samiti* (ZSS)] as an autonomous registered society receiving funds directly from the central and state governments, cutting down delays. The character of the ZSS, with more than 50 per cent NGO representation from district to village level, helped to use the autonomy and flexibility to respond to the urgency of a time-bound programme like the TLC. This would have been impossible in a departmental approach. The ZSS represented both a new agency and methodology to a social intervention programme like the TLC. The triangular structure consisting of the administration, popular committees, and a full-time structure for planning and management of the TLCs and PLCs represented a genuine partnership between the government department and local community representatives.

Some of the strategies adopted in the literacy movement were not only unprecedented, but shaped the approach to similar programmes later. Social mobilization, based on literacy-positive environment building was one. Using, for that purpose, popular and folk art forms of cultural communication—the *kala jathas*—was another. Nucleation of core groups, of activists, resource persons, and volunteers to plan and partner in implementation of TLCs and PLCs was a third. The fourth approach adopted was to develop the literacy movement on a sustainable basis, namely formation of grassroots networks like neo-literate groups, especially women, around savings, thrifts and credits, cooperatives. All these seem

to have acted as role models for other similar programmes. The District Primary Education Programme (DPEP), Siksha Karmi, Mahila Samakhya, Lok Jumbish, and the Education Guarantee Scheme, and the *gurudakshina*-based literacy drive of Madhya Pradesh have all incorporated some of these components of the TLC approach.

Women's participation in the literacy movement not only changed the discourse at policy level about some crucial aspects like content and pedagogy, but also the strategy for social motivation, mobilization, and environment building. Issues like empowerment, solidarity, group formation, and collective assertion were strongly oriented to strengthening women's participation as that represented the mainstay of the literacy movement. Even the discourse in the women's movement, which was ambivalent about literacy, began to recognize the critical nexus between women's literacy and their empowerment.

The transformational potential of the literacy movement was clearly recognized. The Expert Group (known as the Arun Ghosh Committee), for example, noted how (i) many a government functionary, including District Collectors, involved in TLC turned 'activists'; (ii) literacy campaigns tended to promote greater social cohesion and communal harmony; and (c) voluntarism and idealism in civil society exhibited on behalf of the TLCs were unparalleled.

PROBLEMS AND CHALLENGES IN THE LITERACY MOVEMENT

In an analysis of the growth of the literacy movement, a dispassionate treatment of the gains and weaknesses is necessary—neither too romantic nor too pessimistic. The gains, as would be evident, were plenty. But the weaknesses need to be located in the contexts in which these surfaced. One of these was the policy direction with respect to progressive marginalization of the people's movement character of the TLCs in their PL and CE phases. Another was the host of measures taken up by the NLM—measures about which there are divergent perceptions between the NLM and perceptive observers. It is this balance of gains, challenges, and responses as well as the public perceptions about them which gives a totality of NLM endeavours. The evolving policy perceptions in relation to the literacy movement are discussed in the first part of this chapter. The weaknesses witnessed in the movement and the divergent perceptions about NLM measures are examined in the second part.

New Challenges and NLM Measures: Divergent Perceptions

There is a certain trend and pattern in the problems noticed in the literacy movement and the NLM's response, in terms of its perception and measures, in what are called 'new' initiatives. As the NLM sought to come to grips with the problems with new measures at each point of time, a few were on, but many were off, the mark.

Evaluations about the NLM by perceptive observers are generally critical. The NLM, on the other hand, has been far less modest about its record. This section examines the NLM's own position in terms of perception and response regarding problems, challenges, and difficulties, as seen in NLM documents, and those pointed out by the Expert Group and the Ninth Plan Working Group, as well as the assessment of observers.

The First Signs

The 'new initiatives' around 1993–4 included:

• shift of NLM literacy strategy to the 'more difficult', northern Hindi-belt—difficult because of the absence of a voluntary ethos—and therefore, a deliberate decision, as a policy and strategy, to use the administration more decisively and directly (of the 107 projects sanctioned in 1993–4, 55 were in the four Hindi-belt states of Madhya Pradesh, Uttar Pradesh, Bihar, and Rajasthan);

• being alive to the need for PL and CE, and allowing flexibility in aligning PL strategies to learner needs;

• seeking a broader social and institutional support base for literacy—eminent writers, artists, media, and institutions outside adult education like NIEPA, National Book Trust (NBT), Sahitya Akademy;

• ensuring greater transparency as the dominant concern; streamlining monitoring, not merely as a financial or programme audit, but also using other channels of independent non-official assessments;

• attention to the qualitative aspect during evaluation of the campaigns; and

• concurrent evaluation of TLCs for mid-course correction which the NLM was already decided on (see DAE 1994).

Expert Group Plea for Decisive Changes

The Arun Ghosh Committee's assessment of the NLM and its recommendations are pertinent when analyzing the NLM's response to difficulties and challenges faced. Four crucial points and their recommendations are adduced here.

• Minimum Essentials for TLC: In relation to the 'difficult' Hindi-belt states and the compulsion behind using the administration, the Arun Ghosh Committee was particular about the preconditions for sanctioning a TLC. In these states such preconditions consisted of ensuring political commitment, stability of Collectors, adequate pre-launch preparations, selection only of full-timers

with proven dedication and commitment; linking socio-economic development with literacy (see DAE 1994). Scrutiny of TLC proposals by the NLM on the basis of these pre-requisites and rejections on these grounds have been few and far between. Even the few 'rejected' cases came back, promised all, walked away with the sanction and did nothing different, remaining severely deficient in the pre-requisites for TLC and being heavily administration-driven.

• Credibility Crisis of NLM Data: On the periodical progress reports of TLCs Management Information Systems (MIS) on which NLM's Status Reports are based, the Expert Group said that it was

> constrained to note, however, that these progress reports…are not always dependable…. Quite a few of these reports give a picture far removed from the reality, and are apparently oriented to get some funds released from NLM. The problem is systemic…; one has to consider basic systemic reforms. Sometimes *these…reports are based on the internal evaluations which do not always depict the true state of literacy development for diverse reasons*. [DAE 1994, 21, emphasis added]

• Alter Objectives—Forsake 'Total Literacy by 2000' Motto: After surveying the positive effects of TLCs, the Group concluded:

> These transformational effects, as well as the sharp increase in enrolment in primary schools, with consequent pressure for expansion of facilities make the NLM also something of an attempted National Education Mission. The objective of the NLM should now include the promotion, consolidation and development of 'learning society'.
>
> The Expert Group strongly recommends that the objective of fully eradicating illiteracy by the Year 2000 be forsaken, and be replaced by the more sane, feasible, and less manipulable objective of developing and deepening a 'learning society' in which (a) there is accelerated progress in the eradication of basic illiteracy, and (b) in fulfilling both the demand and supply conditions for 'continuing education'. [DAE 1994, 31; emphasis added]

• Abandon 'Total Literacy' Phobia: The Ghosh Committee was most emphatic about 'abandoning the concept "Total Literacy" as it is this which creates urges for conscious or even unconscious "doctoring" of figures'. In this context, about evaluation, the Group noted:

> In making its recommendations as to evaluation procedures, the Expert Group would like to reiterate its view that the literacy campaign has initiated a process of new awareness and change; its success (or failure) has to be gauged in terms of the extent to which this process has taken root (rather than in terms of mere percentages of neo-literates, who may well relapse into illiteracy unless the process is a snowballing one). [DAE 1994, 48]

The NLM picked up the relatively unimportant recommendations of the Committee and left out those that would have altered the very context and salvaged the movement's image and the Mission's credibility.

THE NLM'S HALF-WAY MARK: A FRESH LOOK AT PROBLEMS

The Working Group for Ninth Plan identified four specific aspects needing greater attention:

• provision of adequate technical support and encouragement to voluntary organizations at every step, and evolving both institutional and informal mechanisms to give them an active promotional role in literacy;

• democratic decentralization of literacy efforts and involvement of *panchayats* and urban local bodies through physical and financial devolution of powers and also tapping of resources of technical, industrial, academic institutions, organizations, and set-ups at district level;

• gradual diminution of higher educational institutions' involvement in literacy activities, the genuine contribution they can make in policy making and practical implementation, and the need for their focused, practical and hands-on involvement in literacy; and

• bureaucratization of the programme and the inherent drawbacks in the mode and manner adopted in implementation of the literacy campaign—marginalization of voluntary and non-governmental forces, and the need to evolve 'alternatives' to the 'Collector-centric model'.

The Working Group also referred to the 'new initiatives' taken during the Eighth Plan. One was Operation Restoration (OR). As early as 1993–4, the Arun Ghosh Committee noticed 59 out of the 253 projects 'dragging on for a long time' (see DAE 1994, 21). Such cases shot up, especially in the Hindi heartland. The other was the decision to devolve project sanction powers to states, by releasing block grants through those state literacy missions (SLMs) which had achieved 50 per cent literacy in their state. The third was recognition of the crucial need to strengthen local bodies—the *panchayats*—by specifically delineating their role in the literacy movement at grassroots level. The fourth was about strengthening the State Directorates of Adult Education (SDAE) and Resource Centres. Concurrent evaluation of TLCs by an independent agency nominated by the State Directorate, and external evaluation, by an agency nominated by the NLM were two new measures aimed at ensuring complete transparency and enhancing the credibility of the programme. The last was the scheme of CE, overhauling the existing PL and CE scheme, as found necessary in the emerging literacy scenario.

In the post 1996 scenario of the literacy movement, two questions would seem pertinent: (i) how effectively were the 'new initiatives' pursued by the NLM?; and

(ii) how effective were these measures in checking the problems, that were the purpose of their adoption? In the context of the emerging scenario of the literacy movement, there should be a dialectical relationship between the new challenges or difficulties and the new initiatives and measures. One does not always find such a dialectical nexus; while some problems were expressly addressed, many others were skirted, for sheer inability to address them, as it may not be totally in the NLM's domain, or for sheer lack of zeal and commitment on the NLM's part. But even in respect of the measures undertaken, they were damage control of the declining trend and not a revival of the movement.

An NLM publication in 1997 lists ten challenges that lie ahead (see DAE n.d.a, 6–7). Six of the ten 'challenges' are a reiteration of the Arun Ghosh Expert Committee's express recommendations, namely decentralizing project sanction powers to the states, gender sensitivity in literacy primers and focus on women-related programmes, strengthening the monitoring and evaluation system, linking literacy with development departments and programmes, need-based vocational skills to neo-literates and involvement of the *panchayats*. The list of challenges also includes certain other themes such as to tap electronic media support 'on an unprecedented scale' for sensitization and mobilization of public support. This, and others, were 'new measures' deemed necessary in what the NLM thought to be the needs in the context of the emerging scenario of the literacy movement. There were also certain other 'new' challenges, namely increasing range and depth of non-governmental organization (NGO) involvement in literacy campaigns and strengthening research capabilities to meet changing needs of the movement.

NLM'S 'RECORD': SOME UNEDIFYING FACETS

• Indiscriminate Expansion and Erosion of TLC Credibility: The TLCs initiated in the wake of Ernakulam were marked by the initial zeal and enthusiasm, and were notable for Collector's commitment, a core team of competent and committed social activists, the administration–NGO partnership, voluntarism, large-scale social mobilization, and the NLM's foster care. And as the early TLCs attracted national and international attention and appreciation, there was a sudden rush to take up TLCs everywhere. The problems, however, started with indiscriminate expansion of TLCs during 1991–2 and especially during the Eighth Plan, which pitched a target of covering 345 of the 420 districts in India at a time. This sudden rush for expansion brought in its wake severe problems. The situation became irretrievable when TLCs hit the Hindi states. In a major study of performance of literacy campaigns and their prospects, this trend is tellingly portrayed:

> A major irony in this rapid expansion has been that from 1993 to 1996, the literacy campaigns had been extended to regions where the need was the greatest, but also where the capabilities... were the least prepared to both implement the campaigns in the appropriate style of mass participation... [160 of the 190 districts of Bihar, Madhya Pradesh, Rajasthan and Uttar Pradesh were covered by TLC during 1993–96]. However, the progress of the campaign in this [Hindi] belt is far from satisfactory. The preparatory mobilizational phase prior to the teaching–learning one came to be neglected.
>
> In a context where there are no dramatic changes in the political economy of the country towards more equitous structures of opportunity... the campaigns in the early years had adopted two major strategies primarily at the initiative of the voluntary sector: (i) create a cultural movement for literacy... through environment building programmes... and (ii) create a democratic decentralized structure for implementation that draws together major social resources... Both these strategies were neglected in the race for expansion. [Saldanha 1999, 2029, emphasis added]

• 'Targetitis' Compulsions: Part of the reason for the indiscriminate expansion, as the Arun Ghosh Committee found, was the perceived compulsion within the NLM itself to meet the financial target of spending the Rs 1000 crore for TLCs allotted for the Eighth Plan (see DoE 1996, 18), and covering 345 out of the total 420 districts then in India. More than 50 per cent of these were in the Hindi-belt states.

The success of the early TLCs, coupled with the value attached to literacy in official circles, attracted high media attention and visibility. Not only was political pressure from MLAs, MPs, and other political leaders brought on the NLM and state governments to vie for TLCs, but given the official importance and media attention and visibility, many Collectors and state officials jumped on to the literacy bandwagon thinking it would redound to their credit (see Athreya and Chunkat, 1996, 284; DAE 1994).

• Control and Facilitation: Role of the NLM and SLMAs (State Literacy Mission Authorities): Initially the NLM created SLMAs to encourage states to take interest in the literacy programmes but in many cases it had unanticipated results. This move brought back the old adult education bureaucracy whose opposition to TLCs was scarcely concealed. The SLMAs became an instrument to 'control' and centralize decision making. Standardization and uniformity became the watchwords. Flexibility, autonomy, local initiatives, and innovative process became the casualties.

The DAEs, as secretariats of the SLMAs, taking upon themselves the right to prepare, approve, or print primers, often in lieu of the state share, held the time-bound TLC schedule to ransom, in many cases. The DAE officers were propped up as secretaries of TLCs as an ex-officio right, mocking at the TLC ethos of them being the epitome of commitment and inspiration. Such centralization killed the TLC's energy which lay in voluntarism. The result was that instead of a government-funded programme becoming a people's movement, it only helped to kill the people's movement potential and character and degenerate into a bureaucratic and centralized programme no different from other government programmes (see Athreya and Chunkat 1996).

• Detrimental Gaps between TLC and PLC: The need for continuity, without break, between TLC and PLC was often conceded at policy level but rarely followed in practice. Most TLCs between 1990 and 1993 suffered several months of break before transiting to the PLC stage, resulting in a serious relapse into illiteracy, erosion of voluntarism, and general disillusionment among the public. When PLCs started after several months, not only was the resumption of the TLC atmosphere difficult, but PLCs turned out to be only pale shadows of the vibrant and action-packed TLCs, marked by enormous mass involvement. It took almost till the end of 1994, after the Arun Ghosh Committee severely deplored the gap, before some streamlining came in the procedures to allow TLC's transition to PLC phase without long interregnum.

• Bureaucratization of Programme and Ritualization of Processes: By far the most detrimental trend of degeneration that set in and killed all that was valuable of the literacy movement's mass character was bureaucratization of the programme and ritualization of the processes. The absence of the culture of partnership between administration and NGOs, and non-internalization of the TLC ethos, its principles and processes, or lack of commitment to it, resulted in the whole programme being turned into a bureaucratic one, marked by hierarchism and red tape. The whole range of activities such as popular committee formation, environment building, and surveys, which hinged on decentralization of decision making, encouraging local initiatives, nurturing community involvement and voluntarism was turned into a ritual and done by assertion of official authority and with least regard to the spirit and ethos of TLC as a people's movement.

• Ignoring of Social Audit: A perspective about the literacy movement must evolve based on experience; the initial NLM vision about literacy as a people's movement must necessarily have been solidified, drawing upon the support from experience. The facets of the people's movement character, as emerged in the most satisfying and telling manner, in TLCs implemented in the true spirit and ethos of people's movement, must have become not only the preambles of TLC proposal for the purpose of sanction, but must have remained the basic perspective and yardstick of its audit—MIS—and external evaluation. In the earlier phase of the TLC itself this issue was brought to the fore by observers:

> While an evaluation of the quantitative dimensions...(e.g. number of persons made literate) is surely necessary, an assessment of the qualitative impact on the learners as well as on those involved with them becomes essential in the context of the NLM concept of 'functional literacy' which envisages assertion of rights by the neo-literate poor through organisation and their active role in crucial issues like national integration and movements for women's equality. [Banerjee 1993, 1275]

That the NLM's excessive and one-sided focus on turning evaluation of TLCs into a measurement exercise was a severely deficient perspective of NLM objectives itself. This was pointed out by the Expert Committee on NLM in 1994. That the avowed objectives of 'learning outcomes' also included 'functionality and awareness' was forgotten. The whole process of learning and change noticed by the Expert Group was never the basis in judging the campaign's success.

• Neglecting the Social Gains: The overwhelming women's response seen in the campaign offered a unique and historic opportunity of forging the campaign as a potential force for the mobilization and empowerment of women. While the NLM never missed an opportunity to highlight women's participation, there is scarcely any evidence of this as a barometer of rating a campaign's success or merit.

> Greater self-confidence, a new resourcefulness and presence of mind to tackle complex situations, an enhanced ability to manage inter-personal relationships, effective communication skills, greater gender sensitivity, a more keenly felt humanism—all these and more skills were seen in many a participant in the TLC acquire, as a consequence of the campaign process. [Athreya and Chunkat 1996, 280–1]

This tendency of euologizing the social gains and not reflecting them as express objectives of the projects or in judging the projects, merits, was not confined to the TLCs alone. It became equally true of PLCs as well.

As a commentary on the NLM attitude to the qualitative gains, the observations of a perceptive observer are telling:

> Large scale campaigns impart dynamism and the will to change to their participants and this was more than demonstrated in some districts in the context of TLCs. Traditionally disadvantaged social groups, and women in particular participated with great enthusiasm. It was too good to last. The literacy mission lost in 1993 the momentum it gathered from 1989 to 1992. Campaign managers sitting in Delhi and in state headquarters belied the hopes of thousands. Shoddy planning, red tape and the unfortunate lack of continuity in

the policies and practices of the Government (as represented by senior officers) led to the demise of an otherwise exciting programme. The culture of 'undo what my predecessor did' affected the literacy campaign. The literacy campaign is a story of missed opportunities. Wherever the campaign made an impact women came forward...got a glimpse of a brave new world.... A historic opportunity to use education as a tool to generate and consolidate people's power was lost, as adult educators and campaign managers did not recognize the potential of a village level institutional base for promoting life-long learning and improvement. There was no strategic thinking—either in New Delhi or at the district level. [Ramachandran 1999, 879]

It is in this context that the NLM's euphoria about the NSSO Survey showing a dramatic increase of 10 percentage points in literacy rate between 1991 and 1998 becomes rather confusing. It is confusing because, on the one hand, the NLM's own assessment of performance of different states does not seem vindicated by NSSO Survey results, while, on the other hand, the NLM holds that the 'significantly greater progress...achieved in the 15–35 age-group...the primary target of NLM', as due to its literacy efforts (see DAE n.d.c, 9) (see Table 16.4).

States that are among the worst, in NLM assessment, in target achievement, transition to PLC, and backlog to be covered, are those topping the list with most dramatic increase in literates, by the NSSO and vice versa. Maharashtra and Karnataka are among the better performing states according to the NLM, and the worst according to the NSSO. UP, which ranks fourth best in literacy increase for the NSSO, is for the NLM, a below 25 per cent achievement state. There has been no dramatic change in their UEE record to support the NSSO 'findings' either. The question is not the credibility of NSSO data, but the credulity of the NLM which seems to debunk its own internal assessment.

Looking back, it is evident that three interrelated trends were emerging, namely (i) conceptual evolution—policy perceptions and guidelines, (ii) the trends of decline and distortions noticed in the programme's growth, and (iii) the NLM's response—'new initiatives' in the 'context of emerging scenario of the programme'. First, what is discernible behind the conceptual evolution is a progressive dilution and unmistakable marginalization of the people's movement character of the programme between TLC and PL and CE stages. Even conceptually, the term 'campaign' lost utility to the NLM beyond 1998 and PLC became a 'programme' (PLP) indistinguishable from any other government programme.

In the wake of the Expert Group's recommendations in 1994 or the Ninth Plan Working Group in 1996, the NLM had a historic opportunity to reassess its approach, rescind its 'targetitis' groove, abandon the 'total literacy' phobia and adopt the 'less manipulable, realistic and

TABLE 16.4
NSSO Findings and NLM Claims: Uneasy and Paradoxical

	1998 TLC backlog (thousand)	NLM assessment		NSSO finding	
		1998 Achievement %	Rank in 13 states	Diff. in literacy increase 1991–7	Rank in 13 states
Meghalaya	126	8.42	13	27.1	1
Assam	7594	12.01	12	22.1	2
Rajasthan	6255	31.39	7	16.5	3
Uttar Pradesh	14,289	24.45	8	14.4	4
West Bengal	6039	57.75	2	14.3	5
Madhya Pradesh	8351	33.67	6	11.8	6
Bihar	2900	22.92	9	10.5	7
Andhra Pradesh	6872	51.4	4	9.9	8
Haryana	1879	14.84	10	9.2	9
Maharashtra	2601	59.41	1	9.1	10
Punjab	1706	13.89	11	8.5	11
Karnataka	3518	52.10	3	2.0	12
Orissa	3396	38.17	5	1.9	13

Source: Calculated from the data for different states, in DAE (1999a) and DAE (n.d.c, 15).

saner objective of promoting, developing and consolidating a learning society'. Perceptive observers hardly ever agreed with the NLM's euphoric view. The NGO space within the literacy movement was steadily marginalized and this happened at national and policy levels too. And as the literacy achievement was so unimpressive and fragile, the NLM at least could have valued and legitimated the social gains which promised to keep the movement alive with organizers, volunteers, and learners alike.

THE SOCIAL BALANCE SHEET OF INDIA'S LITERACY ENTERPRISES

Looking back at the sojourn of the NLM in the last ten years in pursuit of its objectives, some important lessons could be abstracted. On the positive side, the following could be noted:

• The initial two to three years of the NLM were also its most crucial and trying period. When literacy had no hopes in a policy milieu which viewed it as trying to 'mop the floor with the taps on' and felt that the priority should be more judiciously shifted to UEE, the NLM was able to establish the value and efficacy of literacy as an important social intervention which, in the long run, had the potential of closing even the leaking tap, of ineffective primary education, leave alone mopping up its spilt water, of illiterates.

• The social momentum that literacy and its driving engine, the NLM, gathered was truly edifying—the

initial TLCs, especially those that adopted and strictly adhered to the ethos and spirit of a people's movement, witnessed a degree of voluntary social action for literacy, unprecedented in Indian history of adult education. All the qualitative or social gains were products of this era of TLCs, which still adorn the front and central pages of NLM literature and policy fora, although they have long ceased to be the prized assets and express objectives in latter-day projects.

• Even conceding all the limitations of exaggeration, the quantitative achievements of literacy, the scale and magnitude of volunteers and social activists mobilized, social mobilization achieved, and innovative methodologies of social motivation and mobilization witnessed were truly unparalleled. These must remain the singular inspirations, especially if we consider the socio-political milieu which did not seem conducive. The only problem was that these ceased to be enshrined in the preambles and objectives of the programmes as condition for sanction or as yardsticks of its merit when it came to evaluation.

• The methodology adopted for implementation of the mass literacy campaigns brought in a breath of fresh air. The creation of the autonomous ZSS, with the District Collector as Chairperson and with more than 50 per cent representation to NGO forces, and directly placing funds under its disposal, and endowing it with flexibility and autonomy, cut out the proverbial hierarchism and red tape which were the bane of the centre-based approach. This single decision, if zealously guarded, valued, and enforced, imbued the necessary commitment, had the potential of aligning administration closely with the people on behalf of the people's movement for literacy. In a limited number of cases, this happened. That was all. In most cases it became ineffective and remained so without the NLM doing its watchdog role.

On the negative side, the following could be abstracted:

• Gradual erosion of political and government priority for literacy.

• The inherent short-lived character of campaign effectiveness and the difficulty involved in sustaining voluntarism, public interest, and involvement and priority of district administration.

• Political instability at central and state levels and the lack of consistency regarding priority to literacy.

• The NLM policy and leadership's inability to come to terms with the erosion of the people's movement character of the literacy enterprise. The NLM's response was largely in the nature of skirting the real issues; relying heavily on administrative streamlining measures. What was called for was candid admission of the decline trends and measures that would uphold the people's movement philosophy and objectives where at least NLM policy could not have been faulted for the decline.

• Indiscriminate expansion, stung by the dramatic success of initial TLCs, but without regard to their contextual constraints, compounded by lack of commitment and preparedness of districts vying for TLCs, and the compulsion of 'targetitis', resulted in overreporting of achievements and erosion of credibility of TLCs. The severely deficient view of assessing the achievement of the campaigns led to the neglect of all that was valuable and self-sustaining in the movement. All these contributed to the steady erosion of credibility and life of the literacy movement.

• As political priority for literacy was dwindling, it was reflected in the sidelining of literacy priority in the agenda of district administration. Dragging TLCs, bureaucratization of the programme, and ritualization of the process, as a result of non-internalization of the TLC ethos and philosophy or commitment to it, went on with impunity as far as the state governments and districts were concerned, and the NLM could, and did, very little about it.

Today, one can hardly find any sympathizers of the NLM even among those who were once its most avowed proponents (activists). This cuts across the entire spectrum of learners, volunteers, activists, NGOs, progressive citizens, the community, and even many within the official machinery. Their disillusionment is not with literacy, but what has happened to the literacy movement. The NLM is, indeed, in need of a moral and ideological renewal or else the literacy achievement will inexorably slide to the margins of civil conscience.

REFERENCES

Athreya, Venkatesh and Sheelarani Chunkat (1996). *Literacy and Empowerment*. Sage Publications, New Delhi.

Banerjee, Sumanta (1993). 'Revisiting the National Literacy Mission'. *Economic and Political Weekly*, vol. XXVIII, no. 25, pp. 1274–8.

———— (1994). 'Flowers for the Illiterate'. *Economic and Political Weekly*, vol. 29, no. 48, pp. 3012–16.

Bordia, Anil and Anita Kaul (1992). 'Literacy Efforts in India'. *The Annals of the American Academy of Political and Social Sciences*. Special Issue on, 'World Literacy in the year 2000'.

Department of Education (1988). *National Literacy Mission*. Ministry of Human Resource Development, Government of India, New Delhi.

———— (1992). *National Policy on Education 1992: Programme of Action 1992*. Ministry of Human Resource Development, Government of India, New Delhi.

———— (1996). *Report of the Working Group of the Planning Commission on Adult Education for the Ninth Five Year Plan 1997–2002*. Ministry of Human Resource Development, Government of India, New Delhi.

Directorate of Adult Education (1993a). *Status of Literacy and Post-Literacy Campaigns*. National Literacy Mission, Ministry of Human Resource Development, Government of India, New Delhi.

———— (1993b). *Status Report of Literacy and Post Literacy Campaigns*. National Literacy Mission, Ministry of Human Resource Development, Government of India, New Delhi.

———— (1994). 'Guidelines for Post-Literacy Campaign— A Summary'. *Literacy Mission*. National Literacy Mission, Ministry of Human Resource Development, Government of India, New Delhi.

———— (1996). *Strategies for Post-Literacy*. National Literacy Mission, Ministry of Human Resource Development, Government of India, New Delhi.

———— (1999a). *Annual Report, 1998–99*. National Literacy Mission, Ministry of Human Resource Development, Government of India, New Delhi.

———— (1999b). *Literacy Campaigns in India—Annual Report 1997–98*. National Literacy Mission, Ministry of Human Resource Development, Government of India, New Delhi.

———— (n.d.a). *Towards a Literate India*. National Literacy Mission, Ministry of Human Resource Development, Government of India, New Delhi.

———— (n.d.b). *A Note on the National Literacy Mission*

Alongwith an Overview of Literacy and Adult Education Activities. National Literacy Mission, Ministry of Human Resource Development, Government of India, New Delhi.

————— (n.d.c). *Literacy Rates: An Analysis Based on National Sample Survey Organisation Survey 1998*. National Literacy Mission, Ministry of Human Resource Development, Government of India, New Delhi.

Mishra, Lakshmidhar (1992). 'Total Literacy Campaign: Still an Unwritten Chapter in Indian History'. Part I & II. *Mainstream*, vol. 30, no. 46, pp. 11–16; and no. 47, pp. 208.

————— (1998). 'National Literacy Mission—Retrospect and Prospect.' *Economic and Political Weekly*, vol. XXXIII, no. 44, pp. 2807–16.

Ramachandran, Vimla (1999). 'Adult Education: A Tale of Empowerment Denied.' *Economic and Political Weekly*, vol. XXXIV, no. 15, pp. 977–80.

Saldanha, Denzil (1999). 'Residual Illiteracy and Uneven Development'. Special Article I–III, *Economic and Political Weekly*, 3–9 July, pp. 1773–82: 10 July, pp. 1907–19; and 17 July, pp. 2019–33.

Shah, S. Y. (1999). *Studies in Indian Adult Education*. Indian Association of Adult Education, New Delhi.

17 Education beyond Literacy
Changing Concepts and Shifting Goals

C. J. Daswani

INTRODUCTION

From the late 1930s to the present, all policy statements and programme strategies for adult education in India mention post literacy (PL) and/or continuing education (CE) as important components. Successive programmes of adult education have reiterated the significance of PL and CE in creating a learning society, yet, no programme has systemically transitioned from basic literacy to PL and CE. Some adult education programmes were obviously initially planned only to achieve the goal of basic literacy, and did not visualize any role for PL or CE. Subsequently, during the implementation of the programme, it was realized that basic literacy by itself was not enough to lead to the goal of creating a learning society, and therefore, PL and CE were appended to the basic literacy component.

Although these two terms recur in many programme documents, there is little consistency in their use. In some cases PL is used synonymously with CE, in other cases CE subsumes PL. This inconsistency can give rise to the perception that the two concepts are perhaps vague or unclear, or poorly apprehended. Nor has there been any consistency in determining the duration of the basic literacy, PL, and CE components. The interlinkages between basic literacy and PL on the one hand, and between PL and CE on the other, have never been clearly enunciated. As a result, it is not clear for how long each component or stage will last. In the process, programmes of adult education seldom go beyond the initial stage of imparting basic literacy skills.

In order to evaluate the role of PL and CE in achieving widespread adult education, it is necessary to understand why programmes of PL and CE have not succeeded so far. Possibly, shifts in the goals of adult education have contributed to the lack of clarity about the place of PL and CE in adult education. Or perhaps, the very concepts of PL and CE have undergone conceptual evolution from one programme of adult education to the next.

When we analyse these underlying causes of changes in the concepts of PL and CE, and the shifts in goals, we may be in a position to understand how the current strategies of PL and CE are different from their forerunners, and what likelihood there is of success for the present programmes of PL and CE.

Adult Education as Part of General Education

In its Report in 1939, the Adult Education Committee of the Central Advisory Board of Education (CABE) recommended that adult education be recognized as an essential component in the system of public instruction. According to the Committee, the function of adult education would be to:

- make adults literate in the narrow sense;
- encourage already literate and newly made literate adults to *continue* (emphasis added) their education; and
- enable adults to proceed to more advanced stages of education.

The Committee recognized the fact that because of lack of stimulus or facilities, newly made literate adults inevitably relapse into illiteracy. In order to avoid such relapse, the Committee recommended that appropriate instructional programmes be provided, which may awaken the interest of the adult and create in her/him the desire to continue her/his education. The Committee felt that interest and desire for further education are best awakened through vocational courses (see Shah 1999).

This is perhaps the earliest extant reference to continuing education in the context of adult education. It is significant to note that where continuing education is concerned, the Committee does not make a distinction between the already literate and the neo-literate. Clearly, this is not CE as it is understood in the present programmes of adult education. In the report, adult literacy is seen as a tool for providing an impetus for further education. Obviously, the intention of the Committee was to underline the importance of creating opportunities (through continuing education, such as vocational courses), which would enable adults to voluntarily continue their education. This is an issue to which we will return in the context of current strategies for PL and CE. It must be noted, however, that the 1939 Committee does not mention PL.

Adult Education as Social Education

Almost ten years after the 1939 Committee, the CABE set up another committee in 1948 to examine 'A Scheme for Adult Education and Literacy' (see Shah 1999). This committee declared that the previous programme of adult education had been confined to 'literacy work'; hence, it recommended that the scheme be rechristened 'A Scheme for Social Education'. The committee felt that while the work of literacy had to continue with the goal of achieving 50 per cent literacy in the country within a period of five years, greater emphasis needed to be placed on social aspects of education. According to this committee, the objectives of social education needed to include, among other things, basic literacy and nume-racy, and continuation of education through libraries, discussion groups, clubs, and institutions like people's colleges. The primary objectives, however, were seen as related to citizenship, democracy, cultural heritage, health, cooperation, moral values, and the like. What is important to note is that this committee links continuing education to libraries and discussion groups, a concept that we find in the latest formulation of CE. Also, the concept of CE as part of social education is basically different from the earlier concept of literacy as a tool for continuing general education.

Interestingly, the 1948 committee recommended that the Government of India should arrange to send educationists for training in social education to foreign countries, particularly the UK, USA, Russia, China, and Mexico. One assumes the committee felt that these countries had already experimented with models of social education, which India could profitably learn from. It is, of course, curious that although 'people's colleges' are mentioned, Denmark is not listed among the important countries where educationists could be trained.

In 1963, another committee, on 'operation of social education' (see Shah 1999), recommended several steps for strengthening the programme of social education. This committee stressed that literacy be given a proper place in the comprehensive programme of social education. Among the various steps recommended for strengthening social education, the Committee wanted proper arrangements to be made for further and continuing education by organizing adult schools, evening colleges, correspondence courses, and refresher courses. It is interesting to note that by 1963, the concept of continuing education had become refined, although the shadow of general education seems to accompany CE, both in the 1948 and 1963 versions.

The shift in emphasis on literacy is clearly discernible in the 1963 version of social education. In 1948, literacy had been relegated to the background, with social education occupying centre stage. In the 1963 version literacy is reinstated and given a 'proper place' in the programme of social education. One gets the impression that the 1963 committee felt that literacy had been denied its role in the scheme of social education. This 'on and off' sentiment with regard to literacy has always influenced adult education in India.

The relationship between literacy and social education was further elaborated in 1965 by the Standing Committee, on social education, of CABE (see Shah 1999). The Standing Committee, ostensibly, wished to underscore the importance of social education, and stated that adult education *is* social education. In the opinion of the Committee, since mere literacy does not interest adults, social education provides a comprehensive concept of adult education. Further and continuing education, therefore, are seen as a part of the numerous activities that are necessary to realize the objectives of social education.

Adult Education for Development

Three decades after the programme of adult education, as social education was mooted, the Government of India formulated in 1978 an adult education programme which was markedly different from the earlier attempts in that it proposed to link adult education to development. Called the National Adult Education Programme (NAEP), it was designed with the objective of providing, to approximately 100 million illiterate persons in the age group 15–35, 'skills for self-directed learning leading to self-reliant and active role in their own development and in the development of their environment' (see Shah 1999). The NAEP, therefore, was seen as a means to bring about a fundamental change in the process of socio-economic development.

Literacy was seen as an indispensable component of the NAEP, which was described as a 'massive programme'. It was envisaged that different types of programmes would be organized as part of the NAEP, including:

• Literacy with assured follow-up.
• Conventional functional literacy.
• Functional literacy supportive of a dominant development programme.
• Literacy with learning-cum-action groups.
• Literacy for conscientization and formation of organizations of the poor.

In addition to basic literacy as an indispensable component, the NAEP included two more components, viz. 'functionality' and 'awareness'. Since literacy was visualized as the primary focus, the NAEP was implemented through literacy centres that provided 350 hours of literacy instruction spread over a period of 9 to 10 months. It was also envisaged that about 35 million illiterate adults would be made literate in the first five years, after which the programmes would be diversified, aimed at creating a learning society with lifelong education as a cherished goal.

In the policy formulation for the NAEP, the concepts of PL and CE do not figure, except by implication, in the context of 'literacy with assured follow-up'. However, in 1979 a Committee on Post Literacy and Follow-up Programmes recommended that post literacy and follow-up programmes were as important as the literacy programme itself, and the agency responsible for the literacy programme should also organize the post literacy and follow-up programmes. In its recommendations, this committee also suggested that a time would come when 'organized groups within the community would take over the responsibility for activities of continuing education and group action for community development' (see Shah 1999).

It may be noticed here that the committee recommendation on PL clearly (and quite rightly) presupposes literacy skills. PL here is not a programme of 'mopping up', or a programme of 'second chance' for those whose literacy skills are fragile.

The progression from the 1939 programme of adult education as part of general education to adult education as social education and then to adult education as development can be viewed from several angles. Despite the rhetoric, the basic orientation in all the programmes has been literacy. In the social education phase the attempt to locate literacy in the larger context of social education was eventually reversed in order to reinstate literacy as the most important component. In the first two programmes, the basic literacy component was not clearly delineated. Only during the NAEP a specific time

frame and total duration of the literacy component were clearly specified.

In the first two programmes, the concept of PL was not included, and continuing education was seen as a positive desideratum, to be achieved after the acquisition of basic literacy skills. PL was introduced for the first time in 1978 as part of the NAEP, where it was seen as a part of the 'follow-up' to succeed acquisition of literacy skills.

The concept of PL was further elaborated in the recommendations of the Review Committee on the NAEP. Set up after only eighteen months from the launching of the NAEP; the Committee submitted its report in early 1980. It said that the provision of PL and follow-up, as envisaged in the NAEP, was not enough. 'This is insufficient for an effective and purposeful adult education programme, especially if its content is to be wider and is to lead to tangible development' (see DAE 1980). The Committee recommended a three-stage programme spread over a period of three years: the first stage of 300–50 hours of basic literacy spread over a period of one year, followed by the second stage of 150 hours spread over a period of one year for reinforcement of literacy skills together with functionality, and the third stage of 100 hours spread over a period of one year for achievement of self-reliance in literacy and functionality. It may be noticed that the three stages actually concentrate on literacy, taking the learners from basic literacy to self-reliant literacy. The focus is literacy, and PL and follow-up stages come after self-reliance in literacy is achieved.

Jan Shikshan Nilayam

After the change in the central government in 1980, the NAEP was greatly trimmed and converted into the National Programme of Adult Education (NPAE), which was linked to the already existing Rural Functional Literacy Programme. The NAEP Review Committee proposal for a three-year literacy programme was shelved. However, in 1982–3 the government commenced funding a PL and follow-up programme with a four-month PL component after the basic literacy component, followed by a year-long follow-up programme.

This programme eventually saw the birth of the *Jan Shikshan Nilayam* (JSN). The JSN was conceived as a permanent institution located in rural areas. It was planned to establish one JSN for a population of about 5000 people, supposed to serve a cluster of 4–5 villages for PL needs of neo-literates who had completed the 300–50-hour one-year literacy programme at an adult education centre.

The intention behind establishing JSNs all over the country in a phased manner was to institutionalise the post literacy and continuing education programme and converge various activities at one nodal centre. JSNs included programmes which were being organized as part of farmers' training programmes, rural radio forum, youth clubs, women's groups (mahila mandal), mobile and village library system and rural reading rooms. [DAE n.d.]

PL AND CE: NATIONAL LITERACY MISSION (NLM) PERSPECTIVE

The Total Literacy Campaign (TLC) or mass literacy campaigns (MLCs) of the NLM were conceived basically as literacy programmes different from the NAEP in implementation. Although the National Policy on Education (see DoE 1986) and Programme of Action (see DoE 1986) had conceived, as in the NAEP, adult education as comprising basic literacy plus PL and follow-up, the TLCs which commenced in 1988 did not include any conscious provision for PL or CE. The mass-based campaign approach experimented with in Ernakulam, and generalized for the TLC model, was the central focus of the NLM. The campaign approach was adopted because, among other things, it supposedly accelerated the acquisition of basic literacy skills, in addition to harnessing 'social forces and channelising the energies of people towards meeting the ultimate objective of effecting a qualitative change in their own lives.' The duration of the literacy component in the TLCs was reduced from 350 to 200 hours, to be completed in 6–8 months.

The PL component, which was visualized in the NPE and POA (1986) and further elaborated in the revised POA (1992), was conceptually incorporated in the programme and was sought to be delivered immediately after the TLC phase. The campaign mode was perceived to be so successful that the PL component was also cast in the campaign mode, leading to the notion of a post literacy campaign (PLC) for twenty-four months following the TLC. The revised POA (1992) also mentioned the necessity of devising a programme of CE.

Unclear Concepts

The foregoing description of the programmes of adult education clearly shows that the twin concepts of PL and CE have undergone several changes in these programmes. In 1939, PL had no place in the programme, and CE carried the wide-ranging connotation of non-formal education (NFE), which neo-literates (and the already literate) could voluntarily pursue. The underlying assumption, it would seem, was that literacy programmes by themselves were enough to equip the neo-literate adult with stable literacy as well as an urge to continue her/his education.

The social education programme, on the other hand, was predicated on the premise that literacy skills are not an essential prerequisite for education in citizenship, personal development, moral-ethical values, nation building, and so on. Basic literacy was seen as only an element in creating complete and socially responsible individuals, who are able to continue their education in a variety of ways, through correspondence, night classes, or in community colleges. The social education model did not assign any place to only PL.

While the first two programmes saw literacy as a tool for continuation of general education, the NAEP perceived literacy as an enabling element in personal, social, economic, and national development. However, although the concept of PL is introduced in the NAEP, the vagueness remains. PL is clubbed with 'follow-up'. Follow-up of what, one may ask. Follow-up of literacy, presumably, or perhaps of PL.

As already noted, the Review Committee on the NAEP was convinced that 350 hours of literacy with assured follow-up were not adequate for self-reliant literacy, and it, therefore, recommended a literacy programme spread over three years. In fact, the Review Committee had stated that since literacy was not effectively linked to PL and follow-up, a large number of neo-literates ran the risk of relapsing into illiteracy. That is the critical issue. How should literacy be linked to PL and follow-up, and to PL and CE?

It would not be unfair to conclude that the concepts of PL and CE in the programmes of adult education before the NLM programme were, at best, hazy. The haziness resulted from the fact that literacy was perceived as the central goal, and anything by way of PL and follow-up was seen as a desirable additionality, without a clear-cut model or strategy for linking literacy with PL and CE. The establishment of the JSNs was a bold and pioneering attempt, but for want of political commitment and administrative support, it remained underdeveloped and undernourished. It was ultimately abandoned for want of clear conceptualization of how PL could be linked to basic literacy.

NLM Perspective on PL and CE

If the concepts of PL and CE were unclear and vague in the earlier programmes of adult education, in the programmes of the NLM, they are constantly changing to the point of having become confused and confusing. Although, as we will see, the NLM has borrowed heavily from the APPEAL (Asia Pacific Programme of Education for All) formulation, the linkage between PL and CE has not been clearly established. Consequently, the relationship between basic literacy and PL/CE continues to be fluid and ambivalent. This fluidity and ambivalence is best reflected in the multiple formulations of PL and CE in NLM documents.

In the past few years, the NLM has issued a number of documents recording the progress of the literacy programmes. Although these documents are very well produced and attractive, not all of them indicate the year of publication. In the occasional document, one may infer the date of publication from the preface, or from the imprint of the Press where the document is published, usually given at the bottom of the back cover in small type. Consequently, it is almost impossible to determine the chronological sequence of these documents. And, since each document reports different sets of statistics, it is not easy to draw clear inferences about the status of the programmes from the data and the information provided in these documents.

As mentioned earlier, the NPE (1986) and the POA (1986, 1992) had visualized programmes of PL and CE as follow-up programmes of the basic literacy programmes. In 1986, the only model for literacy programmes was the centre-based model of the NAEP. The NLM was set up as a Technology Mission whose function was to provide all the essential technological and material inputs without which literacy programmes were likely to languish and fail. The connotation of societal mission was to be added later on, when in 1990 the campaign mode was adopted as the preferred methodology for imparting literacy. The campaign mode necessarily meant mobilization of social forces and involvement of a large number of literate people from the society in the literacy programme. Hence the term 'mission' took on the sense of 'missionary'.

While the NLM was searching, between 1988 and 1990, for a suitable model for its literacy programme, both PL and CE were put on the back-burner, and the JSN model continued to operate half-heartedly. After the success of the TLC in Ernakulam in 1990, the campaign model was adopted as *the* model for the basic literacy programme. From then on, the energies of the NLM were directed entirely towards quickly inundating the country with TLCs in as many districts as possible. As the TLC model succeeded in more and more districts, it was generalized and its components became progressively standardized. Between 1990 and 1993, a large number of districts were declared totally literate. As one looks back, those were heady days, for it seemed that adult illiteracy would soon be eradicated. The main focus was on achieving basic literacy in as many districts in the country in as short a time as possible. In the meantime, the scheme of JSNs continued to exist.

As is customary with educational programmes and schemes, in 1993 an Expert Group was appointed by the Government to 'undertake a Status-cum-Impact Evaluation of Literacy Campaigns launched in different parts of the country since 1990-1.' (see NLM 1994). Chaired by Professor Arun Ghosh, a former member of the Planning Commission, the Group submitted its report in 1994. The Report evaluated not only the TLCs, but also the extant programmes of PL and CE. It sheds light on not only the status and impact of PL/CE, but also on how the concepts of PL and CE were apprehended within the NLM.

Most significantly, the Group felt that

> PL/CE should not be attempted in the campaign mode. New forms of institutionalization, new agencies of organization, new attitudes towards this phase of the programme, fundamentally different from the TLC phase, are required. The term PLC which denotes yet another campaign is therefore a misnomer, and should be replaced by the designation PL/CE. [DAE 1994]

The Group was also of the view that, among other things:

• To begin with, there was no clear conceptual framework for the PL phase.
• Carrying out a successful PL/CE programme is a major problem.
• The TLC and PL/CE phases must be integrated.
• Organizational control of the PL/CE must be different from that of the TLC structure.

At the same time as the Expert Group was constituted, another committee was constituted to study the earlier scheme of JSNs and advise the government on future strategies for PL/CE in the context of TLCs.

Against the backdrop of recommendations of the Expert Group, and the committee on JSNs, an NLM document published in 1998 says, 'Since post literacy programmes also rely considerably on the campaign mode, these are commonly described as Post Literacy Campaigns...' (29). Similarly, a 1996 document of the NLM, declares, '...NLM has visualized PLC as an extension of TLC...' (6). The same document also states, 'Post-literacy is both a part and a process of continuing education.' (18) A little earlier, on the same page (18), it is stated, 'Continuing education goes beyond post-literacy.' Yet another document published at the end of 1999, declares that an integrated 'Literacy Campaign' will amalgamate all the features of the earlier TL and PL phases.

It would not be impossible to reconcile the above seemingly contradictory pronouncements, because the concepts of PL and CE continue to be hazy, and the terms are used ambiguously, if not loosely. The basic confusion can be traced to the separation of post literacy from continuing education. In the APPEAL framework earlier mentioned, PL programmes are part of continuing education. The NLM, on the other hand, for justifiable reasons, has clubbed PL with basic literacy. In a manner of speaking, the NLM formulations on PL and CE have attempted to borrow the APPEAL model without accepting the PL programmes as part of that model.

Why PL

The APPEAL model of CE describes the clientele group of PL programmes as, 'all youth and adults (school dropouts and semi-literates)'. There is no mention of neo-literates among the clientele group.

The justification for PL in the NLM programmes is different:

> While a large number [of learners in TLC] achieve levels laid down by the NLM; a significant number do not, and many remain non-starters. Even those who do achieve the prescribed literacy levels, acquire only 'fragile' literacy. Without a meaningful post-literacy programme, many of these relapse into illiteracy. [DAE 1998, 29]

In 1994, the (Arun Ghosh) Expert Group had voiced a similar sentiment: 'There is real fragility in literacy achievements and thus very serious problem of relapse of neo-literates even in districts where there have been successful TLCs. This problem is aggravated in cases of long time lags between TLC & PL/CE.' (see DAE 1994, 30).

The reason for fragile literacy, however, is not of a time lag between basic literacy and PL. The real reason is that the TLCs were designed to provide only fragile literacy, hence the need for PL. The Review Committee on the NAEP in 1980 had rightly diagnosed the problem and found 350 hours of literacy in the ten-month course insufficient. Therefore, it had recommended 600 contact hours of literacy spread over a period of three years. The NLM, in its wisdom, had cut down the basic literacy component to 200 hours spread over a period of 6–8 months, without the provision of PL for a long time after the TLC.

The NLM went a step further and specified a detailed curriculum in the 3Rs for the TLC. The basis for specifying the levels of competencies in reading, writing and numeracy is not clear, but it is assumed that adult non-literates can achieve these levels.

> There is no research evidence to support the implicit assumption that the TLC curriculum can be acquired within the stipulated time-period. It is well known that children require at least three to four years to achieve independent reading skills. Although adults are believed to have certain advantages of cognitive maturity, it is also believed that they do not necessarily acquire basic reading skills at a more rapid pace. [Daswani 1996]

No wonder, then, that the literacy levels achieved even in the more successful TLCs were fragile.

It must, of course, be pointed out that after the TLC, the NLM had visualized a twenty-four-month PL phase, but in most cases the PL phase did not follow the TLC and the neo-literates actually relapsed into illiteracy. Even now, of the 448 TLC districts only 234 have been sanctioned PL programmes.

Shifting Goals of PL

In the earlier (pre-1999) formulation, each PLC had a life of two years. During this two-year period, the PLC was supposed to fulfil four major goals. These are specified in the 1996 document as under:

- Remediation: To help remedy the deficiencies of learning in the basic literacy phase and to help neo-literates reach the desired level of achievement.
- Continuation: To consolidate and improve the learning skills already acquired by neo-literates with a view to making them self-reliant.
- Application: To help neo-literates attain the ability to use the newly acquired skills and make them adequately functionally literate.
- Communitization: To help neo-literates organize themselves to secure services under programmes related to health, family welfare, child care, nutrition, agriculture, animal husbandry, etc.

The 1998 NLM document lists five major objectives for a PLC:

- Remediation
  - those not covered by TLC to be made literate.
  - those below minimum level of learning to be enabled to achieve it.
- Continuation
  - stabilization, reinforcement, and upgradation of learning.
- Application
  - to living and working conditions.
- Communitization
  - group action for participation in development process.
- Skill training
  - life skills, communication skills, vocational skills.

The latest (November 1999) version stipulates that

> Literacy campaigns would continue to run in those areas where there are large pools of residual illiteracy. At the same time, for those who have crossed the basic learning phase, programmes of consolidation, remediation, vocational skills, integration with life skills and such other aspects would be considered the basic unit.... Therefore, Total Literacy

Campaign and Post Literacy Campaign actually constitute two operational stages on the learning continuum and now under the same scheme will operate in smooth progression. [DAE 1999, 60]

What is significant to note is that, at least for the present, the NLM has delinked PL from CE and linked it inextricably with TLCs.

Programmes of Continuing Education

The NLM had designed a scheme of CE for neo-literates, which came into force on 1 January 1996. This scheme replaced the earlier scheme of JSNs which had been introduced in 1988. It would be interesting to recapture the sequence of events in the provision of CE for neo-literates.

In 1980, the Review Committee on NAEP had recommended a three-year literacy programme. This was not accepted. Instead a four-month literacy programme followed by a year-long follow-up programme was launched in 1982. The NPE and POA in 1986 had stipulated that for a successful programme of adult education, it was important to provide for PL and CE. In response to this JSNs scheme was launched in 1988. Following the adoption of the campaign mode for basic literacy, the JSNs scheme was reviewed in 1993, and it was decided to replace this scheme with a new scheme of Continuing Education Centres (CECs). However, the CECs scheme was launched only in 1996. (Incidentally, the latest NLM document declares that the scheme of CE was launched in 1995!) 'The 1999 Document states that the structure of continuing education programme, launched in 1995 [sic] as a fully funded centrally-sponsored scheme, will be retained and further strengthened and expanded in scope and content' (see DAE 1999).

The main objective of the scheme is to institutionalize CE for neo-literates, which is achieved by establishing CECs. The scheme provides for flexibility in designing and implementation of CE programmes in order to cater to the needs of the neo-literates. More specific objectives of the scheme are:

- provision of facilities for retention and reinforcement of literacy skills;

- application of functional literacy for quality of life improvement;

- dissemination of information on development programmes for participation;

- creation of awareness on national concerns;

- training in vocational skills;

- provision of library;

- organization of cultural and recreational activities.

The responsibility for the implementation of the scheme rests with the *Zilla Saksharta Samiti* (ZSS) headed by the Collector, with assistance from voluntary agencies, *mahila mandals*, *panchayati raj* institutions, *Nehru Yuvak Kendras*, etc. The scheme provides ample freedom to the ZSS to create new structures at grassroots level for effective implementation of the CE programmes.

Under the scheme, CE programmes will be implemented through the CECs. 'A continuing education centre will be set up for a population 2000–2500 so that it caters to the needs of at least 500–1000 neo-literates.' It is also envisaged that a Nodal Continuing Education Centre (NCEC) will be set up for a cluster of 10–15 CECs. Each CEC and NCEC will be run by a *prerak* and an assistant *prerak*, who will together provide the facilities at the centres and coordinate the various activities. The principal function of a CEC will be to provide the following facilities: library; reading Room; learning centre; training centre; information centre; *charcha mandal*; development centre; cultural centre; sports centre.

The scheme, in principle, provides flexibility and freedom to the ZSS for planning and developing CE programmes which are sensitive to the local environment and conditions and needs of the local population, particularly neo-literates. At the same time the NLM has identified four broad programmes areas which can help the CECs develop specific programmes in specific situations. These four programme areas are identical to the CE programmes contained in the APPEAL documents:

- Equivalency programmes (EPs)—designed as alternative education programmes equivalent to existing formal, general, or vocational education.

- Income-generating programmes (IGPs)—designed for acquisition or upgradation of vocational skills for income-generating activities.

- Quality of life improvement programmes (QLIPs)—designed to equip the learners with essential knowledge, attitudes, values and skills, both as individuals and members of the community.

- Individual interest promotion programmes (IIPPs)—designed to provide opportunities for individuals to participate in and learn about their own chosen social, cultural, spiritual, health, physical, and artistic interests.

As is evident, CECs, conceived and planned under the scheme of continuing education, will become nerve centres for lifelong learning. A number of already existing institutions and development departments are expected to lend support to CECs/NCECs. Since vocational training will be an important function of CECs, the government has expanded and strengthened the erstwhile

Shramik Vidyapeeths to serve as support institutions at district level. These institutions have been rechristened *Jan Shikshan Sansthans* (JSS) and charged with the responsibility of addressing the vocational training needs of neo-literates and other rural youth and adults. The JSSs will, of course, continue the vocational training of industrial workers as well as urban youth and adults. The government has also decided that the CE scheme should converge with programmes of Nehru Yuvak Kendras, the National Service Scheme, the National Service Volunteer Scheme, and others at grassroots level. The infrastructure of these institutions will, as far as pos-sible, be utilized to facilitate functioning of the CE scheme.

These are lofty ideas, but there are many fuzzy edges. The central government has decided to finance the scheme fully for three years (or is it five?), and the states will share the costs 50:50 after the third year. In addition to the 60 odd CECs already in operation, only 50 more will be set up during the remaining period of the Ninth Plan. But the scheme is supposed to 'allow for opening of continuing education centres in every major village'. When these CECs are actually set up, the annual running costs should be in the neighbourhood of Rs 5000 crore!

The Prerak

The lynchpin for the CEC is the *prerak* (and the assistant *prerak*). The prerak of the CEC will receive an hono-rarium of Rs 700 per month, and the assistant prerak, Rs 500. Between the two of them, they are supposed to coordinate/run/manage a centre which provides at least nine different kinds of facilities. They will liaise with a variety of institutions and individuals within the official government structures, and NGOs. They will have to run and manage a host of ongoing programmes for about 1000 neo-literates in their catchment area.

Judging by the honoraria determined for these two functionaries, they would have to have some other additional means of livelihood. Consequently, they will be available only part-time, while the CEC is designed to be a full-time centre. Of course, if the CEC is run by an NGO, the two preraks could be employed full-time by the NGO and made available part-time.

But that still leaves the question of the job description for the preraks and their qualifications. It is possible that the NLM has already visualized this problem, and a solution has been devised. Perhaps some of the volunteers from the TLC programmes will be able to handle the job. Yet it would seem to be a difficult task to locate a large number of individuals who fit the bill. And even if 'qualified' individuals were found, how would they relate to the entire 'official' machinery from the District Collector downwards?

THE BOTTOM LINE

It is over sixty years since the notion of CE was first introduced in the context of adult education. The concept has undergone several evolutionary changes and reincarnations. The concept of PL became entwined with CE until it was recently separated. Both PL and CE in India have covered a tortuous journey in the sixty odd years. In the analysis presented here, an attempt has been made to understand the changing connotations and implications of the two concepts. Whether the analysis offered above is tenable or not, several issues need at least to be raised, even if not resolved.

First, what are the preconditions for the success of a PL programme? At a simplistic, or even superficial, level does *post* literacy not imply existence of literacy? Why do we not say 'post fragile literacy', or 'post minimal literacy'? The answer, possibly, is that *literacy* is a prerequisite or precondition for PL. PL can succeed only when the participants have already acquired *stable* literacy. If a person has not acquired stable literacy skills, she/he will not benefit from PL. Of course, one can be euphemistic and use the term 'PL' to mean extension of literacy training. In fact the PL programmes have only been extensions of the basic literacy courses, because the non-literates had not become stable literates, whether through the NAEP or the TLC. Therefore, for a PL programme to succeed, it is necessary to ensure that the non-literate is equipped with stable literacy skills before the basic literacy programme is terminated. The NAEP review committee had stipulated a three-year period. Perhaps that is the critical period for acquiring stable literacy.

Second, do any advantages accrue to a non-literate when she/he becomes a neo-literate? Or what function does minimal literacy have in a society in which a large number of people are illiterate? The answer, probably, is that there is no immediate advantage. There are several notional benefits, which are clear to the literacy activist or a literacy functionary (for different reasons), but to the non-literate learner these are not immediately discernable. In a partially literate society, a large number of non-literate persons function within their socio-economic realities. Unless their newly acquired literacy skills can rapidly ameliorate their conditions, literacy can never become attractive. For any literacy endeavour to succeed, it would seem to be necessary to create conditions where literacy (however minimal) can bring economic and social advantages to the neo-literate. If that were to be ensured, PL and CE programmes would be demanded rather than be provided.

Third, how long does it take for a totally illiterate family to become fully literate? Is it reasonable to expect that a family will become literate in one generation? Experience has shown that it takes two, or even three generations for a family to travel from illiteracy to total literacy. When we are dealing with traditional non-literates, we need to plan an integrated educational package encompassing the adult non-literate, her/his children, and grandchildren. Unless we are willing to support the family through this three-generation saga, all attempts will fall short of the goal. Unfortunately, up until now, all adult education programmes have been in the project mode, coextensive with a Plan period in the form of a scheme, and financial provisions are actually made on annual basis.

Fourth, how is a literate or learning society created? A literate society is seldom created through literacy training. A literate society is one where literacy has become a critical input for all social and economic activities within the society. A learning society is one where the resources of literacy are harnessed for living in peace and harmony, and for the common good.

Fifth, can a mass programme like adult education, which aims at basic changes in the social structure and believes in conscientization, be run by the official government machinery that is by definition committed to the 'status-quo'? And can this machinery actually promote and nurture 'independent' non-governmental action at grassroots level?

The bottom line is that unless programmes of post literacy and continuing education address these issues and more, they will continue to be vague and hazy.

REFERENCES

Daswani, C. J. (1996). 'Total Literacy Campaign in India: Status and Issues'. Paper read at *World Literacy Conference*. Philadelphia.

Department of Education (1986a). *National Policy on Education 1986*. Ministry of Human Resource Development, Government of India, New Delhi.

——— (1986b). *Programme of Action 1986*. Ministry of Human Resource Development, Government of India, New Delhi.

——— (1992). *Revised Programme of Action 1992*. Ministry of Human Resource Development, Government of India, New Delhi.

Directorate of Adult Education (1980). *Report of the Review Committee on NAEP*. National Literacy Mission, Ministry of Human Resource Development, Government of India, New Delhi.

——— (1994). *Evaluation of Literacy Campaign in India, Report of Expert Group*. National Literacy Mission, Ministry of Human Resource Development, Government of India, New Delhi.

——— (1996). *Strategies for Post Literacy*. National Literacy Mission, Ministry of Human Resource Development, Government of India, New Delhi.

——— (1998). *Towards a Literate India*. National Literacy Mission, Ministry of Human Resource Development, Government of India, New Delhi.

——— (1999). *A People's Movement*. National Literacy Mission, Ministry of Human Resource Development, Government of India, New Delhi.

——— (n.d.). *Scheme of Continuing Education—A Write-up*. National Literacy Mission, Ministry of Human Resource Development, Government of India, New Delhi. (Mimeo)

Shah, S. Y. (1999). *Encyclopaedia of Adult Education*. National Literacy Mission.

UNESCO (1996). *Continuing Education for Development*. PROAP, Bangkok.

World Conference on Education for All (1990). *World Declaration on Education for All and Framework for Action to Meet Basic Learning Needs*. Inter-Agency Commission (UNDP, UNESCO, World Bank), New York.

18 Social Mobilization and Total Literacy Campaigns

Anita Dighe

INTRODUCTION

In 1959, the *Gram Shikshan Mohim* (Village Literacy Movement) was initiated in Maharashtra, first on an experimental basis in Satara district, and subsequently extended to all the districts of the state. With the Chief Minister of Maharashtra taking a personal interest, the involvement of the entire government machinery and coordination between different departments at various levels was made possible. But the critical element was the manner in which the entire village community was successfully encouraged to participate in the literacy campaign. Mass meetings were held in village after village, cooperation of the educated people of the village was elicited, and various strategies were used for the successful implementation of the campaign. While the *Gram Shikshan Mohim* was successful in its initial phase, it petered out when it was replicated in the other districts of Maharashtra. What is important for our understanding, however, is that in many ways, the *Gram Shikshan Mohim* anticipated some of the basic elements of the total literacy campaigns (TLCs) which were first taken up by the Kerala Shastra Sahitya Parishad (KSSP) in Ernakulam district of Kerala in 1989.

The Ernakulam experiment was characterized by large-scale mobilization of people from all walks of life through a multipronged communication strategy that highlighted the vital link between literacy and life. The essence of the campaign spearheaded by the KSSP, an NGO working for popularizing science among rural communities, was to generate a positive demand for learning as a tool for social change. Experience showed how an alliance and a partnership could be established between the bureaucracy on the one hand and social activists and volunteer groups on the other. The successful experience of Ernakulam gave birth to the concept of TLCs in the 1990s. The KSSP experience showed that the mass campaigns had to be based on mass mobilization, support of the government (at the centre, state, district, and local levels), involvement of non-government and voluntary organizations, as well as of people from all walks of life, and that a spirit of voluntarism had to be its hallmark.

Interestingly, the experience of the KSSP coincided with the experience of countries that had undertaken literacy campaigns to deal with the problem of mass illiteracy. A study commissioned by UNESCO in the early 1980s, the findings of which were shared at an international meeting in Udaipur in 1982, highlighted some of the basic ingredients that were responsible for the success of the literacy campaigns (see Bhola 1984). On the basis of analysis of case studies of literacy campaigns undertaken in eight countries around the world (these included the USSR 1919–39; the Socialist Republic of Vietnam, 1945–77; People's Republic of China, 1950s–80s; Cuba, 1961; Burma, 1960s–80s; Brazil, 1967–80; Tanzania, 1971–81; Somali Land 1973–5), Bhola (1984) proposed a theory of mass literacy campaigns. One of the major findings of the study related to the importance of political will for the success of the literacy campaigns. Another aspect related to social mobilization of people from different walks of life. While underscoring the commitment of the socialist countries, the study also highlighted how even non-socialist societies were capable of ideological commitment and ability to draw upon the cultural, moral, and spiritual resources of people by challenging them to action and mobilizing them around nationally defined issues.

UNDERSTANDING TLCs

In India, the early 1990s are known for the successful mobilization strategies used by the TLCs in generating political and social support from different sections of society. The (TLCs) strategy subsequently overshadowed and replaced all other previous efforts. The TLC model rests on three basic premises:

• that the entire illiterate population of a district can be identified and made literate through an intensive short-period campaign, preceded by a motivational campaign;

• that the campaign can be given the form of a 'people's movement' by involving and mobilizing volunteers to run literacy classes, as well as elicit larger community support for the entire effort;

• that a motivated, committed, and efficient District Collector can play a major role in mobilizing the entire district administrative machinery, in particular the school education department, to sustain the 'people's movement'.

TLCs begin with a process of consultation and consensus building between government officials, political leaders, teachers and students, activist groups, and cultural troupes. After the setting up of the *Zilla Saksharta Samiti* (ZSS) (District Literacy Committee), a detailed survey is carried out in the district to enumerate and identify the non-literate population. The unique feature of the survey is that it is carried out on the same day throughout the district. This process of conducting the survey also provides opportunities for person-to-person contact and interaction, as well as for identifying literacy volunteers and master trainers. Thus, the process itself results in arousing people's interest and in mobilizing them.

The innovative aspect of the TLC model is the emphasis that it places on the creation of a favourable environment for literacy. The environment-building phase consists of the use of traditional folk media forms and of *kala jathas* that consist of cultural troupes that perform street-corner plays. Conventional media like the electronic media, posters, banners, hoardings, and other non-conventional forms such as *padayatras* and *prabhat pheris*, are all used with great effect. The basic objective of the environment-building phase is to mobilize public opinion, sensitize the educated sections of the community so that they come forward as literacy volunteers, as well as mobilize and motivate non-literate adults to participate as learners in the literacy campaign. Efforts are made to ensure support from all political forces by involving political leaders in the organizational structures that are set up and in the events that are specially organized to sustain the momentum that is generated during the literacy campaign.

CAMPAIGN STRATEGIES AND THEIR RELATION TO SOCIAL MOBILIZATION

It is now more than ten years since the TLC model has been used in India to deal with the problem of adult illiteracy. What has been the TLC experience? How successful have TLCs been in social mobilization? The early 1990s definitely generated euphoria for TLCs and they picked up momentum and spread to district after district so that they now cover more than 450 districts in the country.

It might be useful, for the purpose of analysis, to consider three ways in which TLCs have been implemented. While in three cases, the Collector has played a pivotal role in the implementation process, the degree of commitment and drive displayed by the Collector has varied. In the first category, the Collector was the driving force, the initiator of all programmes and activities, with enormous energy levels and total commitment to the cause of adult literacy. The literacy campaign of Ajmer district is a case in point. Here the Collector was so committed that she mobilized the entire district bureaucracy to the task of eradicating adult illiteracy. A recent attempt to assess the achievements of the Ajmer district campaign (see Saxena 1999), has shown that the district bureaucracy, particularly the teachers who belonged to the education department, were resentful because they had been coerced by the then Collector to participate in the literacy campaign. Mobilization was thus artificially induced and due to pressure from the Collector to show good results, the teachers fudged figures in order to project high literacy achievement.

The second category could be said to be BGVS inspired. The *Bharat Gyan Vigyan Samiti* (BGVS), a national-level NGO was specifically registered to provide academic and technical resource support to the NLM. An offshoot of the KSSP, the BGVS has an ideological commitment to literacy, sees the link between literacy and poverty and believes that people's participation is essential for the success of the campaigns. The BGVS represents a confluence of two streams—its past efforts in the field of people's science movement and its realization of the need for working for the cause of adult literacy. The All-India Jatha of May 1985 in connection with the Bhopal Gas tragedy, the *jatha* of October–November 1987 with the involvement of twenty-six organizations, and that of October–November 1990 covering 304 districts in the country, were major events in the process of creating a national consensus and some voluntary organizational basis for literacy. The BGVS and its fraternal organizations in 18 states and 3 union territories (UTs) thus played a major role in the organizational support that was required by the TLCs. In the early 1990s, a large number of Collectors were influenced by the BGVS activists and worked collaboratively with them. Several Collectors provided leadership to the campaigns in a true spirit of voluntarism and understanding of the ethos of the campaign mode, seeing literacy as a challenge to their administrative innovativeness.

After the success of the TLCs, largely in some of the districts of the southern states as well as Maharashtra and Goa, the model was replicated in the Hindi heartland of the north consisting of the states of Bihar, Uttar Pradesh, Madhya Pradesh, and Rajasthan. This is a region marked by wide caste, class, and gender disparities. This is also a region that is still semi-feudal in nature. In the absence of social movements of any significance, the TLC model became highly bureaucratized. This could be considered the third category of the way TLCs have been implemented. Since the ZSS, of which the Collector is the Chairperson in most cases, could apply for funds directly to the NLM, there was a scramble to prepare hurried district plans and to get the funding for the TLCs sanctioned, bypassing the state government. The ZSS that was created to ensure participation of different sections of society, got reduced to a body consisting mainly of government officials and there were charges of financial misappropriation against the ZSS in some districts. The Collector lacked the commitment and the drive that was necessary to galvanize the support of the district administration. The TLC became routinized, it became a programme like any other government programme.

In retrospect, it could be said that over the years TLCs have been implemented in these three different ways. While these are not mutually exclusive categories, it becomes easier to understand how they have generally fared if we understand the manner in which they have been implemented. It is this difference which has affected every aspect of the campaign—its level of planning, pre-implementation and mobilization strategies, the quality of training, nature of materials prepared, and ways of enlisting people's participation as well as of sustaining it. TLCs that were influenced by committed BGVS activists generally tended to evoke a different response from those that were entirely Collector-driven.

SOCIAL MOBILIZATION AND TLCS—THE PERIOD OF THE EARLY 1990s

Why were TLCs successful in some districts? What were the factors that led to mass mobilization of people? The early 1990s are known for the successes of Nellore and Puddukotai. While these are oft-quoted success stories, it might be useful to capture the mood that prevailed then in order to understand the extent of social mobilization that took place during the literacy campaigns. Unfortunately, the documentation that is available on the TLCs is largely in the form of evaluation studies. These studies have mainly focused on assessing the number of people made literate as a result of the literacy campaign. The excessive preoccupation with determining the percentage

of adults made literate has often resulted in presenting a lopsided view of achievements of the campaign. Some of the documentation that is available on Nellore and Puddukotai, however, has attempted to unfold the processes that were responsible for the success of the campaigns. Shatrugna (1998), in his preamble to the anti-arrack agitation that Nellore is now famous for, describes how the district Collector, who was a Scheduled Caste himself, was the moving spirit behind the campaign and the manner in which, prior to the implementation of the campaign, an elaborate exercise involving the people, political parties, and the bureaucracy was worked out by going into the minutest details of implementation. The mood that prevailed and the extent of people's participation can be gauged from the following description.

> The pre-implementation programme consisted of pamphleteering, wall-postering and a number of padayatras undertaken by the sponsors and others, many times led by the Collector himself. As the main purpose of the campaign was to motivate not only illiterates but also literates who were expected to become volunteers, the kalajathras or cultural teams were formed with a large contingent of 800 artists drawn from all over the district hailing predominantly from the rural areas. The jathras gave about 7000 performances in an idiom and language understood by the village folk. The themes constituted the problems encountered in life because of illiteracy, exploitation of labour, low wages, untouchability, powerlessness in general, social evils like dowry, heavy drinking, wife beating, etc .Usually, after the conclusion of a cultural jathra, a call was given inviting volunteers who were likely to be interested in taking up the literacy work. Those who volunteered were asked to take an oath in the presence of the audience to work for the removal of illiteracy. The method became so popular that about 55,000 volunteers had registered their names when the need was only for 40,000. As a senior official associated with the campaign had put it, not only competence but also a certain ideological framework underscoring the importance of the people's movement in fighting illiteracy, literacy as a key concept in understanding the nature of exploitation, formed the agenda. [Shatrugna 1998]

The main focus of the campaign was not just to teach literacy skills to illiterate adults, but to empower them and enable them to deal with issues of development. As women had participated in the literacy phase in large numbers, *Jana Chetna Kendras* (Centres for People's Awareness) were formed during the post literacy (PL) phase where the problems facing the village were discussed. These Kendras, numbering 6000, became popular with women taking a leadership role in their functioning. These were called 'village parliaments,' and provided an opportunity for women to meet and discuss the general problems faced by the village as well as to discuss their own problems and to share their experiences with fellow women. It was a lesson in the post-literacy primer that later ignited the anti-arrack agitation led by rural women that engulfed the entire district of Nellore and later, the state of Andhra Pradesh, and forced the then Chief Minister to ban the sale of arrack and subsequently, to introduce prohibition.

In Puddukotai, it was once again an enthusiastic Collector who spearheaded the literacy campaign. Athreya and Chunkath (1996) describe in detail the manner in which the literacy campaign in the district went through a process of meticulous planning and pre-implementation strategies for mobilizing people. The extent of people's participation can be gauged when they refer to the district convention that was attended by 10,000 people. The success of the district convention set the stage for organizing block and village conventions. According to them, the district convention was organized 'from above' since the mobilization was achieved with the help of the government machinery. The participatory structures had not yet taken root. But the block- and village-level conventions were different, 'as by then a small cadre of *arivoli* activists were emerging and the programme was slowly becoming more and more participatory'. While an enthusiastic and committed Collector provided leadership to the campaign, the structure upon which the campaign was built consisted of full-time activists, officials, and people's committees.

An innovative feature of the campaign was to provide bicycles to women, and thus, increase their physical mobility. As village women learnt to ride bicycles, they realized they were no longer dependent on their menfolk, and thereby, experienced a sense of autonomy and independence. In another development, the Collector formed a cooperative of women stone-quarry workers and by doing so, eliminated the contractors who had till then reaped huge profits by hiring cheap labour. Likewise, in the lucrative gem-cutting business, for the first time poor women were hired and trained as gem-cutters, thus responding to their economic need. In Puddukotai, as in Nellore, the literacy campaign did not emphasize merely the acquisition of literacy skills but linked literacy to their lives and took up issues that concerned them. As a result, there was unprecedented people's mobilization.

While TLCs are generally known by the successful experiences of Nellore and Puddukotai, there were a large number of other success stories as well. Rao (1993) reported on the progress of the literacy movement in four regions of south India, namely the UT of Pondicherry, Pasumpon Muthuramalinga Therar and Puddukotai districts of Tamil Nadu, and Nizamabad district of Andhra Pradesh. While hers is a field report, it captures the different textures of the literacy movement in each of the four areas. In Pondicherry, the literacy movement had

raised people's expectations about the benefits of literacy. They had begun to expect it to provide solutions to all their problems and hasten the pace of development programmes. However, government policy had brought the PL programme to a virtual standstill. The party and the government in power in Pondicherry saw a campaign that generated mass awareness and sought to make the poorest sections conscious of their rights as being dangerous. The Pondicherry experience showed how a system of governance that has no ideological commitment to educating people and empowering them, can thwart such educational initiatives.

Pasumpon district was the first district in Tamil Nadu to implement the TLC. The programme was developed on the basis of lessons learnt from the Pondicherry experience. Thus, the TLC in Pasumpon district 'concentrated on and developed a network of participatory grassroots village *panchayat* and district level structures to ensure the continuity and sustainability of the movement' (see Rao 1993). A noteworthy feature of the Pasumpon literacy campaign was the programme to train women in karate. The training helped women realize their own strength and lose many of their fears and physical inhibitions. According to Rao (1993), Puddukotai was a further refinement of the TLC. A hallmark of the strategy in Puddukotai was the link the movement for literacy made with the lives and livelihood issues of the people right from the beginning. This provided a constant source of motivation to the learners and, as mentioned earlier, facilitated close cooperation between the district administration, the full-time literacy activists, and the learners.

In Nizamabad district of Andhra Pradesh, the TLC took a different form. Since this is a Naxalite area, the TLC could not take off until the Naxal groups (revolutionary communist groups owing their allegiance to Marxist–Leninist ideas,) announced they would support the programme as it was pro-poor. The TLC created great enthusiasm among the poor and amongst women, especially Muslim women. Celebrations, competitions, and other programmes were arranged at frequent intervals. Various activities such as health camps, cultural programmes, and radio talks provided people the space for expression and social interaction.

Saldanha (1995) has drawn from his experience of conducting evaluation studies in various districts of Maharashtra and Goa. In doing so, once again the unique features of the campaign in different districts have become discernible. According to him, the Nanded district campaign in 1992 was marked by a high degree of social mobilization, the involvement of voluntary organizations in creating an environment for literacy, and designing of innovative supplementary reading materials. The Ratnagiri campaign was able to involve a cross-section of voluntary organizations in creating an environment for literacy and evolving an innovative combination of training and monitoring systems. The literacy drive of the Committee of Resource Organizations (CORO), an NGO working in metropolitan Mumbai, was marked by major involvement of activists from local communities.

Saldanha (1995) then attempted to contextualize the literacy campaigns of Maharasthra and averred that while the selected literacy campaigns of the state drew inspiration from earlier social reform movements, especially among Dalits, they lacked the intensive involvement of the cadre of activists of the trade union and of the peasant movements of Kerala and West Bengal. At the same time, the political economy of Maharashtra was different from that of some of the semi-feudal northern states. The midway position of Maharashtra, according to him, thus provided a useful index of what to expect from literacy campaigns at national level. His study showed that as many as 66.4 per cent of the learners in the selected districts were women. In Goa, women constituted an even higher 81.5 per cent of the learners. Interestingly, the high percentage of women's participation in the literacy campaigns was a uniform pattern across the country. Saldanha's study also showed that in addition to women, the literacy campaigns were able to mobilize the weaker sections and the economically disadvantaged in a major way.

Reflections on the Experiences of the Early 1990s

According to Krishna Kumar, a BGVS activist at the national level, there were several reasons for the success of the TLCs in the initial years.[1] The transformational aspect of literacy had been missing in the earlier literacy programmes. The beginning of TLCs was also the beginning of a new perception about literacy among the masses. As a result, there was growing realization that literacy was not just about reading the word but about transforming the world. The initial success of the TLCs was due to social mobilization becoming an instrument of social change. The mobilization strategies included the forms common people were familiar with. Because of the rich oral culture in rural areas, the *kala jathas* in the form of songs, dance, street plays, became an effective means of communication. The content of these *kala jathas* was not just to do with literacy. Rather, the *kala jathas* dealt with issues of poverty, of oppression, of caste discrimination, of lack of employment opportunities, of gender inequity, and so on. The language used was that which people understood. In places, where

people were encouraged to add on, to contribute, they did so in a creative and enthusiastic manner. According to him, interesting social processes took place in areas where the campaigns were successful. Thousands of learners sat with the literacy instructors and literally hundreds of meetings took place. In villages, it was not uncommon to see 50 to 100 classes going on at the same time in the evenings. Whether adults acquired literacy skills was not all important. The sheer social act of people coming together was an important social phenomenon and had electrifying effect.

Such a massive mobilization resulted in people's initiatives of various kinds. Setting up of cooperative societies in some districts of Maharashtra, of nursery schools in some districts of Assam or the *pani bachao andolan* (Save Water Campaign) again in Maharashtra, are examples of the transformative potential of the campaign as people began to participate in it and developed a sense of ownership over it. Social mobilization was, in effect, expanding the concept of literacy in the minds of the people.

Even the manner in which the youth were mobilized and the spirit of voluntarism that the campaign was able to tap was remarkable. It was not since Independence that youth had been mobilized on such a large scale. This only showed that there was still a lot of idealism in people to work for the underprivileged people in the country. Unfortunately, the National Literacy Mission's (NLM) insistence on evaluating the literacy campaigns and focusing only on numbers made literate, quashed the spirit of voluntarism in people, and left them feeling disenchanted and frustrated.

One of the problems TLCs faced was that in districts that had had successful literacy campaigns, a PL programme should immediately have followed. But since that did not happen, people felt let down and betrayed. They even felt that TLCs had made them false promises.

Had the TLCs been perceived as dynamic and ever evolving, even the Collector-centred model that was followed initially could have changed. Likewise, the role of the ZSS could have changed and the same body could have become a resource agency. Unfortunately, this did not happen. The TLC model was considered replicable without any variation. Boundaries were drawn and a framework established. There was little 'space' left for people to participate.

The early 1990s were heady years, for the BGVS influence on TLCs prevailed. As news started trickling about the successes of the literacy campaigns, pressure started building to expand TLCs rapidly across the states. As district Collectors started vying with one another in preparation of district plans and in getting funding from the NLM, the processes for mobilizing people's

---

[1] Personal communication to the author.

participation got short-changed. In a bid to achieve quick results, it became easier for the Collectors to galvanize the government machinery and to put pressure on the education department, particularly on schoolteachers and students, to volunteer their services for the literacy campaigns. The near exclusive emphasis on literacy attainment in quantitative terms, and measurement of the same through standardized tests, showed that the TLCs had lost their momentum and that the process of bureaucratization of the campaigns had set in.

It is important to understand the politics of evaluation to realize how it exacerbated the process of bureaucratization. The NLM had established the system of external evaluation as it was thought this would lend objectivity and credibility to the literacy campaigns. With the declaration of Ernakulam as a fully literate district, a norm was established for achieving 'total' literacy declaration as a major outcome at the end of the literacy phase of the campaign. This led to frustration among the campaign organizers and to deception with regard to literacy achievements. Campaign districts were categorized into 'A,' 'B', 'C', and 'D' categories on the basis of their literacy attainments, and funds for continuance of the campaigns were determined by this classification. The pilot phase undertaken by the Delhi *Saksharta Samiti* was regarded a 'failure' because despite the successes in mobilization and in eliciting people's participation, the overall literacy achievement was considered poor, and hence, the campaign was slotted in category 'D' and denied funding for continuance. The compulsions of getting validation from literacy evaluation were so great that district after district vied to be declared totally literate and to be in the political limelight. The Arun Ghosh Committee that was constituted in 1993 to review the literacy campaigns, has pointed out to the deleterious effects of such evaluation studies that only encouraged falsification of data to the point that TLCs lost their credibility in the eyes of the public at large.

SOCIAL MOBILIZATION IN LITERACY CAMPAIGNS AFTER 1993: UNRESOLVED DILEMMAS

The recent award of UNESCO Noma Literacy Prize to the NLM (1999) notwithstanding, and apart from sporadic success stories reported from districts such as Dumka in Bihar or Bilaspur in Madhya Pradesh, the fact remains that at present, TLCs have lost the momentum they had gathered from 1989 to 1992. While it is difficult to pinpoint any one single cause for the decline of TLCs, a variety of factors could be identified to explain why the mobilization strategies of TLCs no longer have the same impact. This section attempts to identify what went wrong with TLCs after 1993.

The ideological underpinnings of the TLCs were a unifying vision to those who participated in the campaign in the initial years. As a result of shared understanding, the role of the bureaucracy underwent a change. Collectors became accessible to a majority of common people, probably for the first time. Voices of poor people were heard. District-level officials addressed their development concerns. The campaign thus demanded social activism from the bureaucracy—contrary to the training they have always received of being dispassionate and neutral civil servants. With unprecedented and hurried expansion of TLCs, the process of consensus building and of ensuring a shared understanding among bureaucrats through a constant capacity-building effort got short-changed. Consequently, civil servants started perceiving TLCs as a routine government programme that had set fixed targets that had to be achieved over a period of time. According to Ramachandran (1999), 'The literacy campaign was designed for the exceptionally committed or exceptionally ambitious civil servant. It was beyond the reach of routiners, howsoever competent.'

Bureaucracy was responsible for the slowing down of the TLCs for other reasons as well. The literacy campaigns injected a certain dynamism and the will to change among those who participated in them, but the campaign managers and administrators sitting in Delhi and in state headquarters were unable to respond to that enthusiasm and hence belied the hopes of thousands of people. Literacy classes could not be sustained everywhere and PL and continuing education (CE) programmes were a non-starter, thereby greatly undermining the impact of social mobilization. According to Ramachandran (1999), 'Shoddy planning, red tape and the unfortunate lack of continuity in the policies and practices of the government (as represented by senior officers) led to the demise of an otherwise exciting process.' The bureaucratic culture of 'undo what my predecessor has done' was also responsible for the reverses suffered by TLCs. The literacy campaigns have thus become 'a story of missed opportunities.'

Replicating the TLC model in district after district of the country, irrespective of context and socio-economic development, has also been regarded as one of the reasons for TLCs not doing well largely in the Hindi belt. Saldanhas's study (1995) had shown that the relatively underdeveloped region with a low literacy rate, which formed the hinterland of areas of intensive agriculture, of a market economy, and of the metropolitan region, generally responded well to the campaign approach. The districts included Nanded, Latur, and Ratnagiri in Maharashtra. According to him, national-level data suggested that states that had had a history of social reform movements, peasant organizations, and working class struggles such as Kerala and West Bengal, had also responded effectively to the campaign approach. This was due to the involvement of party cadres, activists from social and mass organizations, and a relatively homogenous political ideology. In the Hindi-belt, on the other hand, the class, caste, and gender divide and semi-feudal relations in agriculture, created a barrier to the literacy campaigns and their mobilizational efforts. Literacy campaigns also did not fare too well in metropolitan cities and in high literacy districts with a high degree of urbanization. Due to high literacy levels, particularly among urban male population, and heterogenous population with varied occupational patterns, the literacy campaigns in metropolitan cities and in high literacy districts did not evoke as much enthusiasm and support as they did in backward districts in the non-Hindi belt. Saldanha (1995) thus concluded that while the essential features of campaign mobilization might be applicable in diverse regions, suitable modifications in the operationalization of the approach would be required on the basis of political economy and the historical context of each region. Quoting Graff who wrote 'there is no one path destined to succeed in the achievement of mass literacy', Saldanha had cautioned that it would be disastrous to uniformly and mechanically apply the so-called Kerala model of literacy campaigns to different regions. What would now seem to be a prophetic warning, Saldanha had anticipated that attempts to short-circuit the essential features of the campaign approach would result in falling back on the strategy of a typical government programme with identified beneficiaries, targets, and declaration of achievements in given periods of time.

A question is always raised whether a government-sponsored programme that uses radical discourse (as TLCs certainly did), can in fact work in the interest of the poor. Given the class and caste interests of the state, how much space can it provide if social mobilization of the masses in the true sense of the term begins to take place. The Nellore experience showed that as the anti-arrack agitation spread from village to village and engulfed the entire district, and later even spread to the rest of the state, the government took certain repressive measures. In districts where the movement was weak, the police swung into action and mercilessly quelled organized action on part of women's groups. The government then withdrew the textbook that contained what it termed, the 'objectionable' lesson that had sparked off the agitation. The functionaries who were in the forefront of the agitation were summarily sent back to their parent departments. Following the anti-arrack agitation, a savings movement was born. By the end of February 1996, about 7000 small thrift and savings groups had been formed across the district and these groups called 'Podupulakshmi groups' had saved around Rs 100 million (see Dighe 1998). Women of the Podupulakshmi groups exuded a new confidence. Earlier, women had found it difficult to save money at home. Membership of the Podupulakshmi groups had helped solve that problem. Women felt empowered as they realized they could stand on their own feet, that their economic dependence on the male members in the family had diminished. 'Our money is our own right now,' they said. The government's response to this development was the gradual takeover of the Podupulakshmi groups by officials of the District Rural Development Agency. Later the government decided to create a women's bank. According to Ramachandran (1999), 'Women who had got used to handling their own money and who had experienced the power of decentralised decision making were reluctant to hand over their savings to an impersonal banking system. The savings movement lost its momentum and gradually petered out.' Nellore's experience with the savings movement shows how the state has ways of co-opting initiatives in which large-scale mobilization takes place. Shatrugna (1998) therefore cautioned that while the government might ignite a movement initially, its class and caste interests would not permit it to support it for long. He concurred with Banerjee (1993) who said, 'Those social activists who seek to use "democratic space" in State-patronized programmes, will have to develop an autonomous interventionist potential that can sustain their activities even if, or when the "space" is withdrawn by the government from them.'

CONCLUSION

In retrospect, one can say that one of the major problems TLCs encountered was the inherent contradiction in the conceptualization of literacy itself. This tension can best be understood if we look at the two models of literacy as defined by Brian Street (1984). One is the 'autonomous' model that assumes a single type of literacy, which is 'neutral' and merely a 'technical skill'. 'The model assumes a single direction in which literacy development can be traced and associated with "progress," "civilisation," "individual liberty," and "social mobility".... It isolates literacy as an independent variable and then claims to be able to study its consequences'. The alternative model is the 'ideological' model that places literacy in a cultural, socio-economic, and political context and emphasizes the ideological and political nature of literacy practice. Being a government-sponsored programme, what prevailed eventually in case of the TLCs was the 'autonomous' model of literacy. In places where some space was provided for the 'ideological' model, there was immediate opposition and censure. This happened in Pondicherry when during the PL phase, the Chief Minister objected to a song in a primer that said, 'Freedom for the country, but why poverty for us?' Key officials who supported the programme were transferred and the voluntary agency which had implemented the TLC was delinked from the PL phase. Experiences from Kerala and Nellore also show that the democratic space that the state had provided quickly shrank when its class and caste interests were threatened. Banerjee (1993) and Saxena (1993) had raised questions about the consequences of regarding literacy as a technical skill and presenting it as a solution to very complex socio-economic and political problems.

As has been noted earlier, the successful campaigns reached out to women, the weaker sections, and the economically disadvantaged classes of society in a major way. They succeeded in penetrating the large politico-economic structures of deprivation due to consensus for literacy that was mobilized through the environment building programmes. However, they failed in changing those structures in any major way due to lack of concurrent processes of organization of the oppressed. While the campaigns generally succeeded in creating an organizational structure of the literate in favour of the majority of the illiterate, they failed to organize the latter towards their wider socio-economic interests. This was an important issue given that the organization of the illiterates was a necessary condition for sustaining the literacy skills that had been acquired (see Saldanha 1995). Except for women's self-help groups, a conscious attempt towards organization building was not made to sustain the momentum generated due to social mobilization. Rao (1993), Banerjee (1993), and Saxena (1993) had anticipated that without mass organizations of the poor and without linking the literacy movement with a larger programme of socio-economic transformation, the literacy campaign could not be sustained.

Presently, the TLC phase is officially over. The NLM is now providing funding only to the PL and CE programmes. So far about 250 PL programmes have been sanctioned by the government as well as about 60 CE programmes. Despite claims about success of the literacy movement, the fact remains that the earlier vision, commitment, and drive that characterized the TLCs are missing. The PL and CE programmes are perceived as government programmes. While there is mention of 'community participation' and 'people's movement', the mere pressure of utilizing funds earmarked for the programme has resulted in the ritualization of the literacy programme. Even the space to attempt an honest stock-taking has shrunk. There is a tendency to hark back to the successes of past campaigns on the one hand. On the other, the process of bureaucratic stranglehold on the literacy programme is increasing. The TLC experience has shown how an educational programme that leans too heavily on leadership by government for its implementation, monitoring, and evaluation can become uninspiring and eventually get routinized.

Bhola (1984) in his memorandum to educational planners and policy makers has enumerated five prerequisites for the conduct of successful mass literacy campaigns. According to him, irrespective of the different labels applied to the political arrangements in various countries, these conditions are absolutely essential. These are the following:

• a political ideology that is humanistic, egalitarian, and democratic;

• a conception of the role of literacy that is not merely economic;

• the articulation of the political will to eradicate illiteracy;

• the ability to mobilize the resources of both the state and the people;

• a commitment to structural reform on behalf of the people.

The initial euphoria about and the subsequent decline of the TLCs can be understood when it is realized that in India these basic prerequisites for the success of the literacy campaigns were not always clearly articulated either in the policies of the government or in the implementation processes. While the resources of the state and of the people were mobilized to some extent during the early 1990s, the other prerequisites were either present to some extent or were not present at all. The ideological underpinnings of the TLCs were thus not clearly enunciated. As a result, the conceptual understanding of literacy shrank until it was reduced to merely a technical skill of reading and writing. The political will to eradicate illiteracy wavered and there was never any uniform commitment on the part of the government to do so. On the other hand, there was never any policy to bring about structural reform on behalf of the people. The uneven implementation of TLCs was, therefore, inevitable.

REFERENCES

Athreya, V. and Sheelarani Chunkath (1996). *Literacy and Empowerment*, Sage, New Delhi.

Banerjee, S. (1993). 'Revising the National Literacy Mission'. *Economic and Political Weekly*, vol. 28, no. 25, 19 June.

Bhola, H. (1984). *Campaigning for Literacy*, UNESCO, Paris.

————— (1988). *World Trends and Issues in Adult Education*. International Bureau of Education, Educational Science, UNESCO.

Dighe, A. (1998). 'A Postscript to Literacy as Liberation: The Nellore Experience.' In Shukla, S. and R. Kaul, (eds), *Education, Development and Underdevelopment*. Sage, New Delhi.

Ramachandran, V. (1999). 'Adult Education: A Tale of Empowerment Denied.' *Economic and Political Weekly*, vol. 34, no. 15, 10 April.

Rao, N. (1993). 'Total Literacy Campaigns: A Field Report.' *Economic and Political Weekly*, vol. 28, no. 19, 8 May.

Saldanha, D. (1995). 'Literacy Campaigns in Maharashtra and Goa: Issues, Trends and Direction.' *Economic and Political Weekly*, vol. 30, no. 20, 20 May.

Saxena, S. (1993). 'Limits and Consequences of Literacy Programmes.' *Economic and Political Weekly*, vol. 28, nos 8 and 9, 20–7 February.

————— (1999). 'A Study of the Literacy Campaign in Ajmer District of Rajasthan.' (Mimeo)

Shatrugna, M. (1998). 'Literacy as Liberation: The Nellore Experience.' In Shukla, S. and R. Kaul (eds), *Education, Development and Underdevelopment*. Sage, New Delhi.

Street, B. (1984). *Literacy in Theory and Practice*. Cambridge University Press, Cambridge.

19

Education and the Status of Women

Vimala Ramachandran

What is the relationship between women's status and women's education? It is universally acknowledged that in societies where women are valued *as women*, they seem to have greater access to education. On the other hand, it has been seen that when women are educated, there is significant improvement in their status within the family and in society. While education can play a positive interventionist role in improving the status of women, the fact remains that low status, coupled with rigid socio-cultural practices, denies women this basic right. It is apparent that education alone does not always lead to higher status. Experience of income-generation programmes has demonstrated that enhancing the income of women alone is also not enough. The critical issue is that of control over income. Similarly, the mere enactment of progressive legislation on property rights, rape, domestic violence, sex selective abortion, 30 per cent reservation in *panchayati raj* institutions and the like remains ineffective in the absence of proactive mobilization to ensure its implementation. The presence of oppressive practices, discrimination, abuse, and violence in all regions of the country and in almost every social class and community points towards a much deeper malaise in Indian society.

At the root of the debate on status is the notion of power. Women's powerlessness stems from their lack of access to and control over resources—material, human, and intangible.[1] This unequal gender relation manifests itself in different ways. Women's work and women's contribution to the economy are either undervalued or outright dismissed. The way work is defined devalues women's contribution to the survival and maintenance of the household and to family occupation (land- cattle-home-based work). As women's work is not 'valued' in

monitory terms, they are perceived as being a drain on family and societal resources. Their skill, knowledge, and abilities are also undervalued. While Dalit and other socially and economically disadvantaged communities in India also experience this kind of powerlessness, there is another dimension to women's powerlessness. Women's reproductive role that ensures the survival of communities is distorted. They are portrayed as being weak and thereby 'dependent' on men. This kind of powerlessness makes women vulnerable. The prevalence of family and societal violence against women is today acknowledged as a sensitive indicator of women's status. Box 19.1 clearly indicates that removal of this degradation and devaluation tops women's list of priorities.

Why have these unequal power relations remained unchallenged for thousands of years? Here we move into another dimension of social organization. Traditionally, women's mobility has been restricted; as a result their knowledge base is also limited. Lack of access to education, mobility, and contact with the larger world has confined women to their immediate environments. Their knowledge base is weak and what they do know (about food, health, cattle, plants, herbs, illness, and the like) is undervalued. The sheer business of survival takes a heavy toll. Education is not perceived as a priority in their daily battle for food, water, fuel, and subsistence chores for the survival of their family. Poor women are caught in a vicious situation where social isolation that stems from lack of mobility and access to information and knowledge beyond their immediate present alienates them from decision-making processes within the family and in the society, which reinforces their isolation. In a social milieu where women are not valued as human beings, they perceive themselves as victims, even of well-intentioned schemes and programmes that purport to address their health, education, employment, and

[1] This framework has been developed in three works: Kabeer (1994), Murty (1994), and Batliwala *et al.* (1998).

Box 19.1

The Essence of Development

A small group of women had come together for a training programme. Talking about the purpose of the workshop, one of the trainers asked: 'Is there something you yearn for?' After some thought, one landless woman answered: 'I want to live in dignity, I do not want to be reduced to a state of helplessness where there is no respect for me as a human being—yes, that's what I want, I want to live in dignity.' This statement left many speechless and forced the group to talk about the essence of development. To come to grips with the essence of what development means to ordinary people, they decided to play a game. They imagined some divine power had given them ten boons and they were supposed to prepare their list in one hour. This is what they asked:

- To live in dignity.
- To able to meet basic needs like clean water, fuel, food for subsistence (two meals a day), employment/income and roofs over our heads.
- Freedom from violence, tensions, and war.
- Justice—a society where right and wrong are recognized.
- Self-sufficiency, not to be dependent for essentials on the outside world.
- Opportunity to know the world outside (mobility, exposure, information, and education).
- A society where every child experiences childhood, where children go to school.
- Equity between men/women and between people.
- Clean environment.
- Good health.
- A government that is within the reach of the people and a say in decisions which affect our lives.

At the top of their list was dignity. The daily struggle for water, fuel, minor forest produce, fodder, and a small daily wage in addition to endless household chores, violence at the hands of drunken husbands, fear of abuse and taunts of being parasites, strips ordinary citizens of this country of their dignity. This lucid list of demands of a mythical divine power tells more than all the great books and theories of development put together. This gut-level response of poor women provides the conceptual framework to understand the issue of women's status and empowerment.

Sources: Author's field notes, 1989–91.

family planning needs. Ultimately, poor women are trapped in their own low self-perception (see Box 19.2).

And the prevailing unequal gender relations perpetuate this perception. Historically, social reformers and radical

Box 19.2

Women's Status and Education

Why has education been inaccessible to rural women for centuries? Part of the answer lies on the supply side—there is clearly a lack of adequate and sensitive educational efforts to mobilize rural women, involve them in the educational process and help them reflect critically on their lives. The other side of the problem lies in women's own inability and lack of will to demand education and to assert themselves. One can begin to understand this inability by a simple analysis of the socio-economic milieu in which a majority of poor rural women exist:

- Caught up in daily struggles for fuel, fodder, and wage, they have no time for anything else.
- Their well-defined social roles and norms of interaction leave little room for education and critical thinking.
- Going about their chores in isolation, they are unable to share their experience of oppression with other women, and are therefore unable to tap their collective strength.
- They are denied access to information and alienated from decision-making processes. Even when they relate to government schemes, they do so as passive recipients.
- Victimized by schemes that purport to address their health, education, and employment needs, they are forced to view their environment with fear and suspicion.
- Systematically robbed of their confidence to think and learn without fear of failure, they are subsequently paralysed by their own low self-image.

As a result of these factors, women are caught in a vicious, self-perpetuating cycle; their inability to educate themselves perpetuates the stereotype that education is irrelevant to women.

Sources: GoI (1989).

movements created environment for change. But in the absence of any social movement, women in India continue to be trapped in the cycle of poverty, powerlessness, and low status.

In India, we are all aware that we can never realize the goal of education for all (EFA) unless we are willing to squarely address the gender dimension of education planning and administration.

MEASURING 'WOMEN'S STATUS'[2]

Educational planners in India have tried a wide range of strategies to bridge the gap between men and women. But, fifty years after Independence we are still grappling with unequal access. The National Policy on Education (NPE) (1986) stated that the government would use education as a means to achieve gender equity and as a tool to correct centuries of discrimination. Yet translating this very radical policy into implementable strategies and activities has been a very difficult task. This is because women's status cannot be altered by the actions of one arm of the government. Education alone cannot become the magic wand. Only coordinated action at several fronts could enable women break out of the vicious cycle of poverty and powerlessness.

Sex Ratio

Box 19.3 and Table 19.1 examine the sex ratio in India, a very sensitive index of women's status in society.

TABLE 19.1
Child Sex Ratio (0–6) in Select 'Red Alert' Districts of India

District	Sex ratio
Bhind, Madhya Pradesh	850 per 1000 boys
Jaisalmer, Rajasthan	851 per 1000 boys
Kaithal, Haryana	854 per 1000 boys
Jind, Haryana	855 per 1000 boys
Salem, Tamil Nadu	859 per 1000 boys

Source: Census 1991.

Women, Work, and their Access to and Control Over Productive Assets and Resources

It is said that women do three-fifths of the world's work, earn one-tenth of the world's income, and own one-hundredth of the world's assets. Women work, but their work is not visible in statistics. The Census of India records that only 27 per cent women in rural areas and 9 per cent in urban areas are formally in the workforce! There are staggering differences across states—while in Andhra Pradesh and Maharashtra 43 and 47 per cent women are reported as being in the workforce in rural areas; Punjab records a mere 4 per cent. As seen in Table 19.2, a clearer picture seems to emerge when data on agricultural labourers and cultivators in different states are examined. The number of women and girl cultivators is large and growing.

BOX 19.3
Sex Ratio

This is perhaps the most sensitive index of women's status. It is determined by a wide range of factors linked to women's access to public and private resources. Sex ratio is an outcome indicator that is a result of higher mortality of girl children in the 0–5 age group, neglect and discrimination in food, health care, and physical well-being at all stages of life. In recent times technology-assisted female foeticide is practised in some pockets—despite prevailing legislation banning the use of diagnostic tests to determine the sex of the child. Similarly, the prevalence of infanticide in some districts sent shock waves throughout the country. There is a temptation to simplify this complex problem. As Drèze and Sen (1995, 143–4) point out:

To begin with, we should deal with two misunderstandings that arise from time to time in popular discussion of the issue of low female–male ratios in India.... First, it is sometimes thought that the main cause of the problem is some phenomenon of hidden female infanticide, not captured in reported death statistics. In fact census figures on female–male ratios are quite consistent with what one would predict based on (1) standard female–male ratios at birth of about 95, and (2) independently recorded age- and sex-specific mortality rates.... It is possible, of course, that recorded child deaths include some female infant deaths due to infanticide, which are reported by parents as due to some other causes. But anthropological evidence suggests that female infanticide, when it does occur, takes place very soon after birth. The bulk of excessive female mortality in childhood, on the other hand, occurs after the age of one, with a less unequal pattern in the first year.... The force of excess female mortality, therefore, lies in mortality rates in age groups beyond female infanticide. The female disadvantage in these age groups is itself due to a well-documented practice of preferential treatment of boys and neglect of female children in intra-household allocation. There is, indeed, considerable direct evidence of neglect of female children in terms of health care, nutrition, and related needs, particularly in North India.

---

[2] This section lists nine indicators that can be used to measure women's status. It has been adapted from Murty (1994), Kabeer (1994), and Batliwala (1998). Recent data have also been used to highlight issues and also point towards gaps in existing database on women.

TABLE 19.2
Women and Girls in Workforce (%)

Select states	Cultivators and agricultural labourers who were women and girls		Women and girls in the workforce who were cultivators or agricultural labourers	
	Cultivators	Agricultural labourers	Cultivators	Agricultural labourers
Andhra Pradesh	29.73	51.13	22.37	60.33
Arunachal Pradesh	50.45	36.27	83.78	5.12
Bihar	11.62	25.59	31.60	59.29
Haryana	11.70	12.81	46.64	25.04
Kerala	10.38	32.28	5.56	36.09
Maharashtra	38.75	53.02	39.07	43.69
Orissa	10.60	34.90	25.84	55.06
Punjab	1.21	4.45	8.72	24.36
Rajasthan	23.16	35.80	69.34	18.23
Tamil Nadu	25.58	47.17	20.92	53.79
West Bengal	7.19	19.42	16.23	37.88
India	20.07	38.12	34.57	44.24

Sources: Census 1991.

Unfortunately we do not have much information on ownership. Women work on land, in looms, take care of cattle and other family assets—but they rarely own them. Similarly, women rarely seem to own the houses they live in; as a result they are always vulnerable. As Agarwal (1994) points out:

> Indeed while the link between property and class relations has been well established in political economy, the link between property and gender relations has remained largely unexamined. Land has been and continues to be the most significant form of property in rural South Asia. It is a critical determinant of economic well-being, social status and political power. However there is substantial evidence that economic resources in the hands of male household members often do not benefit female members in equal degree. Independent ownership of such resources, especially land, can thus be of critical importance in promoting the well being and empowerment of women. [Agarwal 1994]

Material assets like housing, land, tools of production are critical to the survival of poor households. And within the household, women's access to and control over them determines their ability to lead a life of dignity. It also reduces their vulnerability. Developing indicators for ownership and control over assets and resources could be explored. Government programmes for housing, land distribution, and loans for acquiring other productive assets could insist on either sole or joint ownership, thereby safeguarding women's access. Ensuring easy access to credit through self-help groups, credit groups, and the like have made significant difference to women's access to productive assets. Needless to add, other indicators may have to be developed to measure extent of control over these assets.

Women's Access to Public Resources: Forests, Village Commons, Water, Sanitation, Education, and Health

In every democratic society some basic resources are guaranteed by the state. Public resources range from access to village commons, forest produce, water, and fuel at one end of the spectrum to education, training, and health care at the other. Women's inability to access these resources has a profound impact on status. It is well known that lack of basic health care services for pregnant women is responsible for high infant, child, and maternal mortality rates in many parts of the country. It is indeed shocking that only 24.5 per cent of all deliveries are conducted in institutions and trained professionals in India attend only 24.3 per cent deliveries. Regional variations are significant, with Kerala topping the list at 92.3 per cent deliveries in institutions and Rajasthan coming last with deliveries conducted by untrained persons being as high as 75.4 per cent in urban areas and 80 per cent in rural areas (see SRS, GoI 1993). Only 1.3 per cent of India's GDP is spent on health and 88 per cent of pregnant women in the 15–49 age group are anaemic. In 1993 maternal mortality rate was estimated to be as high as 570 per 100,000 live births and infant mortality rate in 1996 as 73 per 1000 live births (Haq 1998) (see Table 19.3 for pregnancy-related death in rural India).

The situation in terms of access to safe water, sanitation, and housing is equally grim. According to *Human Development in South Asia 1998* only 63 per cent of people in India have access to safe water and 29 per cent to sanitation. Even if women technically have access to safe water (piped water, hand pumps, tube wells), the amount of time spent collecting and storing water is quite significant. The situation of Dalit women who are denied access to water sources in their vicinities because of the continuing practice of untouchability is rarely factored in. The experience of organizations working with rural and urban poor women reveals that almost 2–4 hours a day are spent on managing household water resources.

TABLE 19.3
Percentage Distribution of Female Deaths Related to Childbirth and Pregnancy by Specific Cause, Rural India 1990 and 1994

Specific cause	1990	1994
Bleeding and Pregnancy and Puerperium	23.70	23.70
Anaemia	19.40	19.30
Toxaemia	15.20	13.10
Puerperal sepsis	08.10	10.60
Abortion	11.80	12.60
Malposition of child	07.10	06.40
Not classified	14.70	14.20
Total	100	100

Source: Registrar General of India 1994, quoted in GoI (1997).

Women's access (or lack of it) to public resources determines a range of social indicators, like literacy, infant and child mortality, and malnutrition. All these indicators are closely linked, one impacting and influencing the other. In the last thirty years the government has accepted these interlinkages. For example, one of the most popular correlations made in recent times is that between female literacy, fertility, child survival, and child nutrition. As a result of intensive advocacy by women's organizations, the government decided to shift the focus of the Health and Family Welfare programme from method-specific contraceptive targets to a more integrated reproductive and child health approach. Almost every development department of the government provides for formation of women's groups at village level (or in urban settlements) to ensure convergence of different social sector services. Similarly, many development programmes have tried to explore the gender dimension of access. For example, in the last ten years water and sanitation programmes, joint forest management programmes, and primary education projects have tried to provide for the training of women to ensure they become active members of village-level user committees. *Pani panchayats*, village education committees, and *van suraksha samitis* are expected to ensure at least 30 per cent female membership.

Women's access to public resources could be assessed using the following indicators.

• Education: literacy rates over a period, the percentage of boys and girls finishing primary school, middle school, and high school (Board examinations), age-specific school attendance rates of boys and girls and percentage of men and women in post secondary higher education by type of education are indicators of the spread of education. Calculating the gender gap in each of these and plotting the trend over a period of time will enable us to understand the extent of women's access to education.

• Health: Age-specific mortality rate of men and women in the 15–35 age group with causes of death will help us capture a wide range of health-related issues including maternal mortality and death due to unnatural causes (dowry/domestic violence related). Under-5 mortality rate of boys and girls is again a very sensitive index of how much society values its girls and their access to nutrition and health care. The percentage of sterilizations performed on men and women is again an effective indicator of women's status, and taken together with family size and number of girls and boys in the family it can give us an insight into the value society places on women.

• Water and sanitation: Access to safe water and availability of water source by type, distance, and seasonal variations are again an effective indicator of women's access to public resources. Access to proper water disposal systems and toilets is again a sensitive index.

• Percentage of women and men treated in hospitals and clinics, by illness (with the exception of deliveries, abortion, and related problems): In the last twenty years micro studies have revealed gender differences in access to healthcare services. Women seem to have less access to hospital- clinic-based care and greater access to traditional healers and local medical (traditional and rural medical practitioners) practitioners. Girls are often not brought to clinics and hospitals at an appropriate time, with the family first resorting to home-based care, local practitioners, and finally (when it is perhaps too late) to hospitals. On the other hand, son preference in India seems to positively influence health-seeking behaviour for boys

Control Over Labour and Access to Income

Ask any woman what she urgently needs, the first thing that will come to her mind will be employment and income—even when she is already overworked and is shouldering the entire burden of family subsistence work. Innumerable micro studies and life histories have shown that when the family is on the verge of starvation, women take on the responsibility of ensuring survival. Poor women will tell you that children ask them for food, not their fathers. At another level, evidence has also shown that when the income of women goes up there is immediate improvement in the health, nutrition, and education status of children. This does not always hold true when the income of men goes up. Recent reports and documents on the anti-liquor movement in different parts of the country have drawn attention to male alcoholism and family survival. Therefore, women's control over their own labour and the income earned by them is a sensitive index of women's status.

Indicators that help us measure control over labour and income are as follows:

• Women's participation in the labour market: this is captured in work participation rates (main and marginal workers, formal/informal sector/home based, etc.).

• Percentage of male and female non-farm workers among main workers and percentage of male and female agricultural labourers among marginal and subsidiary workers enabling us to capture the economic status of women.

• Agricultural wage rates of men and women and non-farm wage rates of men and women capturing gender differentials.

• Percentage distribution of adult wage earners by duration of employment disaggregated by sex could enrich the previous indicator.

• Women's access to education and skill training.

• Women's access to credit.

Women's Control over their Bodies

One of the most glaring dimensions of gender inequality is women's lack of control over their own bodies. Women's experience of gender injustice is closely linked to a range of body-related issues from age of marriage to access to contraception, abortion, and healthcare: when and whom they marry, when and how many children they have, access to contraception, reluctance of men to take responsibility for their sexuality, sexual abuse, and violence,

and above all the vulnerability of women to sexually transmitted infections including HIV and AIDS. Box 19.4 tells the story in women's own words.

Till recently the only data that influenced policy making were contraceptive prevalence rates. The entire might of India's Health and Family Welfare Programme was geared towards achieving contraceptive targets. The International Conference on Population and Development, Cairo 1994, signalled a major departure in this regard. The Government of India took the initiative to do away with method-specific targets and adopted a more holistic reproductive and child health approach. As a result, today we are more open to looking at a broader range of indicators to determine women's status which include:

• availability of and utilization of ANC and PNC services;

• percentage of institutional deliveries and deliveries assisted by trained personnel;

• contraceptive prevalence rates—spacing methods, male and female sterilization, and abortion;

• fertility rate;

• percentage of male and female sterilizations performed over a period of time and trends thereof;

• prevalence of abortion and resultant mortality and morbidity—access to safe abortion facilities;

• maternal and infant mortality rates;

• recorded numbers of domestic and sexual violence—including rape, sexual abuse, 'eve teasing', and other forms of gender violence. The number of convictions could supplement this information.

Physical Mobility

It is quite surprising that until recently women's physical mobility has not been used as an indicator of status. Mobility is a rather tricky issue. Government programmes

---

BOX 19.4

Women's Control over their Bodies

You ask me about my health—where do I start? I am ill because I do not get adequate food, adequate sleep, and the dust from the stone quarry settles in my lungs. I do not have water to keep clean. My children are exposed to the cold, the heat, and to the rain. My husband gets drunk and beats me and I am bruised all over. I work from dawn to dusk. I produced more children than what my emaciated body could handle—yet I fear how many will actually survive. When I seek doctors, they do not listen to my story. They give me some tablets that make me sick. He never explains what is wrong. When I complain of exhaustion, he says women complain too much. The only time they seek me out is to persuade me to get sterilized. You still want to know what ails me—look at my life, it is the cause of my illness. [Stone quarry worker on the outskirts of Delhi]

From the day I got married it is my husband who takes all decisions. I do not have the freedom or the courage to tell him that I do not want any more children. He wants at least three sons.... Babies do not fall into our wombs on their own, why then are we women chased like animals? Why can't the nurse chase my husband? I have to undergo the pain of pregnancy and childbirth. Why can't my husband undergo the pain of sterlization? [Rural woman from UP Hills]

Source: Author's field notes, 1993–4.

and non-governmental organizations (NGOs) working towards women's empowerment address this seriously. Increased mobility gives women greater access to information and knowledge and helps build self-esteem and self-confidence. The Pudukkottai (Tamil Nadu) total literacy campaign (TLC) enabled thousands of women to learn to ride bicycles. Just the very simple skill of cycling opened a new world to them. The Department of Education's *Mahila Samakhya* programme has built in field trips, *melas*, study visits, and structured exposure to district administration. Similarly NGOs like SPARC, *Swayam Shikshan Prayog*, and SEWA create opportunities to learn from others. But, the basic point is that mobility and autonomy go together. As of now, the only indicator of mobility that could possibly be used is the development of infrastructure and public transport. As the Haryana and Punjab experience amply demonstrates, the mere existence of facilities does not automatically lead to greater use. But it does seem to have made a significant difference to girls' access to schooling beyond primary level.

Access to Intangible Resources

When we debate the relative strength or status of two groups of human beings we invariably use terms like self-confidence, self-esteem, knowledge acquired in the experience of life, and general family environment. These are often dismissed as being intangible, something that cannot be measured or even defined! Therefore, when a government programme known as the Women's Development Programme (WDP) of Rajasthan (1984) talked about improving the self-esteem and self-confidence of women, enabling them to acquire the ability to critically analyse their own life situation, using the information they have, and moving from a state of passive acceptance of their life situation to a more proactive mode, a lot of planners and administrators dismissed the programme as a non-starter. In a short span of four years, the change the programme had engendered was visible and the impact palpable. Based on this experience the Department of Education, Ministry of Human Resource Development (MHRD) launched *Mahila Samakhya*—a women's empowerment programme in 1989 which again proved that such intangibles have to be addressed if we are serious about improving the status of women. Creation of women's collectives (*mahila samooh/mahila sangha*), raising consciousness, enabling women to reach out to information and knowledge, facilitating greater mobility and opportunities to meet and learn from other people—all these have now become accepted processes of empowerment.

Again the indicators that could be used to record and maybe even assess women's access to such intangible resources are by way of documenting the experience of women in forming groups/collectives, the kind of training they have received, exposure to the world outside, and so on.

Law and Mechanisms for Legal Redressal

The constitutional guarantees of fundamental rights and freedom have meant little to millions of women all over India who have been subject to centuries of oppression and all forms of exploitation. Their secondary status in society, coupled with an oppressive caste system and grinding poverty, has effectively robbed them of their rights and a life of dignity. Progressive laws and a women-friendly judiciary theoretically provide women with the opportunity to seek redressal.

Notwithstanding the complex and often contradictory phenomenon, it is necessary to systematically collect information on compliance. Some suggested indicators are as follows:

• Women's access to legal aid and shelters: number of legal aid units and their utilization, quantum of national resources and development aid invested in them over a time period.

• Crimes against women and percentage of registered cases that have lead to conviction. Here we could include unnatural deaths, rape, molestation, and abuse.

• Documenting and compiling reported outcomes of *jati panchayats* (in recent times the media has been reporting horrible cases of community handing out punishments to girls and their parents, even death sentences!) and other traditional fora.

• Civil and property cases against women, cited causes for divorce and desertion, case histories of women confined to mental asylums—systematically gathering information on these issues could be useful.

• Community survey information on prevalence of domestic violence, child marriages, and so on could also be valuable—even though it may be from small studies done by feminist researchers.

Table 19.4 provides percentage distribution of crimes against women in the year 1997.

Women's Access to Decision Making Fora and Political Spaces

India is one of the pioneers in the world in introducing legislation reserving 30 per cent of seats in local self-government institutions and municipal corporations for women. This, by itself, is truly a tremendous achievement. It is now widely acknowledged that this is the outcome of almost two decades of advocacy by the

TABLE 19.4
Percentage Distribution of Various Crimes Against Women in 1997

Crime	Per cent
Molestation	25.30
Torture	30.30
Dowry deaths	05.00
Kidnapping and abduction	12.80
Rape	12.60
Under the Dowry Prohibition Act	02.20
Under the Immoral Traffic (Prevention) Act	06.90
Sexual harassment	04.80
Others	00.10

Source: Statistics from the National Crime Records Bureau, 1997, quoted in Raghavan (1999).

women's movement. The 73rd and 74th amendments to the Indian Constitution are a markers that will eventually have far-reaching implications. However, evidence pouring in from different parts of the country shows that the battle is far from over. Many women have found it difficult to interact with officials at district and block levels, who come across as hostile.

Compiling information at national level could, in the next ten years, become a very effective indicator of improvement in the status of women in India. At this stage, data on elections and subsequent developments, case studies, information on training programmes, and other forms of ongoing support across the country could help us map interesting regional trends. For example, it is said the experiences in Madhya Pradesh and Karnataka are quite encouraging primarily because state governments have played a proactive role in enhancing the capability of women to meet this new challenge. On the other hand, the experiences of Tamil Nadu, Rajasthan, and Uttar Pradesh have been disheartening. The case of Tamil Nadu is of particular interest because it is fast catching up with Kerala on the demographic and educational fronts—but there seems to be a lot of resistance to women's participation in panchayats. A recent case study done in Dharmapuri district revealed that there was a lot of hostility towards women, especially Dalit women, during elections. There were reported incidences of active obstruction by local officials who did not share information on the reserved seats (see Ramachandran and Xavier 1997). In Rajasthan, a large number of women sarpanchs were removed by votes of no confidence. Frivolous financial misappropriation cases were used to remove women who tried to assert their authority.[3]

[3] Information shared by Panchayati Raj Department of Government of Rajasthan, March 1999.

Concluding Remarks

Women's status influences access to a wide range of resources—both within the family and outside. It is now acknowledged that unless we recognize these linkage and design development programmes to ensure some degree of convergence, we will not be able to break out of the current impasse. Even a cursory study of these linkages proves beyond doubt that when we lift the 'statistical Purdah' (see World Bank 1991) it becomes more than evident that women are productive workers whose contribution to the national economy is tremendous. The poorer the family, the greater is their contribution to the household economy. Recognizing this elementary fact is a necessary step towards improving the economic situation of people below the poverty line. In the last twenty-five years small- and large-scale research studies have shown that a major share of the income earned by women goes into maintenance of the family and even a marginal increase in women's income translates into better nutrition, health, and education of children. Despite recognition of this fundamental truth, women continue to have limited access to education, health-care services, credit, employment, training, and so on.

POLICY AND PROGRAMME INITIATIVES TO IMPROVE WOMEN'S STATUS

It is now well known that the Government of India's own understanding of development has changed over the last fifty years. Beginning with a welfare approach in the 1950s, the country gradually moved towards a 'development' approach in the mid-1970s and an 'empowerment' approach in the 1990s. Scanning the Government of India's policy documents it becomes evident that this shift was not confined to women alone. In many ways, the government's policy towards Dalits, tribal communities, and women has evolved in roughly the same direction.

The Community Development Programme (1952) was initiated to promote agricultural development and social welfare. The focus was rural India. In 1954 there was a realization that women workers would be needed to reach out to poor rural women. As a result, each development block in a district was provided with two Gram sevikas working under the overall supervision of one Mukhya sevika. This scheme also provided for the formation of Mahila mandals which were to be the nodal points for creating greater awareness about health and nutrition among women. Welfare programmes for women were focused on widows, deserted women, etc. With the creation of the Central Social Welfare Board (CSWB) in 1954, welfare extension services were introduced to provide 'poor mothers' with supplementary nutrition, health care, and so on. Some social education activities were also initiated and training programmes were limited to sewing, food processing, handicrafts, and so on. The main objective of training programmes was to enable women to 'supplement' family income. This approach to women and development continued almost uninterrupted till the 1970s.

It was in the 1970s that the government constituted a Committee on the Status of Women in India (CSWI). Their report, *Towards Equality*, released and tabled in parliament in 1974 compiled valuable data and information about different dimensions of womens lives—women as agricultural workers, as daily wage earners, as primary providers in poor households, and so on. Women's contribution to the household and to the economy was captured for the first time. This was juxtaposed against the prevalent situation of women—educational achievement, access to health care, mortality rates, intra-household food distribution and resultant poor nutrition status of women and girls, and so on. The report also put together evidence on domestic and societal violence, laws and their enforcement, and women's lack of access to legal or judicial protection. It can truly be said that this report changed the way women were looked at by many economists, planners, and administrators.

As we can see in Box 19.5 it is indeed ironic that when we talk about education, health care, employment and other related issues, the poor status of women in Indian society is cited as a reason for non-fulfilment of our

---

BOX 19.5

Women and India's Population Policy

India's population policy has been a contentious issue for at least thirty-five years. It is well known that since 1952 the rationale, thrust, and objective of India's population policy has been population control and the main vehicle to achieve this has been family planning. The most important indicator has been couple protection rate and the most popular means is method-specific family planning target—i.e. sterlization. Till 1977 men were the main target, but since then it has been women. We have gone through many ups and downs and this dilemma has been captured well in Eighth Five Year Plan document (1992) of the Government of India. The 'containment of population growth through active people's co-operation and effective scheme of incentives and disincentives' is identified as the sixth most important objective of government policy. The government aims to reduce 'the birth rate from 29.9 per thousand to 26 per thousand by 1997.' A reduction in birth rates is to be accomplished by a

holistic approach to social development and population control, integrated programmes for raising female literacy, female employment, status of women, nutrition and reduction of infant and maternal mortality. The younger couples, who are reproductively most active will be the focus of attention, with necessarily a greater emphasis on spacing methods, although the terminal methods would continue to remain the important means of birth control. Medical termination of pregnancy will have to play an important role in the entire scheme of family planning in the Eight Plan. (GoI 1992, quoted in Raghuram and Rahman, 1995)

How did such a self-contradictory policy evolve in India?

1950s and 1960s: India's policy on population dates back to 1952 when the family planning programme was launched. In the early years, the poor (both men and women) were targeted and the mainstay of the programme was male and female sterilization. Spacing methods were still not very popular and the pill had not caught on across the world. Sterilization was the only option for couples who did not want any more children. While it was known that many women resorted to abortion as a means of family planning, and that a large number of women died due to unsafe back-street abortions, the possibility of legalizing abortion was still being explored.

1970s: This decade started with unprecedented initiative by the government—the Medical Termination of Pregnancy Act was passed in 1971. India was one of the few countries that took this bold step. India also was one of the few countries to take a firm stand in the Bucharest Population Conference. Dr Karan Singh declared, 'Development is the best contraceptive'.

1980s: While female sterilization remained the backbone of the family welfare programme, the government acknowledged the need to address infant and maternal mortality. The maternal and child health programme was strengthened and made a part of the overall strategy to promote family welfare. Towards the end of the 1980s, India's population policy started promoting women's education in a big way.

1990s: In 1994 the government passed the Pre Natal Diagnostic Techniques (Regulation and Prevention of Misuse) Act. This was initiated by the Department of Family Welfare, GOI as a response to a growing incidence of female foeticide.

The Cairo Conference held in 1994 signalled a dramatic shift from demographic targets to quality-of-life indicators. The government of India withdrew family planning targets in select districts in 1995 and on 1 April 1996 it declared the entire country 'target-free'. With substantial loan from the World Bank and aid from bilateral and multilateral agencies, the government launched the Reproductive and Child Health programme in April 1997. The main focus is still women, with a few significant differences. The healthcare needs of women in different age groups, especially adolescent girls, and the importance of male involvement and male responsibility in contraception are now integral parts of the new package. Promoting women's and girls' education continues to be an important aspect of the new policy.

goals. But when it comes to birth control, policy makers and administrators conveniently forget that a woman does not have the freedom to decide when she should marry, how many children she should have or how her children should be brought up. Women are not autonomous entities. Acknowledging the roots of women's poor status does not always translate into concrete policies and programme. The schism between government policy, concrete programmes, and their manifestation on the ground increased—creating a big gap between rhetoric and reality.

The Sixth Plan (1980–5) was an important landmark. For the first time the Plan document introduced a chapter on women and development. By the mid-1980s it became quite apparent that credit and employment guarantee schemes work better if women are organized. The importance of programmes that will help women come together in groups, become aware, gain greater confidence, and enhance their ability to access information was acknowledged (see Box 19.6). So in the mid-1980s policy makers and development practitioners started advocating education and awareness programmes for women.

Box 19.6
Revamping the DWCRA—The Andhra Pradesh Experience

By 1992 the DWCRA to become the vehicle for empowerment of the poor to manage resources and productive assets.[*] The state government decided to promote self-help groups starting with savings and credit. A decision was taken to provide DWCRA revolving fund only to those groups who have successfully rotated their own savings for six to eight months. Older groups facilitated the formation of new groups and each village was encouraged to have as many groups as they wish. The objective was to ensure all poor women become members of a group. While revamping the programme some essential characteristics were spelt out, namely:

- Women should be able to come together in homogeneous groups—occupation, economic status, and /or habitation being the common link.
- They must develop group synergy and identity and in the process enhance their ability to negotiate with the world outside. This will also usher self-confidence and collective strength.
- Women must be able to save for a purpose, not necessarily only surplus funds and make a conscious decision to set aside some money.
- Women should have the full freedom to decide who should get a loan, and for what purpose. If a group decides to give precedence to emergency crisis consumption loan, so be it. This 'power' will build their self-esteem.
- The middleman should be eliminated, a government functionary or an NGO as signatory to withdraw DWCRA funds.
- The government should not promise anything. No lollipops, incentives or disincentives.
- The group should be given the right to determine its own criteria for membership.
- The government should build a good information system on the groups. Random sampling could be used to generate information. it is not necessary to generate detailed information on all groups.
- It is important to take the programme to scale and permit multiple groups in a village. Let women decide how many groups they want. Aggressive and sustained effort to take the programme to every single poor woman is the key.
- Administration should focus on social mobilization and make a conscious decision to leave the rest to women.

This strategy led to a sudden spurt in the number of savings/DWCRA groups. In 1987–8 there were only 100 groups in Nellore district. But in 1996–6 there were 5872 groups and there has rotated Rs 84.347 million! This was the only district in India where both DWCRA and IRDP funds were channelled through women's groups. The savings and DWCRA movement together formed an orchestrated development plan for the district. DWCRA become the nerve centre of the community mobilization strategy. It provides a vital link between the people and the administration. It was hoped that women's involvement in development would change the texture of community participation and working towards sustainable livelihood for women would benefit the family with appreciable change in nutrition, health, education, economic and social status. This approach seemed to resonate global understanding that 'development, if not engendered, is endangered', (see UNDP 1995), because a gender sensitive development model widen [sic] choices of both men and women.

Note: * In 1992 established credit groups were encouraged by the government to form new groups, leading to an organic expansion. There are around 6000 groups today, out of which 3500 are said to be good.

Source: Ramachandran (1996b).

In 1984 the Government of Rajasthan introduced a novel programme, the WDP.

> The broad aim of the Women's Development Project (WDP) is to operationalise the policy frame for women's development. In doing so it takes note of the fact that most government schemes are not accessible to women due to lack of receiving mechanisms and that it is possible to create such mechanisms through flexible and diversified structures backed by effective participation of women as the grass roots level. The WDP also takes note of the fact that for too long men have been entrusted the responsibilities of women's development—in the family, government and society—and that a decisive shift is necessary in order to entrust these responsibilities to women at all levels. Yet another aspect of the broad aims of the WDP is the need to encourage and create agencies, groups and individuals to articulate concern towards indignities and discrimination against women. In this sense, the principle aim of the WDP is to empower women through communication of information, education and training to enable them to recognize and improve their social and economic status. [Department of Rural Education and Panchayati Raj 1984]

The programme, in a very real sense, had to be an ongoing exercise in learning organically by doing, 'based on the premise that a development programme has to develop rather than be implemented' (Jain 1986) (emphasis original).

In 1988 the Report of the National Commission for Self-Employed Women and Women in the Informal Sector (NCSW) was tabled. This landmark report gathered first-hand accounts of women at work, analysed the laws affecting women, and made far-reaching recommendations. Ela Bhatt, who had set up the Self-Employed Women's Association (SEWA) in Gujarat, chaired this commission. The valuable data collected by this commission also highlighted the health hazards faced by women and advocated the importance of making women's work safe. It also argued for a more proactive role to promote women's education. Regional variations and the situation of very poor women were highlighted. Unfortunately, this report did not result in any concrete policy or prog-rammes for women. But what it did achieve was to enhance the visibility of women's work and their contribution to the economy.

In the Seventh Plan period (1986–91) Women's Development Corporations (WDCs) were established in may states. The WDCs were intended to promote women's economic advancement. Again, like most programmes, the impact has been patchy. States like Maharashtra, Kerala, and Tamil Nadu took an early lead, while the most backward regions are yet to realize the potential of this institution.

The Mahila Samakhya programme was formulated in 1987–8 as an effort to operationalize a bold new policy statement. The government initiated a participatory planning process to develop a programme concept. The programme essentially revolved around the formation of women's groups (with a focus on poor women), their training in order to build self-esteem and self-confidence, followed by concrete educational and other developmental inputs. One of the basic tenets of the programme was to respect women's existing knowledge and skill, build on their life experience, and enable them to discover their strengths. Education, by way of literacy and other training inputs, was to be provided on demand. This programme is now being implemented in Karnataka, Uttar Pradesh, Gujarat, Madhya Pradesh, Kerala, Assam, and Bihar (see Box 19.7).

The *Rastriya Mahila Kosh* was launched in 1993. Inspired by the *Gramin* Bank of Bangladesh and also the experience of SEWA in India, this programme is intended to enhance poor women's access to credit. NGOs are encouraged to manage and identify women's thrift and savings groups, enhance their managerial skills, and give them a revolving fund to be used by group members for self-employment. Since the inception of the programme, 99,627 women have benefited from this scheme.

Concluding Remarks

From the preceeding brief description of policies and programmes for women in India, it is quite apparent that a wide range of strategies have been tried out. India is not only a vast country, its prevailing diversity and resulting complexity make any national assessment almost impossible. While one strategy may have been effective in some regions, it fails in another. The classic example is the DWCRA. There were 25,071 successful DWCRA groups in Andhra Pradesh and only 175 in Rajasthan, 371 in West Bengal, and 900 in Bihar! Similar experiences have been recorded in almost every programme. What this implies is that the mere introduction of programmes and policies is not enough. The commitment of the state government and the general socio-cultural environment influence implementation. It is generally believed that women's status is quite good in Tamil Nadu, yet the Salem and Dharmapuri districts have become notorious for female infanticide. Rajasthan is popularly believed to be the most gender-unjust society, yet this state has been home to some of the most successful innovations in women's development and primary education. Similar examples could be cited from almost any part of the country. The important issue at stake is that as we stand at the threshold of the new millennium we need to remind ourselves that unless we are willing to grapple with gender inequalities, EFA will remain a distant dream.

Box 19.7
Mahila Samakhya Today

- Recent evaluations report that the programme today reaches out to poor rural women in 2500 villages in the UP, Gujarat, Andhra Pradesh, and Karnataka and 1300 in Bihar (status as of July 1997). This is far less than what was anticipated in 1988. Formation and sustaining of women's groups in the villages covered has not been easy. In some areas women leaders have emerged, but groups have not been consolidated. There is no uniform 'model' and open-ended guidelines of the project were interpreted differently in different regions. For example, Andhra Pradesh does not have any paid worker at village level, and all the 252 villages covered so far have functioning women's groups.

- These women's groups or informal gatherings around rural women leaders are the fulcrum around which the programme revolves. Information, real-life education, demand articulation, monitoring schools, and other government services, struggles—all these take place at this level.

- Education still remains the thrust of the conceptual framework of the programme. Acquiring self confidence, being able to deal with authority, knowledge of one's body and health issues, feeling more in command of one's life (shedding helplessness) and some reading and writing—'education, viewed in this light, permeates all of the MS programme.'* Mahila Samakhya has empowered women all along the line, especially grassroots facilitators, women leaders, and functionaries.

- In the last five years education of children and adolescent girls and women's literacy have intensified. Where feasible, the programme has plugged into the literacy campaign. But the experience of the programme with women's literacy has been mixed. In some areas like Sabarkantha in Gujarat, literacy for women was taken up at an early stage. But in most other areas, women have come to appreciate the relevance of literacy and education, especially for their daughters. One can say with confidence that the programme has created a positive environment for education and learning.

- *Mahila shikshan kendras* (women's education centres)—residential condensed programme for out-of-school girls and for dropouts have been a major success in the last five years. Adolescent girls, young women, and women leaders have responded to this with enthusiasm. Despite increasing demand the programme has not been able to create more residential centres, and this has been acknowledged as a problem area. Recent evaluation reports point to the lack of sustained educational resource support for development of curriculum, teaching and learning material, and training support. *Nirantar*, a Delhi-based education resource group, provides intensive back-up support to the programme in Banda. Similar support organizations do not exist everywhere.

- Mahila Samakhya has mobilized women to send their daughters to school and this is acknowledged as a very significant outcome. Non-formal education (NFE) centres, special coaching classes for girls, and educational fairs for children—these are cited as highlights of the programme.

- One of the major outcomes is women's participation in local self-government institutions. Many women leaders across the country have contested *panchayat* elections and emerged successful.

Note: * Jain and Krishnamurty (1996).

Source: DoE (1989, 1991, 1997b).

WHERE DO WE GO FROM HERE?

Development is about people—men, women, and children. It is about the quality of life of people. It is about ensuring that every citizen can walk with her/his head held high. It is as much about enhancing the capabilities of people as meeting their material needs. And, if this is what we all mean by development, we cannot but address the gender dimension of inequality, oppression, and violence. The deprivation faced by women in this country is quite extraordinary. It is perhaps the most glaring failure of independent India. An improvement in the economic situation or the physical availability of health centres and schools does not lead to greater utilization by women. It definitely does not automatically improve women's status. Therefore, empowering women to become active agents in their own emancipation is perhaps the only way out of this vicious cycle of poverty, powerlessness, and gender discrimination.

Box 19.8 lists the vision of poor women themselves about a gender-just society. It is here that education, meant in the large sense, can play a very significant role. Education in the real sense is about enhancing the capabilities of people to understand and deal with the world they live in. As the NPE states, education can be used as an 'agent of basic change in the status of women'. In order to do that the system would have to 'play a positive, interventionist role in the empowerment of women'. This basically means that we have the mandate to use education as an emancipatory tool. But do we have the political and administrative will to do so?

In the last twenty years, women's programmes and development groups working among poor women have shown that empowerment does not 'happen' automatically. The opportunity to come together as women

Box 19.8

Visions of a Gender-Just Society

A few years after participating in a women's empowerment programme of the government (Mahila Samakhya, Tehri Garhwal, Uttaranchal, 1991) a group of rural women came together to talk about their vision of a gender-just society, This is what they listed:

- Women will be literate and more confident. They will walk upright. They will walk into the *panchayat* office or village *pradhan's* house without fear.
- Women will move around freely. They will dare to drink tea in the village tea-stall, read the newspaper, and discuss politics.
- There will be a more equitable division of responsibilities within the household. Men and boys will also fetch water and fodder. Girls will go to school and boys will share household chores with girls.
- Women will not be beaten and abused. There will be no fear of rape.
- Women will get the same wages as men for the same work.
- Men will act responsibly, use condoms, and women will not have to shoulder the entire burden of contraception and abortion.
- Women will be able to get medical help when they want and will not die during childbirth or after an abortion.
- The births of daughter will be celebrated and husbands will distribute sweets.
- Women will ride cycles and motorcycles, also buses and tractors.
- Husbands will prepare the dough for *roti* and make tea for their wives.
- Women's skills and their knowledge of animals, herbs, household remedies, plants, trees, and land will be respected, and women will also be given the status of farmers.

Source: Author's field notes, 1990–1.

triggers a process of self-reflection. Women also realize that supporting each other is necessary to break out of the isolation they all experience within their homes. Similarly, if mainstream institutions and programmes continue to be dominated by insensitive and hostile service providers, then despite becoming conscious and also despite being organized, they cannot access services like health care, education, credit, and so on. This could then lead to frustration and ultimately undermine the transformatory potential of social mobilization. Finally, if avenues for sustainable livelihood are not created, poor women will sink deeper into a vicious circle of poverty and deprivation.

Central to the search for strategies that could lead to women's empowerment is the need to address the nature of bureaucratic compartmentalization and control. Let us take a very popular strategy of the 1990s—credit for poor women's groups. If the primary objective is to give poor women access to credit for work or even emergency consumption needs in order to prevent them from getting trapped in the vicious circle of debt, then the mechanisms for making this work should start from an appreciation of their existential reality. While designing the credit scheme, governments should not only address credit-related issues, but should simultaneously plan for training of women members and group leaders for a wide range of skills necessary to run a successful credit programme. Starting with a participatory survey of the local market, to availability of raw materials and

mechanisms to transport their goods, a credit programme should also plan for training in managerial skills. Exposure visits to the block and district headquarters, to banks, and also to local fairs and melas—all these should be seen as a necessary inputs to implement a successful credit programme.

What does this imply? An integrated and holistic approach is essential for creating an environment for change. The time has come to fundamentally alter the management of development programmes. We have not only to enhance women's access to credit and productive assets, primary health care, basic education, natural resources management, and the public distribution system, we have to simultaneously enhance their capabilities to negotiate this unequal world from a position of strength. The challenge before us is to work towards a strategy that draws upon the wealth of experience of different sectoral programmes and move towards genuine synergy and convergence, not just of services, but of approaches. EFA cannot become a reality unless we acknowledge this simple truth.

References

Agarwal, Bina (1994). *A field of Ones Own—Gender and Land Rights in South Asia.* Cambridge University Press, Cambridge.

Batliwala, Srilatha *et al.* (1998). *Status of Rural Women in Karnataka.* NIAS, Bangalore.

Committee on the Status of Women in India (1970). *Towards Equality*.

Department of Education (1989). Project Document. *Mahila Samakhya—Education for Women's Equality*. Government of India, New Delhi.

———— (1991 and 1997). *Annual Reports and Indo-Dutch Evaluation Reports*. Government of India, New Delhi.

Department of Rural Development and Panchayati Raj (1984). *Women's Development Project, Rajasthan*. (Project Document, popularly known as the yellow book) Government of Rajasthan, Jaipur.

Dréze, Jean and Amartya Sen (1995). *India Economic Development and Social Opportunity*. Oxford University Press, New Delhi.

Government of India (1992). *Eighth Five Year Plan 1992-97, Volume One (1992)*, quoted in Raghuram, Shobha and Anika Rahman (Editors) (1995), *Rethinking Population—Proceeding of a Consultation on Women's Health and Rights*. HIVOS, Bangalore.

———— (1997). *Annual Report 1994* of Registrar General of India, Quoted in *Women in India—A Statistical Profile*. New Delhi.

———— (1997) *National Crime Records Bureau*. New Delhi. Quoted in Dr R. K. Raghavan 'Figures of crime'. *Frontline*, 30 July 1999.

Haq, Mahbub ul and Khadija Haq (1998). *Human Development in South Asia*. Oxford University Press, New York.

Jain, Sharada (1986). *Exploring Possibilities—A Review of the Women's Development Programme, Rajasthan*. Institute of Development Studies, Jaipur.

Jain, Sharada and Laxmi Krishnamurty (1996). *Mahila Samakhya*. Sandhan, Jaipur.

Kabeer, Dr Naila (1994). *Reversed Realities—Gender Hierarchies in Development Thought*. Kali for Women, New Delhi.

Murty, Ranjani K. (1994). *Gender and Development in India*. IWID, Madras.

Ramachandran, Vimala (1996a). 'Fertility and autonomy in the Indian Family'. *India International Centre Quarterly*, New Delhi.

———— (1996b) *Critical Consciousness, Credit and Productive Assets—Key to Sustainable Livelihood*. UNICEF, New Delhi.

Ramachandran, Vimala and Lucy Xavier (1997). *Internal Review of SEARCH Extension Programme*, SEARCH, Bangalore.

Sample Registration System (1993). *Fertility and Mortality Indicators*. Registrar General of India, New Delhi.

UNDP (1995). *Human Development Report*. New York.

World Bank (1991). *Gender and Poverty in India, A World Bank Country Study*, Washington.

V

Mobilizing Resources for Education

20 Financing Elementary Education in India

Jandhyala B. G. Tilak*

INTRODUCTION

Long before the formulation of the United Nations Educational, Scientific and Cultural Organization (UNESCO) resolutions and the emergence of interest by international agencies like the World Bank, the United Nations Children's Fund (UNICEF) and the United Nations Development Programme (UNDP), the Government of India had recognized the importance of elementary education and had made a resolve in the Constitution of India as long ago as in 1950: 'The State shall endeavour to provide within a period of 10 years from the commencement of the Constitution for free and compulsory education for all children until they complete the age of 14 years (Article 45).' By resolving to provide elementary education 'free' to all, the Government of India has also implicitly recognized the 'public good' and 'merit good' nature of elementary education. Elementary education is, in fact, recognized by many as a 'pure public good' as the benefits from elementary education are immense; they are not confined to the individuals who go to the school; and the rest of the society also benefits considerably. In fact, the neighbourhood or externality benefits of elementary education are believed to outweigh the direct private benefits. Besides, it is a 'merit good,' as the state knows better than individuals availing the benefits of education. Hence, it is necessary that elementary education is fully financed by the government. The Constitutional Directive received a further boost with the human investment revolution in economic thought (see Schultz 1961) and the increasing research evidence that established that the contribution of education to development—in all socio-economic development spheres—is

* The statistical assistance received from Dr Geetha Rani in updating some of the tables presented here is gratefully acknowledged.

very significant (see Psacharopoulos and Woodhall 1985; Tilak 1989, 1994a). Not only are the economic returns to primary education estimated to be positive and high, but they are also estimated to be higher than alternative rates of return. And returns to primary education are higher than returns to secondary and higher education. Returns to primary education of weaker sections (e.g., backward castes and girls) are also found to be sizeable and, in fact, higher than returns to their respective counterparts (viz., non-backward castes and boys), and returns to upper-primary level of education are higher in rural than in urban areas (see Tilak 1987).

The contribution of education is not restricted to economic returns only. Its significant effect on reduction in poverty and improvement in income distribution, improvement in health and nutritional status of the population, its negative relationship with fertility and population growth and positive association with adoption of family planning methods, and its positive relationship with general social, political and economic development and overall quality of life are well recognized. All this has contributed to the rapid growth of education in India, though it is still not adequate.

The National Policy on Education (NPE) 1968 and the NPE 1986 have laid special emphasis on the fulfilment of the Constitutional Directive of universalization of elementary education (UEE). Five Year Plans have repeatedly promised to take the nation towards achieving this goal. Elementary education was also included in the 'National Programme of Minimum Needs' in the Five Year Plans, and this inclusion has significant implications for allocation of resources. This was expected to ensure favourable treatment in the allocation of resources, and to protect it from reallocation of approved outlays away from elementary education. Education was also made an important component of the 'national human development initiative' in the Union Budget of 1999–2000 (see Tilak 1999a).

Thus, much before the Jomtien Conference (1990) and the adoption of the World Declaration on education for all (EFA) at the same conference, the Government of India had repeated its resolve to universalize elementary education in the country as early as possible, and also to increase the public funding of education to at least 6 per cent of national income, so that education, elementary education in particular, does not suffer from paucity of financial resources.

But even after five decades of development planning and four decades after the deadline stipulated by the constitution, and despite several strategies adopted, programmes and schemes launched, this goal is still elusive. It is strongly felt that elementary education suffered in India due to, apart from several other factors, insufficient allocation of financial resources. At the same time, it should be noted that while finances are an important constraint, they are however not the *only* constraint, but one among many. Financial resources provide a necessary but not a sufficient condition in achieving UEE.

So, when national and global reassessments of EFA goals are being made, it would be useful to assess various dimensions relating to EFA in India. This chapter is an attempt to examine one particular aspect, viz., the pattern of financing of elementary education in India, more specifically focusing on the 1990s, i.e. after the Jomtien Conference. It attempts an examination of a few select dimensions relating to financing of education, that too very briefly.

TRENDS IN EXPENDITURE ON EDUCATION IN INDIA

The educational explosion that has taken place in India during the post-Independence period in terms of numbers of students, schools and colleges, and teachers, is also reflected in the growth of expenditure on education (at least at current prices). In absolute terms, the increase in expenditure on education at the national level is very impressive: from Rs 1.1 billion in 1950–1 to Rs 412 billion in 1997–8 (budget estimates), the latest year for which such data are available. The increase is by a staggering 360 times. But this impressive growth is belittled by (i) rapid growth in population, (ii) phenomenal increase in student numbers, and above all (iii) escalation in prices (see Figure 20.1).

While total expenditure on education increased by 360 times, in per capita terms the increase during 1950–1 to 1997–8 has been by about 130 times. In contrast, the expenditure per pupil increased by only 62 times during the same period, from Rs 35.60 to Rs 2224. These figures are at current prices and the impressive picture remains no longer impressive if they are converted into constant prices.[1] After adjusting these figures with the help of national income deflators, it can be noted that the real rates of growth[2] in total per capita and per pupil expenditure on education are very small. For instance, as compared to a rate of growth of 13.5 per cent at current prices, the total expenditure on education at real prices increased at a rate of only 5.8 per cent during the five decades (1950–1 to 1997–8). The real rate of growth in per capita expenditure on education was about one-third the corresponding rate relating to current prices; and in per pupil terms the real growth was less than one-fourth the growth at current prices.

The decadal trends are indeed important. Looking at real rates of growth, one notices that the 1950s were a period of rapid growth in total expenditure on education; and the 1960s were also a very favourable period for education, as in many developing and developed countries of the world. The global disenchantment with education, partly attributable to growing educated unemployment on the empirical scene, and the emergence of screening and credentialism theses on the role of education on the theoretical front, caused a great setback for the growth of expenditure on education during the 1970s in the third world. India has also had a similar experience. The 1980s marked the revival of faith in education. 'Human resource development' became a favourite slogan by the mid-1980s, and education is regarded as an important component of human (resource) development. Expenditure on education increased during the 1980s at a reasonably high rate of growth, particularly compared to the preceding two decades. However, the rates of growth—both in total and per capita—have not reached the levels experienced during the 1950s. The decade of the 1990s experienced the slowest rate of growth. It is a decade when economic reform policies, specifically stabilization and structural adjustment, were introduced in India, and they seem to have their own significant adverse effect. It would be interesting to interpret these trends in the framework of public finance, particularly as a phenomenon of 'displacement effect' (see Peacock and Wiseman 1961), according to which public expenditure on social sectors like education gets displaced due to economic problems and, more importantly, public expenditure levels do not go back to the former levels even several years after the economic crisis.

---

[1] As an aside, it may be noted that very few significant attempts are made at analysing the growth of expenditure on education in real prices in India. As a result, often misleading conclusions are reached on trends in expenditure on education.

[2] The rate of growth is estimated by fitting the semi-log equation.

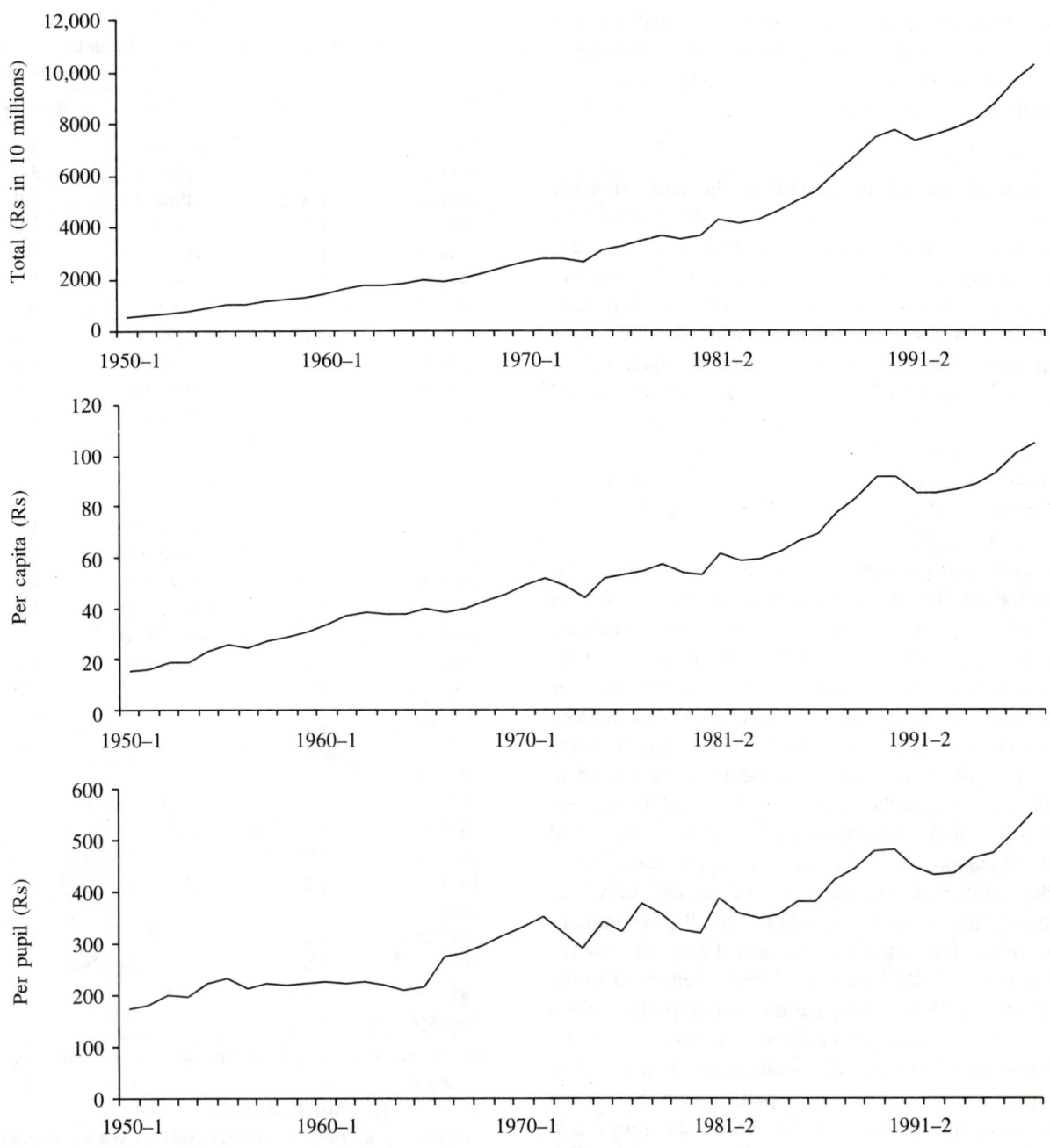

FIGURE 20.1: Public Expenditure on Education in India (in 1980–1 prices)

ALLOCATION OF RESOURCES

There are three important aspects relating to allocation of resources to education: (i) allocation of resources *to* education vis-à-vis other sectors, i.e. inter-sectoral allocation, (ii) intra-sectoral allocation of resources *within* education, i.e. allocation to different levels, and (iii) inter-functional allocation of resources to different activities such as teaching, administrative, and welfare. Yet another important dimension of allocation of resources to education, that is important in a federal system like India, is allocation by the Union government to the states.

These aspects are briefly discussed in the following pages, surveying the existing scanty literature, and with the help of some important indicators using the recent data available. At the outset it may be noted that despite recognizing the contribution of education to economic growth and development, the pattern of allocation of resources to education is still far from satisfactory.

Inter-sectoral Allocation of Resources

First, what is the priority given to education in the national development framework? This question is generally answered in terms of a few select indicators such as the share of education in gross national product (GNP), share of education in government expenditure, share of education in Five Year Plan outlays, etc, some of which are discussed below.

SHARE OF EDUCATION IN GNP

The share of education in GNP is the most standard indicator of national efforts on the development of education in a given society. This reflects the relative priority being accorded to education in the national economy. It is also found to be superior to several other indicators. On the recommendation of the Education Commission (1966), the Government of India (1968) quantitatively targeted investing 6 per cent of national income in education from the public exchequer by 1986. As the goal has not been realized so far, it has repeatedly been reiterated that it will soon be fulfilled. Now the goal is set to be achieved by the end of the Ninth Five Year Plan, i.e. by 2002.

Presently 3.6 per cent of GNP is invested in education in India (1997–8). Compared to the very low level of 1.2 per cent in 1950–1, this marks very significant progress (see Table 20.1). However, it needs to be underlined that this proportion is less than (i) the requirements of the education system to provide reasonable levels of quality education to all the students presently enrolled, (ii) the requirements of the system to provide UEE for eight years to every child in the age group 6–14, and consequent growth in secondary and higher education, as UEE in a comprehensive sense includes universal provision of resources, universal enrolment, and universal retention, (iii) the recommendations of the Education Commission (1966), the resolve made in the NPE 1968 (see DoE 1968), reiterated in the NPE 1986 (see DoE 1986), and the revised policy (1992) to invest 6 per cent of GNP in education,[3] (iv) the proportion of GNP invested in education in many other developing, leave alone developed, countries of the world, including Africa, and (v) finally the proportion invested in India before the Jomtien conference. For instance, 4.9 per cent of Gross Domestic Product (GDP) was invested in education in India in 1990–1. But ever since, it has been consistently declining (see Figure 20.2). It should be noted that it would be a stupendous task to reach a level of 6 per cent of GNP by the end of the Ninth Five Year Plan, as promised by the government, from the current level of 3.6 per cent. Among the countries of the world on which such data are available, India ranked 115th with respect to this

[3] It may, however, be noted that the Education Commission's recommendation assumed a higher economic growth rate than actually realized in the country, in which case, the requirement of education would be more than 6 per cent.

TABLE 20.1
Share of Education in GNP in India

(per cent)

Year	% of GNP	Year	% of GNP
1950–1	1.2	1980–1	2.9
1951–2	1.3	1981–2	3.0
1952–3	1.5	1982–3	3.0
1953–4	1.5	1983–4	3.0
1954–5	1.8	1984–5	3.1
1955–6	2.0	1985–6	3.2
1956–7	1.8	1986–7	3.3
1957–8	2.1	1987–8	3.6
1958–9	2.1	1988–9	3.6
1959–60	2.3	1989–90	4.5
Average	1.8	Average	3.2
1960–1	2.5	1990–1	4.9
1961–2	2.7	1991–2	4.0
1962–3	2.8	1992–3	4.6
1963–4	2.7	1993–4*	4.2
1964–5	2.5	1994–5*	4.0
1965–6	2.8	1995–6*	4.0
1966–7	2.8	1996–7* (R)	3.8
1967–8	2.7	1997–8* (B)	3.6
1968–9	3.0	Average	4.1
1969–70	3.0		
Average	2.8		
1970–1	3.1		
1971–2	3.3		
1972–3	3.2		
1973–4	2.7		
1974–5	2.9		
1875–6	3.2		
1976–7	3.2		
1977–8	3.2		
1978–9	3.5		
1979–80	3.1		
Average	3.1		

Notes: Government expenditure only 1984–5 onwards.
* Quick estimates
R—Revised estimates; B—Budged estimates
Source: Up to 1983–4, MHRD (various years), *Education in India*, after 1983–4.

indicator of national efforts on education, and amongst countries with a population of 100 million or more, India figures at the bottom, except Bangladesh. The need to raise this proportion considerably cannot be emphasized enough.[4] Almost all—from laymen to researchers—plead for the same, though there are no detailed estimates on

[4] Instead of pursuing this goal vigorously, attempts are being made to redefine the target, and play with-not-so confusing terminology, in violation of the spirit and letter of the recommendations made by the national commissions on education, and approved by the Government of India, to show that the target has already been achieved. See Tilak (1999a) for a comment on these trends.

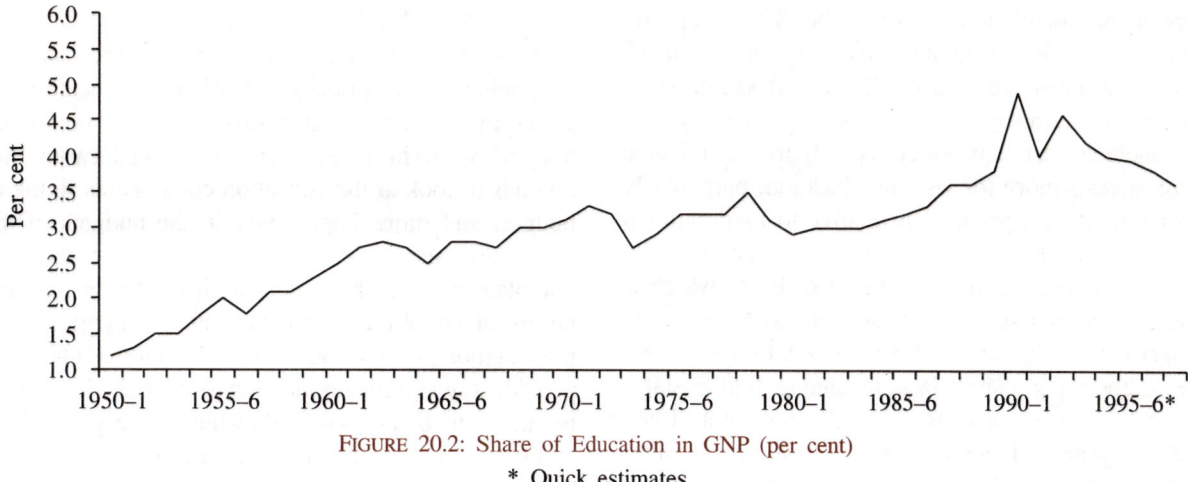

FIGURE 20.2: Share of Education in GNP (per cent)
* Quick estimates

what should be the desirable and feasible proportion of GNP.[5]

However, this proportion has increased considerably in a few states (see Table 20.2) including in some of the backward states. In fact, in some of the backward states like Bihar the proportion was above 6 per cent. This finding is not conclusive; in fact, it raises some questions at the same time. For instance, if the income of the state is low (or declines over the years), even a relatively small amount (or stagnant level) of expenditure on education

TABLE 20.2
Share of Education in State Domestic Product (SDP) by States in India

State	1960–1	1980–1	1983–4	1985–6	1990–1	1995–6
Andhra Pradesh	2.3	3.8	3.7	4.7	4.6	2.4#
Assam	2.2	3.6	3.5	4.8	6.0	6.4#
Bihar	2.3	3.6	4.3	4.2	6.3	6.2#
Gujarat	2.5	3.5	3.1	5.4	4.3	3.1#
Haryana	++	2.7	2.7	3.3	3.1	2.3#
Himachal Pradesh	–	7.3	6.0	7.2	8.8	7.1#
Jammu & Kashmir	2.2	4.5	4.4	6.7	6.7+	4.9
Karnataka	2.6	3.4	3.3	5.2	4.3	3.8#
Kerala	4.2	5.7	4.3	6.5	6.5	6.3#
Madhya Pradesh	2.3	3.3	3.2	4.2	5.0	3.2#
Maharashtra	3.0	3.5	3.3	3.5	3.2	2.8#
Orissa	1.9	3.8	2.9	4.7	5.4	5.1#
Punjab	2.7*	3.5	3.4	3.3	3.5	2.1#
Rajasthan	2.4	3.7	2.8	4.9	5.3	4.1$
Tamil Nadu	2.8	4.3	4.1	4.8	5.0	3.7$
Tripura	NA	7.6	8.3	6.9	11.8+	12.8#
Uttar Pradesh	2.2	3.1	3.0	3.3	4.6	3.8#
West Bengal	2.6	2.9	3.4	3.5	5.4	3.5#

Note: *Includes Haryana; ++ Included in Punjab; + 1989–90; 1985–6 onwards: government expenditure only.
Quick estimates; $ Advance estimates.

Source: For 1990–1, 1995–6: DoE (relevant years), *Analysis of Budget Expenditure on Education,* other years, DoE (relevant years) *Education in India.*

[5] Norm-based estimates (based on cost functions and enrolment projections) by Tilak (1994b) suggest that it should be about 8 per cent by AD 2000. Rao (1992) compared the cost of education in India with developed countries like Singapore, and estimated that about a quarter of our GNP needs to be allocated to education. Seth (1985) felt that provision of appropriate education might require about 10 per cent of GNP.

gives an impression of a high (or increased) proportion of state income being invested in education. Nevertheless this is the best available indicator on the efforts of a state in the development of education.

The variations in the educational efforts of various states do not fall into any systematic pattern. The coefficient of correlation between the SDP spent on education and SDP per capita is estimated to be small, negative, and statistically not significant.[6] Based on similar results on coefficients of correlation for earlier years, it was concluded that it is not necessarily true that a state or nation invests more (or less) in education, particularly when measured as a proportion relative to total national or state income, than others because it is economically rich (or poor). For example, a state like Bihar which is economically a poor state invests as much as 6.2 per cent of its income on education (1995–6) and Punjab which has the highest per capita income among Indian states invests 2.1 per cent, and Haryana 2.3 per cent. Even states like Rajasthan, Jammu and Kashmir, Assam, Andhra Pradesh, and Orissa whose per capita incomes are about half or less than half that of Punjab invest a higher proportion of their incomes on education than does Punjab.

This may mean that level of economic development is not an important determinant of public expenditure on education. It is, in fact, necessary to analyse the determinants of expenditure on education in detail, but it is rarely attempted, and it has been strongly felt that allocation of resources to education is not based on any sound rational principles.

THE EDUCATION BUDGET

Perhaps a more important gauge of what is actually happening is the priority accorded to education in the government budget. Unfortunately there is no 'education budget' *per se* in India. To arrive at an education budget, one has to look at the education components in the union budget, and more importantly in the budgets of all the states and union territories (UTs). Only then can a complete picture of the education budget in the country be presented. We do not have such an 'integrated budget presentation' in our country.[7] The Union Budget fails to provide any significant idea, as its contribution is relative to the state budgets for education is very small.

Further, in the budget framework, resources flow from the government in two forms—in the revenue account of the budget and in the capital account. While in the revenue budget the share of the education sector is reasonably large, in the capital budget the share of education is infinitesimally small, the net result being the pushing down of the share of education in the total budget. If central and state budgets are considered, in terms of both revenue and capital accounts, the total budget resources available for education formed around 11 per cent in 1995–6 (see Table 20.3). Further, we also notice that

TABLE 20.3
Budget Expenditure on Education in India (Education and other Departments)

	1995–6 (Actuals)		1996–7 (Revised)		1997–8 (Budget)	
	Expenditure Rs in 10 million	% in total budget	Expenditure Rs in 10 million	% in total budget	expenditure Rs in 10 million	% in total budget
Centre						
Revenue	5550.5	4.0	6050.6	3.8	7862.5	4.3
Capital	0.0	–	0.0	0.0	0.0	–
Loans and advances	0.5	–	0.5	–	0.0	–
Total	5551.0	3.1	6051.1	2.6	7863.3	3.4
States and UTs						
Revenue	32,627.6	22.3	38,644.9	22.2	43,820.7	22.7
Capital	379.1	2.0	426.5	2.2	507.9	2.2
Loans and						
Advances	211.0	2.6	211.3	2.1	272.7	2.7
Total	33,217.7	19.2	39,282.6	19.2	44,601.3	19.7
Total						
Revenue	38,178.1	13.4	44,695.4	13.4	51,683.3	13.7
Capital	379.1	1.04	426.5	1.2	508.7	1.2
Loans and Advances	211.5	0.6	211.8	0.5	272.7	0.7
Total	38,768.7	10.9	45,333.7	11.1	52,464.6	11.4

Source: DoE (1995–6 to 1997–8) *Analysis of Budgeted Expenditure on Education.*

[6] The coefficient estimated on the basis of the 1990–1 data is (–)0.3739. See also Tilak (1987b) for similar results on an earlier set of data.

[7] In this context, the *Analysis of the Budgeted Expenditure on Education* (Department of Education, MHRD) is a very valuable document, though it is published with a gap of 2–3 years.

while in the central budget the share of the education sector is 3.1 per cent (4.0 per cent in the revenue budget, and nil in the capital budget), it is approximately one-fifth of the budgets of states and UTs (22 per cent in the revenue budgets and 2 per cent in capital budgets) in 1995–6. It may also be noted that even though the share of education in the (revenue) budget oscillated frequently over the years, on the whole, the share in the central budget has increased from 1.6 per cent in 1967–8 to 3.1 per cent in 1995–6, and in the state budgets, it has remained around 20 per cent (see Table 20.4).

TABLE 20.4
Percentage of Education Expenditure on Education to Total Budget

Year	State government*	Union government	All India
1967–8	19.8	1.6	11.9
1968–9	20.2	2.0	12.5
1969–70	20.5	2.3	13.0
1970–1	21.4	2.8	14.1
1971–2	20.3	2.5	13.4
1972–3	19.8	2.4	12.6
1973–4	20.6	2.0	13.0
1974–5	23.2	2.1	14.1
1975–6	22.9	2.0	13.7
1976–7	22.7	2.3	13.8
1977–8	21.4	2.1	12.7
1978–9	21.8	2.2	13.1
1979–80	21.6	2.0	13.1
1980–1	20.9	2.0	12.8
1981–2	20.8	1.9	12.5
1982–3	21.3	1.3	10.8
1983–4	20.8	1.5	11.4
1984–5	23.3	2.7	13.1
1985–6(R)	24.0	2.8	13.4
1986–7(B)	23.8	3.0	13.4
1987–8	–	–	–
1988–9	–	–	–
1989–90	21.3	2.1	9.8
1990–1	20.8	2.2	10.6
1991–2	18.9	2.2	10.2
1992–3	18.9	2.3	10.5
1993–4	19.3	2.6	10.5
1994–5	18.4	2.4	10.3
1995–6	19.5	3.1	10.9
1996–7(R)	19.2	2.6	11.1
1997–8(B)	19.7	3.4	11.4

Note: * includes UTs; R—Revised estimates; B—Budget estimates.
Source: DoE (various years), *Analysis of Budget Expenditure on Education.*

Budgetary resources flow into education from the Departments of Education, and also from other departments (ministries), both at central and state levels. While the share of the Department of Education is substantial, other departments also contribute significant amounts to the education budget. Over the years, the latter has increased in relative proportion from 8.5 per cent in 1971–2 to about 20 per cent of the total education budget in 1997–8.

The share of education in the revenue budget has remained more or less stagnant, around 20–5 per cent, over the years in several states (see Table 20.5). Most states devote roughly one-fifth to a quarter of their revenue budgets to education. According to the latest available statistics, only Kerala and West Bengal devote about 30 per cent of their respective revenue budgets to education (1995–6). In case of Kerala it has been almost consistent though it has marginally declined, while in quite a few states the trends are rather erratic.

If we look at education expenditure levels in various states, in terms of Rs per capita, in Figure 20.3, we note that interstate variations in per capita expenditure on education are indeed very high, though they seem to be declining over the years.

EDUCATION IN FIVE YEAR PLANS

Five Year Plans are an important development strategy in India. Expenditure on education in the Five Year Plans has shown a rapid increase since the inception of the First Five Year Plan in the country. The absolute provision of outlays on education has multiplied by more than 50 times since the First Five Year Plan. The First Plan invested Rs 1.5 billion on education. The expenditure rose to Rs 254 billion in the Eighth Plan. Thus, it seems that increasingly larger resources are being deployed for education (see Table 20.6). But when we look at the figures in real prices,[8] expenditure on education declined from the Third Five Year Plan onwards up to the Fifth Five Year Plan. The expenditure on education in real prices in the Fourth Five Year Plan was less than four-fifths the expenditure in the Third Plan and the expenditure in the Fifth Plan was about three-fourths the expenditure in the Fourth Plan. It is only in the Sixth Plan that this trend was reversed and the expenditure in the Sixth Plan was about double the expenditure in the Fifth Plan and slightly above the expenditure in the Third Plan in real terms; the expenditure in the Seventh Plan was about 1.8 times the expenditure in the Sixth Plan. A major increase was effected in the Eighth Five Year Plan.

The relative importance given to education in the Five Year Plans has declined gradually over the years, from 7.9 per cent in the First Five Year Plan, to 2.7 per cent

[8] The expenditure in the Five Year Plans is spread over five years. Conversion of the actual expenditure into real expenditure in a Plan is made with the help of national income deflators (derived from GNP in current prices and GNP at 1980–1 prices corresponding to the total period of each Five Year Plan).

TABLE 20.5
Share of Education in the Total Budget of the States (Revenue Account)

(per cent)

State	1960–1	1970–1	1980–1	1985–6	1990–1	1995–6	1997–8
Andhra Pradesh	23.2	20.9	25.7	25.6	24.5	20.79	21.1
Assam	21.1	20.8	29.0	23.1	25.5	28.75	29.0
Bihar	18.9	19.5	26.5	27.9	28.1	24.63	28.8
Gujarat	23.4	20.2	23.6	28.3	24.3	23.78	23.2
Haryana	**	19.8	21.2	22.3	18.6	14.47	11.0
Himachal Pradesh	–	24.5	25.7	18.2	22.6	19.86	17.9
Jammu & Kashmir	16.3	13.4	19.3	19.4	13.1	13.1	18.9
Karnataka	21.2	21.3	22.3	22.0	22.1	22.58	21.2
Kerala	36.0	35.7	35.5	31.7	30.4	30.77	27.4
Madhya Pradesh	24.2	24.2	21.4	21.0	24.2	24.47	29.5
Maharashtra	25.2	21.3	24.0	22.4	21.1	23.74	21.3
Orissa	12.8	16.8	22.8	22.2	24.2	23.68	22.7
Punjab	20.6*	22.1	29.3	23.9	22.7	13.07	17.9
Rajasthan	24.5	18.9	26.0	26.4	26.5	21.97	26.3
Tamil Nadu	23.4	22.5	24.3	27.4	23.7	22.71	24.7
Tripura	–	30.7	19.4	19.2	23.5	24.1	26.4
Uttar Pradesh	14.5	18.2	22.0	21.8	24.0	21.49	20.1
West Bengal	37.1	23.0	24.2	25.8	30.4	24.29	24.7
India	22.5	21.4	23.8	24.0	25.4	22.3	22.6
Coefficient of Variation	*28.3*	*22.0*	*15.5*	*14.7*	*16.3*	*20.7*	*20.3*

Note: * includes Haryana; ** included in Punjab.

Source: DoE (various years) *Analysis of Budget Expenditure on Education* and DoE (1994) Annual Report 1993–4, Ministry of Human Resource Development, GoI, New Delhi.

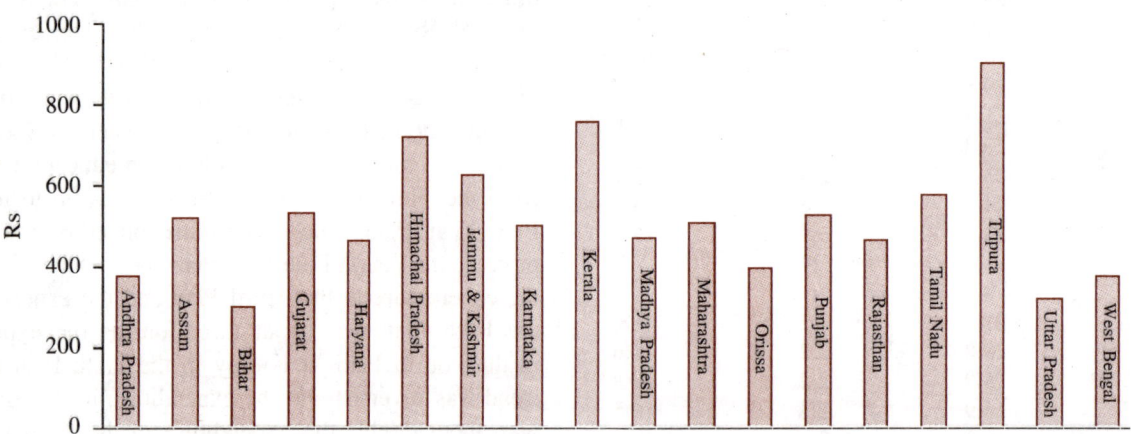

FIGURE 20.3: Per Capita Expenditure on Education in Selected States (1997–8)

in the Sixth Five Year Plan. It was only during the Seventh and Eighth Five Year Plans that this declining trend was reversed.[9] The corresponding figure in the eighth Five Year Plan was high, at 4.5 per cent. Though

the proportion has been increasing after the Jomtien conference, it is interesting to note that it only equals the fourth Plan allocation; and it is still much less than the proportion allocated in the First Five Year Plan.

Not only has the relative importance given to education in Plan expenditure gradually declined until the Sixth Five Year Plan, but also the relative share of education in any Five Year Plan, including the Seventh and Eighth, has been the lowest, despite the hymns sung in praise of education in every Plan document. The closest figure

[9] The declining shares of education in total Plan outlays/expenditure is a phenomenon common to several states also. For example, in Andhra Pradesh the trends were most erratic, and in Uttar Pradesh and Bihar a somewhat consistent declining trend in the relative priority accorded to education in the Five Year Plans can be noted.

TABLE 20.6
Expenditure on Education in the Five Year Plans

(Rs in 10 million)

Five Year Plan	Period	At current prices	At constant prices (1980–1)*	% of total Plan outlay
First Five Year Plan	(1951–6)	153	754	7.86
Second Five Year Plan	(1956–61)	273	1192	5.83
Third Five Year Plan	(1961–6)	589	2076	6.87
Fourth Five Year Plan	(1966–74)	786	1623	5.17
Fifth Five Year Plan	(1974–9)	912	1257	3.27
Sixth Five Year Plan	(1980–5)	2619	2498	2.70
Seventh Five Year Plan	(1985–90)	7633	3549	3.50
Eighth Five Year Plan**	(1992–7)	25,414	9927	4.50

Note: ** Provisional expenditure; * based on National income deflators

Source: Five Year Plan(s), Annual Plan(s), Economic Survey(s) Annual Financial Statistics of Education Sector, 1997–8.

is 3 per cent allocated to health in the Seventh and Eighth Five Year Plans. Several major sectors received much higher allocations than those made to the education sector, as can be noted from Table 20.7.

Thus, it appears that there are three important phases in the allocation of resources to education in the Five Year Plans. During the first three Five Year Plan periods, the allocation to education had been more than 5 per cent. Even though it declined in the Second Plan, the decline was immediately checked in the Third Plan. The second phase, i.e. the post 1968 policy period, consisting of the Fourth, Fifth, and Sixth Five Year Plans, was characterized by a consistent decline in the plan allocation to education. The Seventh, Eighth, and Ninth Five Year Plans form the third phase when efforts are being made to check the declining trend and to substantially increase the allocation to education.

Intra-sectoral Allocation of Resources and the Priority given to Elementary Education

An analysis of intra-sectoral allocation of resources in India during the Plan period shows a lopsided emphasis on elementary education, and also on other layers of education. A clear-cut shift in the priorities is quite obvious from the figures in Table 20.8. In the First Five Year Plan, 56 per cent of the total plan resources to education were allocated to elementary education, 13 per cent to secondary, 9 per cent to university education, and 13 per cent to technical education. The relative importance given to elementary education declined to 35 per cent in the Second Plan, to 34 per cent in the Third Plan, and gradually to 30 per cent in the Sixth Plan. It is only again during the Seventh and Eighth Plans significant efforts were made to increase the allocation

substantially, though the allocation in the Eighth Plan was still less than the corresponding one in the First Plan in percentage terms. The share of other levels, excepting technical education, experienced a significant increase, though the increase is not smooth until the Sixth Plan. In the First Plan only 13 per cent of the total educational expenditure was meant for secondary education and by the Second Plan it had increased to 19 per cent whereas that for university level increased from less than one-tenth to nearly one-fifth in the Second Plan, about one-fourth in the Fourth and Fifth Plans, decreased to about one-fifth in the Sixth Five Year Plan, and then seems to have been drastically reduced to 9 per cent in the Seventh Plan.

Elementary education was given a boost in the Seventh Plan. This boost seems to have been possible with severe cuts in plan resources for secondary and higher education. Elementary education received more favourable treatment in the Eighth Plan (see Figure 20.4).

The Plan period can be divided into four phases depending on the pattern of intra-sectoral allocation of resources to education, viz. phase I: 1951–6 (the First Five Year Plan period), phase II: 1956–69 (the period covering the Second and the Third Five Year Plans, and the Annual Plans), phase III: the post 1968 NPE period up to 1980, or simply 1969–86, and phase IV: the post 1986 NPE period. Phase I witnessed a substantial part, nearly three-fifths, of the total plan educational resources being allotted to elementary education, i.e. high priority was given to elementary education and low priority to higher and technical education. The period favourable to elementary education ended with the end of the First Five Year Plan. Phase II, specifically the Second Five Year Plan marked the beginning of a drastic decline in resources allocated to elementary education and a doubling

TABLE 20.7
Sectoral Outlays in Five Year Plans in India

(per cent)

	First Plan	Second Plan	Third Plan	Annual Plans+	Fourth Plan	Fifteh Plan	Sixth Plan	Seventh Plan	Annual Plans++	Eighth plan	Annual plan 1997-8	Annual plan 1998-9 (R)	1999-2000 (B)
Agriculture and allied	14.8	11.8	12.7	16.7	14.7	12.3	13.7	14.3	13.9	14.7	10.7	12.1	8.8
Irrigation and flood control	22.0	9.3	7.8	7.1	8.6	9.8	10.0	7.5	6.1	7.5	0.4	7.7	0.3
Power/energy	7.7	9.5	14.6	18.3	18.6	18.8	28.3	28.4	28.9	26.6	27.0	23.5	26.4
Industry and minierals	4.9	24.1	22.9	24.7	19.7	24.3	15.8	13.5	12.8	10.8	11.8	6.2	8.4
Transport and communications	26.4	27.0	24.6	18.4	19.5	17.4	16.1	17.4	19.7	18.7	31.6	22.4	23.2
Social sectors of which	24.1	18.3	17.4	14.7	18.9	17.3	16.2	15.8	15.6	18.2	14.7	23.6	19.1
Education	7.9	5.8	6.9	4.6	4.9	3.3	2.7	3.5	3.5	4.5	4.1	5.8	4.5
Health	5.0	4.9	2.9	3.2	3.9	3.2	3.1	3.0	2.9	3.2	3.7	3.6	4.0
Total	100	100.	100	100	100	100	100	100	100	100	100	100	100
	(196)	(467)	(858)	(663)	(1578)	(3943)	(10,965)	(22,292)	(12,737)	(43,410)	(7086)	(15,859)	(10,352)

Note: Figures in (parentheses) are Rs in 100 million.
+ 1966-8 (Three Annual Plans)
++ 1990-1 and 1991-2 (Two Annual Plans)
R—Revised Estimates
B—Budget Estimates

Source: Five Year Plan(s), and Economic Survey(s).

276

TABLE 20.8
Intra-Sectoral Allocation of Plan Expenditure in Education in India in the Five Year Plans

(Rs in 10 million)

Five Year Plan	Elementary*	Adult	Secondary	Higher	Technical	Grand total	% of total Plan outlay
First	85	5	20	14	20	153	7.86
	(56)	(3)	(13)	(9)	(13)	(100)	
Second	95	4	51	48	49	273	5.83
	(35)	(1)	(19)	(18)	(18)	(100)	
Third	201	2	103	87	125	589	6.87
	(34)	(0.3)	(18)	(15)	(21)	(100)	
Annual Plans**	75	N	53	77	81	322	4.86
	(24)		(16)	(24)	(25)	(100)	
Fourth	239	6	140	195	106	786	5.04
	30	1	18	25	13	87	
Fifth	317	33	156	205	107	912	3.27
	(35)	(4)	(17)	(22)	(12)	(100)	
Sixth	883	156	736	530	324	2943	2.70
	(30)	(3)	(25)	(18)	(11)	(100)	
Seventh	2849	470	1829	1201	1083	8500	3.50
	(34)	(6)	(22)	(14)	(12)	(100)	
Annual Plans+	1734	376	1079	595	848	5318	4.20
	(33)	(7)	(20)	(11)	(16)	(100)	
Eighth++	8936	1808	3498	1516	2786	21217	4.50
	(42)	(8)	(16)	(7)	(13)	(100)	
Annual Plan 1992–3	1097.19	195.45	N	N	483.4	2994.23	
	(37)	(7)			(16)	(100)	
Annual Plan 1993–4	1190.12	218.91	835.65	338.01	445.82	3506.17	
	(34)	(6)	(24)	(10)	(13)	(100)	
Annual Plan 1994–5 (E)	1814.22	308.02	N	N	704.06	4681.75	
	(39)	(7)			(15)	(100)	
Annual Plan 1995–6 (E)	2050.84	330.66	409.11	245	867	5811.15	
	(35)	(6)	(7)	(4)	(15)	(100)	

Note: * Includes pre-school education; N—Negligible; ++ Outlay;
E: Estimates by the Planning Commission; ** 1965–6 to 1967–8 (three years)
+ 1990–1 and 1991–2 (two years)
Totals may not add up, as totals include expenditure on other programmes such as art and culture, youth services etc.
Source: Five Year Plan(s), Annual Plans(s), Analysis of Annual Plan, Education Sector (various years), and the Report of the NDC Committee on Literacy, Planning Commission, New Delhi.

or trebling of resources allocated to higher education. It may also be noted that the overall developmental priorities also changed with the beginning of the Second Five Year Plan. Relative emphasis shifted from the agricultural sector in favour of the industrial sector. Industrial development requires manpower, and higher education was looked to for its supply. Accordingly, expenditure on higher education increased considerably. It reached 24 per cent by 1967–8, while the corresponding figures for elementary education showed a decline from 56 per cent in the First Plan to 17 per cent in 1966–7. Phase III, i.e. the period after 1969 showed a slight reversal of these trends. The proportion for elementary education showed an increasing trend and that for university and technical

education a gradual decline. This may be attributable partly to the Education Commission's (1966) concerns, and NPE 1968 that laid emphasis on elementary education. With the formulation of NPE 1986, and with Operation Blackboard (OB) and similar other programmes launched by Union and state governments, after 1986 renewed emphasis on elementary education could be seen. The allocation for elementary education was stepped up significantly during the Seventh Five Year Plan, and the Eighth Five Year Plan continued to lay the same emphasis on elementary education.

Though the third phase showed marginal improvement in allocation so far as elementary education is concerned, it has yet to go a long way to reach the

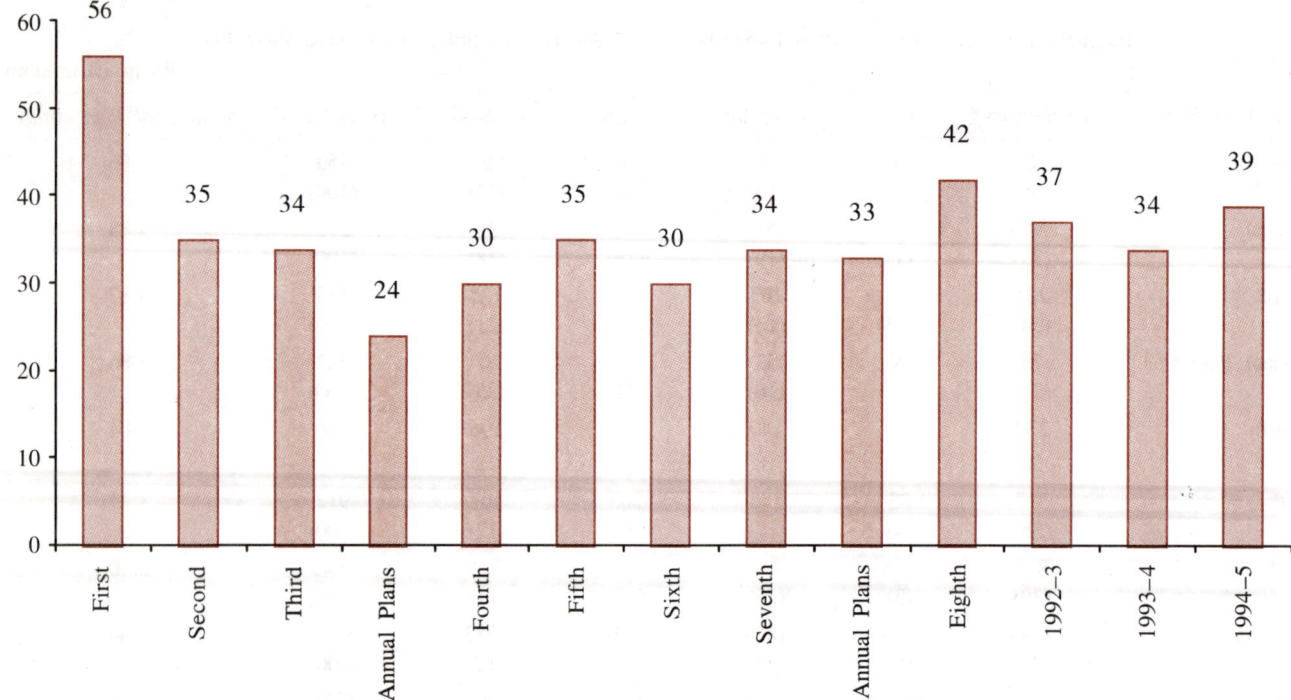

FIGURE 20.4: Share of Elementary Education in Education Expenditure in the Five Year Plans (%)

proportion that it obtained in the First Plan. As has been argued by Tilak and Varghese (1990), had the pattern of intra-sectoral allocation of resources in the education sector adopted in the First Five Year Plan continued, UEE would have been an easy task, if not already accomplished by now.

While UEE has been becoming increasingly tougher and tougher and there has been repeated postponement of the goal, the relative priority given to elementary education in total educational expenditures has gradually declined over the successive five year plans.

PLAN AND NON-PLAN EXPENDITURE ON ELEMENTARY EDUCATION

All this presents only a partial picture because non-plan expenditure on education is equally important. Plan expenditure on education, including elementary education, is relatively small compared to non-Plan expenditure. In fact, non-Plan expenditures form the major chunk of expenditures on elementary education—with Plan expenditure forming only 12 per cent of total expenditure on elementary education presently. Since 1980-1, the proportion of plan expenditure in the total has increased from 5.9 to 7.5 per cent in 1990-1 and then jumped to 24 per cent in 1996-7 (see Table 20.9). It may be emphasized that since non-Plan expenditure is only for maintenance, the smaller the Plan expenditure, the smaller the scope to set new directions of development and to introduce reforms.

TABLE 20.9
Plan and Non-Plan Expenditure on Elementary Education

(per cent)

	Plan	Non-plan	Total	Total Rs in ten million
1980–1	5.9	94.1	100	1537.3
1981–2	6.2	93.8	100	1660.7
1982–3	7.3	92.7	100	2172.1
1983–4	8.8	91.2	100	2475.3
1984–5	9.2	90.8	100	2854.9
1985–6	7.7	92.3	100	3448.3
1986–7	8.9	91.1	100	3881.7
1987–8	11.8	88.2	100	4856.7
1988–9	12.9	87.1	100	5539.8
1989–90	14.0	86.0	100	6888.3
1990–1	7.5	92.5	100	7729.7
1991–2	8.1	91.9	100	8401.4
1992–3	11.2	88.8	100	9477.3
1993–4	12.2	87.8	100	10,821.8
1994–5	14.1	85.9	100	12,638.9
1995–6	18.0	82.0	100	15,217.8
1996–7(R)	20.8	79.2	100	18,047.3
1997–8(B)	22.3	77.7	100	20,781.8

Note: R—Revised estimates; B—Budget estimates.

Source: Analysis of Budgeted Expenditure on Education (various years)

But the trends in total, Plan plus non-Plan expenditure are of the same kind as described in the preceding pages (see Figures 20.5 and 20.6). The share of elementary education in GNP has decreased marginally from 1.53 per cent in 1989–0 to 1.38 per cent in 1995–6 (see Table 20.10). This is the change during the post 1986 NPE decade, though it is generally felt that high priority is being given to elementary education after 1986. The trend is not the same in all states. Himachal Pradesh, for example, allocated 4 per cent of its SDP to elementary education, and Punjab about 1 per cent only (see Figure 20.5).

The share of elementary schools in total 'direct/recurring' expenditure on education, Plan and non-Plan combined, remained more or less stagnant, ranging between 40 and 50 per cent (see Table 20.11).

Though Plan expenditures are relatively small, the increase in them is very important as Plan expenditures allow increase in development activities, including construction of school buildings, recruitment of new teachers, and launching of new development programmes. The significant increase in the relative share of Plan expenditure on elementary education in the 1990s could be due to (i) the massive OB programme that involved

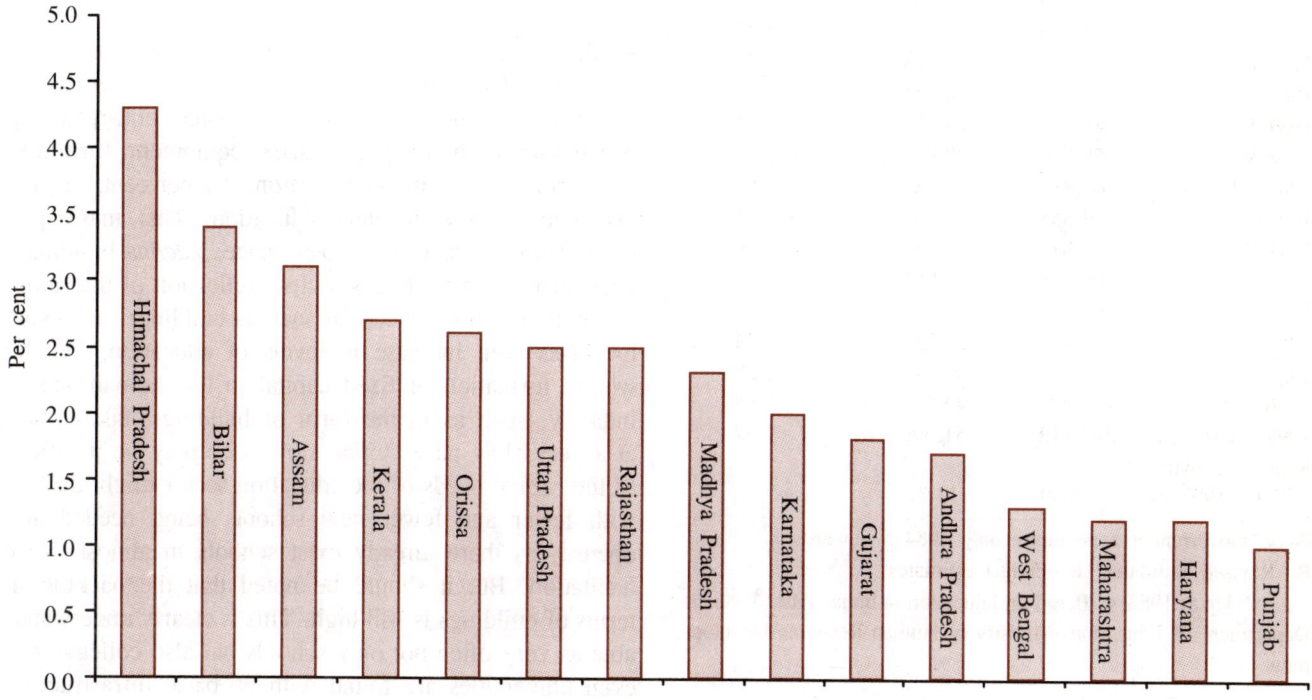

FIGURE 20.5: Share of Expenditure on Elementary Education in State Domestic Product (SDP)

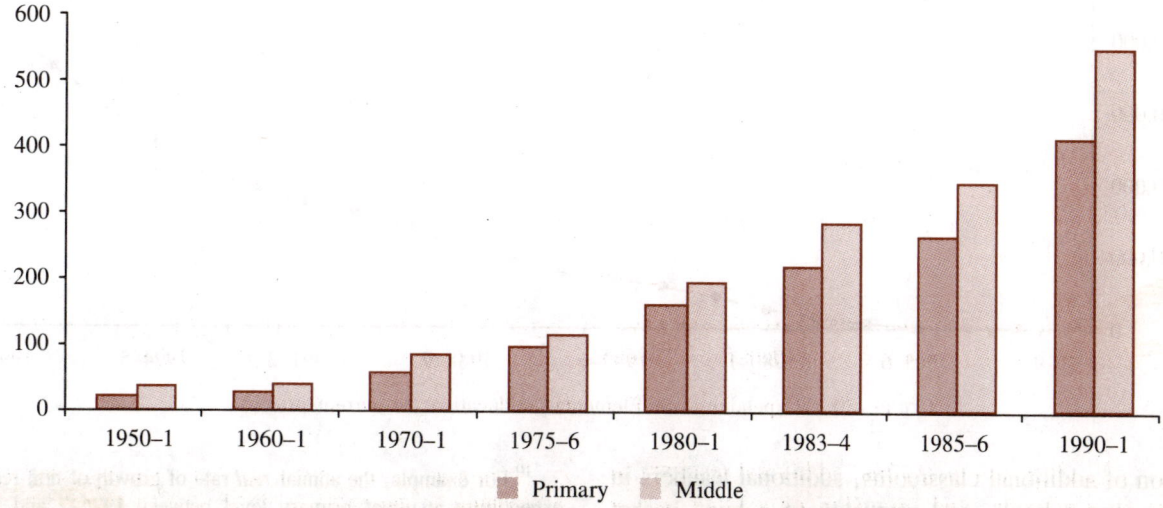

Primary Middle

FIGURE 20.6: Expenditure per Student in Elementary Education (Rs)

TABLE 20.10
Trends in Expenditure on Elementary Education in India
(Rs in million)

Year	Current prices	1980–1 prices	Share of elementary expenditure in GNP (%)
1950–1	463	2261	0.50
1955–6	694	3776	0.68
1960–1	1259	5289	0.78
1965–6	2023	6291	0.78
1970–1	4074	9567	0.95
1975–6	7873	11,663	1.00
1980–1	13,921	13,921	1.02
1983–4	22,016	17,133	1.07
1984–5	28,550	20,670	1.24
1985–6	34,483	23,228	1.32
1986–7	38,817	24,546	1.34
1987–8	48,567	28,290	1.47
1988–9	55,398	29,862	1.42
1989–90	68,883	34,284	1.53
1990–1	79,555	35,693	1.51
1991–2	86,843	34,033	1.44
1992–3	94,773	34,055	1.37
1993–4	108,218	35,963	1.37
1994–5	126,389	37,863	1.34
1995–6	152,177	42,148	1.38
1996–7 (R)	180,473	47,023	1.43
1997–8 (B)	207,818	51,696	1.47
Rate of growth (1950–1/1997–8)	31.0	13.32	

Note: Government expenditure only 1984–5 onwards.
R—Revised estimates; B—Budget estimates
Source: Up to 1983–4: Based on Education in India. After 1983–4: Department of Education, Ministry of Human Resource Development.

significant effects on quality of education, (ii) provision of incentives, particularly noon meals to schoolchildren, and (iii) flow of external aid to education, in the form of the District Primary Education Programme (DPEP) and other projects.

In all, expenditure on elementary education increased significantly at current prices. During the 1990s alone, the public expenditure on elementary education increased by 2.4 times from Rs 7956 crore in 1990–1 to Rs 20,780 crores by 1997–8 (budgeted) (see Figure 20.7). However, at real prices the growth has not been so impressive (as already seen in Table 20.10).

Inter-functional Allocation of Resources

Further, functional classification of expenditure on elementary education given in Table 20.12, though dated, confirms the most prevalent view that non-recurring expenditure on buildings, libraries, equipment, furniture, etc. forms a very small proportion, 2.1 per cent, of total expenditure on elementary education. That many primary schools are run in open space, *kachha* buildings, inadequate rooms, etc., is a clear reflection of the same. Expenditure on fixed capital such as buildings, however, increases with increase in levels of education. On the whole, formation of fixed capital in this human capital industry, such as in the form of buildings, takes place at a very slow pace.[10] The slow pace may be justified, as the capital needs of the education sector might decline with fewer and fewer new schools being needed and opened, as there already exist schools in almost every habitation. But it should be noted that the backlog in terms of buildings is still high. This is clearly understandable as very often not only schools but also colleges and even universities are found with no basic infrastructure

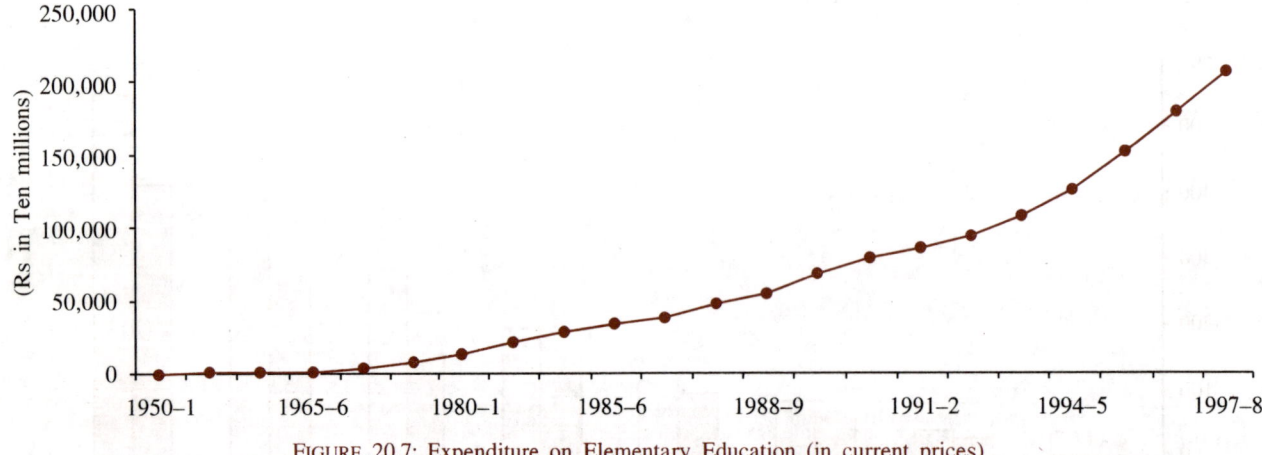

FIGURE 20.7: Expenditure on Elementary Education (in current prices)

provision of additional classrooms, additional teachers in single-teacher schools, and provision of a huge basket of teaching-learning material that is expected to have

[10] For example, the annual *real* rate of growth of non-recurring expenditure at upper primary level between 1976–7 and 1987–8 is 1.85 per cent, compared to 5.6 per cent in recurring expenditure.

TABLE 20.11
Trends in Intra-sectoral Allocation of Total Expenditure on Education in India

(Rs in million)

Year	Direct/recurring expenditure on					Indirect/non-rec. expenditure	Grand total
	Elementary schools	Secondary schools	Professional schools	Higher education	Total		
1950–1	463 (48)	231 (25)	60 (7)	184 (20)	921 (100)	232	1153
1955–6	694 (48)	376 (26)	81 (6)	293 (20)	1148 (100)	449	1897
1960–1	1259 (42)	689 (27)	146 (6)	585 (22)	2573 (100)	870	3444
1965–6	2023 (39)	1504 (32)	105 (2)	1241 (27)	4673 (100)	1192	5853
1970–1	4074 (43)	2700 (28)	128 (1)	2709 (28)	9611 (100)	1572	11,183
1975–6	7873 (44)	4636 (25)	206 (1)	5410 (30)	17,925 (100)	3122	21,047
1980–1	13,921 (41)	10,102 (29)	388 (1)	10,014 (29)	34,425 (100)	1981	36,406
1983–4	22,016 (42)	14,414 (27)	610 (1)	15,068 (29)	52,699 (100)	2539	55,238 (100)
1984–5	28,550 (45)	20,200 (32)	–	14,788 (23)	–	–	63,538 (100)
1985–6	34,483 (46)	22,939 (31)	–	17,148 (26)	–	–	74,570 (100)
1986–7	38,817 (44)	26,011 (30)	–	22,675 (23)	–	–	87,516 (100)
1987–8	48,567 (47)	32,196 (31)	–	23,539 (23)	–	–	104,302 (100)
1988–9	55,398 (44)	39,780 (32)	–	28,909 (24)	–	–	124,087 (100)
1989–90	68,883 (46)	47,215 (31)	–	22,099 (15)	–	–	150,442 (100)
1990–1	79,555 (46)	55,311 (32)	–	23,118 (13)	–	–	171,936 (100)
1991–2	86,843 (46)	61,988 (33)	–	24,437 (13)	–	–	187,576 (100)
1992–3	94,773 (45)	71,780 (34)	–	26,999 (13)	–	–	209,529 (100)
1993–4	108,218 (46)	77,585 (33)	–	31,036 (13)	–	–	234,131 (100)
1994–5	126,389 (46)	90,495 (33)	–	35,253 (13)	–	–	272,321 (100)
1995–6	152,177 (48)	103,440 (33)	–	38,713 (12)	–	–	315,135 (100)
1996–7(R)	180,473 (49)	117,895 (32)	–	44,727 (12)	–	–	370,459 (100)
1997–8(B)	207,818 (50)	123,711 (30)	–	49,097 (12)	–	–	412,459 (100)
Rate of growth (1950–1/1997–8)	31.0	32.1		25.2			29.0

Note: 1984–5 onwards government expenditure only; R—Revised estimates; B—Budget estimates.
Source: Upto 1983–4: Based on Education in India.
After 1983–4: Department of Education, Ministry of Human Resource Development

Table 20.12
Expenditure on Education, by Objects

(per cent)

Item	1983–4		
	Primary	Middle	Elementary
Recurring Expenditure			
Salary of teaching staff	93.6	90.4	92.2
Salary of non-teaching staff	2.8	3.8	3.3
Maintenance of buildings	0.6	0.7	0.7
Maintenance of			
Equipment & furniture	0.2	0.3	0.2
Apparatus, chemicals, etc.	0.1	0.1	0.1
Libraries	0.0	0.1	0.1
Scholarships and other aids	0.5	1.7	1.0
Games and sports	0.1	0.1	0.1
Hostels	0.1	0.2	0.1
Other items	1.9	2.7	2.3
Total recurring	100.0	100.0	100.0
	(1289)	(912)	(2201)
Non-recurring Expenditure			
Libraries	0.8	2.9	1.7
Buildings	55.8	46.5	51.9
Equipment	6.1	7.0	6.5
Furniture	7.1	6.9	7.0
Other items	30.0	36.7	32.9
Total non-recurring	100.0	100.0	100.0
	(27)	(19)	(46)
Distribution of the Grand Total			
Recurring expenditure	98.0	97.9	98.0
Non-recurring expenditure	2.0	2.1	2.0
Grand total	100.0	100.0	100.0
	(1315)	(932)	(2247)

Note: Figures in parentheses are Rs in 10 million.
Source: Based on Education in India 1983–4.

facilities like buildings, furniture, and equipment. Thus, the present pattern of spending does not contribute much to physical capital formation.

Of total recurring expenditure on elementary education, teachers' salaries amount to more than 90 per cent, and expenditure on the salaries of non-teaching staff forms the next largest proportion, about 3 per cent. All other items, including teaching–learning material like apparatus, chemicals, books, and libraries, and others like financial incentives, games, and sports receive negligible amounts. Teachers' salaries increase as a proportion of total recurring expenditure, as one goes down the educational ladder.

Available data for the 1990s allow a brief look at inter-functional classification of expenditure on elementary education, from another perspective (see Table 20.13). The pattern in the 1990s does not show any systematic trends and any significant changes in priorities. This may partly be due to the nature of data available. The available data do not provide a detailed break-up. Trends in expenditure on government schools show a zig-zag pattern—the relative proportion experiencing frequent ups and downs; grants-in-aid to local body schools remaining more or less constant, and grants-in-aid to private schools also experiencing a somewhat zig-zag pattern. Most, if not all, of the aid to government, local body, and private schools is for the salaries of teachers and others. So about 90 per cent of the total expenditure on elementary education could be treated as expenditure on salaries. Quite interestingly, the relative priority accorded to teacher training remained constant. Though there is marginal increase in the share of quality-enhancing inputs like textbooks, the relative proportion continues to be very small, accounting for less than 0.5 per cent in 1996–7. The proportion allocated to financial incentives in the form of scholarships has marginally declined and continues to be rather insignificant—0.3 per cent in 1996–7. This pattern of financing needs to be examined in contrast to research evidence available, though on other countries, that demonstrates significant effects of investment

TABLE 20.13
Intra-sectoral Allocation of Public Expenditure on Elementary Education in India

(per cent)

	1990–1	1991–2	1992–3	1993–4	1994–5	1995–6(R)	1996–7(B)
Direction, inspection, & admn.	2.4	2.6	2.9	2.7	2.5	2.2	2.0
Assistance to govt. schools	37.5	27.1	50.1	36.7	42.9	39.5	39.9
Assistance to private schools	25.9	26.4	17.4	16.3	19.1	21.6	22.3
Assistance to local body schools	22.7	23.0	24.0	23.1	23.3	23.2	22.5
Teacher training	6.5	7.1	1.2	7.7	7.2	7.0	6.9
Non-formal education (NFE)	0.5	9.7	0.6	8.6	0.4	1.0	0.8
Scholarships		0.4	0.4	0.2	0.1	0.2	0.3
Textbooks		0.2	0.5	0.4	0.4	0.5	0.5
Other	4.5	3.5	3.0	4.4	4.2	4.8	4.8
Total	100	100	100	100	0100	0100	0100

Note: R—Revised figures; B—Budgeted figures.
Source: DoE (various years).

in non-salary items such as textbooks and other teaching–learning material on the quality and overall efficiency of education systems in developing countries.

PUBLIC EXPENDITURE ON ELEMENTARY EDUCATION PER STUDENT

The time trends in expenditure on education per student, that is indicative of some aspects of quality of education in terms of physical and human infrastructure facilities available to students on average, presented in Table 20.14 are indeed disturbing. In the four decades after the inception of planning, i.e. from 1950–1 to 1990–1, expenditure per pupil on primary education increased at a very modest rate of 2.1 per cent at real prices; and middle-level education at a rate of growth of less than 1 per cent, even though the trends at current prices are somewhat impressive (see Figure 20.8).

TABLE 20.14
Per Student Public Expenditure by Primary and Middle Levels of Education

(Rs per annum)

Year	Primary	Middle	Primary	Middle
	At current prices		At 1980–1 prices	
1950–1	19.9	37.1	99.5	185.5
1960–1	27.6	40.5	115.0	168.8
1970–1	57.0	84.9	132.6	197.4
1975–6	95.9	114.2	141.0	167.9
1980–1	160.9	193.4	160.9	193.4
1983–4	217.1	285.1	168.3	221.0
1985–6	262.7	344.3	177.5	232.6
1990–1	411.4	547.6	184.5	245.6
Growth Rates (%)				
1950–91	49.18	34.40	2.14	0.81
1950–61	3.9	0.9	1.6	–0.9
1960–71	10.7	11.0	1.5	1.7
1970–81	18.23	12.78	2.14	–0.20
1980–91	15.57	18.31	1.47	2.70

Note: Growth Rate: Simple average annual growth rates.
Source: Based on Education in India (various years).

There are significant decadal variations. During the decade of the 1970s, the expenditure per student on primary education increased rapidly, but during the same period, expenditure per student at middle level registered a negative rate of growth. Middle-level education received favourable treatment only in the 1980s.

RESOURCE REQUIREMENTS FOR UEE

Finding resources to finance UEE is an urgent as well as, contrary to popular fears, an entirely achievable task. On the basis of the recommendation of the high powered Saikia Committee, a group of experts was constituted to estimate the financial requirement for making elementary education a fundamental right in the Constitution. Based on a detailed estimation of costs of each item/programme the group of experts has estimated that UEE requires additionally Rs 136.9 thousand crore during the next ten years (see Table 20.15). While this figure may seem awesome, certainly being much higher than the Rs 40 thousand crore for a five-year period estimated by the Saikia Committee, it has to be noted that additionally it means only Rs 14 thousand crore a year on average, or additionally 0.7 per cent of GDP (if the GDP grows at a modest rate of growth of 5 per cent per annum). This should easily be achievable.

According to the Committee's estimates, this would provide for a reasonably good pupil–teacher ratio of 1:30, improved physical access to schools, provision of instructional material, other necessary incentives, and on the whole a tolerable minimum level of quality of education to every child in India, by the end of the first decade of the twenty-first century. The expert group also felt that if the government is serious about the allocation of 6 per cent of GDP to education, the task becomes much easier 6 per cent of GDP would not only provide the needed resources for UEE, but it also allows provision of additional resources for growth of secondary and higher education. Further, the group showed that

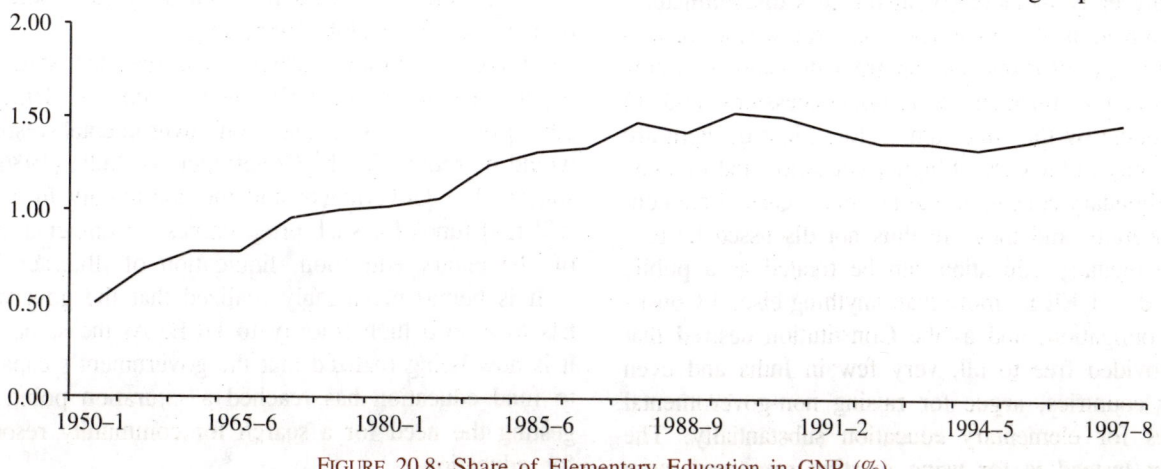

FIGURE 20.8: Share of Elementary Education in GNP (%)

TABLE 20.15
Additional Expenditure Required for UEE in India

(Rs in crores)

	Recurring	Non-recurring	Total	Total as % of GDP
1998–9	100	0	100	0.007
1999–2000	1500	2000	3500	0.24
2000–1	4000	3000	7000	0.46
2001–2	6000	4000	10,000	0.62
2002–3	8500	4000	12,500	0.73
2003–4	10,000	4000	14,000	0.78
2004–5	13,000	4000	17,000	0.90
2005–6	16,000	4000	20,000	1.01
2006–7	20,000	4000	24,000	1.16
2007–8	27,250	1572	28,822	1.32
Total	106,350	30,572	136,922	0.72*

Note: * Average.
Source: Based on DoE (1999).

increasing of total allocation to education to reach 6 per cent of GDP is not at all difficult, given (i) the economy is likely to grow at a rate of growth of above 5 per cent, (ii) the likely increase of tax/GDP ratio from 16 per cent to 18 per cent, and (iii) the likely increase of the non-tax-revenue/GDP ratio from about 3 per cent to 5 per cent during the next ten years. The group also attempted to clear two absurd propositions that are in circulation: (i) that we cannot achieve UEE because it is too costly; and (ii) that the only way to achieve it is to divert funds to it from higher education.

Mobilization of Resources for Elementary Education

In the process of review of NPE 1986, the Government of India (1990) for the first time referred in detail to some of the methods that are nowadays being discussed to generate additional resources for education. These methods largely refer to the higher education sector.

Prominent among the several measures that are discussed presently include: (i) raising fees discriminately, (ii) revitalization of the national loan programme for students, (iii) special taxes such as graduate taxes, (iv) corporate donations through liberal tax concessions, and (v) self-financing by the education sector. Most of them are relevant only in the case of higher education and to some extent secondary education, but not in the case of elementary education, and they are thus not discussed here.

As elementary education can be treated as a public good, and as UEE is, more than anything else, a Constitutional obligation, and as the Constitution desired that it be provided free to all, very few in India and even in other countries, argue for raising non-governmental resources for elementary education substantially. The argument instead is for using existing resources more efficiently, for strengthening the base for local finances, and for generation of voluntary community resources to supplement governmental efforts. The role of local bodies is being expected to be vital in not only generating more resources but also in the context of decentralized planning and management of school education. The 73rd Constitutional Amendment on *panchayati raj* institutions may result in more demands on *panchayats*.

DECENTRALIZATION AND MOBILIZATION OF COMMUNITY RESOURCES FOR FINANCING ELEMENTARY EDUCATION

Quite a few suggestions are being put forward to mobilize additional resources for elementary education. The Government of India (1986, 1990) explicitly favours community financing of elementary education. For example, NPE 1986 stated: 'Resources, to the extent possible, will be raised by mobilizing donations, asking the beneficiary communities to maintain school buildings and supplies of some consumables, raising fees at the higher levels of education, and effecting some savings by the efficient use of facilities' (see DoE 1986, 28).

In contrast to the earlier stand that the state shall provide resources for UEE, now, even for elementary education it is stated that non-governmental resources would be required. The Government of India (1986, 28) states: 'The Government and the community in general will find funds for such programmes as: universalization of elementary education; liquidation of illiteracy.'

It is being increasingly realized that the government has to accord high priority to UEE. At the same time, it is now being realized that the government's capability to fund education has reached a saturation point, suggesting the need for a search for community resources for education.

An important development of the 1990s refers to significant efforts of the government to decentralize educational planning and administration and involve the community at various levels in planning, administration, financing, monitoring, and supervision of the working of the school system. Following the Constitutional amendment in favour of *panchayati raj* institutions, and also the launching of externally aided projects in primary education, village education committees, school development committees, and similar committees at various levels have been set up with the involvement of the local community. With the participation of these committees, efforts are also being made to mobilize physical and financial resources for the village communities to finance elementary education. For example, the School Reform Act in Andhra Pradesh provides for the establishment of committees for people's participation in educational activities at various levels—a school committee, a *panchayat* education committee, a *mandal* education committee, a municipal education committee, a district education committee, and two boards for monitoring the activities relating to education one at district level called the District Education Board and another at state level called the State Advisory Board for School Education. These committees at various levels are expected to comprise parents, community leaders, and teachers, with a fair representation of women. The Committees are vested with several powers including resource generation. Thus a significant move has been made on the part of the government to decentralize the administration of school education in the state. Such experiments have not, however, become widespread.

Financing of Private Schools: Private Enrichment and Public Pauperization

One important issue that has significant implications for financing education, even school education, relates to private schools and the public policy towards private schools. In the present period, characterized by the global wave of privatization, it is being increasingly felt that private schools are an effective answer to the problem of depleting public budgets. The role of the private sector in educational development in India is totally different from that of the private sector in this mixed economy in general. Private education or private schools necessarily mean a privately managed system, not necessarily a privately funded system of education. Thus private schools are of two kinds: private-aided (PA) schools, and pure private or private unaided (PUA) schools. PA schools do not provide any significant financial relief to the government, as more than 95 per cent of the recurring expenditures, and sometimes

some part of the capital expenditures of these schools are met by the government. Private institutions have to survive for 3–5 years before they can qualify for government aid, sometimes even retrospectively.[11] Both during the initial and later periods, they might make profits by underpaying teachers and other staff, charging various types of non-tuition fees, and through other questionable practices. Thus the private sector not only does not necessarily reduce public financial burden, but also may enrich itself at government and social expense.

That the PA schools survive only with public subsidies is an indisputable fact. For example, out of total government expenditure on primary education in the state of Uttar Pradesh, 88 per cent was on PA elementary schools, in the form of grants; this is to be contrasted with the number of schools. Just 1.7 per cent of the primary schools and 14.3 per cent of the secondary schools in Uttar Pradesh are PA, while the rest are run by government or local bodies (in 1993). In other words, an alarmingly disproportionate amount out of government expenditure on elementary education was spent on an infinitesimally small number of the primary and upper primary schools. Similar is the situation in Tamil Nadu, though the degree of unevenness is not as sharp as in Uttar Pradesh (see Table 20.16). Thus, PA schools cause severe inequitable distribution of government expenditure on education.

Thus it seems that the PA sector rarely generates substantial resources on its own, but relies extensively on governmental grants. By taking away disproportionately (in relation to number of schools) large amounts from limited public budgets, the private sector also contributes to pauperization of government schools and misallocation of public resources. It has already been noted in the earlier sections that the contribution of the private sector to public education in the form of voluntary donations and endowments is very small, and further that this share is rapidly declining. Given such evidence, it would be unrealistic to assume that the private sector in education would provide any financial relief to the government.

The unaided primary schools do provide some financial relief, but at huge social and economic cost. The adverse effects include accentuating dualism, elitism, and class inequalities. Tilak (1994b) has analysed the various characteristics of private versus public schools in India, and has found that the private schools cater to the needs of the rich only, their quality of education is not necessarily superior to that of state-run schools, and there are no equity-oriented programmes in these schools.

---

[11] In fact, it may not be appropriate to refer to such schools as 'private' schools.

TABLE 20.16
Government Assistance to Private Schools and
Number of Private Schools—Expenditure on
a Given Level of Education (Revised)

	Government assistant*		% of private schools+(1993)	
	1989–90	1995–6	Primary	Middle
Andhra Pradesh	8.3	7.4	4.19	7.96
Arunachal Pradesh	–	–	1.15	2.20
Assam	1.5	1.2	0.21	3.38
Bihar	0.0	0.0	0.59	1.82
Goa	0.0	0.0	4.15	16.38
Gujarat	0.0	0.0	1.40	5.62
Haryana	1.0	1.2	0.82	1.70
Himachal Pradesh	0.0	0.1	0.53	2.69
Jammu & Kashmir	0.0	0.0	0.28	0.95
Karnataka	3.8	1.5	1.73	11.28
Kerala	53.8	55.9	59.54	65.83
Madhya Pradesh	2.2	5.9	1.65	3.27
Maharashtra	0.1	0.1	4.67	6.04
Manipur	4.6	12.6	16.71	23.50
Meghalaya	69.6	28.8	22.30	91.55
Mizoram	32.6	17.3	10.51	39.75
Nagaland	0.6	0.1	1.82	14.08
Orissa	27.9	1.8	0.76	5.16
Punjab	0.5	3.6	0.53	2.01
Rajasthan	45.6	1.6	1.04	3.17
Sikkim	0.5	0.9	0.38	0.00
Tamil Nadu	80.2	31.7	16.17	32.94
Tripura	0.0	0.0	0.64	1.15
Uttar Pradesh	91.5	87.7	1.65	14.26
West Bengal	0.0	95.1	7.96	73.95
Chandigarh	4.5	0.0	0.00	0.00
Delhi	72.4	0.0	2.76	11.93
Pondicherry	0.0	0.0	1.13	7.95
All India	27.4	25.9	3.94	10.71

Note: * as per cent of total government expenditure on Education at the given level.
+ as per cent of all schools.

Source: Analysis of Budgeted Expenditure on Education 1989–90 to 1991–2 and 1995–6 to 1997–8, Minsitry of Human Resource Development, Department of Education, New Delhi; 1991–2 and 1995–6 to 1997–8, Minsitry of Human Resource Development, Department of Education, New Delhi; 1986–7 and 1990–1 to 1992–3, Minsitry of Human Resource Development, Department of Education, New Delhi.

It has earlier been found that the effects of private schools on income distribution in society are so severe that they even outweigh the positive effects of the vast public (government) school system, the net effect thereby being significantly negative.

The private sector is slowly but steadily growing in size, though its present size is still very small. It is interesting to note that voluntary contributions to government institutions have quite significantly come down, and at the same time the number of profit-making private institutions has increased. These trends reflect a shift from motives of philanthropy and charity on the part of private enterprise to profit and greed.

Lastly, the size of private sector is very small, though it is causing significant distortions in the pattern of financing education. At the same time, its relative size cannot increase significantly, as the benefits attached to private schooling are mostly due to scarcity of places in private schools, and get reduced with expansion of the private sector. It has also been found that the private sector has already reached 'optimum' levels in India, the 'optimum' levels being defined in terms of the share of the private sector in developed countries like the US.

FOREIGN AID FOR EDUCATION[12]

Among the several sources of financing education in India, foreign aid has not been significant during the last four decades. But foreign aid is one important source of finances for education in several developing countries. Its importance gets enhanced in developing countries like India where public budgets for education become very tight with the adoption of the structural adjustment policies. It is, however, too much to expect that foreign aid will be able to substantially deal with the financial shortfall in education in a vast country like India, when it could not contribute significantly even in small countries of Africa, Latin America, and Asia. As Verspoor (1993, 103–4) noted:

International aid has not been able to change the course of events. International meetings have set goals and redefined priorities on a regular basis. Over the past 25 years, a well-established education aid community has developed, with a busy meeting schedule, several newsletters, professional networkers, and aid watchers. It includes also an international education research community with several respectable journals. But the action has rarely been at par with the rhetoric. In fact, it can be argued that *external aid to education has been peripheral to the course of educational development.* [emphasis added]

In the trends on foreign aid for education, a clear shift can be noted, the priority shifting from higher education in the 1960s to secondary education (diversification of secondary education in particular) in the 1970s and up to the mid-1980s, and to primary education since the late 1980s. Relatively more aid began to flow to primary education from the late 1980s. The World Conference

[12] This section partly draws from Tilak (1999b).

on Education for All (see Jomtien, 1990) is also partly responsible for the increased emphasis on foreign aid for primary education.

In India the need for external assistance for education in general, and primary education in particular, was not felt for a long time. Foreign aid was felt necessary only in case of foreign-exchange-intensive, capital-intensive, and foreign-expertise needed sectors. Education in India in general, and primary education in particular, do not belong to either of these categories. The donors also felt the same. But like the rest of the new economic policies relating to liberalization, and structural adjustment, policies on foreign aid for financing primary education have been introduced without any serious debate in the country.

The 1990s is a decade that marks a new phase in developments in education in general, and primary education in particular, in terms of foreign aid. Preceded by a serious economic crisis, the Government of India in 1990 adopted structural adjustment policies which inflicted serious cuts in budgetary resources for education in general, including elementary education. Consequently, a social safety net programme was launched to protect vulnerable but important sectors like primary education and basic health care from the adverse effects of stabilization and structural adjustment policies. Thus began international assistance for primary education in India, which has been a most significant development in education in independent India, as external assistance for a long time was not sought even for other levels of education by the Government of India during the fifty years of Independence. In fact, quite a few international aid organizations were very eager to enter into the primary education scene in India from the mid-1980s onwards. However, the Government of India felt no need of external assistance for primary education then. The foreign exchange crisis in 1989 followed by the adoption of structural adjustment policies, which were regarded as 'a necessary evil', changed the whole situation and thereby the approach of the government. For the first time, the primary education sector was rather reluctantly opened to enthusiastic external aid organizations on a large scale.[13] Starting with World Bank assistance for primary education in ten districts in Uttar Pradesh and that of UNICEF in Bihar, a plethora of international— both multilateral and bilateral—aid organizations are currently in operation in India working for the improvement of primary education system. Some important

organizations are: World Bank, European Community, UNICEF, United Nations Development Programme (UNDP), ODA of England, and the Swedish International Development Agency (SIDA). In order to ensure better coordination from the point of view of the Government of India and governments of various states (provinces) in India on the one hand, and the host of international aid organizations on the other, the Government of India has launched the DPEP, as a broad overall umbrella of international aid programmes in primary education in the country. Quite a few other programmes assisted by external agencies that were in existence before the formation of the DPEP have also been brought under this common umbrella. A couple of projects however, remained separately.[14] In all, starting with 42 districts in seven states in phase I of the DPEP in 1994, the programme has expanded to cover 149 districts, as shown in Table 20.17, and, in fact, it is being planned that soon it will cover 242 districts in fifteen states, out of the total 500-odd districts in the country.

The DPEP: Critical Issues and Emerging Trends

Given the situation in some other countries where a multitude of external agencies work on primary education uncoordinated, even contributing to confusion, if not chaos, with conflicting policies, procedures, approaches, and plans of action, the formation of the overall umbrella of the DPEP by the Government of India can be seen as an important step in a positive direction that facilitated better coordination among the three partners, viz. the Government of India, the states governments and the funding agencies, avoided duplication, and ensured some kind of coherence and consistency in the overall programme. From the point of view of planning and management, this is indeed an important step, though it has also worked as a catalytic force contributing to some weaknesses of the whole programme, will be discussed a little later.

Of all, the most important consequence of the DPEP is a relaxation of resource constraints in planning education. Educational planning under austerity (or under conditions of severe resource constraints) had been the characteristic feature of planning education in India for a long time, as in many developing countries. Perhaps for the first time, the districts in India were told that each district participating in the DPEP would be given about Rs 400 million for a seven-year project period. While Rs 350–400 million is a substantial additional amount for a district, Rs 50–60 million per annum is not really all

---

[13] There were a couple of minor projects in operation earlier. They include NFE projects in a few selected villages financed by United Nations Children's Education Fund (UNICEF) and primary education projects in selected schools in Andhra Pradesh funded by the Overseas Development Administration (ODA).

[14] These are the *Shiksha Karmi* project and the *Lok Jumbish* in Rajasthan—both funded by SIDA, and the *Mahila Samakhya* project financed by the Dutch government.

TABLE 20.17
Geographical Coverage of DPEP (Number of Districts)

States	Phase I	Phase II	Phase III	In process	Total
Assam	4	5	–	–	9
Haryana	4	3			7
Karnataka	4	7			11
Kerala	3	3			6
Tamil Nadu	3	3			6
Maharashtra	5	4			9
Madhya Pradesh	19	15			34
Himachal Pradesh	–	4	–		4
Gujarat	–	3	–	6	9
Orissa	–	8	–	8	16
Andhra Pradesh	–	5	14		19
West Bengal	–	5	–	5	10
Uttar Pradesh	–	15	3	38	56
Bihar	–	–	27	–	27
Rajasthan			10	9	19
Total	42	80	54	66	242

Source: DPEP Moves on.... (New Delhi: Ministry of Human Resource Development, 1997) and DPEP Calling (November December, 1999).

that high compared to the present level of public spending of about Rs 600 million per district in India (1994–5). While there are no detailed and comprehensive estimates on trends in external aid for education, according to the available data, external assistance accounts for about Rs 10,000 million (in the 2000–1 Union Budget), as shown in Table 20.18.

This may be compared to the current level of total expenditure on elementary education in the country (1997–8), which is about Rs 200 billion (thousand million). Thus, despite geographical expansion of the programme as noted earlier, it still cannot be regarded as a large-scale programme of improvement of primary education, as the funds constitute less than 3 per cent of the total expenditure of the government on elementary education. More than the effects of resource availability, the

influence of the DPEP—both positive and negative—on the education scene as a whole is indeed very significant. These effects could either be direct or catalytic in nature.

District planning in primary education has been accorded a respectable place under the DPEP. While there has been much talk about the need for district planning in education in India for a long time ever since Independence, including constitution of a few important national-level committees on district- or block-level planning, few significant efforts could be made until recently in this direction, except for a couple of random district plans in education prepared earlier by researchers and planners. The DPEP has been based on district planning, and accordingly district planning in primary education has become very important. This is the single most important positive contribution of the DPEP.

Table 20.18
Externally Aided Projects in the Union Budget Plan Allocations

(Rs in crore)

Projects	1999–2000(B)	1999–2000(R)	2000–01(B)	% Increase over the revised estimate
Shiksha Karmi	19.3	19.3	26.1	35.2
Mahila Samakhya	7.5	6.0	10.0	66.7
Lok Jumbish	50.3	40.0	56.1	40.3
DPEP	750.0	600.0	969.0	61.5
Total	827.1	685.3	1076.2	57.0

Note: R—Revised estimates; B—Budget estimates.
Source: Expenditure Budget 2000–1.

One of the primary strategies of the DPEP is decentralization of policy making, planning, administration, and implementation of educational policies and plans which is very important in a big country like India, where some of the states and even districts are larger than many countries in the world in terms of population. But when a uniform format was prepared under the DPEP, essentially by the Government of India, some of the fundamental aspects relating to decentralization were obscured. While the plans are formulated at decentralized levels, the formats for the formulation are given by the central government. The formats include detailed procedures and guidelines to be followed at every step. They also include specific limits on the availability of external resources and their broad pattern of allocation between different major items of expenditure, which are same for all districts. It can be said that at best the responsibility for implementation of the programme is decentralized, that too with a limited degree of freedom. The implementation is consistently monitored by the central government and its specially constituted bodies, apart from appraisal and reappraisal missions of the funding agencies. All this could not be avoided not only because the central government and several state governments are involved, but also because, to a great extent, the funding agencies also find it convenient to follow a commonly agreed format. Perhaps it can safely be concluded that such a common format enabled more state governments and new funding agencies to enter the scene and progress fast. The governments as well as the funding organizations find the centralized format convenient, though at the same time they might realize the loss of scope for innovations and experimentation in their activities.

Having noted all this, it should be stated at the same time, that various types and levels of manpower, including planners, administrators, educationists, and community leaders at decentralized levels—the states, the districts, and even lower levels—are involved in the preparation of the plans and their execution, which gives a genuinely rich flavour of decentralization. This is because these several local bodies did not participate in such activities earlier in such a significant way. The 73rd and 74th Amendments of the Constitution of India also strengthened the mechanisms of decentralization with the creation of village- local-level socio-political bodies such as *panchayat* and Village Education Committees.

This is again not free from all weakness. The creation of autonomous 'societies' at national, state, district, and village levels to take active role in the management and implementation of the programme is an important feature of the programme in a framework of decentralization. But simultaneously with the creation of these parallel structures, the government machinery seems to have been slowly sidelined. These parallel structures erode the importance of the government. In short, all this may lead to an increasingly reduced role of the government in education in general, including specifically primary education.

The Programme is in operation in about 150 of the 536 districts of the country. The government and external agencies could run such a massive programme relatively easily without serious problems and constraints, unlike in many other countries, partly because of the existence of highly trained, skilled, and talented manpower, though not sufficiently evenly spread over the country. As a result, the need, on a large scale for consultants from abroad is not felt either by the government or by external agencies. Further, capacity building of manpower at local levels has been an important component of the programme, which gradually fulfils the increasing demand for trained middle-level manpower. In fact, capacity building at local levels has been an important outcome, as it indeed becomes an important prerequisite of preparation of any meaningful district plan in a decentralized framework. As planning has been from above for a long time, expertise also got concentrated at national and state levels. Under the DPEP it has become imperative to train and develop local-level manpower for planning, project preparation, and for execution of the plans and projects. This is another important contribution of the DPEP.

Similarly the massive programme could be run relatively smoothly, as a large amount of research on various aspects of primary education, which can be called in the terminology of the international funding organizations 'sector work', was already available, and the gaps in research could be filled in no time, due to the existence of a large network of universities and research institutions in the country with sufficiently well-trained researchers. In a sense, the external agencies might not have felt the need for extensive technical assistance work to start the project but for collation of research. Further, the programme has a component of strengthening of research capacities of institutions and individuals. After all, elaborate research does greatly help the funding agencies, in addition to helping the recipient governments.

A few more important trends also seem to be emerging, which may have serious long-term implications. In a sense, the whole approach of the DPEP is highly sectarian, instead of being holistic to the cause of education development. First, with different kinds and quantum of inputs being pumped into the DPEP districts, inequalities might be created between DPEP and non-DPEP districts even within a given state. Thus the programme is geographically not holistic. Second, primary education is not approached in a holistic manner. For example, it is surprising to note that EFA, UEE, and the DPEP are perceived by state administrations as different projects/programmes and are in operation in several states in a rather uncoordinated fashion. Further, the upper-primary level, which is part of the compulsory elementary ('basic') education in India, does not seem to have been given sufficient attention. Third, while the DPEP cells/bureaus have been endowed with a higher level of physical, human and financial resources, and are also associated with modernization and efficiency, systemic improvement such as in case of primary education as a whole and in case of directorates of school education (that include primary education), not to speak of the department of higher education and the department of education as a whole, in the states is not noticeable. Fourth, other levels of education, particularly secondary and higher, are increasingly being ignored. Not only are budgetary resources for secondary and higher education either stagnant or declining in recent years, but also the planning and management aspects of secondary and higher education do not seem to be receiving the usual level of attention from the government. Such a sectarian approach causes serious imbalances in education development. The flow of external funds for primary education as 'an adjunct to the structural adjustment operations' (see Ayyar 1996, 352) perhaps complicated the issues, as structural adjustment policies include reduced role of the state in all spheres including education, specifically post-elementary education. Thus, though funding for the DPEP is programme-based, it might work like policy-based lending operations of external organizations.

An immediate fallout of the DPEP can be reduced domestic efforts to finance primary education. The central government could recommend joining the DPEP and go in external financing to the states, so that it can reduce transfers (or additional transfers) of central revenues to states for primary education. Similarly states have been willing to go in for external financing, as it can relieve pressures on them for (i) mobilizing additional resources on their own, and (ii) more efficient reallocation of budgetary resources in favour of primary education. In addition, external assistance has been attractive to states as the central government transfers the external assistance to states as grants, not loans. Fall in domestic efforts to finance primary education is possible despite the condition of 'additionality' in external assistance, as the condition of additionality might refer to the absolute level of expenditure incurred in the base year, and not to the rate of growth in expenditure experienced. On the whole, the states seem to view the programme

essentially as a centrally sponsored programme with generous resources flowing into the states through the central government. What seems to be overlooked both by the central and state governments is the long-term debt burden on the people.

Neither district planning nor capacity building really requires external assistance. It is sad that they could be made possible only under an externally assisted programme of primary education. While the contribution of the DPEP has to be acknowledged, it should be emphasized that the very fact that district planning and capacity building have been revitalized only under an externally assisted programme speaks more about the inability and failure of the government on these two fronts during the last fifty years. Moreover, most, if not all, of the components of the DPEP—whether they relate to quantitative expansion, improvement in quality, improvement in equity, or decentralization—do not actually require foreign exchange. Many of these components could have been funded with the help of domestic resources. Thus a clear and sound rationale for external assistance for primary education does not exit. This is perhaps the most important weakness of the programme. The eagerness of international aid organizations to finance primary education in India on the one hand, and the severely deteriorated general budgetary conditions of the government at the beginning of the 1990s on the other, have been responsible for launching of the programme of external assistance for primary education.

Correspondingly, a very important and damaging consequence of the DPEP (and the economic reform policies introduced since the beginning of the 1990s) has been of a different kind. A view, which has now been widely accepted without much argument is that the government does not have money even for the development of any qualitative or quantitative dimension of primary education. An unfortunate and not necessarily correct impression is being created that improvement in primary education in the country will be possible only with external assistance. As a result, district after district and state after state are eager to enter the DPEP, as the only source available for financing primary education is believed to be external assistance. Resource-poor (as well as resource-rich) states compete with each other to enter into the DPEP arena for external assistance to primary education. This 'dependency' culture, has spread widely in no time both horizontally across all parts of the country in all states, irrespective of political ideologies of the ruling parties, and vertically at all layers of government and administration, and people in general in the whole country. This can be described as a sad and sudden turn in the history of primary education in independent India.

CONCLUDING OBSERVATIONS

The Constitutional Directive of UEE in India is still elusive, even four decades after the expiry of the deadline prescribed by the Constitution. It is feared that unless sufficient resources are devoted to elementary education, and meaningful strategies are adopted, the goal might remain unaccomplished. In this chapter a quick review of a few key dimensions of financing elementary education has been attempted. It should be seen as a modest attempt to present an analytical and descriptive review of major issues in financing education in India. Broad trends in financing education in India are outlined, and the policies discussed. Squeezing data from different sources, an elaborate statistical profile has also been attempted. For this purpose a few important issues have been selected, and on each issue empirical evidence is presented, and the available research is briefly surveyed to highlight the gaps in research and knowledge. But neither are the issues selected exhaustive, nor is the discussion on them in-depth.

The rationale for financing of education is clear. Both economic theory and empirical evidence on returns to investment in education and distribution benefits of investment in education necessitate financing of education. The recognition of the investment nature and the public good characteristic of education are expected to influence the policies and pattern of financing education positively and significantly. The role of the government is found to be justifiably crucial in funding education in India.

Despite recognition of education as an investment, and as a 'crucial investment, for national survival' by the Government of India, the pattern of allocation of resources to education is far from satisfactory, judged in terms of adequacy, efficiency, and equity. The priority accorded to education in the Five Year Plans, total government budget expenditures, and expenditure in GNP need to be improved. There are signs of improvement in intra-sectoral allocation of resources in favour of elementary education.

The beginning of the 1990s is marked by a few significant developments in the socio-economic spheres of the developing countries of the world. The World Conference on Education for All (Jomtien Conference) held in Jomtien, Thailand, in March 1990 has made a few significant contributions in the form of (i) recognition of importance of education for development and (ii) correspondingly a revival of commitment of the governments, the internal organizations, and the societies at large to education in general and to primary education in particular. In a sense, governments became more serious with the goals of EFA.

Parallel to this, unfortunately the 1990s also marked a beginning of serious economic problems in most developing countries, necessitating adoption of stabilization and structural adjustment reform policies. The economic reform policies had a serious adverse effect on public expenditures in general, including education. Public budgets for education, including elementary education, began to seriously suffer. The social safety net programmes and corresponding flow of foreign aid to primary education mitigated the adverse effects of economic reform policies on primary education, but only to a certain extent. As a result, today we find mixed trends in public financing of education in many developing countries.

India is not an exception to these global trends. Though the public expenditures on education, and also as a proportion of the government budgets showed an increase in the 1990s, public expenditures on education as a proportion of national income declined steeply from above 4 per cent to much below 4 per cent. Government expenditure on elementary education as a proportion of national income also declined from 1.6 per cent in 1990–1 to 1.4 per cent in 1996–7. In the last couple of years, allocations to elementary education have increased. But a substantial part of the increase in outlay for elementary education is accounted for by external aid, leading many to warn that the growth in public expenditure on elementary education is largely 'borrowed growth.'

The need to enhance the levels of funding elementary education is obvious. It is estimated that realization of the long-cherished goal of UEE requires additionally Rs 137 thousand crore in the next ten years—about Rs 14 thousand crore a year, or on average about 0.7 per cent of national income per annum. This does not seem to be an unachievable target, nor is it unaffordable. At the end it may, however, be noted that finances are only a necessary, but not a sufficient, condition for achieving UEE in India.

The issue of mobilizing additional resources for education is also briefly discussed here. First, it is concluded that as far as school education, specifically elementary education—a 'pure public' and 'merit' good—is concerned, there are no magic solutions. The government has to 'generously' finance education. Efforts to augment non-government resources may be restricted to higher education. Additional resources that can be generated from the community for financing school education may be viewed as supplementary resources and the government should assume complete responsibility of funding. There are a few developments taking place in funding school education. Two important developments have been reviewed: privatization and international aid. Both have their limitations. The former accentuates socio-economic disparities besides leading to the enrichment of the private sector and the pauperization of government schools, and the latter cannot be an effective solution even if associated anomalies can be eliminated. A strong political commitment to finance the education sector liberally from domestic resources seems to be the only alternative.

To conclude, the new economic policies initiated in 1991 that involve short-term stabilization and long-term structural adjustment policies in India will, it is feared, lead to immediate cuts in public budgets for education, as happened in several developing countries that adopted these policies, as these policies clearly involve reduction in public expenditures and deficits, and in the long run they may result in a drastic change in public policies on financing of education. The higher education sector in India has already experienced drastic budget cuts. It is feared that primary and elementary education might also suffer. However, the DPEP, being launched with external assistance in several states, it is hoped will provide some sort of protection to primary education from the budget squeezes. Nevertheless, the financial crisis in education is transparent, and it is forecasted to continue.

The need for strengthening the resource base for education is obvious. However, the choices seem to be limited as far as school education is concerned. Given the Constitutional Directive, and other considerations, the government should continue to take on complete responsibility of financing elementary education, and other sources can only supplement governmental efforts. There is need to improve the overall allocation pattern in financing education in India.

REFERENCES

Ayyar, R. V. V. (1997). 'Educational Policy Planning and Globalization'. *International Journal of Educational Development*, vol. 16(4), pp. 347–53.

Department of Economic Affairs (various years). *Economic Survey*. Ministry of Finance, Government of India, New Delhi.

Department of Education (1968). *National Policy on Education 1968*. Ministry of Human Resource Development, Government of India, New Delhi.

———— (1985). *The Challenge of Education: A Policy Perspective*. Ministry of Human Resource Development, Government of India, New Delhi.

———— (1986). *National Policy on Education 1986*. Ministry of Human Resource Development, Government of India, New Delhi.

———— (1993). *District Primary Education Programme*. Ministry of Human Resource Development, Government of India, New Delhi.

———— (1993). *Education for All: The Indian Scene*. Ministry of Human Resource Development, Government of India, New Delhi.

———— (1995). *District Primary Education Programme Guidelines*. Ministry of Human Resource Development, Government of India, New Delhi.

———— (1997). *District Primary Education Programme Moves on. . . .* Ministry of Human Resource Development, Government of India, New Delhi.

———— (various years). *Analysis of Budgeted Expenditure on Education in India*. Ministry of Human Resource Development, Government of India, New Delhi.

———— (various years). *Annual Report*. Ministry of Human Resource Development, Government of India, New Delhi.

———— (various years). *Education in India*. Ministry of Human Resource Development, Government of India, New Delhi.

———— (various years). *Selected Educational Statistics*. Ministry of Human Resource Development, Government of India, New Delhi.

Education Commission (1966). *Education and National Development: Report of the Education Commission*. Government of India, New Delhi. [Reprint: National Council of Educational Research and Training, 1971]

Government of India (1990). *Towards an Enlightened and Human Society: NPE 1986: A Review, Report of the Committee for Review of National Policy on Education 1986*. [Chairman: Acharya Ramamurti], Government of India Press, Faridabad.

National Council of Educational Research and Training (1992). *Fifth All India Educational Survey*. New Delhi.

———— (1998). *Sixth All India Educational Survey*. New Delhi.

Peacock, Alan T. and Wiseman (1961). *The Growth of Public Expenditure in UK Oxford*, London.

Psacharpoulos, G. and M. Woodhall (1985). *Education and Development*. Oxford for the World Bank, New York.

Schultz, Theodore W. (1961). 'Investment in Human Capital'. *American Economic Review*, vol. 51(1), (March), pp. 1–17.

Seth, S. C. (1985). *India: The Next 7000 Days*. Wiley Eastern, New Delhi.

Tilak, J. B. G. (1987a). *Economics of Inequality in Education*. Sage Publications, for Institute of Economic Growth, New Delhi.

———— (1987b). 'Educational Finances in India.' *Journal of Educational Planning and Administration*, 1(3–4) (July–October), pp. 132–99.

———— (1989). *Education and its Relation to Economic Growth, Poverty and Income Distribution*. Discussion Paper no. 46. World Bank, Washington, D.C.

———— (1991d). *Financing Education in India: A Review of Trends, Problems and Prospects*. World Bank Resident Mission, New Delhi Office.

——— (1994a). *Education for Development in Asia.* Sage, New Delhi.

——— (1994b). *Resource Requirements of Education in India: Implications for the Tenth Finance Commission.* (Report prepared for the Government of India). National Institute of Educational Planning and Administration, New Delhi.

——— (1994c). 'South Asian Perspectives (on Alternative Modes of Financing, Governing and Managing Educational Systems)'. *International Journal of Educational Research.* (in press)

——— (1999a). 'National Human Development Initiative: Education in the Union Budget'. *Economic and Political Weekly*, 34 (10–11) (6 March), pp. 614–20.

——— (1999b) 'Development Assistance to Primary Education in India: Transformation of Enthusiastic Donors and Reluctant Recipients'. In King, Kenneth and Lene Buchert (eds) *Changing International Aid to Education: Global Patterns and National Contexts.* UNESCO in cooperation with NORRAG, pp. 307–17.

Tilak, J. B. G. and N. V. Varghese (1990) 'Resources for Education for All'. *Journal of Education and Social Change*, 4(4) (January–March), pp. 24–59.

Verspoor, Adriaan (1993). 'More than Business-As-Usual: Reflections on the New Modalities of Education Aid'. *International Journal of Educational Development,* 13(2), pp. 103–12.

VI

Learning from Experience
Recounting Success Stories

21
Primary Education in Himachal Pradesh
Examining A Success Story

Anuradha De, Claire Noronha and Meera Samson

THE TASTE OF SUCCESS

Educational Breakthrough in Himachal Pradesh

From a state that, at the time of Independence, had the lowest literary level, Himachal Pradesh has shown remarkable progress in literacy over time (see Sinha, Tyagi, and Thakur 1997). In terms of rural literacy rates, its progress has been striking (see Table 21.1). Himachal ranked second in literacy among 16 major states as far back as 1981, and it has retained its ranking. This is all the more impressive as there are several factors in Himachal that make educational progress difficult.

TABLE 21.1
Literacy Rates in Himachal Pradesh 1961–97

	Male literacy	Female literacy	Total literacy
1961	32.31	9.49	21.26
1971	43.19	20.23	31.96
1981	64.29	37.72	51.18
1991	75.36	52.13	63.86
1997	87	70	77

Note: Figures for 1961 and 1971 are for population aged 5+: figures for 1981, 1991 and 1997 are for population aged 7+.

Source: Census data for 1961, 1971, 1981, 1991; NSSO for 1997.

In a study of 1991 district-level census data, Saldanha (1996) had noted that districts with higher than average urban population will tend to have higher literacy rates, while districts with higher than average Scheduled Caste (SC) population as well as districts with a higher than average Scheduled Tribes (ST) population will tend to have lower than average literacy rates. Himachal has all three factors tending towards lower literacy: its population is largely rural with none of its 12 districts having

an urban population more than the national average of 25.7 per cent; 11 of its 12 districts have an SC population more than the national average of 16.5 per cent; and 3 of its districts have an ST population more than the national average of 8 per cent. Yet, 3 of its districts are in the high literacy category, i.e. above 70 per cent literacy, and the remaining 9 are in the medium literacy category. There are no districts in the low literacy category, i.e. below 40 per cent.

Just as impressive are the literacy rates for the 10–14 age group—95 per cent for boys and 86 per cent for girls in 1991—very close indeed to the literacy rates for Kerala for this age group—and higher than those achieved by other states (see Table 21.2). It is clear that Himachal Pradesh in 1951 started off very close to the 'BIMARU' states.[1] But by 1991 Himachal was much closer to Kerala than to the BIMARU states. Literacy in this age group is a reflection of the schooling system and it is not surprising that in terms of school attendance rates also— 85 per cent according to NSSO 1996—Himachal ranks very high. In terms of school attendance rates for males as well as for females according to the 1991 Census, at least 8 of Himachal's 12 districts fall under the 50 best districts in India (see Jayachandran 1998).

It is not uncommon for casual visitors to Himachal Pradesh to remark on their surprise at finding an actively functioning school tucked away in what appears to be remote mountain terrain. The PROBE survey[2] of schooling

---

[1] These are the states of Bihar, Madhya Pradesh, Rajasthan, and Uttar Pradesh, which have remained India's problem states in terms of a number of socio-economic indicators.

[2] Clarifications concerning the PROBE survey:

- The sample villages were chosen through stratified random sampling. The districts were chosen after being stratified on the

facilities for the 6–14 age group, which took place in late 1996, also gives evidence of the vitality of Himachal's schooling system (see PROBE 1999).

TABLE 21.2
Comparison of Illiteracy Rates in the 10–14 Age Group 1951–91

	Himachal Pradesh	Kerala	BIMARU states
1951	81	32	86
1961	63	22	69
1971	35	11	63
1981	22	05	57
1991	10	01	43

Source: Calculated from census data.

Himachal Pradesh's terrain is tough and the settlement pattern often scattered,[3] so, even when a village in Himachal has schooling facilities according to country norms (within 1 km of the habitation), very small children can often not join school. Yet, when they do join school, their parents appear particular about school attendance and children persist in school at least till the end of primary school. This picture is corroborated by secondary data. The proportion of population with primary schools within a 1 km radius is the lowest in India. Yet, attendance in both primary and upper-primary sections is far above the average for India as a whole (see Table 21.3).

What is it that makes Himachali parents willing to surmount barriers like access and cost and continue to send children to school? In terms of physical infrastructure, the schooling system is modest. Himachal has few *pucca* or all-weather schools (although the proportion of

TABLE 21.3
Access and School Attendance in Himachal Pradesh

	Primary section			Upper-primary section		
	Proportion of population with school within 1 km of habitation (1993)	Net attendance ratio (1996)	Proportion of children aged 15–19 who have completed class V (1991)	Proportion of population with school within 3 km of habitation (1993)	Net attendance ratio (1996)	Population of children aged 15–19 who have completed class VIII (1991)
Himachal Pradesh	75.97	85	81	78.22	54	51
India	93.76	66	60	85.00	43	45

Note: Net attendance ratio in the primary section is number of persons in the age group 6–10 attending classes I–V expressed as a percentage of the estimated child population in the corresponding age group. Net attendance ratio for upper-primary section is similarly calculated for those children in the 11–14 age group who are in classes VI–VIII.
Source: Census, 1991; NSSO, 52nd round; NCERT (1997).

basis of female literacy rates. Then the villages were chosen from the selected districts at random after excluding villages with census population of more than 3000 and less than 300 (200 for Himachal).

• The main focus of the PROBE survey is primary schooling. Accordingly, information was collected on all schools with a primary section (i.e. classes I–V) in the sample villages.

• While sample schools include both government and private schools, the main focus of the survey is government schools. These make up four-fifths of all sample schools. Unless otherwise stated, the school details presented should be understood to apply to government schools only.

• Sample households consist of a random sample of households residing in the sample villages and with at least one child in the 6–12 age group.

• The findings from the Himachal Pradesh survey are presented separately from the findings on the states of Bihar, Madhya Pradesh, Rajasthan, and Uttar Pradesh. The latter have been grouped together under the commonly used acronym 'BIMARU' states.

[3] According to the 1991 census, as many as 62.87 per cent of villages in Himachal have a population of less than 200 each. The larger villages with a population above 1000 are concentrated in the districts of Una, Kullu, and Kinnaur.

such schools is increasing) but schools on the whole look sturdy, and are often aesthetically appealing. Similarly, the teaching equipment and school facilities do not seem to be very good but there is at least a basic minimum level of infrastructure. Apart from this, children have their textbooks—a vital need, given the educational system. Just as vital is the presence of an adequate number of teachers—the pupil–teacher ratio is 30:1. This means that children are able to get adequate attention. The proportion of single-teacher schools is very small (and these are new schools with only 1 or 2 classes). A system of para-teachers has been introduced where the 'VTs' or voluntary teachers[4] assist the main teachers.

[4] The VT scheme was introduced in Himachal Pradesh in 1984; it was formulated to provide an additional VT to single-teacher primary schools. This was needed because of the increase in enrolment in government schools. Also the scheme was started to provide work to educated unemployed youth. After ten years service, the VTs were to be regularized as JBTs (Junior Basic Trainers). Between 1984 and 1991, nearly 10,000 VT posts had been sanctioned. VTs' salaries were raised to Rs 1500 in 1995.

These teachers, in fact, work hard. The proportion of female teachers is high (41 per cent) considering the remote and rugged nature of the terrain.

One of the chief differences between Himachal Pradesh and the BIMARU states is that in the former there is a functional schooling system. Schooling infrastructure is often minimal, but children have textbooks and enough teachers. Teachers teach and parents send their children to school. In order to explore the reasons the chapter delves into historical, political, and cultural factors in the following section.

THE ROOTS OF SUCCESS

It is inevitable that Himachal's success would spawn a host of questions about its nature and origins, especially when so many areas have been so resistant to the spread of education. Explanations flow easily. The character and nature of hill society are often given the credit for the success by Himachalis themselves and even by outsiders. Is it that hill society is more 'egalitarian' and that caste distinctions are less oppressive than found in the plains, which enable Himachali parents to speak up about problems they face in school? Is it that women have a unique place in Himachali society and this is what has enabled Himachalis to progress? Or is it the fruits of education which have fuelled public motivation for schooling for children—the enormous importance of government jobs in Himachali society? Planned development has also played its part in the educational breakthrough. In addition, the task of spreading education has become easier because of education itself, in a kind of 'virtuous circle' phenomenon. We attempt to look at these and other hypotheses in a little more detail with the preliminary caution that we have suggestions about what actually happened but not enough first-hand information to be anywhere near the final answer or answers.

Education and Development

SUTRA, one of the few large NGOs in the state, though critical of the overall direction and impact of the development process, comments: 'The newly-constituted welfare state of Himachal Pradesh went about its task with missionary zeal' (see SUTRA 1998). The process began much before the state was actually accepted as a full-fledged state and its progress had already attracted favourable attention from neighbouring areas as well as the central government. Two central areas of concern were roads and schooling. The focus on schooling, particularly, was rewarded with spectacular success but there is little doubt that several factors have facilitated this success including the focus on roads. One such factor

may well be the ethnic identity of the Himachali, the sense of cohesiveness, the pride in being Himachali. We will discuss the role of the state in school administration in Himachal Pradesh and then go on to discuss other factors (as well as areas of development which have facilitated the success of primary school education).

THE ROLE OF THE STATE IN EDUCATION

The first Chief Minister of the state is widely credited with creating a 'momentum', that 'established the precedence of primary education on the agendas of the political elites of the state' (see Goyal 1996). Interestingly, primary education has remained a priority of the state government, whichever the party in power. This sustained commitment to schooling has enabled Himachal Pradesh to overcome its initial education at disadvantage.

Figure 21.1 shows 1990–1 literacy rates for different age groups in Himachal Pradesh and India. It is interesting that in the older age groups literacy levels still lag behind the national average: a living reminder of the time when Himachal was below the national average in educational attainments. Other interesting points emerge if we interpret the figure, by backward projection, as showing the literacy rate for the 10–14 age group over earlier periods of time. For example, the literacy rate for the 15–19 age group can be considered as a good approximation to the 10–14 literacy rate in 1985–6 since both groups correspond to the same cohort; similarly, the literacy rate for the 20–4 age group is an approximation for the literacy rate for the 10–14 age group in 1980–1, and so on. This enables us to suggest that literacy in the 10–14 age group has been rising steadily since Independence, at a rate that enabled Himachal to catch up with India in the mid-1950s and subsequently outstrip the country average to an appreciable degree. If we assume that literacy has mainly been achieved through schooling, and not through adult education or non-formal education (NFE) (a legitimate assumption since less than 0.1 per cent of different age groups have attained literacy through non-formal methods, according to the Census 1991b), then the bars can also be interpreted as school participation rate over time. The point that emerges is that Himachal focused early on schooling, and has sustained it over time.

Himachal's progress, then, largely reflects the sustained input into schooling by the Himachal government over the last five decades. Enrolment in Himachal Pradesh schools has been steadily increasing as is shown in Table 21.4 which gives figures from the 1970s onwards. As the DPEP appraisal report on Himachal Pradesh (1996a) says, enrolment is not an issue in Himachal and it remains to mop up the residual 5–10 per cent.

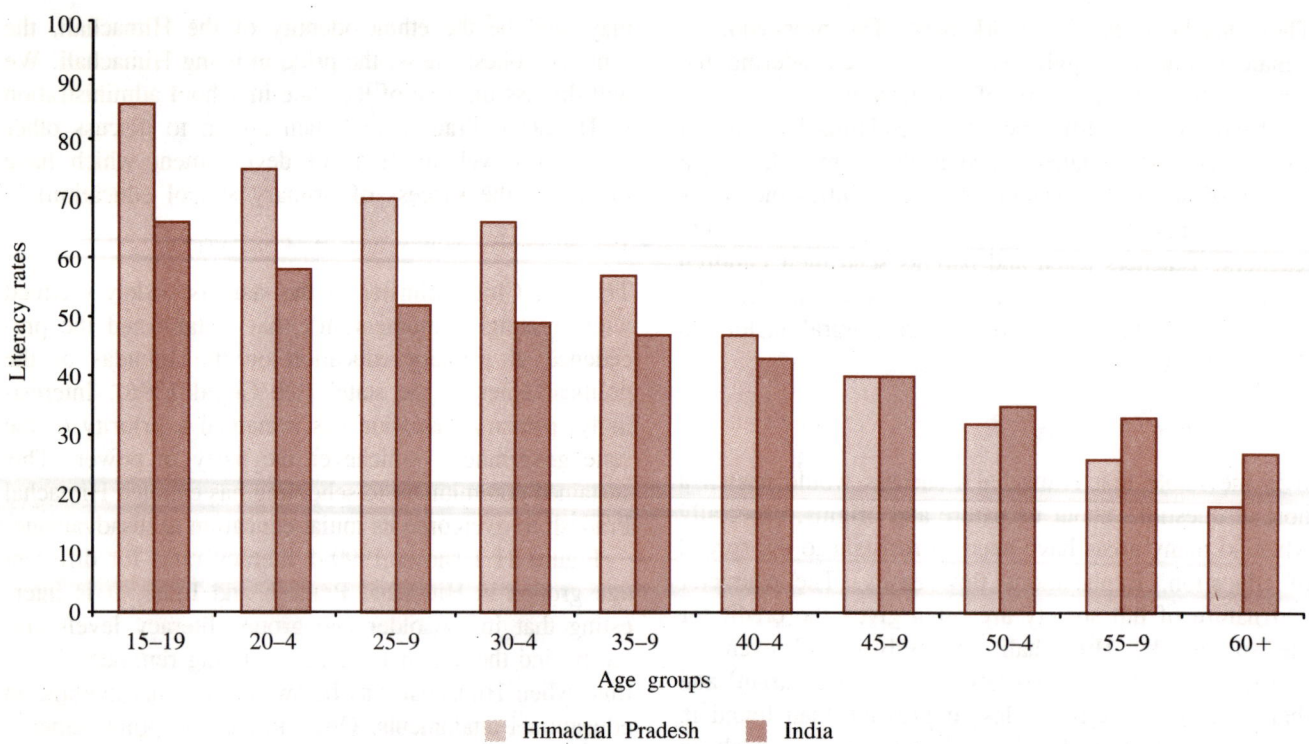

FIGURE 21.1: Literacy Rates in India and Himachal Pradesh

TABLE 21.4
Growth in Enrolment in Himachal Schools

	Primary stage		Upper-primary stage	
	Enrolment (thousand)	Growth rate (%)	Enrolment (thousand)	Growth rate (%)
1973	420		133	
1978	495	3.34	162	4.02
1986	643	3.32	302	8.10
1993	704	1.30	355	2.30
1997	729	0.87	376	1.46

Source: Sinha, Tyagi, and Thakur (1997); NCERT (1997); Selected Educational Statistics. (1997).

Some idea of the seriousness of the Himachal government's approach to school education can be gauged from Table 21.5 which compares state expenditures on education of four states, two of them Himachal's prosperous neighbours Punjab and Haryana, and the less well-endowed Uttar Pradesh. The period chosen is not only the recent past but is also significant because it is both the post National Policy on Education (NEP) (1986) as well as the post-Jomtien period (1991), both stimulants to taking education more seriously. Per capita expenditure on education in Himachal is as strikingly high, as the per capita expenditure in Uttar Pradesh is low, as compared to the Indian average. Haryana is close to the Indian average while Punjab is higher. When it comes to the proportion of SDP spent on education, the figures are even more interesting. While Haryana and Punjab are below the Indian average for both points on the scale, Uttar Pradesh is close to it. Himachal is strikingly above the average for India. This makes the proportion of state expenditure on elementary education significantly higher than for the other states although in terms of the education expenditure the proportion spent by Himachal and the proportion spent by Uttar Pradesh are close. Most important, on every count Himachal shows up much better than its neighbouring states high-lighting the way it is prioritizing education. Many argue that Himachal Pradesh is able to do this because of generous subsidies from the central government. It is a fact that a sizeable proportion of the total revenue of the state comes from these subsidies but in the final analysis spending priorities are determined by the state itself.

Another sign of the willingness of the Himachal government to make consistent effort to educate its people is the way in which it is tackling its inter-district differentials. As has been mentioned earlier the teacher–pupil ratio in the state is good; from Table 21.6 we can see that it is uniformly favourable, and children can get a good deal of teacher attention. Most striking is the teacher–pupil ratio in Lahaul and Spiti which is 4:7. This certainly does not seem cost-effective; it is interesting that Himachal has not used the NFE low-cost alternative to educate children (nor has Punjab or Haryana).

TABLE 21.5
State Expenditure on Education

	Himachal Pradesh	Haryana	Punjab	Uttar Pradesh	India
Per capita expenditure on education (Rs) (1981–2 = 100) 1995–6	215	127	153	71	134
1985–6	138	96	116	55	94
Growth rate	4.5	2.8	2.8	2.6	3.6
State expenditure on education as a proportion of SDP* (%)					
1995–6	7.8	3.0	3.0	3.9	4.0
1985–6	6.6	3.0	3.2	3.4	3.7
State expenditure on elementary education as a proportion of education expenditure (%)					
1995–6	53.5	46.5	30.0	55.5	48.8
1985–6	51.3	40.7	34.3	49.5	46.2

Note: 'Education expenditure' refers to total expenditure on education (by Education Departments and other Departments) on revenue account, plan and non-plan.

*SDP = State domestic product; and for India in place of SDP, gross national product (GNP) is considered.

Source: Economic Survey, relevant years: Budgetary resources for education, relevant years.

TABLE 21.6
Primary Schools and their Facilities—District-Level Variations (1997)

	Literacy rate	School per 1000 persons*	School 100 sq. km*	Teacher–Pupil per ratio*
Hamirpur	86.57	0.51	17	24.7
Una	77.81	1.28	28	26.8
Kangra	70.57	1.18	24	23.4
Bilaspur	67.17	1.29	34	24.1
Shimla	64.61	1.77	21	18.3
Solan	63.30	1.44	29	21.2
Mandi	62.74	1.54	30	20.7
Kinnaur	58.36	2.30	2	16.7
Lahaul and Spiti	56.82	4.00	1	4.7
Kullu	54.82	1.40	8	29.3
Sirmaur	51.62	1.39	8	22.1
Chamba	44.70	1.67	39	21.3
Himachal Pradesh	63.86	2.0	10	22.0

* These figures refer to primary schools only, and not to all schools with a primary section. The variations will therefore be only indicative.

Source: Jagran (1998).

Of course, districts like Lahaul and Spiti and Kinnaur are making gigantic strides in literacy rates, and it seems that proper schools are more efficient in universalizing elementary education in the long run.

Special schemes like Operation Blackboard (OB) seem to have been taken very seriously by the Himachal government and the Himachal government has also contributed some of its own schemes like the immense stress on physical education, the VT system, and flexible response to the agricultural calendar or to climatic conditions. For example, in Lahaul and Spiti, the school calendar is adjusted to give a continuous working period of six months. In the remaining six months the conditions are too harsh and inhospitable for work so teachers and students get a break from school.

It is not surprising that social imbalances are slowly being tackled at least in terms of education. If we look at Table 21.7 which shows the decadal variation in literacy among SCs, STs, and others; among males and females; and in rural and urban areas, we find that the

TABLE 21.7
Decadal Variations in Literacy Rates

(per cent)

	Himachal Pradesh			India		
	1981	1991	Variation	1981	1991	Variation
Community						
SC	40.2	53.2	31.3	30.6	37.4	22.2
ST	34.6	47.1	36.1	25.6	29.6	15.6
Non-SC/ST	56.1	68.6	22.3	48.7	57.7	18.5
Sex						
Male	64.3	75.4	17.3	56.4	64.1	13.7
Female	37.7	52.1	38.4	29.8	39.3	32.3
Region						
Rural	49.1	61.9	26.1	37.1	44.7	20.5
Urban	76.1	84.2	10.6	64.8	73.1	12.8
Total	51.2	63.9	24.8	43.6	52.2	19.7

Source: Census 1981; Census 1991.

differentials show up Himachal very favourably as compared to the all-India averages. Except for urban literacy where the figures for both India and Himachal are very similar (Himachal has a very small and very progressive urban sector where rates are levelling off), on all the other parameters Himachal is doing far better than the rest of India.

Finally, it is important to note that educational development is after all a part of the complex of development and although the state has spent liberally on education, its success has to be viewed as part of a complex whole, some idea of which will emerge from the rest of this section. Gender issues are dealt with in a separate sub-section as they are a subject in themselves.

Other Development Indicators and Educational Advance

ROADS

Roads are especially vital to the development of hilly regions—neither bullock carts nor railways are of much use. As Basu (1985) in his study of the tribal areas of Himachal Pradesh also points out, roads are two to four times as expensive to build in the hills as in the plains. The Himachal government focused on expanding the road system from the start. (see Table 21.8 which records the growth from 1951 onwards).

The effort of the state has been supplemented by the work of the Border Roads Organization which built roads in the most difficult terrain like Lahaul and Spiti because of the strategic importance of these areas. The expansion of the system was immensely valuable in generating jobs in road construction, and in enabling Himachalis to get employment elsewhere as also in facilitating trade and

in allowing the provision of other public services including education. Those districts which had better infrastructure in place early are the ones where literacy rates are higher even today (e.g. Hamirpur, Una, Kangra). However, it must be remembered that the road system even today is nowhere near the level envisaged as desirable, leave alone optimal.

TABLE 21.8
Roads in Himachal Pradesh (1951–91)

Year	Total length (in km)	Increment (in km)
1950–1	288	
1955–6	2559	2271
1960–1	3478	919
1966–7	6941	3463
1970–1	10,617	3676
1975–6	14,345	3728
1980–1	17,433	3088
1985–6	20,038	2605
1990–1	22,445	2407

Source Department of Planning, 1993; 1997.

LAND REFORM

Land reform was aided by the fact that most land holdings in the state were in any case not very large owing to the mountainous nature of the terrain. Even more important, the status of the tenant changed and the *bethu* or serf who was given land in lieu of service to the landowner became a landowner in his own right rather than a tenant of the raja or *jagirdar*. The state government's firm stress on equitable land rights and on land redistribution to the landless paid dividends—the more so because there were two phases of land reform under his tenure—one in the 1950s and one in the 1970s.

When Kangra and Kulu joined Himachal the same rules applied. In spite of this, according to the agricultural census of 1985–6, large and medium holdings occupy large areas in relation to their numbers, an indication that there is still significant unequal distribution of land (see Chathley 1995).

The average landholding is 1.2 hectares according to the 1991 census, but more than about 95 per cent of households own at least a small amount of land (see Thakur 1991). Such a pattern of land distribution means some measure of independence. In agrarian societies like Himachal (Himachal has a very small urban sector: 8.7 per cent) this somewhat even distribution of land allows a more even distribution of power and status. Perhaps it is one reason why even the poorer parents in Himachal did not feel helpless about speaking up about school matters. It is also perhaps a reason that the average parent feels comfortable about sending children to school. Sangeeta Goyal makes a pertinent comment:

> Many observers see social and caste characteristics as major determinants of the quantity and quality of education received by an individual. In agrarian societies generally there is a positive relationship between ownership of land and economic well-being, social status and political power, all of which reinforce each other as sources of influence and advantage. In Himachal Pradesh, a high land–person ratio and a more egalitarian structure of land ownership may have diffused power aligned with these sources. [Goyal 1996]

OTHER PUBLIC SERVICES

Other public services have also received high priority from the Himachal government though not always with the same degree of success as primary education. One difficult, yet vital accomplishment is the communication system. Many remote villages now have telephone connections and Himachal also has the credit of being a state where all villages have been electrified. A look at the same four states which were looked at earlier will show that Himachal is doing fairly well on a number of social indicators (see Table 21.9). State provision of these services has ensured an improved quality of life for the common Himachali. Health, for example, is closely linked with educational advantage as it is with income levels. Although health services are not good (infant mortality rates and maternal mortality rates are still high compared to Kerala, for example), they have improved. According to the National Family Health Survey in 1992–3, 91 per cent of children in Himachal had been vaccinated compared to much lower percentages for the other states.

EXPANSION OF JOB OPPORTUNITIES

This has been cited by many as of immense importance in the economy of Himachal, and, one must note, in the motivation for education. The prospect of jobs is certainly attractive to a people who are mainly marginal farmers.[5] Traditionally, the hillman has always had to look for ways in which to diversify his occupational base. The government is the largest employer in Himachal (one source puts the number of government employees in various departments of the state government at about 400,000). Locational advantage of its contiguity to the prosperous states of Punjab and Haryana and its proximity to the capital city also add to the opportunities for jobs. Many households in Himachal have at least one source of stable service income apart from their agrarian base. Looking at Table 21.10, we see that according to the 1991 Census, a sizeable proportion of men are no longer working in the primary sector, but are employed

TABLE 21.9
Public Services and Social Infrastructure

	Himachal Pradesh	Haryana	Punjab	Uttar Pradesh	India
Proportion of households with electricity connection (1991)	85.9	63.2	77.0	11.0	30.5
Per capita supply of foodgrains through public distribution system (1986–7) (kg/year)	25.0	6.2	4.7	2.9	18.1
Proportion of population receiving subsidized foodgrains through public distribution system (1986–7)	28.2	3.1	0.1	2.1	26.8
Proportion of households having safe drinking water (rural) (1991)	76.7	68.3	94.3	60.1	63.6
Number of hospital beds per million persons (rural) (1991)	102	44	196	23	152
Proportion of children aged 12–23 months, who have not received vaccination (1992–3)	9	18	18	43	30
Proportion of interest-free loans out of total outstanding cash debts	33.8	3.0	8.1	12.6	9.0

Source: Census 1991; NFHS 1992–3; NSSO 42nd round.

---

[5] Only about 11 per cent of land is available for cultivation.

TABLE 21.10
'Main' Workers in Himachal Pradesh (1991)

(per cent)

	Male	Female	Total
Cultivators	54.55	87.23	63.64
Agricultural labourers	3.83	1.99	3.31
Livestock, forestry, fishing, hunting, plantations, orchards, and allied activities	3.17	0.72	2.49
Mining and quarrying	0.36	0.02	0.26
Manufacturing, processing, servicing, and repairs	6.53	1.67	5.17
Construction	6.46	0.79	4.88
Trade and commerce	5.91	0.60	4.43
Transport, storage, and communications	2.63	0.15	1.94
Other services	17.31	7.21	14.49
Total	100.00	100.00	100.00

Note: 'Main' workers are defined as those who spend more than six months in a year in that occupation.
Source: Census, 1991.

in the secondary and tertiary sectors. This must have an impact on increasing parental motivation for education and on their being able to bear the associated costs.

Looking at districtwise variations in Himachal, it is apparent that although the state is mostly rural, the proportion of non-agricultural workers is quite high (Census 1991, cited in Chathley 1995).[6] What is more, the districts which are totally rural have the highest proportion of non-agricultural workers. This is mostly due to the tribal character of these districts—the high and very high proportions are in the eastern and north-eastern parts of the state (Kinnaur: 42.69 per cent; Lahaul and Spiti: 41.84 per cent; and in some scattered tehsils of Chamba, Kangra, Una, and Solan districts).

However, Himachal's economy continues to grow more slowly than that of India as a whole, with per capita SDP in Himachal lagging far behind that of Punjab and Haryana, and even less than the Indian average. Certainly a higher rate of growth would generate a surge in opportunities for jobs and self-employment.

GENDER BIAS

Himachali women, like their sisters in the plains, experience gender bias, as the immense gap between male and female literacy even in 1991 would indicate. As in most of the rest of India, property is not inherited by women. Price (1991) reports that the women of the local *mahila mandal* asked SUTRA to stand collateral as the bank would not lend money to them as they had no assets in their name (the bank refused!). However, the general impression is that gender relations in hill villages are

more equitable than in the plains, and that Himachali women seem more confident and assertive (see Table 21.11). Certainly, the sight of adolescent girls going to school in a neighbouring village would have been very unusual in the PROBE sample villages in the BIMARU states.

There is considerable cultural diversity among subgroups of Himachal's population. Given the tough hilly terrain and poor communication facilties between areas within the state, many pockets have cultural identities which have had limited exposure to outside influences. In general, attitudes to women are defined by strong patriarchal norms.[7]

There are some factors which seem to work against women but which can also give them an advantage. Hill women have a deep involvement in the struggle for survival (see Sutra' 1998, Biswas 1990). This labour-intensive agrarian economy has had to rely on the participation of women as well as men. In a land dominated by small and marginal farmers, women have to actively participate in the fields (97 per cent of female 'main workers' are cultivators according to the 1991 Census). Bhati and Singh (1985) in a study of labour inputs on farm households report that women in Himachal work longer hours than men, on the 'light' non-seasonal work in cultivation (e.g. sowing, weeding, hoeing, harvesting, and cutting of grass for fodder). They also find women spend a lot of time tending animals, a way of supplementing the gains from small plots. Since the terrain is rough and fields are scattered, Himachali women lead

---

[6] Chathley (1995) found literacy to be significantly linked with the percentage of non-agricultural workers and a composite index of social amenities in a district.

[7] There are certain areas, e.g. in Sirmaur in the trans-Giri area, where men share the burden of agriculture, livestock, and domestic work more equitably with women than in the other three districts studied (see SUTRA 1998).

TABLE 21.11
Gender-related Indicators

	Himachal Pradesh	Haryana	Punjab	Uttar Pradesh	India
Females per 1000 males	976	865	882	879	927
Females per 1000 males in the 0–10 age group	956	870	881	892	931
Female labour force participation rate (main workers) (%)	19.4	6.0	2.8	7.5	16.0
Female employment as a percentage of public sector employment	11.1	13.4	4.8	7.7	NA
Proportion of pregnant women (aged 15–49) registered for prenatal care 1995–6 (%)	75.7	42.1	58.5	19.2	45.5
Proportion of children (aged 0–4) registered for pediatric care 1995–6 (%)	85.7	48.7	60.3	26.6	47.0
Female deaths per 100 male deaths, 0-4 age group	88.2	106.7	117.9	115.7	107.4
Married women as a percentage of all women in the 15–19 age group	32	48	13	61	4.6

Source: Census 1991; NSSO 52nd round.

isolated lives as well. And in addition to their farm work, women also bear a heavy burden of domestic work: collection of water and firewood, cooking, childcare are all seen as women's responsibility. Again, since menfolk often work outside the state or district there are also a sizeable number of female-headed households. Most women do not work for wages on construction sites, etc but they may engage in buying and selling (milk or shawls, for example) at the local market.

Himachal has a higher rate of female participation in the labour force[8] compared to the three other states looked at earlier (see Table 21.11). The highest proportion of female workers is in the two tribal districts of Lahaul and Spiti and Kinnaur. Lower female work participation rates prevail all along the western, south-western and southern borders of the state. It increases as we go from the south-west to the north-east of Himachal (see Census 1991, cited in Chathley 1995).

Himachal also has a better female–male ratio than Haryana, Punjab, and Uttar Pradesh. This favourable female–male ratio is partly due to high levels of migration, but Himachal's position remains unchanged even when we compare the female–male ratios across the 0–10 age-group. Under-5 death rates for females as a proportion of under-5 death rates for males are also lower for Himachal than the neighbouring states.[9] Of the four, only Himachali females have a survival advantage, a situation similar to Europe, America, and sub-Saharan Africa (see Drèze and Sen 1995, Ch. 7). In other states

females have a survival disadvantage, an indicator of gender bias in these areas. Though in general health facilities in Himachal are not very good, compared to its neighbours more Himachali women are able to avail of health care for themselves and their children (see Table 21.11).

RISING LEVELS OF FEMALE LITERACY

The state has possibly not targeted the education of women in any direct way but women have benefited enormously from the fact that the government school system is functional. If we extrapolate backwards from male and female literacy rates for different age groups in 1991 we can get an approximation for male and female literacy rates in the 10–14 age group for earlier time periods. We find that female literacy in 1951 in the 10–14 age group lagged far behind male literacy but today the differential is much smaller (see Figure 21.2). The female literacy rate in Himachal has risen so remarkably that today it is the same as the total literacy rate for India as a whole. Another aspect of Himachal's progress in this field is obvious from a comparison of literacy rates for rural SC women. Himachal's achievement is outstanding: not just is it more than twice the rate for India as whole (39.8 vis-à-vis 19.5), it is also way ahead of its affluent neighbours, Punjab and Haryana (see Agarwal 1995). This speaks very strongly of the extent to which Himachal's schooling revolution has spread even among traditionally deprived groups.

However, the progress has not been uniform. If we look at district-level variations in male–female differentials in literacy in 1991 (see Table 21.12), we can see that the differentials are lower and show less variation in the urban areas. In rural areas the differentials are high and greater for those districts with lower levels of literacy. In a study done by the DPEP (see DPEP 1996b), some villages in the trans-Giri area of Sirmaur district

[8] Female labour-force participation rate is the proportion of female 'main workers' to female population, where 'main workers' are those who spend more than 6 months a year in that activity.

[9] Murthi, Guio, and Drèze (1996) have done studies based on statistical analyses of district-level census data which confirm that higher levels of female labour force participation are associated with reduced gender bias in child survival.

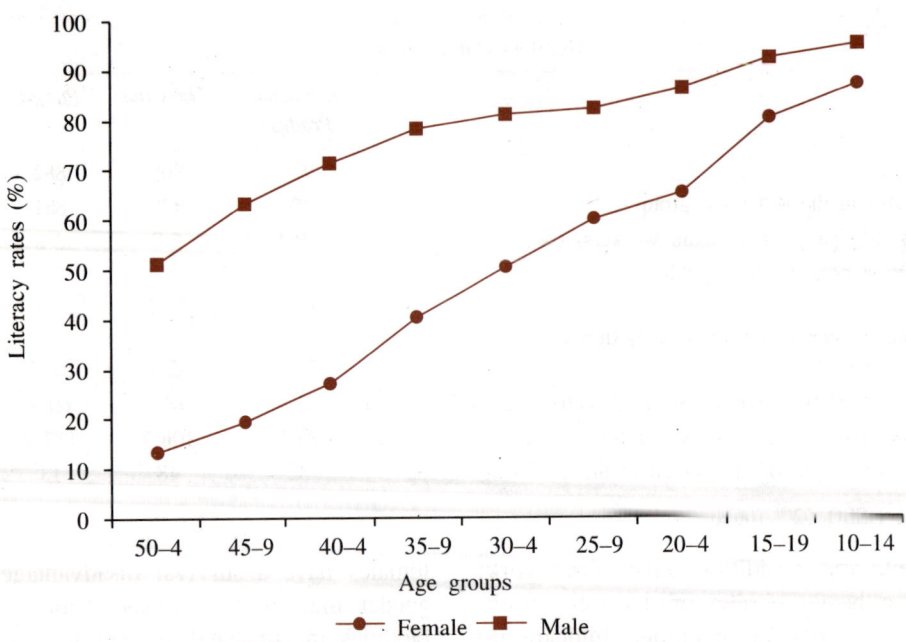

FIGURE 21.2: Growth in Male and Female Literacy*

Note: * This graph shows 1991 literacy rates for males and females for different age groups. This can be used as a good approximation of literacy rates for 10–14 age group in earlier periods. For example literacy rate for 20–4 age group in 1991 can approximate literacy rate for the 10–14 age group in 1981, provided adult literacy schemes did not have a significant impact. By backward projection it seems that the gender gap in literacy rates in 10–14 age group started narrowing from the 1960s and is quite small in 1991.

(an area of extremely rugged topography and economic deprivation) report female literacy below 10 per cent.

TABLE 21.12
Male–Female Differentials in Literacy Rates in Himachal Pradesh 1991

(per cent)

District	All areas	Rural areas	Urban areas
Hamirpur	19.21	19.54	11.31
Una	20.14	20.44	16.40
Kangra	18.73	19.18	9.20
Bilaspur	21.42	21.71	13.29
Shimla	24.21	26.71	8.48
Solan	23.98	25.83	8.23
Mandi	27.43	28.52	11.13
Kinnaur	30.00	30.00	–
Lahaul & Spiti	33.73	33.73	–
Kullu	31.11	32.20	11.59
Sirmaur	24.75	26.23	12.05
Chamba	31.39	32.96	11.30
Himachal Pradesh	23.23	24.10	10.65

Note: The districts have been ranked in order of total literacy rate.
Source: Census, 1991.

HIGH AND RISING ASPIRATIONS FOR GIRLS

The motivation for girls' education is very high according to the PROBE survey, but still lower than that for boys. As the boy is looked upon as the future breadwinner and the security of his family and the girl as one who is to be married off into another family, girls are the first to suffer if there is any problem of access or cost. The PROBE survey came across girls who had been withdrawn after primary school level because of the cost of education.

Continued access to education over time finds girls catching up with boys. This is for two reasons: one, educated boys demand educated girls. 'Who will marry an uneducated girl?' said one parent in Hamirpur. With education spreading throughout the male population, this sentiment becomes increasingly common. Education is seen as important for girls as it helps them in domestic duties and in looking after their children. Today, the PROBE survey suggests, parents also see jobs, access to information, even standing for election as very much potential opportunities for their daughters as well. It is as if new windows of opportunity are opening for girls and women in the state.

Community Involvement

In what has been called a virtuous circle of goodwill, as the community has benefited from education so has education benefited from the community. Each of the factors which have been discussed is isolated in itself and linked in that it offers the individual enhanced life chances and quality of life. Himachal has benefited from good governance which has been committed to various aspects of social sector development,[10] including schooling. Without the provision of a schooling system of reasonable quality no amount of ethnic pride or women's agency could have helped make the school function better. But once it is in place, then gradually the spread of education becomes easier with educated parents being much more used to what is expected by school. When parents are gaining from school then they are willing to contribute to schooling facilities, to see that schools are not closed arbitrarily, and so on. This community involvement is a kind of decentralized management which is vital to Himachal's school system.

SUTRA, an NGO based in Solan district, has done a lot of innovative work which has gone hand in hand with community involvement. It has organized legal literacy programmes and conducted awareness-generation camps for members of mahila mandals (and also for adolescent girls). Over time, women have been effective in launching struggles on common issues such as absenteeism of school teachers, lack of proper facilities at school, and also against liquor, for mobilizing credit and development schemes, for using the legal system to secure justice, and for generating awareness on health.

Mehrotra (1995) observed the vitality of the mahila mandals in Sirmaur, which allowed women to discuss their concerns 'in an empowering and productive environment'. She saw a woman request local leaders and senior government officials that uniforms should not be made compulsory because of the increase in expenditure, another request that a bridge be built over a swiftly flowing stream to enable her children to go to school. On another occasion, she saw members of the mahila mandal vetoing the name of a woman who wanted to stand for election because she had embezzled the funds meant for the local anganwadi. Mahila mandals worked well as a forum through which parents could express their anxieties about the education system to those who had the power and inclination to do something about it. Recently, we heard about a mahila mandal in Kinnaur which has banned video parlours since they interfere with the education of children.

Another good example of community support for the schooling process was provided by the lack of teacher–parent hostility even though the social distance between teacher and taught could be the same as in the plains. Yet the teacher here usually feels a commitment to the children.[11] At the same time, even the good governance can be seen as a factor of ethnic identity and political evolution as well as parent and teacher cooperation.

Himachal's Progress: Achievements and Some Limitations

REAPING THE HARVEST

Himachal Pradesh today is a state where education is the norm for children. The earlier investment on elementary education is now paying off. It is at a stage now where elementary education is within its reach except perhaps in the most difficult pockets. This is an enormous achievement for a state with such a challenging topography.

EDUCATION FOR EQUITY

Education is possibly one of the biggest empowering factors in Himachali society today, enabling most people as it were to reach a certain minimum level. Over time it made the schooling experience easier for Himachali parents: as the first generation became educated they could participate in the schooling of their children. With the functional school system, in time, total literacy has been progressively enhanced till it now far outstrips the national average. The recent total literacy campaign (TLCs) in the 1990s seem to have made some contribution as well.[12] In 1991 the illiteracy rate was 36 per cent for the 7+ age group, in 1997 it was 23 per cent and it could well go down to 18 per cent by 2001, thus meeting the Jomtien target for reducing adult illiteracy. At the same time, as male literacy rates are peaking, the male–female differential is also narrowing. Statistics indicate that Himachal has been attacking and closing the gap between regions and peoples less well served by the education system. Disadvantaged sections of the community have shown a remarkable rise in literacy rates. The DPEP conducted a baseline assessment survey of the four 'difficult' districts in Himachal in 1996 (see DPEP 1996c). Achievements in these areas were fairly respectable; so also was the quality of infrastructure as compared to the BIMARU

[10] Mahila mandals were set up under the panchayati raj Act of 1968. By the 1970s, over 50 per cent of villages had mahila mandals.

[11] Mehrotra (1995) found that teachers in the isolated hilly areas of Himachal (Sirmaur district) were more regular and took a more active interest in children as compared to teachers who worked in the plains of UP (Allahabad district).

[12] One example of the vitality of the TLCs comes from the DPEP, Sirmaur. Great efforts were made by the saksharta team and public representatives, social workers, NGOs, mahila mandals, yuva mandals, etc. Of the 7200 children in the 6–11 age group, some 5200 were admitted into primary schools by motivating their parents and arranging textbooks and fees through donations from voluntary organizations.

states. Again this Himachal has achieved through the formal schooling system, and it began well before the call of Jomtien and the NPE 1986. Dual-track schooling or indifference has not been the automatic response of Himachal to difficult areas. The people of Himachal, therefore, have had enhanced opportunities to live life with dignity.

The Shortcomings

ACCESS

At the same time there are, it must be admitted, several problems. Access to school, both primary and upper-primary, is a tremendous problem in Himachal Pradesh. As Table 21.13 shows, 20–5 per cent of children do not have access to schools according to national norms. If we take into account the topography of the region, then the problem is even greater.

Himachal Pradesh. Similarly the repetition rate is around 11 per cent for each year till class V. This repetition in the primary classes (though it does raise learning achievement) does little for child self-esteem, or family and state finances. The problem needs further investment by the state unit of educational research. Similarly, a good system of early childhood care and education (ECCE) would also enhance learning achievement. Enhancing learning achievement is then a priority area for a state which has already achieved much.

INTERFACE BETWEEN SCHOOL AND SOCIETY

This school-society interface is important when the child is in school but acquires its sharpest edge when the child leaves school. Like other Indian states, Himachal Pradesh has not adequately tackled the issue of the interface between the school-leaver and the training and employment opportunities available.

TABLE 21.13
Access Remains a Problem

(per cent)

	Primary section		Upper-primary section	
	Proportion of habitations with school within 1km	Proportion of population with school within 1 km of habitation	Proportion of habitations with school within 3 km	Proportion of population with school within 3 km of habitation
1978	55	72	58	72
1986	59	77	62	77
1993	59	76	64	78

Source: All-India Educational Surveys, relevant years.

CURRICULUM AND METHODOLOGY

Second, Himachal's educational progress has been hampered by the common ills of the Indian education system. One major problem, just as in the plains, is school quality. The weight of the curriculum, for example, is an issue which plagues children, rich or poor, all over the country. What Professor Yashpal perceptively dubbed the burden of non-comprehension afflicts the poorer sections even more heavily (see Yashpal Committee Report 1993). In Bilaspur, the PROBE investigator found that every child in one particular village had guidebooks for all their subjects even in class III. The curriculum is a straightforward NCERT import from the plains. It needs to be contextualized and made relevant to the Himachali child, apart from keeping the age factor in view. Added to this is the joyless learning system prevalent in schools across the country, as well as in Himachal, where teaching methodology is heavily weighted in favour of rote learning and cramming.

It is not surprising that the 'drop-out rate of scheduled caste children after class v is a matter of concern' in

A visitor to the valley of Bharmour, a remote and difficult area of Himachal Pradesh, was heartened by the vitality of the schooling system but a little discomfited by the number of unemployed youth who spent their time playing cricket. Again, the fact that so many Himachalis are employed in other states (Himachal has been called a 'money order economy'), shows there is much to be done in Himachal itself so that it can utilize the resource pool of educated youngsters that it has created.

ECOLOGICAL IMPLICATIONS

Ecological development needs to be given a key place in future planning. 'For the last two or three decades or so, government policies in the state have been gradually but relentlessly leading towards an environmental catastrophe,' is a common criticism. It is alleged that with growth-oriented policies, the emphasis is on overexploitation rather than conservation. The fragility of Himachal's environment has been disregarded in general, although there are local efforts which are laudable.

IMPLICATIONS OF THE HIMACHAL EXPERIENCE FOR THE UNIVERSALIZATION OF ELEMENTARY EDUCATION (UEE)

Many will hasten to point out that Himachal Pradesh can hardly serve as a model for achieving UEE. It has too many special features like, for example, its combination of ethnic identity and size as a small hill state. All the hill states are spending a great deal on education and it may look like the only source of mobility for both the well-to-do and the poor man. Yet, it must be remembered that hill areas, after all, cover a mere 16 per cent of the country and account for 8 per cent of the population. Himachal's success is also discounted since it is based, apparently, on liberal central subsidies.

On the other hand, prioritizing money resources on primary education has been done by the state government. And not only has money been allocated, it has also been utilized. In addition, Himachal has the unusual credit of overcoming several problems which have been very difficult to surmount in other states. Himachal has a largely rural population and nearly all its districts have higher-than-national-average proportions of SC and/or STs. The rugged terrain and the remote, scattered settlement pattern only add to its problems.

THE POWER OF POLITICAL WILL

What does Himachal Pradesh seem to suggest in terms of achieving UEE? First, the positive power of political will sustained over a long period when tackling any widespread and difficult problem. By prioritizing schooling Himachal has had remarkable success in achieving the type of society where the education of the child becomes a societal norm. By tackling the problem over the lasts fifty years it has now reached the stage where the residual 5–10 per cent (see DPEP 1996a) can be specifically targeted. Its schooling system has got over the humps of access, cost, tough curriculum, first-generation learners, and so on and achieved a society where mass illiteracy is no longer a problem though the system of education still has its drawbacks. Himachal's literacy statistics, improving steadily and impressively, its ability to address region, caste, and gender imbalances particularly in the younger age group show that the government is to a large degree serious about increasing the self-confidence and social opportunities of its younger citizens.

USEFUL ASSETS

One asset which has been useful to Himachal is the broad-based nature of the development process in the state. A good example is the way land reform as well as expansion of the road system have both been taken very seriously. This points the way to the need to tackle education as a subset of society rather than as an isolated entity. Another and equally complex asset is the extent of community involvement which has sustained the schooling system in Himachal. Only further research can show how deep and basic is the contribution of this factor. Let us take up two points. One , Himachal has a less stratified society than is common in the northern plains. This could well mean that politicians, bureaucrats, and common people are all equally clear about the importance of, say, schooling. Not only is the money made available but the administration on its part ensures that teachers are appointed in time, there are enough aids, and so on. Teachers, too, could be feeling more involved with their pupils. A second factor is the very high motivation for education due to the lure of jobs, again felt among all sections of society. It is not clear whether what has happened in this small and cohesive society is easily replicable. But one of the factors, that is high parental motivation for education, is, at present commonly seen all over the country as recent studies indicate. Does this indicate a golden opportunity for states to cash in on the cooperation of the people in sustaining the school system. There is definitely an effort today to involve the community by more institutionalized means like setting up village education committees and if this proves successful it could also be a factor which could help other states. If the states where there are many out-of-school children can now provide a school system which works, they will be able to cash in on the cooperation of their people. The task will become easier once the first-generation pupils have achieved an education, as is found in Himachal.

Himachal has also been able to avoid stratification of the school system by providing government schools of good quality. This has enhanced community accountability.

LOW-COST ALTERNATIVES

Himachal's success also calls into question the present trend towards low-cost alternatives to schooling for children. By maintaining a reasonable quality of schooling it ensures that parents will send children trudging long distances to school and that when a child fails, parents will still continue to sustain the schooling process, inspite of poverty and high cost of schooling.

ADULT LITERACY VERSUS FORMAL SCHOOLS

In keeping with the low-cost alternative formula is the stress on adult literacy, much touted as the low-cost method of the 1990s. Though a better-late-than-never theory would definitely help the adult who has never had a chance, it is no substitute for the empowerment of children. Functional literacy cannot make up for years of lost opportunities and a lack of self-esteem. Added to this is the enormous opportunity cost suffered by adults which often makes them reluctant to engage with such programmes.

This is not to say that adult literacy programmes are not an effective way of dealing with residual illiteracy but to remind us that they are no substitute for a good schooling system. As Saldanha's (1996) study points out, TLCs, for example, work best in medium-literacy or high-literacy districts, and not in low- literacy districts. Himachal's schooling system has enabled it to have no low-literacy districts.

It would in fact be interesting to know which actually works out more expensive, the malfunctioning under-equipped school system in the BIMARU states, with the need for various low-cost alternatives to cope with its by-products like drop-outs/illiterates or the 'costly' school system of Himachal Pradesh with its sustained long-term gains.

QUALITY OF SCHOOLING

Unlike other states where illiteracy is still a problem and non-enrolment still figures as a major issue, Himachal forces us to look at the type of education system which we have put in place, i.e. what are the problems to be faced if all children do achieve basic education. Everything is in place but quality has still to be achieved. This is a prerequisite for an efficient education system where children enjoy their learning and have a good learning achievement. Again it shows up the urgency of curriculum reform and teacher training which will integrate the school-leaver with the opportunities in the society around him instead of creating an underclass of frustrated and alienated young people. If the curriculum and the schooling process are properly contextualized and integrated with pupils' and society's needs, then the concerns in the last two parameters set out in the Jomtien delaration, i.e. education for 'health, employment, and productivity, and a fuller quality of life' would be addressed.

REFERENCES

Aggarwal, Yash (1995). *Literacy Among Scheduled Castes: Trends and Issues*. Occasional Paper No. 20, National Institute of Educational Planning and Administration, Delhi.

Basu, A. K. (1985). *Tribal Development Programmes and Adminisration in India with Special Reference to Bharmour and Pangi Sub-Divisions of Chamba District*. National Book Organisation, Delhi.

Bhati, J. P. and D. V. Singh (1987). 'Women's Contribution to Agricultural Economy in Hill Regions of North-West India'. *Economic and Political Weekly*, vol. XXII, no. 17, 25 April.

Biswas, S. K. (ed.) (1990), *Strategy of Development in the Himalayas*. Institute of Social Research and Applied Anthropology, Calcutta.

Census of India (1991a). *General Economic Tables*. Registrar General of India, New Delhi.

———— (1991b). *Social and Cultural Tables*. Part IV-B, Table C-02, Registrar General of India, New Delhi.

Chathley, Y. P. (1995). *Education, Population and Development: A Regional Perspective of Northwest India*. Centre for Research in Rural and Industrial Development, Chandigarh.

Department of Economic Affairs (various years). *Economic Survey*. Ministry of Finance, Government of India, New Delhi.

Department of Education (1993). *Learning without burden*. Report of the National Advisory Committee appointed by the Ministry of Human Resource Development, Government of India, New Delhi.

District Primary Education Programme (1996a). *Appraisal Aid Memoire*. Himachal Pradesh.

———— (1996b). *Social Assessment Studies of District Primary Education Programme Districts of Himachal Pradesh*.

———— (1996c). *District Primary Education Programme Study Report on Baseline Assessment Study in 4 districts of Himachal Pradesh*. State Council of Educational Research and Training, Solan.

Dréze, Jean and Amartya Sen (1995). *Economic Development and Social Opportunity*. Oxford University Press, Delhi.

Goyal, Sangeeta (1996). 'Primary Education in Himachal Pradesh'. PROBE background paper.

Himachal Pradesh (various years). *Budget Documents*.

Jagran (1998). *Himachal Pradesh at a Glance: Districtwise Statistical Overview*. Jagran Research Centre, Kanpur.

Jayachandran, Usha (1998). 'Understanding School Attendance and Work Participation by Children (5–14 years) in India, Census (1991)', UNDP.

Mehrothra, N. (1995). *Why Poor Children do not Attend School: The Case of Rural India*. University of Chicago, Chicago.

Murthi, Mamta, Anne-Catherine Guio and Jean Drèze (1996). 'Mortality, Fertility and Gender Bias in India: A District-level Analysis'. In Jean Dréze and Amartya Sen (eds) *Indian Development: Selected Regional Perspectives*. Oxford University Press, Delhi.

National Council of Educational Research and Training (1998). *Sixth All-India Educational Survey, National Tables*. All volumes. New Delhi.

National Sample Survey Organisation (1998). *Attending an Educational Institution in India : Its Level, Nature and Cost, 1995–96*. NSS 52nd Round, July 1995–June 1996, Department of Statistics, Government of India, New Delhi.

Planning Department (1997). *Ninth Five Year Plan (1997–*

2002) and Annual Plan (1997–98), Government of Himachal Pradesh, Shimla.

Price, Janet (1991). 'Women in Cattle Care in Himachal Pradesh'. In Punia, R. K. (ed.), *Women in Agriculture*. Northern Book Centre, New Delhi.

PROBE (1999). *Public Report On Basic Education in India*. The PROBE team in Association with Centre for Development Economics. Oxford University Press, New Delhi.

Saldanha, D. (1996). *Residual Illiteracy in Contexts of Uneven Development: Implications for Basic Education*. Tata Institute of Social Sciences, Mumbai.

Sinha, A., R. S. Tyagi, and R. S. Thakur (1997). *Educational Administration in Himachal Pradesh*. National Institute of Educational Planning and Administration, New Delhi.

SUTRA (A. Chhatre, T. Kothiyal, and V. Sharma) (1998). 'Nature in Retreat: Conservation and Development in Himachal Pradesh'. Report for the Biodiversity Conservation Prioritization Project in Himachal Pradesh, August 1996–January 1998.

Thakur, Bimla (1991). *Socio-Economic Analysis of the Weaker Sections: Rural Urban Comparative Study in HP*, Daya Publishing, Delhi.

22

From a Scriptless Status to a Literate Society
The Story of Mizoram's Uphill Journey

S. Hom Chaudhuri

THE STATE: LAND AND PEOPLE

Mizoram, the southernmost state of north-eastern India, covers a total area of 21,081 sq. km. Its 1014 km-long international boundaries touch the neighbouring countries of Bangladesh in the west and Myanmar in the east and the south. The Indian states of Manipur, Assam, and Tripura are located on its north and north-east. According to the 1991 Census, the state had a population of 689,756 with a density of 33 persons per sq. km. The decennial growth rate (1981–91) was 39.70 (see Table 22.1). As a result of the recent reorganization of the original 3 districts, the state has 8 districts, 20 development blocks, and 705 habitations.

The eastern half of the state can be classified as a mountainous terrain province. The overall relief in this province is higher and the slopes are much steeper than in the western half. The altitude here ranges from 400 to 2157 m. The western part of Mizoram, covering half of the area of the state, depicts characteristic ridge and valley type of topography. The relief is low and rises higher towards the east. The flat lands of the state are mostly located in the midst of hills and narrow valleys. These flat lands cannot be grouped as occupying a definite province.

It is the hilly terrain that was known as Lushai Hills till the middle of twentieth century. The Lushais—doughty, dominant tribesmen—lived in their hill-top habitations under the care of their chieftains. Over the ages, they absorbed a number of cognate clans and a larger Lushai society emerged. The British occupation of the land towards the last quarter of nineteenth century and subsequent political arrangement led to the emergence of the Lushai Hills district, geographically the

largest district of Assam. In 1952, the area shed its traditional name and came to be known as the Mizo District. Mizo is a generic term (literally, the highlander), coined to cover all the Lushai and Non-Lushai clans having a broad cultural affinity. On 21 January 1972, the district graduated into the Union Territory (UT) of Mizoram—the abode of the Mizos. Statehood came in 1986.

The Mizos represent a little over 82 per cent of the total population in the state. The two sub-tribes—the Pawis and the Lakhers—account for 7 per cent of population. The Pawi and the Lakher are now known as the Lai and the Mara. The Chakmas, forming 7 per cent of population, are a non-Mizo tribe. All these three minority groups have District Councils in the southern part of the state (see Box 22.1). Riangs (known as Bru) are another semi-nomadic tribe, representing 2.9 per cent of population. Other very small groups make up the rest of the population.

Socio—Economic Scene

The Mizos came under the influence of Christian missionaries in the last decade of the nineteenth century. The society is a close-knit one and attaches importance to kinship, social relations, and coexistence. Among the customary practices, honoured till today, are 'Hnatlang' (Social work) and 'Tlawmngaihna' (self-sacrifice and hard work for others).

Agriculture and allied activities constitute the mainstay of the economy. In 1981, 73.92 per cent of workers depended on this primary sector. In 1991, this proportion came down to 65.99 per cent. The sectoral annual growth rate between 1970–1 and 1984–5 revealed that the rate

TABLE 22.1
Mizoram at a Glance

Population (1991)	Total	689,756
	Male	358,978
	Female	330,778
Percentage of urban population		46.10
Decennial growth rate 1981–91		39.70
Area (sq. km)		21,081
Density of population		33
Sex ratio		921
Literacy rate 1991 (excluding children in age group 0–6)	Persons	82.27
	Male	85.61
	Female	78.60
No. of districts 1999		8
No. of dev. blocks		20
No. of villages	Total	783
	Inhabited	698
No. of towns		22
Sectoral distribution of economy (%)	Primary	37
	Secondary	15
	Tertiary	29
Per cent of educated job seekers to total job seekers 1993		42.4
Per cent of households having basic amenities 1996	Eelectricity	59
	Safe drinking water	16
	Toilet	70
Net sown area		65,000 Hec.
Av. size of operational holding		001.38 Hec.
Forest cover		62%
Crude birth rate 1997–8		21.36
Crude death rate		4.42
Infant mortality rate		21.45
Maternal mortality per thousand 1998		0.80
Marriage age (average)	Male	22
	Female	19
Life expectancy	State	61
	Rural	60
	Urban	62

Box 22.1
Autonomous District Councils

According to the provision of the Sixth Schedule of the Constitution of India, three groups of minorities—Mara, Lai, and Chakmas—were given autonomous District Councils in the southern part of the state to look after their interests and welfare. These District Councils came into existence in 1972 when the Mizo District Council was dissolved and the Pawi—Lakher Regional Council was split into three District Councils, namely Mara, Lai, and Chakma District Councils. The Councils are provided with certain powers by the Sixth Schedule of the Indian Constitution and have full authority over the management of primary education with effect from 1980 and middle-school education with effect from 1995 within their jurisdictions. However, in actual practice, the Education Department of the state continues to play significant administrative and academic roles in the fields of primary and middle-school education in the District Councils. In fact, all educational rules and regulations are also made by the Department and the powers of the District Councils are restricted since the state Education Department exercises control over final allocation of funds.

of growth of the primary sector was (–)0.03 per cent. Shifting cultivation with shortened land-use cycle, and lack of thrust in potential horticultural activities had resulted in stagnation. The state still has to import nearly 70 per cent of its food requirements from other states. Capital formation through generation of surplus in the production of goods and accumulation and investment of the surplus for continuous growth of production are pretty weak.

The political change process since 1972 opened up new avenues of employment. With the expansion of public administration and other services, the demand for various categories of personnel increased and the education system responded by rapid expansion. Between 1970-1 and 1984-5 the annual growth rate of the tertiary sector was 6.21 per cent as against the aggregate rate of growth of 3.69 per cent (see Ganguli 1992). This sector has almost reached saturation point.

Attainment in Literacy

Mizoram stands tall among the states of the Indian Union in the field of literacy. It improved its ranking from third in 1981 to second in 1991. With a literacy rate of 82.27 (male: 85.61; female 78.60) in 1991, Mizoram was ahead of all north-eastern states by a margin of 20 to 30 percentage points. In 1997, the state had the unique distinction of ranking first with a 95 per cent literacy rate, according to NSSO Survey (53rd round 1997).

Table 22.2 shows that during the 1991-7 period, two other north-eastern states have done quite well. Meghalaya has moved 27.9 percentage points forward from 49.1 to 77 per cent; and Nagaland has gone forward by 22.4 percentage points, from 61.1 to 84 per cent. Though, the six north-eastern states other than Mizoram have crossed the 70 per cent mark (except Arunachal Pradesh

with a literacy of 60 per cent) these states have yet to reduce the disparity between male and female literacy rates.

Meghalaya's performance is encouraging with a male–female disparity of 5 percentage points. Mizoram is the only state that has succeeded in virtually closing the gap between male and female literacy. It is a spectacular achievement considering the short history of its literacy movement.

If its population size is considered, Mizoram's rise on the literacy map of India may not be considered extraordinary. But the significance of such growth in literacy from a low of 2.95 per cent in 1901 can be appreciated if one takes into account such factors like the difficult hilly terrain with widely spaced habitations, near inaccessibility of the majority of the habitations during the greater part of the twentieth century, the absence of a written script till the closing years of nineteenth century, the tradition of an exclusive tribal life pattern, insulation from other societies, and the trauma of two-decades-long insurgency.

What are the forces that transformed the Mizos into almost a fully literate society within a span of hundred years? In the next section, an attempt has been made to examine this unique success story.

DYNAMICS OF SUCCESS

There must have been an interplay of a number of factors behind the success story of Mizoram in the field of literacy and basic education. The most cogent factor, cited by many a casual observer of the scene, is the pioneering role of Christian missionaries. it is, no doubt, a factor but not *the* factor. Had it been so, then Meghalaya and Nagaland—the two other states of north-east India with a dominant Christian presence—could have attained a more or less similar commendable

TABLE 22.2
The Literacy Situation in the North-eastern States 1991 and 1997

(per cent)

India/states	Literacy rates (1991)			Literacy rates (1997)		
	All	Male	Female	All	Male	Female
India	52.2	64.1	39.3	62	72	50
Arunachal Pradesh	41.6	51.4	29.7	60	69	48
Assam	52.9	61.9	43.0	75	82	66
Manipur	59.9	71.6	46.6	76	86	66
Meghalaya	49.1	53.1	44.8	77	79	74
Mizoram	82.2	85.6	78.6	95	96	95
Nagaland	61.6	67.6	54.7	84	91	77
Tripura	60.4	70.6	49.6	73	79	67

Source: 1991 Census for 1991 data; NSSO Survey (52nd Round) for 1997 data.

position. In Meghalaya, Welsh missionaries commenced their work by establishing half a dozen schools by 1853. In Nagaland, educational activities had been started by the missionary M. Bronson as early as 1839. Missionary-initiated educational activities, in Mizoram got off to a comparatively late start in 1898. But both the other states are way behind Mizoram in literacy and the universal provision of elementary education (UEE). In 1991, Meghalaya had a literacy rate of 49.10 (rank 23) and Nagaland, 61.65 (rank 13). A study of memoirs and documents and a close examination of the social scene indicate that certain forces have combined in Mizoram to keep up the momentum in the literacy movement. Some of these factors are discussed in the following paragraphs.

People's Initiative

In 1894, two Welsh missionaries stepped into the fort town Aizawl (the present capital) and set about developing Mizo alphabets based on the Mizo phonetic. The first dictionary of the Lushai language followed. A couple of schools came up in 1898. A few more missionaries started their fieldwork in southern part of the hills. By 1904 the number of schools grew to 22. The students were chiefly adult males. They went through the lower primary stage and turned into teachers. 'They brought the rudiments of education to people who had never seen a book and to whom the expression of their thoughts in writing was a completely new and fascinating experience' (see Lloyd n.d., 35). The literacy movement gradually caught on.

The Lushais were very ready to pass on what they had learned, however little. Many who had learnt only the alphabet succeeded in passing on that knowledge to others. It was said at that time that they were eager to master the art of reading but that the ability to write and to produce something themselves gave them vastly greater pleasure'. [Lloyd n.d., 34]

It was a euphoric experience. The initiative passed on from the missionaries to the community teachers. The literacy rate grew four times from 2.95 in 1901 to 12.67 in 1931. From that year, the Lushai Hills remained ahead of the rest of the districts of Assam in literacy rate. Significantly, the literacy rate of the Lushai Hills has been much above the national average since then (see Table 22.3). The passion for learning continued to grow. 'It was attested not only by the growth of literacy and the increase in the number of primary schools...but the amount of free labour given recently for the building of new middle schools and the public collection of pound 2000 made for the erection of a high school in 1944' (see Lloyd n.d., 33). Incidentally, it was the declared policy of the British government 'to prevent expansion of the secondary education' (see McCall 1949, 219) in Lushai Hills. But people, all the same, went ahead to set up the first high school on their own initiative in 1944. They had a new source of inspiration. Young Poet Rokunga (recently declared the greatest Mizo poet) composed a song in which he exhorted one and all to venture into the world of knowledge and wisdom. The lyric touched the right chord.

The urge to preach, to teach, or to occupy positions in the newly opened occupational careers fired the zeal

TABLE 22.3
Growth in Literacy in Mizoram (1901–91)

(per cent)

Year	Literacy rates in Mizoram			M: F	All-India literacy rates		
	Total	Males	Females	Disparity	Total	Males	Females
1901	2.95	6.10	0.14	5.96	5.35	9.83	0.60
1911	4.72	9.64	0.34	9.30	5.92	10.56	1.05
1921	7.43	14.54	1.06	13.48	7.16	12.21	1.81
1931	12.67	23.62	2.78	20.84	9.50	15.59	2.93
1941	23.12	38.89	8.44	30.45	16.10	24.90	7.30
1951	36.51	54.45	19.47	34.98	16.57	24.95	7.93
1961	51.24	62.25	40.34	21.91	24.02	34.44	12.95
1971	62.71	70.15	54.75	15.40	29.45	39.45	18.69
1981	69.90	74.77	64.53	10.24	36.23	46.89	24.82
1991	82.27	85.61	78.60	7.01	52.21	64.13	39.29

Source: Census of India, 1961. Vol. III, Assam, Part I-A General Report
Census of India, 1991 Series—17 Mizoram
Literacy Digest. Directorate of Adult Education, New Delhi—1988.

of the neophyte for education. The parents expected the children to study from Monday to Friday. Monday in Mizo is 'Thawhtanni' (the day the work begins) and Friday, 'Zirtawpni' (day marking the end of study for the week). Very insightful coining indeed!

Five decades of people's initiative resulted in significant improvement in the literacy field. In 1951, the Lushai Hills registered a literacy rate of 36.51 per cent. Male literacy crossed the 50 per cent mark (54.45). The disquieting feature at the time was the low female literacy figure (19.47 per cent). The demand for more formal institutions became more and more pressing.

Role of Government in Universal Access to Education

It was in 1952 that the Government of Assam gradually started taking over direct control of primary education in Mizo hills district and this trend continued till 1961. From 1961 to 1971, the management was handed over to the Mizo District council which could not address itself to the task properly (see Lalchungnunga 1983). In 1972, the government of the newly creased UT took full charge of primary education. In 1977, there were 514 primary schools of which 89 per cent were wholly managed by the government and another 6.6 per cent received recurring aid. The annual average rate of growth of the schools was a modest 2.8 per cent during 1947–77 (see Table 22.4). During the next five years (1977–82) the annual growth rate of schools was a high 12.7 per cent. Almost 97 per cent of schools were either wholly or partly managed by the government. This period of expansion saw wide coverage of habitations (80.86 per cent by 1981). The spread of schools was more or less even in all the three districts. In 1981, 94.59 per cent of rural population were served by primary schools (see Table 22.5).

TABLE 22.4
Growth in Primary Schools 1947–99

Year	Management	District				% increase
		Aizawl	Lunglei	Chhimtuipui	Mizoram	
1947	Govt	–	–	–	NA	
	Aided	–	–	–	NA	
	Private	–	–	–	NA	
	Total	–	–	–	279	
1977	Govt	290(89.0)	72(100.0)	96(82.7)	458(89.1)	
	Aided	25(7.6)	–	9(7.8)	34(6.6)	
	Private	11(3.4)	–	11(9.5)	22(4.3)	
	Total	326(100.0)	72(100.0)	116(100.0)	514(100.0)	84.2
1982	Govt	444(86.6)	135(75.8)	122(81.9)	701(83.4)	16.0
	Aided	60(11.7)	30(16.9)	23(15.4)	113(13.5)	232.3
	Private	9(1.7)	13(7.3)	4(2.7)	26(3.1)	18.2
	Total	513(100.0)	178(100.0)	149(100.0)	840(100.0)	63.4
1986	Govt	539(89.4)	161(79.0)	113(51.9)	813(79.3)	16.0
	Aided	42(7.0)	32(15.6)	48(22.0)	122(11.9)	8.0
	Private	22(3.6)	11(5.4)	57(26.1)	90(8.8)	246.1
	Total	603(100.0)	218(100.0)	218(100.0)	1025(100.0)	22.0
1990	Govt	597(91.4)	164(77.0)	139(57.2)	900(81.2)	10.7
	Aided	19(2.9)	23(10.8)	80(32.9)	122(11.0)	0.0
	Private	37(5.7)	26(12.2)	24(9.9)	87(7.8)	–3.3
	Total	653(100.0)	213(100.0)	243(100.0)	1109(100.0)	8.19
1999	Govt	670(88.0)	186(78.8)	187(70.6)	1043(82.6)	15.9
	Aided	1(0.1)	10(4.2)	60(22.6)	71(5.6)	–41.8
	Private	90(11.8)	40(16.9)	18(6.8)	148(11.7)	70.1
	Total	761(100.0)	236(100.0)	265(100.0)	1262(100.0)	13.8

Note: Figures based on the relevant data from Directorate of School Education, Mizoram.
Figures in parenthesis represent the percentage share of schools under different management type.

TABLE 22.5
Educational Coverage of Villages and Rural Population

| Year | Per cent of villages having primary school within | | | | Per cent of rural population served by primay school (state) |
	Aizawl	Lunglei	Chhimtuipui district	State	
1960	NA	NA	NA	77.26	NA
1981	80	76.4	87.1	80.86	94.59
1986	NA	NA	NA	NA	98.05
1993	83	85	95	87.1	97.74

Source: Directorate of Census Operation, Mizoram
Fifth & Sixth All-India Educational Survey, NCERT.

In 1982–3, gross enrolment ratio (GER) rose to 121 from 103 in 1979–80 (see Ralte 1990). From 1982 to 1999, primary schools grew at a relatively slow average annual rate of around 3 per cent. The state government carried on with its quantitative expansion programme through the twin policy of direct management and grants-in-aid to schools. In 1993, only 88 habitations, representing 12.9 per cent of total inhabited villages, remained unserved. These were small hamlets with an average population of 193. The remaining 87.1 per cent of villages had a primary school within the habitation themselves. Rural population served by primary schools was as high as 97.74 per cent. The gross enrolment ratio (GER) was 152.13 per cent (Girls: 143.35 per cent) (see NCERT 1993). It may be said that the state through its efforts during the last two and a half decades has come close to the goal UEE.

Attitude towards Girls' Education

Till 1960 girls' presence in schools was negligible. No wonder female literacy was below 20 per cent in 1951. Traditional social attitudes served to keep the majority of girls away from schools. Women were perceived to be lazy if their hands were not busy through out the day. Ralte's study (1990, 81–100) shows that girls started participating in the schooling process in a significant manner from 1962 onward. The encouraging trend continued during the next three decades and naturally positively impacted overall growth rate in literacy. Detailed analysis of the participation rate of girls in primary schools shows that in 10 out of 13 educational subdivisions of the state, the number of girls for every 100 boys in school ranged from 90 to 97 in 1999. The overall participation rate was 89 girls per 100 boys. The factor which has played the most crucial role in the girls' increasing participation has to be the progressive change in social attitude towards girls from the earlier attitude that stood in the way of girls' right to be literate. An in-depth study is called for.

Role of Social Organizations

Of the many social organizations that are occupying the social space of the state, two stand out—the Young Mizo Association (YMA) and Mizo Hmeichhe Insuihkhawm Pawl (MHIP). The YMA was born of a collective desire to mobilize youth for social regeneration. It was formed on 15 June 1935 as Young Lushai Association. In response to the social aspiration for a single identity, the association was rechristened Young Mizo Association on 7 October 1947. Over the years it has not only grown in strength but also extended its activities to all spheres of social life. Today it is the largest NGO in the northeastern region with a network of groups, branches, and units reaching out to every corner of the state. This well-knit organization has evolved a unique system of management that allows individual branches adequate functional autonomy. With around 600 branches having a total membership of around 2 lakh, YMA is a social force whose voice is heard, activities appreciated, and advice sought.

In the early 1970s, the YMA started a library movement. In 1994 it was decided to have a library in each branch. There are 460 libraries of which 360 are duly recognized by the central YMA. These branches are run as per the convenience of the branches concerned. Many branches open libraries on alternate mornings so that the librarians (engaged on voluntary basis) are not too pressed. As on 1 November 1996, 238 libraries reported to have a total volume of 147,816 books. An estimated 17,698 persons visited these libraries every week all over the state. Books are received mainly from the Raja Ram Mohan Roy Foundation through the state library, besides contributions from members. These small libraries are in great demand. Very often, young farm hands are found borrowing and carrying books to their 'jhum' fields for 'field reading'. Some books get damaged in the process but the spirit, nevertheless, is encouraged!

In 1976, the YMA started publishing, on a regular basis, a monthly magazine, the *YMA Chanchinbu*. The magazine had first appeared in 1940 but could not be regularly published. In 1985 the YMA got its own Press. Every month 9000–10,000 copies are circulated through branches. It is an excellent medium of dissemination.

The YMA has been involved in the adult literacy programme since 1972. Branchwise effort is made to identify illiterates, and then volunteers take up the literacy programme at homes of the target group. 'We are the chief architects of the adult literacy programme,' said the YMA General Secretary with justifiable pride. On 8 February 2000 a headmaster of a village primary school invited YMA functionaries and other dignitaries to a dinner. It was a thanksgiving. As a poor youngster he had been the beneficiary of the literacy programme of the YMA.

The 50th YMA General Conference declared 1996 as the 'Year of Education'. The following guidelines were drawn up:

- Responsibilities of the Central YMA

 – It shall organize an inaugural function for the declared year.

 – Seminars/training shall be organized on the subject of education.

 – An awareness campaign shall be undertaken by means of Mass Media, visits to groups and branches.

 – More open schools may be set up.

 – Coordination with government, church, and other voluntary organizations may be worked out.

 – It shall oversee the activities of sub-headquarters, groups, and branches.

 – Prizes shall be given to the best performing branches and groups.

 – Every programme shall be organized in a manner that students are least disturbed during study hours.

- Responsibilities of Sub-Headquarters

 – It shall submit a report to the Central YMA before the end of September 1996 as per the constitution.

 – It shall oversee the activities of group and town branches within its area. It shall visit the maximum number of group and branch YMAs.

 – It shall give prizes to the best performing branches and groups within its area.

- Responsibilities of Group YMAs

 – Branches shall ask for help from groups whenever needed.

 – 'Education' shall be the theme of the Group YMA Conference.

 – Report shall be submitted to the Central YMA before September 1996.

 – Prizes shall be awarded to the best performing branches within the group.

- Responsibilities of the Branches

 – Efforts shall be made to send every 'left out' child in the relevant age group to schools. Admissions of children who could not continue studies owing to poverty may be done by the branches.

 – High School Leaving Certificate (HSLC) coaching classes may be established as per requirement.

 – Any problem faced by educational institutions and schools shall be brought to the notice of the government and the authorities of the branch.

 – Visits to schools within the branches to be undertaken.

 – Awards to be given to outstanding students and successful candidates.

 – Teachers of all schools within a branch to be met and exhorted to do their best.

 – Efforts to be made to achieve total adult literacy.

 – The value of work to be emphasized and practical sessions organized.

 – Coordination with other agencies may be sought.

 – Signboards/hoardings to be put up wherever possible.

 – Sanitation and health and preservation of environmental heritage to be emphasized.

 – Improvement of farming and allied activities to be emphasized.

 – Awards and honours to be given to those who implement the programme at individual level within the branches.

 – Every branch may constitute a sub-committee on education to pursue any other requirement felt by the individual branch.

 – Report to be submitted by September 1996.

In conformity with the decision of the General Conference, 1996 was declared the Year of Education. The inaugural function was held on 16 January 1996. A state-level Coordination Committee was set up with the Finance Minister as chair and the Education Minister as the vice chair. The Committee had 9 YMA members and 17 government officials. It organized seminars at twenty-six places in the state.

Here are some of the important achievements of different branches during 1996:

• Extensive survey revealed the following
  – Non-school going males: 5477
  – Non-school going females: 4349
  – Children, dropped out for valid reasons: 5030
  – Unemployed and underqualified: 9320

• Eighty-nine branches succeeded in sending 801 children to school.

• A total of 825 meetings with teachers were organized by 234 branches to understand their problems and to show recognition of their services.

• Besides these meetings with teachers, branches made 903 visits to schools. On some occasions the visiting members taught the children.

• Adult literacy activities were undertaken by 59 branches while 40 branches reported that they did not have any more work because all were literate within their areas.

• Practical sessions on various activities were organized by thirty-two branches.

• West Phaileng (development block) branch employed a science teacher for a private high school on a monthly pay of Rs 1500.

• Zotlang branch made its area a totally literate zone. They had been working for total literacy since 1975. They ran a free coaching class with teachers. During the second-term tests of 1996, YMA members helped those students who had no one to help them out. They admitted nine children to school and paid the admission fee. Children doing well were presented with dictionaries and pens. The branch started a private *anganwadi* centre and the instructor's honorarium was contributed by the YMA. Because of emphasis on better farming, seventy families grew ginger besides their traditional crops that year. The branch had the distinction of winning the first prize for its efforts and achievements.

• Some of the prominent activities taken up by different branches were free coaching classes round the year, home visits, organizing cooking and tailoring classes for girls, courses on the use of electrical appliances for boys, and sponsoring poor students for further studies.

• The central YMA collected used schoolbooks and distributed them to branches for the use of poor students.

As an ongoing programme, YMA branches identify elementary school children from poor families and try to take care of their essential educational expenses. Giving recognition to bright students is another feature. Some branches are engaged in helping adult illiterates in the basics of learning in their homes.

Unlike the YMA, the MHIP, the Mizoram Women's Federation, is a low-profile NGO. Established in July 1974 as the main field agency of the State Social Welfare Advisory Board of Mizoram, this organization focussed on child welfare, women welfare, and education of adult illiterate women. From 1974 to 1988 it concentrated on organizing village women. Urban branches started coming up from 1988 onward. By 1990, as many as 500 village branches came up. Each branch has, on average, 150–200 members. Today all the villages (except Chakma areas) have their MHIP branches. In total, there are 663 branches all over the state.

The following are some of the MHIP's regular activities:

• Running creche and *balwadi* centres.

• Condensed courses for HSLC candidates in the morning and evening for two categories of students: (i) class VIII pass students and (ii) HSLC fail students. For the first category a two-year course and for the second a one-year course is run.

• Running vocational centres for class VIII pass women learners. Centres conduct one-year courses in knitting and tailoring.

In the absence of proper documentation of activities, no clear picture is available on the coverage of various programmes.

Since 1991, the MHIP has been engaged in an orientation training programme (OTP) for social workers every year. The three-day OTP gives orientation to opinion leaders on women and health, childcare, legal status of women, personal hygiene, awareness of development programmes of the government, and accounts keeping.

Annually, two OTPs have been organized so far. Approximately 100–150 women from fifteen villages under a development block attended each OTP. One important message they are exhorted to spread to their villages is, 'Girls must complete the high school course and they should marry only after they cross the age of 18.'

No study has been conducted so far on the impact of the different programmes of the YMA and the MHIP on various categories of target groups. Such a study is needed. Their organizational strength and scale of involvement do give sufficient indication that these NGOs are playing the role of change agents and message carriers in this young society of north-eastern India.

PROGRESS IN PRIMARY EDUCATION: AN ASSESSMENT

In this section an attempt has been made to analyse Mizoram's endeavour in providing education to various target groups, its attempt at improving the quality of education, and the pattern of state financing over the years.

Early Childhood Care and Education (ECCE)

As per the recommendation of National Policy on Education (NPE) 1986, the Government of Mizoram launched an ECCE programme to develop necessary readiness in the child to meet the demands of the primary curriculum. ECCE is a holistic input fostering health, psychological, and nutritional development of children. The Integrated Child Development Service (ICDS) is the largest programme under ECCE, that is being provided through the Department of Social Welfare in collaboration with the Directorate of Health and Family Welfare. Over the years, a total of 1342 *anganwadi* centres have been opened in all the twenty rural development blocks and one urban project area (Aizawl Urban ICDS Project), An estimated 25,000 to 30,000 children in the relevant age group are exposed to preschool experiences under the ECCE programme in the state. Twenty-one Child Development Officers, assisted by 213 Circle Officers are overseeing the activities of these *anganwadi* centres. Table 22.6 presents the GER depicting the expansion of ECCE programmes and the progress made in 1990s in the north-east Indian states.

A close look at the Table shows that compared to the other states of north-east India (with the exception of Assam) Mizoram's efforts in enrolling children in the anganwadi centres have been pretty modest.

The Department of Social Welfare has also undertaken a Special Nutrition Programme (SNP) covering the entire state. However, the national norm of 300 feeding days could not be achieved due to insufficiency of fund resources. The total feeding days for a year are approximately 150 only. Under this programme, pregnant and lactating mothers, adolescent girls, and children of 6 to 72 months are given supplementary feeding (diet supplement and micro-nutrients) through the anganwadi centres. The number of beneficiaries covered during 1998 was 144,090. The SNP programme seems to have had an impact on the health of the children. An all-India study on nutrition in 1997 has ranked Mizoram as the second best in the country on the percentage distrubution of underweight children (1–5) (see Table 22.7).

TABLE 22.6
Comparative picture of GER-ECCE for 1990 and 1997–8

State	GER 1990		GER 1997–8	
	Total	Boys	Girls	Total
Arunachal Pradesh	38.20	75.4	67.7	71.6
Assam	10.11	13.1	12.4	12.8
Manipur	38.81	125.0	126.1	125.5
Meghalaya	129.38	91.0	91.1	91.0
Mizoram	51.38	52.6	53.2	52.9
Nagaland	136.99	151.9	135.7	143.9
Tripura	66.07	81.9	84.1	83.0
India	10.33	17.3	16.4	16.9

Source: EFA Indicators 1999. NIEPA.
Note: GER is gross enrolment ratio.

TABLE 22.7
Percentage Distribution of Underweight Children (1–5) India Nutrition Profile

Sl no.	States	Percentage	Rank
01	Arunachal Pradesh	57.3	17th
02	Assam	46.0	11th
03	Bihar	58.7	18th
04	Chandigarh	37.0	06th
05	Dadra & Nagar Haveli	50.5	14th
06	Daman & Diu	42.2	07th
07	Delhi	42.3	08th
08	Goa	31.6	05th
09	Haryana	51.0	15th
10	Himachal Pradesh	56.8	16th
11	Manipur	28.1	03rd
12	Meghalaya	13.0	01st
13	Mizoram	23.4	02nd
14	Nagaland	29.5	04th
15	Punjab	50.3	13th
16	Rajasthan	46.7	12th
17	Sikkim	43.9	10th
18	Tripura	43.7	09th

Note: The report of the Study 'State DIET Nutrition Profiles' conducted in 1997 by the Protein Foods and Nutrtion Development Association of India, Mumbai, sponsored by Food and Nutrition Board, Department of Women and Child Development, Ministry of MHRD, Government of India.

The study clearly shows that with proper care, adequate infrastructure, allocation of food and nutrition and dissemination of nutritional awareness, and supporting services to increase food production to ensure house-hold food security, Mizoram can achieve drastic reduction in child malnutrition.

The Government of Mizoram is aware of its modest progress in preschool education and has taken a decision to make it an integral part of the primary education system. In its Draft Education Policy, 1998, it made a categorical statement in this regard:

> As the early childhood education centres have a critical role to play by way of providing school readiness programme to pre-school children, a network of ECCE Centres should be established to cater to the needs of 3+ children. The existing *Anganwadis*, forming a part of the network, should be revamped and reinforced.

As a part of this revamping process, the State Council of Educational Research and Training (SCERT), Mizoram has undertaken an evaluative study of the existing *anganwadi* centres of the state.

Progress in Enrolment and Participation Rate in Primary Schools

Till 1981, primary stage included classes A, B, I, II, and III and middle stage covered classes IV–VI. From 1982, primary stage represented classes I–IV and middle stage, classes V–VII. The structural change appears to have

had some impact on total enrolment at primary stage. Table 22.8 shows the trend of enrolment at primary stage from 1972–3 onwards.

The enrolment at primary stage has increased almost two times during the the 1972–99 period. During this period boys' enrolment has grown 1.8 times and that of girls, 2.1 times. The first post UT decade saw rapid growth followed by a slower rate of growth in the subsequent period. The decade witnessed proportionately higher enrolment of girls than that of boys. The trend reversed in later years. The participation rate of girls was a very encouraging 94 girls per 100 boys in 1982–3. In 1999–2000 the participation rate has gone down slightly but the difference has continued to remain very small since 1982–3.

Enrolment Ratio

Enrolment, per se, does not give a clear indication of the proportion of relevant age group children (6–11) already enrolled in primary schools of the state. The most relevant indicator of participation of children in schooling is the enrolment ratio. Table 22.9 presents the gross enrolment ratio which represents school enrolment as a ratio of total population in the age group 6–11.

TABLE 22.8
Trends in Enrolment in Primary Schools

Year	Enrolment			Ratio of girls to total	Number of girls per 100 boys	Growth rate (%)		
	Boys	Girls	Total			Total	Boys	Girls
1972–3	31,580	24,211	55,791	43.4	77			
1982–3	46,228	43,494	89,722	48.5	94	60.8	46.4	79.6
1992–3	51,425	47,346	98,771	48.0	92	10.1	11.2	8.9
1999–2000	56,152	50,152	106,165	47.2	89.3	7.5	9.2	5.9

Source: Statistical Wing, Directorate of School Education, Government of Mizoram.

TABLE 22.9
Statewise Gross Enrolment Ratio (%) (1986, 1993, and 1997)

State	Girls			Total		
	1986–7	1993–4	1997–8	1986–7	1993–4	1997–8
Arunachal Pradesh	78.10	119.87	82.10	94.70	130.96	97.20
Assam	81.21	86.57	104.30	90.10	92.88	109.10
Manipur	86.91	127.64	74.10	93.50	131.88	85.90
Meghalaya	107.08	136.72	86.10	108.61	134.29	93.40
Mizoram	118.45	146.35	104.60	122.53	152.13	113.60
Nagaland	103.92	99.92	86.30	107.76	101.73	94.30
Tripura	112.73	119.92	75.30	124.17	126.73	88.40
India	77.55	85.02	81.50	91.69	95.90	90.30

Source: NCERT 1992 and 1995
EFA Indicators 1999. NIEPA

Between 1986 and 1993 gross enrolment ratio for Mizoram at primary level showed an increase of about 30 percentage points. The figures for girls recorded a high increase of 28 percentage points. Comparative analysis shows that during both the time points the figures for girls as well as those for total enrolled children were much higher than the corresponding figures in respect of all the other six states of north-east India. Arunachal Pradesh had the lowest gross enrolment ratio for girls in 1986–7 (78.10). The figures showed the highest increase in 1993–4 by 41.7 percentage points. The magnitude of increase in the total figures was also very high, next only to that of Meghalaya. Both Assam and Tripura registered marginal increases in gross enrolment ratios during 1986–93. The figures for Nagaland showed negative growth.

The 1997–8 figures for all the states except Assam give a totally different picture from those of previous years. The calculations might have been based on different base population size. Mizoram still heads the list both in respect of total gross enrolment ratio as well as that for girl's. Assam shows vast improvement, almost touching Mizoram figures. Manipur and Tripura have lower gross enrolment ratio than the national average. Based on 1997 figures, it may be said that both Mizoram and Assam are in a position to achieve the goal of universal primary education within a short period. The strong community involvement may make the task of Mizroram in realizing the goal easier.

Retention Rate

It is difficult to get an accurate picture of the retention and drop-out rates of children in the absence of reliable data during the entire primary stage (classes I–IV).

Ralte (1990) in her study made a rough estimate for the entire territory. The apparent Cohort Method was applied to enrolment figures of class I for 1983–4 and that of class IV for 1986–7. The percentage of drop-outs between class I (24,692) and class IV (16,441) over the period 1983–6 was found to be 33.4 and the percentage for girls (35.8) was higher than that for boys (31.3). The figures do give an idea of the magnitude of wastage due to dropout and stagnation. NCERT data for 1993 on drop-out rates for primary schools in Mizoram and those for other north-eastern states resent a disturbing picture (see Table 22.10).

In 1997, the drop-out rate at primary stage in Mizoram showed a declining trend. Based on enrolment figures of class I in 1994–5 and those of class IV in 1997–8, the drop-out rate for the state as whole was found to be 49.7. The situation is not very encouraging despite the declining trend in dropout.

Efforts at Improving Quality of the Primary Schools

Quality of education is an umbrella concept which includes all those aspects of education which make it efficient and good. It includes availability of infrastructure such as buildings, teachers including trained teachers and the quality of instruction, course syllabi etc. What have the Government of Mizoram's efforts at addressing these issues been?

According to the Sixth All-India Educational Survey (1993), 67.5 per cent of the primary schools of Aizawl district had *pucca* buildings. Lunglei and Chhimtuipui districts had 65 per cent and 30 per cent quality buildings respectively. The average number of classrooms in the three districts was found to be 5, 3.86, and 4.5 respectively. With the fund available under the Operation Blackboard (OB) scheme since 1987, 1015 primary schools out of a total of 1262 schools have been provided with teaching-learning equipment. Under the same scheme, single-teacher schools in the interior areas have been provided with a second teacher, 50 per cent of whom are women. The rate of induction of teachers at primary stage during 1992–6 period was much higher than the rate of growth of schools. Against an average 1.8 per cent annual growth rate in enrolment, the rate of growth of teachers was 5.2 per cent, obviously an effort to improve the teacher–pupil ratio (Table 22.11).

This progressive induction of teachers has led to a highly favourable teacher–pupil ratio as can be seen in Table 22.12. The teacher–pupil ratio of 1:26 in 1992–3 has come down to 1:21.7 in 1999–2000. This ratio, however, does not tell the whole story. It, after all, provides a picture of the average number of students to be taken care of by a teacher. A better indicator of quality is the number of teachers present in a school. In 1992–3 there were 3.6 teachers per school. The position remained more or less constant till 1996–7. In 1999, teachers per school were found to be 3.9. Analysis of the teacher strength in primary schools of all the 13 educational

TABLE 22.10
North-eastern States: Dropout Rates at Primary Level (%) (1993)

	Arunachal Pradesh	Assam	Manipur	Meghalaya	Mizoram	Nagaland	Tripura
Girls	61.09	39.55	68.53	34.43	58.58	24.13	66.95
Total	60.05	39.05	68.26	32.26	57.58	37.65	63.49

TABLE 22.11
Teacher–Pupil Ratio, Teachers per School, Pupils per School, and Primary School–Middle School Ratio 1992–9

Year	Primary stage			Middle stage			
	Teacher–Pupil ratio	Teacher per school	Pupil per school	Teacher–Pupil ratio	Teacher per school	Pupil per school	MS–PS Ratio
1992–3	26	3.6	93	13	5.9	76	1.9
1993–4	25	3.6	90	12	6.1	74	1.8
1994–5	24	3.6	86	12	6.1	73	1.8
1995–6	23	3.5	80	11	6.1	68	1.8
1996–7	23	3.7	84	11	6.4	69	1.8
1999–2000	21.7	3.9	84	10.5	6.5	68	1.7

Note: Based on relevant Data of DSE, Mizoram.

subdivisions (including the three autnonomous District Councils) shows that in 3 subdivisions, there are on average 3.9 to 5.8 teachers per school; the remaining subdivisions have lower-than-state-average (3.9) teachers per school figures. The Chakma Autonomous District Council (CADC) schools have the lowerst figure of 2.6 (see Table 22.12).

There has been significant growth in the proportion of trained teachers at the first level of education in recent years. In 1985–6, 50 per cent teachers in primary schools

were trained. The figure came down to 49 in 1990–1 (see Mahajan *et al.* 1994, 25).

The proportion of trained teachers rose to 78.46 in 1996–7 (see Table 22.13). A genderwise, female teachers from 46.6 per cent of total teacher strength at primary stage. Significantly, in 1996–7 trained women teachers (79.8) were proportionately a little higher than their male counterparts (see Table 22.14). Districtwise, Aizawl crossed the 80 per cent mark (81.7) in terms of trained teachers followed by Lunglei (76.9) in 1997–8 (see Table

TABLE 22.12
Teacher–Pupil Ratio, Teachers per School, Pupils per School, and Participation Rate at Primary and Middle Stages (1999)

Sl. no.	Subdivision	Primary stage			Middle stage			Primary stage	Middle stage
		Teacher–Pupil ratio	Teachers per school	Pupils per school	Teacher–Pupil ratio	Teachers per school	Pupils per school	Girls per 100 boys	Girls per 100 boys
01	Aizawl East-I	22.3	5.8	129.7	14.2	7.4	105.1	95	95
02	Aizawl East-II	25.0	3.7	92.2	10.7	6.2	66.5	92	99
03	Aizawl West-I	21.1	4.6	96.9	11.8	6.0	94.1	96	106
04	Aizawl West-II	24.6	3.1	75.9	10.1	6.0	61.1	89	92
05	Aizawl North	28.0	3.0	84.5	10.5	5.8	60.1	91	97
06	Champhai	26.2	3.6	93.3	10.9	6.2	67.8	90	96
07	Kolasib	22.4	4.0	89.0	11.0	6.4	71.1	96	87
08	Serchhip	21.0	4.0	84.8	10.4	6.5	67.7	94	92
	Total of Aizawl district	23.3	4.1	94.7	11.4	6.6	76.0	93	96
09	Lunglei East	20.8	3.9	82.1	9.9	6.5	64.8	92	93
10	Lunglei West	18.9	3.1	58.1	8.6	5.9	50.5	81	87
	Total of Lunglei district	20.0	3.5	69.6	9.3	6.2	57.8	87	90
11	E.O. MADC, Saiha	20.1	4.7	94.2	5.9	6.4	37.5	97	88
12	E.O. LADC, Lawngtlai	13.2	3.7	49.0	7.5	6.6.	49.7	90	88
13	E.O. CADC, Chawngte	25.1	2.6	64.6	NA	NA	NA	49	NA
	Total Chhimtuipui district	18.3	3.6	66.6	6.7	6.5	43.5	78	88
	STATE (Total)	21.7	3.9	84.1	10.5	6.5	68.4	89	94

Note: Worked out from relevant data of DSE, Mizoram.

TABLE 22.13
No. of Trained and Untrained Teachers (1996–7)

Stage	Male		Female		Total		Percentage	
	Trained	Untrained	Trained	Untrained	Trained	Untrained	Trained	Untrained
Primary	1938	570	1749	442	3687	1012	78.46	21.54
Middle	2655	934	666	307	3320	1141	74.42	25.58
High school	945	1004	232	296	1176	1300	47.50	52.50
H. secondary	45	102	25	81	70	0183	28.00	72.00
Total	5583	2510	2672	1136	8253	3636	–	–

TABLE 22.14
No. of Trained and Untrained Teachers—Male/Female (1996–7)

Stage	Teachers		Percentage of female teachers	Percentage of male teachers		Percentage of female teachers	
	Male	Female		Trained	Untrained	Trained	Untrained
Primary	2508	2191	46.6	77.3	22.7	79.8	20.2
Middle	3489	973	21.8	76.1	23.9	68.4	31.6
High School	1947	528	21.3	48.5	51.5	43.9	56.1
H. Secondary	147	106	41.9	30.6	69.4	23.6	76.4

TABLE 22.15
Districtwise Trained Teachers in Elementary School (1997–8)

Stage	Aizawl		Lunglei		Chhimtuipui		Mizoram	
	Total	Percentage trained	Total	Percentage trained	Total	Percentage trained	Total	Percentage trained
Primary	2973	81.7	841	76.9	910	55.6	4724	67.0
Middle	3316	73.6	783	75.3	634	72.4	4733	73.7
Elementary	6289	77.4	1624	76.7	1544	62.5	9457	74.9

Note: Based on Teacher Data from DSE, Mizoram.

22.15). Chhimtuipui district had a relatively low percentage of trained teachers (55.6). The overall trend indicates that efforts are on to improve the situation. How qualified are primary school teachers to teach according to national standards? Table 22.16 attempts to give an answer.

Mizoram is relatively better placed than all the other states of the north-east in this regard (see NCTE 1999, 7). But the fact remains that about one-third of primary school teachers are neither academically qualified nor certified to teach according to national standards even in Mizoram. In fact, all the north-eastern states fare badly on this indicaor compared to the rest of the country i.e. the majority of primary school teachers, these states, with the exception of Mizoram, do not have the minimum academic qualification (10+2) or a proper professional qualification (two-year teaching training course).

Since 1994, in Mizoram a new approach to evaluation of students in their terminal year (class IV) has been adopted. Instead of internal tests, the students (except those of District Council areas) appear at selected centres and answer papers set by the Mizoram Board of Secondary Education (MBSE). After centrewise evaluation of

TABLE 22.16
No. of Trained and Untrained Teachers in the North-eastern States 1996–7

State		Percentage of primary school teachers	
		With academic qualification	Certified to teach
Arunachal Pradesh	Total	50.3	50.3
	Female	50.3	50.3
Assam	Total	47.5	47.5
	Female	47.5	47.5
Manipur	Total	34.8	34.8
	Female	35.5	35.8
Meghalaya	Total	47.5	42.5
	Female	42.5	42.5
Mizoram	Total	67.6	67.6
	Female	67.6	67.6
Nagaland	Total	50.8	50.8
	Female	49.5	49.5
Tripura	Total	33.1	33.1
	Female	33.0	33.0
India	Total	87.7	87.7
	Female	90.0	90.0

papers, answer papers, carrying 70 per cent and above marks, are sent to the MBSE for re-evaluation, leading to selection for merit scholarship. This merit scholarship has been introduced as an incentive scheme.

To improve the quality of schools, the government has recently introduced a grading system for awarding merit grants to best-performing schools.

To tone up the management system, two important decisions were taken: introduction of the comprehensive school system and setting up of school complexes. The objective of the comprehensive schools is to reduce the multiplicity of schools by bringing two to three schools of either first level or first and second levels under one management and one roof, and to improve the functionality of the institutions. The objectives of introducing the school complexes are two: To break the isolation of schools and help them function in small, face-to-face, cooperative groups; and to make a delegation of authority from the Department possible. The comprehensive school scheme has been introduced in a phased manner with effect from academic session 1991. In the same year, 199 school Complexes, formed out of 1490 first and second level schools, were given administrative approval to start functioning. It was a step towards the decentralization of the managment of schools.

Financing of the Primary Education System

An examination of the sectoral allocation of funds during successive plan periods shows that the percentage of educational outlay to total plan outlay in Mizoram has increased during the Seventh Plan (see Table 22.17).

TABLE 22.17
Percentage of Educational Outlay to Total Plan Outlay

(Rs in crore)

Five Year Plan	Total outlay	Educational outlay	% from the total
Fifth	57.73	3.16	5.6
Sixth	149.30	9.61	6.4
Seventh	260.00	21.90	8.4
Eighth	763.00	67.88	8.9
Ninth	1618.51	151.44	9.4

Source: Government of Mizoram: Sectoral Allocation & Plan Budget for Mizoram (Planning Department).

Mizoram's first plan started with the National Fifth Plan period. The educational outlay ratio, i.e. educational outlay as a proportion of total outlay, improved from 5.6. per cent in the Fifth Plan period to 6.4 per cnet in the Sixth Plan, i.e. a relative increase of 14 per cent. In the Seventh Plan, this ratio rose to 8.4 per cent representing a relative increase of 31 per cent over the ratio of the Sixth Plan period. The Eighth and

Ninth Plan proportionate outlay rose by around 6 per cent from the previous outlay ratio. The percentage share of primary education during successive plans does not show an encouraging trend (see Table 22.18).

TABLE 22.18
Ratio Outlay on Primary Education (I–IV) to Total Education Outlay

(Rs in crore)

Five Year Plan	Total education outlay	Outlay on primary education	Percentage from total
Fifth	3.16	1.14	36.1
Sixth	9.61	2.89	30.1
Seventh	21.90	2.64	12.1
Eigth	67.88	13.24	19.5
Ninth	151.44	40.11	6.5

Source: Government of Mizoram: Sectoral Allocation and Plan Budget for Mizoram (Planning Department).

From the Fifth to Seventh Plans there was a steadily declining trend in the percentage share of primary education. The upward trend started again from the Eighth Plan. The proportionate increase has continued till the current plan period. But the shift is not very significant. It is evident that there has been a shift of resources from primary education to other stages of education.

Analysis shows that in 1992–3, education had a 16 per cent share of total state (revenue) expenditure. It rose to 19.6 per cent in 1993–4 and remained more or less at the same level till 1996–7. School education accounted for around 84 per cent of the total educational expenditure. In 1997–8, around 71 per cent of total expenditure on school education was on elementary schools. The share of primary schools (classes I–IV) was 33 per cent and that of middle schools 38 per cent. The 1998–9 revised budget estimate also showed the same pattern. In absolute terms, fund allocation has increased manifold. But it is maintenance expenditure that accounts for more than 95 per cent of total expenditure. Mizoram, in pursuing the policy of taking over full management of an increasing number of schools, under the grants-in-aid system, is burdened with a heavy salary bill. Mid-plan diversion of fund from plan acivities increases the woe of the Education Department.

Adult Literacy

The government-initiated adult literacy programme started in a systematic way in Mizoram from 1979.

During 1979–81, around 4300 adults were made literate annually with a success rate of 56 per cent. A centre-based approach prevailed, wherein adult literacy centres admitted adult learners at the rate of 23–30 learners per centre. The 1982–91 period saw a better annual output (5122) but the success rate was not encouraging. It went down to 44.6 per cent and the government took the decision to change the approach. Two factors influenced the decision. In 1989–90, the Adult Education Wing of the Directorate of School Education had conducted a survey which revealed the presence of 50,637 adult illiterates. As against this there were only 550 adult literacy centres with a total intake capacity of 16,500. The state, in its bid to make Mizoram fully literate, decided to go in for a mass approach (Each-One-Teach-One) to turn the existing iltiterates into literates within a very short period. So the adult literacy centres were wound up and the community was approached. This approach had a better coverage. During 1992–6, annually 12.5 thousand adults were made literate. The annual coverage was 2.4 times more than that during the previous decade. Of course, the success rate was rather low (42.8 per cent). During the last eighteen years, a total of 1.27 lakh adult illiterates h ve been made literate. It is an achievement that was

possible because a decentralized approach was made in which the village community was actively involved. The key agency in this process was the Village Adult Education Committee (VAEC), set up progressively in each village except the three autonomous District Council areas since 1991 (see Box 22.2).

In April, 1999, the Adult Education Wing conducted a survey in all twenty-three Adult Education Circles covering most of the villages except in the CADC area. The survey covered 1.16 lakh households. The population coverage was a little over 6 lakh. 15.83 per cent belonged to 0–6 age group. A total of 10,801 illiterates were identified 44.5 per cent of whom belonged to the 35 and above age group with women forming the majority (63.6 per cent) in this category. Of those identified 49 per cent belonged to 15–35 age group. In this category, too, women were in the majority. Only 6.3 per cent illterates were in the 7–14 age group. The overall picture that emerged from the survey is highly encouraging. Only 2.14 per cent of the population (7+) was found to be illiterate. The Department's efforts at mobilizing the community are showing result.

BOX 22.2

Village Adult Education Committees

A Village Adult Education Committee should be constituted in each and every village. The Committtee, as far as practicabe, should consist of the following as its members:

- Village Council President or representative from the Village Council.
- Representative (at least one each) from any Voluntary Organization available in the locality (YMA, MHIP).
- Representative from Teachers' Association.
- Representative (at least one each) from various church organizations.
- Representative from Service Association.

Functions and Responsibilities of the Village Adult Education Committee

- To conduct illiteracy survey in their jurisdiction/areas and identify all illiterate adults in the age groups 15–35 years and 45 years and above.
- To maintain proper record/register of illiterates stating fathers' names, sex, and age.
- To identify volunteers who would undertake teaching responsibility of the illiterates.
- To make arrangement and matching of the volunteers (known as Animators) with the learners.
- To make arrangements and find suitable place where teaching–learning programme may be carried out.
- To submit report on survey/arrangement concerning teaching–learning requirement of the Village Adult Education Committee/Animators/learners.
- To examine whether there is any duplicacy in teaching carried out by the Animators and how they utilize the teaching–learning materials.
- To supervise the teaching–learning process followed/carried out by the animators and how they utilize the teaching–learning materials.
- To evaluate the learner's progress and literacy competence.
- To submit reports on the achievement of the Animators–learners and make recommendation for award of honorarium to deserving animators.
- To conduct review of their performance and make suggestion for improvement in the subsequent session.

Issues of Concern

Though the system has grown over the years, it has bred certain imbalances and inadequacies that need to be addressed with a sense of commitment.

Mizoram has made great strides in her literacy venture. But the 1991 Census provided a disquieting picture with respect to 5 out of 20 rural development blocks. Chawngte block with a literacy rate of 24.76 (male 36.51; female 11.63) was at the bottom of all the blocks. With the Chakmas forming 90 per cent of its population, this area had not only the highest proportion of illiterate population but also the highest disparity index in 1991. The other four blocks—West Phaileng (53.31), West Bunghmun (55.61), Lungsen (46.40), and Lawngtlai (57.93)—also had high disparity between male and female literacy, ranging from 12 to 21 percentage points. All these are ethnically heterogeneous blocks. Together these depressed areas account for about 17 per cent of the state's population. Four of five blocks are within the District Council areas. Latest information on the literacy front shows that in two of the three District Council areas the situation has vastly changed. It is only the CADC that is still lagging. The 1999 adult literacy survey to the Education Department did not cover this area. The MHIP does not have any village branches here. Other social organizations like the YMA are also largely absent from this area. Even the District Council management appears to lack a sense of commitment. In 1999, the participation rate of girls for every 100 boys in the primary schools of the CADC was 49. There were 2.6 teachers per primary school on average. It is a dismal picture. The area demands priority attention.

The government in the state has been trying to encourage children to complete the four years of primary schooling. Some measures that have been taken are supply of free textbooks and uniforms (on a selective basis), and provision of midday meal to all children of government schools at 3 kg per child per month. But the drop-out rate at the end of the cycle (class IV) is disturbingly high. The problem is acute in the southern part of the state and needs to be addressed.

Around one-third of primary school teachers in the state are neither qualified academically nor certified to teach, according to national standards. Today all the government primary school teachers are trained. They have gone through a one-year Elementary Teachers Training Course. The majority of them have deficiency both in content as well as in the methodology of teaching. The Resource Support Institutes have not addressed themselves to this problem. The latest evaluation of District Institutes of Education and Training (DIETs), as a part of the ongoing national evaluation of DIETs, has found one of the two DIETs virtually non-functional. It has an extremely rickety organizational structure. Both the SCERT and the DIETs, have not yet evolved a systematic plan for recurrent, relevant training programmes for these teachers. An overhaul of these institutes is a must. The quality of academic support to the teachers has its impact on the retentive capacity of schools.

The decentralization process in the form of the School Complex Scheme that the state started with enthusiasm nine years back has lost much its momentum. The enthusiasm was not matched by the needed field-level understanding of this unique scheme through a pilot study or two. A proper planned approach in this regard is called for.

Prospects

Mizoram, through its efforts, has given sufficient indication that it shares the 'expanded vision', proclaimed at Jomtein, Thailand in 1990. The rights of every child have been recognized. The state through its sustained expansion programme has almost succeeded in providing universal access to basic education. The various central schemes have been implemented. The overall impact of the governmental effort on the system is difficult to assess but there are certain indicators of progress. The gap between male and female literacy rates has been bridged. With 95 per cent female literacy against 96 per cent male literacy, the gap is as good as non-existent. There has been considerable improvement too in the functional space of schools and in teacher–pupil ratio.

The adult illiteracy rate has been sufficiently reduced mainly through collaborative efforts of the government and the community. Mizoram has a vast reservoir of public goodwill and energy. It has, in fact, a legacy of public participation. The literacy movement, initiated by the missionaries, was given momentum by young people who had been baptized into learning. The involvement of social organizations like the YMA and MHIP in education for all (EFA) in recent years is sufficient indication of the presence a 'virtuous circle'. Within a span of 100 years Mizoram has achieved much. What is missing is the pursuit of excellence. The state is slowly trying to address itself to the task of qualitative improvement. What is needed is a thorough assessment of the ongoing programmes and a follow-up plan of action for improving the internal efficiency of the school system, establishing linkages with other developmental agencies for a coordinated programme of skill development of youth and adults and forging partnerships with the community organizations for effective management of the formal and non-formal system of education.

The ethnic turmoil that is almost tearing apart the rest of the north-eastern region has not disturbed the social fabric of the Mizo society. The resilience of the society has succeeded in removing the scars of the 1960s insurgency movement. Mizoram has given peace a chance for the last decade and a half. Mizoram is the recent recepient of the 'Peace Bonus'. Central attention to the economic needs of the state is increasingly becoming noticeable. There is greater mobility of people both within and outside the state. The rural economy is slowly looking up. Dissemination media keep people informed about developmental programmes. The information highway has reached urban centres. Synergistic action shall give the needed boost to the state's efforts at EFA. The state's success in adult literacy, in particular, owes substantially to the combined efforts of the community and the state.

REFERENCES

Allen, B. C. *et al.* (n.d.). *Gazatteer of Bengal and North East India.* Mittal Publication.

Census of India (1961). *Assam, Part I-A, vol. III, General Report.* Government of India.

————— (1971). *Mizo Hills District Census Handbook, Assam.* Government of India.

————— (1981). *Mizoram. Part XIII-A&B, Series 31, District Census, Handbook.* Government of India.

————— (1991). *Mizoram. Part XII-A&B, Series 17, District Census Handbook.* Government of India.

Department of Social Welfare (1999). *State Plan of Action for Children.* Government of Mizoram.

Directorate of School Education (1999). *Statistics on School Education (1972–99),* Statistical Wing, Government of Mizoram.

Ganguli, J. B. (1992). *Zonal Planning in Agriculture and Allied Activities* (Planning Perspectives for the North Eastern and Eastern Zone), Lancer Publishers.

Lalchungnunga (1983). 'Progress and Development of Ecuation in Mizoram'. *Historical Journal of Mizoram,* vol. II.

Lloyd, J. M. Rev. (n.d.). *On Every High Hills : Aizawl.* Synod Publications.

Mahajan, Baldev *et al.* (1994). *Educational Administration in Mizoram.* Vikas Publishing House, New Delhi.

Mc Call, A. A. (1949). *The Lushai Chrysalis.* Lusac and Company Limited, London.

Mehta, Arun. C. (1996). 'Reliability of Eduational Data in the Context of National Council of Educational Research and Training Survey'. *Journal of Educational Planning and Administration,* vol. X, no. 3, pp. 281–305.

Ministry of Human Resource Development (1998). *Educational Profile of States and Union Territories.* Government of India.

National Council for Teacher Education (1999). *Teacher Education in Mizoram.* New Delhi.

National Council of Educational Research and Training (1992). *Fifth All-India Educational Survey; A Concise Report.* New Delhi.

————— (1998). *Sixth All-India Educational Survey.* New Delhi.

National Institute of Educational Planning and Administration (2000). *EFA Indicators.* New Delhi.

Ralte, Lalliani (1990). *An Analytical Study of the Primary Education in Mizoram During the Post Independence Period.* An Unpublished Ph.D. Dissertation, North Eastern Hill University, Shillong.

YMA (1996). *YMA in 1996.* Aizawl.

23

Progress towards Education for All
The Case of Tamil Nadu

P. Radhakrishnan and R. Akila

INTRODUCTION

Article 45 of the Constitution of India enjoins that the state shall endeavour to provide, within a period of ten years from the commencement of the Constitution, free and compulsory education for all children until they complete the age of 14 years. While the Constitution thus indicates India's intention to provide universal free and compulsory education, this goal has so far, that is for fifty years, remained elusive. Nevertheless, state, civil, and political support to education as a human right has been gathering momentum, especially since the enunciation of the National Policy on Education (NPE) 1986 which gave very high priority to universalization of elementary education (UEE) and eradication of adult illiteracy.

Education for All (EFA) here is defined as a process of (i) enrolling and effectively retaining all children within the 6–14 age group up to class VIII[1] through either the formal school system or the non-formal system with comparable standards; (ii) expanding early childhood care and developmental activities through both education and welfare centres; and (iii) ensuring functional literacy of adults in the 15–35 age group. EFA is thus taken to mean a blend of literacy and education for creating a fully literate young and adult population. Tamil Nadu's present situation in relation to the goals of EFA should be seen as the outcome of various initiatives over several years.[2]

[1] The reference here is to five years of primary (classes I–V) and three years of upper-primary (classes VI–VIII) schooling, which together make up India's elementary education.

[2] State intervention in public education in Tamil Nadu has a long history, beginning in the late nineteenth century. Most schemes introduced by Christian missionaries and promoted by the British administration included special schools, scholarships, and fee waivers for depressed classes [mostly the present Scheduled

Prior to attempting an assessment of Tamil Nadu's educational efforts, broad clues about certain prerequisites to the success of EFA efforts elsewhere may be useful. Success stories of some of the high achieving developing countries show that both demand and supply initiatives by the state are important for universalizing basic education (see Mehrotra 1998). Most initiatives are based on: (i) speculation in the economics of education—keeping unit costs low, reducing opportunity costs, and generally taking care of direct and indirect costs to parents in a largely poor and illiterate milieu; (ii) welfare approach—given certain culture-specific or contextual peculiarities, through freeships and scholarships to the disadvantaged, and special provisions to minorities; and (iii) a combination of economic and social concerns.

Agencies of civil society have well-recognized roles in democratic societies for their 'voice'.[3] Studies have

Castes (SCs) and Scheduled Tribes (STs), that is the historically suppressed and disabled bottom groups of Indian society], appointing escorts to girl students, and grants-in-aid for teachers and schools, based on performance. Affirmative action was a feature of the recommendations of even the first (1882) Education Commission (for a discussion of this see Radhakrishnan 1990). Issues concerning education as a right and as indispensable to 'self-respect' were important to the non-Brahmin movement of the early twentieth century, followed by the overlapping Dravidian, Self-Respect, and Backward Class movements, which articulated the educational needs and rights of the masses (for a discussion of these movements see Radhakrishnan 1996).

[3] Hirschman's theory (1986) on 'exit and voice' seems relevant here because complaints and criticisms by proactive members or organizations can have an impact on improving schooling process. In Tamil Nadu the 'School Revamping Committees' encourage community participation in this sense, at least to some extent, and are instrumental in collecting funds and other contributions from concerned citizens and agencies for better schooling.

shown that states which have succeeded in their elementary education programmes are those which have overcome, to some extent, official apathy and public disinterest (see, for instance, PROBE 1999). It is, however, important to note that even in such states, traditional patterns of inequality have not been adequately reckoned with. Tamil Nadu is a case in point.

PROGRESS IN LITERACY: TAMIL NADU AND INDIA

Tamil Nadu's Literacy in Regional and All-India Contexts

With a literacy of about 63 per cent in the 7+ population in 1991 and 57 per cent and 62 per cent in the 15+ population in 1991 and 1995–6 respectively, against corresponding national averages of 52 per cent, 48 per cent, and 54 per cent, Tamil Nadu is ahead of many other states.[4] Table 23.1 presents literacy data on 1981 and 1991 for the various age groups for Tamil Nadu and India as a whole.

2 of the 3 northern states (Delhi and Punjab), and 1 of the 2 eastern states (West Bengal) were above the national average by 6 per cent to 38 per cent in the 7+ and 5 per cent to 40 per cent in the 15+ population in 1991. Among these seven states, Tamil Nadu ranked fourth in both 7+ and 15+ literacy, behind Kerala, Delhi, and Maharashtra (90 per cent to 65 per cent in the 7+ and 88 per cent to 60 per cent in the 15+ population). Among these states and also Haryana, where 15+ literacy in 1995–6 was above the national average (54 per cent), Tamil Nadu (along with West Bengal) ranked fifth, behind Kerala, Delhi, Maharashtra, and Punjab (90 per cent to 63 per cent) in overall literacy.

However, the growth rates in Tamil Nadu over the decade 1981–91 in the 7+ and over 1995–6 in the 15+ population were below the national average. Unlike Kerala, where the growth rates were even lower because of the very high literacy in the base year (82 per cent in the 7+ population in 1981; and 88 per cent in the 15+ population in 1991), the lower growth rates in Tamil Nadu

TABLE 23.1
Literacy Rate by Age Group: India and Tamil Nadu

(per cent)

Age group		India		Tamil Nadu		Growth rate	
		1981	1991	1981	1991	India	Tamil Nadu
7–14	Male	60.8	70.3	75.5	88.8	15.7	17.6
	Female	41.3	55.8	60.4	81.2	35.3	34.4
	Total	51.3	63.3	68.0	85.0	23.4	25.0
10–14	Male	66.1	76.9	78.6	89.7	16.3	14.1
	Female	44.7	59.5	61.2	80.6	33.1	31.7
	Total	55.9	68.6	70.2	85.2	22.7	21.4
15–24	Male	66.3	73.5	75.8	81.8	10.8	7.9
	Female	40.3	49.4	49.4	63.9	22.4	29.5
	Total	53.8	61.9	64.8	72.7	15.0	12.2
15–34	Male	63.8	69.5	74.4	78.6	8.9	5.6
	Female	35.4	43.4	47.9	57.6	22.6	20.3
	Total	50.0	56.8	61.0	68.0	13.6	11.5
35+	Male	44.7	53.2	57.0	61.2	19.0	7.4
	Female	14.5	22.9	19.7	28.7	57.9	45.7
	Total	30.2	38.9	38.9	45.4	28.8	16.7

Source: (1) Census of India, India and Tamil Nadu, 1981, 1991, Part IV-A: Social and Cultural Tables.
(2) Census of India, Tamil Nadu, 1981, 1991, Part IV-A: 'Social and Cultural Tables'.

Seen regionwise, 2 of the 4 southern states (Kerala and Tamil Nadu), 2 western states (Gujarat and Maharashtra),

[4] Though the latest literacy data available are for the end of December 1997 in the National Sample Survey (NSS) 52nd Round, these are not used here. However, it may be relevant to point out that according to these data the 7+ literacy in Tamil Nadu was 70 per cent for the total population, 80 per cent for male, and 60 per cent for females against corresponding national averages of 62 per cent, 73 per cent, and 50 per cent.

cannot be attributed to the literacy rates in the base year and should be of concern to the state's efforts in the area of elementary education.

Although Tamil Nadu's 7+ literacy among SCs and Others (the general or total population excluding SCs/STs) was well above the national average, the gap between SCs and Others was almost the same as that at all-India level, a 19 to 21 percentage point difference; literacy among ST males was below the national average;

the literacy gap between STs and Others was wider than that at all-India level; and the gap between SCs and STs though not insignificant at all-India level was wide (see Table 23.2).

The lower literacy among the SCs/STs could be attributed to their entrenched backwardness because of traditional caste prejudices and exclusionary practices against them. However, why they are still so backward, especially after about fifty years of affirmative action by the state to redress their historically accumulated disabilities and bring them to the level of the general population, is an important issue which educational planners' efforts in Tamil Nadu and for that matter in the rest of India will have to address.

The increase in 7+ literacy over the decade 1981–91 was higher among females than males at all-India level by 16 percentage points; in all states with the exception of Madhya Pradesh the increase in female literacy was higher than that in male literacy over 1981–91. With a difference of 19 percentage points, Tamil Nadu (along with Karnataka) ranked sixth among the nine states where the increase was above the national average, ranging from 17 to 33 percentage points.

Of the eight states where 7+ female literacy as a percentage of 7+ male literacy in 1991 was higher than the national average, ranging from 66 per cent to 92 per cent, Tamil Nadu at 61 per cent ranked fourth, behind Kerala, Delhi, and Punjab (92 per cent to 77 per cent). Moreover the percentage point difference in growth rate over 1981–91 (with 8 at national level, and ranging from 3 to 10 in these eight states) was highest in Tamil Nadu (10), indicating an edge over other states in the growth of female literacy.

Female adult literacy as a percentage of male adult literacy in 1991 and 1995–6 though less than in the case of 7+ literacy, broadly conforms to the 7+ pattern: Tamil Nadu ranked fourth (63 per cent) along with West Bengal, behind Kerala, Delhi, and Punjab (90 per cent to 71 per cent) among the eight states where it was above the national average (55 per cent) in 1991, and fifth (66 per cent) in 1995–6 (along with Maharashtra) among the eight states where it was above the national average (61 per cent), behind Kerala, Delhi, Punjab and West Bengal (92 per cent to 69 per cent).

At state level, Tamil Nadu's literacy was as high as 85 per cent in the 7–14 and 10–14 age groups, followed by 73 per cent in the 15–24[5] age group, though in the 35+ population it was only 45 per cent. The all-India percentages were only 63 for 7–14, 69 for 10–14 and 15–24, and 39 for the 35+ population. The higher

[5] The age group 15–24 is one of the EFA indicators for assessing recent outcome of the primary schooling system.

literacy in the younger age groups, especially 7–14, 10–14, and 15–24, and the not too high gender gaps compared to the all-India situation, show not only the not too unequal spread of basic education in Tamil Nadu, albeit in a quantitative sense, but also its rapid literacy and educational advancement.

Inter-district Variations

Considering that the state is one of the more populous (accounting for about 60 million or 6 per cent of India's population), overall figures of percentages do not reveal the variations across regions and among social groups within the state. For instance, by area, in the 7+ population combined literacy in Tamil Nadu in 1991 was:

• low (below the state average by 6 to 17 per cent) in six districts (South Arcot, Thiruvannamalai, Dharmapuri, Salem, Periyar, and Dindigul);

• medium (state average or close to it by 5 per cent) in eleven districts (Chengai-Anna, North Arcot, Tiruchirappalli, Coimbatore, Madurai, Kamarajar, Tirunelveli, Ramanathapuram, Pasumpon Muthuramalinga Thevar, Pudukottai, and Thanjavur); and

• high (6 to 19 per cent above the state average) in four districts (Chennai, Nilgiri, Kanniyakumari, and Chidambaranar).

Among the principal social categories, the variations were wide between STs and Others, followed by SCs and Others, and SCs and STs. The literacy level among these groups also varied considerably across the high and low literacy districts, and the variation was more pronounced among females. These point to the persistence of traditional caste- and gender-based disabilities, and even denial of access to literacy and educational opportunities to the weaker sections (SCs, STs, and women).

However, the state's educational and literacy advancement should again be seen in the context of the literacy status of the younger age groups (see Table 23.3 for data on 7+ age group). Though age-specific data for the SCs, STs, and Others are not available, in most districts variations in total and male–female literacy were not too wide in the 7–14 and 15–24 age groups. While the gender gap was very wide in low literacy districts,[6] it was low

[6] While on gender gap, the following observations by Ammu Joseph (1996) are relevant: (i) Obstacles to girls participation in the educational process are widespread, as reported from Salem and Dharmapuri districts where while a few had never been to school, a larger number had dropped out during or after the primary state; (ii) most drop outs are actually push-outs, driven out of a system which is inherently hostile to children from disadvantaged communities; (iii) many girls claimed that they were forced to discontinue their studies because their economically weak families prioritized their brothers' education over their own,

(per cent)

TABLE 23.2
Literacy Gap in 7+ Population by Social Category and Gender 1991

	India				Tamil Nadu			
	Male	Female	% point difference male and female	Female literacy as % of male literacy	Male	Female	% point difference male and female	Female literacy as % of male literacy
SCs	49.9	23.7	26.2	47.5	58.4	34.9	23.5	59.8
STs	40.6	18.2	22.4	44.8	35.3	20.2	15.0	57.4
Others	69.3	44.6	24.7	64.4	77.7	55.4	22.3	71.3
% point diff. between SCs and others	19.4	20.9	–	–	19.3	20.5	–	–
% point diff. between STs and others	28.7	26.4	–	–	42.5	35.2	–	–
% point diff. between SCs and STs	09.3	05.5	–	–	23.2	14.7	–	–

Source: (1) Census of India, India and Tamil Nadu, 1981, 1991, Part IV-A: Social and Cultural Tables.
(2) Census of India, Tamil Nadu, 1981, 1991, Part IV-A: 'Social and Cultural Tables'.

TABLE 23.3
Literacy Rate in 7+ Population by Social Category in Tamil Nadu, All Areas (1991)

(per cent)

District	SCs			STs			Others			Total		
	Male	Female	Total	Male	Female	Total	Male	Female	Total	Male	Female	Total
Chengai-Anna	63.6	39.8	51.8	29.9	15.9	23.0	82.5	61.3	72.1	77.1	55.3	66.4
Chidambaranar	69.0	45.9	57.3	49.9	31.1	40.4	84.7	68.2	76.1	82.0	64.4	72.9
Coimbatore	46.8	29.1	38.0	30.9	18.2	24.7	82.4	61.0	72.0	76.3	55.5	66.2
Dharmapuri	50.2	27.7	39.2	31.5	17.0	24.6	58.8	35.4	47.4	57.0	34.0	45.8
Dindigul-Quaid-E-Milleth	52.1	27.3	39.8	47.2	28.6	38.1	73.2	47.6	60.5	69.0	43.6	56.4
Kamarajar	56.6	30.3	43.5	49.0	29.2	38.9	79.8	54.4	67.1	75.6	50.0	62.8
Kanniyakumari	83.0	71.7	77.3	59.3	50.2	54.8	85.9	78.8	82.3	85.7	78.3	82.0
Madurai	57.9	32.4	45.3	64.5	40.7	53.0	81.0	58.3	69.8	77.6	54.6	66.3
Nilgiri	75.0	52.9	64.0	40.3	25.5	33.0	86.8	67.0	77.0	81.7	61.3	71.6
North Arcot-Ambedker	67.5	45.0	56.3	32.0	16.8	24.6	74.9	49.7	62.4	72.7	48.2	60.6
Pasumpon Thevar Thirumagan	63.2	35.8	49.3	52.2	27.9	40.0	79.5	52.4	65.6	76.9	49.7	63.0
Periyar	39.9	22.3	31.3	35.0	22.7	28.9	70.9	45.4	58.4	65.4	41.4	53.6
Pudukkottai	63.4	33.7	48.5	63.3	41.0	52.3	73.6	45.7	59.6	71.9	43.7	57.7
Ramanathapuram	59.5	32.5	46.1	33.9	19.1	27.0	78.1	52.1	64.9	74.7	48.6	61.5
Salem	51.6	28.8	40.5	35.7	20.0	28.0	68.2	44.6	56.7	64.3	41.1	53.0
South Arcot	49.7	24.8	37.5	22.2	11.3	16.8	72.0	45.3	58.9	65.5	39.5	52.7
Thanjavur	60.3	34.9	47.7	54.4	33.9	44.2	82.7	60.9	71.8	77.3	54.8	66.1
Tiruchchirappalli	60.7	34.9	47.8	49.5	32.3	41.0	76.5	52.4	64.5	73.4	48.9	61.2
Tirunelveli Kattabomman	61.1	37.4	48.9	60.6	40.0	50.1	80.9	57.7	69.1	77.4	54.1	65.4
Tiruvannamalai Sambuvarayar	55.9	30.5	43.3	26.1	11.3	18.8	71.3	42.7	57.0	66.7	39.2	53.1
Chennai	76.2	58.5	67.6	73.6	52.3	63.3	89.6	77.4	83.8	87.8	74.8	81.6
Tamil Nadu	58.4	34.9	46.7	35.3	20.2	27.9	77.7	55.4	66.7	73.7	51.2	62.6

Source: Census of India, Tamil Nadu, 1991, Part IV-A, Social and Cultural Tables.

in the younger age group of 7–14. This indicates the trend of increasing access to and participation in the education system for the younger population. On the whole, the data point to greater access to literacy and education in urban than rural areas, among males than females, and among Others than SCs and STs.

EXPANSION OF BASIC EDUCATION IN TAMIL NADU

While literacy indicators give a broad idea of the literacy situation and the progress therein and the overall context to delve into the present state of elementary education, understanding the progress of the efforts towards universal free and compulsory education calls for a closer look at education related indicators.

because their labour was needed by the family, or because of parental or fraternal objections to their further education, particularly if it involved travel to another village or town; and (iv) many girls are pulled out of school at or before the advent of adolescence even when they were doing well in their studies, often better than their brothers. See, 'Is Education a Liberating Force?' *The Hindu* (Sunday Magazine) 10 November 1996.

Enrolment and Retention

Enrolment in elementary schools increased from 7.5 million to 9.4 million to 11.6 million over the periods 1983–4, and 1984–93, and decreased from 11.6 million in 1993 to 11.0 million in 1998. While the unprecedented increase by 1.9 million or 25 per cent during 1983–4 is attributed to the Nutritious Noon Meal Scheme introduced in 1982 (on which more shortly), the unprecedented decrease during 1993–8 is attributed to the decrease in the school-age population, from 11.6 million in 1993 to 10.6 million in 1998, as a result of the state's successful family planning programme (see Table 23.4).

Going by the NSS 52nd Round (July 1995–June 1996) (hereafter NSS) which collected educational data for the period July 1995 to June 1996, the average expenditure (Rs) per student pursuing general education was 464 (primary) and 827 (middle), which was next only to Kerala (725 and 849); but enrolment in Tamil Nadu was still below the expected level. Going by the Tamil Nadu government's policy note on education for 1999–2000 (hereafter Policy Note), the gross enrolment ratio for

TABLE 23.4
School-age Population and Enrolment, Tamil Nadu (1982–98)

Year		School-age population in lakhs			Enrolment in lakhs		
		Boys	Girls	Total	Boys	Girls	Total
1984	Primary	26.5	24.9	51.4	38.1	32.3	70.4
	Middle	16.5	15.5	32.0	13.9	9.2	23.2
	Total	43.0	40.4	83.4	52.1	41.6	93.6
1993	Primary	40.5	39.3	79.8	43.1	37.2	80.2
	Middle	18.6	18.1	36.8	19.9	15.5	35.4
	Total	59.1	57.4	116.5	62.9	52.6	115.6
1998	Primary	35.0	33.8	68.8	34.3	32.4	66.7
	Middle	19.0	18.5	37.5	17.6	16.1	33.8
	Total	54.0	52.3	106.3	51.9	48.6	100.4
Growth Rate							
1984–93	Primary	52.8	57.8	55.2	13.0	14.9	13.9
	Middle	12.7	16.8	15.0	42.4	67.6	52.4
	Total	37.4	42.1	39.7	20.9	26.6	23.4
1993–8	Primary	(–)13.6	(–)14.0	(–)13.8	(–)20.4	12.7	(–)16.8
	Middle	2.1	2.2	1.9	(–)11.3	4.1	(–)4.5
	Total	(–)8.6	(–)8.9	8.8	(–)17.5	(–)7.7	(–)13.1

Source: Department of Statistics, Government of Tamil Nadu.

1998–9 was 98 for boys and 96 for girls at primary stage, and 93 and 87 at middle stage. These figures are close to the NSS estimates for 1995–6. According to the NSS, Tamil Nadu's gross attendance rate in general education was 98 in classes I to V and 80 in classes VI to VIII; net attendance rate was 87 in classes I to V and 61 in classes VI to VIII; age-specific attendance was 93 (6–10) and 82 (11–13). The corresponding figures for Kerala were 109/97, 91/76, and 97/97.

Attaining 100 per cent enrolment of girls was one of the items in the state's 15-point programme for child welfare introduced in November 1993. With the cooperation of non-government organizations (NGOs) and local groups the government hoped to fulfil its commitment by launching what it called 'Batch of AD 2000 Graduation Drive'. The scheme envisaged cent per cent enrolment and retention of children in primary schools from 1995–6.

That its progress has been tardy is evident from the following observation in the Policy Note: 'Government considers essential that intensive steps are taken to enroll all children in Primary Schools and ensure that they continue studies without dropping out mid-course.' Tamil Nadu's efforts to prevent stagnation also do not seem to have been effective. The Sixth All-India Educational Survey recorded for 1993, that is a decade after the Noon Meal Scheme was introduced, a larger share of repeaters in classes I to V (14 per cent) and classes VI to VIII (15 per cent) than the national average (8 per cent and 7 per cent), and this is common among the SCs/STs, general population including them, and males and females. The corresponding share for Kerala is small.

Availability of Schools

While school-age population increased by 40 per cent and enrolment by 23 per cent over the 1984–93, the number of schools increased by only 5 per cent, that too at primary level. The data show a decline in the number of middle schools. Though school-age population and enrolment declined considerably during 1994–8, they were still higher than in 1983. Yet the increase over 1983–98 was negligible. This renders the state's repeated claim that in order to achieve UEE, there should essentially be a steady growth in the number of schools, hollow.

The Policy Note shows that about 80 per cent of elementary schools are under the state. But primary and middle schools are unequally distributed across the districts, with the maximum number of primary schools in low-literacy districts like Dharmapuri, and the maximum number of middle schools in medium-literacy districts like Tirunelveli (see Table 23.5).

Lack of any direct correlation between the number of schools in an area and the percentage of enrolment is evident from the NSS. Out of every 1000 persons within each corresponding category, only 6 urban females and 3 males, and 23 rural females and 20 males cited non availability of convenient schooling facilities as the reason for non-enrolment. Data on enrolment ratios in

TABLE 23.5
Schools by Management Tamil Nadu (1998–9)

(per cent)

District	Primary schools					Middle schools				
	Central/state government	Corporation municipality	Panchayat union	Private aided (PA)	Private unaided (PUA)	Central/state government	Corporation municipality	Panchayat union	Private aided (PA)	Private unaided (PUA)
Dharmapuri	1.7	0.9	96.5	0.8	0.2	1.6	3.8	87.6	7.0	0.0
Villupuram	8.4	0.9	77.1	13.4	0.2	4.6	1.1	69.3	25.0	0.0
Vellore	6.0	6.1	75.3	12.4	0.2	2.6	4.5	74.0	18.9	0.0
Thirunelveli	3.0	2.8	37.4	55.9	1.0	1.3	3.7	19.0	74.9	1.1
Erode	1.1	1.5	89.4	7.6	0.5	1.6	5.4	84.4	8.6	0.0
Thiruvannamalai	5.0	2.4	83.8	8.6	0.1	3.7	2.6	82.7	10.5	0.5
Coimbatore	2.7	8.2	79.8	9.1	0.2	0.9	10.7	70.1	16.5	1.8
Salem	4.0	4.7	85.5	5.8	0.0	3.2	8.2	74.1	13.9	0.6
Cuddalore	8.7	3.7	69.7	17.7	0.2	0.5	6.9	58.8	33.8	0.0
Dindigul	3.0	2.2	78.1	16.4	0.2	1.0	1.5	61.0	36.4	0.0
Pudukottai	0.7	1.1	92.7	5.3	0.1	0.0	3.4	81.4	15.3	0.0
Thiruvallur	4.6	5.1	79.0	11.2	0.1	4.1	7.7	69.6	18.6	0.0
Thanjavur	7.9	2.8	73.4	15.9	0.0	1.8	7.6	56.1	34.5	0.0
Virudhunagar	1.9	1.4	61.9	32.7	1.7	0.6	11.0	44.8	43.6	0.0
Thoothukudi	1.0	1.0	46.0	51.9	0.1	0.7	3.5	26.4	69.4	0.0
Kancheepuram	6.0	4.0	77.4	11.6	0.9	4.1	6.9	63.7	24.1	1.2
Trichy	6.5	3.1	72.5	17.8	0.1	2.7	5.7	52.5	38.3	0.8
Madurai	11.1	5.0	67.9	15.2	0.8	3.9	6.8	48.8	39.5	1.0
Ramanathapuram	1.0	1.0	81.6	16.3	0.1	0.6	2.6	61.9	34.2	0.6
Sivagangai	0.2	2.1	85.0	11.3	1.3	0.6	3.2	53.5	40.0	2.6
Nagapattinam	5.0	5.1	63.6	26.4	0.0	1.7	0.6	56.5	41.2	0.0
Namakkal	1.2	3.0	88.3	7.5	0.0	0.0	7.6	66.7	25.8	0.0
Perambalur	6.4	0.0	82.1	11.1	0.4	3.5	0.0	69.3	27.2	0.0
Thiruvarur	3.8	1.3	84.8	10.2	0.0	0.8	4.9	65.6	28.7	0.0
Karur	2.7	0.4	90.9	5.8	0.1	1.2	8.5	80.5	9.8	0.0
Theni	16.7	2.5	51.6	29.0	0.2	4.6	8.5	30.1	52.3	4.6
Udhagamandalam	7.7	4.4	62.5	25.2	0.3	17.7	4.8	58.1	17.7	1.6
Kaniakumari	62.3	0.0	0.0	35.6	2.1	72.0	0.0	0.0	27.3	0.7
Chennai	3.5	46.2	0.0	50.0	0.3	0.9	62.8	0.0	35.9	0.4

Source: Government of Tamil Nadu, Department of Statistics.

Tamil Nadu, though based on gross enrolment (including repeaters and overage children), while corroborating this fact, indicate that increasing the number of schools alone cannot improve enrolments or serve the EFA goals since the percentage of enrolment in a given area is not directly related to the proportion of schools in that area. Areas with fewer schools may have better enrolment than those with more of schools. Examples (based on the assumption that the schooling needs take into account regional, geographical and demographic specificities) are Kanniyakumari which has more than 100 per cent primary school enrolment and less than 1 per cent of the primary schools in the state, and Tiruvannamalai which has enrolment of only 86 per cent with 5 per cent of total primary schools. However, non-availability of schools is still a problem. In some localities children are out of school during rains, floods, etc, and when schooling involves distance and other difficulties, many children, especially SCs/STs children and girls in hilly and remote areas, are at greater disadvantage than the rest of the local population.

As though recognizing this problem, during the five years from 1985 to 1990, despite a policy decision conveyed by the state's slogan 'no more elementary school, no more college', probably to avoid mushrooming of educational institutions and to improve existing institutions, elementary schools were established in locales with predominantly backward population. Table 23.6 presents growth rates in elementary schools and teachers between 1982 and 1998.

TABLE 23.6
Elementary Schools and Teachers in Tamil Nadu (1982–98)

(per cent)

Year		School	Teacher	Growth rate	
				School	Teacher
1982–3	Primary	28,290	114,713		
	Middle	05565	066,299		
	Total	33,855	181,012		
1983–4	Primary	28,543	115,705	0.9	0.9
	Middle	05635	066,399	1.2	0.1
	Total	34,178	182,104	0.9	0.6
1984–5	Primary	28,847	116,305	1.1	0.5
	Middle	05691	066,849	1.0	0.6
	Total	34,538	183,154	1.1	0.5
1993–4	Primary	30,329	116,396	5.1	0.1
	Middle	05593	062,192	(–)1.7	(–)7.0
	Total	35,922	178,588	4.0	(–)2.5
1998–9	Primary	30,844	115,697	1.7	(–)0.6
	Middle	05538	061,719	(–)1.0	(–)0.8
	Total	36,382	177,416	1.3	(–)0.7

Source: Department of Statistics, Government of Tamil Nadu.

The government also introduced some measures exclusively for girls, especially during the 'year of the rights for women' (1989) and the 'year of the girl child' (1995). The 1989 measures included free education for girls up to Bachelor's degree, financial assistance to encourage poor parents to educate daughters at least up to the class VIII and SC girls at least up to class V standard.

The shortage of schools is also addressed by the education department's efforts to start a primary school within a kilometre of hamlets having more than 300 population, and a middle school for every three primary schools.[7]

Dropouts

The official claim that the Noon Meal Scheme considerably increased the rate of literacy, improved the quality of education, and reduced drop-out rates, might have been true in the early 1980s. But this claim is not borne out by the data on drop-outs for subsequent years (see Table 23.7).

Though the 'official' dropout rate for 1998–9 is about 15 per cent in classes I–V and 35 per cent in classes I–VIII, it might have been as high as 30 to 40 per cent in the former and still higher in the latter. This is also evident from the NSS, which recorded a dropout rate of 34.4 per cent and 29.5 per cent for primary and middle schools in Tamil Nadu. State government officials themselves have drawn attention to the anomaly and wide

TABLE 23.7
Dropout Rate by Class in Tamil Nadu

(per cent)

Year	Classes I–V			Classes I–VIII		
	Boys	Girls	Total	Boys	Girls	Total
1990–1	18.3	22.7	20.3	40.2	49.4	44.5
1994–5	15.6	17.7	16.5	30.8	39.4	37.7
1998–9	13.0	16.2	14.5	36.9	33.4	35.2

Source: Department of Statistics, Government of Tamil Nadu.

gap between the official and the actual dropout rates (see *The Hindu*, 21 November 1999). This, and the extensive revision of enrolment and drop-out figures by the government casts serious doubts on the reliability of government data.[8]

The major reasons recorded for dropping out are lack of interest in studies among children and parents, and inability of students to cope with, or failure in, studies. These corroborate the findings by some of the primary education surveys in Tamil Nadu. One such survey, conducted in 1984–9, based on school records of about 7000 students in five districts attributed dropping out mostly to lack of motivation among children and parents, and the overall network of problems in the schooling process (Ramakrishnan 1991). The Directorate of District Teachers Education, Research and Training, cited low achievement and lack of interest as other major reasons. Its finding for the early 1990s that drop-outs in two-thirds of the out-of-school children were for other than economic reasons is still valid (DTERT 1993). Irrespective of the reasons, lack of enrolment and retention has direct bearing on the schooling process, relevance of education, methods of instruction, and suitability of the learning environment.

Infrastructure

That well-equipped schools with basic amenities and ancillary facilities have positive effects on the reach of basic education is well recognized. Though Tamil Nadu is better placed in regard to infrastructure when compared to many other states, if the data available in the Sixth All-India Educational Survey for 1993 are any indication, it still has to cover much ground. According to the Survey only about half the primary schools in the state had adequate number of classrooms; the number of additional classrooms required were 32,400, with about one-fourth of the primary schools requiring one more classroom and one-sixth two more. Even basic facilities like drinking water were not available in one-third of the

[7] According to the Sixth All-India Educational Survey (NCERT 1998) as many as 700 hamlets with 300 population in Tamil Nadu did not have a primary school within a 1 km radius.

[8] Reports indicate that in 1998 about 38 per cent of school-age children, including non-enrolled and dropouts, were outside the educational system in Dharmapuri district (*The Hindu*, 30 November 1998).

rural and one-fourth of the urban schools; provisions for sanitation were even worse, although relatively better in girls' schools; playgrounds, very important for children, were available in only half the schools, that too with serious limitations; students in about one-fifth of the rural and a small but significant proportion of urban primary schools continued to struggle with learning difficulties for want of blackboards. Furniture including mats was not available in about 70 per cent of both rural and urban schools, and to teachers in almost half the rural and one-fourth of the urban primary schools (see Tables 23.8 and 23.9).

Going by the Policy Note, though construction of classrooms in 3060 primary schools had already been taken up, 914 primary schools are identified as still not having *pucca* buildings. This did not include many schools with *pucca* buildings which might have become dilapidated over the years.

In 1990 the state Education Minister said in the Assembly that only about 45 to 50 per cent of schools in the state in dire need of better construction, more space, etc. were actually attended to. Probably as a way out, the government devised a scheme to honour donors by naming the school after them, if they contributed at least

TABLE 23.8
Primary Schools Having Ancillary Facilities and Number of Beneficaries (1993) (%)

State	Area	Drinking water	Urinal	Separate urinal for girls	Lavatory	Separate lavatory for girls	Playgrounds			
							Exclusively for the school	In usable condition	Adequate	Within school premises
Kerala—	Rural	80.1	85.9	59.3	46.4	15.0	44.8	48.1	37.0	51.8
All Schools	Urban	81.3	85.0	63.8	51.7	22.4	46.4	50.6	40.3	54.2
	Total	80.4	85.7	60.2	47.6	16.6	45.2	48.6	37.7	52.3
Tamil Nadu—	Rural	62.4	19.7	12.2	11.3	7.5	42.9	48.8	39.3	45.5
All Schools	Urban	76.9	59.9	44.7	48.6	36.1	39.3	50.4	37.3	46.7
	Total	64.4	25.1	16.6	16.3	11.3	42.4	49.0	39.1	45.6
India—	Rural	44.8	19.4	09.4	09.2	03.8	040.8	039.1	30.6	39.7
All Schools	Urban	72.8	65.6	42.5	54.2	34.2	44.9	47.0	38.7	45.4
	Total	48.5	25.5	13.7	15.1	7.8	41.3	40.1	31.7	40.5
Girls'	Rural	60.2	34.6	27.5	25.0	18.4	–	–	–	–
schools in	Urban	81.1	76.6	69.1	66.3	60.6	–	–	–	–
Tamil Nadu	Total	67.0	48.2	41.0	38.4	32.1	–	–	–	–

Note: Dash indicates data not available.
Source: Sixth All-India Educational Survey, vol. II, 1998.

TABLE 23.9
Lack of Blackboards, Furniture for Teachers and Students (1993)

State	Area	Total no. of sections	In percentage		
			Blackboards	Furniture for teachers	Mats/furniture for students
Kerala	Rural	82,513	22.8	31.2	98.7
	Urban	21,429	18.1	27.7	98.4
	Total	103,942	21.9	30.5	98.6
Tamil Nadu	Rural	207,769	20.9	45.1	71.1
	Urban	49,483	5.7	26.5	72.5
	Total	257,252	18.0	41.6	71.4
India	Rural	3,189,506	33.1	45.6	62.0
	Urban	653,755	11.2	21.4	82.3
	Total	3,843,261	29.4	41.5	65.4

Source: Sixth All-India Educational Survey, vol. II, 1998.

50 per cent of the expenditure for constructing a primary school, or constructed two rooms for a school. In 1995 it announced that an individual, a private or public social service agency, or, even a government institution could similarly adopt a government school and aim to better its infrastructure and overall quality of schooling.

Largely falling under Operation Blackboard (OB),[9] annual schemes for construction of classrooms, buildings, toilets, etc, are implemented with funds available through *Jawahar Rozgar Yojna* and Rural Labour Employment Guarantee programmes.

Teachers

It was mentioned earlier that the spurt in enrolment during 1983–4 was not reflected in the number of elementary schools. This is also true in the case of teachers. Data show a decline in the number of primary and middle school teachers over 1993–8. Though teachers' salaries take away more than 95 per cent of the funds allocated for primary education, their inadequate numbers affects schooling and the expansion of the education system.

As though recognizing this, the Education Minister said in the Assembly in 1990 that children may not be able to study even under the shade of a tree if they do not have a teacher. Nearly a decade after this, following its decision in 1998–9 to appoint at least two teachers in every primary school, the Policy Note indicates that 1385 single-teacher schools have been provided with an additional teacher.[10]

Though there are five classes in primary schools, on average only four teachers were available throughout the period 1990 to 1998. In middle schools the figure was mostly 1:12 (see Table 23.10). The Policy Note shows that the teacher–pupil ratio during the years 1993–8 ranged from 1:49 to 1:38 in primary schools and 1:51 to 1:36 in middle schools. However, this may not reflect the reality because of the wide variations in the numbers of students in different schools. The ratio may be 1:30 in some schools, 1:40 in some others, and even as high as 1:150 in yet others. Since there is no 'average school', an average teacher–pupil ratio can hide much reality.

District Primary Education Programme (DPEP)

The World Bank-aided District Primary Education Programme (DPEP)[11] launched in the mid-1990s is India's most ambitious, internationally assisted, primary education programme, conceived as a 'beachhead' for overhauling the primary education system in the country, and aimed at operationalizing the strategies for achieving UEE through district-specific planning and disaggregated target setting. The DPEP specifically focuses on districts with female literacy below the national average, and where total literacy campaigns (TLCs) have stirred up a demand for elementary education.

In Tamil Nadu, the DPEP districts are Dharmapuri, Tiruvannamalai, Cuddalore, and Villupuram in phase 1, and Perambalur and Ramanathapuram in phase 2. Innovative interventions by the DPEP for improving enrolment

TABLE 23.10
Average Number of Teachers per School, Tamil Nadu (1990–8)

Type of schools	1990–1	1991–2	1992–3	1993–4	1994–5	1995–6	1996–7	1997–8	1998–9
Primary schools	4	4	4	4	4	4	4	4	4
Middle schools	12	12	12	11	11	12	12	12	11
High schools	14	13	13	13	13	13	13	12	11
Higher secondary schools	36	35	34	34	33	32	30	28	29
Total	7	7	7	7	7	7	7	7	7

Source: Department of Statistics, Government of Tamil Nadu.

[9] This scheme, launched in 1987 following NPE 1986, is aimed at improving school environment and enhancing retention and learning achievements of children by providing minimum essential facilities in all primary schools. The Government of India claims that it has brought about remarkable quantitative and qualitative improvement in primary education. However, as it is implemented in phases covering a few districts at a time, by the time some schemes reach certain districts schools may be severely dilapidated and may turn out to be non-functional.

[10] Stating that poor children are deprived of education for want of teachers in backward districts, a report from Dharmapuri in November 1998 cited the plight of one of the elementary schools functioning with just two teachers for 275 students. See *The Hindu*, 20 November 1998.

include flexible school timings, escorts to girls, and organizing programmes for promoting community awareness for basic education and improving enrolment of 5–6 age group children. Assessment of the DPEP interventions has shown that both demand side interventions such as community mobilization for basic education through setting up of Village Education Committees and

[11] The DPEP was introduced in 1994 in select states across the country. Its goals include universalization of primary education, improving learning achievements, and reducing gender and social disparities in literacy.

Mother–Teacher Associations, and supply side interventions such as construction of new schools and provision of infrastructure to existing schools improve access and retention, and reduce repeaters and dropouts (DPEP 1998a).

While gender gaps in dropout were less than 5 per cent even by 1995–6, the trend during the subsequent five years shows that efforts to reduce dropout have been more effective among boys than girls in all the DPEP districts. These apart, both the state and DPEP efforts in general to reduce drop-outs, enhance participation in schooling, and ensure education for all, broadly revolve around the availability of schools, teachers, infrastructure, teaching material, and teaching methods. Of these availability of schools and teachers has already been discussed.

The baseline assessment studies in 46 low literacy districts across 8 states (including Tamil Nadu) by the NCERT in 1992–3 and the National Advisory Committee on reducing curriculum load under Professor Yash Pal in 1993 revealed that even very poor learning achievements of primary school students can be improved by the 'joyful learning' method. A number of states and the DPEP introduced this method in order to ensure retention along with achieving at least minimal levels of learning, as prescribed by the NPE. Through this approach, teaching is made lively through songs, plays, and effective use of learning material. In Tamil Nadu, during 1998–9 training in a phased manner for all teachers was completed in 11 of the 29 districts, and was in progress in 11 districts. According to the Policy Note all primary schools in the state have been supplied with radio-cum-cassette players with lessons for use by the teachers. However, no information on the nature and extent of their use is available.

State Schemes and EFA

Several schemes aimed at universal enrolment and retention, and minimizing stagnation and dropout in Tamil Nadu have been in operation in Tamil Nadu for a long time, though a number of them gained added importance during the last decade. Table 23.11 and 23.12 compare data on the reach of such schemes at Tamil Nadu and all-India levels.

NOON MEAL SCHEME

Probably the most important of all the schemes, has been the Nutritious Noon Meal Scheme. Introduced in July 1982 in child welfare centres in rural areas for preschool children from 2 to 5 years of age and for children from 5 to 9 years of age in primary schools, it was extended to urban areas from September 1982, and to school students from 10 to 15 years of age (classes VI to X) from September 1984. Children in classes I to V are served a meal everyday, those in classes VI to X on working days. From August 1995, under the National Programme of Nutritional Support to Primary Education, the Department of Education, Ministry of Human Resource Development, Government of India, has been supplying rice free of cost for noon meals to primary school children in the state.

According to the Policy Note of the Social Welfare Department for 1999–2000, the state has as many as 37,748 school nutritious meal centres in rural areas and 2059 in urban areas, and the number of beneficiaries from these are 6,000,000 and 460,000 children respectively. The Noon Meal Scheme was well conceived, and well received in the state, by other states, by the centre, and by international agencies such as the United Nations International Children's Education Fund (UNICEF), and has had a positive effect on school enrolment. As though prompted by its outcome, on 15 August 1995 the Government of India launched a nationwide School Meal Programme (National Programme of Nutritional Support to Primary Education) to give a boost to UEE by increasing enrolment, retention, and attendance in primary classes through supplementing nutritional requirements of children attending primary schools.

However, in Tamil Nadu, the scheme has not been free of problems. These include pilferage and poor quality of food supplies, lack of storage and cooking facilities, poor infrastructure, unhygienic surroundings, water scarcity, delayed arrival of materials, and poor pay of staff.[12]

SPECIAL HEALTH PROGRAMME

The Policy Note proposed to implement from 1999 a special School Health Programme, called *vazhvoli thittam* (literally light of life scheme, referring to good health). Under this scheme, a field officer of the health department is supposed to visit schools once a week to examine the children, and if necessary take them to primary health centres for treatment. To make this scheme more meaningful and sustainable, teachers are trained in the symptoms of diseases for reporting to the medical officers visiting the schools, and to teach subjects on health education.

EARLY CHILDHOOD CARE AND EDUCATION (ECCE)

The Integrated Child Development Services (ICDS), the largest ECCE programme in India, was started in 1975 with an integrated approach to reduce malnutrition and related diseases among disadvantaged children and expectant and nursing mothers. The ICDS schemes

[12] For a discussion of these problems, see *Frontline*, 13 June 1997.

TABLE 23.11
Reach of Midday Meals and Free Uniform Schemes to Improve Enrolment and Reduce Dropouts in Tamil Nadu and All India (1993)

Region	Area	midday meals							Free uniforms to children						
		% of schools having the scheme	Number of beneficiaries						% of schools having the scheme	Number of beneficiaries					
			SCs		STs		Others			SCs		STs		Others	
			Boys	Girls	Boys	Girls	Boys	Girls		Boys	Girls	Boys	Girls	Boys	Girls
Tamil Nadu	Rural	96.5	27.8	27.5	1.5	1.3	70.8	71.2	95.5	27.8	23.0	1.5	1.3	70.8	75.7
	Urban	91.1	26.0	25.0	0.8	0.8	73.2	74.2	92.4	26.0	09.3	0.8	0.8	73.2	89.9
	Total	95.7	27.1	26.6	1.2	1.1	71.6	72.3	95.1	27.2	18.1	1.2	1.1	71.6	80.8
All-India	Rural	14.9	16.8	17.1	17.6	15.0	65.6	67.9	30.4	19.8	27.3	16.8	20.9	63.5	90.5
	Urban	15.4	20.7	20.0	4.2	3.8	75.1	76.2	22.4	18.8	14.1	3.9	4.7	38.2	50.5
	Total	15.0	18.2	18.2	12.7	10.6	69.1	71.2	29.3	19.4	22.1	12.1	14.5	54.3	74.7

Source: Sixth All-India Educational Survey, vol. VI, 1998.

TABLE 23.12
Reach of Free Textbooks and Attendance Scholarship for Girls' Schemes to Improve Enrolment and Reduce Dropouts, Tamil Nadu and All India (1993)

Region	Area	Free textbooks to students							Attendance scholarship to girls			
		% of schools having the scheme	Number of beneficiaries						% of schools having the scheme	Number of beneficiaries		
			SCs		STs		Others			SCs	STs	Others
			Boys	Girls	Boys	Girls	Boys	Girls				
Tamil Nadu	Rural	95.3	27.8	27.5	1.5	1.3	70.8	71.2	1.6	43.6	14.0	42.4
	Urban	90.0	26.0	25.0	0.8	0.8	73.1	74.3	2.8	36.2	29.1	34.7
	Total	94.6	27.2	26.6	1.2	1.1	71.6	72.3	1.8	42.0	17.2	40.8
India	Rural	55.8	43.2	41.0	31.5	26.6	133.3	136.0	16.6	28.4	24.3	47.2
	Urban	43.2	40.2	38.7	8.8	7.8	111.6	116.2	8.8	61.3	13.6	25.1
	Total	54.1	42.1	40.1	23.2	19.2	125.4	128.2	15.5	34.4	22.4	43.2

Source: Sixth All-India Educational Survey, vol. VI, 1998.

focus on provision of services towards nutrition, health requirement to the children from the date of conception till the age of 6 years, and physical and mental development. Their package of services through child welfare centres called *anganwadis* includes: supplementary nutrition, non-formal preschool education, health check-up, immunization, and health education. A significant feature of the ICDS's contribution to primary school enrolment among girls is the functioning of the ICDS centres as day-care centres, thus relieving young girls from sibling care at home. *Anganwadi* workers are trained in joyful learning to prepare preschool children for primary education.

Launched initially in 1975–6 on experimental basis in three projects in Chennai, Thalli, and Nilakkottai, in Tamil Nadu, the programme has been expanded and 113 projects implemented (67 projects in rural, 44 in urban, and 2 in tribal areas). Among these, 44 projects are assisted by the Swedish International Development Authority (SIDA).

Each ICDS project covers a population of around 100,000 and is headed by a Child Development Officer, who is assisted by one Medical Officer, four Supervisors, and four Auxiliary Nurse Midwives. The health activities in rural and tribal areas are attended by the primary health centres. Each project has approximately 100 *anganwadis*. Each *anganwadi* covers a population of 1000. At each centre, nearly 100 persons, that is 30 children in the age group 6 months to 2 years, 40 children in the age group 2 to 5 years, and 30 expectant and nursing mothers, are benefitted.

The Tamil Nadu Integrated Nutrition Project (TINP) was implemented with World Bank assistance in 318 blocks covering 24 districts from 1991 to 1997. Its main objectives were to reduce severe malnutrition among children in the age group 6 months to 3 years and to increase the proportion of normal children in this age group, and thus, to contribute towards reduction in infant and maternal mortality rates. The TINP from its inception covered a total of about 4.1 million children in this age group, and 2.1 million pregnant and nursing mothers. Consequent on the closure of the TINP in December 1997, the existing TINP schemes were integrated with the 113 ICDS projects, and the ICDS converted 318 TINP projects to form 431 ICDS projects.

Non-formal Education (NFE) and Adult Literacy

The foregoing discussion indicates a not too unsatisfactory spread of literacy, basic education, and early childhood care. However, it does not reveal the nature and magnitude of the ground realities, concerning the large proportion of out-of-school (both non-enrolled and dropped out) young and adult illiterate population, and the persistence of educational inequalities.

NFE

Considering the high drop-out rate, illiterates in the 6–14 age group in Tamil Nadu may be more than 4 million; more so, when a large chunk of about one million children who attain school age every year do not get into schools. So, NFE, which is rightly seen by the Government of India as a vital aspect of India's current strategy on education as it can reach out to working children, girls, those children who cannot attend full time schools due to several socio-economic compulsions and cultural barriers, is a socio-political imperative and needs to be vigorously pursued until the state succeeds in ensuring free and compulsory universal education.[13] More so, when it is widely recognized that there is a direct nexus between out-of-school children and child labour.

In order to reach the large segment of marginalized children, the Government of India has been running an NFE scheme since 1979, implemented through state governments and voluntary agencies. The main features of the scheme are: short course with duration of about two years; part-time instruction at a place and time convenient to learners in small groups; flexibility in the mode of delivery; special emphasis on girls' education.

The India Status Report, prepared for the second E-9 Ministerial Review Meeting in September 1997, has the following to say about the NFE:

> The NFE was conceived in 1979–80, scaled up in 1987 and revised in 1993 with emphasis on organization, flexibility, relevance of curriculum, diversity in learning activity to suit the needs of the learners through decentralized management. At present, NFE reaches out to nearly seven million children (majority of whom are girls) in the age-group 6–14, and has the potential of enrolling nearly half the number of children enrolled in the formal school system. The NFE scheme is being implemented in 23 states/union territories through 0.29 million centres. Of these, nearly 0.24 million come under the state sector, while the rest are managed by the voluntary sector. Out of the centres under the state sector, 0.12 million are exclusively for girls, covering about

---

[13] While on NFE the following observations by Weiner in *Frontline* (13 June 1997) should sound a note of caution: 'I must say that I am not a supporter of non-formal education programmes. I think non-formal education, which is simply a programme to provide education after children's work hours, is a strategy to perpetuate child labour while at once assuaging the conscience of the elite and the government. I don't see what it is meant to achieve educationally either; how many adults could attend classes after a day of hazardous work and learn something? In the 1830s, the system of non-formal education was experimented with in England as an official strategy precisely to enable the perpetuation of child labour! Today, I don't see how the government or anyone else can promote it as a serious policy.'

2.95 million beneficiaries. The financial allocation in 1996–7 for running these centres was a total of Rs 1582 million. [DoE 1997b]

In Tamil Nadu, NFE schemes are implemented through a number of programmes by the government and voluntary agencies, but largely by the latter. Schemes during 1981–3 included opening NFE centres for child labourers in Sivakasi, and for the STs in Salem, South Arcot, North Arcot and Tiruchirapalli districts. Schemes since 1992 have included employing unemployed local youth to identify and enrol dropouts and adults; and continuing education involving educated youth to teach 6–14 age dropouts in the joyful learning method. Educated women are specially engaged as both field staff and supervisors, in the context of girls dropping out more than boys. A Government Order by the state government issued in December 1998 permits admission in formal schools of alternative schooled children certified by the block-level officer; but only 3 per cent of those in alternative schools were actually admitted during 1998–9.

The DPEP also includes the uneducated and marginalized groups of non-starters and dropouts in 'alternative schooling centres'. These accommodate about twenty learners each in the 10–12 age group. The DPEP data for 1998–9 show that a total number of 1324 centres in 63 blocks of the 7 DPEP districts covered 33,174 learners. Though girls outnumbered boys, they also outnumbered boys among non-starters and dropouts (DPEP 1999).

The Policy Note has the following to say on NFE in Tamil Nadu:

- Seven schemes under the Special Education Project, consisting of 700 centres have been completed in Thuthukudi, Virudhunagar, Vellore, and Chennai districts for the child labourers in the 6–14 age group, with financial assistance both from central and state governments, benefitting 17,500 children. The scheme will be extended to the remaining districts under a phased programme.

- In the districts where literacy level is low, 16 NFE projects with 100 centres each will be started to impart NFE to girls of 6–14 age group during 1999–2000, and priority will be given to SCs and STs.

- Open School System is yet another avenue to provide continuing education for all. This scheme is functioning since December 1997 providing Standard v level education to for the drop out children. Neo-literates who are the products of literacy campaign can attain the third standard level through this scheme. One year course is divided into three terms and examinations are conducted at the end of each term. Promoted persons can join the next higher course in the following year. 2700 persons from six districts have benefited by the scheme. The scheme will be extended to three more districts with 120 centres at the rate of 40 each.

ADULT LITERACY

As at national level, adult literacy efforts in Tamil Nadu date back to the late 1970s. Though the National Adult Education Programme in 1978 was the first official pronouncement treating adult education as a national policy, going by a 1983 publication, a separate department in Tamil Nadu was set up in 1976 for operating the schemes of non-formal and adult education in a concerted manner, and this department was doing yeomen service since 1978 for eradicating illiteracy; but success and reach were limited till the early 1990s, that is till after the Kottayam and Ernakulam experiments in Kerala (in 1989 and 1990), which demonstrated the efficacy of the 'campaign approach' to literacy, as a follow up to the National Literacy Mission (NLM).

Pursuant to the launching of the NLM, Tamil Nadu launched the State Literacy Mission (SLM) in 1990, and its TLC in 1991–2 through *Arivoli Iyakkam* (literally movement for the light of knowledge) at district level guided by District Collectors, with a centre–state fund sharing of 2:1.

According to the Policy Note, to stabilize the literacy status gained by neo-literates, the TLC is followed by a post literacy campaign (PLC) for two years. The PLC, already completed in 19 districts, is being implemented in 6 other districts, and will be extended to the remaining 4 districts. In continuation of the TLC and PLC, continuing education (CE) is implemented in nine districts, and will be implemented in a phased manner in all the districts where the PLC has been completed.

A 1994 publication of the NLM contains districtwise details of Tamil Nadu's adult literacy experience; but it was published just two years after the beginning of the programme. The Directorate of Non-formal and Adult Education prepared a report in 1996 covering all the districts, but as the officials themselves have claimed, the data are not reliable and not used by (even) the government.

The estimate in the Policy Note, of 7.97 million illiterates having been brought into the fold of literates, is close to the figures given in the 1994 publication. This should mean that nothing much was done to wipe out illiteracy since 1994.

Going by the NSS estimate for 1995–6, out of 524 million adults in the country, 239 million (45.6 per cent) were illiterate, with females accounting for 151 million (63 per cent); out of 41 million adults in Tamil Nadu 16 million (38 per cent) were illiterate, with females accounting for 10 million (66 per cent). The Policy Note's estimate of adult illiterates for 1998 is 18 million. This should mean that as at all-India level, Tamil Nadu, like many other states, continues to be a mass producer of illiterates.

As the literacy rates among SCs/STs, the Most Backward classes, and Muslims[14] are very low, a large chunk of the adults among all of them, and among women as a category, also must be illiterate; more so, when traditional inequalities still persist in the state in one form or another with the SCs being victims of recurrent atrocities (through caste clashes), and females of gender prejudices, as evident from among other things repeated reports of female infanticides in Dharmapuri, Erode, and Salem districts.

While the failure of the literacy movement in Tamil Nadu is a reflection of the failure of the NLM, the reasons attributed to it include withdrawal of support extended to NGOs, weak and inadequate political and administrative support, lack of conscientization and motivation, social impediments such as negative attitudes towards education of girls, use of children as cheap labour, excruciating poverty, reification of the existing caste-based social stratification, the fear of politicians that social mobilization for literacy will erode their traditional political support base, bureaucratization of the campaign cutting into voluntarism, and indiscriminate expansion—a bane termed 'targetitis' (see Athreya and Chunkath 1996).

CONCLUSION

While it is evident from the foregoing discussion that the state of Tamil Nadu and the DPEP have addressed most of the goals of EFA, they have not yet fully achieved any of them.

Of the six key goals which the Global Conference on EFA in Jomtien (1990) established, Tamil Nadu's record on expansion of ECCE is mixed. Some indicators of this are available in a UNICEF report:

> (a) under five mortality rate (U5MR)—an indicator of the state of well-being of children—is still as high as 87 (as against Kerala's 32); and (b) infant (0 to 1 age) mortality rate (IMR), despite rapid lowering from 91 in 1981, with a higher rate of reduction (4.6 per cent) compared to all India (3 per cent), is still 56 (as against Kerala's 13). [UNICEF 1996]

Though Tamil Nadu's total fertility rate of 2.2 suggests successful implementation of population control schemes propagating the norm of two children per couple, as parents have to cope with a variety of opportunity costs even in a free-wheeling public delivery system, this decline should have meant better childcare. But despite the plethora of childcare schemes by the state, girls are still at a disadvantage. In the country as a whole, there is a seeming lack of direct correlation between the percentage of out-of-school girls and the number of child workers. This raises the larger issue of 'the missing girls'—those who are neither at school nor in productive labour. Tamil Nadu has a large share of them.

In the absence of follow up measures more schools and infrastructure do not translate into more educated students; nor enrolment for all into EFA. As the DPEP's baseline study mentioned earlier shows, of the students continuing up to the class V only 44 per cent gained the desired skills; the concern of some academics that India is at risk of producing a breed of educated illiterates[15] is not without basis.

Tamil Nadu is already facing this risk. A senior official admitted in a seminar in November 1999 that the state does not have departmentally acknowledged figures as to how many children in the 6–11 age group have acquired the required skills after being through five years of rote learning. Among the 60 per cent of the children who manage to remain in school up to class V, the skill acquisition level was only 40 per cent—75 per cent of the state's investment is going down the drain, and this is a matter of serious concern (*The Hindu*, 21 November 1999). Seen thus, the two other EFA goals, of universal access to and completion of primary education by the year 2000, and of improvement in learning achievement based on an agreed upon percentage of an age group (e.g. 80 per cent of the 14 year olds) attaining a defined level, are still distant dreams.

According to the 1991 Census, the total adult illiterates in Tamil Nadu were 16.6 million, with females accounting for 10.7 million (65 per cent). As against this, the NSS estimate for 1995–6 was 16 million, with females accounting for 10 million (66 per cent). The estimate of adult illiterates for 1998 in the Policy Note is 18 million. Even this figure is probably an underestimate of the adult illiterates. For the official literacy rate is widely seen as misleading for at least three reasons: (i) literacy as defined for the Census is no more than the ability to read and write a simple letter; (ii) the NSS definition is not any better: 'A person is considered literate if he/she can read and write a simple sentence in any language with understanding'; and (iii) relapse of literates into illiteracy is not taken into account by either the Census or the NSS. As there is thus hardly any reduction in adult illiterates over the years, yet another EFA goal, of reduction of the adult illiteracy rate to half its 1990 level by the year 2000, with special emphasis on female literacy, is also far from attainment.

---

[14] Of Tamil Nadu's population SCs and STs account for about 19 per cent and 1 per cent; Muslims account for about 6 per cent; and Most Backward Classes, a sub-category of the population entitled to the state's affirmative action schemes, generally known as reservations, account for about 20 per cent.

[15] See, for instance, 'Education: Half Truths', *Sunday*, 5–11 September 1999.

If the data available in the Policy Note are any indication, the state's inputs to elementary education are enormous: It has more than 36,000 schools, 6.9 million students, 180,000 teachers; its allocation for elementary education is about 19 per cent of its annual budget—Rs 1875 crore out of Rs 18,500 crore; besides offering free education, it provides free uniforms (6.5 million sets), free textbooks, free footwear, free bus travel pass, free slates for children in class I, and one free nutritious meal a day. If the output from the system is hardly commensurate with these and other inputs, as officials have rightly observed, and 75 per cent of the state's investment is going down the drain, EFA in Tamil Nadu will remain a plan gone awry until the state detects the causes, contexts, and sources of this drain, and the loopholes in the delivery systems.

Sustained commitment of the state to child welfare and basic education as evident from the introduction of schemes and the spending priorities, regardless of the party in power, is a unique feature of Tamil Nadu, which others can emulate by plugging likely loopholes. If this uniqueness is expected to make schemes work better in Tamil Nadu more so, when education was part of the movements for self-respect and equality, and for generally coping with the much politicized (and hackneyed) affirmative action (caste reservations), Tamil Nadu's failure to emerge as a 'model' state though its performance cannot be dubbed and dismissed as a failure, is an important issue for consideration.

The educational experience of any state has to be located in its own matrix of bureaucratic, socio-economic, and political complexities and diversities, and replication of successful schemes depends on the nature of this matrix in the region where it is to be replicated. In Tamil Nadu the areas which need close scrutiny for identifying the problems in its education system are the following:

• The state's fast degenerating political culture which looks upon education in a mere quantitative sense and as yet another political constituency, and does not attach the needed importance to education per se in terms of quality and intrinsic values.

• Nexus between the education system, bureaucracy and politics.

• Imperfections and inadequacies in the delivery systems.

• The efficacy of the educational system in terms of teacher effectiveness.

• State's failure to follow up with implementation its enactment on Compulsory Education in the early 1990s as the first-ever legislation in India.

• Persistence of caste, communal, and gender prejudices and inequalities.

• Highly skewed distribution of resources.

• Lack of social awareness, social mobilization, and most important of all, civil space, without which democracy is at best a rhetoric of expectations.

What Tamil Nadu could do for achieving the goals of EFA is also evident from the 'vision' outlined in the Policy Note, which includes the following:

• Formulation of schemes taking into account the characteristics of the uneducated.

• New guidelines for appointment of teachers according to students' strength in primary schools.

• Intensification of steps to enroll all, particularly those from economically weaker sections, and ensure their retention through the special programme called 'Elementary Education Movement'.

• Making lessons and teaching methods and techniques interesting for both the teachers and learners.

• Modification and revision of the teacher training programmes, learning methods, and syllabus so as to enable children to learn enthusiastically.

• Improving the attainment of minimum levels of learning.

REFERENCES

Athreya, Venkatesh, and Sheela Rani Chunkath (1996). *Literacy and Empowerment*. Sage Publications, New Delhi.

Census of India (1981 and 1991). *India & Tamil Nadu*, Part IV-A, *Social and Cultural Tables*. New Delhi.

Department of Education (1997a). *Political and Social Mobilization for Education for All. The Indian Country Paper. Second E-9 Ministerial Meeting, Islamabad, 14–16 September 1997*. Ministry of Human Resource Development, Government of India, New Delhi.

——— (1997b). *Towards the Next Millennium: India—Status Report. Second E-9 Ministerial Meeting, Islamabad, 14–16 September 1997*. Ministry of Human Resource Development, Government of India, New Delhi.

Department Primary Education Programme (1998). *Three Years of District Primary Education Programme and Learners' Achievement: An Overview*. Educational Consultants India Limited, New Delhi.

——— (1998). *Three Years of District Primary Education Programme: Assessment and Challenges*. Educational Consultants India Limited, New Delhi.

District Primary Education Programme (1999). *Tamil Nadu State Mission of Education For All: Status Report for* the 10th Joint Review Mission, 2nd In-depth Review Mission. Chennai.

District Teacher Education Research and Training (1993). *Strategy Plan of Action to Achieve Universal Primary Education in Tamil Nadu by AD 2000*. Government of Tamil Nadu, Chennai.

Hirschman, A. O. (1986). *Rival Views of Market Society and Other Essays*, Viking, New York.

Mehrotra, S. (1998). *Education For All: Policy Lessons from High-Achieving Countries*. UNICEF Staff Working Papers, Evaluation, Policy and Planning Series, No. EPP-EVL-98-005, UNICEF, New York.

National Council of Educational Research and Training (1998). *Sixth All-India Educational Survey. National Tables*, vols 2, 6, 7, New Delhi.

National Sample Survey Organization (1998). *Attending an Educational Institution in India: Its Level, Nature and Cost*. 52nd Round, July 1995–June 1996. Department of Statistics, Government of India, New Delhi.

PROBE (1999). *Public Report On Basic Education in India*. The PROBE team in Association with Centre for Development Economics. Oxford University Press, New Delhi.

Radhakrishnan, P. (1990). 'Backward Classes in Tamil Nadu: 1872–1988'. *Economic and Political Weekly*, 25(10), 10 March.

———— (1996). 'Backward Class Movements in Tamil Nadu'. In Srinivas, M. N. (ed.), *Caste, Its Twentieth Century Avatar*. Penguin, Delhi.

Ramakrishnan, K. (1991). *A Study on Wastage in Primary Education in Tamil Nadu*. Tamil Nadu Council for Science and Technology, Chennai.

School Education Department (1999). *Policy Note on Demand No.17—Education, 1999–2000*, Government of Tamil Nadu, Chennai.

Social Welfare and Nutritious Meal Programme Department (1999). *Policy Note on Demand No. 29—Social Welfare, 1999–2000*. Government of Tamil Nadu, Chennai.

The Hindu. 21 November 1999.

UNICEF (1996). *The Progress of Indian States*.

24

Universal Elementary Education in Rajasthan

A Study with Focus on Innovative Strategies

Sumitra Chowdhury*

RAJASTHAN: LAND AND PEOPLE

Rajasthan is situated in the north-western part of India. With an area of 342,000 sq km, it is the second largest[1] state of India. The state had an estimated total population of 52 million in 1999. Between 1951 and 1991 population has recorded an almost threefold increase. Even then the density of population at 154 persons per sq km is significantly lower than the Indian average of 299 persons per sq km. The Aravalli Hill ranges from the north-west and south-west divide the state approximately into the western arid and eastern semi-arid region, the western part having severe paucity of water. One-third of the state falling in the western and south-western parts is covered by the Thar Desert characterized by extreme temperatures and semi-arid conditions.

Rajasthan has a diverse culture and rich heritage of handicrafts, architecture, music, dance, and folk arts which are the products of a complex and pluralistic society. Yet, feudal values of the past continue to exist in various forms. Caste-based communities and tribes dominate the social structure of the state. Untouchability still persists in the some rural areas and lower ranked castes are socially isolated. The tribes are doubly disadvantaged through living in geographically remote areas. Table 24.1 provides data indicating the abysmally low levels of human development in the state.

A variety of social, cultural, and historical factors have conspired to give rise to a situation in Rajasthan that

may be described as extremely adverse to women. Literacy rate among rural women is 11.59 per cent, the lowest in the country. Although the female literacy rate has increased from 3 per cent in 1951 to 20 per cent in 1991, the gap in literacy rate between males and females has continued to widen in spite of all efforts, even in the 1990s. The enrolment ratio of girls in primary education is adverse compared to boys. Even of those who join primary education, a large number drop out.

Agriculture is the primary economic activity in the state and engages 70 per cent of the population. Animal husbandry is the second major economic activity, especially in the arid and semi-arid regions. Agrarian communities traditionally view children as an economic asset. Thus, a large number of children are engaged in agriculture and animal husbandry, mostly as unpaid labourers. A significantly large number of children also work in gem polishing, carpet making, tobacco processing, and mining industries at less than minimum wages. Many children are also engaged as construction workers and in hotels, restaurants, and petty shops. In western Rajasthan, being a rain-deficit area, a seasonal migration pattern of cattle as well as human beings has evolved over the years. Besides, agriculture being less stable due to uncertain rainfall, a large number of people migrate in search of employment. The large-scale migration due to all these fectors has severe adverse effect on regularity and attendance in schools.

Many villages, especially in the desert and tribal districts, are not connected by approachable roads, as yet. About 30 per cent of rural population live in hamlets, situated at considerable distance from the main villages. One has to walk a distance of 6 to 12 km, sometimes even more, to reach such villages. As per government statistics, 83.42 per cent of villages in Rajasthan are

* The author has immensely benefited from the guidance given by Shri Anil Bordia in the preparation of this paper. Suggestions for reorganization of the paper and editorial help extended by Ms Ratna Mathur is also gratefully acknowledged.

[1] After the carving out of the separate state of Chhatisgarh from Madhya Pradesh on 1 November 2000, Rajasthan is now the largest Indian state.

TABLE 24.1
Indicators of Human Development (1997)

Indicator	Rajasthan	India
Birth rate (per 1000)	33.6	28.5
Death rate (per 1000)	9.3	9.0
Infant mortality rate (per 1000 birth)	85	74
Under-5 mortality (per 1000 birth)	127	119
Maternal mortality (per 1000 birth)	55	45
Children born with low birth weight (%)	39	33
Life expectancy at birth	58.0	59.4
Household access to manmade water sources (%)	56	75
Average radial distance per public health centre (km)	8.3	6.8
Percentage of births by institutional medical attention	8.1	22.3
Domicillary birth attended by untrained persons	67.5	50
Population having access to electricity	31	53
Road length per 100 sq km of area	36.3	62.1
Average age of marriage of girls	14.6	17.2

Source: Lok Jumbish—Phase III—1998–2003, Project Document, June 1998.

electrified. However, only 31 per cent of population has access to electricity.

STATUS OF BASIC EDUCATION IN RAJASTHAN

As one of the educationally underdeveloped states of the country, statistical indicators of educational progress in Rajasthan are not encouraging. However, the past 10–15 years have witnessed a number of special thrusts towards the goal of universal elementary education (UEE).

Early Childhood Care and Development (ECCD)

The Integrated Child Development Services (ICDS) is the main channel of providing early childhood care and education (ECCE) in the state. The ICDS is being implemented in the state since 1975 through centres called *anganwadi* centres (AWCs) which are supposed to remain open for 3 to 4 hours a day and work for early childhood education, immunization of children and pregnant mothers, nutrition, health check-up, and health education. As on 1998–9, 25,701 AWCs were operational. Altogether 1.411 million women including lactating mothers and pregnant women and 634,000 children are the beneficiaries of the scheme. It was originally envisaged that an AWC would invariably be attached to every primary school. However, as most of the primary schools have dilapidated buildings and insufficient space, many AWCs are actually located away from schools and their timings do not match school timings. As a result, there is no linkage with the primary schools and the goal of pre-primary education remains unmet (see Table 24.2 for the status of ECCE and literacy in Rajasthan).

The ICDS is also being implemented by some non-governmental organizations (NGOs) though on a small scale. On the whole, there has not been much progress towards ECCD in Rajasthan. The gross enrolment ratio in ECCE is very low in general in India, and it is even worse in case of Rajasthan.

Adult Literacy

The Government of Rajasthan launched a total literacy campaign (TLC) in 1989 under the National Literacy

TABLE 24.2
Status of ECCE and Literacy in Rajasthan

Indicator	Rajasthan	India
Gross enrolment ratio in ECCE (1997)		
Boys	15.5	17.3
Girls	14.3	16.4
Total	14.9	16.9
Literacy rate 7+ population		
1991 Census		
Male	54.99	64.13
Female	20.44	39.29
Total	38.55	52.21
53rd round of NSSO		
(January–December 1997)		
Male	73.00	73.00
Female	35.00	50.00
Total	55.00	62.00
Literacy rate 15+ population		
1991 Census		
Male	52.50	61.90
Female	16.90	34.10
Total	35.50	48.50
As reported by MHRD: 1997		
Male	69.00	70.00
Female	27.00	43.00
Total	49.00	57.00

Source: MHRD and NIEPA (1999), EFA-2000 Assessment: Core EFA Indicators, Draft Report, Selected Educational Statistics 1997–8, Deptt. of Education, MHRD, GoI (1998).

Mission (NLM) and over a period of time succeeded in securing cooperation of a large section of society. The literacy rate in the 15+ age group population has increased from 35.50 per cent in 1991 to 49.00 per cent in 1997, recording an increase of about 14 per cent. The recorded improvement in Rajasthan indicates better performance than the all-India average. The literacy campaign has certainly brought about awareness among the people regarding the significance of education in development and empowerment, but the performance has mostly been overshadowed by generation of data on literacy rates rather than in developing indicators to capture qualitative changes.

Progress towards UEE

ACCESS

The Sixth All-India Educational Survey (see NCERT 1993) identified 16,259 habitations without primary schools within a distance of 1 km. Accordingly, 74.58 per cent of habitations in Rajasthan were served by primary schools within 1 km and 64.43 per cent of the habitations had upper-primary schools within 3 km (see Table 24.3). After 1993, a number of formal schools and non-formal education (NFE) centres including Rajiv Gandhi *Path-shalas* have been opened in the state.

As per the Annual Report (1998–9) of the Department of Education of the state government, Rajasthan had 34,364 primary schools and 14,548 upper-primary schools in 1998–9, and 7.38 million and 2.31 million children respectively enrolled in these schools. The corresponding enrolment figures in 1991–2 were 4.59 million and 1.43 million. As per the *Selected Educational Statistics 1997–98* (GoI 1998), gross enrolment ratio (see GER) in the state has increased from 67.6 per cent in 1990–1 to 96.9 per cent in 1997–8 in primary classes and from 49.2 per cent to 52.7 per cent in upper-primary classes during the same period. Girls' enrolment has recorded faster growth compared to boys. This has resulted in a

TABLE 24.3
Access to Primary Education (1998)

Indicator	Rajasthan	India
No. of habitations served by primary schools		
up to 1 km	47,711	884,089
(% of total)	74.58	83.36
More than 1 km	16,259	176,523
(% of total)	25.42	16.64
No. of habitations served by upper-primary schools		
up to 3 km	41,219	807,656
(% of total)	64.43	76.15
More than 3 km	22,751	252,956
(% of total)	35.57	23.85
No. of population served by primary schools		
up to 1 km	33,130,093	618,543,482
(% of total)	92.55	93.76
More than 1 km	2,665,588	41,147,566
(% of total)	7.45	6.24
No. of population served by upper-primary schools		
up to 3 km	28,278,241	560,769,550
(% of total)	79.00	85.00
More than 3 km	7,517,440	98,921,498
(% of total)	21.00	15.00
Gross enrolment ratio (I–V)		
Boys	111.30	98.50
Girls	81.00	81.50
Total	97.00	90.30
Net enrolment ratio (I–V)		
Boys	78.50	71.00
Girls	31.80	48.80
Total	56.40	60.30

Source: DoE (1998), *Selected educational Statistics 1997–98*, MHRD, GoI. MHRD, GoI and NIEPA(1999), *EFA-2000 Assessment: Core EFA Indicators*, Draft Report State Institute of Educational Research and Training (1998), *Sixth-All India Educational Survey, State Report—Rajasthan*, Udaipur.

decline in the gap between boys and girls in total enrolment. Further, the GER and net enrollment ratio (NER) for primary level (i.e. classes I–V) are higher in Rajasthan than the all-India average.

EFFICIENCY

The survival rate to class V, calculated from yearwise and gradewise enrolment data compiled from government sources by the State Institute of Educational Research and Training, Udaipur (see SIERT 1998) of children in primary education in Rajasthan is about 16 percentage points less than the all-India average. But the improvement during the 1990s has been better than the all-India aver-

age and retention of girls has improved at a better rate than that of boys (see Table 24.4).

It has been observed that a sizeable number of children continue to repeat the same classes, thereby requiring more than five years for completion of five classes of primary education. Gradewise repetition rates in Rajasthan are approximately half the national average. The years input per graduate of primary education has been worked out to 6.6 years for Rajasthan as against 7.5 years for India as a whole, implying greater efficiency in Rajasthan. The transition rate from highest grade of primary education (i.e. class V) to the lowest grade of upper-primary (i.e. class VI) is also much higher.

TABLE 24.4
Indicators of Efficiency

Indicator	Rajasthan	India
Net attendance ratio: 1996		
I–V	55	66
VI–VIII	35	43
Gradewise repetition rates		
I	4.90	7.70
II	3.00	5.70
III	2.80	7.30
IV	2.20	5.80
V	3.50	5.90
Transition rate from primary to upper-primary (from class V to class VI)		
Boys	95.32	78.57
Girls	80.1	70.39
Total	90.11	75.03
Rates of efficiency		
Survival rate to class V (1990–1)		
Boys	40.79	59.90
Girls	33.20	54.00
Total	38.44	57.40
Survival rate to grade V (1997–8)		
Boys	46.20	62.18
Girls	41.90	58.66
Total	44.65	60.42
Years input per graduate		
Boys	6.2	7.2
Girls	7.5	8.0
Total	6.6	7.5
Status of teaching inputs		
Teacher–pupil ratio (primary level)	51	48
Teacher–pupil ratio (I–VIII)		
1991–2	40.48	50.17
1997–8	42.52	48.09
Percentage of trained teachers	97.6	87.7
Percentage of female teachers	28.8	35.8

Sources: DoE (1998), *Selected Educational Statistics 1997–98*, MHRD, GoI.
NIEPA and MHRD (2000), *EFA 2000 Assessment: Core EFA Indicators*, Draft Report, New Delhi.
Department of Primary and Secondary Education (various years), *Annual Report 1998–9*, GoR.

The reported GER as an indicator of universal enrolment in Rajasthan does not reflect the actual status of enrolment. This is evident from the fact that the reported differential between GER and NER is much higher in Rajasthan than the all-India average, implying that a large number of overage/underage children are enrolled. Corresponding to this, the net attendance ratio (NAR) in Rajasthan is less than the all-India average. This indicates that many of the enrolled children are actually not attending regularly and therefore, even if the reported GER is high, it does not necessarily imply better performance of Rajasthan in a real sense.

Apart from the problem of overreporting of enrolment figures in secondary sources, another very important problem arises from inconsistency of data in various secondary sources (see Table 24.5). This gives rise to serious confusion regarding actual enrolment status and the question arises as to which source of information is to be relied upon as a more accurate assessment.

TEACHER–PUPIL RATIO

The pupil–teacher ratio in Rajasthan works out to slightly worse than the all-India average for the primary section in 1997–8 whereas the percentage of trained teachers is about 97.6 per cent in Rajasthan as against 87.7 per cent for India as a whole. However, teacher–pupil ratio should ideally not be calculated separately for primary level as there are primary sections in upper-primary schools and teachers of upper-primary sections teach primary classes as well. Calculated for elementary level, teacher–pupil ratio for Rajasthan worked out better than the national average in 1997–8.

Intra-state Variation in Performance

The average rates and ratios calculated for a state do not reveal the intra-state variations. Given the diverse circumstances in Rajasthan as already discussed, even if the state average indicates better performance during the

TABLE 24.5
Enrollment Rates from Various Data Sources: Rajasthan

	Boys	Girls	Total
Annual Report, MHRD, GoI, 1992–3			
Age group 6–11	119.5	60.9	91.0
Age group 11–14	76.8	28.9	53.9
Sixth All-India Educational Survey, NCERT, 1993			
Age group 6–11	95.1	53.5	75.4
Age group 11–14	61.9	24.2	44.3
Age group 6–14	83.7	43.7	64.8
HDI survey of NCAER, 1993			
Age group 6–14	78.0	41.9	61.3
National Family Health Survey, 1992–3 (Enrolled and attending school)			
Age group 6–10	72.4	42.4	58.5
Age group 11–14	77.2	37.7	59.3
Age group 6–14	74.3	40.6	58.8

However, based on the primary survey under a study conducted by Lok Jumbish (LJ 1998a), it was found that 14.9 per cent of the enrolled children in classes I–V were repeaters in the same class during the previous year and the percentage of repeaters was highest in class I. To be precise, 30.04 per cent of children were found to be repeating class I. Data on formal schools belonging to the five development blocks, in which the Lok Jumbish project has been operationalized right from the beginning, indicate a still higher repetition rate in class I (42.28 per cent) as the transition rate from class I to class II during the pre-intervention period was found to be 57.88 per cent.

1990s, this is only a half-truth. There are still many areas and disadvantaged groups which need greater attention. On the other hand, performance in some areas have been relatively better than the state average, giving rise to inequality in educational development among different regions/districts within the state. There are, in fact, wide variations across districts.

Persistent Problems in Reaching the Goal of UEE

MAKING PROVISION FOR UNIVERSAL ACCESS

The state government has established a norm of opening a formal primary school in villages having a population of more than 250 (150 in desert and tribal areas). It is difficult to find data reflecting the exact status based on these norms as the Sixth All-India Educational Survey does not separately report the number of habitations having a population of more than 250 but do not have primary schooling facility. Rather, it reports the number of school-less habitations with a population more or less than 300. Based on these data, one could estimate the situation of access as follows in 1998:

• There were 1932 habitations with more than 300 population and no primary schooling facility.

• There were 6582 habitations in the population range of 200–300 not having primary schooling facility.

• There were 3857 habitations in the population range of 100–200 without primary schools.

• There were approximately 7500 habitations having a population of less than 100 and without any primary educational facility.

The 42nd Round of the National Sample Survey (July 1986–June 1987) (see NSS 1993) found that 'non-availability of schooling facilities' accounted for only about 10 per cent of the 'never-enrolled' in rural India and 8 per cent in urban India. As against this, 'disinterest' has been cited by the largest number, accounting for 30 per cent of those surveyed, as the reason for their non-enrolment in school. A study based on a primary survey of 300 children belonging to remote and disadvantaged areas from rural Rajasthan conducted by LJ (1998b) found that the principal reason for low/no enrolment in primary education is that the children are engaged in family economic activities and/or look after younger brothers and sisters and are engaged in household work. Their parents are not in a position to sacrifice the opportunity cost of sending them to school in terms of time and energy for acquiring no education or the irrelevant kind of education that is imparted in schools. Besides, upper-primary education is not available to a large number of children, and girls in particular find it impossible to go to another village to continue upper-

primary education. Nearly one-fourth of the children are also working children who cannot enrol in the school system. Beside patriarchal attitudes come in the way of girls' education.

MAKING SUFFICIENT FUNDS AVAILABLE
FOR ELEMENTARY EDUCATION

The expenditure on education in Rajasthan has increased from Rs 8050 million in 1990–1 to Rs 22,013 million in 1997–8. The corresponding share of educational expenditure in the net state domestic product (NSDP) has increased from 4.40 per cent to 4.75 per cent during the same period. More than 55 per cent of the total allocation of resources for education goes to elementary education. Expenditure on elementary education in Rajasthan has increased from Rs 4478 million in 1990–1 to Rs 12,573 million in 1997–8 (see Table 24.6). But such increase in expenditure does not necessarily imply optimum resource allocation to elementary education by the state government. The per child expenditure in 1997–8 is only 1.96 times more than the per child expenditure in 1990–1 as against the total expenditure on elementary education in 1997–8 being 2.8 times more than in 1990–1. This implies that increase in expenditure has not kept pace with the growing number of children participating in elementary education. Besides, 97 per cent of this expenditure goes only to teachers' salaries. If increased expenditure is intended to upgrade the quality, and benefits expected to reach individual children, per child expenditure has to be increased, thereby implying the need for total investment to be still higher.

Given the funds available to the state government, there appears to be scope for increasing the allocation to elementary education. Out of the per capita NSDP, the proportion of per child expenditure on elementary education has declined from 17.21 per cent in 1990–1 to 15.35 per cent in 1997–8, indicating that the increase in expenditure on elementary education has been less than proportionate to the increase in income, thereby implying that even the available fund has not been optimally allocated.

TABLE 24.6
Financing of Elementary Education in Rajasthan

Indicator	1990–1	1997–8
Expenditure on education (in Rs lakh)		
Total	80,496.69	220,131.15
Elementary education	44,782.69	125,730.72
Expenditure on elementary education as % of total education budget	55.63	57.12
Per capita income in Rs (at current prices)	4191	9215
Per child expenditure on elementary education (Rs)	721.37	1414.61

Source: Annual Report, GoR, Deptt. of Primary and Secondary Education, Ministry of Finance, Economic Survey 1998–9, Economic Division, GoI.

BUILDING UP AN APPROPRIATE DATABASE FOR PLANNING

It has been recognized since long that planning has to be based on appropriate information base. But hardly any effort has been made to build a more reliable, authentic, and relevant information base. Most of the data refer to supply side indicators. For example, data have been generated regarding number of schools per 1000 population to indicate the status of accessibility. Data also show the number of children enrolled in schools, but no data have been generated to show the number of children actually availing the facilities in schools. Similarly, there are data showing teacher–pupil ratio, but no data to indicate to what extent a student avails the teaching input.

To add to the list of inadequacies in data is information regarding learning achievement and the indicator to reflect the impact of learning. Until recently, quality indicators of education used to be the teacher–pupil ratio, pass ratio, availability of physical facilities in schools, etc. Important indicators of quality, viz. relevance of curriculum, teaching method, and the medium of instruction used in school, which are not easily quantifiable, have been left out from any kind of assessment.

Since the adoption of the National Policy on Education (NPE) 1986, measurement of learning levels as an indicator of quality is being accorded importance. But there has not been a systematic attempt to study learning achievement, except some studies which have been undertaken here and there. For example, a study by Shukla and others (1991) indicated that learning achievement of children in both languages and mathematics in Rajasthan is better than the all-India average by about 6 per cent. The baseline achievement study conducted by the SIERT (1997) to study the pre-implementation status of the DPEP in the ten districts of Rajasthan found the achievement score of children in languages and mathematics to be 54.94 per cent and 35.03 per cent respectively. This study noted that mean achievement of students actually varies across the districts and at different grades/classes. As against these, the benchmark study conducted in fifteen blocks to study the pre-implementation status of the LJ project (1998a) indicated much lower achievement levels, the average achievement scores of children in class I and II in both language and mathematics varied from 34.30 per cent to 37.50 per cent.

INNOVATIVE STRATEGIES FOR UEE IN RAJASTHAN

Following the national drive of opening up of schools within a distance of 1 to 3 km from the place of residence of children, primary schools have been opened in most of the revenue villages of Rajasthan. Small school buildings have been constructed and one or two qualified teachers appointed. Qualified teachers appointed by the government invariably belong to the nearby urban/semi-urban area and find it extremely difficult either to stay in the village or commute daily in the absence of proper means of transportation. Consequently, teachers remain absent frequently and the 'schools' provided by the government at an accessible physical distance thus remain inaccessible and are rendered dysfunctional in no time.

Combating this situation demands moving out of the conventional approaches of planning and management. The new planning approach has to be pluralistic, process based, non-homogeneous, and founded on authentic needs as perceived by the community. This cannot be through a centralized and controlled approach. Rather, a decentralized system, permitting autonomy and involvement of the community, NGOs, and people associated with the existing system, becomes indispensable. In fact, the rural community of Rajasthan is largely aware of the importance of education and feels the need for it. However, it feels powerless to intervene in the system.

Keeping the above context in view, an attempt is made in this section to describe two relatively large-scale projects, namely the *Shiksha Karmi* Project (SKP) and the LJ Project, involving a number of innovative strategies, that have been under implementation in Rajasthan during the last decade with a fair amount of success. Both the projects are designed to develop solutions through people's participation and collaboration with NGOs.

The SKP

The SKP is an innovation to transform dysfunctional schools into reasonably efficient schools. It attempts to make provision for quality education with the help of locally available youth in remote rural habitations of the state. The SKP was launched in 1987 with financial assistance from Sweden. With the launching of the SKP, it was necessary to have an implementing structure which could at one level be freed from the government style of decision making and at another level was owned by the government which could give it the power and legitimacy to intervene in the mainstream of education. Thus, the Rajasthan *Shiksha Karmi* Board (SKB) was set up as a registered autonomous society in October 1987 to administer project planning, implementation, coordination, and management.

The basic objectives of the SKP were to achieve:

• universalization of primary education in remote, socio-economically backward villages in those blocks of Rajasthan where existing primary schools have become dysfunctional;

• a qualitative improvement in primary education in

such villages by adapting the form and content of education to local needs and conditions;

- enrolment of all boys and girls in the age group 6–14;
- a level of learning equivalent to the norm for class V.

SHIKSHA KARMI: THE CONCEPT

A 'shiksha karmi', which literally means education worker, is a full-time teacher belonging to the same village in which he or she teaches and substitutes the formally qualified teacher in government primary schools. Shiksha karmis are expected to render voluntary services against a relatively lower payment than the qualified teachers appointed by the government. The concept of shiksha karmi is based on the premise that a change agent, specially in the field of education, can work effectively if he/she belongs to the same locality. More weightage is, therefore, given to his/her willingness and ability to function as a social worker than to only educational qualifications. Thus

> Shiksha Karmis have to have a sense of belonging to their village, to care about children there and to teach them basics of literacy and numeracy. They must help children to be aware of the immediate world around them and the invisible world beyond. They have to be held accountable to the families who send their children to be educated, and to the community which provides the psychological support in such an enterprise. The SKs have to value knowledge and to recognise its value in use, and commit themselves to being continuing learners of both content and communication. Working as a team, cooperatively, is essential. [Anandalakshmy and Jain, 1997]

To inculcate such qualities and values, shiksha karmis have to undergo rigorous induction training. This is followed by regular training aiming at upgradation of their teaching skills at specific intervals. Motivation of shiksha karmis is also sustained through such training and special incentives.

OPERATIONALIZATION OF SCHOOLS BY THE SKB

The field implementation of the SKP starts with identification of remote and backward villages where primary schools opened by the government are not functioning. The next step is to hold a meeting of local self-government officials and the Block Development Officer of the government of Rajasthan. This is followed by a gram sabha (an assembly of all adults in the village). The dysfunctional schools are listed and a resolution of the local self-government body (panchayat) is forwarded to the SKB to take over the identified dysfunctional schools based on the following criteria: extremely low enrolment; low attendance of children; low retention of boys and girls; low academic attainment among children; and pattern of irregular attendance and absenteeism of teacher resulting in frequent closure of school.

If the villagers are found to be willing to extend support for improvement of the school, a decision is taken to take over the school by the SKB and the school made functional through selecting and appointing two shiksha karmis.

SELECTION AND TRAINING OF SHIKSHA KARMIS

The lifeline of the SKP is the selection, education, and training of the shiksha karmis. The minimum qualifications of shiksha karmis are specified at class VIII for male and class V for female candidates. The eligibility age is specified at 18–33 years. After the decision to take up a dysfunctional school is taken, a gram sabha is held. Two persons, with the specified qualifications and age, who are accepted by all villagers, are selected. The selected candidates are required to take tests in writing and oral skills in Hindi (language), handwriting, knowledge of numbers, basic teaching–learning processes, and hygiene and environmental awareness. The selection team for this test consists of representatives from the SKB, a local NGO, the Pradhan (the elected local self-government representative), the Block Development Officer of the Government of Rajasthan, and a woman representative of the village. Preference is given to women candidates.

After the selection, shiksha karmis have to undergo an intensive residential training course. They are trained to handle multi-grade and multi-level teaching, to develop appropriate teaching–learning materials with the locally available materials, and to teach and behave with girls with special care and retain them in school till they complete primary level of education. Following this initial training, an induction training of forty-one days is given to each shiksha karmi. Even after appointment as shiksha karmis, effort to improve their capability is sustained through recurrent and rigorous training throughout their career. During a span of eight years, a shiksha karmi receives about 350–400 days of individualized and group training. Flexibility and innovation combined with professional rigour and cooperative learning may be said to be the hallmarks of shiksha karmi training.

FOCUS ON GENDER ISSUES IN THE SKP

Shiksha karmi schools were able to attract a very limited number of girls initially because there were few women shiksha karmis. There is a shortage of village women with required education and self-confidence to become a shiksha karmis. Mahila Prashikshan Kendras (MPKs), i.e. Women Training Institutes, were, therefore, set up with women trainers where young women take basic education required for becoming shiksha karmis. The trainees stay in the MPKs for 6 months to 2 years depending on their original education and the progress they make. Most of these women are mothers of young children. To facilitate their studies and training, a creche and childcare unit with a woman helper, is attached to every MPK. As of now, 14 MPKs spread over 13 districts are functioning, and till now 345 women have been trained successfully at these centres to become shiksha karmis.

Many children in Rajasthan, especially girls, cannot attend school as they take care of younger siblings or social customs do not allow them to attend schools. *Mahila sahyogis* (female escorts), who are local women, are appointed to collect children from their homes, escort them to school, and take care of young siblings during school hours. Experience reveals that appointing female escorts has proved to be a major breakthrough in enabling girls to attend *shiksha karmi* schools.

EVOLUTION OF NEW PROGRAMMES

With the expansion of the SKP, changes have evolved in its functioning and implementation strategies:

• Initially, the SKP did not envisage opening of new *shiksha karmi* schools. During phase I, it was observed that there was a demand and need for opening of new schools in habitations where there were no facilities for primary education due to geographical or social barriers to access. The opening of new schools is based on the following criteria:

 – population of the village;
 – number of out-of-school children in the 6–14 age group;
 – primary schools situated within a radius of 2 km;
 – preparation of village maps indicating educational status;
 – the availability of educated local youth for selection as *shiksha karmis*;
 – willingness of villagers to provide land for establishment of a new school and to make temporary accommodation available until a school building is constructed by the government.

Of late, the government has been disallowing taking up of dysfunctional government schools by the SKP. Instead, only new schools were opened during the past three years and operationalized under the SKP.

• On the basis of the review of the project in 1991, *prahar pathshalas* (schools of convenient timings) have been started to reach children who are unable to attend day school. The *prahar pathshalas* run for two hours every evening. The same *shiksha karmis* who run the day schools run the *prahar pathshalas* as well which are run either in the same buildings used for the day schools or at other convenient places in the village. Each centre is expected to cater to twenty-five learners in the 6–14 age group. Decisions regarding place and timings are taken in consultation with parents and the community members. *Prahar pathshalas* are seen as a stepping stone to the transfer of children to day school.

• To attract more girls to schools, the concept of *aangan pathshalas*—'courtyard schools'—was introduced in 1992–3. A rural woman, who has passed class V and is willing to teach girls, is engaged to teach a group of at least fifteen girls in the 6–14 age group in her neighbourhood. She is given training and academic support. Recent studies have shown that aangan pathshalas are proving to be an effective contextual intervention to encourage sustained participation of girls in primary education. *Aangan pathshalas* are usually started in villages where there are no formal schools or other facilities for the education of children.

COVERAGE AND ACHIEVEMENT OF THE SKP

The SKP has completed two phases. As of now, coverage of the SKP extends to 2697 villages with a population of 761,000. The project has engaged and trained 6285 shiksha karmis who are providing primary education to 216,084 children in 2697 day schools and 4335 *prahar pathshalas*. Fourteen MPKs have successfully trained 345 women to become *shiksha karmis*. Each village has been able to constitute a village education committee. Twenty-eight NGOs and voluntary agencies are working with SKB as partners in various aspects of the programme.

Evaluations and studies have indicated marked achievement of the project.

• In SKP villages, 83 per cent of children in the 6–14 age group have been enrolled. Of these, 70 per cent are first generation learners.

• Of girls in the age group, 78 per cent are enrolled in day schools and *prahar pathshalas* taken together.

• In 25 per cent of the SKP villages, there has been universal enrolment (with cent per cent enrolment ratio).

• Of the children studying in *shiksha karmi* schools, 67 per cent belong to disadvantaged population groups.

• Average attendance in *shiksha karmi* schools is as high as 85 per cent.

• Retention in *shiksha karmi* schools is 65 per cent now as against 19 per cent when the dysfunctional schools were taken up.

• Gender gap in enrolment has reduced.

The SKP has proved that quality education for unprivileged children is feasible through *shiksha karmis* and establishing a strong support system. It offers a successful model of para-teachers which is being adopted and adapted in many states of India.

COST

The SKP is considered to be a cost-effective project. Per child cost under SKP is Rs 1065 per annum as against Rs 2170 per annum in government schools (see Thakur and Methi 1999). Of this, the project spends 25 per cent on items like training and teaching–learning materials. In the government system this constitutes only about 4 per cent of total expenditutre.

THE LOK JUMBISH PROJECT

The LJ is a bold attempt to develop and implement a new decentralized planning approach for universalization of quality primary education which conforms to the aspirations of the community. The LJ process of planning and management is based on authentic grassroots-level information, community participation, government–NGO collaboration and gender equity. The LJ has attempted to make education a people's movement ensuring active and sustained participation of people at every level. The special emphasis of the LJ is on education of girls and children belonging to the disadvantaged sections. The long-term goals of the LJ include the following:

• Providing access to primary education to all children between 5 and 14 years of age.

• Ensuring that all enrolled children regularly attend school or non-formal centres and complete primary education.

• Ensuring that quality of education is improved by emphasizing active learning, child-centred processes and achievement by all children at least of minimum levels of learning.

• Making modifications in the content and process of education to better relate it to the environment, to people's culture and to their living and working conditions.

• Involving people in the planning and management of education.

• Creating structures and setting in motion processes that would empower women and make education an instrument of women's equality.

• Pursuing the goal of equity in education—between boys and girls, between socially or educationally disadvantaged sections and the rest of the society and between children with disabilities and others.

THE LJ PROCESS OF FIELD OPERATIONS

The unit of decentralized planning in the LJ is the village and the unit of decentralized management is the block. Between the village and the block, there is a crucial structure of the LJ called cluster consisting of 25 to 35 villages with similar geographical and socio-economic conditions.

Each development block is divided into 5 to 7 (sometimes more) compact clusters. A block steering group (BSG) of 5 persons is appointed at block level and a team of 4 persons at cluster level. The role of the cluster personnel is to translate the ideas of the LJ into action in villages. They are responsible for penetrating rural areas, earning the confidence of the village community, providing necessary support as facilitators through active participation in the activities, and coordinating with the BSG. The cluster personnel take up environment-building activities through personal contacts and traditional and modern media. The environment building aims at creating a stir among people for pursuing the common goal of UEE.

When the villagers come forward, a core team called *prerak dal* (motivational group), in every village is set up with women members constituting nearly half the membership. A separate women's group is also set up. The members of these groups are trained and empowered through sharing of information. The emphasis in training is on confidence building, creating genuine interest in children's, particularly girls', education, on learning the techniques of preparing the village map, household survey, survey of the school or NFE centre, if any, and analysing the educational status of the village. After training, the core teams undertake the responsibility of reviewing the educational status of their respective villages through preparation of the village map, information gathered from house-to-house contact, preparing statistical summary of all information, and discussing the matter in the village assembly.

In the meantime, the women's group engages the community on issues of the girl child—her status and education. Women's groups also mobilize the women of the village in bringing about a change in perception regarding education of girls and their role in the family and society. Women's groups also raise voice collectively against social injustice towards their fellow women in the village.

Based on the analysis of educational status of the village, the core team makes proposals with necessary assistance of the LJ's cluster and block personnel for improvement of the educational facilities of the village. The proposals thus prepared are taken to the Block Educational Management Committee (BEMC). The state government has empowered this committee to review the situation and take decisions regarding the creation of educational facilities based on specified norms approved by the state government. The plans approved by the BEMC for improvement in formal schooling facilities are implemented by the state government whereas those for NFE are implemented by the LJ.

Simultaneously, a Building Construction Committee (BCC) is set up in those villages where repair of existing school buildings has to be undertaken. The members of the BCC are also imparted training regarding the process of management of the building construction work, maintenance of the buildings, opening up of a bank account in the name of the BCC, record keeping, etc. A certain amount of money is collected by the BCC from villagers towards their contribution to the school building and a bank account is opened with this money. The LJ transfers money to this account. The proper utilization of the money for construction work then becomes the responsibility of the BCC.

Members of the village-level core team, the women's group, and the BCC, who give evidence of dedicated work, subsequently become a part of the Village Education Committee (VEC). The VEC undertakes microplanning to ensure enrolment of all children and their regular attendance and retention till they complete primary education.

SCHOOL MAPPING

The series of processes, starting from environment building to submission of proposed village education plan to the BEMC and formation of the VEC, is known as School Mapping (SM) in the LJ. The LJ has used SM as the principal instrument for people's participation and generation of childwise authentic information.

The generation of database through SM follows some steps:

• Creation of the initial *naksha nazri* (village map) based on initial information about the village.

• Establishing contact and generating genuine information through actual survey of each family, filling up a performa containing details of every child in the age group of 3 to 14 years in the family and their educational status, noting down the reasons if not participating in education.

• Preparation of a Village Education Register (VER) by putting together the survey sheets of every household. The VER thereafter becomes a source of authentic information regarding the actual participation of children in primary education. It is actually an alternative to mere enrolment data collected from the school register.

• Survey of schools or NFE centres, if any, in the village.

• Creation of the final *naksha nazri*. All schoolgoing and non-schoolgoing boys and girls from every family are shown through symbols and different colours on the map. The symbols and colours get easily communicated even to an illiterate person. Thus, this map serves as a visual database. Any villager can locate his/her house on the map and can also compare the status of his/her children regarding primary education in the context of overall status of the village and also in comparison to the children of other families.

A village education plan prepared initially by the core team becomes a basis for continuous follow-up by the VEC. The village education plan is repeatedly reviewed and improved upon by the VEC with special attention to improvement of enrolment, retention, and quality of education, and suggestions for further improvement are presented to the BEMC for consideration.

FOCUS ON GENDER EQUITY

The LJ aims at providing access to education to every girl child. Girls' enrolment and retention are seen as the principal indicator of the project's performance. The LJ also believes that education serves as an instrument of women's equality. Gender equity is attempted to be established through 'feminization of the education system'—appropriate mode of education accessible to girls, curriculum content, teachers' training, facilities in schools, improvement in school environment, recruitment of women at every level, empowerment of women teachers and students.

Gender equity in the LJ is a goal as well as principal strategy. Gender sensitivity permeates all programmes and processes. Working conditions in the field are very difficult and women workers face serious problems that are rooted in the patriarchal tradition of Rajasthan. The LJ management takes cognizance of this issue. The status of gender equity in the LJ is constantly reviewed. Based on this analysis, the LJ management has devised appropriate strategies to interweave gender in management as well as in all programme components. At block level, out of a team of 5, 1 position, *samyukta*, is reserved for a woman. Her responsibility is to interpret the idea of gender equity in every action and management in the field. At cluster level, 3 out of 4 personnel are women. Besides, a field centre is established in every cluster to facilitate women-centred development activities and mobilization.

Two Women's Residential Institutes for Training and Education or *Mahila Shikshan Vihars*, have been established for education and training of prospective workers of the LJ. These institutes are located at Jalor, the lowest rural female literacy district, and Jhalawar, where more than one-third of the villages have no literate female. More than 100 women have already received education up to Class VIII and vocational training. About twenty of them have already been engaged as field workers of the LJ.

SAHAJ SHIKSHA (NFE) PROGRAMME

The *Sahaj Shiksha* Programme (SSP) is the NFE programme of the LJ developed as a parallel and complementary system to formal education. The SSP aims at providing education to

- children residing in small habitations,
- working children,
- girls who have to look after their siblings and attend to other domestic chores, and
- children who are 9 years old and above and cannot, therefore, be admitted to school.

Consequently, three principles were evolved to govern the SSP. First was to establish equivalence with the formal school system. This is attempted in two ways. By encouraging children to transfer from *sahaj shiksha* centres to schools and by making efforts to ensure that the quality of instruction in *sahaj shiksha* is equivalent to the school system. Second was to ensure that both the formal education and NFE systems learn from each other and benefit from each others strengths. The third was to allow flexibility in all organizational aspects.

BALIKA SHIKSHAN SHIVIRS (BSS)

BSSs are short-term residential camps for adolescent girls who have missed the opportunity of schooling at the right age of school entry due to lack of access and family compulsions. From January 1997 to May 1997, four camps were organized on experimental basis. About 400 girls joined these camps, about 20 per cent of them achieved education of class IV and 45 per cent completed education up to class III. The rest of them mostly completed class II and a few struggled around class I. Besides acquiring the laid down competencies in the 3 Rs, these girls also learnt about health and sanitation and became self-confident and better informed.

Inspired by the success of first series of camps, a second series of fourteen camps was started in November–December 1997. Experience of the first series of camps showed that the camps needed to be six months long to enable girls to reach class IV or V. The duration of the second series of camps was accordingly six months. But at the end of six months about 20 per cent of the girls had completed education upto class V and another 12 to 15 per cent of the girls were at a stage nearing completion. The camps were therefore extended by one more month to enable these girls to complete at least the level of primary education. About 1400 girls received education in this series of camps. This time, 84 per cent of the girls completed education up to class III and above, 32.5 per cent, in fact, completed the basic primary stage education up to class V. Six more camps were organized during 1998–9, two of which were follow-up camps for girls who had completed up to classes III and IV in earlier camps and needed some more time to complete education up to class V.

Each of the BSSs attracted girls from 12 to 20 villages located within a radius of 25 km or so. None of them was literate, not to speak of being associated with any formal or non-formal schooling system earlier. They belonged to educationally very backward areas and low-income families. Except in a few cases, their parents were also illiterate, but given a chance for meaningful education under proper security conditions, the parents, especially the mothers, were found to be very keen for them to study. These camps have been organized basically in desert and tribal areas of Rajasthan.

Urdu Education

Several blocks of Rajasthan have a large Muslim population. This is particularly true of the blocks in Alwar and Bharatpur districts falling in the Mewat region dominated by Meos—a Muslim community of agriculturists and cattle breeders.

School mapping in 1993–4 undertaken by LJ workers revealed that nearly 60 per cent of boys and 90 per cent of girls belonging to the Meo community were not attending school. But a large number of them were going to local mosques for religious instruction. Such instruction did not include any modern Indian language or mathematics, resulting in exclusion of these children from the educational mainstream. Interaction of LJ functionaries with the Meo families in the villages revealed that no real effort had been made to draw these children to schools. There was lack of mutual confidence between the teachers and the village community. The Meos wanted their children to learn Urdu which was not a part of the syllabus in formal schools.

With effect from July 1995, a new programme of *madrassah* education was initiated in thirteen schools. In each of these schools, the building was repaired, necessary equipment provided, and Urdu introduced as a subject of study by appointing a trained Urdu teacher called *Urdu shiksha karmi*. Academic qualifications for *Urdu shiksha karmis* were the same as laid down by the Director of Primary & Secondary Education for a primary-level Urdu teacher. Selections were made through open competition. Three supervisors were also appointed. The medium of instruction in these schools continues to be Hindi but Urdu has been introduced from class I as an additional subject.

The response to this initiative has been very positive. The impact on enrolment has been dramatic. The participation rate of Meo boys in primary education has increased from 42.19 per cent to 82.21 per cent within a period of three years. The impact on girls' enrolment has been even more encouraging, the participation rate in case of girls has increased from only 11.05 per cent to 57.00 per cent during the same three-year period. There has been tremendous demand for the scheme. Consequently, the scheme has now been extended to eighty schools of Kaman block of Bharatpur district.

LJ Management

When the LJ project was being planned, no clear design or structure of management was thought of. Only a few principles and postulates were spelt out. The management system evolved as a response to the needs which emerged and also pose challenges for programme improvement. As of now, the LJ offers a design of administration of education which enables people to manage, and wherever necessary, modify the delivery system. This is in contrast to a centrally designed, hierarchically controlled, tradition-governed system, with in-built inflexibility, which eliminates the weaker sections of society from effective access to the opportunities which can improve their lot. To begin with, it was visualized that the organizational manifestation of the LJ would be the VEC. People connected with the basic education system would be reoriented to perceive a shift of accountability from a hierarchical system of a line of inspectors appointed by government departments to an organized forum of the village community. A systematic effort has, therefore, been made to inform and train all people concerned and to ensure that people who can facilitate implementation of the programme are co-opted into it.

Right from the beginning, the *Lok Jumbish Parishad* (LJP) has been set up as an autonomous and independent organization headed by a Director and a team of 15–20 faculty members. The style of management is characterized by a matrix system which implies that each faculty member has responsibility for one or more subject areas and also has to deal with all aspects of LJ processes in a geographical area. At state level, there is an advisory and policy-making council headed by the Chief Minister of Rajasthan and an Executive Committee chaired by an experienced educational administrator/an eminent educationist. The Executive Committee has full administrative and financial powers. Members of the Executive Committee include representatives of the government and a number of educationists.

The LJ management is characterized by in-built review and planning processes. Review and Planning meetings (RPM) are held at every level where LJ functionaries collectively observe, measure the progress, and transform the whole process into a problem solving. Representatives of partner NGOs participate in the planning and review process in the LJ at every level. RPMs take place at state level once every quarter. At block and cluster levels RPM is a monthly phenomenon. Over the years, RPMs have helped the LJ in the creation of a new, participatory culture of management, which is based on collective review and systematic and practical evolutionary planning processes.

To facilitate decentralized management, a very well-thought-out Management Information System (MIS) has been developed over the years through interactive meetings among cluster and block level functionaries. The MIS is expected to be used as a ready-reckoner for re-viewing the working status as well as processes at every level. Both qualitative and descriptive information generated through the MIS are used as tools for consensus building among the group members at every level; improvement of quality of the processes involved; enhancing involvement of every individual concerned with the activities; monitoring the progress made; creating a data base for both ready reference and analytical purposes; and preparing the monthly and quarterly action plans.

FINANCE AND COST

A distinguishing feature of the LJ's investment is that expenditure is not uniformly distributed in each block. In fact, different blocks of the LJ are at different stages of operationalization. Expenditure is allocated to each block as per their respective requirement. Activity-based unit costs have been calculated separately for each programme. Based on this standard unit costs and the respective action plans, every block has to calculate its financial requirements.

COST-EFFECTIVENESS

It is not easy to calculate cost-effectiveness of the LJ project. Calculating per student cost does not appear to be a meaningful exercise in view of the fact that the LJ intervenes not only in schools or NFE centres but also in the community. Realizing the complexity, an attempt has been made to analyse the details of LJ investment in one of the oldest blocks of LJ (called *Garhi* in Banswara district) vis-à-vis the amount of investment by the state government on primary and upper-primary schools in the same block. This revealed that over the period 1992–8, the state government has invested an amount of Rs 390.7 million, on primary and upper-primary schools, of which 85.4 per cent has been spent on teachers' salaries. In addition to this, the LJ has invested another Rs 58 million approximately during the same period. Of this 22.3 per cent has been invested for repair and construction of school buildings, 46.2 per cent for creating additional facilities, 13.8 per cent for social mobilization, 13.3 per cent for quality improvement, and 4.4 per cent for creating and maintaining a decentralized management structure.

As against this investment, three-fourths of all existing school buildings in the block have been repaired involving the local community. Forty-five new primary schools have been opened and 13 primary schools upgraded to upper-primary level, 77 additional teachers have been appointed and 273 *sahaj shiksha* centres opened. School mapping has been done in all the villages. Core Groups and Women's Groups have also been formed which undertake micro-planning regularly. Intervention in all the 269 schools of the block has been done with the quality improvement programme. Ninety-one per cent of the teachers have been trained. Teaching–learning materials and school equipment have been supplied to all the schools; the students have also received textbooks and other learning materials like slates, bags, and pencils.

All these interventions have resulted in creation of additional facilities to accommodate another 15,500 children in the primary education system in this block. Participation rate (enrolment rate) of children in primary education has improved by 36 per cent and in case of girls, by 46 per cent. The retention rate of children in formal schools has improved by 7 per cent, learning achievement of children has improved by 7 to 11 per cent in classes I and II for which tests have been conducted in mathematics and Hindi (language). Besides, establishment of a BSG at block level and cluster staff in all the five clusters of the block has helped develop a system of effective monitoring and supervision for the overall activities in the block.

Calculation of cost per child per annum has been done for the five blocks taken up by the LJ right from its initiation in 1992. This calculation shows that per child expenditure of the LJ per annum varies from Rs 229 to Rs 248 as against the per student expenditure of Rs 1177 for the state of Rajasthan as a whole and Rs 1209 for India as a whole in the year 1996–7. The cost calculation as mentioned above, has not taken into account the indirect cost and the opportunity cost of the voluntary work and financial contribution made by individuals and the villagers.

LESSONS LEARNT FROM INNOVATIONS: STRATEGIES AND FACTORS CONTRIBUTING TO THE SUCCESS OF THE SKP AND THE LJP

Collaborative Model with Autonomy for the Implementing Structure

The SKP and LJP are strategically based on collaborative models with four sets of actors: (i) villagers, (ii) grassroots workers, who are capable of local mobilization and flexible planning and management; (iii) the Government of Rajasthan which provides wherewithal and machinery for scale and sustainability; (iv) academics and NGOs that facilitate the training and curriculum development, make mid-term corrections, and guide the revisions in planning.

The creation of the SKB and LJP as autonomous bodies to manage the projects, has been an important step. The SKB and LJP are neither the inside the system nor are they parallel or outside systems. These autonomous bodies have both the space and stability to devise, implement, and monitor, at the same time the government has the responsibility of funding the programme and the authority to intervene in the delivery system. State-level resource institutions, local voluntary organizations, district-level officials, block and *panchayat samiti* members are all linked together in a web and a delicate balance is maintained between autonomy and linkage.

Giving Recognition to the Talent and Emphasis on Continuous Training of Workers and Teachers

Appointment in various positions under the SKP and LJP has not been identified with employment schemes. Rather, the potential of unemployed and underemployed youth has been recognized, nurtured, and supported through a network of institutions. For maintaining the motivation, the SKP and LJP devote tremendous time, energy, and effort to providing continuous training and support to staff at all levels. This has enabled them to meet the high expectation of the community.

Using New Vocabulary for Altered Functions

A shift in the position and style of a single function in a large system necessitates shifts in all related functions. Such shifts are seldom internalized by the functionaries concerned. Hence, in order to reinforce the initiated process for change, the intended alterations in functioning patterns need to be demonstrated by the use of fresh vocabulary giving new role descriptions. The SKP has systematically adopted this process. The new names are suggestive of this. '*shiksha karmi*'—education worker— rather than *gram shikshak*—village teacher, '*shiksha karmi* sahyogi' rather than supervisor; *mahila sahyogi*— a woman who escorts girls to schools are all symbolic of internalization of the new role. Learning from the success of the SKP, the LJ has also adopted this principle. Thus NFE has been renamed '*sahaj shiksha*'. Similarly, the various designations, using Hindi terms, of staff at different levels connote their functions.

Limited Claims and Demonstration of Results

The SKP and LJ did not start with radical targets. These were modest in aim, gradual in practice, with the approval of the concerned community as a constant. One step at a time has been the motto. Identification and training of staff and *shiksha karmis/anudeshaks* was the major focus.

Willingness to Learn from Others

The SKP and LJ have shown a welcome willingness to learn from contextual experiences and to work in coordination with holistic initiatives. Both these projects also work in coordination with each other. The SKP responds to the critical issues of teacher absenteeism, dysfunctional schools, and school-less distant habitations even within the LJ project area. The introduction of new textbooks based on the concept of minimum levels of learning and micro-planning based on school mapping and improvement in the quality of learning in *prahar pathshalas* are illustrations of the SKP's interface with the LJ. Besides, the SKP has adopted the idea of RPMs and democratization of decision making from the LJ. The SKP provides some of the human resources for the LJ and works with the LJ towards increased access, retention, and learning achievement of children in the primary education system of Rajasthan.

Incentives and Career Opportunities of Shiksha Karmis and Other Staff

To be a *shiksha karmi* itself brings prestige and a special position in the community. Although appointment of *shiksha karmis* is not identified with an employment scheme, appropriate financial and career incentive schemes have been introduced. They are paid a monthly honorarium of Rs 1800 for running both day schools and *prahar pathshalas*. A *shiksha karmi* who completes eight years of tenure in a satisfactory manner, attends all training programmes, and has attained a matriculation certificate is eligible to be elevated to the status of regular teacher with concomitant benefits of salary and other service conditions. Besides, *shiksha karmis* are also given motivational and financial support to acquire higher educational qualifications through reimbursement of expenditure incurred on books and examination fees and duty leave for taking examinations. Many *shiksha karmis* have availed of these incentives and passed the secondary and senior secondary examinations after becoming *shiksha karmis*. In the LJ as well, workers at all levels can expect elevation if their work is good.

Understanding the Basis of Innovations

From the insight of success of the two specific projects meant for achieving the goals of universal primary education, what appears important is to understand and recognize the factors which have contributed to the success of these innovations. Often, the success of an innovative effort is measured in terms of its replicability and cost-effectiveness. For instance, based on the encouraging results emerging from some innovative actions, the state government decided to uniformly implement these programmes throughout the state. While this could be considered as a welcome step, it is necessary to guard against mechanical implementation without emphasizing the basic spirit of the innovation. The following two examples illustrate this point.

School mapping under the LJ has come to be recognized a successful process of initiating participatory planning at grassroots level. Learning from the experience of the LJ, the state government instructed the teachers of all schools to conduct school mapping of the respective villages in which the schools were located. The teachers were given two-days' training to carry out the task. After going back from the training, school mapping was done by all these teachers within a specified period of one week. They have all produced a visual map on a chart sheet and a register which lists out the details of the families and the children of 6–14 age group participating or not participating in primary education. The household survey proforma developed by the LJ was used for the purpose. However, the very strengths of the school mapping process, to be used as a means of community participation and preparing a base for micro-planning to follow, have been missed out in the midst of generating only information and database.

Coverage of the SKP has gradually extended to 2697 villages over a period of eleven years. Following the idea of shiksha karmi, para-teachers have been trained and appointed in many other states. *Guruji* under the Education Guarantee Scheme of Madhya Pradesh, para-teachers under the Mabadi Project of Andhra Pradesh, Education Activists under the MV Foundation of Andhra Pradesh, volunteer teachers in Himachal Pradesh, *anudeshaks* under the *Sahaj Shiksha* Programme of the LJ, 'Saraswati *behan*' under the Saraswati Yojana of Rajasthan, teachers of alternative schools under the District Primary Education Project are all examples of para-teachers. Experience of all these projects/programmes reveals that the idea of employing para-teachers has been effective only in cases where very strong training and supervisory support have been extended. Besides, all successful programmes involving para-teachers have been tried out on a smaller scale. Their implementation on a larger scale is yet to be tested.

Emerging Issues and Specific Lessons

Experience of the past planning process in India reveals that reliance has been placed for too long on techno-bureaucratic solutions that have treated the people as beneficiaries, masses to whom certain benefits are given by those who know better and who control economic resources, social privilege and information channels. Planning for primary education is no exception.

Till the mid-1980s, attempts have been made to achieve the goal of universal primary education only through supply-side intervention, i.e. opening of schools, appointing teachers, and supplying basic teaching–learning materials. This was based on the implicit assumption that children do not join primary education because the schooling facilities are not available to them. However, this involved a lot of complexity. First, the needs of children belonging to small clusters and isolated, scattered habitations are not served by such schools. Second, appointed teachers, usually belonging to distant places, cannot be regular in such schools. Third, most of the out-of-school children are working either in agriculture, go for animal grazing, are engaged in the family business, working as child labourers, or have to do household work. Hence, school timings do not suit them. Fourth, the social and caste groupings in some places prevent the children of one caste from attending the same school that children belonging to another caste group go to. Experiences of the LJ and SKP reveal that these barriers can best be removed through adoption of an appropriate process of school mapping that helps removal of social, cultural, and economic barriers in addition to solving the problem in terms of physical distance. The SK and LJ projects offer models to assess the exact educational needs of children, provide necessary support to fulfil the needs, and create an environment for people to take care of their educational needs themselves. For this to function, decentralized planning and implementation become indispensable.

To sum up, the operationalization of both the SK and LJ projects point towards some common lessons:

• If schools of good quality are functional, parents will send their children to them and children will learn. This minimum requirement has to be met.

• UEE has to be understood in the context of diversity. The requirements of the children and the community differ from place to place. Therefore, any strategy used for universal primary education must be context-sensitive and therefore need not be uniform everywhere. Every such effort must precede proper diagnosis of the situation to understand the contextual diversity in which the children are living and plan of action determined accordingly.

• Problems of the state-managed delivery system can best be solved by moving out of the defined system of planning, implementation, and evaluation. This could be through reaching out to the body of knowledge and skills in the non-government sector rather than being confined to the government sector alone, because the state authorities may be insensitive and unable to grasp the aspirations of the common people. Sometimes the state authorities could even be oppressive. Such a harsh face can be made people oriented or even people centred only through frequent interaction with civil society. Therefore, application and sustenance of fresh approach to planning, implementation, and evaluation in the existing system requires not only ongoing collaboration of different actors, but also creation of new forums of decision making supported by political will and administrative acceptance.

• A delivery system can run efficiently over a stretch of time if an appropriate self-correcting process of management is designed and set into action. Building this process (such as RPM in the LJ) makes it possible to question the concepts of the project planning, because in such a process, rather than beginning with predetermined project parameters, the parameters are allowed to evolve through action and reflection of the concerned role actors. Second, the idea of evaluation is altered in the process. Rather than evaluation becoming an external and distrustful exercise, it becomes a continuous process of self-reflection, problem-solving, planning, and implementation. This is very important, especially in view of the fact that changes take place continuously in the basic environment in which the intervention is conceived and applied. Continuous rethinking and allowing for evolution of the entire planning thus become of utmost necessity. In the absence of review, the gains achieved in one phase may get converted into stagnated schemes mismatched with contextual requirements in the next phase.

• There is a need to develop processes for institutionalizing community participation and to create a system in which the community feels empowered and is able to take initiatives. Any social development programme can be successful if the concerned people themselves can be inspired to kindle their idealism, and if they can be aroused to work for a cause which they also perceive as in their interest.

REFERENCES

Anandalaksmy, S. and Sharada Jain (1997). *Shikshakarmi: A Paradigm Shift in the Delivery of Primary Education.* Sandhan Research Centre, Jaipur.

Department of Economic Affairs (1999). *Economic Survey 1998–99*. Ministry of Finance, Government of India, New Delhi.

Department of Education (1998). *Selected Educational Statistics 1997–98*. Ministry of Human Resource Development, Government of India, New Delhi.

Department of Primary and Secondary Education (various years). *Annual Reports—1993–94 to 1998–99*, Government of Rajasthan.

Education Department (1997). *A Report on Status of UEE in Rajasthan*. Government of Rajasthan.

Lok Jumbish Parishad (1998a). *Reaching the Unreached: Innovative Strategies for Providing Access to Basic Education to out-of-school Children—Case of India*. Paper submitted to PROAP, UNESCO, Bangkok.

————— (1998b) *The Project Document for Phase III (1998–2003)*, Jaipur.

National Council of Applied Economic Research (1994). *Non-Enrolment, Dropout, and Private Expenditure on Elementary Education: A Comparison Across States and Population Groups*. New Delhi.

National Council of Educational Research and Training (1998). *Sixth All-India Educational Survey*. New Delhi.

National Institute of Educational Planning and Administration and Ministry of Human Resource Development (2000). 'EFA 2000 Assessment: Core EFA Indicators'. New Delhi.

National Sample Survey Organisation (1993). *Results of Participation in Education for Major States*. NSS 42nd Round (July 1986–June 1987) Department of Statistics, Government of India, New Delhi.

————— (1993). *Sarvekshana*. Journal of the National Sample Survey Organisation, 56th Issue 17(1), Department of Statistics, Ministry of Planning and Programme Implementation, Government of India, New Delhi.

Shukla, Snehlata, V. P. Garg, V. K. Jain, Sarla Rajput and O. P. Arora (1994). *Attainments of Primary School Children in Various States*, National Council of Educational Research and Training, New Delhi.

State Institute of Educational Research & Training (n.d.). *Rajasthan Mein Prarambhik Shiksha Mein Shaikshik Apavyya*. Educational Planning and Administration Division, Udaipur. (In Hindi)

————— (1998). *Sixth All-India Educational Survey, State Report—Rajasthan*, Udaipur.

Thakur, P. and S. N. Methi (1999). 'Shiksha Karmi Project-Rajasthan'. (India: The key to locked schools, paper presented at *Human Development Week*, The World Bank, Washington, D.C.).